Excavating Mormon Pasts

Excavating Mormon Pasts:
The New Historiography of the Last Half Century

Edited by

Newell G. Bringhurst

and

Lavina Fielding Anderson

GREG KOFFORD BOOKS
SALT LAKE CITY 2004

© 2004 Greg Kofford Books, Inc.

Cover design copyrighted 2004 by Greg Kofford Books, Inc.

Published by Greg Kofford Books, Inc.
Salt Lake City, Utah

All rights reserved. No part of this book may be reproduced in any format or in any medium without the written permission of the publisher, Greg Kofford Books, Inc., P.O. Box 1362, Draper, UT 84020. The views expressed herein are the responsibility of each author and do not necessarily represent the position of Greg Kofford Books, Inc.

2013 12 11   5 4 3

Visit us at www.koffordbooks.com

The illustrations used the book are from the publisher's personal collection, with the exception that the following are courtesy Lavina Fielding Anderson: 35, 55, 93, 222, 250, 314, 318, 368

The printer's device on the title page was slightly modified from the original form. The orignal was drawn by Glen Strock for the book *Land Grants and Lawsuits in Northern New Mexico* by Malcolm Ebright (University of New Mexico Press, 1994). It is used by permission of Malcolm Ebright who holds the copyright thereto.

Library of Congress Cataloging-in-Publication Data

Excavating Mormon pasts : the new historiography of the last half century / edited by Newell G. Bringhurst and Lavina Fielding Anderson.-- 1st ed.
    p. cm.
 Includes bibliographical references and index.
 ISBN 1-58958-115-6

 1. Mormon Church--Historiography. I. Bringhurst, Newell G. II. Anderson, Lavina Fielding, 1944-
BX8611.E93 2004
289.3'072'2--dc22
                              2004006572

Contents

Introduction ... ix
Newell G. Bringhurst

Chapter

1   Mormon History and the Conundrum of Culture: American and Beyond ... 1
Klaus J. Hansen

2   The Search for Cultural Origins of Mormon Doctrines ... 27
David L. Paulsen

3   Mormon Origins: The Church in New York and Ohio ... 53
Roger D. Launius

4   The Mormon Experience in Missouri, 1830-39 ... 87
Stephen C. LeSueur

5   The Nauvoo Experience ... 113
Glen M. Leonard

6   Mormonism on the Frontier: The Saints of the Great Basin ... 137
Craig L. Foster

7   Mormonism in Transition, 1890-1945 ... 165
M. Guy Bishop

8   The LDS Church in the United States since 1945 ... 179
Jessie L. Embry

9   Growth and Internationalization: The LDS Church since 1945 ... 199
Kahlile Mehr, Mark L. Grover, Reid L. Neilson, Donald Q. Cannon, and Grant Underwood

Excavating Mormon Pasts

10	Studies of Mormon Fissiparousness: Conflict, Dissent, and Schism in the Early Church *Danny L. Jorgensen*	229
11	"Travelers on the New Mormon History Trail": Community of Christ Contributions to the New Mormon History Movement *Mark A. Scherer*	253
12	The New Mormon Women's History *Todd Compton*	273
13	Out of the Closet and into the Fire: The New Mormon Historians' Take on Polygamy *Martha Sonntag Bradley*	303
14	Mormon Biography: Paradoxes, Progress, and Continuing Problems *Newell G. Bringhurst*	323
15	Mormon Society and Culture *Davis Bitton*	351
16	Fictional Pasts: Mormon Historical Novels *Lavina Fielding Anderson*	367
	Index	395

Illustrations

Fawn M. Brodie, *No Man Knows My History: The Life of Joseph Smith the Mormon Prophet*	2
Whitney R. Cross, *The Burned-Over District: The Social and Intellectual History of Enthusiastic Religion in Western New York, 1800-1850*	7
Klaus J. Hansen, *Quest for Empire: The Political Kingdom of God and the Council of Fifty in Mormon History*	11
Klaus J. Hansen, *Mormonism and the American Experience*	13
Thomas O'Dea, *The Mormons*	15
Ethan Smith, *View of the Hebrews,* 2d ed.	29
Richard T. Hughes and C. Leonard Allen, *Illusions of Innocence: Protestant Primitivism in America*	35
Dan Vogel, *Religious Seekers and the Advent of Mormonism*	38
John L. Brooke, *The Refiner's Fire: The Making of Mormon Cosmology, 1644-1844*	43
Paul M. Edwards, *Our Legacy of Faith: A Brief History of the Reorganized Church of Jesus Christ of Latter Day Saints*	55
Kenneth H. Winn, *Exiles in a Land of Liberty: Mormons in America, 1830-1844*	56
Richard L. Bushman, *Joseph Smith and the Beginnings of Mormonism*	65
James B. Allen and Glen M. Leonard, *The Story of the Latter-day Saints*	67
D. Michael Quinn, *Early Mormonism and the Magic World View*	70
Stephen C. LeSueur, *The 1838 Mormon War in Missouri*	91
Alexander L. Baugh, "A Call to Arms: The 1838 Mormon Defense of Northern Missouri"	93
Roger D. Launius, *Alexander William Doniphan: Portrait of a Missouri Moderate*	94
William G. Hartley, "My Best for the Kingdom": History and Autobiography of John Lowe Butler, A Mormon Frontiersman*	100
Robert Bruce Flanders, *Nauvoo: Kingdom on the Mississippi*	115
John E. Hallwas and Roger D. Launius, eds., *Cultures in Conflict: A Documentary History of the Mormon War in Illinois*	122
Glen M. Leonard, *Nauvoo: A Place of Peace, and People of Promise*	125
Carol Cornwall Madsen, ed., *In Their Own Words: Women and the Story of Nauvoo*	128
Milton V. Backman Jr., *People and Power of Nauvoo: Themes from the Nauvoo Experience*	134
Leonard J. Arrington, *Great Basin Kingdom: An Economic History of the Latter-day Saints: 1830-1900*	138
Thomas G. Alexander and James B. Allen, *Mormons and Gentiles: A History of Salt Lake City*	147
Leonard J. Arrington, Feramorz Y. Fox, and Dean L. May, *Building the City of God: Community and Cooperation Among the Mormons*	150
Juanita Brooks, *The Mountain Meadows Massacre*	154
Will Bagley, *Blood of the Prophets: Brigham Young and the Massacre at Mountain Meadows*	156
Thomas G. Alexander, *Mormonism in Transition: A History of the Latter-day Saints, 1890-1930*	166
Edward Leo Lyman, *Political Deliverance: The Mormon Quest for Utah Statehood*	169
David L. Bigler, *Forgotten Kingdom: The Mormon Theocracy in the American West, 1847-1896*	171

Excavating Mormon Pasts

Robert C. Freeman and Dennis A. Wright, eds., *Saints at War: Experiences of Latter-day Saints in World War II*	175
Mark P. Leone, *Roots of Modern Mormonism*	182
Leonard J. Arrington, *Adventures of a Church Historian*	185
Susan Buhler Taber, *Mormon Lives: A Year in the Elkton Ward*	197
Richard O. Cowan, *The Latter-day Saint Century*	202
Marjorie Newton, *Southern Cross Saints: The Mormons in Australia*	206
Bruce A. Van Orden, D. Brent Smith, and Everett Smith Jr., eds., *Pioneers in Every Land: Inspirational Stories of International Pioneers Past and Present*	209
F. LaMond Tullis, *Mormons in Mexico: The Dynamics of Faith and Culture*	214
Douglas J. Davies, ed., *Mormon Identities in Transition*	222
Steven L. Shields, *Divergent Paths of the Restoration*	235
D. Michael Quinn, *The Mormon Hierarchy: Origins of Power*	239
Roger D. Launius and Linda Thatcher, eds., *Differing Visions: Dissenters in Mormon History*	242
Davis Bitton ed., *Lamoni Wight: Life in a Mormon Splinter Colony on the Texas Frontier*	250
Richard P. Howard, *Restoration Scriptures: A Study of Their Textual Development*	255
Wayne Ham, *"Publish Glad Tidings": Readings in Early Latter Day Saint Sources*	256
F. Mark McKiernan and Roger D. Launius, eds., *An Early Latter Day Saint History: The Book of John Whitmer Kept by Commandment*	259
Roger D. Launius, *Joseph Smith III: Pragmatic Prophet*	261
Juanita Brooks, ed., *Not By Bread Alone: The Journal of Martha Spencer Heywood, 1850-1856*	276
Annie Clark Tanner, *A Mormon Mother: An Autobiography*	278
Maureen Ursenbach Beecher, *Eliza and Her Sisters*	282
Jill Mulvay Derr, Janath Russell Cannon, and Maureen Ursenbach Beecher, *Women of Covenant: The Story of the Relief Society*	285
Linda King Newell and Valeen Tippetts Avery, *Mormon Enigma: Emma Hale Smith, Prophet's Wife, "Elect Lady," Polygamy's Foe*	290
Todd Compton, *In Sacred Loneliness: The Plural Wives of Joseph Smith*	312
Kathryn M. Daynes, *More Wives Than One: Transformation of the Mormon Marriage System, 1840-1910*	314
Martha Sonntag Bradley, *Kidnapped from That Land: The Government Raids on the Short Creek Polygamists*	318
Lawrence Foster, *Religion and Sexuality: Three American Communal Experiments of the Nineteenth Century*	320
Donna Hill, *Joseph Smith: The First Mormon*	325
Leonard J. Arrington, *Brigham Young: American Moses*	330
Samuel W. Taylor, *The Kingdom or Nothing: The Life of John Taylor, Militant Mormon*	332
Davis Bitton, *George Q. Cannon: A Biography*	335
Boyd Jay Petersen, *Hugh Nibley: A Consecrated Life*	337
Dean L. May, *Three Frontiers: Family, Land, and Society in the Far West, 1850-1900*	354
F. Ross Peterson, *A History of Cache County*	356
Brent D. Corcoran, ed., *Multiply and Replenish: Mormon Essays on Sex and Family*	359
Marie Cornwall, Tim B. Heaton, and Lawrence Young, eds., *Contemporary Mormonism: Social Science Perspectives*	365
Orson Scott Card, *A Woman of Destiny*	368
Gerald N. Lund, THE WORK AND THE GLORY, Vol. 1: *Pillar of Light*	371
Dean Hughes, CHILDREN OF THE PROMISE, VOL. 1: *Rumors of War*	382
Margaret Blair Young and Darius Aidan Gray, STANDING ON THE PROMISES, Book 2: *Bound for Canaan*	384

Introduction

Newell G. Bringhurst

Over the past sixty years a growing body of historical literature has emerged, examining diverse aspects of Mormon history. In 1952, Fawn M. Brodie noted "the phenomenon of the Mormon writer" or "new group" of writers having "the ambition to be serious . . . historians [striving] earnestly if not always successfully for impartiality."[1] In 1969, Moses Rischin called this scholarship the "New Mormon History." In the quarter-century that followed, a vigorous debate has waxed and waned over whether there is, in fact, a "New Mormon History,"[2] its characteristics, and the pros and cons of scholarship produced under its rubric. Senior Mormon historian Marvin S. Hill, for example, said in "The 'New Mormon History' Reassessed in Light of Recent Books on Joseph Smith and Mormon Origins," *Dialogue* 21, no. 3 (Autumn 1988): 116-27, that he did not "believe that there actually exists an entirely 'new Mormon history'" (115), even though he conceded that "certainly the quantity of scholarly studies has greatly increased, and often the quality as well" (116). Among the heaviest critiques are Boyd K. Packer, "The Mantle Is Far, Far Greater Than the Intellect," *BYU Studies* 21 (Summer 1981): 259-78; David Earl Bohn, "No Higher Ground: Objective History Is an Illusive Chimera," *Sunstone* 8 (January-March 1983): 26-32; his "Our Own Agenda: A Critique of the Methodology of the New Mormon History," *Sunstone* 14 (June 1990): 46-54; and Louis Midgley, "Which Middle Ground," *Dialogue: A Journal of Mormon Thought* 22 (Summer 1989): 6-8.

It is not my intention to become involved in either debate. Rather, I accept the historiographical fact that a body of scholarship has emerged in Mormon studies that differs in significant ways from its predecessors. One of these distinctive characteristics of recent Mormon scholarship, has been its sheer volume. "The years stretching from the 1950s on," note Davis Bitton and Leonard J. Arrington, *Mormons and Their Historians* (Salt Lake City: University of Utah, 1988), 126, "saw an incredible volcano burst: dozens, scores, of historians [taking] up the subject of Mormon history, writing more books, articles, and dissertations than ever before." Mormon studies by the late 1960s, had attracted "an array of sophisticated scholars" that "had no parallel in the history of any other religious group in America—with the single exception of the Puritans," noted Moses Rischin (49). But the

---

1. Fawn M. Brodie, "New Writers and Mormonism," *Frontier Magazine,* December 1952, 17.
2. Moses Rischin, "The New Mormon History," *American West* 6, March 1969, 49.

Excavating Mormon Pasts

flood had barely begun. In their editors' introduction, James B. Allen, Ronald W. Walker, and David J. Whittaker, *Studies in Mormon History, 1830-1997: An Indexed Bibliography with A Topical Guide to Published Social Science Literature on the Mormons* (Urbana: University of Illinois Press, 2000), ix, list almost 15,000 items.

Also writing in the 1960s, P. A. M. Taylor, "Recent Writing on Utah and the Mormons," *Arizona and the West,* August 1962, 252, identified a second characteristic of recent Mormon scholarship—its growing "professionalization." This characteristic has also only intensified as new generations of academically trained historians have taken up their tools. Robert Bruce Flanders, "Some Reflections on the New Mormon History," *Dialogue* 9, no. 1 (Spring 1974): 35, observed that "most of the new historians are professionals whose work exhibits critical-analytical techniques." True, Paul M. Edwards, "The Irony of Mormon History," *Utah Historical Quarterly* 41, no. 4 (Autumn 1973): 408, noted that "in history as in no other discipline the amateur is vital. For it is the interest, the love of the past, the willingness to become half lost in the imagination of previous days that is the historian's first tool and the one which few graduate students learn to use." Still, he also characterized the "large majority" of New Mormon historians as "professional," and, in "The New Mormon History," *Saints' Herald,* November 1986, 474, listed as evidence: the 1972 appointment of Leonard J. Arrington, trained scholar and noted author, as the LDS Church's first professional appointment to the office of Church Historian; followed by the calling of Richard Howard, also professionally trained, to a similar position over the Historical Department of the Community of Christ (then Reorganized Church of Jesus Christ of Latter Day Saints). Further facilitating professionalization was the creation of "networks of historical-minded persons" enabling scholars and interested students to discuss, debate, and exchange information. Edwards noted the Mormon History Association formed in 1965, followed the next year by the appearance of *Dialogue: A Journal of Mormon Thought,* and *Courage: A Journal of History, Thought, and Action* (1970), and the creation of the John Whitmer Historical Association (1972).

Recent Mormon scholarship has reflected a third outstanding characteristic: use of heretofore unavailable and/or unused manuscript source materials. Important in this process is the availability of primary materials in the LDS Church Archives in Salt Lake City. For the decade of Arrington's tenure as LDS Church Historian, archival materials, including papers of General Authorities and official minutes and records, were relatively open to scholars. It was a period Davis Bitton, one of Arrington's Assistant Church Historians, commemorates in "Ten Years in Camelot: A Personal Memoir," *Dialogue* 16 (Autumn 1983): 9-33. Arrington explained his approach to the historical enterprise in "Historian as Entrepreneur: A Personal Essay," *BYU Studies* 17 (Winter 1977): 193-209.

By the mid-1980s, and particularly after the Mark Hofmann forgeries and murders, such access became more restrictive with particular caution applied to the papers of Mormon General Authorities. However, most reputable and patient scholars have continued to be granted access to various other manuscript and documentary materials. Also somewhat offsetting Mormon Church restrictions has been the publication of important manuscript collections, particularly those of Joseph Smith, thanks to such scholars as Dean C. Jessee, Scott H. Faulring, Andrew F. Ehat, Lyndon W. Cook, Dan Vogel, and others.[3] A

---

3. Notable examples include Dean C. Jessee, ed., *Autobiographical and Historical Writings,* Vol. 1, *The Papers of Joseph Smith* (Salt Lake City, Deseret Book, 1989); Jessee, ed., *The Papers of Joseph Smith, Journal, 1832-*

recent and welcome development is the digitalized image publication in *Selected Collections from the Archives of the Church of Jesus Christ of Latter-day Saints,* 2 vols. (Provo, UT: Brigham Young University Press, [Dec. 2002]), of more than 400,000 manuscript pages of archival material, including journals of Joseph F. Smith, J. Golden Kimball, Franklin D. Richards, and others. Another is the multi-volume effort to collect and publish all of Joseph Smith's papers, private and public, being undertaken as a joint effort of the Joseph Fielding Smith Institute for Latter-day Saint History at BYU (the successor unit of Arrington's History Division at Church headquarters), the LDS Church Archives, and a somewhat revived BYU Press.

A fourth characteristic of recent Mormon scholarship has been the expanded variety of techniques and methodologies in research and writing. D. Michael Quinn, "Editor's Introduction," *The New Mormon History* (Salt Lake City: Signature Books, 1991), vii, noted that Mormon scholars "have adopted new techniques and emphases in reexamining familiar topics," mirroring wider trends in the writing of other types of history since the 1950s. Mormon scholars have begun to consider the "experiences of 'common people'" and of other heretofore neglected groups, including "women, children, families and ethnic minorities." Another important technique is what Quinn termed "cross cultural comparisons" (vii). Such efforts began with Whitney Cross's foundational *The Burned-Over District: The Social and Intellectual History of Enthusiastic Religion in Western New York, 1800-1850* (Ithaca, NY: Cornell University Press, 1950; paperback reprint, Harper Torchbook, 1965), which considered the origins and development of early Mormonism within the broad context of antebellum American society. Efforts to contextualize the Mormon experience are evident in such works as David Brion Davis, "The New England Origins of Mormonism," *New England Quarterly* 26 (June 1953): 147-68; Mark Leone, *Roots of Modern Mormonism* (Cambridge, MA: Harvard University Press, 1979); Lawrence Foster, *Religion and Sexuality: The Shakers, the Mormons, and the Oneida Community* (New York: Oxford University Press, 1981); Klaus J. Hansen, *Mormonism and the American Experience* (Chicago: University of Chicago Press, 1981); Jan Shipps, *Mormonism:The Story of a New Religious Tradition* (Urbana: University of Illinois Press, 1985); D. Michael Quinn, *Early Mormonism and the Magic World View* (1987; rev. ed., Salt Lake City: Signature Books, 1998); John L. Brooke, *The Refiner's Fire: The Making of Mormon Cosmology, 1644-1844* (New York: Cambridge University Press, 1994); and Dean L. May, *Three Frontiers: Family, Land, and Society in the American West, 1850-1900* (New York: Cambridge University Press, 1994).

Furthermore, as Quinn noted in his editor's introduction, recent Mormon historical scholarship has become increasingly sensitive to "methods and theories of the social sciences," including those of sociologists, political scientists, economists, anthropologists, and psychologists (vii). Flanders characterized Mormon studies as "a modern history, informed by modern trends of thought, not only in history but in other humanistic and scientific disciplines as well, including philosophy, social psychology, economics, and religious studies" 35). Edwards, in "The New Mormon History," 12-13, found it "more wholistic" (*sic*) in its approach with its practitioners more willing to acknowledge that

---

1842, Vol. 2, *The Papers of Joseph Smith* (Salt Lake City, Deseret Book, 1992); Scott H. Faulring, ed., *An American Prophet's Record: The Diaries and Journals of Joseph Smith* (Salt Lake City, Signature Books, 1989); Andrew F. Ehat and Lyndon W. Cook, eds., *The Words of Joseph Smith* (Orem, UT: Grandin Book Company, 1993); Dean C. Jessee, ed., *Letters of Brigham Young to His Sons* (Salt Lake City: Deseret Book, 1974).

Excavating Mormon Pasts

"Mormonism did not arise unaffected by the people who brought it forth or the environment in which it originated."

A conscious quest for objectivity represents a fifth characteristic evident in recent Mormon historical writing. As early as Flanders's 1966 essay, he noted a "trend to detach the Mormon past from American mythology or hagiography" (27). Eight years later in "Some Reflections on the New Mormon History," Flanders added: "Their point of view might be described generally as interested, sympathetic detachment." Such writers were "interested in more than the narrowly sectarian experiences of Latter-day Saints" or "morality play" of good versus evil—a "cast of characters" composed of "White Hats and Black Hats." Such writers, Flanders concluded, are "more aware of and sympathetic toward the ambivalence of the human condition" (36).

Similarly, William Mulder, "Mormon Angles of Historical Vision: Some Maverick Reflections," *Journal of Mormon History* 3 (1976): 13-14, observed that "Mormon scholars have come of age: they have learned the tools of their trade and have achieved a certain objectivity and composure in dealing with their extraordinary history." Or as Quinn put it more colorfully in his introduction: Mormon historians have tried "to avoid using history as religious battering ram," instead approaching "their task from the perspective of functional objectivity." But Quinn also conceded that "ultimate 'historical objectivity' is an impossible task because the observer historian brings his or her own limitations to the study of the past" (viii). Thomas G. Alexander, "Toward the New Mormon History: An Examination of the Literature of the Latter-day Saints in the Far West," in *Historians and the American West*, edited by Michael P. Malone (Lincoln: University of Nebraska, 1983), 344-68, made perhaps the most acute observation about the parameters of the New Mormon History: "It derived from a belief that secular and spiritual motivation coexist in human affairs and that a sympathetic but critical evaluation of the Mormon past, using techniques derived from historical, humanistic, social-scientific, and religious perspectives, could help in understanding what was at base a religious movement" (345).

The genesis of what became the New Mormon History can be deduced from the work of five important writers of the 1940s: Bernard DeVoto, Dale L. Morgan, Juanita Brooks, Wallace Stegner, and Fawn McKay Brodie. Their influence forms the thesis of Gary Topping's foundational study, *Utah Historians and the Reconstruction of Western History* (Norman: University of Oklahoma Press, 2003), esp. 331-40. Brodie and Brooks were, in Topping's words, "the spearheads of a thrust toward a new Mormon historiography"—Brodie by her controversial 1945 biography on Joseph Smith, *No Man Knows My History* and Brooks in her 1950 *Mountain Meadows Massacre* chronicling "the darkest deed of Mormon history." Less than a decade later, the publication of Leonard J. Arrington's *Great Basin Kingdom: An Economic History of the Latter-day Saints* was, as Topping put it, "probably the greatest single forward leap in Mormon historiography" (333).

This volume of essays attempts to critically evaluate the general body of recent Mormon scholarship—that is, historical books, monographs, articles, and other scholarly works published over the past sixty years—reflecting the emergence of a "new" Mormon history. This work provides a general overview of what has been accomplished, while at same time noting areas in need of further exploration. Such a "progress report" is inevitably a moving target, largely conditioned by the reading interests and awarenesses of their respective authors. Some works will have been slighted or overlooked altogether, while some will, viewed from the judicious perspective of another decade or two, have been given too much weight. .

Because each chapter was prepared as a stand-alone survey of the topic and an analysis of it, we have made no attempt to reduce repetition of citations between essays. Indeed, many works, such as Leonard J. Arrington's *Great Basin Kingdom: An Economic History of the Latter-day Saints, 1830-1900* (Cambridge, MA: Harvard University Press, 1958; reprint ed., Lincoln: University of Nebraska Press, 1966), is so foundational in the field of the New Mormon History that it is relevant even to surveys of literature that begin decades later and that cover fields far distant from economic history.

Furthermore, the project has its own historical development. It originated in about 1990 in the fertile minds of Roger D. Launius and Paul M. Edwards, who saw the usefulness of tracking our own historiography. They did the initial organizational work, and a significant number of these essays have existed in draft since at least 1992. A number of roadblocks delayed the project, necessitating various revivals and resuscitations. When first Paul, then Roger succumbed to the pressure of other projects, Roger turned existing manuscripts over to Craig Foster and Newell Bringhurst in the fall of 1996; and they began encouraging completions and updates of the existing manuscripts. Newly organized Greg Kofford Books showed enthusiasm for the project; and when Craig's other commitments became overwhelming, Lavina Fielding Anderson came on board to chivvy authors and copy edit the results. The authors, all of whom agreed about the importance of the project and manifested commendable professionalism in looking up recently published works, lamented, even as they complied with the deadlines, the landscape of "what I could have done with two more weeks." As both an editor and a contributor to this volume, I can only express my sympathy; but it seemed quite clear that another delay would mean only another period of updating later. It seemed better to provide a Polaroid of the Mormon history field as of February 2004 than to linger over the brushstrokes of a master piece that might never be completed.

Despite the very real limitations imposed by these working conditions, these sixteen essays trace the exciting youth and early maturation of the New Mormon History. Each is an original work, published here for the first time, by scholars chosen for their expertise on a particular topic. Two essays—Klaus J. Hansen's "Mormon History and the Conundrum of Culture: American and Beyond" and David Paulsen's "The Search for Cultural Origins of Mormon Doctrines"—provide two different perspectives on scholarship concerned with Mormon origins as it interfaced with American culture and society during the early nineteenth century.

Three essays evaluate scholarly writings concerned with the early Latter-day Saint experience in New York and Ohio, in Missouri, and in Illinois, during 1830-46. They are Roger D. Launius, "The Church in New York and Ohio: Writing the History of Mormonism's Early Period"; Stephen LeSueur, "The Mormon Experience in Missouri, 1830-1839"; and "The Nauvoo Experience" by Glen M. Leonard.

Another cluster of four essays evaluates scholarship concerned with the Mormon experience among those Latter-day Saints who accepted the leadership claims of Brigham Young following the death of Joseph Smith. Presented within a chronological framework, the four, taken together, cover from 1846 to the present. The first, "Mormonism on the Frontier: The Saints of the Great Basin, 1846-1890" is by Craig L. Foster, and the second

Excavating Mormon Pasts

by M. Guy Bishop is "Mormonism in Transition, 1890-1945." Jessie L. Embry's "The LDS Church in the United States Since 1945," is an insightful interpretation of the Church's "headquarters" response to both internal and external pressures since World War II. In "Growth and Internationalization: The LDS Church Since 1945," Kahlile B. Mehr, Mark L. Grover, Reid L. Nielson, Donald Q. Cannon, and Grant Underwood look beyond the borders of the United States to chronicle the historiography on the LDS Church as an international movement.

Focusing on division and dissent is Danny L. Jorgensen in "Studies of Mormon Fissiparousness: Conflict, Dissent, and Schism in the Early Church." Mark A. Scherer, "Travelers on the New History Trail: Community of Christ Contributions to the New Mormon History Movement," focuses on the historiographical contributions of historians in the Community of Christ (formerly the RLDS Church), the major group that emerged following the death of Joseph Smith to reject Brigham Young's leadership. These contributions are especially significant since the rise of the New Mormon History coincided with a general theological liberalization in the RLDS Church, something that did not happen to anywhere near the same degree in its Utah-centered counterpart.

The remaining essays deal with scholarship on particular topics important in the broader sweep of Latter-day Saint history. Todd Compton explores "The New Mormon Woman's History." Evaluating writings on the highly controversial topic of plural marriage is Martha Sonntag Bradley in "Out of the Closet and Into the Fire: The New Mormon Historians' Take on Polygamy." I examine what is arguably the largest sub-genre in the New Mormon History: "Mormon Biography: Paradoxes, Progress, and Problems." Davis Bitton's essay is concerned with scholarship on "Mormon Society and Culture," and Lavina Fielding Anderson evaluates the role of Mormon historical fiction in "Fictional Pasts: Mormon Historical Novels."

This volume is intended not only for individuals directly involved in the research and writing in Mormon history but also is a basic, readily accessible reference guide for scholars in the larger fields of American studies, the history of the American West, and the history of religions.

Chapter 1

Mormon History and the Conundrum of Culture: American and Beyond

Klaus J. Hansen

In a spirited letter to Dale Morgan discussing Fawn Brodie's biography of Joseph Smith, Bernard DeVoto took aim at the notion—implied in Brodie's work—that the study of the relationship between Mormonism and American culture was an enterprise of significance or importance. "Practically everyone who writes about Mormonism," he argued, overstates "the importance and the typicalness of Mormonism in the United States of its time. It was not typical of American life at that time and it was, even in sum total, of exceedingly minute importance in or to American life. It is at best a minor thing in America as a whole, and at best an aberration of the principal energies involved in it."[1] Though Morgan, not surprisingly, took exception to such strong opinions, DeVoto had hit upon a major issue in Mormon historiography: the significance of Mormonism's place in American culture.

Excellent overviews of this topic are the "Introduction" to *Mormonism and American Culture,* edited by Marvin S. Hill and James B. Allen (New York: Harper & Row, 1972): 1-9; and Thomas G. Alexander, "The Place of Joseph Smith in the Development of American Religion: A Historiographical Inquiry," *Journal of Mormon History* 5 (1978): 3-17. Important for the early period is Howard Clair Searle, "Early Mormon Historiography: Writing the History of the Mormons, 1830-1858" (Ph.D. diss., University of Southern California, 1979). My own study inevitably overlaps somewhat not only with these studies but also with others in this volume because the theme of culture is such a broad one. Although it would be desirable for this essay to achieve comprehensiveness, such a goal is compromised less by space limitations than by my idiosyncratic reading in Mormon and American history.

Although DeVoto's eruption of temper resulted primarily in hyperbole, ironically, he was at least in partial agreement with a group of writers for whom he professed noth-

---

1. 28 December 1945, in Wallace Stegner, ed., *The Letters of Bernard DeVoto* (New York: Doubleday, 1975), quoted in William Mulder, "Preface," *Dale Morgan on Early Mormonism: Correspondence and a New History* (Salt Lake City: Signature Books, 1986), 4. Morgan had taken exception to some of DeVoto's comments in his review of Brodie, which was on the whole favorable, published in the *New York Herald Tribune,* on December 16, 1945.

No man knows my history

The Life of JOSEPH SMITH

THE MORMON PROPHET

by FAWN M. BRODIE

New York. Alfred A. Knopf. 1945

ing but contempt—orthodox Mormons who saw their religion as *sui generis,* beyond culture, though the nature of extra-cultural inspiration for the two was radically different, in the one case divine inspiration or revelation, in the other psychopathology.

DeVoto, however, was hardly the first to make such an argument. Some of the very first attacks on Mormonism, while lacking more sophisticated modern psychological insights, called Joseph Smith deluded. For instance, Alexander Campbell, Philastus Hurlburt, and Eber D. Howe also placed great emphasis on social and cultural factors influencing Mormonism.[2] It was three quarters of a century later, after the study of psychology had become academically respectable, that I. Woodbridge Riley attempted a more ambitious psychological interpretation in his Yale dissertation published as *The Founder of Mormonism: A Psychological Study of Joseph Smith, Jr.* (New York: Dodd, Mead, 1902). Riley's conclusion that Joseph Smith was an epileptic, derived from the physiological psychology of Krafft-Ebing, has not stood the test of time. Indeed, all attempts at psychological interpretation, whether positive or negative have had the same result. Fawn M. Brodie, *No Man Knows My History: The Life of Joseph Smith the Mormon Prophet* (1945; 2d ed. rev., New York: Knopf, 1971), 418-19 offers an "impostor" hypothesis, borrowed from psychiatrist Phyllis Greenacre. T. L. Brink, "Joseph Smith: The Verdict of Depth Psychology," *Journal of Mormon History* 3 (1976): 73-83, proposed a Jungian version—that Smith had tapped "the vast reservoir of creative energies within the collective unconscious." After I read Julian Jaynes, *The Origin of Consciousness in the Breakdown of the Bicameral Mind* (Toronto: University of Toronto Press, 1978), 361-78, I speculated in *Mormonism and the American Experience* (Chicago: University of Chicago Press, 1981), 18-21 whether the bicameral brain hypothesis might work as a metaphor to explain the sincerity with which Joseph asserted the reality of his visions.

Another Jungian interpretation is Jess Groesbeck, "Joseph Smith and the Shaman's Vision: A Psychoanalytic Exploration of Mormonism," Sunstone Symposium, Salt Lake City, August 1985, He has since switched to birth order and family dynamic theories ("The Smiths and Their Dreams and Vision," *Sunstone* 12 [March 1988]: 22-29), shaping scanty clues about Joseph's childhood into clues about the origin of Smith's religious creativity. Intrigued by these possibilities, Lawrence Foster has proposed in "The Psychology of Religious Genius: Joseph Smith and the Origins of New Religious Movements," *Dialogue: A Journal of Mormon Thought* 26 (Winter 1993): 1-22, a theory that Joseph Smith was a manic-depressive. Because these works are highly speculative their persuasiveness depends on the receptivity of respective readers to these arguments. The same goes for the more ambitious works of William D. Morain, *The Sword of Laban: Joseph Smith Jr. and the Dissociated Mind* (Washington, DC: American Psychiatric Press, 1998) and Robert D. Anderson, *Inside the Mind of Joseph Smith: Psychobiography and the Book of Mormon* (Salt Lake City: Signature Books, 1999). In my critique of *Inside the Mind of Joseph Smith* at the Sunstone symposium the following year, I commented that anyone capable of believing in Freudian speculations regarding Smith's claims should have no difficulty believing Joseph's own autobiographical version. Finally, Dan Vogel, *Joseph Smith: The Making of a Prophet* (Salt Lake City: Signature

---

2. Alexander Campbell, *Delusions: An Analysis of the Book of Mormon* . . . (Boston: Benjamin H. Greene, 1832); reprinted from the *Millennial Harbinger,* February 7, 1831); Eber D. Howe, *Mormonism Unvailed; or, a Faithful Account of That Singular Imposition and Delusion* (Painesville, OH: Howe, 1834). Philastus Hurlburt provided Howe with the defamatory affidavits collected from Joseph Smith's New York neighbors that appeared in *Mormonism Unvailed.*

Excavating Mormon Pasts

Books, 2004) also treats the origins of Mormonism and devotes considerable space to reading the Book of Mormon as autobiography.

It is true that, with the exception of DeVoto, these commentators do not privilege psychological explanations to the exclusion of cultural influences, but rather express a need to come to terms with the phenomenon of revelation through a secular orientation. Riley, for example, connected many of Smith's ideas to the surrounding evangelical, Protestant culture, while at the same time granting him sincerity derived from mystical insights and conjecturing that Mormonism's more systematic theological developments were added by Mormon believers like Orson Pratt. A major achievement, however, was Riley's decisive break with the theory that the Book of Mormon was plagiarized from a novel by the Rev. Solomon Spaulding. Richard L. Bushman called *The Founder of Mormonism* "the most original and important non-Mormon work [on Mormonism] of the twentieth century."[3]

In his 1977 presidential address to the Mormon History Association, "The Secular Smiths," Paul M. Edwards used some of Riley's ideas as a catalyst for an imaginative and suggestive attempt to bridge revelation and culture. Joseph was a mystic, but not as mysticism was understood in the West. Mormon theology "was born full-grown through the minds and talents of some Burned-Over District supernaturalists of whom Parley Pratt was a prime example, if not the actual culprit," asserted Edwards, while the Mormon church was "a product of the organizational mind of Hyrum Smith and a host of inspired secular leaders." In the same spirit, but putting it somewhat differently, Langdon Gilkey in his 1984 Tanner Lecture to the Mormon History Association cautioned against the tendency of secular scholars to see religion as merely a human projection. "The religious community . . . is not identical with its cultural environment. . . . It arises from beyond history . . . in response to the revelation from God."[4] Of course, at this juncture the historian is either silenced or else thrown back into a world where religion and culture are inevitably yoked in an uneasy relationship.[5]

Thus, rather than losing too much sleep over an intractable conundrum, most historians have devoted their energies to the question of just how Mormonism and culture are connected, usually making an inauspicious start with Alexander Campbell. Of the Book of Mormon, Campbell complained that it touched upon "every error and almost every truth discussed in New York for the last ten years"—deciding "all the great controversies—infant baptism, ordination, the trinity, regeneration, repentance, justification, the fall of man, the atonement, transubstantiation, fasting, penance, church government, religious experience, the call to the ministry, the general resurrection, eternal punishment, who may be baptized, and even the question of freemasonry, republican government, and the rights of man."[6]

Unaware that Campbell by 1834 had dropped his earlier environmental explanation to adopt the Spaulding theory being disseminated by Eber Howe, many subsequent commentators used Campbell's work as a foundation for environmental explanations of Mormonism, especially those linking it to the cultural matrix of evangelical religion

---

3. Richard L. Bushman, *Joseph Smith and the Beginnings of Mormonism* (Urbana: University of Illinois Press, 1984), 191.
4. Langdon Gilkey, "Religion and Culture: A Persistent Problem," 1 *Journal of Mormon History* 12 (1985): 30, 40.
5. For a discussion about how a believing Mormon may write history that respects the canons of scholarship, see Richard L. Bushman, "Faithful History," *Dialogue* 4 (Winter 1969): 11-25.
6. Campbell, "The Mormonites," *Millennial Harbinger* 2 (February 1831): 93.

and such antebellum influences as anti-Catholicism, anti-Masonry, and Hebraic Indian origins[7]—themes picked up and elaborated on with varying emphases by numerous authors over the ensuing hundred years, most of them pejorative and condescending.

As Thomas G. Alexander summed it up, "By Joseph Smith's death, many positions taken since that time on Mormonism and American religion had been outlined. For Mormons it was *sui generis*—a religion for all the world designed to restore pristine Christianity."[8] In the words of Richard Bushman, "Mormons have felt little incentive to strive for a deeper understanding in cultural and social terms when they believe Joseph Smith himself disclosed the deepest meaning of his work in religious terms."[9] Continues Alexander: "For some critics like Alexander Campbell, it [Mormonism] was a sect, developed in the Protestant tradition of English and American millennialists and Christian primitivists with claims like the rest to new revelation and special authority. For those in the Hurlbut-Howe tradition it was fraudulent—developed by a facile, creative, but unscrupulous mind, and in part the creation of Sidney Rigdon or Parley P. Pratt."[10]

An exception to this general trend was Jules Remy and Julius Brenchley, *A Journey to the Great Salt Lake City, with a Sketch of the History, Religion, and Customs of the Mormons*, 2 vols. (London: W. Jeffs, 1861). Eschewing a crude environmental approach, these travelers conceded the originality and genius of Joseph Smith's eclectic brand of Christianity. Twelve years later, Mormon apostate T. B. H. Stenhouse likewise combined culture and spirituality in his *The Rocky Mountain Saints: A Full and Complete History of the Mormons, from the First Vision of Joseph Smith to the Last Courtship of Brigham Young* (New York: D. Appleton & Co., 1873). His perspective persisted even in Riley's psychological study of 1902. Also in 1902 appeared William A. Linn's immensely popular *The Story of the Mormons: From the Date of Their Origin to the Year 1901* (New York: Macmillan, 1902). Though well-written and entertaining, it was a facile pastiche, repeating old clichés and even infusing the Spaulding theory with new life, until Fawn Brodie finally gave it the coup de grace in *No Man Knows My History*.

In the seven decades between Campbell's charges and the 1902 productions by Riley and Linn, Mormonism had acquired a thoroughly un-American image as a result of practices not even hinted at in Campbell's catalogue—a theocratic kingdom of God, plural marriage, and a program of economic self-sufficiency and cooperation. These practices had evolved from embryonic stages in Kirtland and Independence to experimentation in Nauvoo until they flourished in the Mormon kingdom in the Rocky Mountains. An anti-Mormon crusade lasting more than two generations produced a mountain of literature branding Mormons as religious and cultural outcasts who had more in common with Islamic beliefs and practices than with the values of North American society—a comparison intended to be entirely pejorative: both Mormonism and Islam were autocratic and despotic, as well as sensual and promiscuous.[11] However, a number of legitimate orientalists familiar with Islam, such as Richard F. Burton and German scholar Eduard Meyer,

---

7. For an excellent modern overview of this topic, see Dan Vogel, *Indian Origins and the Book of Mormon* (Salt Lake City: Signature Books, 1986).
8. Alexander, "The Place of Joseph Smith," 5.
9. Bushman, *Joseph Smith and the Beginnings of Mormonism*, 192.
10. Alexander, "The Place of Joseph Smith," 5.
11. See, for example, Jennie Fowler Willing, *Mormonism: The Mohammedanism of the West* (Louisville, KY: Picket Publishing, 1906); and Bruce Kinney, *Mormonism: The Islam of America* (New York: Revell, 1912); Arnold H. Green and Lawrence Goldrup, "Joseph Smith, an American Muhammad?: An Essay on the Perils

made comparisons between the two religions and cultures that cannot be dismissed as being motivated by anti-Mormon animus. Meyer saw significant cultural similarities between the historical development and the social conditions of nineteenth-century frontier America and seventh-century Arabia, both resulting in the birth of prophetic leaders and new religions.[12] Meyer wrote his book based on research he conducted as a visiting professor in the United States in 1911 at a time when Frederick Jackson Turner's frontier hypothesis had become the reigning paradigm of academic American historians. However, if Meyer encountered Turner's writing, he did not mention it.

At about the same time, a generation of young Mormons were taking opportunities for graduate education in major eastern, midwestern, and western universities, where they were exposed to Turner's frontier hypothesis. For example, Andrew L. Neff, working on his Ph.D. in American history at Berkeley, wrote to his former BYU teacher George Brimhall that he saw Mormonism as participating in a great westering pageant of American history.[13] To him, as well as several of his contemporaries, the Turner hypothesis in fact provided a ready-made vehicle for the Americanization (or perhaps better, re-Americanization) of Mormon history. Neff's *History of Utah, 1847-1869*, edited by Leland H. Creer (Salt Lake City: Deseret News Press, 1940), Creer's own *The Founding of an Empire: The Exploration and Colonization of Utah, 1776-1856* (Salt Lake City: Bookcraft, 1947), and Levi Edgar Young, *The Founding of Utah* (New York: Scribner's, 1923), were all in this tradition. Significantly, all of these works incorporated the story of the Mormons in the secular framework of Utah history. Only Dean D. McBrien's unpublished doctoral dissertation, "The Influence of the Frontier on Joseph Smith" (George Washington University, 1929) pursued a more religious theme. Thomas Weldon's M.A. thesis, "The Turner Thesis and the Mormon Frontier" (Stetson University, 1964), appeared late enough that academic fashion was turning against the frontier hypothesis.

Although it is doubtful that these works were responsible for rehabilitating Mormonism, they unquestionably reflected a changing *zeitgeist* that accepted Mormons as respectable Americans.[14] Historiographically, this change in image was accompanied by a shift in emphasis from the visionary (and perhaps un-American) Joseph Smith to the practical frontiersman and colonizer Brigham Young, the "American Moses." Even the vitriolic Bernard DeVoto, who all but loathed Joseph

---

of Historical Analogy," *Dialogue* 6 (Spring 1971): 46-58. For a discussion of anti-Mormon literature, see Terryl L. Givens, *The Viper on the Hearth: Mormons, Myths, and the Construction of Heresy* (New York: Oxford University Press, 1997), and Leonard J. Arrington and Jon Haupt, "Intolerable Zion: The Image of Mormonism in Nineteenth-Century American Literature," *Western Humanities Review* 22 (Summer 1968): 243-60.

12. Richard Francis Burton, *The City of the Saints and Across the Rocky Mountains for California*, edited by Fawn M. Brodie (1861; reprint ed., New York: Alfred Knopf, 1963), 428. *Ursprung und Geschichte der Mormonen . . .* (Halle, Germany: Max Niemeyer, 1912); translated by Heinz F. Rahde and Eugene Seaich as *The Origins and History of the Mormons with Reflections on the Beginnings of Islam and Christianity* (Salt Lake City: University of Utah, 1961), esp. i-ix, 44-56. For an interesting and informative discussion, see Arnold H. Green, "The Muhammad-Joseph Smith Comparison: Subjective Metaphor or a Sociology of Prophethood," in *Mormons and Muslims: Spiritual Foundations and Modern Manifestations*, edited by Spencer Palmer (Provo, UT: BYU Religious Studies Center, 1983), 63-84.

13. Neff, Letter to Brimhall, April 1, 1906, George H. Brimhall Papers, L. Tom Perry Special Collections, Lee Library, Brigham Young University, Provo, Utah.

14 See Jan Shipps, "From Satyr to Saint: American Attitudes toward the Mormons, 1860-1960," paper presented at the annual meeting of the Organization of American Historians, Chicago, 1973; published in her Sojourner in the Promised Land (Urbana: University of Illinois Press, 2000), 51-97.

The Burned-over District

THE SOCIAL AND INTELLECTUAL HISTORY

OF ENTHUSIASTIC RELIGION IN

WESTERN NEW YORK, 1800-1850

BY WHITNEY R. CROSS

West Virginia University

Cornell University Press

ITHACA, NEW YORK, 1950

Excavating Mormon Pasts

Smith to his dying day, managed to express grudging admiration for Brigham in his sweeping saga of *The Year of Decision: 1846* (Boston: Little, Brown, 1943). Alice Felt Tylor, *Freedom's Ferment: Phases of American Social History to 1860* (Minneapolis: University of Minnesota Press, 1944), 96, depicted Joseph Smith condescendingly but made Brigham Young the frontier thesis centerpiece of her breezy narrative: "Only the American backwoods in the mid-nineteenth century could have produced such a conglomeration" of "miracles, visions, the gift of tongues, and . . . 'a queer hodgepodge of Campbellite dogma, perfectionism, paganism, and Oriental philosophy, with a strong admixture of sex'" (96). The theme of Young as westering American, which had been first introduced in M. R. Werner's *Brigham Young* (New York: Harcourt, Brace, & Co., 1925), also characterized secular Mormon Ray B. West, *Kingdom of the Saints: The Story of Brigham Young and the Mormons* (New York: Viking Press, 1957), Leonard J. Arrington's magisterial *Brigham Young: American Moses* (New York: Alfred A. Knopf, 1985), as well as Newell Bringhurst's *Brigham Young and the Expanding American Frontier* (Boston: Little, Brown, 1986).

Fawn M. Brodie's influential *No Man Knows My History*, published in 1945, was less an exception to this trend than the transformation of the founder of Mormonism from a visionary, mystic, and dreamer into an American prophet—a man of both imagination and action who, having absorbed the cultural milieu of his environment translated it into a syncretic religion with a powerful appeal to the disinherited and disaffected. Brodie's environmental assumptions were shared by her friend and mentor Dale Morgan, who aspired to write a grandly conceived history of Mormonism from a "primarily sociological viewpoint."[15] He never completed this work, although seven heavily annotated chapters, including an appendix of important sources (such as Smith's 1826 Bainbridge trial) were published in 1986, fifteen years after Morgan's death. Unfamiliar with Morgan's ambitions, it was Thomas F. O'Dea who completed a respected study of Mormonism, *The Mormons* (Chicago: University of Chicago Press, 1957). Taking a sociological, environmental perspective, O'Dea recognized, more seriously than Alexander Campbell, the importance of the Book of Mormon for understanding Joseph Smith's religious thought. While Brodie, Morgan, O'Dea, and their contemporaries did not structure their works self-consciously along Turnerite assumptions, their environmental framework explicitly recognized the importance of frontier conditions in explaining the rise of Mormonism.

Yet even before a new generation of historians began to question American exceptionalism, and with it both the Turnerian and liberal paradigms of American history, scholars began to have second thoughts on the symbiosis of religion and the frontier. Analyzing this complex relationship theme had been the lifelong enterprise of William Warren Sweet who, more than any other scholar, had "Turnerized" American religion.[16] Ironically, S.

---

15. Morgan, Letter to Fawn Brodie, in Walker, *Dale Morgan on Early Mormonism*, 16.

16. Sweet was a prodigious scholar who produced numerous volumes of major denominations on the American frontier. The summation of his scholarly labors can be found in *The Story of Religions in America* (New York: Holt, 1930). No doubt the Mormon fellow-Turnerites who encountered his judgment of their religion would have been discomfited: "Many of these strange religious movements were the unhealthy offspring of the revivals of the thirties, forties and fifties. But along with the rise of Mormonism, Adventism, Perfectionism and all the other 'isms,' the great Protestant churches were adding tens of thousands of *sane* Christians to their membership" (411; emphasis mine).

George Ellsworth, a graduate student at the University of California, which produced a significant number of Mormon Turnerites, was the first of a postwar generation of Mormon historians to raise questions about Mormonism as a frontier religion in his doctoral dissertation "A History of Mormon Missions in the United States and Canada, 1830-1860" (1951). At almost the same time, Whitney R. Cross, *The Burned-Over District: The Social and Intellectual History of Enthusiastic Religion in Western New York, 1800-1850* (Ithaca, NY: Cornell University Press, 1950), likewise attempted to refute the concept of Mormonism as a frontier religion. The rural New Englanders who had settled western New York had brought their social and cultural baggage with them. Schools and churches served a literate community. Palmyra even had a library. The region was in the early days of the market revolution, benefitting from the newly opened Erie Canal. Though a more youthful community, it was "less isolated and provincial, more vigorous and cosmopolitan, than Vermont," asserts Cross (140). Such traits did not necessarily make the Mormons any less American. However, David Brion Davis, at the time a graduate student at Yale, argued in his much-discussed "The New England Origins of Mormonism," *New England Quarterly* 26 (1953): 147-68, for a reconsideration of Mormon origins. Employing an implicitly anti-Turnerian paradigm, he proposed that Mormonism, far from being a frontier manifestation, "ran against the main stream of American thought" by representing an "anachronistic residue of seventeenth century New England."

Taking issue with both of these approaches, Mario S. De Pillis, while no disciple of Turner, published two articles: "The Quest for Religious Authority and the Rise of Mormonism," *Dialogue* 1 (Spring 1966): 68-88; "The Social Sources of Mormonism," *Church History* 37 (1968): 50-79. In them he argued that western New York was indeed a frontier of New England and thought that Whitney Cross was wrong to emphasize the peculiarities of Mormonism and to link them to the cultural environment of the time. Challenging Davis, he averred that many of the new ideas had their origins in the "west," not New England. What made the new religion unique was the doctrine of priesthood authority—providing a powerful appeal, an anchor for Americans bemused and disoriented in a modernizing world. Another attempt to refute Cross about the same time is Alexander Evanoff, "The Turner Thesis and Mormon Beginnings in New York and Utah," *Utah Historical Quarterly* 30 (Spring 1965): 157-73.

In the 1960s and 1970s when running against the mainstream became respectably American, labeling the Mormons as dissenters or as representative of a counterculture no longer put them beyond the pale. Robert Flanders was the first to do so, arguing in "To Transform History: Early Mormon Culture and the Concept of Time and Space," *Church History* 40 (March 1971): 109, that Mormonism represented "an alternative view of American history and an alternative way for Americans." I went further in my "Mormonism and American Culture: Some Tentative Hypotheses," in *The Restoration Movement: Essays in Mormon History*, edited by F. Mark McKiernan, Alma Blair, and Paul M. Edwards (Lawrence, Kans.: Coronado Press, 1973): 1-25, suggesting "that the suspicion of nineteenth-century Americans that Mormonism posed an internal threat to the established order had a basis in fact." I thus challenged David Brion Davis, "Some Themes of Counter-Subversion: An Analysis of Anti-Masonic, Anti-Catholic, and Anti-Mormon Literature," *Mississippi Valley Historical Review* 47 (September 1960): 205-24, which attempted

Excavating Mormon Pasts

to explain anti-Mormonism as an expression of countersubversive paranoia. In 1987, D. Michael Quinn made perhaps the strongest argument for Mormon radicalism in "Socioreligious Radicalism of the Mormon Church: A Parallel to the Anabaptists," in *New Views of Mormon History: Essays in Honor of Leonard J. Arrington,* edited by Davis Bitton and Maureen Ursenbach Beecher (Salt Lake City: University of Utah Press, 1987), 363-86.

Providing evidence for this interpretation of Mormonism as deliberately in conflict with Americanism was a rediscovered secret organization, the Council of Fifty, which Joseph Smith set up as the governing body for an embryonic Mormon theocratic state. It had been hinted at in works as diverse as Brodie's *No Man Knows My History* (356-66), O'Dea's *The Mormons* (166-67), and G. Homer Durham, "A Political Interpretation of Mormon History," *Pacific Historical Review* 12 (1944): 136-50. Although Hyrum Andrus, *Joseph Smith and World Government* (Salt Lake City: Deseret Book, 1958), was the first book-length treatment on the Council of Fifty, it deemphasized conflict, characterizing the council as the millennial projection of a theocratic world government. In 1960, I presented an alternative interpretation in "The Political Kingdom of God as a Cause for Mormon-Gentile Conflict," *BYU Studies* 2 (1960): 241-60, then explored the theme further in *The Political Kingdom of God and the Council of Fifty in Mormon History* (East Lansing: Michigan State University Press, 1967). As expected, such a controversial interpretation did not remain unchallenged. It met its most visible critique in Marvin S. Hill, *Quest for Refuge: The Mormon Flight from American Pluralism* (Salt Lake City: Signature Books, 1989). Hill summarized the difference between his *Quest for Refuge* and Hansen's *Quest for Empire* as follows: "It may be that the Mormon quest for political power came not from a rising estimation of man's capabilities to usher in his own millennium, as Hansen supposed, but rather from a terrible fear that the people could not govern themselves without divine direction" (xvi). The disagreements between Hansen and Hill were, however, secondary to their fundamental agreement on the this-worldly significance of the theocratic kingdom as a major expression of the anti-pluralistic nature of Mormonism. In 1980 D. Michael Quinn published "The Council of Fifty and Its Members, 1844-1945," *BYU Studies* 20 (Winter 1980): 163-97, and Andrew E. Ehat published "'It Seems Like Heaven Began on Earth': Joseph Smith and the Constitution of the Kingdom of God," *BYU Studies* 20 (Spring 1980): 253-79. Both articles revived Andrus's position, with Quinn taking essentially the same position in his later *The Mormon Hierarchy: Origins of Power* (Salt Lake City: Signature Books, 1994), 105-42.

Economic experiments and polygamy were other cornerstones of the conflict interpretation—though these were no less controversial and were likewise incorporated into the American mainstream by advocates of cultural consensus. A number of important studies assumed a mediating position, such as Leonard J. Arrington, Feramorz Fox, and Dean L. May, *Building the City of God: Community and Cooperation Among the Mormons* (Salt Lake City: Deseret Book, 1976), which followed essentially Leonard J. Arrington's landmark work on the Brigham Young era, *Great Basin Kingdom: An Economic History of the Latter-day Saints, 1830-1900* (1958; reprint ed., Lincoln: University of Nebraska Press, 1966). Two original and imaginative works on plural marriage—Lawrence Foster, comparative *Religion and Sexuality: Three American Communal Experiments of the Nineteenth Century* (New York: Oxford University Press, 1981), and B. Carmon Hardy, *Solemn Covenant: The Mormon Polygamous Passage* (Urbana: University of Illinois Press, 1992), saw Mormon sexual norms

QUEST FOR EMPIRE

The Political Kingdom of God and the Council of Fifty in Mormon History

By Klaus J. Hansen

MICHIGAN STATE UNIVERSITY PRESS
1970

as less antagonistic to Victorian American values than anti-polygamy crusaders did. But at this point, thematic consistency has pushed chronology ahead of the story.

In the mid-seventies, when conflict had replaced consensus as the reigning frame of reference in American college classrooms, David Brion Davis popularized the newly fashionable paradigm in a widely disseminated American history text, *The Great Republic: A History of the American People,* with Bernard Bailyn, David Herbert Donald, John L. Thomas, Robert H. Wiebe, and Gordon S. Wood (Lexington, MA: D. C. Heath, 1977), 386-91, in which he applied the Mormons as a test case to the limits of dissent. His chapter on "Dissent, Protest, and Reform" was, in fact, the most extensive treatment of Mormonism in any general American history textbook. In keeping with the temper of the times, this approach significantly shortened the distance between dissenters and the mainstream. R. Laurence Moore pushed this line of reasoning even further in his intriguing chapter on the Mormons in *Religious Outsiders and the Making of Americans* (New York: Oxford University Press, 1986), in which he argued that "outsiders" were in fact a quintessentially American phenomenon. He thus placed Mormonism at the very center of the making of modern America.

I had been suitably cautious in titling my 1973 essay "Mormonism and American Culture: Some Tentative Hypotheses." In 1981, I moved to a more nuanced interpretation in my *Mormonism and the American Experience* (Chicago: University of Chicago Press, 1981), which was part of Martin Marty's HISTORY OF AMERICAN RELIGION series. I argued that, if Mormons were dissenters from what became the dominant cultural norm of competitive individualism, they could not for that reason be labeled "un-American" because the conflicting claims of antebellum Americans to define the meaning of America were far from settled (51-54). Even if evangelicals supported an emerging pluralism, numerous groups opposed this trend. As Marvin Hill has argued in *Quest for Refuge,* Mormons were among those most determined to resist the pluralist tide because they were among those most alienated from the emerging modern, competitive order of society. My student Gordon Douglas Pollock took issue both with me and with Hill in *Northern Voices: A Folk History of Mormonism Among British Americans, 1830-1867* (Halifax, Nova Scotia: Kelso Associates, 1995). He marshalled evidence to show that British American converts, at least, were ordinary folk buying into the American dream, a revisionist interpretation too recent to have influenced the literature discussed below.

According to Charles Sellers, *The Market Revolution: Jacksonian America, 1815-1867* (New York: Oxford University Press, 1991), and Paul E. Johnson, *A Shopkeeper's Millennium: Society and Revivals in Rochester, New York, 1815-1837* (New York: Hill & Wang, 1978), the struggle lay between evangelicals who supported the market revolution and anti-evangelicals who opposed it, even as in political culture the division was between Democrats and Whigs. Sellers and Johnson equated the Finneyites with the winning middle class, while Mormons and eccentric radicals like the Prophet Matthias were losers in the market.[17] However, by calling the struggle a *Kulturkampf,* Sellers imposed a manichean dichotomy on a conflict that requires a less polarized interpretation, one without the advantage of hindsight. Steven C. Harper, "Missionaries in the American Religious Marketplace: Mormon Proselyting in the 1830s," *Journal of Mormon History* 24, no. 2 (Fall 1998): 1-29, is an insight-

---

17. Paul E. Johnson and Sean Wilentz, *The Kingdom of Matthias* (New York: Oxford University Press, 1994).

Mormonism and the American Experience

Klaus J. Hansen

The University of Chicago Press   Chicago and London

ful appraisal of Mormonism's success in its first decade. As for the relationship of Mormonism to the market revolution in its formative period, our understanding is still quite limited.

An important contribution toward understanding the relationship between economic factors and religion is the revisionist work by Marvin S. Hill, C. Keith Rooker, and Larry T. Wimmer, "The Kirtland Economy Revisited: A Market Critique of Sectarian Economics," *BYU Studies* 17 (1977): 391-475, demonstrating that the economic debacle was not nearly as serious as critics have argued. They also corrected the view that the crisis was the result of the Panic of 1837 and attributed it more to external causes. Peter Temin, *The Jacksonian Economy* (New York: W. W. Norton, 1969), concurs with the larger point that the Panic of 1837 was caused not by Andrew Jackson's economic policies but by major stresses in the world market.

Because the nature of evangelical culture is itself contested ground, sorting out the relationship of Mormonism with its opponents is no easy task. Robert Baird may well have been the first to set up this dichotomy in his influential *Religion in America: Or, an Account of the Origin, Relation to the State, and Present Condition of the Evangelical Churches in the United States* (1844; reprint ed., New York, 1856). R. Laurence Moore quotes Baird in his *Religious Outsiders and the Making of Americans,* 5-6, noting that Baird divided the American churches of his day into evangelical and non-evangelical. In the latter were Mormons, along with Catholics, Unitarians, Universalists, Jews, Swedenborgians, Shakers, atheists, deists, and socialists, whom he located "at the fringes of American respectability." He heaped special scorn on the Mormons: "The annals of modern times furnish few more remarkable examples of cunning leaders, and delusions in their dupes, than are presented by what is called Mormonism." Still, if Baird had little respect for Mormons, he had included them in an important cultural dialogue that has persisted to this day.

The most serious recent attempt to position Mormonism in relation to evangelical matrix of antebellum America is Clyde R. Forsberg Jr., "In Search of the Historical Nephi: The Book of Mormon, 'Evangelicalism' and Antebellum American Popular Culture c. 1830" (Ph.D. diss., Queen's University, Ontario, 1994). I discuss its published revision in the "Postscript." He argues convincingly that the new religion was very much at odds with the evangelical mainstream. In a perceptive analysis of the Book of Mormon that includes original interpretations of race and class, it is particularly through gender that he identifies cultural issues separating Mormons and evangelicals. Johnson and Wilentz, *The Kingdom of Matthias,* also place gender at the center of their analysis of relationship between Mormonism and evangelicalism, though much more superficially.

That is not to say, however, that the conflict interpretation has swept all before it. A significant article was Gordon Wood, "Evangelical America and Early Mormonism," *New York History* 61 (October 1980): 351-86, delivered as one of the inaugural Tanner lectures at the Mormon History Association's annual meeting in Canandaigua, New York, in 1980, Mormonism's sesquicentennial year. Wood saw early Mormonism responding to the fears and anxieties besetting the post-Revolution early Republic in a fashion not unlike that of its evangelical contemporaries. Even as "evangelical Christianity and the democracy of these years . . . emerged together and were interrelated," Mormons were no strangers to such events. Inspired by Wood, Mark Thomas, "The Meaning of Revival Language in the Book of Mormon," *Sunstone* 8 (May/June 1983): 19-25, sees important connections

THE MORMONS

By

Thomas F. O'Dea

THE UNIVERSITY OF CHICAGO PRESS

between the contemporary revivals and the Book of Mormon. Also taking his cue in part from Wood, Nathan Hatch included Mormonism in that broad cultural religious movement from the bottom up that he called *The Democratization of American Christianity* (New Haven, CT: Yale University Press, 1989). Harking back to Wood's republican theme, Kenneth H. Winn, *Exiles in a Land of Liberty: Mormons in America, 1830-1846* (Chapel Hill: University of North Carolina Press, 1986), argues that the acrimonious conflict between Mormons and their adversaries resulted less from opposing world views than from competing interpretations of shared republican values.

Like Gordon Wood, Timothy Smith, who also delivered one of the two Tanner lectures in 1980, adopted a consensus approach. In "The Book of Mormon in a Biblical Culture," *Journal of Mormon History* 7 (1980): 3-21, he argued that Mormonism's deep-seated biblicism made it more alike than different from Protestants. More complex is Philip L. Barlow, whose intensive study *Mormons and the Bible: The Place of the Latter-day Saints in American Religion* (New York: Oxford University Press, 1991), links the Saints "sometimes with Catholics, sometimes with Jews, sometimes with more exotic groups like the Jehovah's Witnesses, and sometimes with others of the world's religions." He "links them often with evangelical Protestants," although he also sees "enduring differences" (228). Yet he also makes the point that "compared to the Bible," early Mormons used the Book of Mormon "surprisingly little" (44). A work with an implicit subtext of Mormon apologia is Grant Underwood, *The Millenarian World of Early Mormonism* (Urbana: University of Illinois Press, 1993), and his "Re-Visioning Mormon History," *Pacific Historical Review* 55 (1986): 403-26. Underwood regards neither theocracy nor polygamy as examples of radical cultural differences but insists that the Mormons always remained part of the dominant culture yet simultaneously sees Mormonism as essentially *sui generis,* propositions that may well appear contradictory.

If such viewpoints are more than academic, it is because Mormonism, having evolved significantly in its relation to American culture over the 180 years sees its history as mediating between the present and the future. To this end, consensus is more congenial than conflict as a historical model. Central to the debate is the question of historical continuity. Numerous commentators, from both the conflict and consensus schools, agree that modern Mormonism has indeed much in common with evangelical Protestantism. However, they do part company over the question of whether it has always been thus. For example, are the McLellin journals representative of early Mormonism, or does the contemporary emphasis on their importance represent a historical distortion?[18]

It follows logically that the conflict historians argue that Mormonism is increasingly accommodating itself to the modern world. One of the earliest scholars to use this framework was sociologist Ephraim E. Ericksen, *The Psychological and Ethical Aspects of Mormon Group Life* (Chicago: University of Chicago Press, 1922), in which he couched accommodation in terms of withdrawal and return. O'Dea developed a similar perspective extensively in his influential *The Mormons*. The theme of accommodation is also evident in the comprehensive and objective James B. Allen and Glen M. Leonard, *The Story of the Latter-day Saints* (1976; 2d ed. rev., Salt Lake City: Deseret Book, 1992), written with a Mormon audience in mind. The same theme informs the well-written standard history for

---

18. *The Journals of William E. McLellin, 1831-1836,* edited by Jan Shipps and John W. Welch (Urbana/Provo, UT: University of Illinois Press/BYU Studies, 1994).

the general public by Leonard J. Arrington and Davis Bitton, *The Mormon Experience: A History of the Latter-day Saints* (New York: Alfred A. Knopf, 1978).

For a more detailed and nuanced treatment of the theme, serious students should turn to two superb works by Thomas G. Alexander, *Mormonism in Transition: A History of the Latter-day Saints, 1890-1930* (Urbana: University of Illinois Press, 1986), and *Things in Heaven and Earth: The Life and Times of Wilford Woodruff, a Mormon Prophet* (Salt Lake City: Signature Books, 1991). Other important examinations by Alexander are his "'To Maintain Harmony': Adjusting to External and Internal Stress, 1890-1930," *Dialogue* 15 (Winter 1982): 44-58, and his "The Reconstruction of Mormon Theology: From Joseph Smith to Progressive Theology," *Sunstone* 5 (July-August 1980): 24-33.

In the opinion of some scholars, the trend toward accommodation has accelerated in the post World War II period. According to O. Kendall White Jr., *Mormon Neo-Orthodoxy: A Crisis Theology* (Salt Lake City: Signature Books, 1987), "a quest for respectability, the pursuit of converts, and expansion of Mormonism throughout the world tempt contemporary Mormons, especially officials, to present Mormonism as mainline Christianity" (174-75). Supporting evidence for this assertion comes from the work of Gordon and Gary Shepherd, who have documented an increasing emphasis on "Christian" themes in LDS general conference talks by Church authorities in their *A Kingdom Transformed: Themes in the Development of Mormon* (Salt Lake City: University of Utah Press, 1984), and "Mormonism in Secular Society: Changing Patterns in Official Ecclesiastical Rhetoric," *Review of Religious Research* 26 (September 1984): 28-41.

This trend has led to some ironic developments, including the "neo-orthodox" backlash that White documents as well as a concerted movement among a loose coalition of conservative Protestants and former Mormons to charge that the "Christianization" of Mormonism is only a deceptive veneer to hide the "true" nature of a religion that is the very essence of anti-Christ.[19] However, Mormon sociologist Armand Mauss has issued a demurrer in *The Angel and the Beehive: The Mormon Struggle with Assimilation* (Urbana: University of Illinois Press, 1994), arguing that he has detected a retreat from accommodation to the Protestant mainstream and a return to traditional Mormon values, although this reaction against assimilation clearly does not entail a revival of polygamy, the political kingdom, or communitarian experiments. Other studies of resistance to or retreat from assimilation are Mario S. De Pillis, "The Persistence of Mormon Community into the 1990s," *Sunstone* 15 (October 1991): 28-49, and Larry M. Logue, "Modernization Arrested: Child-Naming and the Family in a Utah Town," *Journal of American History* 74 (1987): 131-38.

Indeed, whether it is, in fact, Mormonism's conspicuous departures from national norms characteristic of the nineteenth century that made Mormonism distinctive, "a peculiar people," is a matter of considerable debate. Some scholars argue that what has made Mormons distinctive—as a people, a subculture, even an ethnic group (and there is no agreement on the definition) is less a matter of theology or ideology than of historical, social, or geographic experience.[20] Mormonism, at least in the American West, has assumed

---

19. See especially ex-Mormons Jerald and Sandra Tanner, *The Changing World of Mormonism* (Chicago: Moody Press, 1980); and Ed Decker and Dave Hunt, *The God Makers* (Eugene, OR: Harvest House, 1984). Decker made his exposé into two motion picture/videos that circulated widely in fundamentalist Christian circles. For a perceptive analysis, see Massimo Introvigne, "The Devil Makers: Contemporary Evangelical Fundamentalist Anti-Mormonism," *Dialogue* 27 (Spring 1994): 153-69.

20. See, for example, Dean L. May, "A Demographic Portrait of the Mormons, 1830-1980," in *After 150 Years: The Latter-day Saints in Sesquicentennial Perspective*, edited by Thomas G. Alexander and Jessie L. Embry

Excavating Mormon Pasts

a regional identity that is analogous, in its idiosyncratic way, to the American South.[21] Some representative works, approaching this topic from various perspectives, are Nels Anderson, *Desert Saints: The Mormon Frontier in Utah* (Chicago: University of Chicago Press, 1942); Edward A. Geary, "For the Strength of the Hills: Imagining Mormon Country," in *After 150 Years: The Latter-day Saints in Sesquicentennial Perspective,* edited by Thomas G. Alexander and Jessie Embry (Provo, UT: Charles Redd Center for Western Studies, 1983), 73-94; Mark Leone, *Roots of Modern Mormonism* (Cambridge, MA: Harvard University Press, 1979); Larry M. Logue, *A Sermon in the Desert: Belief and Behavior in Early St. George* (Urbana: University of Illinois Press, 1988); Dean L. May, *Three Frontiers: Family, Land, and Society in the American West, 1850-1900* (New York: Cambridge University Press, 1994), which discusses Alpine, Utah, as one of the three (185-243); Donald W. Meinig, "The Mormon Culture Region: Strategies and Patterns in the Geography of the American West, 1847-1964," *Annals of the Association of American Geographers* 55 (June 1965): 191-220; and Charles S. Peterson, *"Take Up Your Mission": Mormon Colonizing Along the Little Colorado River, 1870-1900* (Provo, UT: Brigham Young University Press, 1973).

In Peterson's "A Mormon Town: One Man's West," *Journal of Mormon History* 3 (1976): 3-12, his presidential address to the Mormon History Association in 1975, he asserted that the Mormon village pattern of settlement represented isolation from the larger world and allowed—even encouraged—the creation and maintenance of a Mormon identity that was less influenced by the forces of modernization than in the ecclesiastical center of Salt Lake City. Thus, the Mormon village culture at the periphery—in Cache Valley or in southern Utah—became the quintessential Mormon heartland characterized by a social type Dean May has called the "Deseret Mormon" in his *Three Frontiers* (185-243). Formation of culture was less a top-down process directed by ecclesiastical superiors than an indigenous development of local custom dictated by local needs in a local environment—though monitored by the hierarchy in Salt Lake City.

This shift in emphasis and focus also signaled a dissatisfaction with the bi-polar sociological assumptions of much of the twentieth-century literature on Mormonism and American culture: traditional and modern, sect and church, *Gemeinschaft* and *Gesellschaft,* contentment and anomie. These polarized positions were heavily influenced by the important works of Max Weber, Emile Durkheim, Rudolf Toennies, and Ernst Troeltsch, as well as some of their American descendants, including H. Richard Niebuhr and Talcott Parsons. Larry Logue, for example, quotes Robert R. Dykstra and William Silog in calling for an "eclectic empiricism" and content with lower-order generalizations."[22]

In spite of the great diversity in interpretations discussed thus far it could be argued that most of them conform to William Mulder's graphic image that Mormonism was "as native to the United States as Indian corn and the buffalo nickel."[23] Paradoxically,

---

(Provo, UT: Charles Redd Center for Western Studies), 65, and his "Mormons," *Harvard Encyclopedia of American Ethnic Groups,* edited by Stephen Thernstrom (Cambridge, MA: Harvard University Press): 720-31.
    21. Some representative works on Southern history and culture are W. J. Cash, *The Mind of the South* (New York: Alfred A. Knopf, 1941); C. Vann Woodward, *The Burden of Southern History* (Baton Rouge: Louisiana State University Press, 1960); William R. Taylor, *Cavalier and Yankee: The Old South and American National Character* (New York: George Braziller, 1961); Carl Degler, *Place over Time: The Continuity of Southern Distinctiveness* (Baton Rouge: Louisiana State University Press, 1977); Bertram Wyatt-Brown, *Southern Honor: Ethics and Behavior in the Old South* (New York: Oxford University Press, 1982).
    22. Logue, *A Sermon in the Desert,* xii.
    23. Mulder, *The Mormons in American History* (Salt Lake City: University of Utah Reynolds Lecture, 1957).

it was Mulder who also wrote *Homeward to Zion: The Mormon Migration from Scandinavia* (Minneapolis: University of Minnesota Press, 1957), a superior study of Mormon immigration from Scandinavia as part of a dramatic saga that had, by 1900, brought some ninety thousand converts to the Mormon Zion from Britain and western and northern Europe. Nevertheless, in spite of the high percentage of European immigrants, Dean May has argued that the "social, cultural, and religious norms were set by . . . [the] American elite . . . . Most immigrants came to Zion with a heart prepared—eager to abandon Babylon and to learn from those having priesthood authority and status within the Mormon kingdom."[24] Lowry Nelson pointed out early that Utah immigrants adopted English as their primary language more readily than immigrants to other states—such as Minnesota, implying that the Mormon kingdom served as a more effective melting pot than other regions of the United States.[25] However, an important exception to this generalization is the Godbeite movement of the late 1860s and early 1870s, led by a group of British intellectuals who challenged Brigham Young's theocratic leadership in what they regarded as areas of personal choice. As Ronald W. Walker has argued, cultural differences played a major role in the conflict.[26]

At this point it may be appropriate to reflect on an important distinction between the origins of Mormonism and the cultural influences that impinged on the new religion. As a historiographical problem, interpretations of how Mormons responded to their environment are inextricably connected to interpretations of Mormon origins and do not fall into place in predictable or easily recognizable patterns. Sorting out these complexities clearly requires another essay. In spite of the multiplicity of interpretations discussed so far, they all appear to refer to one monolithic entity—Mormonism—when in fact the Mormon religion is a conglomerate of numerous sects.[27] It is only because of space limitations that I have concentrated in this essay on the Church of Jesus Christ of Latter-day Saints headquartered in Salt Lake City, but it is important to acknowledge that Mormonism before 1844 was the source of many other religious groups, most prominent among them the Community of Christ (formerly Reorganized Church of Jesus Christ of Latter Day Saints) headquartered in Independence. I regret that space precludes a discussion of the cultural accommodation of these other groups to larger American society. However, it is important to recognize the argument made by Jan Shipps that, while both movements differ from traditional Christianity, the Community of Christ "is primarily a movement of reformation rather than radical restoration," as is the Utah church. "The RLDS church embraces a theology and practice much closer to traditional Christianity."[28] In addition to doctrinal and familial reasons for the split, I believe that differences rooted in diverging responses to the American cultural environment also played a major role in the schism. At the risk of oversimplification, I argue that, on balance, those alienated from American pluralism were more

---

24. May, "Demographic Portrait," 64.
25. Quoted in Mulder, *Homeward to Zion,* 346, n. 3.
26. Ronald G. Walker, *Wayward Saints: The Godbeites and Brigham Young* (Urbana: University of Illinois Press, 1997).
27. See Dale Morgan's essay on the "Churches of the Dispersion" Coe Collection, Beineke Library, Yale University; Robert Bruce Flanders, *Nauvoo: Kingdom on the Mississippi* (Urbana: University of Illinois Press, 1965), v-vi, and Danny L. Jorgensen, "Studies of Mormon Fissiparousness: Conflict, Dissent, and Schism in the Early Church," in this volume.
28. Shipps, *Mormonism: The Story of a New Religious Tradition* (Urbana: University of Illinois Press, 1985), xiv, 192.

likely to join Brigham Young in the exodus to the Rocky Mountains, while those comfortable with an emerging Protestant evangelical culture were more likely to remain behind.[29]

The story of assimilation is thus more the story of the Utah church than of its cousins in Independence. So is the problem of Mormonism as a world religion. Having reinvented itself as a conservative Christian peace church, beginning in the 1960s, the Community of Christ blends well into the Protestant missionary tradition, with its respect for and accommodation to local cultures. Clearly, the Community of Christ faces less of a cultural conundrum than the Utah church. How to export Independence culture, certainly, is less of a cultural conundrum than that faced by the expansion of the Utah church. Among documents along the path of international culture and acculturation of Utah Mormonism are F. LaMond Tullis, *Mormonism: A Faith for All Cultures* (Provo, UT: Brigham Young University Press, 1978); Spencer J. Palmer, ed., *Mormons and Muslims: Spiritual Foundations and Modern Manifestations* (Provo, UT: Brigham Young University, Religious Studies Center, 1983); and Steven Epperson, *Mormons and Jews* (Salt Lake City: Signature Books, 1992). A thoughtful discussion is James B. Allen, "On Becoming a Universal Church," *Dialogue* 25, no. 1 (Spring 1992): 13-36. Armand L. Mauss, "The Mormon Struggle with Assimilation and Identity: Trends and Developments since Mid-Century," *Dialogue* 27 (Spring 1994): 148-49, argues that, if Mormonism is to become a world religion, it must be purged of its American peculiarities and "become a minimal Mormonism; that is, a religion which can jettison all forms of American influence and reduce its message and its way of life to a small number of basic ideas and principles." Of course, such a trend would have major implications for Mormon ethnicity, quite possibly leading to the demise of "Deseret Mormons" and the relegation of the concept of "Mormon Country" to historical and geographical nostalgia, while "cultural" Mormons such as Sterling McMurrin or Wayne Booth would no longer be welcome within the community of Saints.[30] For the time being, however, the internationalization of Mormonism is still being negotiated. By no means are all General Authorities committed to Mauss's "minimalist" Mormonism, since most of them still have a "Deseret Mormon" background. At the moment international Mormonism is best represented by the Community of Christ, while the expansion of Utah Mormonism seems to go hand in hand with the Americanization of the world.

However, although Mormons might have less of a public-relations problem if their religion were not as American as Indian corn and the buffalo nickel, recent studies decoupling Mormonism from American culture by suggesting earlier Old World influences are seen as problematic, especially for Utah Mormons. John Brooke, *The Refiner's Fire: The Making of Mormon Cosmology, 1644-1844* (New York: Cambridge University Press, 1994), states explicitly that he dissents "from the notion of the essential 'Americanness' of Mormonism" and observes that Mormon historians, both believers and nonbelievers, have for the most part approached that history from a functionalist perspective "that discouraged a serious examination of the content—and possibly earthly origins—of Mormon thought" (xiv-xv). According to Brooke, "unless one rests one's argument on revelation, Jungian archetypes, or simple reinvention, . . . we have to ask from whence these ideas came, we have to take seriously the problem of the transmission and reformulation of

---

29. Klaus J. Hansen, "The World and the Prophet," *Dialogue* 1 (Summer 1966): 103-7.

30. University of Utah political scientist J. D. Williams, a fifth-generation Mormon and former bishop, coined the term "birthright" Mormons to identify those who resist the flattening out of Mormon doctrine and culture.

memory and of text.... Joseph Smith's cosmology becomes comprehensible only when it is placed in a setting broader than that of antebellum America ... [reaching] back to the extreme perfectionism forged in the Radical Reformation from the fusion of Christianity with the ancient occult hermetic philosophy" (xiv-xvi).

While Brooke's work is the most recent and most single-minded in its genetic approach, D. Michael Quinn has made an important contribution in his 1987 essay, "Socioreligious Radicalism of the Mormon Church: A Parallel to the Anabaptists," in Bitton and Beecher, *New Views of Mormon History,* 363-86; but especially in his massive volume *Early Mormonism and the Magic World View* (1987; 2d ed. rev., Salt Lake City: Signature Books, 1998). In this work and its subsequent revision, he made the most sustained argument for a radical kinship shared by Anabaptists and Mormons, which posits a modern, rationalistic outlook juxtaposed to a premodern Mormon past of folk magic rooted in both American and European folk traditions. Brooke attempted to make these connections even more explicit by arguing for a fusion of hermeticism and religious radicalism in the English Revolution and a transmission of these ideas to the fringes of nineteenth-century American culture and their subsequent reenactment in Mormonism.[31]

To orthodox Mormon scholars who eschew American environmentalism and evolution, extensions of cultural horizons would be viewed as a change in degree but not in kind. Those who take the Book of Mormon literally as an ancient doctrine seek an understanding of its text in the culture of the ancient Near East. Hugh Nibley popularized the work of Eduard Meyer in the modern Mormon scholarly community with his early Book of Mormon studies: *Lehi in the Desert* (Salt Lake City: Bookcraft, 1952); *An Approach to the Book of Mormon* (Salt Lake City: Deseret Book, 1964); and *Since Cumorah: The Book of Mormon in the Modern World* (Salt Lake City: Deseret Book, 1967). Both Nibley and Meyer had an interest in the origins of Christianity and Islam, and saw Mormonism as an ideal contemporary laboratory for studying the emergence of new religions, although their motives for doing so differed drastically. While Nibley and his disciples have focused their attention on Near Eastern and early Christian history, a few scholars have been willing to pick up the "stick of Joseph," as it were, and explore the ramifications for American culture.

Richard L. Bushman, "The Book of Mormon and the American Revolution," *BYU Studies* 16 (Autumn 1976): 3-20, was based on his acceptance of the Book of Mormon as an authentic historical document and attempted to refute the idea that the political ideas of the Book of Mormon mirrored American republican values, thus implying that these ideas must have their origins elsewhere. While not tracing the millenarian world of early Mormonism to the ancient Near East, Grant Underwood in *The Millenarian World of Early Mormonism* made an ambitious attempt to decouple it from the cultural environment of antebellum America and identifies what he sees as early Christian connections. A careful reading of Philip Barlow's *Mormons and the Bible* likewise leaves no doubt that, in his view, the Mormon understanding of the Bible cannot be subsumed by modern American cultural influences alone. It is perhaps possible to generalize that, while in theory it might have

---

31. See also Alexander, "The Place of Joseph Smith," 16-17; and R. Laurence Moore, "The Occult Connection? Mormonism, Christian Science, and Spiritualism," in *The Occult in America: New Historical Perspectives,* edited by Howard Kerr and Charles L. Crow (Urbana: University of Illinois Press, 1983): 135-61. Harold Bloom, acknowledging Joseph Smith as a "religious genius" traces his ideas to gnosticism and the Kaballah in *The American Religion: The Emergence of the Post-Christian Nation* (New York: Simon & Schuster, 1992): 77-128.

taken a great deal of effort for believers to adopt an environmentalist framework, functionalism served them as a convenient bridge. An example is Milton Backman Jr., *American Religions and the Rise of Mormonism* (1965; 2d rev. ed., Salt Lake City: Deseret Book, 1970). Secular historians may have found it as difficult to move beyond environmentalism as believing historians have found adopting this view. Partly in response to the Nibley approach, which they reject, a number of younger scholars have made concerted efforts to explore the relationship of the Book of Mormon to American culture. The most important of these studies have been collected in Brent L. Metcalfe, ed., *New Approaches to the Book of Mormon: Explorations in Critical Methodology* (Salt Lake City: Signature Books, 1993), with interesting further explorations in his *American Apochrypha: Essays on the Book of Mormon,* with coeditor Dan Vogel (Salt Lake City: Signature Books, 2002).

A cursory reading of Fawn Brodie suggests that even she, reputedly a dyed-in-the-wool American cultural environmentalist, perceived the impossibility of confining Mormonism within such boundaries. It is intriguing to speculate what she had in mind when she cryptically wrote: "It is exciting and enlightening to see a religion born. And Joseph's was no mere dissenting sect. It was a real religious creation, one intended to be to Christianity as Christianity was to Judaism: that is, a reform and a consummation."[32] It would be interesting to know whether she agreed with Mario De Pillis that the "special status of Mormonism as a fourth major religion is generally accepted in American society."[33] If so, perhaps she saw this status as more than an extension of American denominational pluralism in the tradition of Will Herberg's Protestant/Catholic/Jew,[34]—as a more radical innovation.

One scholar who does not leave us guessing is Gordon Pollock, who picked up the idea of religious innovation in a more systematic fashion, arguing that Mormonism had pushed beyond the confines of American Christian culture "by shifting goals, no longer seeking sinlessness but rather godliness."[35] Such a view does not appear incompatible with Richard Bushman's assertion that "Joseph Smith is best understood as a person who outgrew his culture."[36]

Thus, Jan Shipps's influential and undeniably brilliant *Mormonism: The Story of a New Religious Tradition,* rather than being a supernova appearing out of nowhere, is in fact the climax of a body of "new religious tradition" scholarship. On rereading O'Dea's *The Mormons,* I am particularly impressed how much he anticipated Shipps. Like her, he identifies the Mormons as a "modern Israel" who "had chosen to emulate the example of a holy nation—and in so doing had found themselves in circumstances that rendered such emulation more than mere symbolic commemoration," bringing "into existence a new American religion." Shipps, however, goes beyond O'Dea by arguing that rather than "a peculiarly American *subculture*" [O'Dea's words, her emphasis], "the Latter-day Saints . . . have acquired an ethnic identity so distinct that it sets the Saints apart in much the same fashion that ethnic identity sets the Jews apart."[37] O'Dea, clearly, is not willing to follow

---

32. Brodie, *No Man Knows My History,* viii.
33. De Pillis, "The Quest for Religious Authority and the Rise of Mormonism," *Dialogue* 1 (Autumn 1966): 75.
34. Will Herberg, *An Essay in American Religious Sociology* (Garden City, NY: Doubleday, 1955).
35. Quoted in Pollock, *Northern Voices,* 208, n. 5. He develops this idea further in *In Search of Security: The Mormons and the Kingdom of God on Earth, 1830-1844* (New York: Garland Publishing, 1989), 256-66. Pollock had first expressed these ideas in his doctoral dissertation by the same title (Queen's University, 1977).
36. Bushman, *Joseph Smith and the Beginnings of Mormonism,* 7.
37. O'Dea, *The Mormons,* 115, 56; Shipps, *Mormonism,* 23, 187 note 23. 112.

Shipps this far. At the risk of misreading her, I hear another echo of Richard Bushman: just as Joseph Smith had outgrown his culture, so have his people. To O'Dea, however, Mormonism's "typical American quality is no less real" but is in fact "one of the great paradoxes of the Mormon experience. The Mormon group came closer to evolving an ethnic identity on this continent than did any other comparable group. . . . Yet it also has been 'an America in miniature.'" This "strange combination of peculiarity and typicality stands out as the most striking Mormon characteristic." Thus, the Mormon drama replicated not only the experiences of the Israelites of old but also "the chief processes of American history."[38] With a backward glance to Brooke, I see in the works of both Shipps and O'Dea marriages of memory and text, though deriving from radically differing assumptions about "culture."

Perhaps it may strike readers as curious that only now, at this juncture, I am finally including B. H. Roberts in my narrative, although his magisterial *A Comprehensive History of the Church of Jesus Christ of Latter-day Saints* was first published serially in *The Americana,* from July 1909 to July 1915, with a revised edition appearing in six volumes from Deseret News Press in 1930. Strictly speaking Roberts does not really belong in these pages because, unlike just about everyone else in my discussion, he does not pose the question of how Mormonism fits with its American cultural setting. Rather, his history is the implicit answer to a very different question: where and how does Mormonism fit into the larger world-historical scheme of human events? He formulates his answer within a religious/dispensationalist framework that he takes for granted and which apparently requires no analysis or explanation. While his internal history of Mormonism is remarkably detailed and objective, the modern reader is left guessing at just how Roberts might fit his religion into a world-historical tradition.

Two authors who have moved beyond Roberts in attempting this daunting task are Richard Bushman, a believing Mormon, and Jan Shipps, a sympathetic nonbeliever. While most historians, myself included, continue to seek answers to cultural questions, such as "How does Mormonism relate to American culture and vice versa?" Bushman and Shipps are asking religious questions. As I remarked above, according to Bushman, Joseph Smith moved beyond culture, while to Shipps, Joseph sacralized culture in the tradition of someone like Moses or Mohammed. The difference between Shipps and believing Mormons might be that, to the latter, Mormonism is *the* religious tradition, while to Shipps it is *a* religious tradition. Ultimately, the question of who is right, the cultural historian or the student of religious tradition, has no simple answer. We are dealing with two different questions that cannot be resolved by an either/or approach. No doubt cultural historians are not likely to give up anytime soon, convinced as they are that historical questions, including religious ones, are rooted in culture. At the same time, those who insist on separating religion from culture will continue to flourish, especially as Mormonism is expanding more and more into a world religion that might well perceive too close a link to American cultural origins as an impediment to its continued growth.

Postscript

Since I first wrote this essay in 1998, the stream of Mormon studies pouring off the presses has continued unabated. Although lack of time and space do not allow for a

---

38. O'Dea, *The Mormons,* 116-17.

Excavating Mormon Pasts

thorough and systematic discussion of this vast new literature, key works that seem to fit into the theme of my essay merit brief consideration. Consequently, I have selected those studies that, in my opinion, transcend the questions and concerns of the majority of works representing what by general agreement has been labeled the New Mormon History, flourishing from the 1950s until the present. A useful and perceptive overview and interpretation of the New Mormon History is Ronald W. Walker, David Whittaker, and James B. Allen, "The New Mormon History: Historical Writing since 1950," in their *Mormon History* (Urbana: University of Illinois Press, 2000), 60-112. There is, of course, a substantial historiography of the New Mormon History, but it is not central to my essay. Among the sharpest critics cited is Charles S. Peterson, who argued that the new history "had helped create a nonmainstream 'exceptionalist' history that ultimately was self-defeating" (94). Community of Christ historian Roger Launius is reported as arguing that many of the New Mormon history scholars were motivated by self-discovery, eager "to understand their religious and cultural heritage," but producing "a history that could be introspective and self-confining" (94).

A major criterion for my choice of works in this section is that they should be outward-looking, engaged in exploring Mormonism within its larger cultural context. Perhaps some future scholar, taking a broad view of Mormon historiography, will perceive this period as the beginning of a post-New Mormon History school: outward-looking, comparative, cosmopolitan. Of course, historical trends don't appear full-blown overnight. Clearly, the work of scholars such as Thomas Alexander and Jan Shipps point in this direction.

Shipps picked up the stick from the other end, so to speak, in "Gentiles, Mormons, and the History of the American West," in her *Sojourner in the Promised Land: Forty Years Among the Mormons* (Urbana: University of Illinois Press, 2000), 21. Here she launched a critique of the New Western History for its own parochialism by ignoring the history of the Mormons—circling around the topic as if it were a hole in a doughnut. These New Western historians, privileging *process* as their frame of reference, tend to identify Mormon culture as *place,* and thus beyond the purview of their investigation. In a stimulating recent study: *Transformation of the Mormon Culture Region* (Urbana: University of Illinois Press, 2003), historical geographer Ethan Yorgason has brokered a marriage of place and process that is truly impressive, leading to a sophisticated understanding of a crucial period in the transformation of the Mormon culture region, 1880-1920. Unlike more traditional studies, he does not see the accommodation between Mormons and Gentiles as entirely one-sided, but rather the result of a dialogue (if an acrimonious one) between the two cultures.

In contrast, even a recent comparative study of *The Americanization of Religious Minorities: Confronting the Constitutional Order,* by political scientist Eric Michael Mazur (Baltimore: Johns Hopkins University Press, 1999), argues that, in their power struggle with the American "Constitutional Order," the Mormons' political accommodation was achieved through conversion to the American "formula for pluralism" (92). The "traditional" sources he cites for his interpretation are Arrington and Bitton, *The Mormon Experience,* and my *Mormonism and the American Experience.* Earlier studies focusing more specifically on the victory-defeat paradigm are Gustive O. Larson, *The "Americanization" of Utah for Statehood* (San Marino, CA: Huntington Library, 1970), and Mark P. Leone, *Roots of*

Modern Mormonism (Cambridge: Harvard University Press, 1970). Writing from a "marxist" perspective, Leone saw Mormons as "colonized" victims of a victorious American empire.

Another study transcending (like Yorgason's) the paradigm of federal victory and Mormon defeat is Sarah Barringer Gordon's sophisticated, magisterial *The Mormon Question: Polygamy and Constitutional Conflict in Nineteenth-Century America* (Chapel Hill: The University of North Carolina Press, 2002). As Gordon makes clear, the Constitutional conflict had far-reaching consequences not only for the Mormon place in the Constitutional order, but for the Constitutional order itself. A work that focuses on political and social issues is Jeffrey Nichols, *Prostitution, Polygamy, and Power: Salt Lake City, 1847-1918* (Urbana: University of Illinois Press, 2002). Nichols shows how, through a transformation of gender systems, the moral standards of Mormons and Gentiles had converged. Kathryn M. Daynes, *More Wives than One: Transformation of the Mormon Marriage System, 1840-1910* (Urbana: University of Illinois Press, 2001), describes a profound cleavage between the Mormon patriarchal system of marriage and companionate marriage that had emerged as the ideal of middle-class America by the end of the nineteenth century. Approaching related issues from a broader perspective of cultural history, not unlike Gordon, Kathleen Flake, *The Politics of American Religious Identity: The Seating of Senator Reed Smoot, Mormon Apostle* (Chapel Hill: the University of North Carolina Press, 2004), 11, sees Mormonism's transformation from un-American to American "not [as] its story alone, but the story of the changing relation of churches to the state in the early twentieth century." Also distancing herself from the victory-defeat paradigm, Flake argues that "the Mormon Problem was solved not by legal force but by political negotiation that satisfied the principal interests of both the nation and the L.D.S. Church" (181 note 13).

If I have anything to add to this discussion, it is that "negotiation" has had a long history in the conflict between Mormonism and its American adversaries. As I argued in *Mormonism and the American Experience,* the Saints had played an active role in the struggle over the definition of the meaning of America from the very inception of their religion, so that the labeling of the Mormons as un-American merely had propaganda value. What I have learned from the literature under discussion is that I underestimated the continuing significance of "negotiation" into the twentieth century, giving in too easily to the "capitulation" paradigm at the conclusion of my book. I would have benefited from Thomas Alexander's insights. He rejected a simplistic "capitulation" framework in *Mormonism in Transition: A History of the Latter-day Saints, 1890-1930* (Urbana: University of Illinois Press, 1986), especially 16-27.

The most recent book arriving on my desk to merit discussion in this collection of outward-looking, culturally oriented works is *Equal Rites: The Book of Mormon, Masonry, Gender, and American Culture* by Clyde R. Forsberg, Jr. (New York: Columbia University Press, 2004). Full disclosure requires acknowledgment that I directed an earlier version of this book as a doctoral dissertation in the Department of History at Queen's University:

---

39. Selected important works are Stephen C. Bullock, *Revolutionary Brotherhood: Freemasonry and the Transformation of the American Social Order, 1730-1800* (Chapel Hill: University of North Carolina Press, 1996); Mark C. Carnes, *Secret Ritual and Manhood in America* (New Haven: Yale University Press, 1989); Mary Ann Clawson, *Constructing Brotherhood: Class, Gender, and Fraternalism* (Princeton, NJ: Princeton University Press, 1989); Lynn Dumenil, *Freemasonry and American Culture, 1830-1930* (Princeton, NJ: Princeton University Press, 1984); Paul Goodman, *Towards a Christian Republic: Antimasonry and the Great Transition in New England, 1826-1836* (New York: Oxford University Press, 1988); and Dorothy Ann Lipson, *Freemasonry in Federalist Connecticut, 1789-1835* (Princeton, NJ: Princeton University Press, 1877).

Excavating Mormon Pasts

"In Search of the Historical Nephi: The Book of Mormon, 'Evangelicalisms' and Antebellum American Popular Culture, c. 1830" (1994). However, Forsberg's imaginative linking of Mormonism and Masonry is entirely his own, without benefit from his former supervisor, but richly contextualized by a growing literature linking Freemasonry and American culture,[39] and transcending an out-of-date, traditional body of scholarship on Masonry and Mormonism represented by James C. Bilderback, "Masonry and Mormonism: Nauvoo, Illinois, 1841-1847" (M.S. thesis, State University of Iowa, 1937); Samuel H. Goodwin, *Additional Studies in Mormonism and Masonry* (Salt Lake City, 1927); and E. Cecil McGavin, *Mormonism and Masonry* (Salt Lake City: Stevens and Wallis, 1947). Even those skeptical of a direct linkage between Freemasonry and Mormonism should appreciate how an understanding of Masonry in American culture provides at the very least a catalyst for the complex chemistry of race, class, and gender contributing to the violent reaction between Mormonism and American culture. Perhaps even more important, Forsberg's original and imaginative foray into cultural connections previously underexplored provides, in the words of Alfred Bush, "not only a new view of Mormonism but . . . a new view of America" (dust jacket).

By way of conclusion, I wish to make an analogy between the question of whether or not Mormonism is an *American* religion and an old debate over the role and position of science in America. There were those who argued that science was beyond culture, that there was no such thing as "*American* science," only "science *in* America." Nowadays, most scholars agree that to some extent even "pure science" has a cultural component. The same, I think, is true of religion. Even God accomplishes his ends through "culture."

KLAUS J. HANSEN taught the history of American thought and culture at Queen's University, Ontario, from 1968 to 2001. He regards as his proudest achievement the distinguished work of his students on Mormonism, Masonry, gender, American culture, Emerson, Perry Miller, racial thought, and the historiography of slavery to name a few of the most important. His own work on Mormonism was always part of his larger interest in the central focus of his seminar on American culture, exemplified by his *Mormonism and the American Experience* (Chicago: University of Chicago Press, 1981). Among his retirement projects are a new edition of *Quest for Empire: The Political Kingdom of God and the Council of Fifty in Mormon History* (1967; Salt Lake City: Greg Kofford Books, forthcoming), and a comparative study of the religious thought of Karl Marx and Alexis de Tocqueville.

Chapter 2

The Search for Cultural Origins of Mormon Doctrines

David L. Paulsen

For those interested in Mormonism's singular belief system, the question of origins has always posed a particular challenge. Historians, believers, and critics have turned to a variety of sources—natural and preternatural—in an effort to explain from whence this uncommon theology came. For many of the faithful, an appeal to divine revelation, or maybe even providence, has sufficed. Revelation has also satisfied a number of critics, though they disagree with believers as to the identity of the preternatural source. Others have concentrated on seeking natural sources of Mormon doctrines.

The first of these explanatory theories explains Mormon doctrine in terms of the psyche of the founding prophet Joseph Smith. They include Fawn Brodie, *No Man Knows My History: The Life of Joseph Smith, the Mormon Prophet* (1945; 2d ed. rev., New York: Alfred A. Knopf, 1971), esp. the "Supplement" to the 1971 edition, 405-21; T. L. Brink, "Joseph Smith: The Verdict of Depth Psychology," *Journal of Mormon History* 3 (1976): 73-83; C. Jess Groesbeck, "The Smiths and Their Dreams and Visions," *Sunstone*, March 1988, 22-29; Lawrence Foster, "The Psychology of Religious Genius: Joseph Smith and the Origins of New Religious Movements," *Dialogue: A Journal of Mormon Thought* 26, no. 4 (Winter 1993): 1-22; William D. Morain, *The Sword of Laban: Joseph Smith, Jr. and the Dissociated Mind* (Washington, DC: American Psychiatric Press, 1998); Robert D. Anderson, *Inside the Mind of Joseph Smith* (Salt Lake City: Signature Books, 1999); and Dan Vogel, *Joseph Smith: The Making of a Prophet* (Salt Lake City: Signature Books, 2004). The comment of Newell G. Bringhurst, *Pacific Quarterly Review* 70, no. 2 (May 2001): 319-21, though reviewing Anderson, may be said to apply to the others as well—a point Bringhurst himself makes about Brodie: "It presents a secular portrait of a religious man, making it a fundamentally flawed work" (321).

The second approach sees Mormon doctrine as a functional solution to the social stresses of the new republic and/or the issues of the Age of Jackson. Among significant works in this category are Mario S. De Pillis, "The Quest for Religious Authority and the Rise of Mormonism," *Dialogue: A Journal of Mormon Thought* 1, no. 1 (Spring 1966): 68-88; Gordon S. Wood, "Evangelical America and Early Mormonism," *New York History* 61, no. 4 (October 1980): 359-86; Lawrence Foster, *Religion and Sexuality: The Shakers, the Mormons, and the Oneida Community* (1981; reprint ed., Chicago: University of Illinois Press, 1984); Nathan O. Hatch, *The Democratization of American Christianity* (New Haven, CT: Yale University Press, 1989); Marvin S. Hill, *Quest for Refuge: The Mormon Flight from American Pluralism* (Salt Lake City: Signature Books, 1989); Kenneth H. Winn, *Exiles in a Land of Liberty: Mormons in America, 1830-1846* (Chapel Hill: University of North Carolina Press, 1989). For treatments of early Mormonism and its doctrines as functional solutions on grander scales than American history, see D. Michael Quinn, "Socioreligious Radicalism of the Mormon Church: A Parallel to the Anabaptists," in *New Views of Mormon History: A Collection of Essays in Honor of Leonard J. Arrington,* edited by Davis Bitton and Maureen Ursenbach Beecher (Salt Lake City: University of Utah Press, 1987), 363-86; John G. Gager, "Early Mormonism and Early Christianity: Some Parallels and Their Consequences for the Study of New Religions," *Journal of Mormon History* 9 (1982): 53-60; and Jan Shipps, *Mormonism: The Story of a New Religious Tradition* (Urbana: University of Illinois Press, 1985).

A third and more traditional approach, which has not lost any steam, has been to demonstrate cultural and intellectual borrowings—whether direct, divergent, or syncretic. It is on this final category of cultural continuity that I provide a historiography.

Students of Mormon history in the past half century have searched far and wide in their quest for cultural explanations of the faith's theology. This search has led them not only into Joseph Smith's immediate environs such as western New York, but down such diffuse and divergent cultural trails as New England Puritanism, the Bible, Christian primitivism, millennialism, folk magic, masonry, and most recently, the occult philosophy of Renaissance hermeticism. While the trails mapped by these historians crisscross and overlap, I will attempt to traverse them individually, reviewing the works of their proponents and adversaries.

I begin my travels with Fawn Brodie's controversial 1945 biography of Joseph Smith, *No Man Knows My History*.[1] While her approach seems highly biased, writing off the Mormon faith and trying to interpret Joseph only to a non-Mormon audience, her importance in accelerating the search for cultural antecedents is apparent. Thorough historiographical essays on the response to and influence of *No Man Knows My History* appear in Newell G. Bringhurst, "Applause, Attack, and Ambivalence: Varied Responses to Fawn M. Brodie's *No Man Knows My History,*" *Utah Historical Quarterly* 59 (Winter 1989): 46-63 and his *Fawn McKay Brodie: A Biographer's Life* (Norman: University of Oklahoma Press, 1999). He does not discuss Brodie's approach of seeking for cultural explanations of Mormon doctrine. However, he ironically turns her psychoanalytic approach back upon herself, concluding, "Fawn's obsession with problems of sexuality not only affected her early relationship with [her husband] but would apparently also influence her later biographical writing, where the sexuality of her subjects would emerge as a major theme" (68). Bringhurst also highlights Brodie's tensions with her family, whom she loved but had severe differences with, especially her father. She apparently saw her book as something detrimental to her family's faith and felt acute guilt over the matter, at one point saying, "Sometimes I wish to God I'd never started the book" (93).

Gary Topping, *Utah Historians and the Reconstruction of Western History* (Norman: University of Oklahoma Press, 2003), clearly sees Brodie's naturalistic approach as stemming from personal motives: "She came to the conclusion that Smith's stories of angelic visitations, scriptural writings on golden plates translated magically by various occult devices, and his eventual claim to have been a prophet of God were all an immense fabrication. Brodie felt cheated—violated—by Smith and his successors in the Mormon Church who had led her to believe in its divine origin. . . . Even the energetic labors of Bernard Brodie and Dale Morgan in mitigating the harshness of Brodie's tone throughout most of her narrative could scarcely conceal the fury of a woman scorned (she had been, as a girl, a victim of Smith's deception) in her summation of the significance of Joseph Smith and his church" which was that Smith "was as much a product" of New England "as Jonathan Edwards" (287, 289, 292). Several significant concepts in Brodie's work (including rejecting the Spaulding theory, advancing the *View of the Hebrews* hypothesis, psychological explanations for Joseph, and Joseph's "dependence on local theology") were first discussed forty-three years earlier by I. Woodbridge Riley in *The Founder of Mormonism: A Psychological Study*

---

1. There are no significant retractions or revisions in her 1971 second edition, even though she acknowledges new discoveries in Mormon history as well as advances in psychology. Still she says, "The new discoveries do not necessitate important revisions in this biography. On the contrary, I believe that the new data tend on the whole to support my original speculations about Joseph Smith's character" (xi).

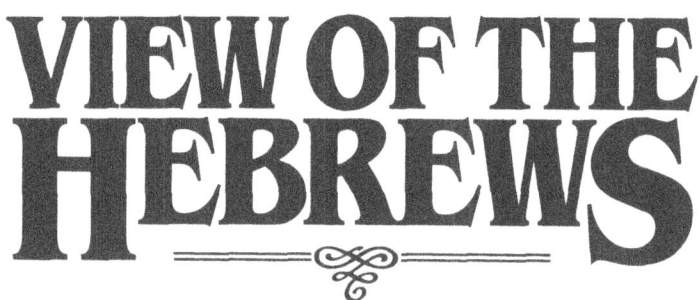

VIEW OF THE HEBREWS

1825 2nd EDITION

Complete Text by
Ethan Smith

Edited with an Introduction by Charles D. Tate, Jr.

Volume Eight
in the Religious Studies Center
Specialized Monograph Series

Religious Studies Center
Brigham Young University
Provo, Utah

of Joseph Smith Jr. (New York: Dodd Mead & Company, 1902). However, it is Brodie's synthesis and arguments that have drawn the most attention and response.

Leonard J. Arrington and Davis Bitton, *Mormons and Their Historians* (Salt Lake City: University of Utah Press, 1988), 115 observed: "Bernard DeVoto may have been exaggerating only slightly when he wrote, 'It is her [Brodie's] distinction that she has raised writing about Mormonism to the dignity of history for the first time.'" Furthermore, as Marvin Hill, "Secular or Sectarian History? A Critique of *No Man Knows My History*," *Church History* 43 (March 1974): 78, recorded, Brodie's book "quickly became the most influential book on early Mormonism, a status it has retained."

By provoking Mormon historians and other scholars interested in the Mormon past, Brodie's book acted as a catalyst to start the New Mormon History. As Robert Bruce Flanders, "Some Reflections on the New Mormon History," *Dialogue* 9, no. 1 (Spring 1974): 35, wrote, "A new era dawned with her book. All subsequent serious studies of early Mormonism have necessarily had Brodie as a referent point." Similarly, Sterling McMurrin, "A New Climate of Liberation: A Tribute to Fawn McKay Brodie, 1915-1981," *Dialogue* 14 (Spring 1981): 74-75, called *No Man Knows My History* "a watershed in the treatment of Mormon history by Mormon historians" because thereafter, "Mormon history produced by Mormon scholars moved toward more openness, objectivity, and honesty." Richard S. Van Wagoner, "Fawn Brodie: The Woman and Her History," *Sunstone* 7, no. 4 (July-August 1982): 37, reflected, "Though we may disagree with [Brodie's] assessment of the truth respecting Mormonism, *No Man Knows My History* may be the major impetus in the quest for a less apologetic, more objective Mormon history." Louis C. Midgley, "F. M. Brodie—'The Fasting Hermit and Very Saint of Ignorance': A Biographer and Her Legend" *FARMS [Foundation for Ancient Research & Mormon Studies] Review of Books* 8, no. 2 (1996): 229, commented: "Though it was certainly not her intention, Brodie almost single-handedly managed to focus the attention of Latter-day Saints on the crucial historical foundations of their faith. She has thereby helped an entire generation of Latter-day Saint historians to devote careful attention to what can be found about the Mormon past in libraries and archives. Topping concurs: "Few biographies in American historiography have had the dominance and staying power of *No Man Knows My History*" (297).

The Burned-Over District

Laying aside the possibility of divine revelation as a source of Joseph Smith's ideas, Brodie looked primarily to his immediate cultural environs, starting with western New York, or the "burned-over district" for explanations. And eschewing the idea of just one principal source (e.g., Christian Primitivism), she hypothesized a potpourri of isolated and apparently unrelated sources. On the doctrinal content of the Book of Mormon, for instance, Brodie adopted Alexander Campbell's claim (which he later modified by endorsing the Spaulding theory) that the book contained "every error and almost every truth discussed in New York for the last ten years."[2] As Topping put it, "Brodie's thesis was that all the materials an imaginative young man would need to create the *Book of Mormon* were present in the cultural environment of upstate New York in the 1820s" (290). Brodie is specific: Joseph Smith drew his Indians/lost tribes theory primarily from Ethan Smith's *View of the Hebrews;* his anti-secret society doctrine from the anti-Masonic mood in western New York; many of his *Book of Mormon* stories from the Bible; his concept of a plurality of Gods from his classes in Hebrew; his belief that the earth was organized out of preexisting materials and his astronomy (Kolob, God's time, intelligences of various levels engaged in evolution) all from Thomas Dick's *Philosophy of a Future State;* his ideas concerning the

---

2. According to Campbell, "Delusions," *Millennial Harbinger*, 2, no. 2 (February 1831), 85-96, these issues included infant baptism, ordination, the trinity, regeneration, repentance, justification, the fall of man, the atonement, transubstantiation, fasting, penance, church government, religious experience, the call to the ministry, the general resurrection, eternal punishment, permission to baptize, and even questions of free masonry, republican government and the rights of man.

origin of Negroes from Thomas Smiley's *Sacred Geography;* his attitude on slavery from the "prevailing opinion of the time"; his teachings concerning the premortal life from "the old story, ennobled by Milton of the war in heaven"; the temple theology from freemasonry; his theory of dual priesthood from James Gray's *Dissertation on the Coincidence between the Priesthoods of Jesus Christ and Melchisedek*"; and the Word of Wisdom from the temperance and health reform movements of the times (47, 65, 36, 171, 173, 176).

Brodie's claim that Mormonism is entirely a nineteenth-century product of Joseph Smith's psyche and cultural environs has been extensively and vigorously challenged, beginning in 1946 with an official but unsigned review produced by a Church committee of which Apostle Albert E. Bowen was the principal author. The review charged that Brodie's work was "a composite of all anti-Mormon books that have gone before pieced into a pattern conformable to the author's own particular rationale and bedded in some very bad psychology."[3] Beyond criticizing Brodie's assumptions, adductions, and conjectures, the review focused mostly on discrediting three primary sources for several of Brodie's claims concerning Smith's character and early money-digging activities: affidavits, the Dogberry articles, and his "alleged" journal admissions and an "alleged" court record, all of which the committee suggested were "unworthy of mention in a work of scholarly research." The review also challenged Brodie's thesis that Smith used *View of the Hebrews,* pointing out that it cannot be shown that he ever saw the book.

In *No Ma'am, That's Not History: A Brief Review of Mrs. Brodie's Reluctant Vindication of a Prophet She Seeks to Expose* (Bookcraft: Salt Lake City, 1946), Hugh Nibley examined Brodie's methodology, logic, and sources, challenging her claim that many of Smith's ideas came "directly" from Dick. Nibley showed that the "later teachings" (which Brodie claimed came from Dick) were simply a continuation of earlier teachings, presented before Smith had access to Dick's works. As to her claimed connection between *View of the Hebrews* and the Book of Mormon, Nibley acknowledged the "striking parallels" between the two works but denied that they prove derivation. Similarly, Nibley argued that Mormon-Masonic parallels do not show that Smith borrowed from Masonry, since the two institutions differ totally "in form and meaning" (17). Further, he asserted that temple rituals were well established before Smith became a Mason and rejected Brodie's implicit assumption that parallels between belief-sets constitutes evidence of cultural borrowing, pointing out that "there is no such thing as a completely original religion. Every religion, including classical Christianity, is full of things that may be found elsewhere" (14, 17, 34, 45). Nibley also criticized in detail Brodie's evolutionary framework, her penchant for insinuation, and her psychological speculations. According to Topping, Brodie dismissed Nibley's critique, calling it "as shallow and superficial a piece as has yet appeared" (293). As late as 1996, Roger D. Launius, a Community of Christ historian, quoted Nibley's claim (46, 57-68, 61-62) that none of Joseph Smith's doctrines had ever undergone the "slightest change" and called it "one of the most asinine statements ever written about Mormon history" (qtd. in Topping, 293).

Marvin S. Hill, "Critical Examination of *No Man Knows My History,* by Fawn M. Brodie," manuscript, [n.d., ca. 1959?] L. Tom Perry Special Collections, Lee Library, Brigham Young University, Provo, Utah, challenged several of Brodie's claims about doctrinal origins. For example, Smith's concept of dual priesthood could not have derived from Gray's dissertation, since Gray's concept was not dual (17-18). As another, the 1835 edition of Doctrine and Covenants contained the revelation that matter is eternal while 1832 revelations announce the central throne, the existence of numerous peopled worlds, and the gradation of intelligences. Thus, Smith could not have derived these concepts from a December 1836 reading of Dick as Brodie claimed. Furthermore, Brodie dates this hypothesized reading from a "Sidney Rigdon" quotation from Dick in a *Messenger and Advocate* arti-

---

3. [Unsigned], *Appraisal of the So-Called Brodie Book* ([Salt Lake City]: The Church of Jesus Christ of Latter-day Saints, n.d.), pamphlet reprinted from the *Church News,* May 11, 1946. On Apostle Albert E. Bowen's authorship, see Bringhurst, *Brodie,* 289 note 113, and John Phillip Walker, ed., *Dale Morgan on Early Mormonism: Correspondence and a New History* (Salt Lake City: Signature Books, 1986), 125.

cle in December 1836 when, in fact, Oliver Cowdery was quoting Dick (22, 25-28). Hill painstakingly enumerates a lengthy list of "remarkable" similarities between Smith's and Dick's ideas but without taking a position on whether there was a direct influence. Hill's "Secular or Sectarian History? A Critique of [the 1971 ed.] *No Man Knows My History*," *Church History* 43 (March 1974): 78-96, did not probe doctrinal origins but instead found that Brodie's secular orientation and Mormon background tainted her conclusions. As a result, she "overstate[d] her case," "depend[ed] heavily on hearsay," and succumbed to the either/or fallacy (Smith is a prophet or an imposter). Hill proposed that we search for a middle ground, a position Midgley, "F. M. Brodie," 210-25, pointedly critiqued. Edward T. Jones, "The Theology of Thomas Dick and Its Possible Relation to that of Joseph Smith" (M.A. thesis, Brigham Young University, June 1969), concluded that the two "theologies" showed "insufficient similarity . . . to justify the assertions Mrs. Brodie makes" (95-96).

Although Hill did not undertake to resolve the question of whether *View of the Hebrews* was a source for the Book of Mormon, he mapped three possible responses: (1) the similarities are not as significant as Brodie maintains, (2) Smith was not familiar with *View of the Hebrews,* or (3) the Book of Mormon is conclusively of ancient Hebrew origin. All of these approaches have in fact been taken in Mormon apologetics. A thorough example of the first is John W. Welch, "An Unparallel" ([Provo, UT]: Foundation for Ancient Research and Mormon Studies, 1985), who concluded that "the Book of Mormon differs from VH far more than it resembles it" (1). While not always explicitly responding to Brodie's claims about *View of the Hebrews,* Nibley has done much work supportive of the third possibility—attempting to establish an ancient setting for the Book of Mormon. FARMS and the *Journal of Book of Mormon Studies* continue to publish work prodigiously in this vein. Spencer J. Palmer and William L. Knecht, "*View of the Hebrews:* Substitute for Inspiration?" *BYU Studies* 5, no. 2 (Winter 1964): 105-13, also found the parallels unconvincing.

Charles D. Tate Jr. wrote an introduction for Ethan Smith, *View of the Hebrews,* 2d ed. (Provo, UT: Brigham Young University, Religious Studies Center, 1996), and listed fifty-two books and articles that discuss alleged connections between *View of the Hebrews* and the Book of Mormon. Tate invited readers, with the aid of these materials, to resolve the issue for themselves.

Following Brodie's lead, Whitney R. Cross, *The Burned-Over District: The Social and Intellectual History of Enthusiastic Religion in Western New York, 1800-1850* (Ithaca, NY: Cornell University Press, 1950), contended that Smith's cultural environs in western New York ("the burned-over district") were crucial to understanding not only the vitality of Mormonism as a movement but also the content of its beliefs. For example, he asserted that early Mormonism stressed and concretized the "doctrines which thirty years of revivalism had made most intensely interesting to the folk of western New York" (146). Mario S. De Pillis, "The Social Sources of Mormonism," *Church History* 37, no. 1 (March 1968): 50-79; and Marvin S. Hill, "The Rise of Mormonism in the Burned-over District: Another View," *New York History* 61, no. 4 (October 1980): 411-30, both critiqued Cross at length.

Sociologist Thomas O'Dea, *The Mormons* (Chicago: University of Chicago Press, 1957), 21, 31, 54, 57, also claimed that Mormonism inherited its basic ideas and values from its cultural background, though eventually transforming them. He saw the Book of Mormon as an American work addressing American concerns with unconcealed American patriotism, and he also repeated Brodie's charges that Thomas Dick may have influenced Smith's theology. William Mulder, in his important essay, "The Mormons in American History," *Utah Historical Quarterly* 27, no. 1 (January 1959), 59-77, explained Mormonism as "a dynamic reworking of the diverse elements of American culture." Its theology constitutes "a fairly complete cross section of the American mind in the early nineteenth century," with the Mormon doctrines of eternal progress and perfectionism reflecting the "go ahead" spirit of progress and industry in Jacksonian America (60). Mulder, like Brodie and Cross, cast the net broadly across Joseph Smith's America. In the last three decades, historians have concentrated their investigative efforts on more specific sources of more specific doctrines.

New England Puritanism

David Brion Davis, "The New England Origins of Mormonism," *New England Quarterly* 26, no. 2 (1953): 147-68, questioned Smith's immediate cultural environs as the primary source of his theological ideas. Instead, while acknowledging the possibility of multiple cultural sources, Davis saw Mormonism as "a link in the Puritan tradition, asserting a close and personal God, providential history, predestination, an ideal theocracy, the importance of the Christian calling, and a church of saints. . . . Finally, the Latter Day Saints represented an outburst of mysticism and superstition, the belief in continued revelation and the perfectibility of man, which was at least a latent facet of American Puritanism" (158).

De Pillis mildly challenged Davis in his 1968 article "The Social Sources of Mormonism," arguing that much of what became distinctively Mormon after 1830 was actually contrary to Puritanism (6). Grant Underwood in "The New England Origins of Mormonism Revisited," *Journal of Mormon History* 15 (1989): 15-26, called Davis's argument into question on nearly every front, countering four of Davis's alleged Puritan-Mormon shared beliefs: "a close personal God," providential history, eschatology, and communitarianism.

Concerning the nature of God, Underwood asserted that Mormon beliefs matched only very loosely with the Puritans who "certainly did not teach a corporeal theology, though they did believe in a close, interventionist God." He also rejected Davis's claim that Mormonism's providential worldview was a revival of the Puritan doctrine of God. Instead, Mormons believed that "God presided over the most minute happenings" and that "ordinary sequences of cause and effect were meaningful only in light of the overall system." These beliefs, according to Underwood, were common among nineteenth-century American farmers, tradesman, and merchants (16-17). Similarly, the "commonplace assumption of a generation ago of the nineteenth century's ebullient optimism and sense of constant, inevitable progress," which led Davis to conclude that the Saints' pessimistic evaluation of the society around them was "the ghost of another era," was also erroneous. Recent research, Underwood said, established that the broad cross-section of Americans shared a more negative outlook. Indeed, from the perspective of eschatology, Underwood claimed that Mormon pessimism resembled apocalyptic millenarian movements which, while not the dominant view of nineteenth-century America, were nonetheless hardly atypical. Indeed, when differences as well as similarities were taken into account, Underwood contended, one could show at best only "a rather tenuous connection" between Puritan and Mormon eschatology (17-19).

Finally, with regard to Puritan and Mormon communitarianism, Underwood argued that "most Latter-day Saints seem to have imbibed the prevailing ethos of economic liberalism a little too fully to fit the description of being the 'antithesis' to the age of Jackson." And even among Church leaders, communitarian views differed greatly, as the contrasting economic programs of Brigham Young and John Taylor demonstrate. He concluded: "LDS attitudes . . . in the nineteenth century seem less countercultural, and communitarianism and theocracy more superficial than Davis and others have assumed" (19-21). While not denying genuine similarities, he found "more reason to comfortably situate Mormons within the nineteenth century than to view them as [the] 'anachronistic residue' of the seventeenth century" (20-22). Karl C. Sandberg returned briefly to the Puritan thesis in "Mormonism and the Puritan Connection: The Trial of Mrs. Anne Hutchinson and Several Persistent Questions Bearing on Church Governance," *Sunstone* 16, no. 8 (February 1994): 21-22.

Excavating Mormon Pasts

The Bible and Christian Primitivism

Perhaps a more promising trail explored by historians in search of the origins of Mormon doctrines leads back to Christianity's text: the Bible. For instance, Philip L. Barlow proposed:

> Nothing—not the early pioneer experience of the Saints, not the geography of Mormon headquarters, not Mormon political behavior, not the famous attempts to establish a polygynous or theocratic or communal society, not Mormon millennialism or Mormon social make-up, not the alleged contemporary corporate wealth, not former charges of racism or still-current accusations of sexism, not the quasi-religious interest of some early Mormons in folk magic; in sum, none of the more dramatic aspects of the Mormon experience often spotlighted by observers—captures the evolving but enduring religious quintessence of Mormonism and its relationship to the balance of American religion better than a firm, comparative grasp of the Bible's place among the Latter-day Saints. This assertion applies even to Mormon theology and revelation, which, as we shall see, is inextricably enmeshed with and dependent on prior and often unconscious biblical perspectives.[4]

In particular, Barlow claimed that, in the Church's first years when Joseph Smith made his inspired revision of the Bible, the good book acted as a catalyst for many of his doctrinal revelations. These revelations include the general resurrection, the three degrees of post-mortal glory, oral scripture, pre-mortal existence, polygyny, and divine embodiment (43, 62-65). Beside the direct influence of the Bible text, Barlow notes the influence of Joseph Smith's biblical culture, especially the elements of an "imminent Millennium" and "Christian primitivism" (11).

Originating in Reformation Europe, Christian primitivism asserted that Christ's church had been corrupted through the ages and that the truth of God's religion could be found only by returning to the "primitive church." The movement spread widely in antebellum America because of anti-Catholic sentiment, dissatisfaction with the old mainline denominations, and sectarian competition. Many of the settlers remained content with their denominations and sects, or felt that reform was needed, but that the corruption was not serious enough to require a separation. Others, called "Seekers," left their organized religions in search of a restoration. In "The Free Seekers: Religious Culture in Upstate New York, 1790-1835," *Journal of Mormon History* 27, no. 1 (Spring 2000), Alan Taylor provides an illuminating portrait of "seekers" in upstate New York. He argues that the environment of the burned-over district created an enormous number of "free seekers," many of whom were early converts to Mormonism— including the Joseph Smith Sr. family.

In the late 1980s, three works appeared presenting Christian primitivism (especially in its more radical expressions) as a primary precursor to the emergence of Mormonism. These three were Richard T. Hughes, ed., *The American Quest for the Primitive Church* ((Urbana: University of Illinois, 1988), Richard T. Hughes and C. Leonard Allen, *Illusions of Innocence: Protestant Primitivism in America* (Chicago: University of Chicago Press, 1988), and Dan Vogel, *Religious Seekers and the Advent of Mormonism* ((Salt Lake City: Signature Books, 1988). All three were deeply indebted to Marvin S. Hill, "The Role of Christian Primitivism in the Origin and Development of the Mormon Kingdom: 1830-1844" (Ph.D. diss., University of Chicago, 1968). In this influential and widely quoted but still unpublished dissertation, Hill examined the primitivist tendencies that permeated the culture out of which Mormonism arose and concluded that they profoundly shaped Mormon theology and its ideal of the kingdom of God.

---

4. Philip L. Barlow, *Mormons and the Bible: The Place of the Latter-day Saints in American Religion* (New York: Oxford University Press, 1991), x-xi. See esp. chaps. 1-2: "Before Mormonism: Joseph Smith and the Bible, 1820-1830," 11-42, and "From the Birth of the Church to the Death of the Prophet," 43-73.

ILLUSIONS *of* INNOCENCE

Protestant Primitivism in America, 1630–1875

•

Richard T. Hughes
and C. Leonard Allen

Foreword by Robert N. Bellah

The University of Chicago Press
Chicago and London

Excavating Mormon Pasts

Hill traced Christian primitivism up to the "Christian" movement of Barton Stone and the Campbells (19-32). As the movement expanded, many joined the Disciples of Christ and similar groups, but a number of New Englanders and New Yorkers, dissatisfied with these new movements, pondered how the true faith might be restored. Some "awaited the coming of a new prophet who would usher in the prophesied events preceding the millennium. Here, on the fringes of the main body of Christian primitivists, acting independently of the others, were the future Latter-day Saints" (35-36). Joseph Smith's own primitivism sprang more directly from his immediate progenitors. For instance, Hill pointed out that Lucy Mack Smith's narrative had a "persistent primitive gospel motif" and that her brother, Jason, also sought for primitive gifts and signs. When Joseph Smith Sr. became religiously interested in 1811, he sought the "ancient order" established by Christ (48-50). Even young Joseph's 1838 account of the first vision was firmly rooted in primitivist principles. Though Joseph's account of the first vision was most revolutionary in its claims about the nature of the Godhead, he does not emphasize that aspect but rather "his disgust with the contradictory creeds of the contending sects, his conviction that the churches had strayed from divine truth and had lost 'the power of God' or the ability to perform healings through faith which characterized early Christianity" (55). Yet Smith was not alone in this view; Hill finds it common among the disinherited of the time. Many early members of Mormonism expressed primitive gospel convictions.[5] For Hill, "primitive gospel principles provided the central core of motivation among the Mormons" (56-60, 92).

In *Illusions of Innocence*, Hughes and Allen saw the quest for the primitive church as a specific manifestation of a broader American yearning for pure origins. Mormonism and other sects began and grew "precisely when numerous factors converged to make the appeal to pure beginnings a powerful dimension of American popular culture" (21). The authors also tie primitivistic tendencies in Mormonism to the problem of pluralism. Profoundly bothered by the competing sects, Joseph Smith, like Roger Williams and many of his day, concluded that the sects were "all wrong together" and that Christ's church was no longer on the earth. Also like Williams, Smith looked for a divine restoration of the original church by a latter-day prophet: "But there the similarities break down, for Smith and Williams differed profoundly in two major respects. Most obvious is that Williams died a seeker, still longing and searching for the prophet and the restoration. In contrast, Smith himself became that prophet and by 1830 claimed that God, through Smith, had restored the Church of Christ again to the earth" (136). Because of Mormonism's anti-pluralist posture, its restorationism was more encompassing (including, for example, the gifts of the Spirit and revelation) than that of others who sought to merely emulate the faith and practices of the ancients. Indeed, referring to their vision of "the restoration of all things" (17), Mormons embraced a scheme of restoration that was cosmic in its scope and that encompassed time from its very beginning to the end.

Jan Shipps wrote "The Reality of the Restoration and the Restoration Ideal in the Mormon Tradition," which appeared in Hughes's *The American Quest for the Primitive Church*. She similarly argued that Mormonism is not merely a restoration of the primitive church, it is *the* restoration of direct communication between God and man. The Mormon dispensation did not "supersede all previous dispensations, it fulfilled them" (183, 191). These characteristics are largely responsible for Mormonism's growth. Shipps adds, "The Mormon conviction that they were directly connected to both Old and New Testament restoration promises . . . proved to be a motive force powerful enough to bring a new religious tradition into being" (183).[6]

---

5. For example, Hill lists Joel Johnson, Wilford Woodruff, Hosea Stout, Oliver Huntington, Newel K. Knight, Edward Hunter, Parley P. Pratt, John Taylor, Daniel Tyler, Willard Richards, Nathaniel Henry Felt, and Lorenzo Snow.

6. This article was reprinted as "The Prophet Puzzle: Suggestions toward a More Comprehensive Interpretation of Joseph Smith," in *The New Mormon History*, edited by D. Michael Quinn, (Salt Lake City: Signature Books 1999). This compilation contains fifteen essays from believers and non-believers alike attempting to further explain the enigma that was and is Joseph Smith. Another essay in the same volume, Samuel S.

Paulsen: The Search for Cultural Origins of Mormon Doctrines

In *Religious Seekers and the Advent of Mormonism,* Dan Vogel argued that "Seekerism," the most extreme expression of Christian primitivism, must be factored into any complete understanding of Mormon origins (218). He distinguished Seekerism from other modes of primitivism, detailed the similarities between Seekerism and Mormonism, and concluded that Joseph Smith's early revelations were significantly impacted by Seeker beliefs, especially as mediated to him through his own parents.

According to Vogel, many Mormon converts were attracted to the new religion's radical authority claims because Mormonism was congruent with their literalistic expectation of an apostolic restoration. Contrary to less radical primitivists, Seekers believed that the apostasy was so complete that only a new dispensation could remedy the situation (52). Other parallels between Seeker and Mormon doctrine also run long and deep. These include the view that both Catholic and Protestant churches were equally misled; the rejection of scripture as a sure means of salvation because the original manuscripts have been lost; the rejection of Puritan Calvinism because of its "intellectual and 'heartless' doctrines"; the belief that the atonement was for all but that it was not unconditional; the beliefs, countering the Calvinistic tenets of "irresistible grace" and "total depravity," that someone who had been saved could fall from grace and that individuals had freedom to choose between good and evil; and the belief that human beings could overcome the depravity of the fall (perfectionism). The Mormon doctrine of deification, though more extreme than most Seeker expectations, was certainly in line with their optimistic view of human nature. Mormonism also fulfilled the Seeker quest for "a spirit filled ministry" replete with gifts and manifestations of the Holy Spirit (61-62, 67-68, 70-71, 169). Vogel added to this list: "Direct revelations from God—the desire of Seekers—especially in restoring the true church and true doctrine of Christ, was the promise of Mormonism. The Book of Mormon—echoing the gospel according to Seekers—criticizes rational religion for denying the operations of the spirit while at the same time criticizing revivalism for not embracing a radical enough concept of spiritual gifts" (90).

Vogel's analysis provoked mixed reviews. Mark Thomas, "The Ideal Apostasy and Restoration," *Sunstone,* June 1989, 46, criticized him for attributing too much influence to the Seekers, indicating, for instance, that there is no mention in Mormon doctrine of the Seeker split between a visible and invisible church. David J. Whittaker, Review, *Western Historical Quarterly* 21 (August 1990): 378, complained that Vogel used the term *Seeker* so loosely that it consequently had little meaning. Grant Underwood, Review, *BYU Studies* 30 (Winter 1990): 120, charged that Vogel reified "Seeker" into a sect or movement that in reality never existed. While "seeker" (lower-cased) described the "spiritual nomads of [any age] for whom institutional Christianity was effete and who awaited a recrudescence of genuine religion," Vogel used the term as a catch-phrase that magically collected people with diverse beliefs under one name, then became the *movement* that most contributed to the rise of Mormonism. Similarly, Daniel Peterson, *Journal for the Scientific Study of Religion* 30, no. 1 (March 1991): 130, pointed out that "once it is realized that Vogel's American 'Seekerism' is an article construct, unknown to history, and one moreover which has been *designed* for comparison with Mormonism, the fact that some 'Seeker' beliefs are comparable to certain Mormon beliefs becomes, well, rather unimpressive." But Thomas, Gerald E. Jones, "Review of *Religious Seekers and the Advent of Mormonism,* by Dan Vogel," *Church History* 59, no. 4 (December 1990): 571-72, and Roger D. Launius, Review, *American Historical Review* 95, no. 4 (October 1990): 1286, concluded that Vogel's work not only merits serious examination but even provides a useful model for examining other influences on Mormonism.

Hill Jr., "Comparing Three Approaches to Restorationism: A Response," concurs that Mormonism was much different from most Christian primitivist movements: "Mormonism is not in essence a derivation or a deviation or a reactionary response. In fact, it is even more than a configuration of components found elsewhere. It is a *sui generis* religious tradition (with parallels of course)" (232).

Religious Seekers
and the
Advent of Mormonism

BY DAN VOGEL

Signature Books
Salt Lake City
1988

Underwood, *The Millenarian World of Early Mormonism*, 2, wrote, "Previous studies of Mormonism have correctly identified the first Latter-day Saint as Christian primitivists . . . but the undergirding essence was the Mormons' millennial worldview." He demonstrates that Mormon millennialism was driven by Bible literalism. Augmenting the Bible's apocalyptic message and the resulting Christian tradition, "biblicist respect for the social categories of antiquity, such as 'Gentile,' or the scriptural devices of boundary maintenance, such as cursing, reinforced the dualism of a millenarian mindset" (74-75). Underwood held that this "mindset" was the most important aspect of early Mormon biblicism.

Underwood saw many of the early revelations as "standard millenarian fare" (24) and the content of Joseph Smith's inspiration as "profoundly Millenarian in character" (23) and outlined five characteristics of early Mormonism's particular version of apocalyptic millenarianism: Salvation was (1) collective, to be enjoyed by the faithful as a group; (2) terrestrial, to be realized here on earth; (3) total, to completely transform life on earth; (4) imminent, to come soon and swiftly rather than gradually; and (5) miraculous, to be accomplished by, or with the help of, supernatural agencies (5). As for other doctrines, Underwood argued that LDS biblical millenarianism influenced the doctrine of the restoration of ancient Israel, which in turn influenced the doctrines of the gathering and polygyny (58-75). He thus made a strong case that biblicism with its related doctrine of Christian primitivism and millenarianism shaped the way in which early Mormonism emerged and developed.

Dan Erickson, like Underwood, has also analyzed LDS intellectual history through a millennialist lens in his book *As a Thief in the Night* (Salt Lake City: Signature Books, 1998). However, his millennialist explanation of Mormon origins goes a step further than Underwood's, as Erickson seemingly argues for the millennialist worldview as the major shaping force behind the emergence and evolution of LDS theology. Erickson's book begins with a brief history of millennialist beliefs in nineteenth-century New England and ends with "the Manifesto and Mormon Capitulation" (229); but despite some very in-depth and careful research, it seems obvious that Erickson has overlooked more plausible explanations for certain LDS doctrines. As should be apparent from this historiographical survey, the cultural trail down which he retraces the Mormon past is far too narrow to account alone for the broad expanse of Mormon doctrinal understanding.

Magical Worldviews

The historiography of Mormon theological origins includes a considerable body of recent works concerned with magical beliefs and practices attributed to Joseph Smith and his family during the 1820s, several of which argue that some Mormon theological ideas derive from a magical worldview. These works have struggled with the difficult task of clarifying exactly what magic is. Unfortunately, both scholars and laymen have far too often used *magic* pejoratively, implying that it is inherently bad while religion is inherently good. Understood as inherently bad, the claim that magical ideas contributed to Mormon doctrine has caused some to recoil and protest. More neutrally, scholars have defined magic as a supernatural belief system that emphasizes manipulation and coercion, as contrasted with religion, which is a supernatural belief system emphasizing supplication or submission. According to this understanding, since all supernatural belief systems involve a mixture of magic and religion, a more technical and nonpejorative definition of *magic* is needed.

A helpful model for this purpose has been provided by Massimo Introvigne, professor of religious studies at the Pontifical University Regina Apostolorum, Rome, and director of Center for Studies of New Religions (CESNUR), who describes magic by use of the metaphor of a three-story palace. Folk-magic, which inhabits the first floor, consists of informal and generally coercive magic. Introvigne calls the inhabitants of the second floor "neo-magical movements," organized systems of supernatural belief and practice that use magical concepts and rituals. Floor 3 is the realm of esoterica. Here elites study and discuss refined systems of theosophy such as hermeticism and Rosicrucianism. (One might envision a religious temple with three corresponding floors: folk religion, organized religion, and theology.) Because of its usefulness, and because both LDS and non-LDS historians generally accept Introvigne's work, I will adopt his metaphor of the "magical palace."[7]

Contemporary works that explore the possibility of magic as a source of Mormon theology continue to be informed by E. D. Howe, *Mormonism Unvailed: Or, A Faithful Account of That Singular Imposition and Delusion, from Its Rise to the Present Time. With Sketches of the Characters of Its Propagators, and A Full, Detail of the Manner in which the Famous Golden Bible Was Brought Before the World* (Painesville, OH: E. D. Howe, 1834). This is the book that opened the canon of anti-Mormon literature and which has attained the status of a classic. Howe's work clearly situates Mormonism on the first floor of the magical palace, containing, as it does, affidavits by former acquaintances of Joseph Smith that charge him with being a superstitious treasure-seeker and that allege he used magical rituals (such as drawing magic circles) and using divinatory devices (e.g., divining rods and seer stones) to help him in his quest for buried treasure. Howe argued that Joseph Smith's claims to be a prophet followed directly from his use of divinatory devices within the folk-magical context of the treasure quest (43). "Joseph Smith, Jun.," he asserted, "was well skilled in legerdemain, and the use of the divining-rods, which afforded him great facilities in translating [the golden plates]. He doubtless had become acquainted with mystifying every thing, and collected that class of people about him, who were willing dupes, and anxious devotees to the marvelous. To establish the truth of any pretension, however ridiculous and absurd it might be, required nothing but some little necromancy, and it would be received as of divine inspiration by them" (43, also 11-12, 17-18, 31-32). Howe originated the tradition among evangelical pamphleteers of arguing that Mormonism originated from black magic—that it was, in fact, inspired by the devil. A twentieth-century example is W. J. Mck. McCormick,, *Occultism: The True Origins of Mormonism* (Belfast, Ireland: Raven Publishing, 1967).

Dale Morgan's work on early Mormonism, unfinished at his death in 1971, but subsequently published in 1986 as *Dale Morgan on Early Mormonism,* contains important insights into Mormonism's origins based on meticulous research in primary sources. If this manuscript, which he worked on regularly from the 1930s to the early 1950s, had been published earlier, it would no doubt have hastened similar examinations. Morgan, like Eber Howe, concluded that Smith's role and views grew directly out of his participation in folk magic.

Historians have reiterated Howe's thesis, beginning with Protestant minister Wesley P. Walters, "New Light on Mormon Origins from the Palmyra (N. Y.) Revival," *Bulletin of the Evangelical Theological Society* 10, no. 4 (Fall 1967): 227-44. Walters argued, on the basis of newspaper notices and church records in the Palmyra area, that the revival which provoked the First Vision experience took place in 1824, not in 1820 as portrayed in Joseph Smith's autobiography in his "story" canonized in the Pearl of Great Price. Walters's article, which generated a flurry of intensive research on Mormon origins, was later reprinted in *Dialogue* 4 (Spring 1969): 60-81. Walters also attacked the authenticity of Joseph Smith's first vision story, arguing that it capped a long series of magical treasure quests. According to Walters, Joseph Smith initially sought to propitiate a spirit guardian of buried treasure, then later transformed the golden treasure into golden plates of scripture and the treasure's guardian into an angel. Still later, Smith inflated this angel into Christ himself and, finally, into both the Father and the Son (71-73). In sum, Walters maintained, magic influenced the Mormon theology of God and revelation.

In *Mormonism, Magic, and Masonry* (1983; 2d ed., Salt Lake City: Utah Lighthouse Ministry, 1988), 22-23, Jerald and Sandra Tanner followed Howe and Walters in claiming

---

7. Massimo Introvigne, "Mormonism and the Occult Connection," paper presented at "Mormons as Americans: A Symposium Co-sponsored by the Sunstone Foundation and Boston University's American and New England Studies Program," Boston, November 1995; audiocassette 1995 NE-3 produced by the Sunstone Foundation, Salt Lake City, 1995, side A.

that Joseph transformed necromancy into the doctrine of ministering angels, without arguing that he later inflated it into the First Vision.

Mark Hofmann's forgeries in the mid-1980s, especially his "White Salamander" letter, redirected the attention of historians to the folk-magical elements in the culture in which Mormonism emerged. Alan Taylor, in two 1986 articles—"The Early Republic's Supernatural Economy: Treasure Seeking in the American Northeast, 1780-1830," *American Quarterly* 38, no. 1 (Spring 1986): 6-34; and "Rediscovering the Context of Joseph Smith's Treasure Seeking," *Dialogue* 19, no. 4 (Winter 1986): 18-28—suggested that Mormonism's ontology (including its doctrine of divine embodiment) derived from the materialistic worldview of magic in general and of treasure seeking in particular. Taylor's work was followed by D. Michael Quinn's *Early Mormonism and the Magic World View* (Salt Lake City: Signature Books, 1987), the most comprehensive book yet on the relationship between magic and Mormonism even before he published a greatly enlarged second edition in 1998. Though developing a magical perspective of the Mormon past, Quinn recognized that magic was only "one of the components of a complex mix that also included the common American's emphasis on pragmatism and common sense, together with devotion to the Bible, an intensely personal relationship with God, the belief in the reality of divine and diabolic intervention in daily life, expectations that God's true church should be like apostolic Christianity, and a conviction that the glorious return of Christ to the earth was imminent" (228).

Quinn drew parallels between Mormon theology and the hylozoism of the magical worldview, both of which held that animals, plants, and even planets had spirits and were living beings—and that all materiality was full of life. In such a universe, a multitude of natural and supernatural beings are subject to physical (or metaphysical) laws and may be manipulated by employing those laws (xii). Given manipulation as the defining aspect of magic, Quinn argued that Mormon theology incorporated the concept of manipulation and thus is an expression of a magical worldview, citing, as an example, "I, the Lord, am bound when ye do what I say; but when ye do not what I say, ye have no promise" (D&C 82:10; pp. 71, xiii-xiv, 190-91, figs. 51-52).

More specifically, Quinn developed the relationship between folk-magical divination and the theology of revelation, amassing evidence that both Joseph Sr. and Joseph Jr. used a divining rod, particularly to locate buried treasure according to the folk magical lore of the treasure quest. He documents that Joseph Jr. was a scryer before Moroni's visits and shows how snugly Smith's seer stones fit within a folk-magic historical and cultural setting. (A scryer divines by using a reflective surface like a crystal ball or seer stone.) Quinn shows that Joseph was not the only owner and operator of a seer stone; in fact, he found his first seer stone by looking into the stone of another village seer (38-40). Joseph used these stones to search for buried treasure and later to find the golden plates of the Book of Mormon and to translate them. He also points to the connection between the doctrine of ministering angels or angelic messengers and necromancy, specifically, the ceremonial magic of spirit invocation. He conjectures that the Smiths used ceremonial magic in an attempt to enlist the aid of or to overcome the spiritual beings who guarded treasure in the magical tradition of the treasure quest. Thus, Joseph Smith would have initially seen Moroni and his golden plates in the context of a treasure guardian and his golden treasure. Finally, Quinn notes that Joseph received several revelations—including many of the first revelations in the church—through a stone (27-52). Quinn thus emphasized a smooth transition from the magical world of seer stones to the religious world of Joseph Smith as a prophet and seer with a theology of revelation (143-45, 195-200, 204-5).

Quinn's book also offers numerous parallels of a weaker nature. In particular, he discusses the similarities between (1) a medallion Joseph owned and the doctrine of a Heavenly Mother, (2) baptism for the dead in Christian occult communities and Mormonism's vicarious soteriology of proxy ritual, (3) magical and mystical texts concerning three degrees of postmortal glory and the Mormon version of afterlife, and (4) the possible influence of astrological beliefs on polygamy (65, 74, 181, 172-205). Magic affected not only Mormonism's earliest years, according to Quinn, but the entire founding period. He argues, for example, that temple ordinances and theology, particularly the concept of the ascent into heaven, have much more in common with the Eleusinian mysteries than with Freemasonry (184-90).

More recently Grant H. Palmer has used the magical worldview to present what he calls *An Insider's View of Mormon Origins* (Salt Lake City: Signature Books, 2002). Specifically, Palmer argues that Joseph Smith's account of the retrieval of the golden plates was actually a revamped version of E. T. A. Hoffmann's children's tale entitled "The Golden Pot," which Palmer claims was transmitted to Joseph by one Luman Walters (139-40). In his book Palmer places Hoffmann's story next to Joseph's 1832, 1835, 1838, and 1842 accounts of the plates' retrieval in an attempt to show the similarities between the two accounts. Palmer concludes: "What do these parallels mean? Clearly, there are similar motifs, descriptions, and occasionally the same terminology in both the New York and 'Golden Pot' narratives. Moreover, how could Joseph control the many detailed events and descriptions that are clearly beyond his power to duplicate and which are common to both narratives? It would stretch credulity to believe that this could be a coincidence, and I therefore think that a debt is owed to E.T.A. Hoffmann and the European traditions for at least some of the details" (171).

The *FARMS Review* 15, no. 2 (2003) received Palmer's book unenthusiastically. Steven C. Harper commented: "[Palmer] presents a partisan polemical argument. In addition, he is guilty of censorship, and . . . repeatedly privileges late hearsay over early eyewitness accounts" (278). Mark Ashurst-McGee noted, "As a historian, I find that the book fails to follow the *basic* standards of historical methodology" (312; emphasis his). Other reviews in this number also found Palmer's scholarship less than adequate for a book of this character.

The claimed connection between magic and Mormonism has not gone unchallenged. In a landmark article, Ronald W. Walker, "Joseph Smith: The Palmyra Seer," *BYU Studies* 24, no. 4 (Fall 1986): 461-72, accepts the claim, "with or without" the suspected Hofmann documents, that the Smith family had been involved in "soothsaying," "predicting the future," and using seer stones. He acknowledged that these activities were causally connected with the early Mormon doctrines of prophecy and revelation. But instead of arguing for a naturalistic evolution from Joseph's magical practices and beliefs to revelation and prophecy, he suggests that Joseph eventually transcended these culturally acquired antecedents. He "required some time and effort to separate religious truth from [his] own sincerely held, culture-derived ideas. . . . [But] with Providence's intervention, [Joseph] transformed himself from 'Joseph, the Palmyra Seer,' who likely understood his early religious experiences in one way, to the mature 'Joseph, the Mormon Prophet,' who saw them in quite a different light" (470).

In delivering his presidential address to the Mormon History Association in 1986, Richard L. Bushman, "The Book of Mormon in Early Mormon History," *New Views of Mormon History: A Collection of Essays in Honor of Leonard J. Arrington,* edited by Davis Bitton and Maureen Ursenbach Beecher (Salt Lake City: University of Utah Press, 1987), 3-18, joined Walker in challenging the prevailing historiography relating Mormon doctrine to magic. While admitting that "even with the Hofmann letters out of the picture, magic is now entrenched in the story of Mormonism's founding" (3), he nonetheless rejected the idea "that Joseph Smith was essentially and above all a magician and that magical beliefs lay at the very heart of nineteenth-century Mormonism." He cautioned historians that they "should not forget the Book of Mormon":

> In that volume, we have over five hundred pages of source material, incontestably produced before 1830, that also relate to Smith's character and culture. Furthermore, most of the evidence about magic comes from the minds of others and bears the mark of their preconceptions; the Book of Mormon came from Joseph Smith's own lips giving it a spe-

The Refiner's Fire
The Making of Mormon Cosmology, 1644–1844

JOHN L. BROOKE
Tufts University

cial claim on our attention. There seems to be little question that Smith did follow practices that we would call magic, but before we sum him up in that one idea, we should weigh the few hundred words on that theme against the tens of thousand of words in the Book of Mormon. (4)

Bushman contended that the Book of Mormon, a fundamentally religious work that condemns magic (Morm. 1:19; 2:10), significantly influenced Joseph Smith and stands as compelling evidence against a magical influence strong enough to shape core elements of Mormon theology. Richard L. Bushman, "Treasure Seeking Then and Now," *Sunstone* 11, no. 5 (September 1987): 5-6; and his "Joseph Smith's Family Background," in *The Prophet Joseph: Essays on the Life and Mission of Joseph Smith,* edited by Larry C. Porter and Susan Easton Black (Salt Lake City: Deseret Book, 1988), both acknowledge the link between scrying and the Mormon doctrine of modern revelation and prophecy, but, in an interpretation not unlike Walker's, argued that God "redirected" Joseph Smith from the former to the latter ("Treasure," 5-6).

The year 1994 proved important for this area of Mormon historiography. H. Michael Marquardt and Wesley P. Walters, *Inventing Mormonism: Tradition and the Historical Record* ([Salt Lake City]: Smith Research Associates, 1994), is the culminating work of these two widely known anti-Mormon authors who devoted years of research in primary documents. *Dialogue* published a special issue (Vol. 27, no. 3, Fall 1994) featuring Mormonism and magic, while then Tufts University professor John L. Brooke published *The Refiner's Fire: The Making of Mormon Cosmology, 1644-1844* (Cambridge, UK: Cambridge University Press, 1994).[8]

In *Inventing Mormonism,* Marquardt and Walters continued the project of connecting Mormonism with nineteenth-century folk magic. They saw the transformation of scrying into prophecy as one of the processes by which Mormonism was "invented." Joseph's treasure scrying led "two widely separated communities [Manchester-Palmyra and Bainbridge-Harmony] to associate him with divination and necromancy." Those close to Joseph confirm that he "located the gold plates from which he dictated the Book of Mormon by gazing into his seer stone. He also used this stone to obtain the text of the book as well as to receive instructions from God for his early followers" (75). Marquardt and Walters thus located original Mormonism squarely on the first floor of the magical palace. Scott H. Faulring, Review, *Journal of Mormon History* 21, no. 2 (Fall 1995): 203-8, points out that, while the authors should be commended for their dogged research and their generous quotation of primary documents, they are unwilling to cross-examine possible contradictory sources and that they avoid exploring or discussing alternative analyses of many key events.

Dialogue's special issue on magic contained articles on Mormon origins that pointed to each floor of the magical palace. Dan Vogel, "The Locations of Joseph Smith's Early Treasure Quests," 197-231, presents a folk-magic approach. Michael W. Homer, "'Similarity of Priesthood in Masonry': The Relationship Between Freemasonry and Mormonism," 1-113, describes Mormonism as a neo-magical movement, while Lance S. Owens, "Joseph Smith and Kabbalah: The Occult Connection," 117-94, takes an esoterica approach.

Vogel's article reinforces the Marquardt-Walters thesis, concluding that

> . . . a clear distinction between Smith's role as treasure seer and religious seer cannot be made. In fact, Smith's use of the same stone and the same modus operandi (i.e., placing the stone in his hat) in translating the gold plates are simply two sides of the same coin. It is impossible to understand fully the mature Joseph Smith without coming to terms with

---

8. In 2000, Brooke was awarded the Arthur Jr. and Lenore Stern Chair in American History at Tufts. However, in 2001 he took a position teaching history at Ohio State University and was named an OSU Humanities Distinguished Professor in 2003.

his early role as treasure seer. Indeed, Smith's failure as a treasure seer leads us to a greater understanding of his success as a religious leader. (231)

Reed C. Durham Jr. had broached the subject of magic in his presidential address to the MHA, "Is There No Help For the Widow's Son?" published in an unauthorized edition, with an introduction and notes by Mervin B. Hogan of the Utah Masonic Lodge, as "Reed C. Durham, Jr.'s Astounding Research on the Masonic Influence on Mormonism," *Mormon Miscellaneous* 1, no. 1 (October 1975): 11-16. Michael Homer, like Durham, opened up the second floor of the magical palace as a possible source of Mormon theology by arguing that, after Joseph Smith joined a newly created Masonic lodge in 1842, Freemasonry's neo-magical elements influenced not only temple rituals, but also doctrines of premortal existence and a political kingdom of God (16-17, 92-93). He concluded that it is far more likely that Masonry, and not the Eleusinian mysteries, influenced the Mormon temple endowment, although the extent to which it influenced Mormon theology is less clear (88-89, 92-93, 106-8).

For his part, Owens declares that "Smith's concepts of God's plurality, his vision of God as *anthropos,* and his possession by the issue of sacred marriage, all might have been cross-fertilized by . . . intercourse with Kabbalistic theosophy—an occult relationship climaxing in Nauvoo" (119). Sprinkled throughout the article are suggestions that all of the following Mormon doctrines derived from or were influenced by what he called "the Hermetic-Kabbalistic World View": the coeternality of spirit and matter, a spirit creation that preceded the material creation, eternal marriage, modern revelation, the ministry of angels, humankind's ability to know God and to become divine, the plurality of gods, that gods exist in hierarchized lineages, that God was once a man, and Brigham Young's Adam-God theory. In short, Owens supposes that Mormonism's cosmology, soteriology, and distinctive doctrines of God and man can be traced in some ways back to early modern esoteric thought, the third story of the magical palace (163, 132, 149-50, 131, 178-79, 182-84). Another version of this paper appeared as "Joseph Smith: America's Hermetic Prophet," *Gnosis,* no. 35 (Spring 1995): 56-64.

William Hamblin, "'Everything Is Everything': Was Joseph Smith Influenced by Kabbalah?" *FARMS Review of Books* 8, no. 2 (1996): 251-325, examined nearly every facet of Owens's study, including his sources, methodology, and logic, and concluded: "Owens's thesis cannot bear the weight of critical scrutiny" (319). Among the failings he found were unrestrained speculation, imprecise definition, semantic equivocation, unfamiliarity with recent relevant scholarship, and misreadings of the King Follett Discourse and the *Zohar,* a kabbalistic text Owens posits as a source of Joseph's teachings. He also found problematic the lack of any "*uniquely* kabbalistic ideas in the writings of early Mormons, the methodological imperative if Owens's case is to be substantiated" (320). Many of Smith's ideas that Owens attributes to Alexander Neibaur's kabbalistic tutoring actually antedate Neibaur's arrival in Nauvoo. Further, since those same ideas are also found in biblical texts, Hamblin queries: "Why do we need kabbalism to explain the development of his thought?" (320). Ultimately, Hamblin opines, Owens's theory can be seen "as another attempt in the grand tradition of Quinn and Brooke at *historia ex nihilo*—the creation of history out of nothing. His efforts to pull a magic rabbit out of his hat to bolster environmental explanations of Joseph Smith's revelations are simply smoke and mirrors" (321).

No doubt stirring up the most controversy in recent Mormon historiography is John Brooke's award-winning 1994 history *The Refiner's Fire: The Making of Mormon Cosmology, 1644-1844,* which staked out a new area of research on esoterico-magical Mormon origins. As his main thesis, Brooke argued that Mormonism borrowed the inner logic of its theology from the top floor of the magical palace—in particular, from the esoteric traditions of hermeticism and alchemy.

Brooke rejected the Puritan origins of Mormon doctrine. While Puritanism is "firmly situated in the Magisterial Reformation of Calvinistic theology," Mormonism "springs from the sectarian traditions of the Radical Reformation, in fact from its most extreme fringe" (xv). While the sixteenth-century Reformation separated the European Christians into Protestants and Catholics, Protestants themselves were separated into two distinct groups, reformers and radicals. According to Brooke, both the reforming clergy and laity of Protestantism and the Catholic reformers of the Counter-Reformation "shared a common antipathy for contrary and disorderly voices, most obviously those of prophetic, millenarian, and utopian radicals who challenged the spiritual hegemony and civil privilege that both parties struggled to assert" (5). Radical Protestants posed a threat to the agendas of both reforming Protestants and Catholics. "But the Protestants were divided similarly into two broad camps, reformers and radicals. The first, the Magisterial Reformation of Lutherans, Calvinists, and Anglicans, limited biblical primitivism to a restoration of Augustinian piety and retained a central place for predestination, a restricted human will, and the state's role in upholding a true faith. The advocates of a Radical Reformation, divided in northern Europe broadly between Anabaptists and Spirituals, rejected the state's role in a Christian commonwealth and advanced doctrines of a restoration of a pure apostolic church, free will and universal salvation, human powers of prophecy, and an impending millennium or new dispensation" (6).

Brooke's book is fundamentally a presentation of an hermetic interpretation of Mormonism. Hermeticism is the view that matter, including humankind, emerged from the divine spirit at creation. Unlike the classical Christian account in which Adam fell because he sinned, the hermetic Adam was a divine androgynous being who voluntarily submitted himself to a material world and transformed into two beings—the first couple. Since humankind was divine by origin and imbued with divine potentiality, the hermetic quest focused on recovering the divine power and perfection lost at the Fall. This recovery was achieved through alchemical marriage (*conunctio*), in which Adam's offspring fused dyadic pairings (spirit and matter, male and female) to restore divine immortality. By use of divine powers, human beings could rise to the status of "magus," an exalted level at which the hermetic adept's use of divine power enabled him to be coequal with God—a belief which Brooke calls "divinization" or "perfectionism" (11).

Brooke identifies several parallels between this occult tradition and Mormonism: the coeternality and mutuality of spirit and matter; the perfectibility and even divinization of humankind; the symbolic and religious efficacy of marriage and sexuality; a *felix culpa* ("fortunate fall") and hence a rejection of original sin; an emphasis on human free agency; a denial of the efficacy of grace alone; a differentiated afterlife sometimes expressed as three degrees of glory; an Adam who is prominent and sometimes even divine; a legacy of ancient, hidden books; and racist doctrines concerning Africans.

Brooke devotes the first portion of his book to locating the crossroads at which sectarian Christianity fused with ancient occult hermeticism to produce the perfectionism found much later in Joseph Smith's Mormon message. From the Radical Reformation when this cosmology emerged, Brooke traces hermeticism across the Atlantic into antebellum America, where, he hypothesizes, the message found its way into Joseph Smith's intellectual environs. Brooke fails, however, to provide evidence that the ideas were, in fact, present in these environs.

In the second portion of his book, Brooke shows how Joseph Smith himself underwent a sort of alchemical transmutation as his Mormon theology developed. Joseph Smith began as a "treasure-diviner" or "village conjuror." Although the Book of Mormon is overwhelmingly Christian, "the accounts of the discovery of the plates, the language and narrative structure of the Book of Mormon itself," and various elements of the Book of Mormon story all derive from hermetic influences (149-83). Then with its publication, Smith transformed himself from village conjuror to a "prophet" of the "Word." Finally, Smith matured into a Christian-hermetic magus, teaching the mysteries of co-participation with God. While admitting that his work is "a selective reinterpretation of the founding story of Mormonism" (xvi), Brooke claimed that it is useful to consider 1844 Mormonism as a "hermetic restoration" (4).

The Refiner's Fire gained much attention among historians, receiving not only the prestigious Bancroft Prize in American History, but also the Book Prize of the Society of Historians of the Early American Republic, and the New England Historical Association's Annual Book Award. Most New Mormon Historians, however, found it less than persuasive. Davis Bitton, for example, reviewing it in *BYU Studies* 34, no. 4 (1994): 182-92, wrote: "Add magic and folk culture, mix a bit of quantification, get advance recommendations from scholars who should know their subject, land a respected press to publish your work, and then have it reviewed by people whose mastery of the whole range of subject matter is lacking, and a prize should be in sight. But is this fire, or only smoke?" (182) For Bitton, the answer was smoke only. I found twenty reviews, about half generally positive. The other half, invariably written by New Mormon Historians, were generally negative.[9] Few, if any, of those who positively reviewed *The Refiner's Fire* could be considered specialists on either Mormon or hermetic history.

Of the positive reviews, all praise Brooke's work in tracing the movement of European hermeticism across the Atlantic to early American culture, unquestionably a contribution to American history. Jan Shipps, while noting the weakness of his central thesis, acknowledged in a newspaper interview Brooke's contribution in uncovering more of the unorthodox side of early America's religious past (Stack, C-2); and later, in *Sojourner in the Promised Land: Forty Years Among the Mormons* (Chicago: University of Illinois Press, 2003), she speculated that it was for this reason that *Refiner's Fire* received both the SHEAR and Bancroft Prizes (209). Martin Marty and John Saillant also acknowledged this contribution, although Saillant challenged Brooke's rejection of Mormonism's Puritan roots and his identification of Joseph Smith as a direct heir of the Radical Reformation: "Brooke presupposes a sharp divide between 'magisterial' Puritanism on the one hand and the Radical Reformation and occult beliefs and practices on the other," but in fact, Saillant argues, the world of the occult permeated the barrier between the radical reformation and orthodox Puritanism (233).

The Johnson reviewers lauded Brooke's "extensive [use] of primary research," and his "intricately marshaled evidence" (Curtis Johnson, 684; see also Owens, 187). Paul Johnson added admiringly, "Brooke's approach is refreshingly old-fashioned: he simply stayed in the library until he had read everything that pertained to Smith's spiritual and religious ideas and their antecedents" (47). Also praising Brooke's seemingly exhaustive research were Cohen, Frost, Marty (26), and Stein (168, 169, 172).

---

9. Kenneth Anderson, "The Magi of the Great Salt Lake," (London) *Times Literary Supplement*, March 24, 1995, 10-11; Philip L. Barlow, "Decoding Mormonism," *Christian Century*, January 17, 1996, 52-55; Philip L. Barlow, "Decoding Mormonism," *John Whitmer Historical Association Journal* 16 (1996): 123-31; Richard L. Bushman, "The Mysteries of Mormonism," *Journal of the Early Republic* 15, no. 3 (Fall 1995): 502-8; Richard L. Bushman, "The Secret History of Mormonism," *Sunstone* (March 1996), 66-70; Charles L. Cohen, Review, *William and Mary Quarterly* 53, no. 1 (January 1996), 213-15; Douglas Davies, Review, *Journal of Ecclesiastical History* 46 (October 1995): 745; Douglas Davies, Review, *Scottish Journal of Theology* 49, no. 2 (1996): 235-37; Paul M. Edwards, "The Salting of Mormon History," *John Whitmer Historical Association Journal* 16 (1996): 120-23; Rachelle E. Friedman, Review, *Journal of Interdisciplinary History* 27, no. 2 (1996): 329-31; J. W. Frost, Review, *Choice: Current Reviews of Academic Books*, March 1995, 1137 (one paragraph long); William J. Hamblin, Daniel C. Peterson, and George L. Mitton, Review, *BYU Studies* 34, no. 4 (1994-95), 167-81; Curtis D. Johnson, Review, *Journal of American History* 82, no. 2 (September 1995), 684-85; Paul E. Johnson, "The Alchemist," *New Republic*, June 12, 1995, 46-48; Bill Martin, "Prophetic Communitarianism: A Synthesis of Hermetic and Sociological Analyses of the Origins of Mormonism," Sunstone Symposium, Salt Lake City, August 1995, audiocassette SL95 153 in my possession; Martin E. Marty, "Saints for these Latter Days," *Commonweal*, March 10, 1995, 26-27; "Mormonism in American Historiography: John L. Brooke's *The Refiner's Fire* and Competing Versions of Mormon Origins," panel by Clyde R. Forsberg, Bill Martin, and D. Michael Quinn, with comments by John L. Brooke, at "Mormons as Americans," a symposium cosponsored by the Sunstone Foundation and Boston University American and New England Studies Program, Boston, November 1995, audiocassette by the Sunstone Foundation, 1995 NE-4; Lance S. Owens, "The Divine Transmutation," *Dialogue* 27, no. 4 (Winter 1994), 187-191; John Saillant, Review, *Vermont History* 63 (1995); Peggy Fletcher Stack, "Book Explores Joseph Smith and Alchemy," *Salt Lake Tribune*, April 15, 1995, C-1, C-2; Stephen J. Stein, *Journal of Mormon History* 22, no. 2 (Fall 1996): 168-72; Grant Underwood, *Pacific Historical Review* 65, no. 2 (May 1996), 323-34; and Paul L. Owen, Institute for Religious Research, http://www.irr.org/mit/Refiner's-Fire.html (2000).

Excavating Mormon Pasts

Yet FARMS reviewers William J. Hamblin, Daniel C. Peterson, and George L. Mitton sharply criticized the "utter lack of primary sources written by early Latter-day Saints, manifesting any clear connection to alchemy, hermeticism, or magic" (16). Furthermore, they did a representative, though not exhaustive, computer search of early LDS writings and documented that references to the occult are always negative in tone. Examples include Orson Pratt's lament that "alchemists tried for generations to transmute the coarser materials into gold, and hundreds have spent all their time in pursuit of that vain phantom" (16-17); four negative references to the Salem witch trials (17); Book of Mormon and Doctrine and Covenants disapproval of "sorceries, witchcraft, and magics" (18); and examples of official condemnation of occult practices including church discipline for "using magic and telling fortunes" (18-19). The reviewers also note that "Brooke's key terms, such as 'alchemy,' 'astrology,' 'hermeticism,' 'androgyny,' and 'cabala' are never mentioned in LDS scripture" (18).

Also while Curtis Johnson (685) and Paul Johnson (47) praised Brooke for his "balanced" approach, Brooke himself conceded that his book is "not necessarily a well-rounded approach to early Mormonism" (xvii); and Philip Barlow observed: "Brooke so regularly overreaches his evidence, overstates his parallels, misconstrues his subject, indulges his speculations, exaggerates the centrality of hermetic analogue for Mormon thought, depends upon suspect authorities, and ignores alternative (and simpler) explanations that he finally undercuts himself" (126).

Other criticisms have scored *The Refiner's Fire*'s methodological leaps, factual errors, forcing of evidence, and "often remarkable misreadings of texts" (Hamblin, Peterson, Mitton, 58). Borrowing Samuel Sandmel's term, Underwood asserted that the book suffered from "'parallelomania' . . . the tendency to exaggerate similarities and the assumption that parallels prove provenance" (323). Hamblin, Peterson, and Mitton agreed, charging that Brooke had committed the "fallacy of perfect analogy, which consists in reasoning from a partial resemblance between two entities to an entire and exact correspondence" (45). Bushman wrote that Brooke "cannot point to a single site where Joseph Smith could have learned about the ideas that supposedly influenced him most"; thus, his need to fit everything Mormon into some aspect of hermetic philosophy makes him ever more "determined to find a precedent somewhere for every Mormon idea, even if he must reach back a century or two" (68). Marxist philosopher Bill Martin agreed that Brooke "can, at most, only speak of the possible implications of Smith's background for what emerged in Smith's visions and revelations, not to absolute connections . . . . and he is in danger of allowing his own cultural continuity model, as he puts it, to become an overdetermined framework" (audiocassette). Paul Edwards criticized Brooke's heavy dependence upon *post hoc ergo prompter hoc* reasoning—the assumption that "if X comes before Y then X must somehow be responsible for Y" (123). Hamblin, Peterson, and Mitton devoted a lengthy section to the same point (43-52). Underwood observed disapprovingly that Brooke's "ear is clearly more attuned to the hermetic 'community of discourse' than the Mormon" (324; see also Barlow, 128). Consequently, Brooke does not allow for antecedents outside of hermeticism—not even the Bible.

As to factual errors, Davis Bitton wrote that spotting them was "child's play." For example, contrary to Brooke, Joseph Smith never claimed he was Enoch (185). Brooke fell victim to his own enthusiasm by urging: "If we widen our definition of alchemy to include counterfeiting, the ranks and the chronology of the alchemical tradition are extended mightily" (162). I question the advantages of abandoning solid definitions in favor of a particular hypothesis. In an otherwise positive review, Charles Cohen conceded that *The Refiner's Fire* "is marred perhaps by . . . a tendency to oblique explanations" (215). In addition, Underwood points out the book is "marred by a lack of source criticism." That is, by avoiding primary sources and relying heavily on secondary and even anti-Mormon sources, Brooke, in spite of his wide-ranging research, "does little to help readers identify source biases or weigh their relative merits" (324). Underwood also criticizes Brooke's failure to pay sufficient "attention to the contextual and situated nature of meaning" (323).

In the same year that Cambridge published *The Refiner's Fire, The Journals of William E. McLellin, 1831-1836,* edited by Jan Shipps and John W. Welch appeared in a co-published edition (Provo, UT: BYU Studies/Urbana: University of Illinois Press, 1994). Reviewers Barlow and Bushman compared the two books, concluding that the McLellin journals showed a biblicist Mormonism that refuted Brooke's thesis. This point was not lost on McLellin's editor, Jan Shipps, who wrote in "Another Side of Early Mormonism," her introduction to the journals:

> Many . . . expected—and some feared—that any contemporaneous documents in a collection of McLellin's papers would be filled with information that would add to a perception of early Mormonism as a hotbed of occultism and hermetic hocus-pocus. Instead, what these narratives from the 1830s depict is a struggling missionary band preaching not only a millenialist message that, to be sure, reflected the importance of the coming forth of the Book of Mormon as a signal that the end was near, but also a message whose true anchor was nonetheless the Christian scriptures. (3)

Barlow, (125-26), Bitton (187), Quinn (side A), and Hamblin, Peterson, and Mitton (39-43), united in contending that Brooke's failure to acknowledge the Bible meant either that he did not know the Bible well or that he purposely ignored it. Brooke countered that he had not ignored the Bible and its tremendous influence upon Joseph Smith and early Mormonism. However, he stressed that early Mormon use of the Bible was vastly different than general Protestant use of the Bible, and that what people brought to the good book was more important than the text itself. Furthermore, he asserted, Joseph Smith performed a hermetic reading of the Bible (side B).

The historiographical impact of *The Refiner's Fire* has already been felt in part. How long it will haunt Mormon history remains to be seen. Roger D. Launius has speculated that *The Refiner's Fire* may become the fourth historiographical heavyweight[10]—the first three being Brodie, *No Man Knows My History,* Arrington, *Great Basin Kingdom: An Economic History of the Latter-day Saints, 1830-1900* (1958; reprint ed., Salt Lake City: University of Utah Press and the Tanner Trust Fund, 1993) and Flanders, *Nauvoo: Kingdom on the Mississippi.* However, Paul M. Edwards predicted that it "will quickly drift from center stage" (121); and Jan Shipps has recently written that "despite what Brooke has added to our knowledge of important features of the early LDS story, I think it is unlikely the *Refiner's Fire* will become a standard work, one of those about which a scholarly consensus develops regarding whether it is essential to the study of American religion or the study of Mormonism. . . . Readers wanting to understand the beginnings of Mormonism are still likely to turn to older works: Fawn McKay Brodie's *No Man Knows My History*, Donna Hill's *Joseph Smith, the First Mormon* and Richard Bushman's *Joseph Smith and the Beginnings of Mormonism*" (*Sojourner,* 213). It remains to be seen what part Brooke's hermetic thesis of Mormon doctrinal origins will play historiographically.

Returning to Massimo Introvigne's metaphor of the magical palace, it can be seen that historians have seen Mormon theology generated on all three floors. There are two possibilities for comprehensive analysis that will incorporate all of this history. Introvigne explains that the floors of the palace are connected by stairways on which the inhabitants (concepts) move up and down. If Mormon origins truly involve elements from all three levels of magic, then perhaps Mormonism itself could be viewed as an entire palace, or adjacent temple, rather than a mere inhabitant of a single floor. However, I doubt that a comprehensive approach of this sort would succeed. Stacking up a group of already weak arguments would produce an edifice so rickety that even a reinforcing stairwell could not save the structure.

---

10. Roger D. Launius, participant on a panel, "Fawn McKay Brodie's *No Man Knows My History:* A Fifty Year Perspective," with Lavina Fielding Anderson, Newell G. Bringhurst, Todd Compton, Mario S. De Pillis, and Maricio Mazon, Sunstone Symposium, Salt Lake City, August 1995, audiocassette SL 95 001, tape 1, side B.

Introvigne may be hinting at another approach, which lies in the nature of neo-magical movements. Residents of the middle floor reach up and seize esoteric ideas, popularizing them so that they can be used to organize new syntheses with material from the ground floor. Such an image may explain why Introvigne, a sociologist who studies new religions and neo-magical movements, has paid attention to Mormonism, even though he has not specifically identified any intellectual transmissions from magic to Mormonism. Cast as a neo-magical movement, early Mormonism would connect the three floors of the magical palace, allowing historians to synthesize the full spectrum of the historiography under review. This approach, if taken, would also be fraught with problems; but historians will likely continue to identify magical ideas hitherto unconsidered as antecedents of Mormon theology and argue over them.

Conclusion: Not "Laying aside Revelation"

Where are we now after a half-century of historical probing for the cultural origins of early Mormon doctrines? I believe a plausible answer to this question might run something like this: Our awareness of cultural antecedents (and, hence, of possible cultural explanations) of several Mormon doctrines has increased significantly; yet all explanations to date are, at best, partial, neither individually nor collectively even beginning to account for all Mormon doctrines considered severally let alone for their unique synthesis in the teachings of Joseph Smith. For this comprehensive and coherent synthesis, there is no cultural antecedent; it must thus be explained in some other way. Furthermore, as my historiographical survey clearly reveals, competent and candid historians have arrived at little by way of consensus regarding any specific claim of cultural reductionism. And so, the work must continue—perhaps indefinitely.

At this point, let us engage in a simple thought experiment. Let us suppose that cultural reductionists realize their fondest dream—that is, that they uncover a cultural antecedent (and, hence, a possible cultural explanation) for every specific Mormon doctrine. What would this hypothetical development portend for the veracity of Mormon claims of divine origin for their doctrines? Little or nothing.

First, as any logician would immediately remind us, the inference that a particular Mormon belief must have been derived from some demonstrated cultural parallel is a non sequitur. Second—and this is a point often overlooked—considerable *direct* cultural borrowing is perfectly consistent with Mormon self-understanding. Joseph Smith saw his work as the literal fulfillment of biblical prophecies pertaining to the latter-day "times of restitution of all things" (Acts 3:21)—"the dispensation of the fulness of times" when "all things" would be "gathered together in one" (Eph. 1:10). Of it, President Gordon B. Hinckley has said: "This is the dispensation of the fullness of times when God has moved His hand to bring about a restoration of all previous keys, authorities, and blessings of His gospel."[11]

Although Joseph Smith understood, to be sure, that God was superintending the work of restoration, he also understood that in the process God expected concurrent human initiative—not only in seeking and receiving direct revelation from God, but also in seeking, recognizing, and appropriating "truths" from others, wherever found. For instance, on March 22, 1839, Joseph wrote to Isaac Galland from Liberty Jail: "Mormonism is truth, in other words the doctrine of the Latter Day Saints, is truth. . . . Now, sir, you may think that it is a broad assertion that it is truth; but sir, the first and fundamental principle of our holy religion is, that we believe that we have a right to embrace all, and every item of truth, without limitation or without being circumscribed or prohibited by the creeds or superstitious notions of men."[12]

At least three times in Nauvoo, Joseph asserted the Saints' right to embrace every discoverable truth. On January 22, 1843, he declared: "We don't ask any people to throw

---

11. *Teachings of Gordon B. Hinckley* (Salt Lake City: Deseret Book, 1998), 157.
12. Dean C. Jessee, ed., *Personal Writings of Joseph Smith* (Salt Lake City: Deseret Book, 2002), 458.

away any good they have got; we only ask them to come and get more."[13] Seven months later on July 9, 1843, the Prophet taught: "One of the grand fundamental principles of 'Mormonism' is to receive truth, let it come from where it may."[14] Then two weeks later on Sunday, July 23, 1843, Joseph added: "Have the Presbyterians any truth? Yes. Have the Baptists, Methodists, etc., any truth? Yes. They have a little truth mixed with error. We should gather all the good and true principles in the world and treasure them up, or we shall not come out true 'Mormons.'"[15]

Though Joseph understood that God was providentially guiding the restoration process, he also made clear that much of the responsibility for truth-gathering rested first with the Saints. Thus, it seems that direct cultural borrowings, if such there were, square perfectly with Mormon self-understanding and in no way rule out divine direction.

However, Richard Bushman in "The Secret History of Mormonism" raised some serious questions about the sufficiency of the project as currently conceived, quoting America's foremost literary critic, the Gnostic Jew Harold Bloom, *The American Religion: The Emergence of the Post-Christian Nation* (New York: Simon and Schuster, 1992). Bloom concluded that Joseph Smith was an "authentic religious genius," whose "genius for restoration exceeded that of Muhammed" and of whom "the religious necessity and sincerity of [his] vision are beyond doubt" (80-82, 104). However, Bushman warned that "introducing the word 'genius' is admittedly a dangerous game for secular writers, for works of genius are by their nature, inexplicable. Genius, by common admission, carries human achievement beyond the limits of simple historical explanation, just as revelation does. To say that the Book of Mormon could only be written by a genius is logically not much different from saying God revealed it. In both cases, we admit that historical analysis fails us" (69).

Bushman also acknowledged that purely cultural explanations had failed him as well in his own search for Mormon origins. Instead, he discovered that, while culture may have shaped the questions Joseph Smith asked, it does not explain the answers he gave. In his *Joseph Smith and the Beginnings of Mormonism* (Urbana: University of Illinois Press, 1988), he explained that he had originally planned to title the book *Joseph Smith and Origins of Mormonism* but found that "an attempt to trace all the images, ideas, language, and emotional structure of a movement as elaborate as Mormonism became more evidently elusive and futile as the work went on." Indeed, historical works that "depict persons and ideas as the sum total of the historical forces acting on them" tend to exaggerate similarities between a subject and its supposed origins, while suppressing differences. "We can understand Mormonism better if it is seen as an independent creation, drawing from its environment but also struggling against American culture in an effort to realize itself." Although "there is no denying that many of [Joseph Smith's] ideas are not new" ("Secret," 66), he concluded that Joseph "is best understood as a person who outgrew his culture" (*Joseph*, 7). As Bushman saw Joseph's relation to his cultural milieu: "The teaching of the religious world around him, questions from his followers, and incidents of everyday life moved Joseph to seek answers which then grew in unforeseen directions, blossoming into explications of doctrine that went far beyond the original stimulus. In a sense, Joseph Smith as revelator could be said to have had a green thumb: from the smallest seed he grew mustard trees" ("Secret," 67).

And I believe that perhaps it is this "green thumb" of revelation that will, in the end, doom attempts at naturalistic reduction to failure, for, as Terryl L. Givens *By the Hand of Mormon: The American Scripture that Launched a New World Religion* (New York: Oxford University Press, 2002), points out: "Ironically, the exact same evidence [adduced] to invalidate the [*Book of Mormon's*] ancient origin is adduced by believers to confirm its prophetic qualities," Indeed, "to the Mormon orthodox, then, the Book of Mormon's status would

---

13. Joseph Smith Jr. et al., *History of the Church of Jesus Christ of Latter-day Saints*, edited by B. H. Roberts, 7 vols. (Salt Lake City: Deseret News Press, 1902-12, vols. 1-6, Vol. 7 published 1932; 1976 reprinting), 5:259.
14. Ibid., 5:499.
15. Ibid., 5:516-17.

be suspect if it did *not* evince remarkable relevance to the context in which it has been read" (166). My personal conviction is that the same statement could be made of any doctrine taught by any prophet in any dispensation.

Leonard J. Arrington, former Church Historian, former director of the Joseph Fielding Smith Institute for Latter-day Saint History and arguably the founder of the New Mormon History, perhaps foresaw our contemporary dialogue on naturalistic or cultural explanations for the origins of Mormon doctrine. In his preface to *Great Basin Kingdom* in 1958, he explained, to readers troubled by his naturalistic treatment of sacred historic themes:

> The Church holds, of course, that it is based on divine revelation. The body of revealed knowledge, however, at least to the Latter-day Saint, is not static, but constantly changing and expanding. Revelation is continuous and expedient—"suited to the people and the times." Moreover, it is impossible to separate revelation from the conditions under which it is received: "We have this treasure in earthen vessels." Or, as Brigham Young expressed it, "the revelations which I receive are all upon natural principles." The true essence of God's revealed will, if such it be, cannot be apprehended without an understanding of the conditions surrounding the prophetic vision, and the symbolism and verbiage in which it is couched. Surely God does not reveal His will except to those prepared, by intellectual and social experience and by spiritual insight and imagination, to grasp and convey it. A naturalistic discussion of "the people and the times" and of the mind and experience of Latter-day prophets is therefore a perfectly valid aspect of religious history, and, indeed, makes more plausible the truths they attempted to convey. While the discussion of naturalistic causes of revelation does not preclude its claim to be revealed or inspired of God, in practice it is difficult, if not impossible, to distinguish what is objectively "revealed" from what is subjectively "contributed" by those receiving the revelation. (1958 ed., ix; 1993 xxiv; emphasis mine)

The New Mormon History, characterized by a spirit of broad methodologies and nondogmatic investigation, has been and should remain open—indeed, sympathetic—to the possibility that divine revelation was an important or even the most important explanation of Mormon doctrine.

DAVID L. PAULSEN is a professor of philosophy at Brigham Young University, with special interests in the philosophy of religion and LDS intellectual history. His scholarly writings have appeared in international, national and local venues including the *Harvard Theological Review*, the *International Journal for the Philosophy of Religion*, *Analysis*, the *Journal of Speculative Philosophy*, *Faith and Philosophy*, and *BYU Studies*. He expresses appreciation to the Richard L. Evans Chair for Religious Understanding, which funded the research for this paper, and especially to Mark Ashurst-McGee, staff member of the Joseph Fielding Smith Institute for LDS Church History. Mark made a very substantial contribution to this essay: first as research assistant and finally as a professional consultant. The following student assistants have each contributed significantly to the research for this paper: Spencer Anderson, Greg Call, Darren Mitchell, Abraham Skousen, Tyler Stoehr, and Nathan Westbrook. To all of these, but especially to Mark, Paulsen acknowledges his deep indebtedness.

Chapter 3

Mormon Origins: The Church in New York and Ohio

Roger D. Launius

From almost the beginning of what has been called the New Mormon History a debate has been raging in Mormon intellectual (and in some not so intellectual) circles about the nature of Mormon history. Beginning with Richard L. Bushman's 1969 article, "Faithful History," and continuing to D. Michael Quinn's "On Being a Mormon Historian (and Its Aftermath)," the stresses and strains of Mormon historical inquiry have been an important subtext of every Mormon historical publication.[1] These tensions essentially revolve around Mormonism's long-standing merger of history and theology and the inevitable problem this situation creates when historical interpretation does not always matching previous faith perceptions. When historians have found that Mormon historical evolution has not been nearly so cut and dried as the faith story suggests, it has the potential of creating a theological crisis of conscience in thinking Mormons. The difficulties of navigating the shoals of faith and history are tellingly discussed in Leonard J. Arrington's memoir, *Adventures of a Church Historian* (Urbana: University of Illinois Press, 1998). An interesting further exploration of this issue is Jan Shipps, *Sojourner in the Promised Land: Forty Years among the Mormons* (Urbana: University of Illinois Press, 2000), an insightful account of an outsider's observation of the subject. In my presidential address before the Mormon History Association, "Mormon Memory, Mormon Myth, and Mormon History," *Journal of Mormon History* 21 (Spring 1995): 1-24, I explored some of the challenges of being a historian of Mormonism.

This essay will examine these themes as they have been played out in the New Mormon History during the last thirty years and will conclude with some suggestions for continued exploration of the early Mormon experience in New York and Ohio.

General Works

All of the overviews of Mormon history have included the early Mormon experience as foundational in the development of the religion. The best general treatment of the era among survey histories is four chapters in James B. Allen and Glen M. Leonard, *The Story of the Latter-day Saints* (1976; 2d ed. rev., Salt Lake City: Deseret Book, 1992). They

---

1. Both of these articles, as well as others dealing with this subject have been conveniently reprinted in George D. Smith, ed., *Faithful History: Essays on Writing Mormon History* (Salt Lake City, UT: Signature Books, 1992). See also the historiographical essay, James B. Allen, "Since 1950: Creators and Creations of Mormon History," in *New Views of Mormon History: Essays in Honor of Leonard J. Arrington,* edited by Davis Bitton and Maureen Ursenbach Beecher (Salt Lake City: University of Utah Press, 1987), 407-38; Ronald W. Walker, David J. Whittaker, and James B. Allen, *Mormon History* (Urbana: University of Illinois Press, 2001).

offer important analyses on such episodes as the First Vision, the coming forth of the Book of Mormon, the organization of the Church, and the development of early theology and polity. The Reorganized Church of Jesus Christ of Latter Day Saints (now Community of Christ) also has a contemporary one-volume history, Paul M. Edwards, *Our Legacy of Faith: A Brief History of the Reorganized Church of Jesus Christ of Latter Day Saints* (Independence: Herald Publishing House, 1991), with chapters on New York and Ohio; but they follow closely the themes outlined by Allen and Leonard. Also interesting for this aspect of Mormon history is Richard P. Howard, *RLDS Beginnings to 1860,* Vol. 1 of *The Church Through the Years* (Independence: Herald Publishing House, 1992). Surprisingly, the analytical synthesis of Leonard J. Arrington and Davis Bitton, *The Mormon Experience: A History of the Latter-day Saints* (New York: Alfred A. Knopf, 1979; 2d ed., Urbana: University of Illinois Press, 1992), does not provide the kind of sustained analysis of these episodes in Mormon history expected from a work of its type written by two esteemed and knowledgeable historians.

Two additional and exceptionally significant historical interpretations of early Mormonism also contain new discussions of founding activities of Mormonism. Appearing almost simultaneously, Marvin S. Hill, *Quest for Refuge: The Mormon Flight from American Pluralism* (Salt Lake City: Signature Books, 1989), and Kenneth H. Winn, *Exiles in a Land of Liberty: Mormons in America, 1830-1844* (Chapel Hill: University of North Carolina Press, 1989), analyze Mormonism as a movement steeped in disgust for American society that attempted to build a refuge against the great apocalypse that would soon come upon the earth. Those who embraced Mormonism, Hill argued, saw little of worth in American civilization. "They wanted a society that would exclude unnecessary choices and would exclude pluralism. Above all, they wanted to diminish the secular influences that pluralism engendered" (14). The Latter Day Saint movement was founded on a paranoia that the world had gone awry and would subvert or coopt them if it had the chance. They reacted with an effort to close off the outside world, "to revitalize this magical world view [of medieval society, to] combine it with elements of more traditional Christianity, and [to] establish a theocratic society where the unconverted, the poor, and the socially and religiously alienated could gather and find a refuge from the competing sects and the uncertainties they engendered" (17). Hill explored this same theme in "Counter-Revolution: The Mormon Reaction to the Coming of American Democracy," *Sunstone* 13 (June 1989): 24-33. Winn's book complements *Quest for Refuge* by showing how Mormons used the ideology of republicanism as justification for their retreat from pluralistic America. A study with similar overtones is Richard T. Hughes and C. Leonard Allen, *Illusions of Innocence: Protestant Primitivism in American, 1630-1875* (Chicago: University of Chicago Press, 1988), chap. "Early Mormons and the Eclipse of Religious Pluralism."

Two important specialized works sought to synthesize the development of Mormonism in the East. The first was *Joseph Smith and the Beginnings of Mormonism* (Urbana: University of Illinois Press, 1984), written by prize-winning colonial historian Richard L. Bushman. It was originally conceived as one of the sixteen volumes on Mormon history the LDS Church planned to sponsor in commemoration of its sesquicentennial in 1980; the Church later abandoned the series, leaving authors who completed their volumes to seek publication on their own. This book is an elegant, eloquent, exacting, and exasperating analysis of the origins of Mormonism through the end of 1830. In it Bushman dealt in an exceptionally faithful manner with the rise of the Church, despite the very real historical difficulties that had to be addressed. While it is an important synthesis, it has been acceptable mostly to believing Mormons and was one of the few books along with the scriptures which the Mormon Church placed in thousands of media kits and public libraries in the United States and abroad as part of a public relations effort related to the 1997 sesquicentennial of the trek across the plains and the Winter Olympics held in Salt Lake City in 2002.

Also begun as part of the same sixteen-volume history is the most detailed and probably the most significant general history of the Kirtland experience, Milton V. Backman Jr., *The Heavens Resound: A History of the Latter-day Saints in Ohio, 1830-1838* (Salt

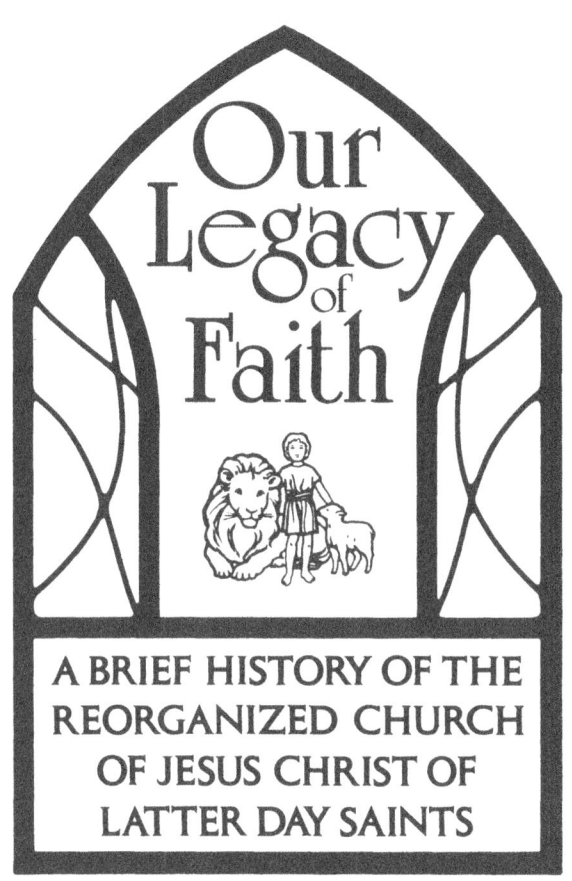

Our Legacy of Faith

A BRIEF HISTORY OF THE REORGANIZED CHURCH OF JESUS CHRIST OF LATTER DAY SAINTS

Paul M. Edwards

Exiles in a Land of Liberty
Mormons in America, 1830–1846

by Kenneth H. Winn

The University of North Carolina Press

Chapel Hill and London

Lake City: Deseret Book, 1983). It provided an exceptionally rich base of detailed information about early Kirtland, but it too suffered from an inability to view Mormonism from any perspective but one of reverent faith. The Saints in both books were presented as saints in every respect, the non-Mormons were mostly enemies motivated solely by blind hatred of the always dignified and noble-minded Joseph Smith, and the Mormons were unjustly persecuted. Both works concentrated on the sacred story of the Church's development, the religious activities of leading men, the revelations of the founding prophet, the doctrines espoused, and the spiritual manifestations taking place in the era. Bushman's and Backman's commitment to telling the sacred story was both honest and obtrusive. They saw events only through the eyes of faith, explaining events from the perspective of the institutional church. Too often they acted as Joseph Smith Jr.'s, defense attorney, arguing the case on behalf of the prophet to revise revelations as he saw fit, to implement policy and doctrine flexibly, to deal harshly with both rivals and followers who held honest differences of opinion, and to activate structures and decisions in seemingly incongruous patterns. They consistently depicted Smith as a persecuted innocent, pursued by evil conspirators who brought "vexatious lawsuits" out of sheer malice. They never gave alternative positions equal time, and they never challenged either Smith's motives or his actions. Writing earlier, Ivan J. Barrett, *Joseph Smith and the Restoration: A History of the LDS Church to 1846* (Provo, UT: Brigham Young University Press, 1973), had taken the same approach. Backman as editor continued it in *Regional Studies in Latter-day Saint History, Ohio* (Provo, UT: Department of Church History and Doctrine, Brigham Young University, 1990).

H. Michael Marquardt and Wesley P. Walters took an entirely different perspective, focusing on the lapses and unexplained aspects of early Mormonism, in *Inventing Mormonism: Tradition and the Historical Record* (Salt Lake City: Signature Books, 1994). Their account emphasized the Smith family's poverty, shifty activities, and Joseph Smith Jr.'s involvement with money diggers on a desperate hunt for buried Spanish treasure. Marquardt and Walters also emphasized the difference between the Mormon faith story and the contradictory evidence that has emerged. The publisher's advertisement (http://www.signaturebooks.com/inventin.htm, accessed March 7, 2004) describes the book: "During this turbulent time Joseph Smith was brought to court three times for crystal gazing, eloped with a former landlord's daughter, watched as his mother and siblings were excommunicated from the Presbyterian church, published his translation of the hieroglyphs, founded the Church of Christ, saw a potential convert forcibly abducted by her minister, and eventually sought refuge in Ohio where he changed the name of his church and its place of origin." Not exactly a litany of virtuous behavior!

The best short introductions to Mormonism in New York and Ohio are still two essays that appeared in 1973: Larry C. Porter, "The Church in New York and Pennsylvania, 1816-1831," and Max H. Parkin, "Kirtland: A Stronghold for the Kingdom," in *The Restoration Movement: Essays in Mormon History,* edited by F. Mark McKiernan, Paul M. Edwards, and Alma R. Blair (Lawrence, KS: Coronado Press, 1973), 27-61, 63-98. Porter's article, drawn from his "A Study of the Origins of the Church of Jesus Christ of Latter-day Saints in the States of New York and Pennsylvania, 1816-1831" (Ph.D. diss., Brigham Young University, 1971), has been reprinted (Provo, UT: Joseph Fielding Smith Institute for Latter-day Saint History and BYU Studies, 2000). In both the Porter and Parkin articles, they outlined major themes that have been explored about the Saints in New York and Ohio during the 1820s and 1830s. They relate the story of Mormon beginnings, the revelatory experience, the coming forth of the Book of Mormon, the organization of the Church, the first conversions, the conversion of Sidney Rigdon, the settlement of New York Mormons in Ohio, the evolution and enlargement of Church government, the doctrinal development and scriptural additions that took place there, the continued missionary fervor, the problem of Mormon/non-Mormon relations and persecution, political and economic issues, the building and use of the Kirtland Temple, and the dissension and declension of Mormon Kirtland. While not particularly interpretive, the strength of these essays is that they draw together the major themes that have been discussed relative to the period and provide a brief, readable, and quite useful survey of the era.

While these publications collectively provide a serviceable history of the Mormon experience in the era—although most emphasize a sacred story that will satisfy the needs only of rank-and-file Saints—there is a pressing need for a more sophisticated, balanced, and interpretive full-length treatment of this experience. What is probably required at this point is a overall study that moves beyond the well-worked themes, most of which emphasize the aspirations and actions of leaders of the institutional church, to explore some very significant topics in Mormon history that could reinterpret the entire episode. Such topics could include a serious dissertation on the theological development of the Church, especially bringing in the thinking of the larger Christian community and analyzing the far-ranging intellectual currents of the era that formed the backdrop of Mormon conceptions. Additionally, there is much yet to be learned about the social, political, and economic history of the Church's eastern sojourn. Future historians should raise new questions about the nature of power and influence and their role in the early Church, especially about who was in control and how and why. They could also ask some of the questions of the "new social history" and investigate themes of class, ethnicity, race, and gender. I suggested some of these avenues for exploration in my "The 'New Social History' and the 'New Mormon History': Reflections on Recent Trends," *Dialogue: A Journal of Mormon Thought* 27 (Spring 1994): 109-27.

Published Primary Sources

One of the boons of the New Mormon History has been the sustained attention of those who are dedicated editors of documents dealing with the Mormon experience. Publications emerging from their efforts have made it possible for nonprofessionals to investigate much more fully the period than ever before, guided to key documents by scholars working in the field. Excellent introductions to the sources available on these fields include, in addition to the bibliographies in the works already cited, Peter Crawley, "A Bibliography of the Church of Jesus Christ of Latter-day Saints in New York, Ohio, and Missouri," *BYU Studies* 12 (Summer 1972): 465-537; Stanley B. Kimball, "Sources on the History of the Mormons in Ohio, 1830-1838," *BYU Studies* 11 (Summer 1971): 524-40; David J. Whittaker, *Mormon Americana: A Guide to Sources and Collections in the United States* (Provo, UT: BYU University Publications, 1994); James B. Allen, Ronald W. Walker, and David J. Whittaker, comps., *Studies in Mormon History, 1830-1997: An Indexed Bibliography* (Urbana: University of Illinois Press, 2000), and their companion volume of essays, Walker, Whittaker, and Allen, *Mormon History* (Urbana: University of Illinois Press, 2001).

Perhaps the most important of the published source materials is Scott Faulring, *An American Prophet's Record: The Diaries and Journals of Joseph Smith* (1987; 2d ed., Salt Lake City: Signature Books in association with Smith Associates, 1989), since it provides the perspective of the prophet. Dean C. Jessee's three edited works, *The Personal Writings of Joseph Smith* (Salt Lake City: Deseret Book, 1984), and the two volumes of *The Papers of Joseph Smith* (Salt Lake City: Deseret Book, 1989, 1992), publish some of the same items as Faulring, but go much further to include autobiographical materials and letters from the era. A third volume of *The Papers of Joseph Smith* was prepared, but did not secure approval for publication from the LDS Church General Authorities and the project ended at that point. There is a new effort underway to publish a broad-based multi-volume collection of Joseph Smith's papers, jointly administered by the Joseph Fielding Smith Institute at Brigham Young University and the LDS Church Archives. Although the first volume has not yet appeared as of this writing, all historians of Mormonism anticipate it with relish. Perhaps there will also be an electronic version of this work, thereby enhancing its use in the future.

Collectively these papers are a much-needed replacement to Joseph Smith Jr. et al, *The History of the Church of Jesus Christ of Latter-day Saints, Period One*, edited by B. H. Roberts (Salt Lake City: Deseret News Press, 6 vols. published 1902-12, Vol. 7 published 1932, with various reprintings by Deseret Book. It also takes a documentary approach and includes a version of Smith's diaries along with many other items, many of them originally by other authors but recast to give the impression of Smith's authorship. Dean C. Jessee, "The Writing of Joseph Smith's History," *BYU Studies* 11 (Summer 1971): 439-74; Dean C. Jessee, "The Reliability of Joseph Smith's History," *Journal of Mormon History* 3 (1976): 34-69; and Howard C. Searle, "Authorship of the History of Joseph Smith: A Review Essay," *BYU Studies* 21 (Winter 1981): 101-22, outline some of the difficulties of dealing with this work. A critical document dealing with early Mormonism is the autobiography of Lucy Mack Smith, the prophet's mother, which has been published in three editions by the LDS Church (1853, 1902-03, 1945) and in two by the RLDS Church (1880, 1912), each with continuous reprints. It contains a wealth of detail about Mormonism's early years, some of it contradictory. Lavina Fielding Anderson, ed., *Lucy's Book: Critical Edition of Lucy Mack Smith's Family Memoir* (Salt Lake City: Signature Books, 2001), has made a contribution toward opening this information to broader use.

Another resource useful in the early history of Mormon history is the outstanding collection of primary documents contained in Dan Vogel, ed., *Early Mormon Documents*, 5 vols. (Salt Lake City: Signature Books, 5 vols., 1996-2003). Volume 1 dealt with the Smith family and Vermont. Volumes 2 and 3 concerned the experience of the Smith family in Palmyra, New York, and environs. Volume 4 focused on Colesville, New York, and South Bainbridge and Harmony, Pennsylvania; while the most recent volume contains documents relating to Fayette, New York, and the organization of the Church. Each volume gathers, collates, and correlates more than a hundred documents each. These documents represent a wide view and a fair and balanced approach to events that were mysterious, strange, or wondrous.

During the Mormon sojourn in the East the Church's organizational structure became increasingly complex and expanded in its role in local society. This development is reflected in several records of worth to students of the era. *The Far West Record: Minutes of the Church of Jesus Christ of Latter-day Saints, 1830-1844* (Salt Lake City: Deseret Book, 1983), edited by Donald Q. Cannon and Lyndon W. Cook, is a record of ecclesiastical meetings during the first generation of the Church. It provides background for institutional decisions and revelations. Likewise, Lyndon W. Cook and Milton V. Backman Jr., eds., *Kirtland Elders' Quorum Record, 1836-1841* (Provo, UT: Grandin Book Co., 1985), reproduces the minutes of an important priesthood quorum in the city. It provides a unique opportunity to view the rise of esoteric rituals associated with the temple as well as the lives of Saints in Kirtland. The Church's first historian, John Whitmer, also wrote a manuscript history that has appeared as *An Early Latter Day Saint History: The Book of John Whitmer,* edited by F. Mark McKiernan and Roger D. Launius (Independence: Herald Publishing House, 1980). Whitmer, who became disaffected from the Church in 1837-38, told in this account about a sacred unfolding of history until his own dissension, then switches his emphasis to a description of how Joseph Smith and his new Church had gone awry. Bruce N. Westergren, ed., *From Historian to Dissident: The Book of John Whitmer* (Salt Lake City: Signature Books, 1995), has also published an edition of this work.

Several enticing accounts written about early Mormonism have been edited and published in recent years. They include M. Hamlin Cannon, "Contemporary Views of Mormon Origins (1830)," *Mississippi Valley Historical Review* 31 (September 1944): 261-66; Reed C. Durham, "Joseph Smith's Own Story of a Serious Childhood Illness," *BYU Studies* 10 (Summer 1970): 480-82; Dean C. Jessee, ed., "Howard Coray's Recollections of Joseph Smith," *BYU Studies* 17 (Spring 1977): 341-46; Dean C. Jessee, ed., "Joseph Knight's Recollection of Early Mormon History," *BYU Studies* 17 (Autumn 1976): 29-39; D. Michael Quinn, ed., "The First Months of Mormonism: A Contemporary View by Rev. Diedrich Willers," *New York History* 54 (July 1973): 317-33; Leonard J. Arrington, "James Gordon Bennett's 1831 Report on 'The Mormonites,'" *BYU Studies* 10 (1970): 353-64; Leonard J. Arrington, ed., "Oliver Cowdery's Kirtland, Ohio, Sketchbook," *BYU Studies* 12 (Summer 1972): 410-26; Dean C. Jessee, ed., "The Kirtland Diary of Wilford Woodruff," *BYU Studies*

12 (Summer 1972): 365-99; Scott G. Kenney, ed., *Wilford Woodruff's Journals: 1833-1898*, 9 vols. (Midvale, UT: Signature Books, 1987); Karl R. Anderson, ed., *Joseph Smith's Kirtland: Eyewitness Accounts* (Salt Lake City: Deseret Book, 1989); Dennis Rowley, ed., "The Ezra Booth Letters," *Dialogue* 16 (Fall 1983): 133-37; Milton V. Backman Jr., ed., "Truman Coe's 1836 Description of Mormonism," *BYU Studies* 17 (Spring 1977): 347-55.

These edited works written by early Mormons reveal a myth of Mormon innocence (or infallibility) in the face of what appears to be an unbelieving and evil society. They disclose that the Mormon retreat from American religious pluralism to the theocratic separatist community at Kirtland represented an escape from moral ambiguity, from the fear of making the wrong choices.[2] As a religious entity under ever-tightening control, the Church became a haven where the followers of Joseph Smith had their most important choices—what they should do to serve God—made for them. They went on missions, engaged in business, and served in various Church offices at the prophet's direction. Also, their devotion to the Mormon millennium was defined by Smith, and their identity as God's chosen people was assured through him. Their innocence (i.e., infallibility) was thus guaranteed, and their sense of potential for evil was minimized. They projected evil onto others—in this case the Gentiles, who were regarded as ungodly enemies.[3] Another way of saying the same thing is that a chosen people always defines itself against an unchosen opposite and that, through that mythic dichotomy, differences in human culture (beliefs, values) are transmuted into differences in human nature (the good versus the evil). Hence, the innocent children of God began to realize their identity through their perceived struggle against the evil followers of Satan, who dominated American society everywhere else except in the city of the Saints.

Biographical Studies

The central figures in early Mormonism have always been considered the family of Joseph Smith, Jr. The two best biographies about Smith—Fawn M. Brodie, *No Man Knows My History: The Life of Joseph Smith* (1945; 2d ed. rev., New York: Alfred A. Knopf, 1971), 98-207; and Donna Hill, *Joseph Smith: The First Mormon* (Garden City, NY: Doubleday, 1977), 129-220—are also critical analyses of early Mormon history. A new, short biography of Joseph Smith by Robert V. Remini, *Joseph Smith* (New York: Viking, 2002), seeks to place Smith's life into the larger context of Jacksonian America. A somewhat marginal work overall, J. Christopher Conkling, *A Joseph Smith Chronology* (Salt Lake City: Deseret Book, 1979), is useful for tracing where Smith was on certain days.

Perhaps the most interesting recent study of Joseph Smith—and certainly a highly speculative work—is William D. Morain, , *The Sword of Laban: Joseph Smith Jr. and the Dissociated Mind* (New York: American Psychiatric Press, 1998). A psychological study of Smith, it makes much of the trauma of his childhood illness and its effect on his later life. The author suggests that he wrote this book more for psychiatric clinicians, in the hope that it would serve as a model for studying psychiatric illness. Accordingly, it takes an entirely naturalistic approach to exploring Smith's remarkably creative mind, an approach that comes with its own limitations as well as its strengths. Morain's is certainly not the first instance of psychological analysis of Joseph Smith nor will he be the last; but none of the earlier works exploring Smith's psyche, including this one, have proven particularly useful. Two of these other efforts are I. Woodbridge Riley, *The Founder of Mormonism* (1903; reprint

---

2. For a discussion of this psychological process, see Rollo May, *Freedom and Destiny* (New York: W.W. Norton and Co., 1981), esp. 121-22, 227-28. Also relevant is Erich Fromm's classic study, *Escape from Freedom* (New York: Holt, Rinehart, and Winston, 1941). This escape from pluralism is the theme of Hill, *Quest for Refuge*, 51-67.

3. A similar psycho-social process had been at work during the Middle Ages, which provides some interesting parallels. See Norman Cohn, *The Pursuit of the Millennium* (Fairlawn, NJ: Essential Books, 1957), 69-74. For discussions that focus on repression, pseudo-innocence, scapegoating, and similar matters from a Jungian perspective, see Connie Zweig and Jeremiah Abrams, eds. *Meeting the Shadow: The Hidden Power of the Dark Side of Human Nature* (Los Angeles: Jeremy Tarcher, 1991), especially the essays in Pt. 7, "Devils, Demons, and Scapegoats: A Psychology of Evil."

ed., Whitefish, MT: Kessinger Publishing, 2003); and Robert D. Anderson, *Inside the Mind of Joseph Smith: Psychobiography and the Book of Mormon* (Salt Lake City: Signature Books, 1999). The most recent is Dan Vogel, *Joseph Smith: The Making of a Prophet* (Salt Lake City: Signature Books, 2004), which goes further than the other psychobiographies in reading the Book of Mormon as autobiographical.

Joseph Smith remains an enormously significant figure who continues to appeal to biographers. The potential for powerful reinterpretations of his life and career are present in an exciting project underway by Richard Bushman, buttressed by perhaps the most extensive research ever conducted by JFS Institute interns and graduate assistants to understand the context of the early republic. This biography of Joseph Smith is intended to appear in 2005, the bicentennial of Smith's birth. Scheduled for the same date is a three-volume history of Joseph Smith sponsored by the Smith-Pettit Foundation and Signature Books. Richard S. Van Wagoner is writing about the New York experience, Scott G. Kenney is working on Kirtland and Missouri, and Martha Sonntag Bradley is taking on the Nauvoo experience. Each of these books—by seasoned, skillful, and well-respected historians of Mormonism—promises to be a major benchmark in the historiography of early Mormonism.

The life of the prophet's wife has been well told and ably interpreted in Linda King Newell and Valeen Tippets Avery, *Mormon Enigma: Emma Hale Smith, Prophet's Wife, "Elect Lady," Polygamy's Foe* (Garden City, NY: Doubleday, 1984), which has several chapters on the New York and Kirtland eras. Other biographies of members of the Smith family are less useful both in terms of what they have to say about Kirtland and for their largely saccharine approach toward dealing with episodes in Church history. Pearson H. Corbett, *Hyrum Smith: Patriarch* (Salt Lake City: Deseret Book, 1963), has been updated but not professionalized by Jeffrey S. O'Driscoll, *Hyrum Smith: A Life of Integrity* (Salt Lake City: Deseret Book, 2003); Richard L. Anderson, "What Were Joseph Smith's Sisters Like?" *Ensign*, March 1979, 42-45; Leonard J. Arrington and Susan Arrington Madsen, "Lucy Mack Smith," in *Mothers of the Prophets* (Salt Lake City: Deseret Book, 1987), 3-26; and Maurice L. Draper, *The Founding Prophet: An Administrative Biography of Joseph Smith, Jr.* (Independence: Herald Publishing House, 1991).

The three most important early Mormon figures after the Smiths—the witnesses to the Book of Mormon—have not received acceptable historical treatment. Richard L. Anderson, , *Investigating the Book of Mormon Witnesses* (Salt Lake City: Deseret Book, 1981), amasses a mountain of information about the characters of these individuals but all of it is aimed toward buttressing the crumbling wall of support for the divinity of the Book of Mormon.[4] The most work has been done on Oliver Cowdery, who has been profiled in two books, each containing information on Kirtland. Stanley R. Gunn, *Oliver Cowdery: Second Elder and Scribe* (Salt Lake City: Bookcraft, 1962), avoids difficult issues, and Philip R. Legg, *Oliver Cowdery: The Elusive Second Elder of the Restoration* (Independence: Herald Publishing House, 1989), tries to interpret Cowdery's defection during the crisis years in Kirtland in 1837-38. Neither David Whitmer nor Martin Harris has received full-length biographical attention, although a good article is Ronald E. Romig, "David Whitmer: Faithful Dissenter, Witness Apart," in *Differing Visions: Dissenters in Mormon History*, edited by Roger D. Launius and Linda Thatcher (Urbana: University of Illinois Press, 1994), 23-44. Of all of the issues raised by these individuals, most pressing are questions about how and why these three

---

4. Debates on this subject may be found in Dan Vogel and Brent Lee Metcalfe, eds., *American Apocrypha: Essays on the Book of Mormons* (Salt Lake City: Signature Books, 2002); Terryl Givens, *By the Hand of Mormon: The American Scripture that Launched a New World Religion* (New York: Oxford University Press, 2002); David Persuitte, *Joseph Smith and the Origins of the Book of Mormon* (Jefferson, NC: McFarland Co., 2000 ed.); Mark D. Thomas, *Digging in Cumorah: Reclaiming Book of Mormon Narrative* (Salt Lake City: Signature Books, 2000); Daniel H. Ludlow, S. Kent Brown, and John C. Welch, eds., *To All the World: The Book of Mormon Articles from the Encyclopedia of Mormonism* (Provo, UT: Foundation for Ancient Research and Mormon Studies [FARMS], 2000); B. H. Roberts, *Studies of the Book of Mormon*, edited by Brigham D. Madsen (Urbana: University of Illinois Press, 1985; reprinted with new editor's "Afterword" by Salt Lake City: Signature Books, 1992); and Stan Larson, ed., *Quest for the Gold Plates: Thomas Stuart Ferguson's Archaeological Search for the Book of Mormon* (Salt Lake City: Freethinker Press, 1996).

dominant characters in the formation of the Church were removed from the power center of Church governance in the mid-1830s and what role that fact might have played in their dissent in the latter part of the decade.

Members of the ruling priesthood quorums that emerged in the mid-1830s, especially the First Presidency and the Council of Twelve Apostles, have been studied in some detail. The members of the First Presidency, besides Joseph Smith, all have acceptable biographical studies. First counselor Sidney Rigdon, the 1830 Disciples of Christ convert who was probably more responsible than any other person for the establishment of Church headquarters in Kirtland, has been studied in F. Mark McKiernan, *The Voice of One Crying in the Wilderness: Sidney Rigdon, Religious Reformer* (Lawrence, KS: Coronado Press, 1971); and in Richard S. Van Wagoner, *Sidney Rigdon: A Portrait of Religious Excess* (Salt Lake City: Signature Books, 1994). Other studies are F. Mark McKiernan, "The Conversion of Sidney Rigdon to Mormonism," *Dialogue* 5 (Summer 1970): 71-78; F. Mark McKiernan, "The Uses of History: Sidney Rigdon and the Religious Historians," *Courage: A Journal of History, Thought, and Action* 2 (September 1971): 285-90; and Hans Rollmann, "The Early Baptist Career of Sidney Rigdon in Warren, Ohio," *BYU Studies* 21 (Winter 1981): 37-50.

Some articles have appeared on the shadowy second counselor, Jesse Gause, who walked out of Mormonism in 1832, and his replacement Frederick G. Williams. Among them are Robert J. Woodford, "Jesse Gause: Counselor to the Prophet," *BYU Studies* 15 (Spring 1975): 362-64; D. Michael Quinn, "Jesse Gause: Joseph Smith's Little-Known Counselor," *BYU Studies* 23 (Fall 1983): 487-93; and Frederick G. Williams, "Frederick Granger Williams of the First Presidency of the Church," *BYU Studies* 12 (Spring 1972): 243-61.

Many members of the Twelve have also received historical analysis, part of it dealing with their time in Kirtland. They include Leonard J. Arrington, *Brigham Young: American Moses* (New York: Alfred A. Knopf, 1985); Newell G. Bringhurst, *Brigham Young and the Expanding American Frontier* (Boston: Little, Brown, 1986); Thomas G. Alexander, *Things in Heaven and Earth: The Life and Times of Wilford Woodruff, a Mormon Prophet* (Salt Lake City: Signature Books, 1991); Howard H. Barron, *Orson Hyde: Missionary, Apostle, Colonizer* (Bountiful, UT: Horizon Publishers, 1977); Myrtle Stevens Hyde, *Orson Hyde: The Olive Branch of Israel* (Salt Lake City: Agreka Books, 2002); Stanley B. Kimball, *Heber C. Kimball: Mormon Patriarch and Pioneer* (Urbana: University of Illinois Press, 1981); Richard S. Van Wagoner and Steven C. Walker, "The Return of Thomas B. Marsh," *Sunstone* 6 (September-October 1981): 57-63; Irene M. Bates, "William Smith, 1811-1893: Problematic Patriarch," *Dialogue* 16 (Summer 1983): 11-23; Paul M. Edwards, "William B. Smith: The Persistent 'Pretender'," *Dialogue* 18 (Summer 1985): 128-39; on-going research on William Smith by William Shepard; John Quist, "John E. Page: An Apostle of Uncertainty," *Journal of Mormon History* 12 (1985): 53-68; Breck England, *The Thought of Orson Pratt* (Salt Lake City: University of Utah Press, 1985); Keith Perkins, "A House Divided: The John Johnson Family," *Ensign,* February 1970, 54-59; and Bruce A. Van Orden, "W. W. Phelps: His Ohio Contributions, 1835-1836," in *Regional Studies in Latter-day Saint Church History, Ohio,* edited by Milton V. Backman Jr. (Provo, UT: Department of Church History and Doctrine, Brigham Young University, 1990), 45-62.

There is a great need, however, for biographical treatments of women, other individuals who were not among the top ranks of the Church hierarchy, and non-Mormons who interacted with the Saints in New York State and Kirtland. A helpful beginning is Dale W. Adams, "Grandison Newell's Obsession," *Journal of Mormon History* 30, no. 1 (Spring 2004): 159-88 exploring the role of a man who prided himself on hounding the Mormons out of Kirtland.

The Making of a Prophet

One of the most critical sets of concerns in early Mormon history is the rise of Joseph Smith as a religious leader, the coming forth of the Book of Mormon, and the meaning of the Church for its membership in the 1830s. The importance attached to these questions revolves largely around the fact that the Latter-day Saints do not so much have a theology as they have a history. Confusing theology with history, therefore, requires that believing Saints accept a specified set of affirmations that are grounded in the "pure" thoughts and actions of past individuals, especially Joseph Smith. One sophisticated exposition of this position is Louis Midgley, "The Challenge of Historical Consciousness: Mormon History and the Encounter with Secular Modernity," in *By Study and Also by Faith, Vol. 2,* edited by John M. Lundquist and Stephen D. Ricks (Salt Lake City: Deseret Book/Provo, UT: Foundation for Ancient Research and Mormon Studies, 1990), 503-51, boiled the issue down to the answers that had to be given of two related questions: "Was Joseph Smith a genuine seer and prophet, and is the Book of Mormon true? If either one or the other is true, because both are linked, the truth of the other is thereby warranted" (510). The current LDS Church president added a third element to the equation recently by stating "without equivocation that God the Father and His Son, the Lord Jesus Christ, appeared in person to the boy Joseph Smith," adding, "Our whole strength rests on the validity of that vision. It either occurred or it did not occur. If it did not, then this work is a fraud. If it did, then it is the most important and wonderful work under the heavens."[5] Without acceptance of these truths, advocates of this position would argue, Mormonism could and probably should fall of its own weight. The perception of truth or falsity about the religion, therefore, rests on what historians say about those who have gone before.

The First Vision

No Man Knows My History, Fawn Brodie's biography of Joseph Smith, systematically dealt with three issues that related directly to the rise of the young prophet and in the process framed much of the historical debate that has followed. One of the most important was Joseph Smith's First Vision. Brodie emphatically denied that there was any valid evidence for this vision and that Smith fabricated it in 1838. He began dictating his history to provide a starting point for his prophetic career that would counter charges that he was involved in treasure seeking, she claimed. A second was about treasure seeking itself and its relationship to Smith and Mormon origins. Third, many questioned the origins and content of the Book of Mormon, asserting that it was a product of Joseph Smith's vivid imagination and not an actual history of any groups of people who came from Palestine to America.

The first major controversy over Joseph Smith is the skepticism of many about the visitation of God the Father and Jesus Christ to the youthful Smith about 1820, in which he was instructed to join no church because all were corrupt but that he would and reestablish the gospel in its ancient purity. The First Vision has been a linchpin of Mormon faith since at least the 1850s. Historian James B. Allen, "Emergence of a Fundamental: The Expanding Role of Joseph Smith's First Vision in Mormon Thought," *Journal of Mormon History* 7 (1980): 43-61, concluded: "Next to the resurrection of Christ, nothing holds a more central place in modern Mormon thought than that sacred event of 1820" (43). Challenging the legitimacy of this event, Brodie wrote matter-of-factly: "When in later years Joseph Smith had become the revered prophet of thousands of Mormons, he began

---

5. Gordon B. Hinckley, "The Marvelous Foundation of Our Faith," October 2002 LDS general conference address, retrieved from www.lds.org March 2004. Speaking on "Loyalty" at the April 2003 LDS general conference, he similarly but more generally stated, "Either the Church is true, or it is a fraud. There is no middle ground. It is the Church and kingdom of God, or it is nothing." Ibid. Apostle Jeffrey R. Holland, addressing seminary and institute teachers in the annual Church Educational System Religious Educators' Symposium at BYU in 1994, stated: "Accept Joseph Smith as a prophet and the book as the miraculously revealed and revered word of the Lord it is or else consign both man and book to Hades for the devastating deception of it all, but let's not have any bizarre middle ground about the wonderful contours of a young boy's imagination or his remarkable facility for turning a literary phrase. That is an unacceptable position to take—morally, literarily, historically, or theologically. . . . Nothing in our history and nothing in our message cuts to the chase faster than our uncompromising declaration that the Book of Mormon is the word of God. On this issue we draw a line in the sand." Elder Jeffrey R. Holland, "True or False," *New Era,* June 1995, 64, 66.

writing an official autobiography, in which his account of his adolescent years differed surprisingly from the brief sketch he had written in 1834 in answer to his critics" (21). While this 1838 autobiography contained a detailed account of a "First Vision," she noted, an 1834 autobiography did not mention the incident. Brodie also commented that the Palmyra newspapers failed to note anything about this incident, in spite of the fact that Smith described persecution when he told others of it. "The awesome vision he described in later years was probably the elaboration of some half-remembered dream stimulated by the early revival of excitement and reinforced by the rich folklore of visions circulating in the neighborhood," she concluded. "Or it may have been sheer invention" (25).

Brodie's contention that the beloved First Vision was the result of a psychosomatic condition or outright lies could not be ignored by those accepting the Mormon faith. Soon historians were quartering the New York countryside trying to find evidence refuting Brodie's allegations. They found proof that Joseph Smith did indeed record this event prior to 1838, and that it was not a significant religious issue for the Latter-day Saints of the 1830s. Only later did it reach its central place in the history/theology of the movement. Those historians accepted that the vision had occurred, even as they presented more nuanced versions of it in James B. Allen, "The Significance of Joseph Smith's First Vision in Mormon Thought," *Dialogue* 1 (Autumn 1966): 29-46; his "Emergence of a Fundamental"; Milton V. Backman, Jr., *American Religions and the Rise of Mormonism* (Salt Lake City: Deseret Book, 1965); Richard Lloyd Anderson, "Circumstantial Confirmation of the First Vision Through Reminiscences," *BYU Studies* 9 (Spring 1969): 373-404; Richard P. Howard, "Joseph Smith's First Vision: The RLDS Tradition," *Journal of Mormon History* 7 (1980): 23-29; Richard Lloyd Anderson, "Confirming Records of Moroni's Coming," *Improvement Era*, September 1970, 4-9.

But they also found that the eight extant accounts of the First Vision have numerous discrepancies. The first to develop this problem was Paul R. Cheesman, "An Analysis of the Accounts Relating Joseph's Smith's Early Visions" (M.A. thesis, Brigham Young University, 1965), but he did not publish his dissertation. Only after the divergent accounts were ballyhooed as evidence of Smith's fraudulent claims—most notably in Jerald and Sandra Tanner, *Joseph Smith's Strange Account of the First Vision* (Salt Lake City: Modern Microfilm Co., 1965)—did Mormon scholars begin to grapple seriously with the differences. Even forty years afterward, a vigorous discussion continues, this time on the internet rather than in print, concerning the various accounts of the First Vision. As only one example see, "Joseph Smith's Changing First Vision Accounts," http://www.irr.org/mit/First-Vision-Accounts.html, accessed on March 7, 2004.

Numerous articles have been dedicated to dealing with the problem of the divergent accounts of the First Vision and what that might mean for the Saints, specifically trying to refute any possibility of duplicity on the part of Joseph Smith in providing different accounts. These efforts include James B. Allen, "Eight Contemporary Accounts of Joseph Smith's First Vision—What Do We Learn from them?" *Improvement Era,* April 1970, 4-13; Dean C. Jessee, "The Early Accounts of Joseph Smith's First Vision," *BYU Studies* 9 (Spring 1969): 275-94; Richard P. Howard, "An Analysis of Six Contemporary Accounts of Joseph Smith's First Vision," in *Restoration Studies I,* edited by Maurice L. Draper and Clare D. Vlahos (Independence: Herald Publishing House, 1980), 95-117; and Neal E. Lambert and Richard H. Cracroft, "Literary Form and Historical Understanding: Joseph Smith's First Vision," *Journal of Mormon History* 7 (1980): 31-42. In *The Mormon Experience* historians Leonard J. Arrington and Davis Bitton summarize the problems and reconciliation of the various accounts in a way that would be acceptable to most Mormons: "If the later version was different, this was not a result of inventing an experience out of whole cloth, as an unscrupulous person might readily have done, but rather of reexamining an earlier experience and seeing it in a different light" (8).

A new twist was placed on the First Vision controversy in 1967 when Wesley Walters, a Presbyterian minister and anti-Mormon, questioned whether there had even been a Palmyra revival in the 1819-21 time period. The sectarian revivals, Smith said, had been

JOSEPH SMITH
AND THE BEGINNINGS
OF MORMONISM

RICHARD L. BUSHMAN

UNIVERSITY OF ILLINOIS PRESS
Urbana and Chicago

the catalyst for his own questions, his visit to what is now known as the Sacred Grove, and the visitation of God the Father and the Son. However, Wesley Walters, "New Light on Mormon Origins from the Palmyra (N.Y.) Revival," *Bulletin of the Evangelical Theological Society* 10 (Fall 1967): 227-44, found no evidence of revivals in Palmyra during this period, once again suggesting that Joseph Smith might have invented the event to legitimize his prophetic role. Because this publication received little circulation in the Mormon community, Walters also submitted the paper simultaneously for publication to *Dialogue,* where it appeared in the spring of 1969. The journal had delayed publication until a sympathetic historian, Richard L. Bushman, could write a reply. Relevant articles are "Roundtable: The Question of the Palmyra Revival," 59-100, including Walters, "New Light on Mormon Origins from the Palmyra Revival," 60-81; Bushman, "The First Vision Story Revived," 82-93; and Walters, "A Reply to Dr. Bushman," 94-100.

Coincident with this renewal of concerns about the First Vision's veracity in 1967, five Mormon historians met in Salt Lake City to organize a research effort on Mormon origins in New York. Headed by Truman G. Madsen, director of the Institute of Mormon Studies at Brigham Young University, it helped fund literally hundreds of researchers looking for, among other things, evidence to repel the challenge. The resulting papers resulting from this effort were published in a special issue of *BYU Studies* 9 (Spring 1969), and include Truman G. Madsen, "Guest Editor's Prologue," 235-40; James B. Allen and Leonard J. Arrington, "Mormon Origins in New York: An Introductory Analysis," 241-74; Allen and Arrington, "Mormon Origins in New York," 241-74; Dean C. Jessee, "The Early Accounts of Joseph Smith's First Vision," 275-94; Milton V. Backman Jr., "Awakenings in the Burned-Over District: New Light on the Historical Setting of the First Vision," 301-20; Larry C. Porter, "Reverend George Lane—Good 'Gifts,' Much 'Grace,' and Marked 'Usefulness,'" 321-40; T. Edgar Lyon, "How Authentic Are Mormon Historic Sites in Vermont and New York?" 341-50; Marvin S. Hill, "The Shaping of the Mormon Mind in New England and New York," 351-72; and Richard Anderson, "Circumstantial Confirmation of the First Vision Through Reminiscences," 373-404.

Others have sought to deal with the same issue since that time, primarily from the perspective of strengthening the case that there was, in fact, such a vision. See particularly Milton V. Backman, Jr., *Joseph Smith's First Vision: The First Vision in Historical Context* (1971; 2d ed., Salt Lake City: Bookcraft, 1980); Peter Crawley, "A Comment on Joseph Smith's Account of His First Vision and the 1820 Revival," *Dialogue* 6 (Spring 1971): 106-9; Marvin S. Hill, "A Note on the First Vision and Its Import in the Shaping of Early Mormonism," *Dialogue* 12 (Spring 1979): 90-99; Bushman, *Joseph Smith and the Beginnings of Mormonism,* 53-59; Hill, *Joseph Smith: The First Mormon,* 41-54; Marvin S. Hill, "The First Vision Controversy: A Critique and Reconciliation," *Dialogue* 15 (Summer 1982): 31-46. A useful introduction to sources is David J. Whittaker, "Joseph Smith's First Vision: A Source Essay," *Mormon History Association Newsletter,* No. 42 (November 1979), 7-9.

One of the great problems with following this course on the First Vision is that it focuses historical research into an "either-or" mode. Mormon historiography has enough problems with this anyway; the Mormon Church is always seeking to buttress its religious mission through its history. In this instance, it crippled historical inquiry for more than forty years by enticing scholars into answering questions that were inappropriate for historians to begin with and were often distorted beyond validity. Did Joseph Smith actually see God and Jesus Christ in a First Vision or did he invent the story after the fact to legitimate his religious work? That question, it seems to me, is both far less interesting and significant than a related one: What kind of religion is it that Smith brought into being and how did the First Vision relate to it? Marvin S. Hill, "A Note on the First Vision," 95-96, insightfully emphasizes that Joseph Smith was anti-pluralistic and that the First Vision validated a firm view of religion as either right or wrong. God tells Smith to "join none of them" (meaning other churches), because while all have a form a godliness they deny the power thereof. He was told to restore the "true" gospel of Jesus Christ to the earth and to demand repentance of all peoples. Smith's anti-pluralism is exhaustively documented in Marvin S.

James B. Allen and Glen M. Leonard

Published in Collaboration
with the Historical Department of
The Church of Jesus Christ of
Latter-day Saints

Deseret Book Company
Salt Lake City, Utah
1976

Excavating Mormon Pasts

Hill, "Counter-Revolution: The Mormon Reaction to the Coming of American Democracy," *Sunstone* 13 (June 1989): 24-33, and especially his *Quest for Refuge*. Also helpful are Hill, "The First Vision Controversy," 31-46; and Dan Vogel, *Religious Seekers and the Advent of Mormonism* (Salt Lake City: Signature Books, 1988).

Equally suggestive is a fact emphasized by non-Mormon scholar Jan Shipps, *Mormonism: The Story of a New Religious Tradition* (Urbana: University of Illinois Press, 1985), 30-33, that the First Vision was a means of keeping Joseph Smith, the founding prophet, center stage in the movement when it would have been quite easy to emphasize other aspects of the religion. This symbolic emphasis has shaped the direction of Mormonism to the present. Such issues are more interesting and, ultimately more illuminating, than the narrow "either-or" dichotomy.

Money-Digging and Magic

A second great question raised about Joseph Smith's early career is the nature of treasure seeking in the early republic and Joseph Smith's role in it. Several early affidavits and other information that implicated Joseph Smith in efforts to use folk magic to recover buried treasure. Specifically, an 1826 account emerged about a court case filed against Joseph Smith for defrauding a Josiah Stowell of money in a treasure hunting scheme. Joseph Smith's accusers charged that he was a "glass looker" and a money digger. He could have been, if this account was legitimate, nothing more than a frontier scryer who found a way to make money digging pay in the only way it could—as a scam, which is how Brodie assessed it (16-33).

For many years, major Mormon historians denied Smith's connection with these types of activities, asserting that the affidavits had been prepared as anti-Mormon statements designed to drum up opposition to Smith in the 1830s and that the 1826 court record was possibly a forgery and at best questionable as a document.[6] But other records emerged in the 1970s and 1980s confirming that Smith had been involved in money digging. Feeling the need to answer the charges, Mormon historians, at first hesitantly but then with more openness, began to construct an interpretation of Mormon origins that allowed for Smith to have been involved in treasure seeking. Perhaps the first serious attempt to wrestle with this challenge can be found in Marvin S. Hill, "Joseph Smith and the 1826 Trial: New Evidence and New Difficulties," *BYU Studies* 12 (Winter 1972): 223-33. Also relevant Richard Lloyd Anderson, "Joseph Smith's New York Reputation Reappraised," *BYU Studies* 10 (Spring 1970): 283-314; Wesley Walters, "From Occult to Cult with Joseph Smith, Jr.," *Journal of Pastoral Practice* 1 (Summer 1977): 121-31; Wesley Walters, "Joseph Smith's Bainbridge, N.Y., Court Trials," *Westminster Theological Journal* 36 (Winter 1974): 123-55; James B. Allen and Glen M. Leonard, *The Story of the Latter-day Saints* (1976; 2nd ed. rev., Salt Lake City: Deseret Book, 1992), chaps. 1-2; Arrington and Bitton, *The Mormon Experience*, 10-11.

One particularly adventurous explanation suggested that Smith was imbued with a magical worldview and that evidence of magic could be found in all manner of Mormon theology and institutions, as explored in Reed C. Durham, Jr., "Is There No Help for the Widow's Son," in *Joseph Smith and Masonry: No Help for the Widow's Son: Two Papers on the Influence of the Masonic Movement on Joseph Smith and his Mormon Church,* edited by Jack Adamson and Reed C. Durham Jr. (Nauvoo, IL: Martin Publishing Co., 1980), 15-28. This was the 1974 presidential address of the Mormon History Association, and Durham was disciplined because of his statements. Three years later, Paul M. Edwards, "The Secular Smiths," *Journal of Mormon History* 4 (1977): 3-17, suggested that Joseph Smith was a mystic in the eastern pattern and did not separate magic from the broader world. Since that time, much additional work has documented the importance of magic and the occult in Smith's life and the early history of the Church. Relevant sources, among others, are Max Nolan, "Joseph Smith and Mysticism," *Journal of Mormon History* 10 (1983): 105-16; Alan

---

6. John A. Widtsoe, *Joseph Smith—Seeker after Truth* (Salt Lake City: Deseret Book, 1951), 78, 267; Hugh Nibley, *The Myth Makers* (Salt Lake City: Bookcraft, 1961), 142.

Taylor, "Rediscovering the Context of Joseph Smith's Treasure Seeking," *Dialogue* 19 (Winter 1986): 18-28; Lance S. Owens, "Joseph Smith and Kabbalah: The Occult Connection," *Dialogue* 27 (Fall 1994): 117-94; both editions of D. Michael Quinn, *Early Mormonism and the Magic World View* (1987; rev. ed., Salt Lake City: Signature Books, 1998); and John Brooke, *The Refiner's Fire: The Making of Mormon Cosmology, 1644-1844* (New York: Cambridge University Press, 1994).

Like the First Vision, the money-digging issue got an enormous boost from challenges by newly discovered records that appeared to tie Joseph Smith closely to folk magic and treasure seeking in the 1820s. Two letters, one supposedly from Joseph Smith to Josiah Stowell in 1825 and a second supposedly from Martin Harris to W. W. Phelps in 1830 placed treasure seeking squarely at the origins of the Book of Mormon and the birth of the Church. Both of these documents later turned out to be modern forgeries by Latter-day Saint documents dealer Mark W. Hofmann,[7] but they opened a pandora's box of concern about the subject. A special issue of *BYU Studies* 24 (Fall 1984) was dedicated to repelling the challenge, including Dean C. Jessee, "New Documents and Mormon Beginnings," 397-428; Ronald W. Walker, "The Persistent Idea of American Treasure Hunting," 429-59; his "Joseph Smith: The Palmyra Seer," 461-72; Marvin S. Hill, "Money-Digging Folklore and the Beginnings of Mormonism," 473-88; and Richard Lloyd Anderson, "The Mature Joseph Smith and Treasure Searching," 489-560. As a result Richard L. Bushman—perhaps the quintessential practitioner of what he called "Faithful History," *Dialogue* 4 (Winter 1969): 11-28, an approach that emphasizes the sacred nature of the history of Mormonism—felt the need to attempt an integration of Smith's folk magic tradition with his later career in Bushman's award-winning *Joseph Smith and the Beginnings of Mormonism* (64-76). Perhaps the ultimate in an exhaustive approach was Quinn's revised edition of his book on Mormonism and magic, in which he interprets the two as being inextricably intertwined during Mormonism's first generation.

Once again, the either-or dialectic wrapped up some very talented historians who might have explored other aspects of this subject had they not been consumed with the desire to refute and later explain away Brodie's arguments. The folk magic context in early Mormonism is truly an interesting area of exploration, but a broad-based analysis divorced from the question of Mormon legitimacy would have been more useful. An investigation that employed the argument of paradigm shift and *weltanschauung* that Thomas S. Kuhn developed in *The Structure of Scientific Revolutions* (New Haven, CT: Yale University Press, 1957) could easily have spanned a broad spectrum of social issues involving Mormonism with the rational/irrational world being only part of a much larger exploration. Such an approach would have been especially rewarding. Moreover, the problem of money-digging took historians away from other worthwhile studies; and, like the "Dutch boy" plugging the dike, they sacrificed their services to a perceived immediate public relations and theological/historical problem. A good example is Ronald W. Walker who had projects underway on the Godbeite protest in Utah, a valid historical topic if ever one existed. It was interrupted by the money-digging question, with Walker writing three articles on the subject. (In addition to the two cited above in the fall 1984 issue of *BYU Studies,* he also published "Martin Harris: Mormonism's Early Convert," *Dialogue* 19 [Winter 1986]: 29-43.) His *Wayward Saints: The Godbeites and Brigham Young* (Urbana: University of Illinois Press, 1998), did not see the light of day for more than a decade.

An example of what might be accomplished by historians who move beyond the initial framework of the question is the recent masterful analysis of Mormon cosmology by John L. Brooke. Bringing together an analysis of Mormonism's occult origins in folk magic and money-digging with its later expression in unique theological ideals, *Refiner's Fire*

---

7. See Linda Sillitoe and Allen Roberts, *Salamander: The Story of the Mormon Forgery Murders* (Salt Lake City: Signature Books, 1988); Steven Naifeh and Gregory White Smith, *The Mormon Murders: A True Story of Greed, Forgery, Deceit, and Death* (New York: Weidenfeld and Nicolson, 1988); Robert Lindsey, *A Gathering of Saints: A True Story of Money, Murder, and Deceit* (New York: Simon and Schuster, 1988); and Richard E. Turley Jr., *Victims: The LDS Church and the Mark Hofmann Case* (Urbana: University of Illinois Press, 1992).

EARLY MORMONISM AND THE MAGIC WORLD VIEW

D. Michael Quinn

Signature Books
Salt Lake City, Utah
1987

goes beyond these earlier concerns with Brodie's dialectical approach to show how Smith unified Mormon thought using the opposing forces of European hermetic purity and danger.

The Coming Forth of the Book of Mormon

The Book of Mormon of course, has been a controversial work since it first appeared in 1830.[8] Numerous publications, therefore, either defend or condemn the book; but in some way or another, almost all of these bear the fingerprints of Fawn Brodie and her erudite handling of the subject in her biography of Joseph Smith. The first and most central question was whether the book was an authentic history of a group of religious pilgrims who came to America (which was Joseph Smith's claim for it), or whether it was a product of frontier mythology written either by Smith or some other author. Fawn Brodie eloquently challenged the conventional Mormon perception of the coming forth of the Book of Mormon and, in the process, undermined the legitimacy of the work as scripture. She charged that Smith had originally intended the book as a secular history of ancient America, but his own treasure-seeking opportunism led him to transform it into a religious history with attendant angelic visitations, "gold plates," and the "Urim and Thummim" which enabled him to "translate" these "ancient records" through by the "gift and power of God" (50-66).

Specifically, Brodie argued that frontier America was consumed with interest about the origins of American Indians and that a favorite theory was that they were remnants of the lost tribes of ancient Israel. Smith was as curious as anyone else and enjoyed speculations about the development and eventual extinction of the moundbuilders, a perceived ancient and extinct aboriginal people.[9] The Book of Mormon, Brodie charged, was basically the history of two rival moundbuilder groups, one a "fair and delightsome people" of refinement, the other a "wild and ferocious, and a bloodthirsty people; full of idolatry and wandering about in the wilderness, with a short skin girded about their loins, and their heads shaven," skilled with "the bow, and the cimeter and the axe."[10]

Smith started out wanting to write a history of the moundbuilders, Brodie concluded, but gradually came to the decision to describe only the "peregrinations of two Hebrew families, headed by Lehi and Ishmael, who became the founders of the American race. He began by focusing upon a single hero, Nephi, who like himself was peculiarly gifted of the Lord. This device launched him smoothly into his narrative and saved him from having bitten off more than he could chew" (49). Joseph Smith drew his Indian information, conjectures Brodie, from Ethan Smith's 1825 edition of *The View of the Hebrews* that argued that the Indians were descendants of Hebraic peoples. Spencer J. Palmer and William L. Knecht, "View of the Hebrews: Substitute for Inspiration?" *BYU Studies* 5 (Winter 1964): 105-15; and Roy E. Weldon, "Masonry and Ethan Smith's 'View of the Hebrews,'" *Saints Herald* 119 (September 1972): 26-28, defend Joseph Smith's contention that it was a sacred record and not a product of frontier mythology like *A View of the Hebrews*. The whole religious angle, Brodie speculated, was dreamed up after 1828 when Smith had gathered around him a small group of believers who accepted him as a prophet of God (35-55). She cites supporting statements from Abner Cole, who wrote under the pseudonym Obadiah Dogberry,[11] and affidavits by Palmyra neighbors. Richard Lloyd

---

8. An important new edition is Grant Hardy, ed., *The Book of Mormon: A Reader's Edition* (Urbana: University of Illinois Press, 2003).
9. Curtis Dahl, "Mound Builders, Mormons, and William Cullen Bryant," *New England Quarterly* 34 (1961): 178-90; Dan Vogel, *Indian Origins and the Book of Mormon: Religious Solutions from Columbus to Joseph Smith* (Salt Lake City: Signature Books, 1986); Robert N. Hullinger, "The Lost Tribes of Israel and the Book of Mormon," *Lutheran Quarterly* 22 (August 1970): 319-29; Grant H. Palmer, *An Insider's View of Mormon Origins* (Salt Lake City: Signature Books, 2002).
10. These quotations are from *Book of Mormon* (Palmyra, NY: E.B. Grandin, 1830), 72, 144-45; Brodie's analysis is in *No Man Knows My History*, 34-49.
11. Joseph W. Barnes, "Obadiah Dogberry: Rochester Free-Thinker," *Rochester History* 36 (July 1974): 1-24; Russell R. Rich, "The Dogberry Papers and the Book of Mormon," *BYU Studies* 10 (Spring 1970): 315-20.

Excavating Mormon Pasts

Anderson, "Joseph Smith's New York Reputation Reappraised," *BYU Studies* 10 (Spring 1970): 283-314, challenges the reliability of the Palmyra neighbors and further but indirectly elaborates on Smith's good character by analyzing his ancestry in *Joseph Smith's New England Heritage: Influences of Grandfathers Solomon Mack and Asael Smith* (Salt Lake City: Deseret Book, 1971). In contrast, Rodger I. Anderson, *Joseph Smith's New York Reputation Reexamined* (Salt Lake City: Signature Books, 1990), argued that the neighbors were reliable and that Brodie's conclusions were justified.

Not long after the organization of the Church in 1830, and especially because of the attraction that the Book of Mormon held for members of its rival Disciples of Christ, the Disciples' leader, Alexander Campbell, published one of the earliest criticisms of the book, commenting that it dealt with "every error and almost every truth discussed in New York for the last ten years."[12] Brodie latched upon Campbell's critique as *the* explanation of the book's message and concluded that Smith, as he fully grasped his prophetic role, was extraordinarily responsive "to the provincial opinions of the time." She did not entertain any other hypothesis about the Book of Mormon except that it was a modern work written by Joseph Smith (69, 86). Also taking Campbell's observation as her departure point, Susan Curtis Mernitz concluded in "Palmyra Revisited: A Look at Early Nineteenth Century America and the Book of Mormon," *John Whitmer Historical Association Journal* 2 (1982): 30-37, that the "Book of Mormon offered ideas that were familiar to New Yorkers in 1830 when distribution of the book began. Though the Book of Mormon tells us much about its author, it also illuminates ideas and social phenomena that characterized the generation of 1830." Other historians who found Smith intrigued by and sensitive to the major theological questions of the day include essayists in Brent Lee Metcalfe, ed., *New Approaches to the Book of Mormon* (Salt Lake City: Signature Books, 1993); Mark D. Thomas, *Digging in Cumorah: Reclaiming Book of Mormon Narratives* (Salt Lake City: Signature Books, 2000); and Persuitte, *Joseph Smith and the Origins of the Book of Mormon*.

Grant Underwood, "Book of Mormon Usage in Early LDS Theology," *Dialogue* 17 (Autumn 1984): 35-74, discussed the book's centrality in the life of the Church, while Richard L. Bushman argued that the republican tendencies everywhere present in the early American nation were tellingly absent from the Book of Mormon and that the scripture was strangely distant from the social and political milieu of the United States in 1830. He saw more "Old World" perspectives than early American thought in the book. He developed this position in "The Book of Mormon and the American Revolution," *BYU Studies* 17 (Fall 1976): 3-20, reprinted in Noel B. Reynolds, ed., *Book of Mormon Authorship: New Light on Ancient Origins* (Provo, UT: Brigham Young University Religious Studies Center, 1982), 189-211; his "The Book of Mormon in Early Mormon History," in Davis Bitton and Maureen Ursenbach Beecher, eds., *New Views of Mormon History: A Collection of Essays in Honor of Leonard J. Arrington* (Salt Lake City: University of Utah Press, 1987), 3-18; and his "The Character of Joseph Smith: Insights from his Holographs," *Ensign,* April 1977, 11-13; Bushman, *Joseph Smith and the Beginnings of Mormonism*, 115-42. Hyrum L. Andrus also examines republic influences in his earlier "The Second American Revolution: Era of Preparation," *BYU Studies* 1-2 (Autumn 1959-Winter 1960): 71-100. Marvin S. Hill, "Counter-Revolution," offered a slightly different perspective by concluding that the Book of Mormon presented a nondemocratic position with government by judges and kings, suggests that individuals are unable to govern themselves, and that hierarchical structure (which inhibits pluralism) is necessary. "The Book of Mormon," he observed, "is thus an ambivalent spokesman for republicanism." He saw Joseph Smith taking an antipluralistic, nondemocratic approach toward life and concluded that Mormonism retreated from the Jacksonian era to one of more order (24-33).

Mormon and non-Mormon scholars have debated these points about the origins of the Book of Mormon to the point of tedium but without resolution, for, to a very

---

12. Alexander Campbell, *Delusions: An Analysis of the Book of Mormon* (Boston: Benjamin H. Greene, 1832),

real extent, one's conclusion depends on whether one is a believing member of the Church and not on evidence. Like attorneys arguing a case, each side amasses evidence to either buttress or destroy the foundations of the Book of Mormon as ancient scripture and convinces only those who already hold preconceptions in that direction. Participants in this debate include Wayne Larson, Alvin C. Rencher, and Tim Layton, "Who Wrote the Book of Mormon? An Analysis of Wordprints," *BYU Studies* 20 (Spring 1980): 229; Hugh Nibley, *Since Cumorah: The Book of Mormon in the Modern World* (Salt Lake City: Deseret Book, 1967); Gayle Goble Ord, "The Book of Mormon Goes to Press," *Ensign,* December 1972, 66-70; David Brion Davis, "Some Themes of Counter-Subversion: An Analysis of Anti-Masonic, Anti-Catholic, and Anti-Mormon Literature," *Mississippi Valley Historical Review* 47 (September 1960): 205-24; Blake Ostler, "The Book of Mormon as a Modern Expansion of an Ancient Source," *Dialogue* 20 (Spring 1987): 66-124; Robert Paul, "Joseph Smith and the Manchester (New York) Library," *BYU Studies* 22 (Summer 1982): 333-56; Larry C. Porter, "The Colesville Branch and the Coming Forth of the Book of Mormon," *BYU Studies* 10 (Spring 1970): 365-85; Larry C. Porter, "William E. McLellin's Testimony of the Book of Mormon," *BYU Studies* 10 (Summer 1970): 485-87; Noel B. Reynolds, ed., *Book of Mormon Authorship: New Light on Ancient Origins* (Provo, UT: Religious Studies Center, Brigham Young University, 1982); Noel B. Reynolds, "Nephi's Outline," *BYU Studies* 20 (Winter 1980): 131-49; Russell R. Rich, "Where Were the Moroni Visits?" *BYU Studies* 10 (Spring 1970): 255-58; B. H. Roberts, *Studies of the Book of Mormon,* edited by Brigham D. Madsen (1985; reprint ed., Salt Lake City: Signature Books, 1992); Timothy L. Smith, "The Book of Mormon in a Biblical Culture," *Journal of Mormon History* 7 (1980): 3-21; John L. Sorenson, "The 'Brass Plates' and Biblical Scholarship," *Dialogue* 10 (Autumn 1977): 31-39; Geoffrey F. Spencer, "Anxious Saints: The Early Mormons, Social Reform, and Status Anxiety," *John Whitmer Historical Association Journal* 1 (1981): 43-53; Geoffrey F. Spencer, *The Burning Bush: Revelation and Scripture in the Life of the Church* (Independence: Herald Publishing House, 1975); Geoffrey F. Spencer, "Mormonism in the Historical Setting of 19th Century America," *Commission,* September 1979, 12-19; Ernest H. Taves, *Trouble Enough: Joseph Smith and the Book of Mormon* (Buffalo, NY: Prometheus Books, 1984); John A. Tvedtnes, "Composition and History of the Book of Mormon," *New Era,* September 1974, 41-43; John A. Tvedtnes, "Hebraisms in the Book of Mormon: A Preliminary Survey," *Sunstone* 12 (January 1988): 8-13; Grant Underwood, "Book of Mormon Usage in Early LDS Theology," *Dialogue* 17 (Autumn 1984): 35-74; Dan Vogel, ed., *The Word of God: Essays on Mormon Scripture* (Salt Lake City: Signature Books, 1990); Steven C. Walker, "More Than Meets the Eye: Concentration in the Book of Mormon," *BYU Studies* 20 (Winter 1980): 199-205; John W. Welch, "Chiasmus in the Book of Mormon," *BYU Studies* 10 (Autumn 1969): 69-84; and Douglas Wilson, "Prospects for the Study of the Book of Mormon as a Work of American Literature," *Dialogue* 3 (Spring 1969): 29-41.

These scholarly attacks and ripostes are so much sound and fury signifying nothing. As non-Mormon scholar Mario S. De Pillis has astutely observed in "The Social Sources of Mormonism," *Church History* 37 (March 1968): 50-79, "Since Mormonism as a religion developed mostly after 1830 in Smith's revelations, Campbell—and the historians who so avidly quote him instead of the Mormon sources—was premature and wrong in equating the Book of Mormon with Mormonism" (62).

While Campbell's challenge to the ancient origin and divinity of the Book of Mormon made during the Kirtland era has been of interest to modern historians, Eber D. Howe, *Mormonism Unvailed* (Painesville, OH: n.p., 1834), 278-89, put forth the theory of Book of Mormon origins that held sway for nearly a century among non-Latter Day Saints. In a conspiracy theory of outlandish proportions, Howe, a newspaper editor in nearby Painesville, Ohio, suggested that Solomon Spaulding, a minister and would-be novelist from Conneaut, Ohio, had written a manuscript (the Book of Mormon) and sent it to a publisher in Pittsburgh where Sidney Rigdon discovered it, stole it, and passed it on to coconspirator Joseph Smith. Smith brought in additional conspirators as witnesses to the book's divinity, published it, and began to masquerade as a prophet.[13]

Unfortunately, Spaulding was long since dead and his manuscript could not be found. The account was mostly hearsay and recollection and had all the veracity of the tabloids. It was not until the 1880s, when Spaulding's papers were discovered in Hawaii and his manuscript compared to the Book of Mormon, that it became apparent to a larger community that there was no relationship between the two. This story has been ably documented in Lester E. Bush Jr., "The Spaulding Theory: Then and Now," *Dialogue* 10 (Autumn 1977): 40-69; and Charles H. Whittier and Stephen W. Stathis, "The Enigma of Solomon Spaulding," *Dialogue* 10 (Autumn 1977): 70-73.

Other aspects of Book of Mormon origins have also interested Mormon historians. These have included the story of the so-called Anthon transcript, supposedly a sheet of paper on which Smith copied some of the "reformed Egyptian" characters from the golden plates. Martin Harris took this sheet to an accomplished linguist for verification, an incident that may have given Smith an inkling of insight into his role as a prophet, according to Danel W. Bachman, "Sealed in a Book: Preliminary Observations on the Newly Found Anthon Transcript," *BYU Studies* 20 (Spring 1980): 321-45; Ariel L. Crowley, "The Anthon Transcript: An Evidence for the Truth of the Prophet's Account of the Origin of the Book of Mormon," *Improvement Era* 45 (1945): 14-15, 58-60, 76-80, 124-25, 150-51, 182-83; Stanley B. Kimball, "The Anthon Transcript: People, Primary Sources, and Problems," *BYU Studies* 10 (Spring 1970): 325-52; and Edward H. Ashment, "The Book of Mormon and the Anthon Transcript: An Interim Report," *Sunstone* 5 (May-June 1980): 29-31.

Other aspects that have interested researchers include the method of translation and the role of the seer stone, which bore more relationship to treasure seeking than to Christian religious activity. Examinations of the translation process include James E. Lancaster, "By the Gift and Power of God," *Saint's Herald* 109 (15 November 1962): 798-802, 806, 817; reprinted with minor revisions in the *John Whitmer Historical Association Journal* 3 (1983): 51-61; Ronald W. Walker, "Joseph Smith: The Palmyra Seer," *BYU Studies* 24 (Fall 1984): 461-88; Richard S. Van Wagoner and Steven C. Walker, "Joseph Smith: The Gift of Seeing," *Dialogue* 22 (Summer 1982): 48-68; Dean C. Jessee, "Lucy Mack Smith's 1829 Letter to Mary Smith Pierce," *BYU Studies* 22 (Fall 1982): 457-58; Clair E. Weldon, "Two Transparent Stones: The Story of the Urim and Thummim," *Saints' Herald* 109 (1 September 1962): 616-20, 623.

The nature, development, and disposition of the texts of the Book of Mormon has also attracted some scholarly studies including Dean C. Jessee, "The Original Book of Mormon Manuscripts," *BYU Studies* 10 (Spring 1970): 259-78; Stan Larson, "Textual Variants in Book of Mormon Manuscripts," *Dialogue* 10 (Autumn 1977): 8-30; Richard P. Howard, "Latter Day Saint Scriptures and the Doctrine of Propositional Revelation," *Courage: A Journal of History, Thought, and Action* 1 (June 1971): 209-25; and his major *Restoration Scriptures: A Study of Their Textual Development* (1969; rev. ed., Independence: Herald Publishing House, 1994).

But the most interesting area explored here is the role of the witnesses to the divinity of the Book of Mormon. The three key figures—Martin Harris, Oliver Cowdery, and David Whitmer—were excommunicated in 1838, but none ever denied his testimony that the scripture was of God. This is a remarkable record, and Brodie suggests that Smith became adept at hypnosis to convince the three that they had seen what she fully believed were nonexistent golden plates (67-82). Such a hypothesis seems somewhat farfetched against David Whitmer's powerful *An Address to All Believers in Christ* (Richmond, MO: n.p.,

---

13. For a discussion of this quotation's harmful influence on Mormon history, see Mario S. De Pillis, "The Quest for Religious Authority and the Rise of Mormonism," *Dialogue* 1 (Spring 1966): 68-88, esp. 79. Brodie, *No Man Knows My History,* 442-56; Hans Rollmann, "The Early Baptist Career of Sidney Rigdon in Warren, Ohio," *BYU Studies* 21 (Winter 1981): 37-50; McKiernan, *Voice of One Crying in the Wilderness: Sidney Rigdon,* 36-40.

1887), which confirms his belief in the Book of Mormon despite his disaffiliation. Richard Lloyd Anderson has attacked Brodie's hypothesis in his *Investigating the Book of Mormon Witnesses*; his "David Whitmer: Unique Missouri Mormon," in *Missouri Folk Heroes of the Nineteenth Century,* edited by F. Mark McKiernan and Roger D. Launius (Independence: Independence Press, 1989), 45-59; and Romig, "David Whitmer," 22-44.

The reaffirmation of this testimony, as well as that of the Cowdery and Harris, has been important for Mormons and has led to all manner of historical explorations into the question as a means of shoring up the book's sacred origin and message, with Anderson's *Investigating the Book of Mormon Witnesses* leading the way. Other studies include Richard Lloyd Anderson, "Martin Harris, The Honorable New York Farmer," *Improvement Era,* February 1969, 18-21; his "Reuben Miller: Recorder of Oliver Cowdery's Reaffirmations," *BYU Studies* 8 (Spring 1968): 277-85; Wayne Cutler Gunnell, "Martin Harris, Witness and Benefactor to the Book of Mormon" (M.A. thesis, Brigham Young University, 1971); Preston Nibley, comp., *The Witnesses of the Book of Mormon* (1968; reprint ed., Salt Lake City: Deseret Book, 1973); Walker, "Martin Harris; and Stanley R. Gunn, *Oliver Cowdery: Second Elder and Scribe* (Salt Lake City: Bookcraft, 1962).

Unfortunately the mountain of information amassed about these individuals, designed as it is to buttress the wall of support for the divinity of the Book of Mormon has been a blind alley down which Brodie led Mormon historians. The central questions still to be asked are how and why these three dominant characters in the formation of the Church were removed from the power center of Church governance in the mid-1830s and what role that fact might have played in their dissent in the latter part of the decade. Brodie did not raise these important questions, and they have gone begging ever since, with the exception of Legg, *Oliver Cowdery: The Elusive Second Elder of the Restoration;* and Romig, "David Whitmer: Faithful Dissenter, Witness Apart."

Recently, a few Mormon historians have begun to get away from the either-or type of questions about the Book of Mormon's coming forth. For instance, the question of the historicity of the Book of Mormon has been under attack from without since nearly the formation of the Church in 1830 and within Mormonism for much of the twentieth century in some form or another. This situation has sparked a concern for finding a way to deal with the book as a nonhistorical sacred text similar to the approach that has developed for some parts of the Bible. There is some evidence that B. H. Roberts, perhaps the greatest Mormon intellectual, began in the early part of the twentieth century to question the book's historicity as an actual document portraying the record of people calling themselves Nephites. Roberts's biographer, Truman G. Madsen, presented him as uniformly orthodox in "B. H. Roberts and the Book of Mormon," *BYU Studies* 19 (Summer 1979): 427-45; but Roberts's unpublished manuscript was printed in B. H. Roberts, *Studies of the Book of Mormon*. Springing to the defense of this General Authority were an anonymous writer, "New B. H. Roberts Book Lacks Insight of his Testimony," *Deseret News,* December 15, 1985; and John W. Welch, "B. H. Roberts, Seeker After Truth," *Ensign,* March 1986, 56-62; with Madsen's response in "B. H. Roberts's Studies of the Book of Mormon," *Dialogue* 26 (Fall 1993): 76-86.

More recently, the approach taken by essayists in Brent Lee Metcalfe, ed., *New Approaches to the Book of Mormon,* seriously questions the historicity of the Book of Mormon. One essayist, Anthony A. Hutchinson, "The Word of God Is Enough: The Book of Mormon as Nineteenth-Century Scripture," bluntly summarized the central issue: "Members of the Church of Jesus Christ of Latter-day Saints should confess in faith that the Book of Mormon is the word of God but also abandon claims that it is a historical record of the ancient peoples of the Americas" (1).

There has been considerable concern about such statements, and the forces of traditional truth claims about the book are now engaged in a struggle about how Latter-day Saints should interpret the scripture. While some of those questioning the book's historical origins have suggested that the Church should formally repudiate the Book of Mormon, many people wisely have seen such a response as an overreaction. Contrary to the position that the Book of Mormon must be an authentic history of a central group of ancient peoples in America or it must be a hoax, a more "catholic" middle position can be adopted that emphasizes the powerful message for the present-day LDS Church and the world as a whole. Proposing such interpretations are Wayne Ham, "Problems in Interpreting the Book of Mormon as History," *Courage: A Journal of History, Thought, and Action* 1 (September 1970): 15-22; and William D. Russell, "History and the Mormon Scriptures," *Journal of Mormon History* 10 (1983): 53-63. If there is one central theme in the book, it is the continual covenanting together of God and humanity in a cyclical pattern of covenant-righteousness-turning from the gospel-falling away-covenanting anew. The conclusion of non-Mormon William Collins, "Thoughts on the Mormon Scriptures: An Outsider's View of the Inspiration of Joseph Smith," *Dialogue* 15 (Autumn 1982): 53, seems appropriate here: "When I examine the Book of Mormon for truth rather than facticity, my reading reveals powerful, eternal, and relevant truths which are capable of changing and guiding men's lives."

The Mormon Approach to Scripture

The 1830s were a fertile period for the development of Mormon doctrine and it was reflected in the various Mormon scriptures: revisions to the Bible, the Book of Mormon, the Book of Commandments (Doctrine and Covenants), and the Book of Abraham. These were analyzed in a single outstanding volume, Richard Howard's *Restoration Scriptures: A Study of Their Textual Development* (Independence: Herald Publishing House, 1969, rev. ed. 1994), followed by a useful collection of essays Dan Vogel, ed., *The Word of God: Essays on Mormon Scripture*. Additionally, some very important noncanonical doctrinal writings emerged, such as the "Lectures on Faith," which were either written by Sidney Rigdon or prepared because of Rigdon's pressure on Smith to systematize his theological writings. (See discussion below.)

Joseph Smith's imaginative religious thinking led directly to a revision of the King James version of the Bible beginning in the early 1830s. An outstanding investigation of the place of the Bible in Smith's thought can be found in the early portions of Philip L. Barlow, *Mormons and the Bible: The Place of the Latter-day Saints in American Religion* (New York: Oxford University Press, 1991). A fine discussion limited to Smith's revision is Robert J. Matthews, *"A Plainer Translation:" Joseph Smith's Translation of the Bible, A History and Commentary* (Provo, UT: Brigham Young University Press, 1975). Specific discussions are Gordon Irving, "The Mormons and the Bible in the 1830s," *BYU Studies* 13 (Summer 1973): 473-88; and Robert J. Matthews, "The 'New Translation' of the Bible, 1830-1833: Doctrinal Development during the Kirtland Era," *BYU Studies* 11 (Summer 1971): 400-22. Discussions of Smith's prophetic license in revising the Bible include Kevin L. Barney, "The Joseph Smith Translation and Ancient Texts of the Bible," *Dialogue* 19 (Fall 1986): 85-102; Anthony A. Hutchinson, "The Joseph Smith Revision and the Synoptic Problem: An Alternate View," *John Whitmer Historical Association Journal* 5 (1985): 47-53; his "LDS Approaches to the Holy Bible," *Dialogue* 15 (Spring 1982): 99-125; Robert L. Millet, "Joseph Smith's Translation of the Bible and the Synoptic Problem," *John Whitmer Historical Association Journal* 5 (1985): 41-46; and William D. Russell, "History and the Mormon Scriptures," *Journal of Mormon History* 10 (1983): 53-63.

Also during this period, Smith took action to collect, edit, and publish revelations to the Latter Day Saint movement. These were printed in 1835 in the *Doctrine and Covenants of the Church of the Latter Day Saints* (Kirtland, OH: F. G. Williams and Co., 1835). Several good commentaries on the revelations and the Doctrine and Covenants's development include Lyndon W. Cook, *The Revelations of the Prophet Joseph Smith* (Provo, UT: Seventy's Mission Bookstore, 1981); Richard O. Cowan, *Doctrine and Covenants: Our Modern Scripture* (Provo, UT: Brigham Young University Press, 1978); F. Henry Edwards, *A New Commentary on the Doctrine and Covenants* (Independence: Herald Publishing House, 1985); Geoffrey F. Spencer, *The Burning Bush: Revelation and Scripture in the Life of the Church* (Independence: Herald Publishing House, 1975); H. Michael Marquardt, *The Joseph Smith Revelations: Text &*

Commentary (Salt Lake City: Signature Books, 1999); Robert J. Woodford, "The Historical Background of the Doctrine and Covenants" (Ph.D. diss., Brigham Young University, 1974); and Maurice L. Draper, "The 1835 General Assembly and the Doctrine and Covenants," *Saints Herald* 132 (August 1985): 12-13, 16.

A persistent issue in the publication of the Doctrine and Covenants has been how to handle the variant readings published in Mormon periodicals or in the Book of Commandments that was in the process of being printed in Missouri in 1833 when the Saints were expelled from Jackson County. Howard's *Restoration Scriptures* provides a compelling discussion of this subject, as do Melvin J. Petersen, "A Study of the Nature of and Significance of the Changes in the Revelations as Found in a Comparison of the Book of Commandments and Subsequent Editions of the Doctrine and Covenants" (M.S. thesis, Brigham Young University, 1955); his "Editing the Revelations for Publication," *Courage: A Journal of History, Thought, and Action* 1 (March 1971): 172-79, and Karl F. Best, "Changes in the Revelations, 1833 to 1835," *Dialogue* 25 (Spring 1992): 87-122. All document the changes, some editorial in nature and others more substantive, and seek to demonstrate the evolution of Joseph Smith's theological insight as reflected in the textual alterations made for the 1835 Kirtland publication. Earl E. Olson, "The Chronology of the Ohio Revelations," *BYU Studies* 11 (Summer 1971): 329-49, pins down important details on when and where Joseph Smith gave his many Ohio revelations.

In 1835 Michael Chandler sold to the Saints several Egyptian mummies, some of which had papyri containing hieroglyphics. This odd episode is chronicled in Thomas M. Tinney, "Michael H. Chandler and the Pearl of Great Price: 1986 Update," *Genealogical Journal* 15 (Fall 1986): 128-61; his "Michael H. Chandler and the Pearl of Great Price Update," *The Report* [Ohio Genealogical Society], 27 (Fall 1987): 132-40; Christopher C. Lund, "A Letter Regarding the Acquisition of the Book of Abraham," *BYU Studies* 20 (Spring 1980): 402-403; Charles M. Larson, *By His Own Hand Upon Papyrus: A New Look at the Joseph Smith Papyri* (San Francisco: Institute For Religious Research, 1992); and, most definitively, Stanley B. Kimball, "New Light on Old Egyptiana: Mormon Mummies, 1848-71," *Dialogue* 16 (Winter 1983): 72-90. Joseph Smith, who had gained renown for his foreign language skills because of his work with the Book of Mormon, began to translate them in Kirtland, claiming that they were sacred writings from Abraham while in Egypt. This translation was published in 1842 as the Book of Abraham and later canonized by Latter-day Saints in Utah. General commentaries for the Latter-day Saint audience are Keith Terry and Walter Whipple, *From the Dust of Decades: Saga of the Papyri and Mummies* (Salt Lake City: Bookcraft, 1968); and Jay M. Todd, *The Saga of the Book of Abraham* (Salt Lake City: Deseret Book, 1969).

In the late 1960s some of the papyri that had been used to translate the Book of Abraham presumed lost for all time, was rediscovered. It naturally created a furor among those interested in Mormon scripture. Retranslating the papyri, modern Egyptologists found that their translation bore no relationship to what Joseph Smith said he translated. Orthodox Mormon scholars have sought to explain how this could be the case while still maintaining Smith's prophetic identity and the sacred stature of the Book of Abraham. Some have engaged in complex scholarly exercises as a means of seeking to understand Joseph Smith and his fertile theological perception in light of this development. Some of the more sophisticated and useful of these studies include, Richard P. Howard, "The 'Book of Abraham' in the Light of History and Egyptology," *Courage: A Journal of History, Thought, and Action* 1 (April 1970): 33-47, which offers a Reorganized Church perspective; Hugh Nibley, *The Message of the Joseph Smith Papyri: An Egyptian Endowment* (Salt Lake City: Deseret Book, 1975), which presents an LDS apologist's position; and Karl C. Sandberg, "Knowing Brother Joseph Again: The Book of Abraham, and Joseph Smith as Translator," *Dialogue* 22 (Winter 1989): 17-38, which seeks to understand Joseph Smith's thinking as he wrote the Book of Abraham.

Mormonism's early era was a very creative periods for defining theological conceptions. Indeed, the seeds of the unique theological speculations that emerged in Nauvoo were planted and nurtured near the shores of Lake Erie. From its vague identification with the beliefs of American Protestantism in 1830, the Church evolved a highly distinctive set of beliefs during its Ohio experience. These included ideas about the nature of God, an existence before this life, a plurality of worlds each with its own life forms, the concept of a progressive God, a set of rituals that prepared the Saints for an afterlife of glorification, dietary strictures, and a three-part system of rewards for the righteous Saints.

Some recent studies of these theological questions include Charles R. Harrell, "The Development of the Doctrine of Preexistence, 1830-1844," *BYU Studies* 28 (Spring 1988): 75-96; Blake Ostler, "The Idea of Pre-existence in the Development of Mormon Thought," *Dialogue* 15 (Spring 1982): 59-78 (he is now preparing a three-volume work on Mormon theology of which the first volume, *Exploring Mormon Thought: The Attributes of God* [Salt Lake City: Greg Kofford Books, 2001] has appeared, see also his *Refractions on Light: Essays on Mormon Theology* [Salt Lake City: Greg Kofford Books, forthcoming]); Robert Paul, "Joseph Smith and the Plurality of Worlds Idea," *Dialogue* 19 (Summer 1986): 13-36; Garland E. Tickemyer, "Joseph Smith and Process Theology," *Dialogue* 17 (Autumn 1984): 75-85; David John Buerger, "The Development of the Mormon Temple Endowment Ceremony," *Dialogue* 20 (Winter 1987): 33-76; Robert L. Millet, "Beyond the Veil: Two Latter-day Revelations," *Ensign* 15 (October 1985): 8-13 (the Kirtland visions of celestial kingdom and redemption of the dead); Gary James Bergera, ed., *Line Upon Line: Essays on Mormon Doctrine* (Salt Lake City: Signature Books, 1989); Gary J. Bergera, "Has the Word of Wisdom Changed Since 1833?" *Sunstone* 10 (July 1985): 32-33; Lester E. Bush Jr., "The Word of Wisdom in Early Nineteenth Century Perspective," *Dialogue* 14 (Fall 1981): 47-65; Paul H. Peterson, "An Historical Analysis of the Word of Wisdom" (M.A. thesis, Brigham Young University, 1972); Robert T. Divett, "Medicine and the Mormons: A Historical Perspective," *Dialogue* 12 (Autumn 1979): 16-25; and E. Robert Paul, *Science, Religion, and Mormon Cosmology* (Urbana: University of Illinois Press, 1992).

Some of these ideas were taught in the School of the Prophets, later called the School of the Apostles, at Kirtland in the mid-1830s but others were reserved for special gatherings of the priesthood. While there is a need for intensive investigation of the School of Prophets, Orlen C. Peterson, "A History of the Schools and Educational Programs of the Church of Jesus Christ of Latter-day Saints in Ohio and Missouri, 1831-1839" (M.A. thesis, Brigham Young University, 1972); and Bruce Westergren, "A Time of Preparation: The Kirtland School of the Prophets," *The Thetean: A Student Journal of History,* May 1984, 91-113, provide an introduction.

Central to understanding the theological concepts being publicly taught is the information contained in the "Lectures on Faith," bound as a part of the Doctrine and Covenants in 1835. They reflected a transliteration of Protestant doctrine and were certainly much more theologically moderate than Mormon thought in the 1840s. At the same time they demonstrate some of the nascent uniqueness of Mormon doctrine that became apparent later, but not enough for the Latter-day Saint Church to see them as valuable and maintain them in its canon, as recounted in Leland H. Gentry, "What of the Lectures on Faith?" *BYU Studies* 19 (Fall 1978): 5-19; and Richard S. Van Wagoner, Steven C. Walker, and Allen D. Roberts, "The 'Lectures on Faith': A Case Study in Decanonization," *Dialogue* 20 (Fall 1987): 71-77. Another important activity associated with the School of the Prophets was the employment in early 1836 of Jewish scholar Joshua Seixas to teach Hebrew to Joseph Smith and other members of the Mormon leadership. His role has been studied in Louis C. Zucker, "Joseph Smith as a Student of Hebrew," *Dialogue* 3 (Summer 1968): 41-55; and Michael T. Walton, "Professor Seixas, the Hebrew Bible, and the Book of Abraham," *Sunstone* 6 (March/April 1981): 41-43.

The Development of a Mormon Community

Most students of Mormon history are aware of the remarkable expansion of the Church from a small, tightly knit group in upstate New York to a larger, but still tightly knit, organization in both Kirtland, Ohio, and Missouri. (See "The Mormon Experience in Missouri, 1830-39" by Stephen C. LeSueur in this volume.) The context for this expansion is described in several publications. One question centers on Mormonism's appeal, generating much scholarly debate on whether Mormonism was a frontier or an eastern-focused religion. Such a debate was probably inevitable in the first half of the twentieth century when Frederick Jackson Turner's frontier thesis strongly influenced American historians.[14] Whitney R. Cross, *The Burned-Over District: The Social and Intellectual History of Enthusiastic Religion in Western New York* (Ithaca, NY: Cornell University Press, 1950) challenged Mormonism's frontier foundations as the dominating influence, substituting instead evangelicalism fomented by revivals. Others have weighed in on this interpretation, and the most comprehensive view presently espoused comes from the work of Marvin Hill whose interpretation of Mormonism's appeal as a counter-revolutionary movement holds particular attraction for many modern students of the Church's origins. Hill argues this thesis in "Quest for Refuge: An Hypothesis as to the Social Origins and Nature of the Mormon Political Kingdom," *Journal of Mormon History* 2 (1975): 3-20; "The Rise of Mormonism in the Burned-Over District: Another View," *New York History* 61 (October 1980): 411-30; "The Shaping of the Mormon Mind in New England and New York," *BYU Studies* 9 (Spring 1969): 351-72; and, of course, his *Quest for Refuge*. Also relevant are David Brion Davis, "The New England Origins of Mormonism," *New England Quarterly* 27 (June 1953): 147-68; James B. Allen and Leonard J. Arrington, "Mormon Origins in New York: An Introductory Analysis," *BYU Studies* 9 (Spring 1969): 241-74; Leonard J. Arrington, "Mormonism: From Its New York Beginnings," *New York History* 61 (October 1980): 387-410; Milton V. Backman Jr., "The Quest for a Restoration: The Birth of Mormonism in Ohio," *BYU Studies* 12 (Summer 1972): 346-64; Backman, *American Religions and the Rise of Mormonism* (Salt Lake City: Deseret Book, 1965); Mario S. De Pillis, "The Quest for Religious Authority and the Rise of Mormonism," *Dialogue* 1 (Spring 1966): 68-88; De Pillis, "The Social Sources of Mormonism," *Church History* 37 (March 1968): 50-79; and Dan Vogel, *Religious Seekers and the Advent of Mormonism* (Salt Lake City: Signature Books, 1988).

One of the first issues that the young Mormon movement faced was finding a viable economic order. One, especially influential in Ohio, was modeled on the New Testament passage indicating that the early Saints "held all things in common." Sidney Rigdon had instituted a communal group known as the "Family." The system worked imperfectly at best, and Joseph Smith revamped it into the law of consecration and stewardship. The evolution of this doctrine has been studied intensively, and an important overview of this subject is offered in Leonard J. Arrington, Feramorz Y. Fox, and Dean L. May, *Building the City of God: Community and Cooperation Among the Mormons* (Salt Lake City: Deseret Book, 1976). Other interpretive studies include Arrington, "Early Mormon Communitarianism: The Law of Consecration and Stewardship," *Western Humanities Review* 7 (Autumn 1951): 341-69; Lyndon W. Cook, *Joseph Smith and the Law of Consecration* (Provo, UT: Grandin Book, 1985); Mario S. De Pillis, "The Development of Mormon Communitarianism, 1826-1846" (Ph.D. diss., Yale University, 1960); Rex Eugene Cooper, *Promises Made to the Fathers: Mormon Covenant Organization* (Salt Lake City: University of Utah Press, 1990); and Milton V. Backman Jr., "Clothed with Bonds of Charity: The Law of Consecration and Stewardship in Ohio, 1830-1838," in (no editor) *Hearken, O Ye People: Discourses on the Doctrine and Covenants*, Proceedings of the 1984 Sidney B. Sperry Symposium, Brigham Young University (Sandy, UT: Randall Books, 1984) 93-104.

Many within Mormonism viewed the law of consecration and stewardship as the first necessary step in establishing God's millennial kingdom on earth. The logical result of

---

14. See Frederick Jackson Turner, "The Significance of the Frontier in American History," first published in 1893 but conveniently reprinted in *The Frontier in American History* (New York: Holt, Rinehart, and Winston, 1920). For critiques of this approach and the final burying of the frontier thesis, see Patricia Nelson Limerick, *The Legacy of Conquest: The Unbroken Past of the American West* (New York: W. W. Norton and Co., 1987); William Cronon et al., eds., *Under the Open Sky: Rethinking America's Western Past* (New York: W. W. Norton and Co., 1992); Richard White, *"It's Your Misfortune and None of My Own:" A New History of the American West* (Norman: University of Oklahoma Press, 1991).

such thinking was the creation of a theocracy that, while it might not be *of* this world, was very much *in* it. The zionic ideal created difficulties throughout Mormonism's early history. Although all of the following works provide a broad coverage, they also offer useful analyses of what Zion meant to the early Mormons in the context of American society: Ken Driggs, "The Mormon Church-State Confrontation in Nineteenth Century America," *Journal of Church and State* 30 (Spring 1988): 273-89; Steven L. Olsen, "Zion: The Structure of a Theological Revolution," *Sunstone* 6 (November/December 1981): 21-26; Miriam Elizabeth Higdon, "Eyes Single to the Glory: The History of the Heavenly City of Zion," in *Restoration Studies I,* edited by Maurice L. Draper (Independence: Herald Publishing House, 1980), 269-77; Geoffrey F. Spencer, "Symbol and Process: An Exploration into the Concept of Zion," in *Restoration Studies I*, 287-95; Hyrum L. Andrus, *Joseph Smith and World Government* (Salt Lake City: Hawkes Publishing, 1972); Richard L. Anderson, "Joseph Smith and the Millenarian Time Table," *BYU Studies* 3 (Spring-Summer 1961): 55-66; Edward A. Warner, "Mormon Theodemocracy: Theocratic and Democratic Elements in Early Latter-day Saint Ideology, 1827-1846" (Ph.D. diss., University of Iowa, 1973); and John F. Wilson, "Some Comparative Perspectives on the Early Mormon Movement and the Church-State Question," *Journal of Mormon History* 8 (1981): 63-78. Klaus J. Hansen, *Quest for Empire: The Political Kingdom of God and the Council of Fifty in Mormon History* (East Lansing: Michigan State University Press, 1967), is the classic study of the Zionic quest in Mormonism, but its emphasis is on the Nauvoo and Utah experience.

As soon as a Mormon group began to emerge in 1830 a series of problems surfaced, for the Saints were a clannish and politically homogeneous group who alarmed those around them. The non-Mormons in the area early concluded that Mormonism was a revolutionary theology that created political, economic, and social upheaval. Max H. Parkin, "Mormon Political Involvement in Ohio," *BYU Studies* 9 (Summer 1969): 484-502, and especially his broader study, *Conflict at Kirtland: The Nature and Causes of Internal and External Conflict of the Mormons in Ohio between 1830 and 1838* (Provo, UT: BYU Religious Studies Department, 1967), provide valuable analyses of these strains in Ohio, but there are no comparable works on the New York period. Now outdated is Willis Thornton, "Gentile and Saint at Kirtland," *Ohio State Archaeological and Historical Quarterly* 63 (January 1954): 8-33.

The tendency toward the development of theocracy was a very real concern. Even had the early Mormons wanted to do so—and there is little reason to believe that Joseph Smith understood the potential dangers theocracy would conjure up among outsiders—the difficulties associated with avoiding secular issues once a Church community has taken root were very real. Alma R. Blair, "A Loss of Nerve," " *Courage: A Journal of History, Thought, and Action* 1 (September 1970): 29-36, argued persuasively in another context that, although the "Saints were not always conscious of it, and would certainly have denied it, they were in fact a very 'political' group. The reason they were is simple: Certain values they held important enough to act on were also of concern to others outside the church" (34). While the full impact of Mormonism theocracy would not be realized until later, the discontent it engendered when dealing with nonbelievers was already visible in Kirtland in the mid-1830s.

The Development of Church Organization and Doctrine

Without question one of the significant unfoldings that took place in New York and Ohio was the emergence of a complex organizational structure. Evolving from a remarkably simple system of Church governance and polity in 1830 to an exceptionally intricate hierarchy by 1835, Joseph Smith created a series of priesthood quorums and councils to oversee various aspects of the Church. The classic discussion of this process is D. Michael Quinn, "The Evolution of the Presiding Quorums of the LDS Church," *Journal of Mormon History* 1 (1974): 21-38, elaborated in his "From Sacred Grove to Sacral Power Structure," *Dialogue* 17 (Summer 1984): 9-34. The creation of the administrative unit of the Quorum of Twelve Apostles has been described in Alfred L. Bush, "A Quorum Called Out of the Kingdom," *Princeton University Library Chronicle* 42 (Autumn 1980): 55-59; Ronald K. Esplin, "The Emergence of Brigham Young and the Twelve to Mormon Leadership, 1830-

1846" (Ph.D. diss., Brigham Young University, 1981); and Wilburn D. Talbot, "The Duties and Responsibilities of the Apostles of the Church of Jesus Christ of Latter-day Saints, 1835-1945" (Ph.D. diss., Brigham Young University, 1978).

Research has also been conducted about the function of other offices in the Church, as well as the role of the general conferences of the Church, notably Robert L. Marriott, "History and Functions of the Aaronic Priesthood and the Officers of Priest, Teacher, and Deacon in the Church of Jesus Christ of Latter-day Saints, 1829 to 1844" (M.A. thesis, Brigham Young University, 1976); Robert Glen Mouritsen, "The Office of Associate President of the Church of Jesus Christ of Latter-day Saints" (M.A. thesis, Brigham Young University, 1972); and Jay R. Lowe, "A Study of the General Conferences of the Church of Jesus Christ of Latter-day Saints, 1830-1901" (Ph.D. diss., Brigham Young University, 1972).

Much work remains to be done on the development of organizational structures and power relationships in the Kirtland church, as well as both before and after that period. Especially important in this study is how issues of power and influence have been played out in the history of the institution. How did individual members obtain and maintain high office in the early movement? How did individual officials fare as the ecclesiastical system evolved? How did others once in positions of power, such as the three witnesses to the Book of Mormon, fall from favor? What have been the interrelations of this aristocracy and how have these interactions unfolded in the history of the Church? Moreover, what are its relationships *vis à vis* both other leaders and the rank and file? Only D. Michael Quinn's suggestive but massive and difficult study, *The Mormon Hierarchy: Origins of Power* (Salt Lake City: Signature Books, 1994) and *The Mormon Hierarchy: Extensions of Power* (Salt Lake City: Signature Books, 1997), and Gregory A. Prince's monograph, *Having Authority: The Origins and Development of Priesthood During the Ministry of Joseph Smith* (Independence: John Whitmer Historical Association Monograph Series, 1993) and *Power from On High: The Development of Mormon Priesthood* (Salt Lake City: Signature Books, 1995), have attempted to tackle any of these questions. Consequently, much remains to be done, especially since the Church experiences in the East were so fertile for organizational transformation, promising instructive insights from a deep study of power strategies.

Life Among the Saints

One of the very significant areas that has been largely unexplored in relation to Mormonism's sojourn in the East is the way in which individuals and families lived and interacted. There is only a little on this subject in any of the larger studies available, and almost nothing of a specialized nature. This has largely been the case because of the historical concentration on Joseph Smith and the activities of the institutional Church. To resolve this problem in the historiography, historians will want to explore the issues of race, ethnicity, class, and gender—the four cornerstones of the "new social history"—in the context of early Mormonism. Until such time as this social history is pursued the important studies include Linda King Newell and Valeen Tippets Avery, "Sweet Counsel and a Sea of Tribulation: The Religious Life of the Women in Kirtland," *BYU Studies* 20 (Winter 1980): 151-62; Newell B. Weight, "The Birth of Mormon Hymnody," *Dialogue* 10 (Spring 1975): 40-48; and the first part of Michael Hicks, *Mormonism and Music: A History* (Urbana: University of Illinois Press, 1989).

It was while the Church was headquartered in Ohio that the first rumors of experimentation with family relationships began to be heard. During the summer of 1835, for instance, gossip about marital irregularities swirled around the community and led to the decision to place a special section in the Doctrine and Covenants affirming that the law of the Church was monogamy. It seems reliably established that Joseph Smith had an affair with Fanny Alger, then living in his home as a hired girl. An incensed Oliver Cowdery wrote to his brother, Warren, on January 21, 1838, that he had confronted Joseph Smith about "a dirty, nasty, filthy affair of his and Fanny Algers" (holograph, Mormon Collection, Huntington Library, San Marino, CA). Cowdery's outrage was apparently the catalyst behind the statement's inclusion, giving it canonical status and providing the Reorganized Church with a powerful weapon later in the century to fight polygamy among the Mormons, as recounted in Richard P. Howard, "The Changing RLDS Response to Mormon Polygamy: A Preliminary Analysis," *John Whitmer Historical Association Journal* 3 (1983): 14-29; Alma R. Blair, "RLDS Views of Polygamy: Some Historiographical Notes," *John Whitmer Historical Association Journal* 5 (1985): 16-28; Roger D. Launius, "Methods and Motives: Joseph Smith III's Opposition to Polygamy, 1860-90," *Dialogue* 20 (Winter 1987): 105-20.

While the affirmation of monogamy was one development, the Kirtland period also seems to have generated an early discussion of eternal marriage, for W. W. Phelps wrote to his wife in September 1835 that he had learned from Joseph Smith the law of "celestial marriage" and that his wife would be Phelps's "in this world and in the world to come; . . . This is the reason why I have called you at the commencement of this letter, *My Only One* because I have no right to any other woman in this world nor in the world to come according to the law of the celestial Kingdom."[15] Furthermore, almost certainly Joseph Smith was discussing his disruptive innovation of celestial/plural marriage in certain settings as early as 1831 and perhaps seeing its limited practice by 1835. Important examinations are Lawrence Foster, *Religion and Sexuality: Three American Communal Experiments of the Nineteenth Century* (New York: Oxford University Press, 1981); Danel W. Bachman, "A Study of the Mormon Practice of Plural Marriage before the Death of Joseph Smith" (M.A. thesis, Purdue University, 1975); Richard S. Van Wagoner, *Mormon Polygamy: A History* (1985; 3rd ed., Salt Lake City: Signature Books, 1992); B. Carmon Hardy, *Solemn Covenant: The Mormon Polygamous Passage* (Urbana: University of Illinois Press, 1991); and Todd Compton, *In Sacred Loneliness: The Plural Wives of Joseph Smith* (Salt Lake City: Signature Books, 1997). All discuss this early experience as a prelude to the Nauvoo and Utah periods. Danel W. Bachman, however, focuses on the Kirtland period in "New Light on an Old Hypothesis: The Ohio Origins of the Revelation on Eternal Marriage," *Journal of Mormon History* 5 (1978): 19-31.

Without question, the center of life for Mormons in Kirtland, from 1833 until the body of the Church migrated to Missouri in 1837-38, was the temple constructed and used over a five-year period. This building, which the early Saints imbued with so many of their hopes and dreams, has been the subject of several interesting historical, architectural, and theological studies. A broad study, emphasizing the role of architecture in all nineteenth-century Mormon temples is Laurel B. Andrew, *The Early Temples of the Mormons: The Architecture of the Millennial Kingdom in the American West* (Albany: University Press of New York, 1978). My *The Kirtland Temple: A Historical Narrative* (Independence: Herald Publishing House, 1986), is a historical study that presents a biography of the building from its conception to the present, amplified in my "The Dream Shattered: The Abandonment of the Kirtland Temple, 1837-1862," *Restoration* 5 (April 1986): 13-18; and my "Joseph Smith III and the Kirtland Temple Suit," *BYU Studies* 25 (Summer 1985): 110-16.

An important recent study of the history and architecture of the building may be found in Elwin C. Robison, *First Mormon Temple: Design, Construction, and Historic Context of the Kirtland Temple* (Provo, UT: BYU Press, 1997). Lauritz G. Petersen's short article, "The Kirtland Temple," *BYU Studies* 12 (Summer 1972): 400-409, is a suggestive piece that asks important questions about the meaning of the temple in the theology of Mormonism. Other articles include Nancy J. Break, "A Mormon Temple in the American Rural Tradition," *Lake County Historical Quarterly* 31 (September 1989): 17-26; Walter C. Kidney, *Historic Buildings in Ohio* (Pittsburgh: Ober Park Associates, 1972); Robert Winter, "Architecture on the Frontier: The Mormon Experiment," *Pacific Historical Review* 43 (1974): 50-60; and Richard Price and Pamela Price, "The Building of the Kirtland Temple," *Restoration Voice,* November/December 1981, 22-25.

The dedication of the temple at Kirtland on March 27, 1836, brought an outbreak of pentecostal enthusiasm, the likes of which had never been seen before within Mormonism. Positive descriptions of these activities can be found in Stephen D. Ricks,

---

15. Quoted in Richard S. Van Wagoner, "Mormon Polyandry in Nauvoo," *Dialogue* 18 (Fall 1985): 67-83, quotation p. 72. Despite the title, this article has as much to say about Kirtland as Nauvoo.

"The Appearance of Elijah and Moses in the Kirtland Temple and the Jewish Passover," *BYU Studies* 23 (Fall 1983): 483-86; Richard Bullard, "Dedication of Kirtland Temple," *Restoration Voice* January/February 1982, 26-28; and Jacob Heinerman, *Temple Manifestations* (Salt Lake City: Hawkes Publishing Co., 1975). However, LaMar Petersen, *Hearts Made Glad: The Charges of Intemperance Against Joseph Smith the Mormon Prophet* (Salt Lake City: n.pub., 1975), includes a chapter suggesting that the spiritual experiences reported at the time of the dedication were the result of drunkenness on the part of Joseph Smith and other key members of the Church leadership.

The Mormon Economy

The tightly knit community of Latter Day Saints, a poor group, also created unique social and economic problems. The institutional church went to great lengths to purchase land and businesses as a means of employing those who had no other means of support. The construction crews for the temple, for instance, received assistance in the form of food and shelter, making the project a public works program. But Joseph Smith needed capital to finance his community efforts, and money was always in short supply among the Saints. He decided in 1836 to charter a bank in Ohio and issue his own paper money, thereby inflating the local economy and making it possible to leverage out of the community's debt. He created a wildcat bank, the Kirtland Safety Society Anti-Banking Company, after the state legislature refused a banking charter, and it functioned through most of 1837. Critics of Joseph Smith and the Mormons have invariably challenged the viability of the whole economy and the bank in particular, chalking the episode up to greed and stupidity. Since the bank was suspect from the beginning and eventually failed, perhaps in response to the general economic crisis coming with the Panic of 1837, they had powerful evidence for these conclusions. The result was a crisis of the first magnitude that led directly to the Mormon exodus of 1838. This is the general story of the economic activities of the Saints in Kirtland, as recounted with varying degrees of skill in the general surveys already cited by Allen and Leonard, Arrington and Bitton, Edwards, and Howard.

The subtleties of the Kirtland economy, which are rarely explored in these more general treatments, have received their most important examination in Marvin S. Hill, C. Keith Rooker, and Larry T. Wimmer, *The Kirtland Economy Revisited: A Market Place Critique of Sectarian Economics* (Provo, UT: Brigham Young University Press, 1977). Hill, Rooker, and Wimmer argue convincingly that the Mormon economy was a viable entity but that the Panic of 1837 was not the reason behind the failure of the Mormon bank and the collapse of the Kirtland economic bubble. The collapse rested squarely on operating a bank without a charter, since without legal status all businesses that had been dealing with the Saints hesitated to continue. This was all the more true when rumors of slipshod management of the bank's assets began to circulate. An outstanding example of what talented scholars can accomplish when focusing on objectively testable economic hypotheses, *The Kirtland Economy Revisited* should be read in conjunction with Peter Temin, *The Jacksonian Economy* (New York: W.W. Norton, 1969), for the broader conception of economics in the 1830s, and Robert Kent Fielding, "The Mormon Economy at Kirtland, Ohio," *Utah Historical Quarterly* 27 (October 1959): 331-56.

Several fine articles, most assuming that the Kirtland bank failed as a result of the Panic of 1837, have appeared in recent years: Dale W Adams, "Chartering the Kirtland Bank," *BYU Studies* 23 (Fall 1983): 467-82; Dean A. Dudley, "Bank Born of Revelation: The Kirtland Safety Society Anti-Banking Co.," *Journal of Economic History* 30 (December 1971): 848-53; Scott H. Partridge, "The Failure of the Kirtland Safety Society," *BYU Studies* 12 (Summer 1972): 437-54; and D. Paul Sampson and Larry T. Wimmer, "The Kirtland Safety Society: The Stock Ledger Book and the Bank Failure," *BYU Studies* 12 (Summer 1972): 427-36. Larry Schweikart, "Making Money the Old-Fashioned Way: Banking before the Civil War," *Timelines* December 1989-January 1990, 33-43, is insightful background on the climate in which the Mormon bank at Kirtland operated.

Excavating Mormon Pasts

Declension and Movement West

Concurrent with the collapse of the Church's economy in Ohio in 1837 dissension began to be seen everywhere. Joseph Smith described it as religious persecution by apostates and evil men who filed "vexatious lawsuits." This was the position taken by Edwin Brown Firmage and Richard Collin Mangrum, *Zion in the Courts: A Legal History of the Church of Jesus Christ of Latter-day Saints, 1830-1900* (Urbana: University of Illinois Press, 1988), 48-58; however, the authors' comments on this dicey episode are superficial at best. They use Smith's *History of the Church* to suggest that the bank failure caused the dissent, even though Marvin S. Hill, "Cultural Crisis in the Mormon Kingdom: A Reconsideration of the Causes of Kirtland Dissent," *Church History* 49 (September 1980): 286-97, demonstrates the complexity caused by differing approaches of Church leaders to the secular world. Firmage and Mangrum's characterization of "vexatious lawsuits and persecution" (38) is a simplistic and generalized assessment connoting unjust actions but ignoring alternative positions which could be fully justified from a different perspective. While suggesting that it was sad that good people became dissenters from the Church, the authors argued that those individuals "could not be tolerated if the vision of a unified religious community was to survive the persecution from without" (39-40). Other simplistic views are Richard Price and Pamela Price, "The Kirtland Crisis: The Division of 1837-1838," *Restoration Voice*, March/April 1983, 21-24; and Backman, *The Heavens Resound*, 310-41.

In fact there was very little religious persecution, and the dissent was predicated more on questions about the proper role of religion in American life. Hill, "Cultural Crisis in the Mormon Kingdom," offers a compelling analysis of the complicated and nuanced dissent demonstrated in Kirtland. He found that the Saints' complaints about specific issues were only symptoms of a larger discontent over the fundamental nature of the Church: "In the upheaval at Kirtland, which carried over into Far West, Missouri, the degree of control to be possessed by the church and its leaders, the degree of consolidation in the kingdom was at stake. Dissenters like the Cowderys, the Whitmers, Burnet, McLellin and Brewster, wanted a more open society, closer to the values and traditions of evangelical Protestantism, while those who supported Smith tolerated a more closed society based on higher law, where the Saints were of one mind an[d] one heart, ready to do battle against the ungodly" (296).

Precursors of this crisis had been seen following the disastrous Zion's Camp expedition to Missouri in 1834, when several Church officials in Kirtland challenged Smith's role in the Church and brought charges against him. These episodes are explored in Peter Crawley and Richard L. Anderson, "The Political and Social Realities of Zion's Camp," *BYU Studies* 14 (Summer 1974): 406-20; Roger D. Launius, *Zion's Camp: Expedition to Missouri, 1834* (Independence: Herald Publishing House, 1984); and Wilburn D. Talbot, "Zion's Camp" (M.A. thesis, Brigham Young University, 1973).

In short, the conflict resulted from passionate concerns about the fundamental shape of the Church and whether it would be a part of American religion or outside of it. The rift was a significant philosophical and theological difference, not just the dismissal of a few disgruntled individuals. It culminated in the withdrawal or expulsion of the three witnesses to the divinity of the Book of Mormon—Oliver Cowdery, Martin Harris, and David Whitmer—more than half of the Quorum of Twelve Apostles, and the ranking bishop, Edward Partridge. An unquantifiable number of members of lesser stature also withdrew or were excommunicated. There is considerably more to be done on this subject, although Hill's work charts an important path of exploration, for the Kirtland dissenters raised fundamental questions that went far beyond the details of the events involved to consider the nature of Church government and the direction of institutional development. In addition to other works, Davis Bitton, "The Waning of Mormon Kirtland," " *BYU Studies* 12 (Summer 1972): 455-64, explores the community's dissension-racked demise and the departure of those faithful to Smith to Missouri. A journeyman discussion of the primary group of Mormons to leave Kirtland can be found in Gordon O. Hill, "A History of Kirtland Camp: Its Initial Purpose and Notable Accomplishments" (M.A. thesis, Brigham Young

University, 1975). By the end of 1838, only a handful of Mormons remained in Kirtland, contending among themselves for control of the temple, whose legal status has received what may well be the definitive treatment in Kim Loving, "Ownership of the Kirtland Temple: Legends, Lies, and Misunderstandings," *Journal of Mormon History* 30, no. 2 (Fall 2004): forthcoming, with a commentary about "The Kirtland Temple Suit and the Utah Church" by Eric Paul Rogers and R. Scott Glauser (ibid.).

Conclusion

The New York and Ohio eras of early Mormonism are still fertile fields for study. The foundations of some truly exciting work has been laid, as shown by this survey. Earlier historians have defined relatively well the general contours of the subject and touched on many of the institutional aspects of the Church during its sojourn in the East. Yet several themes and areas remain to be explored. The most important of these is the social history of the Saints. Who were the early Saints, and what were their priorities, dreams, ideas, and ambitions? What was it like to live among the Mormons in their stronghold in Kirtland during the mid-1830s? The themes of race, ethnicity, class, and gender so prevalent in the new social history hold remarkable promise for the New Mormon History, and many can be undertaken using sources that are not restricted in the LDS Archives since they are not as dependent on the papers of high Church officials. Their study could well restructure the understanding of the Church in Kirtland and its evolution. Useful models for such a history might include J. Milton Yinger, *Religion in the Struggle for Power: A Study in the Sociology of Religion* (Durham, NC: Duke University Press, 1946); Rowland Berthoff, *An Unsettled People: Social Order and Disorder in American History* (New York: Harper and Row, 1971); Mario S. De Pillis, "Trends in American Social History and the Possibilities of Behavioral Approaches," *Journal of Social History* 1 (Fall 1967): 38-60; Stuart Blumin, "The Historical Study of Vertical Mobility," *Historical Methods Newsletter* 1 (September 1968): 1-13; Stephen Thernstrom, *Poverty and Progress: Social Mobility in a Nineteenth Century City* (Cambridge, MA: Harvard University Press, 1964); Philip J. Greven, Jr., *Four Generations: Population, Land, and Family in Colonial Andover, Massachusetts* (Ithaca, NY: Cornell University Press, 1970); Michael Kamman, ed., *The Past Before Us: Contemporary Historical Writing in the United States* (Ithaca, NY: Cornell University Press, 1980); David J. Russo, *Families and Communities: A New View of American History* (Nashville, TN: American Association of State and Local Historians, 1974); and David Levine, *Family Formation in an Age of Nascent Capitalism* (New York: Academic Press, 1977).

While new perspectives might shake up the discipline and offer strikingly different conclusions from those presently accepted, they should also instill a wider appreciation of the diversity and the complexity of the religion. There is also much work to be done on religious dissent, which individuals were involved on each side, and why they made the choices they did. There has been little investigation of this subject in Mormonism, probably because of a basic belief held both by the early Saints and present-day believers that Smith and the Church were persecuted innocents. As a result, men of integrity who criticized the prophet, such as Oliver Cowdery, could be defamed as enemies of the people and instantly denounced in the most damning terms. There seems to be considerable evidence that dissenters, by their very act of expressing dissent, were cast out of the ranks of the inherently innocent and were transmuted, in the Mormon mind, into the inherently evil. Dissenters were always characterized as demon-driven, woeful malcontents whose arguments were without foundation. The problem was always with the dissenters' characters, never with the Church or its leadership. Gordon D. Pollock notes this dynamic in "In Search of Security: The Mormons and the Kingdom of God on Earth, 1830-1844" (Ph.D. diss., Queen's University, 1977), 292-93. An intensive investigation of the nature and causes of internal conflict in the Church, with an honest survey of the charges of the dissenters might allow historians to move beyond the stock morality play that has characterized so much writing about this issue.

While there are other suggestive areas worthy of exploration—the role of women in the community, the nature of Mormon/non-Mormon interaction and disagreement, and the creation and evolution of institutional power—a final area that should be especially singled out for investigation is the history of Mormonism in the East *after* the 1838 decamping for Missouri. A small colony of Mormon dissidents remained in Ohio and continued to function in Kirtland after that time, among them Martin Harris. Different Mormon factional groups used the temple and some had substantial followings, at least for a time. The continued history of the temple and the Saints, even though they might not have been identified with the main group of Mormons, deserve sustained attention. There were also members in New York State after 1838. What happened to them?

With the perspectives that might be gained from inquiry into these themes, among others, a new synthesis of the early Mormon experience could be prepared. A new history of early Mormonism could draw together the insights made in the best work from the "new Mormon" and "new social" histories. It could also balance the stresses and strains of Mormon historical inquiry to achieve the goal of nonjudgmental observation that seeks to understand the past on its own terms rather than to judge its actors.

What should emerge from this effort, in the words of Paul M. Edwards, one of the leading historians of Mormonism, in "The New Mormon History," *Saints Herald* 133 (November 1986): 13, is "a decided shift away from polemics designed as either attacks on or defense of the Mormon movement." This history should embrace a view that directs the inquirer beyond the assumptions of faith. I would agree with Edwards that "this is not to be understood as lacking faith, being unfaithful, or going beyond faith. Rather it is an affirmation that one moves through reason and understanding to a larger faith. It suggests that doubt and unanswered questions are not issues of weak faith but the consideration of faithful persons seeking to know that which they do not understand. This assumption arises within historians and is based on their understanding of humans, and their own personal relationship with God. Thus they work fully aware that their faith is personal, not historical" (13). Mormon historians still await the undertaking of such a comprehensive history.

ROGER D. LAUNIUS is chair of the Division of Space History at the Smithsonian Institution's National Air and Space Museum in Washington, D.C. Between 1990 and 2002, he served as chief historian of the National Aeronautics and Space Administration. His books on Mormon history include *Kingdom on the Mississippi Revisited: Nauvoo in Mormon History* (Urbana: University of Illinois Press, 1996), coedited with John E. Hallwas; *Cultures in Conflict: A Documentary History of the Mormon War in Illinois* (Logan: Utah State University Press, 1995), coedited with John E. Hallwas; *Differing Visions: Dissenters in Mormon History* (Urbana: University of Illinois Press, 1994), coedited with Linda Thatcher; *Let Contention Cease: The Dynamics of Dissent in the Reorganized Church of Jesus Christ of Latter Day Saints* (Independence: Graceland/Park Press, 1991), coedited with W. B. "Pat" Spillman; *Father Figure: Joseph Smith III and the Creation of the Reorganized Church* (Independence: Herald Publishing House, 1990); *Joseph Smith III: Pragmatic Prophet* (Urbana: University of Illinois Press, 1988); *Invisible Saints: A History of Black Americans in the Reorganized Church* (Independence: Herald Publishing House, 1988), *Zion's Camp: Expedition to Missouri* (Independence: Herald Publishing House, 1984); and *An Early Latter Day Saint History: The Book of John Whitmer* (Independence: Herald Publishing House, 1980), coedited with F. Mark McKiernan. He has also published more than fifty articles on Mormon history. Portions of the material appearing in this essay were previously published in Roger D. Launius, "From the Old to New Mormon History: Fawn Brodie and the Legacy of Scholarly Analysis of Mormonism," in *Reconsidering No Man Knows My History: Fawn M. Brodie and Joseph Smith in Retrospect,* edited by Newell G. Bringhurst (Logan: Utah State University Press, 1996), 195-233, and Roger D. Launius, "The Latter Day Saints in Ohio: Writing the History of Mormonism's Middle Period," *John Whitmer Historical Association Journal* 16 (1996): 31-56.

Chapter 4

The Mormon Experience in Missouri, 1830-39

Stephen C. LeSueur

Fifty years of exhaustive research have not altered the historical consensus about Mormons during the Missouri period: The Mormons were unjustly and unlawfully expelled from their homes in western Missouri. The Mormons lost land, crops, possessions, and lives in Jackson County, Clay County, and northwestern Missouri, while their non-Mormon persecutors suffered very little in comparison. Beginning in 1833, when the anti-Mormon violence first began, the Saints petitioned the state and local governments to resolve the hostilities through legal, peaceful means. Their petitions continued until late 1838, when Mormon leaders, despairing that Missouri authorities would protect them from continuing abuses, went on the offensive to defend themselves. Mormon soldiers seized the initiative, plundering and burning homes of suspected enemies as open warfare erupted for a two-week period in the upper counties. Missouri authorities, who had seemed virtually powerless against the anti-Mormon vigilantes, moved swiftly to halt the Mormon violence, ordering that the Saints be expelled from the state and their leaders tried for crimes committed during the conflict. Soon after the Saints surrendered, some of their enemies rushed to settle Mormon lands, creating the impression, as a St. Louis newspaper observed, that the Missourians "got up this crusade in order to obtain possession of the houses and lands of their victims."[1]

Although historians do not question the essential unfairness of the Mormons' expulsion, they have significantly altered their views regarding the causes of conflict and the participants' motivations and actions. Historians, for example, have looked more closely at the non-Mormons, reconstructing a much less monolithic view of their attitudes and actions. Some were rabidly anti-Mormon, but many were not. Historical accounts also have reexamined the role of Mormon dissenters and of the Danite organization, created in 1838 to stamp out dissent within the Church. Such findings have prompted historians to reevaluate teachings and developments within Mormonism that contributed to the antagonism of their neighbors. Perhaps most important, historians have tried to understand how the Mormon experience, in Missouri and elsewhere, fits within the broader American religious and social experience. Why did a movement that many now consider the quintessential American religion arouse such fierce opposition? And why would government officials and law-abiding citizens accede to the Saints' expulsion from their homes? There is still disagreement on many of these issues, but the debate has broadened our understanding of the Mormons' attempt to establish a New Jerusalem in western Missouri and of the conflict that ensued.

---

1. *Missouri Republican Daily* (St. Louis), 13 December 1838, quoted in Leland H. Gentry, "The Land Question at Adam-ondi-Ahman," *BYU Studies* 26 (Spring 1986): 52.

Excavating Mormon Pasts

Jackson County: Building the City of God

When Joseph Smith told his people to establish the New Jerusalem along the Indian frontier in the West, he laid claim to one of New England's oldest religious traditions. The Mormons, like the Puritans, viewed themselves as a chosen people, commissioned by God to build the city of Zion in America. Explorations of this topic are Gustav H. Blanke with Karen Lynn, "'God's Base of Operations': Mormon Variation on the American Sense of Mission," *BYU Studies* 20 (Fall 1979): 83-92; and H. Michael Marquardt, "The Independence Temple of Zion," *Restoration: The Journal of Latter Day Saint History* 5 (October 1986): 13. James B. Allen and Glen M. Leonard, *The Story of the Latter-day Saints* (1976; Salt Lake City: Deseret Book, 1992), chap. 1, also set this Puritan ideal as context for nascent Mormonism. Some of the early Puritan leaders, in fact, speculated that the New Jerusalem would be established in the West, beyond the New England territory.[2] This concept was a central theme of early Mormonism, invigorating their efforts to proselytize and gather, build cities and temples, and create a new socioeconomic order. Because of the violent opposition they faced, the Missouri Saints had little opportunity to put into practice Smith's evolving blueprint for building Zion. Nevertheless, Mormons since that time and to the present have looked to the Missouri experience for clues to the Prophet's original social and religious teachings.

One such teaching is the law of consecration and stewardship, a topic that has been explored in Leonard J. Arrington, "Early Mormon Communitarianism: The Law of Consecration and Stewardship," *Western Humanities Review* 7 (Autumn 1953): 341-69; his "Religion and Economics in Mormon History," *BYU Studies* 3 (Spring and Summer 1961): 15-33; Arrington, "Joseph Smith, Builder of Ideal Communities," in *The Prophet Joseph: Essays on the Life and Mission of Joseph Smith,* edited by Larry C. Porter and Susan Easton Black (Salt Lake City: Deseret Book, 1988), chap. 7; Arrington, Feramorz Y. Fox, and Dean L. May, *Building the City of God* (Salt Lake City: Deseret Book, 1976); and Lyndon W. Cook, *Joseph Smith and the Law of Consecration* (Provo, Utah: Grandin Book Company, 1985). Kent W. Huff, "The United Order of Joseph Smith's Times," *Dialogue: A Journal of Mormon Thought* 19 (Summer 1986): 146-49, is an interesting discussion of a related topic.

Embedded in the law are the principles for establishing the cooperative, harmonious religious community—the New Jerusalem—that, according to Smith, would usher in the millennium. He first outlined the law of consecration in a February 9, 1831, revelation directing the Saints to "consecrate" or deed all of their possessions to the Church bishop. The bishop would then give back to each Mormon family an "inheritance" or "stewardship," which was determined by the family's "wants and needs." Members might be granted a stewardship over a farm, store, mill, or workshop; or they might be asked to serve as teachers or in some other community position. The wealthier Saints likely would receive back a stewardship that was considerably less than what they consecrated, while the poor would receive more. The surplus that accumulated each year could be used to invest in community projects—both secular and religious—and to give stewardships to new or younger members. Individual stewards retained the authority to operate their businesses as they believed best, but the principle of consecration ensured a rough equality of wealth in the community. "The law was a prescription for transforming the highly individualistic economic order of Jacksonian America into a system characterized by economic equality, socialization of surplus incomes, freedom of enterprise, and group economic self-sufficiency," wrote Arrington, Fox, and May (15).

---

2. During the Revolutionary War period, ministers from many religions preached an apocalyptic and millennial vision of a New Jerusalem that foreshadowed Mormonism's key themes: the conversion of the Indians, which would lead to the restoration of Eden in the unspoiled regions of the western world; the gathering of Israel; the fullness of the Gentiles; the New World as the scene of Christ's second coming; and America as a land of religious and political destiny. Blanke and Lynn, "'God's Base of Operations,'" 91, observed: "The Mormon church stands today as a preserver of many original aspects of the American sense of mission which have now been transformed or dropped by most other Americans, claiming as their own certain convictions that were once widespread among all Americans. In many respects, the American sense of mission has become the Mormon sense of mission."

A chief benefit of this new practice was that it enabled the Saints to pool their resources to migrate to Zion. Smith identified Jackson County as the New Jerusalem in July 1831, and the Saints who gathered there immediately entered into the new order, working cooperatively to build homes and plant crops with their new inheritances. Consecration, in fact, was compulsory for all Mormons who gathered to Missouri. Observes Cook, those who did not "consecrate all to the Lord" through the bishop would not receive an inheritance, nor would they be recognized as Saints or have their names recorded on any Church records (16). As the new community began to take root, Mormon leaders sent out glowing reports of the economic prospects for Jackson County and the surrounding area, encouraging the faithful to gather swiftly and build up the New Jerusalem.

The law of consecration, however, faced several obstacles. First, a large number of those who migrated to Missouri were poor. Consequently, the Church's resources were stretched to the limit as the bishop tried to give each member an adequate inheritance. "Redistribution of property thus resulted in a leveling down rather than a leveling up of the stewards' living standard . . . ," writes Cook. "Clearly the stewards consumed more than they produced, and new techniques to enhance productivity were either too expensive or totally unavailable on the frontier" (22). Arrington, Fox, and May also concluded that, "From the frequent exhortations in the *Evening and Morning Star* and in the revelations of Joseph Smith, one would also gather that idleness was a problem" (22). In addition, one Mormon changed his mind after deeding his property to the bishop and successfully sued for its return in the spring of 1833, thus undermining the Church's absolute control over consecrated property. Finally, Cook (21) and Arrington, Fox, and May (32) agree that the requirement that the Saints consecrate all their property to the bishop and then reconsecrate their annual surpluses undermined incentive and prompted members to withhold possessions and pursue economic activity outside the system.

But the law of consecration was never truly tested in Jackson County because the Mormon community had grown to only 1,200 to 1,500 when non-Mormon vigilantes drove the Saints from their homes in November 1833. After the Saints fled to neighboring Clay County, Smith suspended the law while the Saints petitioned local and state authorities to restore them to Jackson County. The cooperative economic system was not reestablished until July 8, 1838, when Smith issued the law of consecration and tithing. The new law was similar to the 1831 law of consecration except that it required the Saints to consecrate only their surplus property—not all their property—to the Church. This provision allowed individual Mormons to retain an amount sufficient for their stewardships and for their families' needs. In addition, the Mormons were required to consecrate only one-tenth of their annual surplus to the Church. As was the case in Jackson County, the Saints were warned that those who did not obey the new law "shall not be worthy to abide among you" (LDS D&C 119:5).

The Mormons have traditionally viewed the law of consecration and tithing as inferior to the original law of consecration because it did not require the consecration of all property and surplus income. Arrington, Fox, and May adopted this view, saying, "This 'inferior' law, as it was called, was introduced because 'the people had polluted their inheritances' while in Jackson County" (34). Lyndon Cook disagrees, asserting that the new law of consecration and tithing was just another program to carry out the basic principle of consecration (viii). Cook contends that Mormon leaders devised various economic systems in Ohio, Missouri, and Illinois to implement this principle, which he defines as "the act of setting apart or devoting one's self and his possessions for sacred purposes" (viii). Each of these economic systems in its own time became an official Church program, but none represented the "real" or "true" law of consecration; rather, they were different ways of implementing the principle, which "became a fundamental law of the Church in 1831 and was never rescinded" (viii). Cook cites two less familiar applications of the principle of consecration to demonstrate his point. In March 1838, for example, more than 500 Mormons pooled their resources to create the Kirtland Camp, a large wagon train that journeyed from Ohio to western Missouri. Similarly, in January 1839, nearly 400 Mormons signed an agreement placing their property at the disposal of a Church committee directing the removal of the Saints from Missouri. In both instances, the Saints were consecrating their property to ensure equality and harmony in the Church (73-74, 85-86).

Another important topic of historical inquiry has been Mormon plans for building a temple, even multiple temples, in Zion. Community of Christ Archivist Ronald E. Romig and John H. Siebert, "The Genesis of Zion and Kirtland and the Concept of Temples," *Restoration Studies IV* (Independence: Herald Publishing House, 1988), argue that the dual concept of building the New Jerusalem and a temple had its roots in the Book of Mormon (99). Oliver Cowdery mentioned it as early as October 1830. But they also show that the Prophet's concept was continually evolving and that "each month of each year . . . presented a changing picture of the building process" for both Zion and the temple (286). Smith may have initially envisioned using the temple for the School of the Prophets and other educational purposes. Later descriptions by Church leaders suggest that the temple would be primarily a place of endowment for preparing men for the ministry. Romig and Siebert also document that there is little indication how much land was originally consecrated for the temple site. In June 1833, Smith and his counselors completed a draft of Zion that had twenty-four temples sitting in the center of a city that was a little more than a mile square. The temples would be located on two fifteen-acre blocks situated beside another fifteen-acre section set aside for storehouses. Farmers would have their homes in Zion but their farms surrounding the city. In this way, all Mormons would share in the city's religious and cultural benefits. But as Romig and Siebert point out, the Church did not own all of the property outlined in the plan, which had Zion spilling into Independence. They suggest that this ambitious plan may have contributed to local opposition against the Saints; trouble erupted about the time the plan for Zion was delivered to Church leaders in Jackson County (295-98).

Additional investigations of this topic are Ronald E. Romig, "Temple Lot Discoveries and the RLDS Temple," in *Regional Studies in Latter-day Saint Church History: Missouri,* edited by Arnold K. Garr and Clark V. Johnson (Provo, UT: Department of Church History and Doctrine, Brigham Young University, 1994), 313-35; and Romig and Siebert, "Jackson County, 1831-1833: A Look at the Development of Zion," *Restoration Studies III* (Independence: Herald Printing House, 1986), 286-304; their "Historic Views of the Temple Lot," *John Whitmer Historical Association Journal* 7 (1987): 21-27; and "First Impressions: The Independence, Missouri, Printing Operation, 1832-33," *John Whitmer Historical Association Journal* 10 (1990): 51-66.

Only two months later in August 1833, this plan again changed. The two temple blocks were reduced from fifteen to ten acres each, and the fifteen acres reserved for storehouses were removed altogether. This change may have been designed to increase the number of lots available for Mormon families, thus allowing for a population of about 13,000, instead of 4,800. "In light of the changing nature of the early Church's plan for the development of Zion," Romig and Siebert conclude, "no one view, or snapshot, of the correct or precise physical and scriptural method of developing Zion is comprehensive. It was a time of rapid change and much revision" ("Genesis," 302).

A Richer View of Non-Mormons

One of the most important contributions of recent Mormon histories is that they have focused attention on non-Mormons, helping us view the conflict from a different perspective. Some non-Mormons welcomed the Mormons into their communities and assisted them by providing credit at local stores and lending them horses to cultivate their land, as documented in my *The 1838 Mormon War in Missouri* (Columbia: University of Missouri Press, 1987), 24-27. During the 1838 crisis in northern Missouri, many Missourians initially refused to support the vigilantes because representatives sent to investigate the disturbances reported that the Mormons were not causing trouble. In Jackson County, local authorities were largely aligned with the vigilantes against the Saints; but in northern Missouri, some officials made genuine efforts to quell the anti-Mormon violence. In the

The 1838 Mormon War in Missouri

Stephen C. LeSueur

University of Missouri Press
Columbia, 1987

end, however, deeply felt animosities and prejudice overwhelmed the Missourians' meager law-enforcement resources and skills.

Among the non-Mormons in Missouri who played a particularly significant role was Governor Lilburn W. Boggs, a figure examined in Warren A. Jennings, "Zion Is Fled: The Expulsion of the Mormons from Jackson County, Missouri" (Ph.D. diss., University of Florida, 1962); Leland H. Gentry, "A History of the Latter-day Saints in Northern Missouri from 1836 to 1839" (Ph.D. diss., Brigham Young University, 1965);[3] Richard L. Anderson, "Clarifications of Boggs's 'Order' and Joseph Smith's Constitutionalism," in *Regional Studies in . . . Missouri*, 27-70; Alexander L. Baugh, "A Call to Arms: The 1838 Mormon Defense of Northern Missouri" (Ph.D. diss., Brigham Young University, 1996, also published in the JFS Institute/BYU Studies series). While the Mormons were in Nauvoo, tensions and attempts to extradite Joseph Smith persisted, recounted as a theme in Glen M. Leonard, *Nauvoo: A Place of Peace, a People of Promise* (Salt Lake City: Deseret Book/Provo, UT: BYU Press, 2002). Monte B. McLaws, "The Attempted Assassination of Missouri's Ex-Governor Lilburn W. Boggs," *Missouri Historical Review* 60 (October 1965): 50-62, discusses how Joseph Smith was blamed for ordering the attempt and Porter Rockwell was charged with the crime.

As a resident of Jackson County in 1833, Boggs, who was then lieutenant governor, supported efforts to oust Mormons from the county. In 1838 as the state's governor, he issued the infamous "extermination order" declaring that the "Mormons must be treated as enemies, and must be exterminated or driven from the state if necessary for the public peace." Early Mormon histories typically painted Boggs as a rabid anti-Mormon who, after plotting with western Missourians to expel the Saints, seized the first opportunity to call out state troops against them. Historian Richard L. Anderson, "Clarifications of Boggs's 'Order,'" largely agrees with this view, arguing that Boggs was a "tool" of anti-Mormon settlers and a "power center for the expulsionists" (27, 32). Anderson gives credence to Hyrum Smith's claim, reportedly told to him by his Missouri jailer and a local judge in Liberty in the winter of 1838-39, that "the whole plan [to expel the Saints] was concocted by the governor down to the lowest judge in the upper country early in the previous spring" (61). There is no question that Boggs strongly disliked the Mormons and that this attitude colored his interpretation of reports describing the developing disturbances. He appeared inclined to let local authorities handle the difficulties when Mormons were under attack but to act when non-Mormons were on the defensive. Still, the governor's actions likely resulted as much from weakness and poor judgment as from invidious intent. The anti-Mormons in western Missouri were his political allies as well as personal friends; supporting the Mormons would have alienated many of his most loyal supporters. In addition, state and local officials were ill equipped to handle the large-scale disturbances in the western counties. Some militia units rebelled when asked to quell the anti-Mormon vigilantes. The crisis demanded greatness from the governor, a willingness to stand up to the anti-Mormon vigilantes, and the political ability to extract compromises from both sides. Even then, a peaceful resolution satisfying all parties might have defied the most courageous and skillful of politicians. It eluded Boggs altogether.

While Boggs failed the test of statesmanship, two Missourians, Alexander W. Doniphan and David R. Atchison, did not. Roger D. Launius, *Alexander William Doniphan: Portrait of a Missouri Moderate* (Columbia: University of Missouri Press, 1997, examines extensively Doniphan's interaction with the Mormons in the book's early chapters. Gregory Maynard, "Alexander William Doniphan: Man of Justice," *BYU Studies* 13 (Summer 1973): 462-472, also examines Doniphan's relationship with the Mormons, while Richard L. Anderson, "Atchison's Letter and the Causes of Mormon Expulsion from Missouri," *BYU Studies* 26 (Summer 1986): 3-47, treats Atchison's relationship with the Saints. In addition,

---

3. This work has been reprinted (Provo, Utah: Joseph Fielding Smith Institute for Latter-day Saint History and BYU Studies, 2000), while a revised edition is forthcoming: Leland Homer Gentry and Todd Compton, *Fire and Sword: A History of the Latter-day Saints in Northern Missouri From 1836 to 1839* (working title) (Salt Lake City: Greg Kofford Books, 2004).

A Call to Arms: The 1838 Mormon Defense of Northern Missouri

A Dissertation Presented to the
Department of History
Brigham Young University

In Partial Fulfillment
of the Requirements for the Degree
Doctor of Philosophy

by
Alexander L. Baugh

Alexander William Doniphan

Portrait of a Missouri Moderate

ROGER D. LAUNIUS

UNIVERSITY OF MISSOURI PRESS
Columbia and London

Missouri Folk Heroes of the Nineteenth Century, edited by F. Mark McKiernan and Roger D. Launius (Independence: Herald Publishing House, 1989), contains short biographies of Atchison, Doniphan, and Sterling Price, a prominent politician and soldier who crossed paths with the Mormons.

After the Saints were expelled from Jackson County, Doniphan and Atchison joined a team of lawyers in 1833 that attempted to secure the Saints' return to their homes. In June 1834, when mobs threatened to expel the Mormons by violence from Clay County, where both men resided, they spoke out on behalf of the Saints. Doniphan, a state legislator, subsequently helped to push through legislation creating Caldwell County for the Mormons. As generals in the state militia, Atchison and Doniphan tried to halt the escalating violence during the 1838 conflict. Both again expressed sympathy for the Saints' plight. Following the Mormons' surrender at Far West in November 1838, Doniphan refused an order to execute Joseph Smith and other Mormon leaders, threatening to hold his superior officer responsible if the Mormons were harmed. After the war, Doniphan served as a defense lawyer for Mormons accused of crimes, while Atchison took up the Mormons' cause in the state legislature, where he denounced the governor's order expelling the Saints from the state.

Although there is no doubt that Doniphan and Atchison befriended the Mormons in significant ways, closer studies have documented that their relationships with the Mormons were not always amicable.[4] For example, when Doniphan and Atchison signed on to take the Mormons' case in Jackson County, Mormon leaders complained that the lawyers were extorting a high price because they knew the Saints had nowhere else to turn for legal advice. Similarly, Michael S. Riggs, "The Economic Impact of Fort Leavenworth on Northwestern Missouri 1827-1838. Yet Another Reason for the Mormon War?" *Restoration Studies IV* (Independence: Herald House, 1988), argued that Doniphan and Atchison helped establish "the dross prairie country" of Caldwell County for the Saints, perhaps partially to prevent the Mormons from settling on "the choice bottomlands" in Missouri's Platte region, an attractive tract of Indian territory just west of Clay County that Clay's non-Mormons wanted for themselves (129). In September 1838, when Doniphan and Atchison, acting as generals of their militia units, dispersed vigilantes in Daviess County, Mormon leaders protested because they did not arrest and punish the non-Mormons. At the same time, some non-Mormons complained that the generals, perhaps courting the Mormon vote in future elections, were not taking sufficiently strong action against the Mormon soldiers. When full-scale war broke out in the upper counties in October 1838, Doniphan and Atchison condemned both sides, blaming the non-Mormon mobs for starting the conflict but asserting that the Mormons, whom they called "a community of fanatics," had been "goaded into a state of desperation" that made them the aggressors (Launius, 57-58).

Despite their efforts on behalf of the Mormons after the war, Mormon leaders continued to criticize both men. They accused Doniphan of deceiving his clients, asserting that the Mormon prisoners could have been released earlier had it not been for their attorneys' bad advice and cowardice. "They have done us much harm from the beginning," accused Smith. "They are co-workers with the mob."[5] Although the Mormons later changed their minds about Atchison and Doniphan, at the time these men were caught in the middle of two opposing sides, satisfying neither the Mormons nor the non-Mormons with their efforts to resolve peacefully the conflict. Launius concedes that Doniphan profited handsomely from his service to the Mormons, both monetarily and from the notoriety he gained taking on the high-profile Mormon cases (23, 71). He further concludes that, while Doniphan sought justice for the persecuted Saints, "he came to loathe their anti-democratic tendencies" (14).

---

4. See Launius, *Doniphan,* 14, 69. LeSueur, *The 1838 Mormon War in Missouri,* 97, 130, 245, 257.

5. Joseph Smith et al., "The Prophet's Epistle to the Church," March 25, 1839, in Joseph Smith Jr., *History of the Church of Jesus Christ of Latter-day Saints,* edited by B. H. Robert (6 vols. published 1902-12, Vol. 7 published 1932; reprint ed., Salt Lake City: Deseret Book, 1978 printing), 3:292.

Excavating Mormon Pasts

A less well-known Missourian who also has received attention in recent years is Isaac McCoy, a Baptist missionary whom the Mormons accused of spearheading anti-Mormon persecution in Jackson County. Historian Warren A. Jennings, "Isaac McCoy and the Mormons," *Missouri Historical Review* 61 (October 1966): 62-82, documents that, before the Mormons' arrival in Jackson County, McCoy had been a driving force behind the 1830 Indian Removal Bill, which provided for the transfer of all Indians living east of the Mississippi River to lands west of Missouri. McCoy, who spent many years among various Indian tribes, was subsequently appointed an agent to select sites for Indian resettlement and to assist in their removal. He hoped to segregate all Indians from what he considered to be the pernicious influence of the whites, after which the Indians could be educated and converted to Christianity. He envisioned the formation of a federation of Indian tribes that eventually would be amalgamated into a separate Indian state.

McCoy shared the prevailing prejudices against the Mormons and opposed their interaction with the Indians, asserting that Mormon leaders were "ignorant of the laws regulating intercourse with the Indian tribes" (73). McCoy was apparently correct in his assessment of the Mormons' knowledge of the laws pertaining to the Indian tribes, since Ronald E. Romig, "The Lamanite Mission," *John Whitmer Historical Association Journal* 14 (1994), concluded that these first Mormon missionaries to the Indians "had obviously either been unaware of or had chosen to ignore the federal laws regulating commerce and communication with the Indians" (29). Romig also puts forward the interesting thesis that, had the initial Mormon mission to the Lamanites been successful, Zion might have been located in present-day Kansas, rather than in Missouri (32-33). McCoy's attitudes were guaranteed to bring him into conflict with the Jackson County Saints, who, because of Joseph Smith's revelations and the Book of Mormon, saw the hand of the Lord in the gathering of Indians just across the Missouri border. They believed the Indians would join the Church in droves if allowed to hear the restored gospel.

When trouble in Jackson County erupted in late 1833, several Mormons said McCoy led a company of about seventy men that marched through the Mormon settlements, threatening and disarming the Saints prior to their expulsion from the county a few days later. But Jennings says the Mormons may have misunderstood McCoy's role in these events. McCoy's diary records that, while journeying to Independence in early November 1833, he met two companies of men planning to disarm Mormon settlers. Upon learning that some of the men "were determined to kill," McCoy said he went along to "regulate the conduct of the rash." At several houses, McCoy said he intervened to prevent the Missourians from shooting and beating Mormons, eventually persuading the men to let him act as spokesman. "I prevailed upon the company to stop a little from houses, and allow me with one or two only to approach and ask for their guns, &c.," he wrote. "Had it not been for this measure, the alarm and injury to the Mormons would have been much beaten [sic] and the injury considerable" (Jennings, 71).

McCoy's role in the conflict, from his own perspective, was that of a peacemaker who risked his life to prevent Mormons from being harmed. According to Jennings, McCoy "personally found the Mormons repugnant but disliked violence. However, like moderates before and after him, when extremists have forced an issue and the middle ground has dissolved, he had to pick a side" (81). And, like nearly all Missourians, when compelled to choose, McCoy sided against the Saints and endorsed their expulsion from the community.

The Role of Mormon Dissenters

Just as historians have looked more closely at the Missourians' actions and motivations, so too have they reexamined the role of Mormon dissenters during the 1838 conflict. Early Mormons viewed dissension as a chief cause of their troubles. They believed, for example, that God had allowed them to be driven from Jackson County because the Saints there lacked sufficient unity and commitment. Similarly, Joseph Smith told them that the 1834 expedition known as Zion's Camp (discussed below) had failed to restore the exiled Saints to Jackson County because of dissension and iniquity. Furthermore, dissenters played the chief role in driving Joseph Smith from Church headquarters in Kirtland, Ohio, to Missouri. Consequently, after Joseph Smith arrived in Far West in early 1838, he and other Mormon leaders vowed that dissension would not undermine their kingdom building efforts in northern Missouri.

In June 1838, a number of Mormons organized themselves into a vigilante group, called the Danites, to weed out dissent within Mormonism. Shortly afterward, the Danites forcibly expelled from Far West several prominent Mormon dissenters, including David Whitmer, John Whitmer, Oliver Cowdery, and their families. Dissent, however, continued to grow. During the summer and fall, other dissenters left Mormon communities in northern Missouri, warning their non-Mormon neighbors that a growing militant spirit among the Mormons threatened the western counties. After the surrender of Far West, even more dissenters turned up at the Richmond preliminary hearing, testifying that Mormon soldiers had committed numerous crimes, including the sacking and burning of Gallatin and Millport in Daviess County. All three major sources on Mormonism in Missouri—Baugh, *A Call to Arms;* Gentry, *A History of the Latter-day Saints in Northern Missouri;* and LeSueur, *The 1838 Mormon War*—describe the interplay between Danites and dissenters, and the dissenters' testimony at the Richmond preliminary hearing following the conflict.

At the time, Mormon leaders condemned the dissenters' testimonies and statements as exaggerations and outright lies, motivated largely by the dissenters' hatred of Mormonism and fear of the mob. This interpretation of the dissenters' motives and actions is presented consistently in the letters, affidavits, documents, and historical narrative compiled in Joseph Smith's *History of the Church,* which in turn formed the basis for Mormon histories that followed well into the twentieth century. Histories such as B. H. Roberts, *A Comprehensive History of the Church of Jesus Christ of Latter-day Saints,* 6 vols. (Salt Lake City: Deseret News Press, 1930); Joseph Fielding Smith, *Essentials in Church History* (Salt Lake City: Deseret News Press, 1940); Ivan J. Barrett, *Joseph Smith and the Restoration: A History of the Church to 1846* (1968; 2d ed., Provo, UT: Brigham Young University Press, 1973); and William E. Berrett, *The Restored Church* (1937, rev. and enl. ed., Salt Lake City: Deseret Book, 1973), were widely used in Mormon Sunday schools, seminary classes and college courses and rarely strayed from this interpretation of dissenters and their controversial testimony about the Danites and Mormon military operations. Inez Smith Davis, *The Story of the Church* (Independence: Herald Publishing House, 1989) presented a similar view for the Reorganized Church of Jesus Christ of Latter Day Saints (now the Community of Christ). In recent years, however, historians have questioned this traditional view. Historians have studied the dissenters more objectively, reading the dissenters' testimonies and accounts with skepticism but also with empathy and a desire to understand.

This new approach has revealed that men such as John Corrill had an important story to tell in his *A Brief History of the Church of Christ of Latter Day Saints* (St. Louis: Author, 1839). Kenneth H. Winn, "'Such Republicanism as This': John Corrill's Rejection of Prophetic Rule," in *Differing Visions: Dissenters in Mormon History,* edited by Roger Launius and Linda Thatcher (Urbana: University of Illinois Press, 1994), 45-75, presents Corrill as a forthright, sincere seeker after truth, a cautious, deliberate man who investigated Mormonism thoroughly before deciding to join. A champion of freedom of speech and inquiry, Corrill admired Mormonism because of what he viewed as its intellectual, rational approach to the Bible and religion. As one of the key Mormon leaders in Missouri, he demonstrated great courage and diplomatic skills in dealing with the hostile non-Mormon community. In Jackson County, Corrill and several other Mormon men offered their lives to the mob in exchange for the safety of other Church members; in Clay County, he helped negotiate with Missourians the creation of Caldwell County exclusively for the Mormons; and in Caldwell, the Mormons elected him their representative to the state legislature. Corrill's falling out began when the Mormons formed the Danites and expelled dissenters from Far West. He perceived this action as contrary to the spirit of republicanism and Christian teachings. After attending two of the initial Danite meetings in which action was planned against Mormons who were out of favor, he secretly warned the Whitmers and other dissenters to flee. He was also alarmed by the Mormons' military operations, especially by their attacks on non-Mormon towns and cabins in Daviess County. Corrill opposed the reintroduction of the law of consecration in Far West; but after he publicly expressed this view, Joseph Smith rebuked him for "unbecoming" conduct. Following the Mormon War, Corrill was one of several dissenters who testified against the Mormons at the Richmond hearing.

Traditional Mormon histories typically painted Corrill as an apostate who betrayed the prophet into the hands of the mob and then testified to falsehoods about the Danites and Mormon military operations.[6] But these histories fail to explain why Corrill, after years of loyalty, would suddenly turn against the Church. The picture Winn draws, however, helps us to see that Corrill dissented because of Mormonism's growing authoritarianism and militancy. Corrill contends that he warned Joseph Smith and other Mormon leaders that their activities would bring the entire state down upon them (*Brief History*, 36). Ironically, after Corrill's prediction came true, Mormon leaders angrily denounced Corrill and other dissenters, blaming them for instigating much of the trouble in northern Missouri. "We have waded through an ocean of tribulation and mean abuse, practiced upon us by the ill bred and the ignorant, such as Hinkle, Corrill, Phelps, Avard, Peck, Cleminson, and various others, who are so very ignorant that they cannot appear respectable in any decent and civilized society, and whose eyes are full of adultery and cannot cease from sin," Joseph Smith wrote in a December 16, 1838, letter to the Church (*History of the Church*, 3:232).

Corrill and other dissenters were further discredited in Mormon histories by being lumped together with Sampson Avard, the Danite leader who testified against the Mormons after the war. This association, however, is misleading. A primary reason these men dissented was because they objected to Avard's extensive influence within Mormonism. Corrill, for example, said Avard was "as grand a villain as his wit and ability would admit of."[7] But because Mormon leaders did not share this view, Avard remained influential until the end of the Mormon War. It was not until Avard turned state's evidence against his former brethren that Mormon leaders denounced both the man and his teachings.

One of the most persistent myths about dissenters is that they benefited financially from their alleged perfidy. George Hinkle, for example, reportedly accepted a large bribe to betray Church leaders into the hands of the mob. While it is true that the Missourians allowed many of the disaffected Saints to remain, many others left in the Mormon exodus. Corrill, who remained, sold all of his property and distributed the proceeds, about $2,100, to nearly 160 needy Mormon families.[8] Other dissenters also deeded their land for the use of the poor. The once wealthy Hinkle left the state a destitute man, according to his son: "I am told [he] had to walk out and carry some of the smaller children in his arms, with the Gentiles persecuting him and the Saints shunning him as they had been warned."[9]

The Danites

This reinterpretation of the dissenters' role has also been accompanied by a reexamination of the Danite organization. The traditional Mormon view held that a renegade Mormon, Sampson Avard, organized the Danites near the end of the Mormon War without the knowledge or approval of Joseph Smith.[10] Traditional historians said that, while it

---

6. See, for example, Roberts, *Comprehensive History*, 1:500; and Barrett, *Joseph Smith*, 334.
7. Quoted in LeSueur, *The 1838 Mormon War in Missouri*, 41.
8. Winn, "'Such Republicanism as This,'" 67.
9. Quoted in LeSueur, *The 1838 Mormon War in Missouri*, 223.
10. The foundation for this view can be found in Joseph Smith, *History of the Church*, 3:178-82, which was generally adopted in subsequent Mormon histories. See, for example, Roberts, *Comprehensive History of the*

was true Avard encouraged the Danite recruits to commit crimes in the name of the Lord, the Mormon men rebelled immediately at Avard's outrageous teachings and brought Avard's activities to Joseph Smith's attention with Avard's excommunication following promptly. This action would have eliminated the Danites except that, after the war, Avard turned state's evidence and testified that Smith and the First Presidency had been the driving force behind the Danites. In addition, Avard said the Danites, who wielded great influence among the Mormons, were bound together by secret signs and oaths of allegiance to their prophet, making them part of a treasonous plot by Mormon leaders to establish a theocratic government in western Missouri. The presiding judge at the hearing deemed Avard's testimony, which was backed by Corrill and other dissenters, as sufficient evidence to jail Mormon leaders pending a formal trial. Mormon historians, relying on denials by Smith and other Church leaders, labeled this testimony as false.

This traditional view of the Danites, however, has undergone significant revision. Leland H. Gentry, "The Danite Band of 1838," *BYU Studies* 14 (Summer 1974): 421-50, documents a three-stage evolution in the Danite organization. The first stage began in June 1838, not near the end of the Mormon War, when the Danites organized to rid the Mormon community of dissenters. The Danites, he said, played a prominent role in driving the Whitmers and other dissenters from Far West after Sidney Rigdon's Salt Sermon of June 17. Following the flight of the dissenters, Gentry says the Danites moved to a second stage of seeking to protect Mormon families from mob violence. Although Avard organized the Danites and directed their activities, Gentry said that Smith and the first presidency knew of these initial Danite activities and even attended at least one meeting. But Smith, who did not understand the full extent of Avard's teachings, "may have felt that the society had a legitimate basis for existence in that it was organized for protective purposes" (444).

In time, however, the Danites evolved into a third purpose, which was "to retaliate against those who committed depredations against defenseless Saints" (428). William G. Hartley, *"My Best for the Kingdom": History and Autobiography of John Lowe Butler, A Mormon Frontiersman* (Salt Lake City: Aspen Books, 1993), concurs that the Danites evolved through three stages, but he said that Danite activities in the second and third stages are understandable "only if it is recognized that Latter-day Saints by mid-1838 had adopted a wartime mentality. They felt they were being pushed into war and, fearing attack, they determined to defend themselves" (49). According to Gentry, Avard assembled his Danite soldiers and told them that the conflict presented them with the opportunity to prove their faithfulness and courage, told them to obey only their Church leaders rather than civil authorities, and that it was permissible to lie, steal, and even murder, if necessary, to establish the Kingdom of God in the latter days (428-32). Gentry says that Smith did not approve or have knowledge of the teachings presented in this third stage of Danite development. At this point, his interpretation corresponds with the traditional Mormon view, since he said that the Danite men rebelled against Avard's more radical teachings and that Joseph Smith did not learn of it until the preliminary hearing at Richmond in November 1838 where Avard blamed Smith for the group's treasonous teachings and activities. Writing from Liberty Jail, Smith condemned Avard's "false and pernicious" teachings "which the Presidency never knew were being taught in the Church by anybody until after they were made prisoners" (444).

More recent historians have concluded that Gentry, while moving in the right direction, underestimated the extent of the Danites' influence among the Mormons and the extent of Smith's involvement with the group. These studies include my *The 1838 Mormon War in Missouri*, 43-47; John E. Thompson, "A Chronology of Danite Meetings in Adam-ondi-Ahman, Missouri, July to September 1838," *Restoration* 4 (January 1985): 11-14; Hartley, *"My Best for the Kingdom,"* 41-80; D. Michael Quinn, *The Mormon Hierarchy: Origins of Power* (Salt Lake City: Signature Books, 1994), 92-103; Baugh, *A Call to Arms*, 33-46; and

---

Church, 504-5; Joseph Fielding Smith, *Essentials in Church History*, 227 note d; and Barrett, *Joseph Smith and the Restoration*, 314-15.

MY BEST FOR THE KINGDOM

HISTORY AND AUTOBIOGRAPHY OF

JOHN LOWE BUTLER

A MORMON FRONTIERSMAN

WILLIAM G. HARTLEY

ASPEN BOOKS
Salt Lake City, Utah

Quinn, "National Culture, Personality, and Theocracy in the Early Mormon Culture of Violence," *John Whitmer Historical Association 2002 Nauvoo Conference Special Edition* (Kansas City, MO: John Whitmer Historical Association, 2002), 172-78.

This newer interpretation defines the Danites as a secret organization, but in the same way that the Mormon temple ceremony is secret. Everyone knows it exists, but only its practitioners—those deemed worthy to participate—know its precise teachings and secret oaths and signs. To support this thesis, these historians point to the accounts of loyal Mormons who report that the Danites were leading and honored participants at many key events during this period. For example, the Danites helped drive Mormon dissenters from Far West in June 1838; Danite soldiers marched in the Mormons' Fourth of July parade; the Danite generals, including Avard, were given a place of honor with Joseph Smith on the parade reviewing stand; the Danites met regularly at Adam-ondi-Ahman; Daviess County Danites were the primary Mormon combatants at the August 6 election battle in Gallatin; Joseph Smith led a company of Danites to Adam-ondi-Ahman to protect Mormon families after the Gallatin battle; and the Danites played a prominent role in implementing the law of consecration among the Saints. All of these activities were well known to Smith and his followers. In fact, many of the Church's staunchest men in Far West and Adam-ondi-Ahman belonged to the group, including Elias Higbee, George W. Robinson, Reynolds Cahoon, Anson B. Call, Allen J. Stout, Hosea Stout, Moses Clawson, John L. Butler, and Luman Shurtliff.[11] Contemporary evidence simply does not support the assertion that the Danites operated in secrecy. Besides, there was no reason for them to do so. Joseph Smith and the Mormons looked with favor upon the Danites, who sought to obey the Prophet and implement his policies, and encouraged other Mormons to do the same.

But what about Danite teachings? Did Joseph Smith advocate that the Danites disobey the law, if directed to do so by their leaders, and to steal from the Missourians if necessary? Here the evidence from loyal Mormon sources is more circumstantial. Nevertheless, it still indicates that Smith approved many of the Danites' more questionable teachings for which Avard received the blame. For example, the Danites, with Smith's knowledge and with no recorded expression of disapproval, used threats of violence to unlawfully expel dissenters from their homes in Far West in June 1838. Richard Anderson, "Clarifications of Boggs's 'Order,'" defends the expulsion of dissenters on the grounds that Joseph Smith and the Mormons were exercising "prior restraint of defamation in times of danger." The dissenters were planning to publish a rival newspaper that would be, Anderson said, "an invitation to persecution if twisted images of the presidency were continually thrown to non-Mormon enemies seeking expulsion pretexts" (63). Mormon leaders, including Smith, also announced on several occasions that they would not allow their enemies to initiate "vexatious lawsuits" against them, another example of placing the preservation of the Church above civil law. Similarly, in October 1838, Smith instructed Mormon soldiers to live off the land during the conflict—that is, to steal the livestock, crops, and property of their enemies. The Mormons subsequently burned two non-Mormon towns in Daviess County, Gallatin and Millport, taking as the "spoils of war" wagonloads of plunder, which they deposited in the bishop's storehouse at Adam-ondi-Ahman. Smith also declared that Mormon men who refused to fight the Missourians would have their property confiscated and turned over to those who did. Given the past persecution suffered by the Saints, Smith's pronouncements are quite understandable; but there is no compelling reason to conclude that Avard's teachings, if they really were his own, differed significantly from Smith's. Like Avard, the Mormon prophet advocated militant and occasionally illegal methods to rid the Church of dissenters and to defend his people against persecution. D. Michael Quinn, *Origins of Power*, concluded that Joseph Smith essentially proclaimed that his priesthood authority was superior to secular authority and that

---

11. LeSueur, *The 1838 Mormon War*, 46. The evidence identifying these men as Danites comes from loyal Mormon sources. Quinn, *Origins of Power*, Appendix 3, "Danites in 1838: A Partial List," 479-90, has an extensive list of Danites.

gentile law had no power over actions authorized by the priesthood. As early as November 1835 in Kirtland, Ohio, Smith espoused a doctrine of "theocratic ethics" which, according to Quinn, "justified LDS leaders and (by extension) regular Mormons in actions which were contrary to conventional ethics and sometimes in violation of criminal laws" (88). Quinn also pointed out that in 1836, Joseph Smith and his counselors signed a petition along with dozens of other Mormons warning a non-Mormon justice of the peace to "depart forthwith out of Kirtland" (91). In 1837, Smith hinted that killing anti-Mormon Grandison Newell would be justified in God's sight, according to the testimony of Apostles Orson Hyde and Luke S. Johnson. These incidents, Quinn argued, presaged Danite teachings and activities of a similar nature.

It is impossible to identify the precise level of Smith's involvement with the Danites—such as how many meetings he attended or how actively he directed their activities. Baugh, for example, says Danite activities during June, July and August of 1838 "received at least tacit support and approval from the First Presidency," but Joseph Smith "may not have necessarily known of their private teachings and the conduct of their leaders until sometime later" (42). While I agree that Smith may not have known everything that Avard taught, I contend that the evidence overwhelmingly suggests that he knew and approved of a large portion of their teachings and activities, including the secret signs and oaths to support Church leaders, which were well-known throughout Missouri long before the Mormons surrendered (LeSueur, *The 1838 Mormon War,* 43-47). Michael Quinn, in fact, argues that Smith himself was a Danite, most likely initiated into this secret, oath-bound society by future apostle Lyman Wight (96-97, 337 note 77).

Although Smith supported the Danites throughout 1838, it is easy to see why he later sought to disassociate himself from the group. Following the Mormon War, the Missourians believed the Danites were primarily responsible for the burning and plundering in Daviess County. In addition, the Missourians believed the group represented a treasonous effort by the Mormons to overthrow the civil government in western Missouri. Some loyal Mormons, not just dissenters, had also grown weary of what they considered Danite excesses. Consequently, when the Mormon prophet was charged with Danite crimes at the Richmond hearing after the war, he denied any knowledge of or connection with the group's illegal activities. He could not defend the Danites without implicating himself further in the charges already leveled against him, a scenario I reconstructed in my "'High Treason and Murder': The Examination of Mormon Prisoners at Richmond, Missouri, in November 1838," *BYU Studies* 26 (Spring 1986): 3-30.

Dean C. Jessee and David J. Whittaker, "The Last Months of Mormonism in Missouri: The Albert Perry Rockwood Journal," *BYU Studies* 28 (Winter 1988): 5-41, took a different view of the Danites. They concurred with the assertion that the Mormons, including Smith, knew the Danites well, but they contended that the group's nature and purpose has been misunderstood. Quoting the journal of Albert P. Rockwood, a Mormon who arrived in Far West in September 1838, they describe the Danites as a community service group involved in all aspects of Mormon kingdom building. Their military activities thus represented only one part of their overall function within the community. "Some groups of Danites were to build houses; others were to gather food or care for the sick, while still others were to help gather the scattered Saints into the community," asserted Jessee and Whittaker. "There can be no doubt that Rockwood is describing the total activities of a covenant community that viewed itself in the same terms as ancient Israel. Working in groups, these Danites served the interests of the whole" (13).

Jessee and Whittaker further argued that Avard, because of his Richmond testimony, was responsible for the "dark" view of the Danites that still persists. Avard, realizing that the Missourians wanted evidence to convict Mormon leaders, gave them what they needed by concocting the false story of treasonous Danite oaths and activities. Corrill and other dissenters, seeking to discredit Smith and the Church, were merely building on Avard's testimony—in other words, lying—when they presented corroborating evidence at the hearing. Jessee and Whittaker acknowledged that some Danites may have burned and plundered as Avard described but that they were only the "more radical fringe" that such activities represented an "aberration" from the group's true principles.

Historiographically, Jessee and Whittaker thus returned full circle to the traditional Mormon interpretation: Joseph Smith had no knowledge of, nor did he approve of, the Danite teachings that Avard described at the Richmond hearing. The chief difference is that the Mormons originally claimed the Danites existed only briefly. In contrast, Jessee and Whittaker contend that a "good" Danite organization existed for several months, while the "bad" Danite organization, if it existed at all, was a mere fringe group. Jessee and Whittaker also restored the traditional Mormon interpretation that lumped John Corrill and other dissenters in with Sampson Avard. In reality, as already discussed, Corrill and the others had dissented because they opposed Avard and his influence in the Mormon leadership.

The Jessee and Whittaker thesis, however, does not hold up. I found their argument unconvincing and challenged it in "The Danites Reconsidered: Were They Vigilantes or Just the Mormon Version of the Elks Club?" *John Whitmer Historical Association Journal* 14 (1994): 35-51. Marvin Hill, *Quest for Refuge: The Mormon Flight from American Pluralism* (Salt Lake City: Signature Books, 1989), 225 note 65; and Quinn *Origins of Power*, 336 note 68, 339 note 83, also remained unpersuaded. The Jessee and Whittaker argument relied almost exclusively on Rockwood's journal, but they took his account out of context. The Danites were organized in June 1838, but Rockwood's key journal passage was written October 22, during the height of the Mormon War, and quoted in a letter to his parents on October 29. Even though Jessee and Whittaker discuss the different versions of the journal/letter (15-17), they apparently failed to realize that Rockwood was actually describing a Danite meeting held October 20 in Far West under the leadership of Sidney Rigdon and Sampson Avard (LeSueur, "The Danites Reconsidered," 44). Expecting the armed conflict to continue, Rigdon and Avard organized the Danites into companies to gather crops and supplies, tend the sick, carry express messages for Mormon military leaders, and spy on their Missouri enemies. These Danite responsibilities were tied directly to the war effort, not to general kingdom building.

Jessee and Whittaker also incorrectly assert that Avard was the first person to promulgate the dark view of the Danites. As early as September 1838, Missouri newspapers began publishing statements by Mormon dissenters warning of the growing influence of the Danite organization among the Mormons. As tensions reached a crescendo in late October, the Missourians were inundated with dissenters' reports, including an affidavit signed by Apostles Thomas B. Marsh and Orson Hyde on October 24 asserting that the Danites "have taken an oath to support the heads of the church in all things that they say or do, whether right or wrong."[12] When Avard testified at the Richmond hearing, his general description of the Danite organization differed little from what already had been widely reported. By dismissing the negative view of the Danites as primarily the creation of Sampson Avard, Jessee and Whittaker ignored a wide body of evidence that the Danites engaged in militant and even illegal activities. Similarly, the Mormon soldiers who plundered and burned the homes of Missourians were not extremists, hotheads or a fringe element within Mormonism but were among the Church's most loyal men, including Apostle David W. Patten, future apostle Lyman Wight, and other stalwarts such as Dimick Huntington and Benjamin F. Johnson. Michael Quinn concluded that the Jessee-Whittaker argument for discounting the dissenters' testimony "strains credulity." The evidence from the journals and reminiscences of loyal Mormons, Quinn said, "should persuade LDS historians to accept the basic accuracy and honesty of Danites who became dissenters" (*Origins of Power*, 339 note 83).

Marvin Hill also rejected the Jessee-Whittaker thesis in his *Quest for Refuge*: "Most of the negative view of the Danites comes not from Avard but from Joseph Smith, Orson Hyde, Thomas B. Marsh, [George W.] Robinson, and Rockwood, to name the most reliable. Nor can John Corrill be ignored" (225 note 65). Hill contended that Jessee and Whittaker overlooked Joseph Smith's explicit warnings that, if persecution continued, the Mormons

---

12. Quoted in LeSueur, "The Danites Reconsidered," 12.

would retaliate. "He acted on this, exactly as he and Rigdon said they would. The Saints were on the defensive at DeWitt, but after this they went on the offensive and raided Missouri towns. If the Danites were but a small, divergent group Joseph Smith would have stamped them out before March 1839" (225 note 65).

Quinn added another dimension with his assertion that, although the Danites disbanded after the Saints' expulsion from Missouri, the organization's influence persisted for decades. Some of Joseph Smith's most trusted bodyguards in Nauvoo were former Danites, as were many members of the city's police force. In addition, Quinn viewed the Danite group, with its passwords and oath of secrecy, as a precursor to Nauvoo's Council of Fifty. Former Danites, in fact, accounted for one-third of the men Smith admitted into the Council of Fifty. "The Danites," Quinn concluded, "forecast a path the LDS church would increasingly take in Illinois and later Utah: creating its own alternative civil and political institutions as the basis of theocracy" (103; see also 102, 129, 218).

Mormon Military Activities

Related to the controversy surrounding the Danites are questions regarding Mormon military operations during the Mormon War. Both dissenters and non-Mormons, including non-Mormon friends like Atchison and Doniphan, acknowledged that Mormon troops burned towns, looted stores, and drove settlers from their homes. After the Mormons surrendered at Far West, authorities charged Joseph Smith and some fifty Mormons with treason, murder, riot, and numerous other crimes allegedly committed during the conflict. The Mormon defendants strongly denied these charges. Parley P. Pratt, for example, said Joseph Smith "never bore arms or did military duty, not even in self-defense."[13] The Prophet's brother, Hyrum Smith, said the Missourians burned their own homes and then blamed the Mormons to inflame public opinion against them.[14] Traditional Mormon histories present this same view, describing the Mormons as innocent victims of Missouri violence. While traditional historians did not deny that the Saints took up arms, they asserted that the Mormons fought only in self-defense, never struck the first blow, acted according to the laws regulating the state militia, and did not commit any of the crimes attributed to them at the Richmond Court of Inquiry.[15]

In recent years, however, historians have modified these conclusions, sparking debate about the nature and extent of Mormon aggression. Historians have examined whether Mormon militancy was an outgrowth of persecution or was, at least to some extent, inherent in the religion itself. In addition, they have debated whether Joseph Smith condoned or encouraged these aggressive tendencies and whether Mormon troops may have acted illegally in some of their operations.

There appears to be universal agreement among historians that the Saints, while in Jackson County in 1833-34, took up arms in self-defense and only after non-Mormon vigilantes started a campaign of destruction and abuse. On November 4, 1833, a battle at the Mormon Big Blue settlement resulted in the deaths of two Missourians and one Mormon. Lt. Gov. Lilburn W. Boggs called out the local militia; at the command of local authorities, the Mormons surrendered their arms, thinking the vigilantes would be required to do the same. This, however, was not the case; and within a week the vigilantes had driven the unarmed Mormons to neighboring Clay County. Warren A. Jennings, the most prolific writer about the Jackson County conflict, has published in addition to the works already cited, "The Army of Israel Marches into Missouri," *Missouri Historical Review* 62 (Winter 1968): 107-35; "The Expulsion of the Mormons from Jackson County, Missouri," *Missouri Historical Review* 64 (October 1969): 41-63; "Factors in the Destruction of the Mormon Press in Missouri, 1833," *Utah Historical Quarterly* 35 (Winter 1967): 57-76; "The First Mormon Mission to the Indians," *Kansas Historical Quarterly* 37 (Autumn 1971): 288-99; and

---

13. Quoted in LeSueur, *The 1838 Mormon War in Missouri,* 209.
14. Ibid., 207.
15. See, for example, Roberts, *Comprehensive History of the Church,* 463-464; and Joseph Fielding Smith, *Essentials in Church History,* 222-223; Barrett, *Joseph Smith and the Restoration,* 318.

"Importuning for Redress," *Bulletin of the Missouri Historical Society* 27 (October 1970): 15-29.

The Ohio Saints were appalled when they received word of the expulsion. The next month, on December 16, 1833, Joseph Smith received a revelation that God had allowed the Saints to be driven from Zion because of their transgressions. Later the same day, another revelation called Smith to march to Missouri with a force of up to five hundred to escort the exiled Saints back into Jackson County as a supplement to state troops promised by Governor Daniel Dunklin. Furthermore, Zion's Camp would remain to protect the Jackson County Saints from further attacks. This expedition of two hundred armed volunteers reached western Missouri, but Smith cancelled the march when local citizens gathered a larger force and when the governor's reinforcements failed to materialize. The most comprehensive treatment is Roger D. Launius, *Zion's Camp: Expedition to Missouri, 1834* (Independence: Herald Publishing House, 1984).

Traditional Mormon historians blamed Dunklin: "Had Governor Dunklin possessed the courage to enforce the law of the State; had he called out the militia of Missouri to reinstate the exiles to their homes as at one time he expressed a willingness to do, the history of Zion's Camp might have had a different ending," wrote B. H. Roberts in a footnote to Joseph Smith's account in *History of the Church* 2:123. Peter Crawley and Richard L. Anderson, "The Political and Social Realities of Zion's Camp," *BYU Studies* 14 (Summer 1974): 420, said that, had Dunklin ordered Missouri troops to escort the Mormons back to their land, "a second violent confrontation would have erupted, with the Mormons at a disadvantage." But they asserted that Dunklin, not Smith, decided against the military escort.

More recently, however, Max H. Parkin, "Latter-day Saint Conflict in Clay County, Missouri," in *Regional Studies in . . . Missouri*, 241-60, said that Dunklin told Mormon leaders he would call out the militia if they made a formal request, but the governor was reluctant to take this step because he foresaw that it would result in civil war. Joseph Smith decided not to request the escort largely for the same reason: to avert bloodshed and resolve the conflict through peaceful negotiations (252-54). Consequently, Smith disbanded his troops, prophesying on June 22, 1834, that Zion would be redeemed after a "little season" (D&C 105:9). Parkin interpreted this revelation as a call for the Saints to overwhelm western Missouri with immigrants, but also instructing the Saints to enter quietly and in small groups over a long period of time, keeping their plans to themselves so as to not excite the Missourians. The primary goal was to create a community of Mormons—and a force of Mormon soldiers—large enough to restore the Saints to Jackson County. "Though the Lord stated in the revelation that 'my elders should wait for a little season for the redemption of Zion,' the Lord said that the 'little season' was to give the Saints in Clay County time 'to gather up the strength of my house' to that place," Parkin says. "They were to gather and purchase land in Clay County and otherwise fortify their position until their 'army became very great'" (253). Later that summer, Smith told the Saints that the date appointed for the redemption of Zion was September 11, 1836.

Other historians, including Marvin Hill (53), Michael Quinn (87-88); and Romig and Siebert, "Contours of the Kingdom: An RLDS Perspective on the Legions of Zion," *Restoration Studies V* (Independence: Herald Publishing House, 1993), 25-40, also concluded that the Mormons began preparing at once for conflict in Missouri. On September 24, 1835, at a secret meeting in his Kirtland home, Smith organized the Army of Israel, appointing David Whitmer "captain of the Lord's host" while he was head of the "war department," and several other Church leaders received military titles. John Whitmer's brief account lists Frederick G. Williams, Sidney Rigdon, W. W. Phelps, John Corrill, Hyrum Smith, and Oliver Cowdery among those attending. According to Quinn, Smith "proposed 'by the voice of the Spirit of the Lord' to raise another Mormon army 'to live or die on our own lands, which we have purchased in Jackson County, Missouri'" (87). He also launched an ambitious recruiting effort for the spring of 1836: "I ask God in the name of Jesus that we may obtain Eight hundred men or one thousand well armed [men] and that they may ac[c]omplish this great work."[16] In March 1836, as the appointed time neared, Smith resolved with his people "that if any more of our brethren are slain or driven from their lands in Missouri, by the mob, we will give ourselves no rest until we are avenged of our enemies to the uttermost."[17] In short, as the Saints hoped to resolve their dispute with Jackson County peacefully, they simultaneously prepared for war.

Parkin, Hill, and Romig and Siebert agree that Mormon immigrants began flooding Clay County, but so rapidly that the old settlers reacted with immediate alarm. Dan Vogel, *Religious Seekers and the Advent of Mormonism* (Salt Lake City: Signature Books, 1988), 200-202, also describes this incendiary situation. The Mormons armed in self-defense after a few of their men were brutally whipped, but the Missouri legislature created Caldwell County solely for the Mormons, defusing the crisis. The Mormons began settling Caldwell in 1837 and also fanned out into Daviess, Carroll, Clinton, and other sparsely settled northwestern counties, living in relative peace until hostilities started anew in the summer of 1838.

One of the most controversial conclusions by recent historians is that Mormon soldiers acted aggressively in the 1838 conflict and that their aggression contributed to the violence against them. Starting with Leland Gentry's influential dissertation on northwestern Missouri, Mormon historians have shown that Mormon soldiers burned and plundered homes during the Mormon War. While this view is universally accepted, the chief point of contention now is the extent and purpose of destruction. Richard L. Anderson, "Atchison's Letters and the Causes of Mormon Expulsion from Missouri," *BYU Studies* 26 (Summer 1986), 3-47, admitted that the Mormons looted Gallatin and Millport, burning about two dozen buildings, and plundering and burning an unspecified number of non-Mormon cabins. But he cast these activities as part of a defensive strategy: "The preemptive strikes south of Adam-ondi-Ahman were intentionally destructive, but it appears that any burning elsewhere was selective" (29). Alexander Baugh, "A Call to Arms," and William Hartley, *My Best for the Kingdom,* essentially agreed. When Mormon officials and military leaders made their final plans at Adam-ondi-Ahman, Baugh says, "they determined that the course of action should be aggressive in nature but selective in focus, and that Mormon troops were expected to confine their militant plunderings to mob-characters and destroy 'those places that harbored them'" (192-93). Hartley explained the Mormon activities: "In peacetime, such acts are arson, vandalism, and robbery—clearly crimes. But in wartime they are military actions serving strategic purposes" (68-72).

While Anderson, Baugh, and Hartley correctly emphasized the defensiveness of Mormon military operations, they essentially changed the focus from whether Mormon soldiers destroyed property to questions about whose property was destroyed and how much. I estimated in *The 1838 Mormon War in Missouri,* 124, that the Mormons burned about fifty cabins and stores, while Anderson, "Atchison's Letters," 29, concluded that "aside from the two dozen structures burned in the Gallatin-Millport area, no one can give an accurate figure" (29), although in his later "Clarifications of Boggs's Order," 44, he gave an estimate of perhaps three dozen buildings. These conclusions, regardless of the numbers, contradict the fervent denials of Joseph Smith, Hyrum Smith, Lyman Wight, and other Mormon leaders. Anderson and Baugh, for example, say that Mormon soldiers were guided by a defensive strategy that targeted only enemy homes, buildings, and property. Such a strategy, which involved hundreds of soldiers operating in at least four different companies, would have required careful planning by Mormon leaders. But Joseph, Hyrum, Wight, and other Church leaders who were present during the Daviess operations denied that Mormon soldiers burned homes or plundered property, claiming instead that the Missourians torched their own homes and blamed it on the Mormons. Thus, the very men who would have devised the strategy described by Anderson and Baugh denied that such a strategy existed. Smith, in fact, stated that he personally had nothing to do with the burn-

---

16. Quoted in Quinn, *Origins of Power,* 87. See also Parkin, "Latter-day Saint Conflict in Clay County," 253-54.

17. Quoted in Romig and Siebert, "Contours of the Kingdom," 28.

ings in Daviess County and that he made public proclamations against such activities. In short, the claims of nineteenth-century Mormon leaders contradicted Anderson's and Baugh's conclusions, but neither historian addressed this discrepancy.

Equally significant, the basic claims that Mormons engaged in burnings and destruction in northern Missouri were precisely the claims made by Mormon dissenters and Missourians. Most dissenters and many non-Mormons would have agreed that the Mormons were fighting in self-defense, but the point at issue was whether the Mormons' military operations went too far. Doniphan, Atchison, Hinkle, Marsh, Corrill, and others believed that, regardless of who started the conflict, the Mormons had become the aggressors. And although Mormon leaders may have intended to expel only mobbers from the Daviess County, innocent Missourians, including women and children, were also driven from their homes, further inflaming public opinion against the Saints (LeSueur, *1838 Mormon War*, 118-20). The Mormons' motives are not unimportant, but defining their military operations as defensive does not recognize the complexity of motives that lay behind their actions, nor does it explain why burning and plundering was the defensive strategy adopted, especially when it was apparent to many that such a course would bring them into conflict with the entire state.

The attitude of Lyman Wight, the fiery Mormon leader at Adam-ondi-Ahman, provides important insights. He and his family had already been driven from Jackson and Clay counties, suffering repeated hardship and economic loss. When the Prophet reintroduced the law of consecration, Wight enthusiastically embraced the principle, exulting that its participants would be "tied with cords of love & disinterestedness" (LeSueur, *1838 Mormon War*, 34). But the years of persecution also hardened Wight against his Daviess County neighbors, whom he later described as "an ignorant set, and not very far advanced before the aborigines of the country in civilization or cultivated minds." A Mormon dissenter said that Wight, the reputed head of the Danite organization at Adam-ondi-Ahman, regularly denounced the Missourians from the pulpit, referring to them as "hypocrits, long-faced dupes, devils, . . . [who] ought to be damned, and sent to hell, where they properly belonged." Others said that Wight boasted of what the Mormons would do if their enemies did not let them alone, seemingly inviting an attack (LeSueur, 59, 86).

When the conflict broke out, Wight, a colonel in the state militia and head of Mormon forces in Daviess County, taught the Mormon soldiers "to pray for our enemies that God would damn them and give us power to kill them," while another said Wight promised his men that "we will hew them [the Missourians] down like old stumps." John D. Lee summarized: "Wight's manner of address struck terror to his enemies, while it inspired his brethren with enthusiastic zeal and forced them to believe they were invincible and bullet proof" (LeSueur, 86-87). According to Corrill, Wight "meant to winter" in St. Louis, while Hinkle related that Wight declared that his sword "should not be sheathed until he had marched . . . into Jackson county, and into many other places in the state."[18] Wight led the expedition in October 1838 to Millport, where Mormon soldiers plundered and burned the town.

One of Smith's most loyal and courageous followers, Lyman Wight was fighting on the defensive in Daviess County, but he was also motivated by anger, righteous indignation, a desire for revenge, and an apocalyptic vision of the kingdom of God. Many of the Mormon soldiers who marched with Wight shared these complex feelings. Joseph Smith probably did as well, because he subsequently selected Wight to replace David W. Patten, slain at Crooked River in October 1838, as a Mormon apostle.

New Interpretations

The closer examination of events also has produced other new interpretations and insights. For example, Mormon historians have traditionally argued that the Missouri

---

18. Corrill, *A Brief History*, 38; Testimony of George M. Hinkle, *Document Containing the Correspondence, Orders, &c. in Relation to the Disturbances with the Mormons; and the Evidence Given Before the Hon. Austin A. King, Judge of the Fifth Judicial Circuit of the State of Missouri* (Fayette, MO: Boon's Lick Democrat, 1841), 129.

troops that attacked Haun's Mill were taking it upon themselves to carry out Boggs's extermination order. B. H. Roberts said the "butchery" that left seventeen Mormons dead and more than a dozen wounded "was doubtless the first fruits of Governor Boggs' Exterminating Order."[19] But Baugh persuasively argued in "Call to Arms" that the governor's order, issued October 27, could not have reached the militia unit in time for the attack three days later (127). Rather, he saw the attack as retaliation for Mormon raids in Daviess County and (false) reports that Mormon soldiers had nearly annihilated state troops at Crooked River.[20]

William G. Hartley, "'Almost Too Intolerable a Burthen': The Winter Exodus from Missouri, 1838-39," *Journal of Mormon History* 18 (Fall 1992): 6-40, took a closer look at the Mormon exodus from Missouri during the winter of 1838-39. While the general facts of the Saints' plight have been well known, Hartley assembled a vast array of sources on their evacuation routes (mostly to Illinois) and about their treatment by Missourians. Many Mormons lacked adequate food, clothing, or shelter. "The [Levi] Hancock family slept nightly on the ground despite the snow. One night, perhaps typically, their bed was leaves covered with a quilt. Levi cut down a basswood tree for the horses to eat from, and the family supplemented their corn with 'elmbark and buds'" (27). The "helplessness and suffering of the exodus, help explain why the Saints formed a self-defensive city state in Nauvoo, why some Saints justified retaliation, why many gladly left the United States to head into the Mexican Territory, why many felt such loathing for federal judges, courts, deputies, laws, and military officials, and even why the Mountain Meadows Massacre was in part an act of revenge" (40).

The Nature of Opposition to Mormonism

At the time, the Mormons believed their Missouri persecutors were motivated primarily, if not solely, by religious prejudice. Considerable evidence supported their view. Anti-Mormon broadsides attacked their religious beliefs; the Saints' enemies stated flatly that they could not abide the new, obnoxious religion; the Saints were condemned as fanatics, duped by Joseph Smith; Mormons were often attacked for no other reason than that they were Mormons; and many were told they could escape punishment—and even remain in Missouri—if they denied their faith. Furthermore, much of the anti-Mormon violence was incited by ministers and preachers, who could often be found at the head of the mobs. "Ultimately, then, it was religious differences that drove the settlers to expel the Mormons," concluded Richard L. Bushman, "Mormon Persecutions in Missouri, 1833," *BYU Studies* 3 (Autumn 1960): 11-20. "From the beginning until the last decade of the century, the fear of religious aliens in power lay at the heart of gentile hatreds and fears" (18, 20).

But even if religious prejudice provoked anti-Mormon persecution, such a view still raises several important questions. Why did Mormonism elicit such strong hatred? And what was it about American society that would allow—and perhaps even encourage—the violent reaction against the new religion?

One of the most interesting revisionist interpretations of Mormonism is Marvin Hill's *Quest for Refuge: The Mormon Flight from American Pluralism*. Hill argued that Mormonism was largely a reaction against the religious and social pluralism that flourished in Jacksonian America. The early nineteenth century was marked by a growing number of diverse religious, social, and political philosophies, and by a breakdown in the social ties that characterized America's agrarian, pre-industrial society. This pluralism, although celebrated by most Americans today as symbolizing democratic tolerance and individualism, troubled

---

19. Roberts, *Comprehensive History of the Church*, 1:483. See also Joseph Fielding Smith, *Essentials in Church History*, 234.

20. At least one Missouri participant gave a statement supporting this conclusion. Charles Ashby, a state legislator, said the Missourians attacked because Mormon dissenters fleeing into Livingston warned them that the Haun's Mill Saints were planning to invade Livingston. "We thought it best to attack them first. . . . What we did was in our own defence, and we had the right to do," Ashby said. Quoted in LeSueur, *The 1838 Mormon War*, 164.

Joseph Smith and his followers. The Mormons viewed with alarm the democratic spirit awakened in Jacksonian America—Smith, for example, opposed the abolitionist movement as subversive—and regarded it as evidence of social and moral chaos. Hill saw this theme running throughout the Book of Mormon, where dissent and diversity "were always atheistic and destructive" precursors to social disintegration (xii). Similarly, the Book of Mormon stressed that even a democratic society will fail if it is not led by righteous prophet-rulers. "This understanding helps us better understand why so many Americans at the time opposed Mormonism so strongly," Hill observed in his "Counter-Revolution: The Mormon Reaction to the Coming of American Democracy," " *Sunstone* 13 (June 1989): 24-33. "There was a set of assumptions among the Mormons about man and his government that ran counter to the liberalizing, democratic views sweeping the northern and border states during the first half of the nineteenth century" (29).

Although their anti-pluralism ran counter to the nascent spirit of Jacksonian America, the Mormons saw themselves as the true defenders of American republican values. Kenneth Winn, *Exiles in a Land of Liberty: Mormons in America, 1830-1846* (Chapel Hill: University of North Carolina Press, 1989), argued that the Mormons and anti-Mormons justified their own positions by appealing to the same set of values: good citizenship, civic virtue, responsibility, and self-reliance. Similarly, each side accused the other of anti-republican values: materialism, mobocracy, tyranny, and corruption. "Smith considered the entire American mainstream of society as an aberration that had deserted the republican morality of its forefathers," Winn writes. "In the guise of a prophet of the coming millennium, Smith in effect posed as the conservative defense of an older America crumbling under the social pressures of Jacksonian America" (39). Winn saw republican values in the Book of Mormon, but Hill, "Counter-Revolution," argued that Winn overstated his case, pointing out, for example, that Book of Mormon chief judges were church officials or members, their positions often hereditary. Asserting that there was little religious freedom or separation of church and state in Book of Mormon society, Hill found the Book of Mormon "an ambivalent spokesman for republicanism" (25).

To escape the impending social and religious disorder, the Mormons sought to establish communitarian societies where economic and social differences were mitigated, where Church members worked for both individual and group needs, and where dissent was quickly stifled. The Mormons' blueprint for the ideal community was the biblical city of Enoch. Social harmony and unity prevailed there to such a high degree that God "translated" the earthly city directly into heaven. In short, Mormons were not trying to build a separate community, but a competing community—one that eventually would overthrow and replace all Gentile political and religious organizations, including the United States. It was this kind of community the Mormons sought to establish in Missouri, and it was this kind of community that Missourians found so threatening to their own.

Despite these differences, the Mormons enjoyed short periods of relative peace during their stay in Missouri. Whatever their personal views regarding Mormonism, many Missourians tolerated the Mormon presence, and many befriended the Saints and sought business relationships with them. But the friendly relations ended—in Jackson County, in Clay County, and finally in the northwestern counties—when Mormon numbers grew too large relative to their non-Mormon neighbors. From the Missourians' perspective, the burgeoning Mormon population meant that the Mormons would control local politics and, probably more important, dominate their economy. The Mormons used Church funds to buy land throughout the western counties and, in 1838, pooled their resources to form large commercial and agricultural cooperatives. The collective Church group could easily outcompete and outproduce the non-Mormon farmers and businesses, relegating them to secondary positions in the local economy and society as Michael Riggs points out in "The Economic Impact of Fort Leavenworth," 124-33. Because the Mormons sought to create a self-sufficient community of believers, non-Mormons were often shut out of the Mormon economy and the benefits of mutual trade. The non-Mormons' fears of exclusion, said Clay County resident Joseph Thorpe, were heightened by Mormon boasts that "this country was theirs by gift of the Lord, and it was folly for them [the Missourians] to improve their lands, they would not enjoy the fruits of their labor, that it would finally fall into the hands of the saints."[21]

But whatever the primary cause of antagonism—whether religious, cultural, or economic—an important question remains: Why did the conflict result in the violent expulsion of the Mormons from their homes? Historians of American violence, as referenced in LeSueur, , *The 1838 Mormon War,* 275, and Quinn, "National Culture, Personality, and Theocracy," 159 note 3, point to several unifying themes. First, since colonial times, Americans have shown a willingness to take the law into their own hands to enforce the will of the majority. Vigilante justice has often been an expression of community values. Similarly, vigilante violence has tended to be conservative in nature, designed to protect the community and its values from individuals or groups perceived as inimical to the community. Consequently, local leaders are often found heading vigilante organizations, keeping them from disintegrating into disorganized mobs, but also keeping them moving toward the community's goal of expelling the unwanted group. Nineteenth-century law enforcement officials, even if so inclined, lacked the resources or training to quell large-scale riots. Thus, the Mormon experience was similar, at least in a broad sense, to the experience of Catholics, free blacks, Indians, Chinese, and others who appeared to threaten community values. In the case of the Mormons, Missouri citizens held meetings, published the minutes of those meetings, issued ultimatums to the Saints, and eventually resorted to violence to achieve their ends. The precise dynamics were different in Jackson County, Clay County, and northwestern Missouri, largely because the Mormon response differed each time. But the outcome was always the same. The Mormons were expelled from the community.

And so we return to the assertion made at the beginning of this chapter: The Mormons suffered greatly and were treated unfairly in Missouri, a point largely agreed upon by both traditional historians and New Mormon historians. But many new historians also contend that Mormon militancy contributed to the anti-Mormon violence, an assertion that disturbs some historians who resist the implication that Mormons are largely to blame for their troubles in Missouri.

At one time, the issue of blame was very important for both the Missourians and the Saints. After the 1838 conflict, Missouri authorities put the Mormons on trial to fix blame on them for the hostilities; meanwhile, the Mormons wrote affidavits, letters, and petitions seeking to absolve themselves of blame and to demonstrate that the Missourians were at fault. The historians' primary task, however, is not to assign blame but to understand why people acted the way they did and why events turned out as they did. And while a historical work that seeks to explain cause and effect may also attempt to assign blame, cause is not synonymous with blame. The assertion that Mormon military operations alarmed Missouri citizens and prompted them to call out state troops against the Saints does not imply that the Mormons were at fault; it only explains the effect of the Mormons' action (which, of course, was influenced by a variety of factors, including earlier persecution by non-Mormons). In trying to downplay the question of blame, R. J. Robertson, "The Mormon Experience in Missouri, 1830-1838," *Missouri Historical Review* 68 (April and July 1974): 280-98, 393-415; said, regarding the conflict in Missouri: "In reality, it was the social characteristics of both sides that determined that tension would surface, and it was the failure of either side to compromise that determined that violence would result. . . . In a more fundamental sense, each group's only 'guilt' lay in their being different from each other" (415).

Conclusion

There still is much history to be written. While recent histories showed the actions and motives of the non-Mormons to be more complex than previously acknowledged, the time now is ripe for a reexamination of the roles played by major players like Governor

---

21. Quoted in Parkin, "Latter-day Saint Conflict in Clay County," 254.

Boggs and digging deeper into the lives of average citizens. Similarly, we know more about the Danites and Mormon dissenters, yet the debate about their roles in Mormon society has only intensified. The Jackson County or Clay County periods have been the subject of dissertations, but no monograph treatments have been published. The two most recent published works examining the northern Missouri experience are my *1838 Mormon War in Missouri* and Alexander Baugh's dissertation, *A Call to Arms: The 1838 Mormon Defense of Northern Missouri*, but both focus largely on the conflict between the Mormons and Missourians, and so leave unexplored many developments within Mormonism.

This does not mean, however, that scholars are ignoring this period. Several individuals and organizations are devoted to uncovering new source materials and cataloguing a multitude of information about both the Mormons and their Missouri neighbors. The non-profit Missouri Mormon Frontier Foundation (MMFF) in Independence, founded in 1992, has been especially active in the geographical history of the Mormon experience, examining land records, photographs, artifacts, and memorabilia, in locating, preserving, and marking important historical sites, old homes, and trails, gathering genealogical information of the affected area, and publishing tour guides and other items of interest.[22] At the same time, the Far West Cultural Center, established in 2002 by Michael Riggs five miles south of Far West, is restoring a log house built in 1837 by Charles C. Rich, a future apostle. Riggs and Romig have been instrumental in bringing together a diverse group of professional and lay historians who are continually uncovering new source materials and information on the Missouri period. Under editor Maurine Carr Ward and Alex Baugh, assistant editor, *Mormon Historical Studies* has begun devoting a significant percentage of its pages to Missouri history.[23] But journals are not the only places Mormon historians are publishing these days. The internet has proved a valuable tool for historians to share information and publish new insights and discoveries, as well as make more widely available previously published work.[24] Finally, an impressive set of maps is forthcoming from mapmaker John Hamer and others who have been working with these new materials.

This new research could lead to the creation of a searchable database of information that would allow historians to tie together different pieces of information, such as the property holdings or home sites of Mormons who fought in the Crooked River battle. The database also could shed light on the Saints' everyday life, both secular and religious. An important resource for such a database would be the Johnson and Romig *Index to Early Caldwell County, Missouri, Land Records*, a 2002 revision of Johnson's 1994 limited edition.

Johnson's *Missouri Redress Petitions: Documents of the 1833-1838 Missouri Conflict* (Provo, UT: Brigham Young University Religious Studies Center, 1992), is likewise a valuable cultural resource. *Mormon Redress Petitions* reprints more than eight hundred affidavits and petitions submitted by the Mormons to the federal government after their expulsion. Although many Mormons later described the Missouri experience in their reminiscences, the petitions are an important historical resource because they were written soon after these events and within a two-year period. Some participants offered little information, simply listing the land and possessions they lost when expelled from their homes; but others wrote

---

22. Among MMFF's publications are Ronald E. Romig, *Early Independence, Missouri "Mormon" History Tour Guide*, illustrated by Henry K. Inouye Jr. (1994); Romig, *The "Mormon" Settlement on the Big Blue River*, illustrated by Inouye (1996); Clark V. Johnson and Ronald E. Romig, eds., *An Index to Early Caldwell County, Missouri, Land Records* (2002); and William J. Curtis, *Jackson County, Missouri Mormon Sites* (2002).

23. Among recent articles are, in the spring 2001, issue: William G. Hartley, "Missouri's 1838 Extermination Order and the Mormons' Forced Removal to Illinois," 5-27; Alexander L. Baugh, "'We Took Our Change of Venue to the State of Illinois': The Gallatin Hearing and the Escape of Joseph Smith and the Mormon Prisoners from Missouri, April 1839," 59-82; and Baugh, "Not Every Missourian Was a Bad Guy: Hiram G. Parks' 1839 Letter to James Sloan in Quincy, Illinois," 163-72; also Baugh, "A Relic of the Missouri Mormon Period: The Haun's Mill Stone at Breckenridge, Missouri," 2 (Fall 2001): 211-15; and Gary J. Bergera, "The Personal Cost of the 1838 Mormon War in Missouri: One Mormon's Plea for Forgiveness," 4 (Spring 2003): 139-44.

24. Among active websites are the Missouri Mormon Frontier Foundation (www.mmff.net), the Far West Cultural Center (www.farwesthistory.com), and www.tungate.com, run by Mel Tungate, a lay historian who maintains a scholarly interest in Mormon history, particularly the Missouri experience.

narrative accounts that give details about the wrongs they suffered at the hands of the Missourians. Taken as a whole, they present a unique glimpse into the Latter-day Saints' lifestyle and their view of the conflict that engulfed them.

For example, Kenneth W. Godfrey, "New Light on Old Difficulties: The Historical Importance of the Missouri Affidavits," *Regional Studies in . . . Missouri,* 201-17, uses the petitions to reconstruct the diet of Missouri Mormons: ham, chicken, eggs, milk, honey, butter, boiled maize and hot wheat bread, supplemented at times with elk, deer, and wild turkey. The petitions contain similar information about the Saints' tools, weapons, and other possessions. Other articles drawing on the petitions include Clark V. Johnson, "Missouri Persecutions: The Petition of Isaac Leany," *BYU Studies* 23 (Winter 1983): 94-103; his "The Missouri Redress Petitions: A Reappraisal of Mormon Persecutions in Missouri," *BYU Studies* 26 (Spring 1986): 31-44; his "A Profile of Mormon Missouri, 1834-1839," in *Regional Studies in . . . Missouri,* 219-31; his "Government Responses to Mormon Appeals, 1840-1846," in *Regional Studies in Latter-day Saint Church History: Illinois,* edited by H. Dean Garrett (Provo, UT: Department of Church History and Doctrine, Brigham Young University, 1995), 183-204; and Paul C. Richards, "Missouri Persecutions: Petitions for Redress," *BYU Studies* 13 (Summer 1973): 520-43.

As the body of published research grows, this period awaits a history that examines the entire scope of the Mormon experience in Missouri, from the Saints' first efforts to settle Jackson County to their expulsion from the state. Such a history would be a major contribution both to Mormon history and to the history of the American West.

STEPHEN C. LESUEUR, an independent scholar and magazine editor, resides in Washington, D.C. He has written extensively on the Mormon experience in Missouri and, in addition to his articles, published *The 1838 Mormon War in Missouri* (Columbia: University of Missouri Press, 1987).

Chapter 5

The Nauvoo Experience

Glen M. Leonard

Nauvoo's church historians contributed to the prominence of Nauvoo on the map of Mormon history through diligent efforts in collecting and compiling a record of the 1839-46 period. In a format resembling a first-person diary of the first prophet's life, the resulting compilation, known as "The History of Joseph Smith," became the foundation stone on which later historians would build.

During recent decades, historians have introduced new data, asked new questions, and reworked old understandings in their retelling of the familiar story of Nauvoo. My task in the discussion that follows is to examine those innovations. At times, I will illustrate influences and contrasts with references to the "old" Nauvoo history as it was told between the dramatic dispersal of 1846 and the emergence of the New Mormon History in the mid-twentieth century. Important topical bibliographies are Richard D. Poll, "Nauvoo and the New Mormon History: A Bibliographical Survey," *Journal of Mormon History* 5 (1978): 105-23; Glen M. Leonard, "Recent Writing on Mormon Nauvoo," *Western Illinois Regional Studies* 11 (Fall 1988): 69-93; Roger D. Launius and John E. Hallwas, "Bibliographical Essay," in *Kingdom on the Mississippi Revisited: Nauvoo in Mormon History*, edited by Launius and Hallwas (Urbana: University of Illinois Press, 1996), 251-67. Basic sources are also listed in Robert Bruce Flanders, *Nauvoo: Kingdom on the Mississippi* (Urbana: University of Illinois Press, 1965): 342-50; James B. Allen and Glen M. Leonard, *The Story of the Latter-day Saints* (1976; 2d ed., Salt Lake City: Deseret Book, 1992), 714-20; and Glen M. Leonard, *Nauvoo: A Place of Peace, a People of Plenty* (Salt Lake City: Deseret Book, 2002/Provo, UT: Brigham Young University Press, 2002), 767-86. A comprehensive tool for historical researchers is now available in James B. Allen, Ronald W. Walker, and David J. Whittaker, *Studies in Mormon History: A Bibliography, with Index, and a Guide to Further Research* (Urbana: University of Illinois Press, 1999). Another historiographical essay is Kenneth W. Godfrey, "Telling the Nauvoo Story," *Mormon Historical Studies* 3 (Spring 2002): 5-28, a careful analysis of the major Nauvoo books through 2000 and an updated list of articles, with suggestions for topics needing further attention.

Excavating Mormon Pasts

The New Nauvoo

Robert B. Flanders established a new benchmark in Nauvoo history with his thoughtfully organized and handsomely written *Nauvoo: Kingdom on the Mississippi* (Urbana: University of Illinois Press, 1965). In the first New Mormon History of Nauvoo, Flanders set aside the moralizing tone of books written for his parents' generation and moved beyond the pseudo-scholarship of critics of Mormonism. Instead, with sympathetic detachment, he applied analytical skills honed through university training to create a balanced political and economic perspective on the Nauvoo years.

Flanders noted the importance of religious developments. He did not intend to offer (nor did he offer) a religious perspective on doctrinal and ecclesiastical changes. Instead, he crafted his presentation to spotlight the more secular aspects of Nauvoo's history. In his book, the topics of government, the military, the land business, commerce, industry, and finance took center stage. Descriptive adjuncts included city-building, missionary work, and construction of a temple. For more than thirty-five years Flanders's notable achievement stood without challenge as the most satisfactory book-length interpretation of Joseph Smith's Nauvoo. Reviews of this work include George R. Gayler, *Journal of American History* 53 (June 1966): 131; Klaus Hansen, "The World and the Prophet," *Dialogue: A Journal of Mormon Thought* 1 (Summer 1966): 103-7; Stanley B. Kimball, "Taking Flanders Too Seriously," *Dialogue* 1 (Autumn 1966): 177-81; and Rex Snydergaard, *Journal of the Illinois State Historical Society* 59 (Winter 1966): 433-34.

Flanders adopted and developed the idea of an independent Mormon nation-state as a precursor to corporate Mormonism in Utah. He further explored the themes of nationhood, political unity, and the authoritarian rule of Nauvoo in "Nauvoo: Dream and Nightmare," in *The Restoration Movement: Essays in Mormon History,* edited by F. Mark McKiernan, Alma R. Blair, and Paul M. Edwards (Lawrence, KS: Coronado Press, 1973), 144-66. It was the nation-establishing aspects of Nauvoo that members of the Reorganized Church rejected, preferring instead the theology of restorationist Kirtland (v-vi, 92-93). Flanders echoed as well the tradition of measured neutrality found in the Nauvoo interpretation of Hubert Howe Bancroft, *History of Utah, 1540-1886* (San Francisco: History Company, 1889), chaps. 6-8. Like Bancroft and sociologist Thomas F. O'Dea, Flanders spoke sympathetically from outside the Utah Mormon tradition. He examined both strengths and weaknesses of Mormon leaders and institutions in a spirit of frankness and fairness. He presented a reasoned interpretation based in secular assumptions. All three of these writers sought to understand but go beyond the Utah perspective on Nauvoo. From his vantage point within the Restoration movement, Flanders had the additional benefit of an insider understanding.

During that time Flanders's closest competitors as Nauvoo's modern story-tellers were University of Utah historian David E. Miller and his wife, Della S. Miller, authors of *Nauvoo: The City of Joseph* (Santa Barbara, CA: Peregrine Smith, 1974). This supplemental telling is a modestly revised version of a 1963 report prepared at the behest of Nauvoo Restoration Incorporated (NRI). The Millers addressed a Utah Mormon audience with a "brief but factual history" (v) presented as a descriptive overview of familiar themes in the religious and social history of Nauvoo. Their contributions include new material and instructive maps on land purchases, a rather detailed recounting of the operation of city government, and a few other tidbits of fresh information. Illustrations emphasize the built environment in a restored Old Nauvoo. Somewhere between an in-house history for the faithful and a full-blown treatment for specialists, this study fell short of being a much-needed complete history of Nauvoo, as noted by Francis Henry Touchet, Review, *Annals of Iowa,* 3rd series, 44 (Summer 1978): 412. Other reviews are Glen M. Leonard, *BYU Studies* 17 (Autumn 1977): 126; T. Edgar Lyon, *Western Historical Quarterly* 6 (October 1975): 448-49; and Melvin R. Smith, *Utah Historical Quarterly* 43 (Fall 1975): 425-26.

Flanders published his well-received analysis and the Millers completed their initial report during an era of good feelings and increasing openness in Mormon studies. The new inquiries into Nauvoo's past were part of a trend toward a tolerant but rigorous scholar-

Robert Bruce Flanders ✹

NAUVOO ✹ Kingdom on the Mississippi

UNIVERSITY OF ILLINOIS PRESS ✹ URBANA, 1965

ship. Setting the standard for such probes were two popularly received and widely influential works published by distinguished university presses in the late 1950s. While neither book focused on Nauvoo, both recognized the pivotal importance of the period. More importantly, these works reflected the spirit and approach that made possible a fresh look at Nauvoo.

The first was produced by the Catholic sociologist Thomas F. O'Dea. His close look at the Utah church, *The Mormons* (Chicago: University of Chicago Press, 1957), helped outsiders understand the internal stresses of a people seeking acceptance and understanding in the broader world. O'Dea's fifteen-page Nauvoo section centered on community—the qualities of a separatist, self-sufficient, self-determining people. Robert S. Michaelson, "Thomas F. O'Dea on the Mormons: Retrospect and Assessment," *Dialogue* 11 (Spring 1978): 44-57, assesses O'Dea's insights. As an outsider, but as one who had both taught and lived in Utah, O'Dea moved beyond the sensationalist narrative of William A. Linn, *The Story of the Mormons: From the Date of Their Origin to the Year 1901* (1902; reprint ed., New York: Macmillan, 1923), who had attempted somewhat unsuccessfully to write a balanced, "factual" account. Linn was among the twentieth-century's earliest scholars to write critical for a national audience and one of the most influential.

O'Dea and economic historian Leonard J. Arrington helped make the story of the Mormon experience more compatible with the mainstream story of American life. In its pre-Utah chapter, Arrington's *Great Basin Kingdom: An Economic History of the Latter-day Saints, 1830-1900* (Cambridge, MA: Harvard University Press, 1958), traced "the formulation of an economic creed which was at once distinctive, yet peculiarly American" (6). Arrington legitimized post-Nauvoo Mormon history among students of the American West. He identified the faith-motivated, organized cooperation of the Mountain West settlers as a case study in religious, economic, and institutional history. For Arrington, Nauvoo represented "a phase of what might be called nation-building" (17).

The approaches taken by Flanders and the Millers reflected in somewhat different ways the framework of American frontier history, with its interest in varied peoples in regional settings. Nauvoo as a jumping-off place for the trek to the Great Basin is especially evident in the Millers' initial draft, tellingly titled "Westward Migration of the Mormons, with Special Emphasis on Nauvoo" (Salt Lake City: Typescript report, submitted to the National Park Service, 1963). David Miller's career was anchored in the history of the American West (the common grounding for Utah Mormon historians of his time), which shored up Nauvoo Restoration's predisposition to see Nauvoo as an incubator of Utah Mormon values. As a western Williamsburg, Nauvoo also represented for NRI an exemplar of American patriotism and courage—values in tune with the mid-century political ethos.

Flanders accepted the continuity between his Nauvoo boom-town and the West, while pointing out the presence of a minority who opposed the more radical of the Nauvoo developments. A Midwesterner, Flanders wrote his Nauvoo book after first completing what might be called a "Contra-West" study, "The Mormons Who Did Not Go West: A Study of the Emergence of the Reorganized Church of Jesus Christ of Latter Day Saints" (M.A. thesis, University of Wisconsin, 1954). It is possible to read *Nauvoo: Kingdom on the Mississippi* as a prequel to Arrington's *Great Basin Kingdom*. Both of these "Kingdom of the World" texts examine the economics of religion within the context of a general history. They share an organizational outline that begins with a definition of the economic dreams of a geographically gathered people and that ends with conflict. For Arrington, friction precipitated the Retreat of the Kingdom, for Flanders, the Fall of the Kingdom.[1]

In "Writing on the Mormon Past," *Dialogue* 1 (Autumn 1966): 52-53, Flanders chided Utah Mormon historians for their western bias in seeing "the early formative period of the movement in the Midwest . . . as *merely* preliminary to the Great Basin experience" (emphasis mine). From his own perspective, "the frames of reference for early Mormon

---

1. For additional discussion of this and other points noted above, see Hansen, "The World and the Prophet," 103-7.

history traditionally set by Mormons themselves have been far-western rather than Midwestern or national, religious and social rather than economic or political, polemical rather than critical, defensive rather than objective." By reaching beyond conventional Utah perspectives, Flanders adopted an academic model for his study that placed Nauvoo in the larger context of Jacksonian America. By critically examining the political and economic developments of a Midwestern people, Flanders succeeded in creating a balanced treatment acceptable to readers from a variety of backgrounds. After forty years, *Nauvoo: Kingdom on the Mississippi* retains its usefulness as an economic and political analysis. In September 2002, Flanders reflected on his personal religious trek and its relationship to his book in an evocative John Whitmer Historical Association paper at Nauvoo: "Nauvoo on My Mind," *John Whitmer Historical Association Journal* 23 (2003): 13-20.

Defining the New History

A number of important historiographical essays during the 1960s and '70s examined what the new ways of explaining the past meant for Mormon history. Of concern to many Latter-day Saint historians was the trend toward the secularization of what in preceding decades had been a faith-promoting history. While lauding the shift away from polemics, these students of the past often cautioned against the paucity of a purely secular approach. Practitioners of the New Mormon History sought a middle ground that invited frankness tempered by fairness. According to Flanders, "Some Reflections on the New Mormon History," *Dialogue* 9 (Spring 1974): 34-41, they infused the actors in their histories with agency, wrapped the religious story with its political dimensions, and began the process of acceptance and understanding of diversity. Leonard J. Arrington, "The Search for Truth and Meaning in Mormon History," *Dialogue* 3 (Summer 1968): 55-66, encouraged a meaning-filled interpretive history that reflected personal and cultural values, the role of women, intellectuals, and grass-roots members, along with variety in Mormon life. Richard D. Poll, "God and Man in History," *Dialogue* 7 (Spring 1972): 101-9, offered thoughts toward the definition of a philosophy of history based in religious beliefs. Adding a note of reality to these dreams for a new perspective, Richard L. Bushman, "The Future of Mormon History," *Dialogue* 1 (Autumn 1966): 23-26, predicted that future Mormon historians would not find a distinctive voice in their search for meaning, but would follow standard historiographical trends of American history. Additional essays on this topic are collected in George D. Smith, ed., *Faithful History: Essays on Writing Mormon History* (Salt Lake City: Signature Books, 1992).

Earlier Nauvoos

Those who wrote about Nauvoo after the publication of Flanders's new history were influenced not only by discussions of how to write history, but also by earlier interpretations, especially some widely read educational histories published for members of the Salt Lake City and Independence churches. Among the titles enjoying the imprimatur of "official" or at least "accepted" works, were the Nauvoo and general Church histories created by B. H. Roberts, E. Cecil McGavin, William E. Berrett, and Inez Smith Davis. Mid-twentieth-century historians moved beyond these existing mainline works and left behind the hostile criticisms as well to create middle-ground histories that responded to contemporary needs.

The earliest and perhaps most broadly influential of the authorized writers was the English emigrant Brigham H. Roberts, whose influence in defining the themes of Nauvoo's history are summarized in Launius and Hallwas, *Kingdom on the Mississippi Revisited*, 6-8, 13. For a younger generation of Utah Latter-day Saints, Roberts penned *The Rise and Fall of Nauvoo* (1900), first serialized in 1886-87 in a Church periodical. This selective restatement of Joseph Smith's "History of the Church" from the *Millennial Star* offered clear characterizations of historical figures and teased out moral lessons from the choices they made.

Roberts also wrote for adult readers, not just to strengthen faith, but to defend the Church of Jesus Christ of Latter-day Saints as a legitimate world religion. In his "History of the Mormon Church," serialized in the nationally circulated *Americana* magazine (1909-

15), Roberts sought credibility by adapting Bancroft's technique of citing non-Mormon sources as a foil against a positive narrative. An expanded version of these articles appeared in *A Comprehensive History of the Church of Jesus Christ of Latter-day Saints, Century I*, 6 vols. (1930; reprint ed., Provo, UT: BYU Press, 1965), written in the pattern of the literary Romantic historians. Nauvoo occupies the second volume of this carefully crafted history. Included are a balanced profile of Joseph Smith as man and prophet and a philosophical treatise of Mormon doctrine, which he labels a theology of "Eternalism." Roberts emphasized Nauvoo's potential for economic and population growth and praised the Saints' striving for truth and knowledge through doctrinal expansiveness and formal education. He lamented the city-state's failure through errors of judgment by Nauvoo's leaders, non-Mormon jealousies of Mormon power and prosperity, and the actions of traitors to the cause. Interested in candor but anxious to preserve Joseph Smith's role as prophet of the new dispensation, Roberts invited his readers to measure Smith, not by the strengths and weaknesses of his humanity, but by his work as a religious leader.

Roberts is also remembered for bringing the serialized "History of Joseph Smith" to a broader Utah audience. As edited for republication, the Nauvoo sequence of Joseph's "History" and the "Apostolic Interregnum" through early 1846 occupy more than four volumes of the *History of the Church of Jesus Christ of Latter-day Saints . . .*, 7 vols. (Salt Lake City: Deseret News Press, 1902-12, 1932). In introductions to each volume, Roberts discusses the major topics to be covered, providing a useful analysis of key points pertinent to any general Nauvoo history. The book preserves the memories of Old Nauvooers who witnessed the rise and fall of the City Beautiful, the transition in leadership from Joseph Smith to Brigham Young, the completion of the temple, and removal to the West. Dean C. Jessee, "The Writing of Joseph Smith's History," *BYU Studies* 11 (Summer 1971): 439-73; and "The Reliability of Joseph Smith's History," *Journal of Mormon History* 3 (1976): 23-46, describes the history's compilation in the 1840s-50s and its limitations as a primary source.

A Midwestern version of the "History" had appeared earlier, and with a different take on Nauvoo. The compilation, edited by the Reorganization's president and historian, Joseph Smith III and Heman C. Smith, *History of the Church of Jesus Christ of Latter Day Saints,* 4 vols. (Lamoni, IA: Herald Publishing House, 1897-1903), depicts Nauvoo as a place of ecclesiastical disorganization whose temple remained unfinished, as Brigham Young influenced doctrine, usurped authority, and led a small minority to Utah. Meanwhile, a faithful remnant followed the traditional paths of Joseph Smith's original church.

The new historians of Nauvoo have been more accepting of Roberts's intellectually rigorous work than the sentimental narrative of E. Cecil McGavin, *Nauvoo the Beautiful* (1946; reprint ed., Salt Lake City: Deseret Book, 1962). McGavin's topical history emphasized the suffering and personal tragedy of the Smith family, a strong thread in Lucy Mack Smith's narrative, *Biographical Sketches of Joseph Smith and His Progenitors for Many Generations* (Liverpool: S. W. Richards, 1853), reissued in a revised format as *History of the Prophet Joseph Smith by His Mother, as Revised by George A. Smith and Elias Smith* (Salt Lake City: Improvement Era, 1902). McGavin created emotionally powerful images of betrayal, persecution, martyrdom, exodus, expulsion, and the desolate city.

The impact of Joseph Smith's "History" was likewise evident in Joseph Fielding Smith, *Essentials in Church History* (Salt Lake City: Deseret News, 1922), written as an adult study manual, kept in print through its twenty-sixth edition (Salt Lake City: Deseret Book, 1973, and updated and republished by Deseret Book in 1979 in its CLASSICS IN MORMON LITERATURE series. William E. Berrett, *The Restored Church: A Brief History of the Growth and Doctrines of the Church of Jesus Christ of Latter-day Saints* (1936; 15th ed., rev. and enl., Salt Lake City: Deseret Book, 1973), was first prepared as a text for seminary students. For members of the Reorganization, the standard popular reference was a loose collection of articles by Inez Smith Davis, *Story of the Church: A History of the Church of Jesus Christ of Latter Day Saints, and of Its Legal Successor, the Reorganized Church* (Independence: Herald House, 1934), still in print as late as 1985.

It was against this historiographical background that Fawn McKay Brodie published her controversial work *No Man Knows My History: The Life of Joseph Smith* (1945; 2d ed. rev., New York: Alfred A. Knopf, 1971). This transitional study was widely accepted outside Mormon circles but generally rejected within the Church. Brodie's treatment of Nauvoo, occupying more than half of the biography's pages, resurrected many of the issues hammered by the older antagonistic works and refined by critical writers T. B. H. Stenhouse, *The Rocky Mountain Saints: A Full and Complete History of the Mormons . . .* (New York: D. Appleton and Co., 1873), James H. Kennedy, *Early Days of Mormonism: Palmyra, Kirtland, and Nauvoo* (New York: C. Scribner's Sons, 1888), and Linn's 1902 *Story of the Mormons*. In effect, Brodie turned B. H. Roberts's Nauvoo on its head. Where Roberts vindicated Joseph Smith as an authentic spiritual leader, Brodie defined him as a counterfeit and fraud who was motivated by greed, passion, and a hunger for power. Herself an insider turned unbelieving outsider, Brodie satisfied outsider needs for a history that lacked faith claims.

Perspectives on Nauvoo's History

Even though historians did not offer monographs centered on Nauvoo in the quarter century following the appearance of Flanders's work, they did contribute new ways of looking at topics pertinent to Nauvoo's history. Seeking a truce in the battles between faith and folly, some writers approached their subject with broad interpretive analyses of political, social, or intellectual themes. Others merely challenged traditional answers to factual questions. A few joined the discussion of how to write history. Local history and biography attracted others. Some applied scholarly models to the study of Mormonism's religious manifestations. Fourteen of the most cogent articles (most of them cited in the present essay from their original sources) have been collected for convenient access in Roger D. Launius and John E. Hallwas, eds., *Kingdom on the Mississippi Revisited: Nauvoo in Mormon History* (Urbana: University of Illinois Press, 1996).

Moses Rischin, "New Mormon History," *The American West* 6 (March 1969): 49, had lamented the parochial approach of Church history in all denominations and applauded O'Dea, Arrington, Flanders, William Mulder, P. A. M. Taylor, B. Carmon Hardy, Mario De Pillis, and Klaus Hansen for their "candor, depth and intellectual poise." As he put it, "A giant step from church history to religious and intellectual history seems in the offing." Another critique of traditional histories and suggestions on finding meaning in the past for contemporary readers is Paul M. Edwards, "The Irony of Mormon History," *Utah Historical Quarterly* 41 (Autumn 1973): 393-409. And for the most part, the new histories—books, theses, and articles—moved beyond the extremes of the earlier, polarized works. The spectrum narrowed by becoming less didactic, less polemic, and less controversial. While the old labels of "faithful" and "unfaithful" apply to some writing, many scholars sought moderation by avoiding naturalism and other secular overtones. Klaus Hansen, "Jan Shipps and the Mormon Tradition," " *Journal of Mormon History* 11 (1984): 135-37, pointed out that the middle-ground scholars have found balance by using a behavioralist approach that looks at Mormon history through the perspective of the participants, people who were believers in the religious experiences of the time. Jan Shipps, "The Mormon Past: Revealed or Revisited?" *Sunstone* 6 (November-December 1981): 55-57, and Thomas G. Alexander, "Historiography and the New Mormon History: A Historian's Perspective," *Dialogue* 19 (Fall 1986): 25-49, concur. These approaches dominated the writing of Nauvoo's new history in the 1970-90 period, after which a more partisan approach began to appear.

Even though the new historians of Nauvoo shared much in common, by the late 1980s it was apparent that significant differences in viewpoint persisted. Historians brought to their investigations varying interests, concerns, and assumptions. A useful measure of those distinctions appeared in four essays published in *Journal of Mormon History* 16 (1990). Richard P. Howard's examination of the "Nauvoo Heritage of the Reorganized Church," 41-52, summarized his Church's painful shift after 1965 from a denial of Nauvoo's real history to an acknowledgment of Joseph Smith's role in doctrinal innovations, plural marriage, and temple ordinances. Regional historian John E. Hallwas, "Mormon Nauvoo from a Non-Mormon Perspective," 53-69, echoed Robert Flanders in encouraging historians to place Nauvoo into the context of Jacksonian America. It was political history that best explained the Hancock County conflict for Hallwas—as a standoff between republican individualism and theocratic cooperativeness. Two Utah historians examined Nauvoo's meaning as religious fountainhead and magnet. In the tradition of B. H. Roberts, Ronald K. Esplin identified "The Significance of Nauvoo for Latter-day Saints," 71-88, as its temple-centered teachings and ordinances. In "Remembering Nauvoo: Historiographical Considerations," 25-40, I examined four ways of savoring Nauvoo's history—through reminiscences, in journalistic and travel writings,[2] with historic sites, and through interpretive writings.

Nauvoo in General Histories.

The traditional institutional texts that defined Nauvoo early in the twentieth century were supplanted in the late 1970s in Salt Lake City and early 1990s in Independence with New History syntheses. Among the general histories of Mormonism, James B. Allen and Glen M. Leonard, *The Story of the Latter-day Saints* (1976; 2d ed. rev., Salt Lake City: Deseret Book, 1992), chaps. 5-6, offered a balanced textbook treatment of Nauvoo written for an internal audience seeking the latest research. Another useful synopsis for institutional use is Paul Edwards, *Our Legacy of Faith: A Brief History of the Reorganized Church of Jesus Christ of Latter Day Saints* (Independence: Herald House, 1991), chap. 6-7, which included a new reading for the Community of Christ of plural marriage in Nauvoo. Addressing a national audience, Leonard J. Arrington and Davis Bitton discussed major themes topically in *The Mormon Experience: A History of the Latter-day Saints* (New York: Alfred A. Knopf, 1979). They made the rise and fall of Nauvoo—its strengths and weaknesses, triumphs and tragedies—their focus in chapters 4-5. . *Mormon Experience* found dissent a natural consequence of new revelation and Brigham Young's succession a pragmatic (and legitimate) solution to the vacuum of leadership. A contrasting topical approach is found in the two-volume treatment of the Reorganized Church by Richard P. Howard, *The Church through the Years,* 2 vols. (Independence: Herald House, 1992, 1993). The Nauvoo chapter in volume 1 gently acknowledged Joseph Smith's role in starting plural marriage, embracing militarism and a political agenda, and initiating esoteric rituals. Howard's negative view of Nauvoo describes a church undergoing a metamorphosis that diverted it from its original (Kirtland-era) purposes, an interpretation he again treats in "Themes in Latter Day Saint History," *John Whitmer Historical Association Journal* 2 (1982): 22-29. Dealing with the relation of history and identity are notable essays by W. Grant McMurray: "The Reorganization in Nineteenth-Century America: Identity Crisis or Historiographical Problem?" *John Whitmer Historical Association Journal* 2 (1982): 3-11; his "'As Historians and Not as Partisans': The Writing of Official History in the RLDS Church," *John Whitmer Historical Association Journal* 6 (1986): 43-52, and his "A 'Goodly Heritage' in a Time of Transformation: History and Identity in the Community of Christ," *Journal of Mormon History* 30, no. 1 (Spring 2004): 59-74. See also Danny L. Jorgensen, "Dissent and Schism in the Early Church: Explaining Mormon Fissiparousness," *Dialogue* 28 (Fall 1995): 15-39; and his "Studies of Mormon Fissiparousness: Conflict, Dissent, and Schism in the Early Church," in this volume.

Political History

The analysis of political ambition and goals, the excitement of elections, and the operations of governments—mainstays in much traditional history—has also dominated the histories written of nineteenth-century Mormonism. Klaus J. Hansen, "The Metamorphosis of the Kingdom of God: Toward a Reinterpretation of Mormon History," *Dialogue* 1 (Autumn 1966): 64 notes 1-2, lists key political studies completed during 1945-55. Nauvoo possessed the additional intrigue of politics mixed with religion and laced with

---

2. For a first analysis of visitors' and residents' descriptions, see William Mulder, "Nauvoo Observed," *BYU Studies* 32 (Winter/Spring 1992): 959-118.

conflict. Rather than emphasizing persecution, historians in recent decades have centered their discussions on political conflict, a theme explored in Robert Flanders, "Some Reflections on the New Mormon History," *Dialogue* 9 (Spring 1974): 37-39.

The exploration of causes and consequences of political opposition has attracted the attention of numerous students attracted by the tension, contention, and violence of the Nauvoo period. Building upon George R. Gayler, "The Mormons and Politics in Illinois, 1839-1844," *Journal of Illinois State Historical Society* 49 (Spring 1956): 48-66, recent students have broadened the scope conceptually and geographically. Robert B. Flanders, and Marvin S. Hill offered contrasting explanations for the conflict. Flanders, "The Kingdom of God in Illinois: Politics in Utopia," *Dialogue* 5 (Spring 1970): 26-36, found its genesis in the differences between Nauvoo's millennialist-oriented, theocratic approach to worldly issues and Hancock County's traditional Jacksonian political climate. Hill, "Religion in Nauvoo: Some Reflections," *Utah Historical Quarterly* 44 (Spring 1976): 170-80, countered with a socio-religious argument—that the kingdom of God served more as an answer to members' frustration with social disorder. The Saints, he said, were seeking refuge from this chaos rather than political power, and their neighbors misunderstood this religious motive. Drawing from neglected Midwestern sources, Annette P. Hampshire, *Mormonism in Conflict: The Nauvoo Years* (New York: Edwin Mellen Press, 1985), traced how extralegal violence was legitimized as state authority waned. Introducing a new factor into the discussion was Kenneth H. Winn, *Exiles in a Land of Liberty: Mormons in America, 1830-1846* (Chapel Hill: University of North Carolina Press, 1989), whose study of the rhetoric of "republicanism" in Jacksonian America found both Mormons and their opponents at odds over differing applications of shared republican values.

Readers can draw their own conclusions from ninety documents in John E. Hallwas and Roger D. Launius, *Cultures in Conflict: A Documentary History of the Mormon War in Illinois* (Logan: Utah State University Press, 1995). Even though the documents offer views from various perspectives, the editors bias the readings with their commentary, which is grounded in the 1840s non-Mormon view that the Latter-day Saints wrongly perceived themselves as persecuted innocents. The interpretive framework surrounding the documents in *Cultures in Conflict* triggered a disagreement among reviewers who both praised and criticized it, evidence of an increasing polarization in the writing of Mormon history. These appraisals include my review, *BYU Studies* 36 (1996-97): 235-40; Donald G. Godfrey, *Journal of Mormon History* 26 (Spring 2000): 227-29; and Elden J. Watson, "Cultural Conflicts: History Served on the Half Shell," *FARMS Review of Books* 12, no. 1 (2000): 355ff. Two other recent volumes that have drawn sharply divided reviews are Todd Compton, *In Sacred Loneliness: The Plural Wives of Joseph Smith* (Salt Lake City: Signature Books, 2000); and my *Nauvoo: A Place of Peace, and People of Promise* (Salt Lake City: Deseret Book/Provo, UT: BYU Press, 2002). Another important political document is Governor Thomas Ford's 1854 *A History of Illinois: From Its Commencement as a State in 1818 to 1847,* annotated and introduced by Rodney O. Davis (Urbana: University of Illinois Press, 1995).

While others have glanced beyond Nauvoo, it was not until late in the twentieth century that students offered sustained contextual examination for Nauvoo in its setting. An exemplary model for examining conflict in other Mormon clusterings in western Illinois is Susan Sessions Rugh, "Conflict in the Countryside: The Mormon Settlement at Macedonia, Illinois," *BYU Studies* 32 (Winter/Spring 1992): 149-74, and her *Our Common Country: Family Farming, Culture, and Community in the Nineteenth-Century Midwest* (Bloomington: University of Indiana Press, 2001). Another look within Hancock County is Marshall Hamilton, "'Money-Diggersville'—The Brief, Turbulent History of the Mormon Town of Warren," *John Whitmer Historical Association Journal* 9 (1989): 49-58, which explains how distrust and persecution ended Mormon expansionist plans in Illinois. Hopefully, examinations of outlying towns will continue.

Governor Ford acknowledged that lawlessness was a common problem along the Mississippi River frontier, but the issue for historians has been whether Nauvoo's citizens themselves sponsored illegal activities. Kenneth W. Godfrey demonstrated that Nauvoo

CULTURES IN CONFLICT

A DOCUMENTARY HISTORY OF THE MORMON WAR IN ILLINOIS

John E. Hallwas – Roger D. Launius

Utah State University Press
Logan, Utah
1995

was not a significant haven for counterfeiters and other criminals as claimed by critics in "Crime and Punishment in Mormon Nauvoo, 1839-1846," *BYU Studies* 32 (Winter/Spring 1992): 195-227. The subject continues to attract attention. Marshall Hamilton has explored attempts to arrest Joseph Smith, in "The People Versus the Prophet: Joseph Smith and the Criminal Law in Illinois," in John Whitmer Historical Association, *2002 Nauvoo Conference Special Edition* (Kansas City, MO, 2002), 121-27. William Shepard examined perceptions and realities before and after June 1844 in "Stealing at Mormon Nauvoo," *John Whitmer Historical Association Journal* 23 (2003): 91-110. The role of a non-Mormon county official during Nauvoo's troubling times is unfolded in Omer (Greg) W. Whitman and James L. Varner, Sheriff Jacob B. Backenstos: 'Defender of the Saints,'" *Journal of Mormon History* 29 (Spring 2003): 150-78.

The events surrounding the murders of Joseph Smith and Hyrum Smith in 1844 have attracted mostly Latter-day Saint writers striving to understand this pivotal event and to sort fact from folktale. The landmark reinterpretation of the plotting and trial by Dallin H. Oaks and Marvin Hill, *Carthage Conspiracy: The Trial of the Accused Assassins of Joseph Smith* (Chicago: University of Illinois Press, 1975), offered authoritative answers to questions that had remained unsettled since the publication of the problematic tract by William M. Daniels (pseud. of Lyman O. Littlefield), *A Correct Account of the Murder of Generals Joseph and Hyrum Smith at Carthage on the 27th Day of June, 1844* (Nauvoo: John Taylor, 1845). Oaks and Hill also resolved misconceptions popularized in N. B. Lundwall's compilation *Fate of the Persecutors of the Prophet Joseph Smith* (Salt Lake City: Bookcraft, 1952). Keith Huntress offered a more sympathetic rendering of Ford's role in "Governor Thomas Ford and the Murderers of Joseph Smith," *Dialogue* 4 (Summer 1969): 41-52. Yet more work is needed to sort out conflicting details surrounding the attack on the jail. Joseph L. Lyon and David W. Lyon have illuminatingly analyzed the forensic evidence about the attack on the jail in "Physical Evidence at the Carthage Jail," *Let the Artifacts Speak!*, edited by Glen M. Leonard (Provo, UT: BYU Press, forthcoming).

Other reexaminations explore how the story has been presented in histories, reminiscences, newspapers, and illustrations by both Mormon and non-Mormon authors, including, Dean C. Jessee, "Return to Carthage: Writing the History of Joseph Smith's Martyrdom," *Journal of Mormon History* 8 (1981): 3-19; Davis Bitton, *The Martyrdom Remembered: Reactions to the Assassination of the Prophet Joseph Smith* (Salt Lake City: Aspen Books, 1994); Kenneth W. Godfrey, "Non-Mormon Views of the Martyrdom: A Look at Some Early Published Accounts," *John Whitmer Historical Association Journal* 7 (1987): 12-20; Richard C. Poulsen, "Fate and the Persecutors of Joseph Smith: Transmutations of an American Myth," *Dialogue* 11 (Winter 1978): 63-70; Roger D. Launius, "Anti-Mormonism in Illinois: Thomas C. Sharp's Unfinished History of the Mormon War, 1845," *Journal of Mormon History* 15 (1985): 16-45; and Paul D. Ellsworth, "Mobocracy and the Rule of Law: American Press Reactions to the Murder of Joseph Smith," *BYU Studies* 20 (Fall 1979): 71-82.

Three newer studies look at details. Richard Van Wagoner and Steven C. Walker discuss "The Joseph/Hyrum Smith Funeral Sermons," *BYU Studies* 23 (Winter 1983); 3-18. Barbara Hands Bernauer, "Still 'Side by Side': The Final Burial of Joseph and Hyrum Smith," *John Whitmer Historical Association Journal* 11 (1991): 17-33, recalls the 1938 exhumation and reburial of the bodies. Shannon M. Tracy, *In Search of Joseph* (Orem, UT: KenningHouse, 1995), recreated the faces of Joseph and Hyrum through digital manipulation of visual and forensic information.

For the largely neglected period known as the "peaceful interlude" following the death of Joseph Smith, Marshall Hamilton offered a fresh view of the newspaper debates in "From Assassination to Expulsion: Two Years of Distrust, Hostility, and Violence," *BYU Studies* 32 (Winter/Spring 1992): 229-48. Future probes of those critical years should examine the political, economic, social, and religious aspects of the Quorum of the Twelve's interregnum leadership in Nauvoo. The final Battle of Nauvoo in September 1846 has likewise been neglected for what it tells of the relationship between the Mormon urbanites and their neighbors. Laying the groundwork for further study of both subjects is my *Nauvoo: A Place of Peace, A People of Promise,* chaps. 16-19; and responding to that base, Kenneth W. Godfrey has offered an expanded narrative in "The Battle of Nauvoo Revisited," *2002 [JWHA] Nauvoo Conference Special Edition,* 133-46.

The dramatic events of political conflict have dominated the stories of Nauvoo's government, but some work since 1965 has challenged traditional assumptions about the Nauvoo city charter and militia and added new details to knowledge of city and military management. Most notably, James L. Kimball Jr. qualified claims of the city charter's uniqueness with evidence of borrowings from other Illinois cities: "The Nauvoo Charter: A Reinterpretation," *Journal of the Illinois State Historical Society* 64 (Spring 1971): 66-78; and his "A Wall to Defend Zion: The Nauvoo Charter," *BYU Studies* 15 (Summer 1975): 401-97. In *Nauvoo: City of Joseph,* the Millers sampled city legislation to further illustrate Nauvoo's typicality. An excellent recent analysis is Richard E. Bennett and Rachel Cope, "'A City on a Hill': Chartering the City of Nauvoo," in *2002 [JWHA] Nauvoo Conference Special Edition,* 17-42. Offering a look into municipal government as a tool for self-protection is Arnold K. Garr, "Joseph Smith: Mayor of Nauvoo," *Mormon Historical Studies* 3 (Spring 2002): 29-46. On the Nauvoo Legion, Hamilton Gardner, "The Nauvoo Legion, 1840-1845: A Unique Military Organization," *Journal of the Illinois State Historical Society* 65 (Summer 1961): 181-97, found that the militia's large size was its only uniqueness—and a major factor behind the first settlers' distrust. John Lee Allaman, "Uniforms and Equipment of the Black Hawk War and the Mormon War," *Western Illinois Regional Studies* 13 (Spring 1990): 5-18; and Glen M. Leonard, "Picturing the Nauvoo Legion," *BYU Studies* 35, no. 2 (1995): 95-135, concur that the volunteer militia had origins and accouterments typical of the times.

Despite the work on Joseph Smith's perplexing run for the presidency done thirty years ago by Richard D. Poll, "Joseph Smith and the Presidency, 1844," *Dialogue* 3 (Autumn 1968): 17-21, the debate over Smith's intent and expectations persist. A recent summary of the story that also examines the authorship of *General Smith's Views* is Arnold K. Garr, "Joseph Smith: Candidate for President of the United States," in *Regional Studies in Latter-day Saint Church History: Illinois,* edited by H. Dean Garrett (Provo, UT: Department of Church History and Doctrine, Brigham Young University, 1995), 151-68. Margaret C. Robertson has examined "The Campaign and the Kingdom: The Activities of the Electioneers in Joseph Smith's Presidential Campaign," *BYU Studies* 39, no. 3 (2000): 147-80. Opinions on the meaning of the campaign appear in numerous general treatises on Nauvoo politics and await a definitive study. A thoughtful new analysis is Timothy L. Wood, "The Prophet and the Presidency: Mormonism and Politics in Joseph Smith's 1844 Presidential Campaign," *Journal of the Illinois State Historical Society* 93, no. 2 (Summer 2000): 167-93. And a discussion of the topic by five panelists was summarized by Newell G. Bringhurst, "Reflections on a Roundtable Colloquium Dealing with Joseph Smith's 1844 Campaign for U.S. President," in *2002 [JWHA] Nauvoo Conference Special Edition,* 153-58.

Rising above the traditional discussions of operational politics, Klaus J. Hansen offered a political interpretation of Mormon religious objectives in *Quest for Empire: The Political Kingdom of God and the Council of Fifty in Mormon History* (1967; rev. ed., Salt Lake City: Greg Kofford Books, forthcoming). Hansen's thesis that Nauvoo's Council of Fifty, organized as a preparatory step toward a millennial world government, was more important as a cause of conflict than polygamy has been accepted. But, as noted above, Marvin Hill and others have challenged the notion that Joseph Smith's motivation was political power. Also contributing to the discussion is D. Michael Quinn, who discusses theocracy in Nauvoo in *The Mormon Hierarchy: Origins of Power* (Salt Lake City: Signature Books, in association with Smith Research Associates, 1994), chap. 4. For another development to the story, see Matthew S. Moore, "'Joseph's Measures': The Continuation of Esoterica by Schismatic Members of the Council of Fifty," *Journal of Mormon History* 25 (Fall 1999): 70-100.

Economic History

Because *Nauvoo: Kingdom on the Mississippi* centered on the economic life of Nauvoo, historians have apparently assumed that the topic had been exhausted, except for

NAUVOO

A PLACE OF PEACE, A PEOPLE OF PROMISE

GLEN M. LEONARD

DESERET BOOK COMPANY
SALT LAKE CITY, UTAH
AND
BRIGHAM YOUNG UNIVERSITY PRESS
PROVO, UTAH

a handful of specialized articles, all published in *BYU Studies:* Dennis Rowley, "Nauvoo: A River Town," 18 (Winter 1978): 255-72; his "The Mormon Experience in the Wisconsin Pineries, 1841-1845," 32 (Winter/Spring 1992): 119-48; Donald L. Enders, "A Dam for Nauvoo: An Attempt to Industrialize the City," 18 (Winter 1978): 246-54; his "The Steamboat *Maid of Iowa*: Mormon Mistress of the Mississippi," 9 (Spring 1979): 321-35; and Dallin H. Oaks and Joseph I. Bentley, "Joseph Smith and Legal Process: In the Wake of the Steamboat *Nauvoo*," 19 (Winter 19979): 167-99.

Future river town studies will benefit from the context provided for Nauvoo by Robert P. Sutton's test of an economic thesis of urban growth, "Illinois River Towns: Economic Units or Melting Pots," *Western Illinois Regional Studies* 13 (Fall 1990): 21-31. However, most needed for understanding Nauvoo's economy are thorough inquiries into agriculture (land, crops, and livestock), the trades unions, the residential construction industry, and the job market in and beyond Nauvoo. Resources also exist for a better understanding of commerce, personal finance, and the role of the Church in Nauvoo's economy (including the land business and construction industry).

Social History

An intriguing question is the extent to which the Latter-day Saints were different from their neighbors. Social historians in recent decades have explored that issue both at the theoretical and practical levels. The most comprehensive interpretation, and one that recognizes the importance of religious beliefs, is Marvin S. Hill, *Quest for Refuge: The Mormon Flight from American Pluralism* (Salt Lake City: Signature Books, 1989), an alternative to Klaus Hansen's emphasis on the political kingdom in *Quest for Empire*. Hill suggests that, in their retreat from a world of political and theological pluralism, early Saints found a hope for salvation in Joseph Smith's promise of both secular and religious sanctuary in a theocratic community defined by equality and unity. At Nauvoo, according to Hill (chaps. 6-7), Smith's use of political means stirred opposition from people committed to individualism and pluralism. Another approach to this topic is Richard T. Hughes and C. Leonard Allen, "Soaring with the Gods: Early Mormons and the Eclipse of Religious Pluralism," in *Illusions of Innocence: Protestant Primitivism in America, 1630-1875,* edited by Richard T. Hughes (Chicago: University of Chicago Press, 1988), 133-52.

One of the popular recent approaches to American history has been to examine ordinary people doing ordinary things. (For example, see the "everyday life" series published by the University of Arkansas Press.) In 1984, Kenneth W. Godfrey responded to his own earlier call for a comprehensive social history with a preliminary look at occupations, trade associations, demographic patterns, disease and death, schools and libraries, recreation and entertainment, patterns of worship, clothing, food, home furnishings, civil marriages, city ordinances, and crime. Godfrey's outline of "The Nauvoo Neighborhood: A Little Philadelphia or a Unique City Set Upon a Hill," *Journal of Mormon History* 11 (1984): 78-97, found Nauvoo much like other American communities of the time. George W. Givens offered a large descriptive collection of social data confirming this view in *In Old Nauvoo: Everyday Life in the City of Joseph* (Salt Lake City: Deseret Book, 1990), but to date no one has tackled an "everyday life" interpretive history. Broader comparative studies, drawing from the sources identified by Godfrey and other, more recent examinations of the topics he identified, would likely confirm Godfrey's preliminary findings. (Also see Davis Bitton, "Mormon Society and Culture," in this volume.)

Also useful would be an examination of the interface between the ideal and the practical—a look at how religious beliefs and practices made a difference in the way Nauvoo's Saints viewed the mundane activities of ordinary life. Grant Underwood, "Re-visioning Mormon History," *Pacific Historical Review* 55 (August 1986): 403-26, proposed both a bottom-up study of Mormon society with an emphasis on continuity. Carol Cornwall Madsen, *In Their Own Words: Women and the Story of Nauvoo* (Salt Lake City: Deseret Book, 1994), offers glimpses into domestic and religious life. So do a fair number of primary sources edited for academic journals.

Leading the way in examining the influence of religious views on sickness and death is M. Guy Bishop, who has drawn three articles from his dissertation, "The Celestial Family: Early Mormon Thought on Life and Death, 1830-1846" (Ph.D. diss., Southern Illinois University, 1981). Another look at the topic is H. Dean Garrett, "Disease and Sickness in Nauvoo," in *Regional Studies in . . . Illinois,* 169-82.

Although Susan Easton Black offered a corrective with answers to the question "How Large Was the Population of Nauvoo?" *BYU Studies* 35 (1995): 91-94, little has been accomplished in understanding that population. James E. Smith's first, tentative demographic look, "Frontier Nauvoo: Building a Picture from Statistics," *Ensign* 9 (September 1979): 17-19, opened the door; but no one has followed with needed analyses of migration, population, marriage, family, and wealth. Beyond the social histories noted above, anecdotal data on family life during the Nauvoo years can be found in many biographies and family histories, plus personal letters and diaries, including such published diaries as Maureen Ursenbach [Beecher], "Eliza R. Snow's Nauvoo Journal," *BYU Studies* 15 (Summer 1975): 391-416; her "'All Things Move in Order in the City': The Nauvoo Diary of Zina Diantha Huntington Jacobs," *BYU Studies* 9 (Spring 1979): 285-320; Dean C. Jessee, ed., *John Taylor: Nauvoo Journal* (Provo, UT: Grandin Press, 1996); Eugene England, "George Laub's Nauvoo Journal," *BYU Studies* 18 (Winter 1978): 151-78; and Gregory R. Knight, "Journal of Thomas Bullock," *BYU Studies* 31 (Winter 1991): 15-75.

Community History

While political, economic, and social history remain for many historians valid avenues for communicating the meaning of Nauvoo's history to a broad audience, Charles S. Peterson, "Beyond the Problems of Exceptionalist History" in *Great Basin Kingdom Revisited: Contemporary Perspectives,* edited by Thomas G. Alexander (Logan: Utah State University Press, 1991), 133-51; and Gary Topping, "Reappraisal of a Classic [*Great Basin Kingdom*]," *Dialogue* 25 (Summer 1992): 165-66, have advocated a regional or national context for Mormon history (including, by inference, the Nauvoo period). Before 1965, college-trained Utah historians paid little attention to anything but the post-Nauvoo western phase of Mormon history. Out of this context came Arrington's *Great Basin Kingdom,* which Peterson and Topping cite as a successful example of their model for Mormon history. In thoughtful essays extolling the virtues of regional history, they have chided LDS historians for taking an insular approach, which, they suggest, severely limits the usefulness of Mormon studies for an outsider audience.

Because of geographical spread and chronological persistence, the Great Basin seems a better fit for regional Mormon history than the Upper Mississippi River Valley. If attempted for the Nauvoo period, a history placed into a broader geographical context would require familiarity with state history and community studies. Launius and Hallwas identify useful sources for such an approach in their 1996 bibliography in *Kingdom on the Mississippi Revisited,* 252-53, as does James E. Davis, *Frontier Illinois* (Bloomington: Indiana University Press, 1998). Twenty years ago, Don Harrison Doyle, *The Social Order of a Frontier Community: Jacksonville, Illinois, 1825-70* (Urbana: University of Illinois Press, 1978); and John Mack Faragher, *Sugar Creek: Life on the Illinois Prairie* (New Haven: Yale University Press, 1986), may have offered appropriate models for examining Nauvoo's past. But Mormonism attracted few demographers, and the number-crunching approach has received less emphasis by American historians in recent years. Traditional community history remains a possibility, an approach that intrigued T. Edgar Lyon in his early work on Nauvoo. Commendable examples today might include the holistic local history of a Southern community by Christopher Morris, *Becoming Southern: The Evolution of a Way of Life, Warren County and Vicksburg, Mississippi, 1770-1860* (New York: Oxford University Press, 1995), or the historical geographical approach to frontier Illinois by Douglas K. Meyer, *Making the Heartland Quilt: A Geographical History of Settlement and Migration in Early-Nineteenth-Century Illinois* (Carbondale: Southern Illinois University Press, 2000). Other excellent examples of local history are Robert A. Gross, *The Minutemen and Their World* [Concord, Mass.] (New

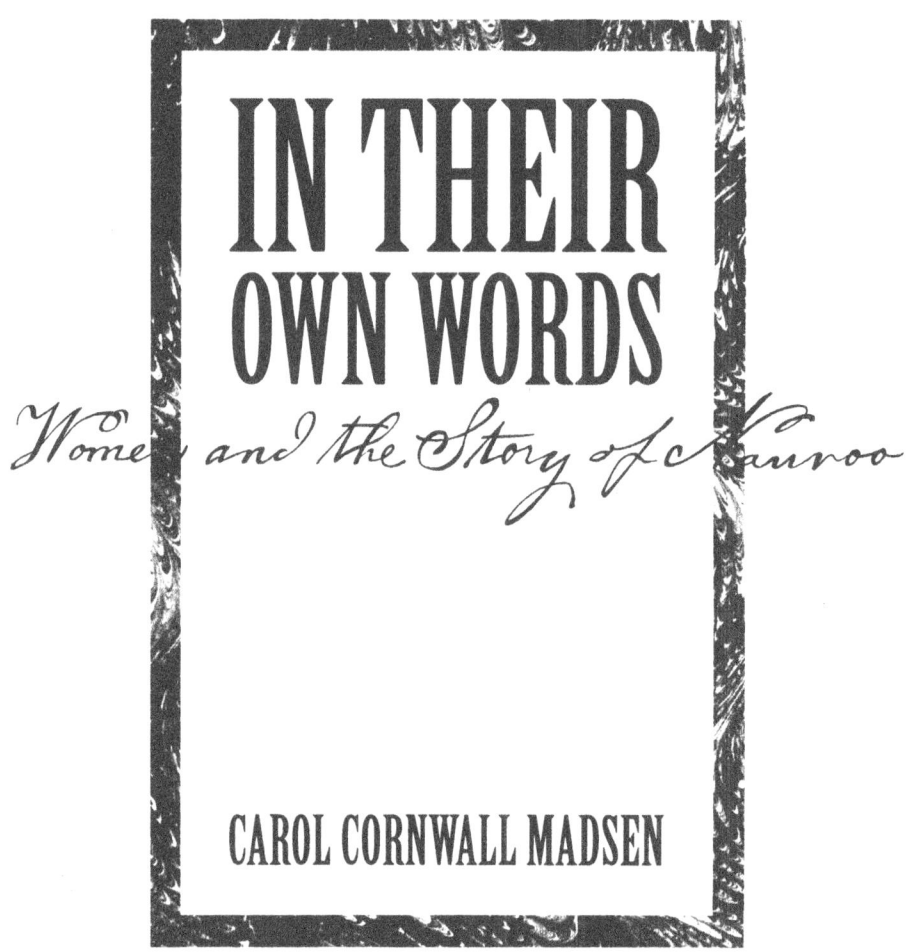

Deseret Book Company
Salt Lake City, Utah

York: Hill and Wang, 1976), and Paul E. Johnson, *A Shopkeeper's Millennium: Society and Revivals in Rochester, New York, 1815-1837* (New York: Hill and Wang, 1978). Also useful is the historical geography by James T. Lemon, *The Best Poor Man's Country: A Geographical Study of Early Southeastern Pennsylvania* (Baltimore, MD: Johns Hopkins University Press, 1972).

If the study of the Nauvoo period were enlarged geographically, Mormon settlements beyond Nauvoo would be an essential part of the equation. Donald Q. Cannon, "Mormon Satellite Settlements in Hancock County, Illinois, and Lee County, Iowa," in *The Iowa Mormon Trail: Legacy of Faith and Courage*, edited by Susan Easton Black and William G. Hartley (Orem, UT: Helix Publishing, 1997), 21-34; and Donald L. Enders, "Spokes on the Wheel: Latter-day Saint Settlements in Hancock County, Illinois, *Ensign*, February 1986, 62-68, follow-up Stanley B. Kimball, "Nauvoo West: The Mormons of the Iowa Shore," *BYU Studies* 18 (Winter 1978): 132-42; and his "The Saints and St. Louis, 1831-1857: An Oasis of Tolerance and Security," *BYU Studies* 13 (Summer 1973): 489-519.

A history of Nauvoo's Mormon Country would require historical probing into all of these settlements. Good beginnings are the case studies of Macedonia and Warren by Susan Sessions Rugh and Marshall Hamilton (in articles noted earlier), though both authors emphasized political conflict. Rugh has also examined the pre-Mormon setting in "Creating a Farm Community: Fountain Green Township, 1825-1840," *Western Illinois Regional Studies* 13 (Fall 1990): 5-20. Keith A. Erekson and Lloyd D. Newell examined a clustering closer to Chicago than to Nauvoo, in "'A Gathering Place for the Scandinavian People': Conversion, Retention, and Gathering in Norway, Illinois (1842-1849)," *Mormon Historical Studies* 1 (Summer 1999): 21-36. Another important town that figured in Nauvoo's history is celebrated in Susan Easton Black and Richard E. Bennett, eds., *A City of Refuge: Quincy, Illinois* (Salt Lake City: Millennial Press, 2000). While these works point to town histories, they are a necessary prelude. If more settlement stories were told with the right questions being answered, the Nauvoo period could then be examined in the context of midwestern development by some future regional historian.

For Church historians, the examination of Mormon communities within (and outside of) Nauvoo's sphere of influence might include administrative processes and personal interactions within smaller branches or groups of branches scattered around the United States and in Great Britain. Stanley B. Kimball offered glimpses in his report on "The Saints and St. Louis, 1831-1857: An Oasis of Tolerance and Security," *BYU Studies* 13 (Summer 1973): 489-519. Another step in this direction is David L. Clark, "The Mormons of the Wisconsin Territory: 1835-1848," *BYU Studies* 37, no. 2 (1997-98): 57-85. The byproduct of multiple congregational studies might be a broadened understanding of Mormon ecclesiastical history during the Nauvoo years, including the role of the presiding elder as pastor over the flock.

Religious History

For more than a century, historians have acknowledged the need to consider religious belief and behavior to understand Mormon history. Approaches to the question varied, depending on the author's position along the spectrum of belief. In the nineteenth century, defenders of the faith and critics of Mormonism battled over the issue of the ultimate truth of Joseph Smith's experiences. Forms of this polemic approach survive today, but practitioners of the New Mormon History seek a middle ground. Muting their desire to defend or to challenge the faith, they strive from their differing perspectives to understand, as articulated in Roger D. Launius, "Whither Reorganization Historiography?" *John Whitmer Historical Association Journal* 19 (1990): 24-38.

In 1966, Mario S. De Pillis set the stage for a conversation between Mormon historians and secular historians with his path-breaking "The Quest for Religious Authority and the Rise of Mormonism," *Dialogue* 1 (Summer 1966): 68-88. De Pillis pointed out the centrality for early Latter-day Saints of the search "for the religious authority of one true church, i.e., for divine authority"—found in priesthood and revelations. This same issue of *Dialogue* included a "Roundtable" discussion of De Pillis's article by Richard L. Bushman and William A. Clebsch, with a response by De Pillis (89-97). Richard L. Bushman, "The Historians and Mormon Nauvoo," *Dialogue* 5 (Spring 1970): 51-61, invited historians within the faith to write Mormon history as a quest for salvation and specifically challenged historians of Nauvoo to move from merely describing religion within a framework of social conflict to an inclusion of its spiritual dimensions. Marvin S. Hill, "Mormon Religion in Nauvoo," (cited earlier) suggested that "everything that occurred at Nauvoo of a social or political nature was to the Saints essentially religious" (174). The implications of his holistic approach would be to include the so-called "secular" activities as integral parts of the all-encompassing community of faith. Though Robert Flanders did not explore religious meaning in *Nauvoo: Kingdom on the Mississippi,* in "Dream and Nightmare," he later acknowledged that "the only way to understand religious life in Nauvoo is to understand that religion *was* life" (157). Furthermore, he said, the true meaning of Mormon Nauvoo was found in the temple—"a building to link heaven and earth" (159).

In recent years, historians trained in the discipline of religious studies have considered the spiritual aspects of Mormon history. These writers have found inspiration in such works as H. Richard Neibuhr, *The Kingdom of God in America* (New York: Harper & Row, 1937); John G. Gager, *Kingdom and Community: The Social World of Early Christianity* (Englewood Cliffs, N.J.: Prentice-Hall, 1975); Mircea Eliade, *The Quest: History and Meaning in Religion* (Chicago: University of Chicago Press, 1975); Eliade, *Cosmos and History: The Myth of the Eternal Return,* translated by William R. Trask (New York: Harper, 1959); and Eliade, *The Sacred and the Profane: The Nature of Religion,* translated by William R. Trask (New York: Harcourt, Brace & World, 1959). Some practitioners of New Mormon History have sought to weave both theological ideas and religious practices into their explanations of Mormon history, a possibility perceptively discussed by Edwin S. Gaustad, "Historical Theology and Theological History: Mormon Possibility," *Journal of Mormon History* 11 (1984): 99-111.

The new religious historians revived interest in an old view that positioned Mormonism apart from both Catholic and Protestant forms of Christianity. H. H. Bancroft, *History of Utah, 1540-1886* (San Francisco: History Company, 1889), x-xi, said of Utah's religious community, "Theirs was not an old faith, . . . but professedly a new revelation, . . . a new religion, with all its attendant trials and persecutions." In chapters 6-8, he told the Nauvoo story with a perspective that allowed unbelievers to set aside the polemical definition of Mormonism as fraud. Instead, investigators could examine the experiences of the believers and the process by which a new religious tradition emerged. Endorsing this approach were such twentieth-century outsiders as O'Dea, *The Mormons;* De Pillis, "The Quest for Religious Authority and the Rise of Mormonism"; and Jan Shipps, *Mormonism: The Story of a New Religious Tradition* (Urbana: University of Illinois Press, 1985). Klaus J. Hansen, "Jan Shipps and the Mormon Tradition," 144-45, noted that Fawn Brodie, who depicted Mormonism as delusion, used the idea of a new religion as well; but unlike the unbelievers, truth questions did matter for her. O'Dea consulted both Frederick Jackson Turner, *The Significance of the Frontier* (1893) on the character-molding influence of the frontier and Whitney R. Cross, *The Burned-Over District: The Social and Intellectual History of Enthusiastic Religion in Western New York, 1800-1850* (Ithaca, NY: Cornell University Press, 1950), in constructing an explanation for the emergence of Mormonism. The new explanation of Mormonism as born in the social chaos of post-Puritan America impact Nauvoo history, for it was in the 1840s that Joseph Smith implemented the penultimate stage of his religious restoration. Geoffrey F. Spencer, "Anxious Saints: The Early Mormons, Social Reform, and Status Anxiety," *John Whitmer Historical Association Journal* 1 (1981): 43-53, follows this sociological approach.

Two challenges to the idea that Mormonism originated as a response to social stress in New England and upstate New York have spawned much recent discussion. Harold Bloom tethered the new faith in Gnosticism in *The American Religion: The Emergence of the Post-Christian Nation* (New York: Simon & Schuster, 1992), while John L. Brooke, *The Refiner's Fire: The Making of Mormon Cosmology, 1644-1844* (New York: Cambridge University Press, 1994), found its intellectual roots in the hermeticism of Radical Reformation. It was in Nauvoo, these interpreters posit, that Joseph Smith unfolded the ultimate Mormon expression of Gnostic and hermetic ideas by merging restorationism with Gnostic thought (Bloom) or with hermetic perfectionism (Brooke).

Despite similarities in overall structure with other interpretive histories, the central premises set forth by Bloom and Brooke have been rejected by mainstream Mormon historians as uncharacteristic of historical Mormonism. Similarly, American historians of religion have viewed Bloom's work as idiosyncratic and have been puzzled at his neglect of mainline churches.[3] (See Klaus J. Hansen, "Mormon History and the Conundrum of Culture: American and Beyond," in this volume.) Despite these challenging new explanations, as the twentieth century opened, the search to understand the "new religion" remained centered in American socio-religious history. Supporting that approach is Rex Eugene Cooper, *Promises Made to the Fathers: Mormon Covenant Organization* (Salt Lake City: University of Utah, 1990), which uses anthropological and sociological concepts to demonstrate that the Saints developed a group identity for their united religious community against the backdrop of Puritan New England.

Whatever the attraction of other approaches for presenting Nauvoo's history to an academic, general, or national audience, many writers have continued their focus on Church history, written for informed Church members and founded on a presumption of faith. In the past, those intent on writing faithful history (i.e., "church history" with a revelatory perspective) have followed the lead of B. H. Roberts. For example, in a challenge to Bancroft's thesis, Roberts argued that Mormonism was not so much a new religion as a new dispensation, a restoration of original Christianity.[4] Richard L. Bushman, "Faithful History," *Dialogue* 4 (Winter 1969): 11-25, has noted that, in the past, some of these faithful historians have pitted the Church against the world, while others have described Mormonism as a restoration of original Christianity. Some who see God's hand in history have proposed a scriptural pattern to define the history of a chosen people. Perhaps some future historians will respond to Bushman's call for a faithful history couched in an interpretive language of souls seeking for salvation within a community of peace and union. For a perceptive analysis of Bushman's faithful approach to history in *Joseph Smith and the Beginnings of Mormonism* (Urbana: University of Illinois Press, 1984), see Marvin Hill, "Richard L. Bushman—Scholar and Apologist," *Journal of Mormon History* 11 (1984): 125-33. Challenging advocates of the scriptural pattern is Eric Olson, "The 'Perfect Pattern': The Book of Mormon as a Model for the Writing of Sacred History," *BYU Studies* 31 (Spring 1991): 5-18. For discussions of denominational history generally, see Henry Warner Bowden, "Ends and Means in Church History," *Church History* 54 (March 1985): 74-88; and Sydney E. Ahlstrom, "The Problem of the History of Religion in America," *Church History* 57 (1988 Supplement): 127-28.

Thus far, much of the internal writing has continued its providential or restorationist approach. As such it serves an expanding Latter-day Saint audience who seeks engaging denominational history. In addition to the themes attractive to the scholarly disciplines listed earlier, the Nauvoo depicted by Church historians has followed and will likely continue with traditional subjects: the gathering of the Saints, the unfolding of doctrines, the construction and uses of the temple, the development of Church government, the question of presidential succession, and the dispersion from Nauvoo.

---

3. Bloom is critiqued by Richard Dilworth Rust, *Journal of Mormon History* 19 (Fall 1993): 144-47; Eugene England, Truman G. Madsen, Charles Randall Paul, and Richard F. Haglund, "Four LDS Views on Harold Bloom: A Roundtable," *BYU Studies* 35 (1995): 173-204; Clare D. Vlahos, *John Whitmer Historical Association Journal* 13 (1993): 105-10; and Martin E. Marty, "All Gnostics Here," *Christian Century* 109 (May 20-27, 1992): 545-48. A useful comparison of Gnostic and Mormon belief is Bertrand C. Barrois, "Gnosticism Reformed," *Dialogue* 27 (Spring 1994): 238-52. See reviews of Brooke by William J. Hamblin, Daniel C. Peterson, George L. Mitton, and Davis Bitton in *BYU Studies* 34, no. 4 (1994-95): 167-92; and by Paul M. Edwards and Philip Barlow, *John Whitmer Historical Association Journal* 16 (1996): 120-30. More favorable toward Brooke are Lance S. Owens, *Dialogue* 27 (Winter 1994): 187-91; and Stephen J. Stein, *Journal of Mormon History* 22 (Fall 1996): 169-72.

4. For comments on this point, see Brooke, *Refiner's Fire*, 279; Shipps, *Mormonism*, chap. 5; and Hansen, "Shipps and the Mormon Tradition," 142-43.

Excavating Mormon Pasts

A necessary component of future understandings of religious practices during the Nauvoo period will be missionary efforts such as those explored in James B. Allen, Ronald K. Esplin, and David J. Whittaker, *Men with a Mission, 1837-1841: The Quorum of the Twelve Apostles in the British Isles* (Salt Lake City: Deseret Book, 1992). Similar histories are needed for less prominent missions and less prominent missionaries. Many of the archived Nauvoo-period diaries record missionary journeys. These sources offer insights into methods, messages, and the experiences of the messengers. Ronald W. Walker, "Seeking the 'Remnant': The Native American during the Joseph Smith Period," *Journal of Mormon History* 19 (Spring 1992): 1-33, examines an important relationship with missionizing implications.

The story of ocean crossings prompted by the spirit of the gathering to an American Zion continues to attract researchers. Fred E. Woods used eyewitness narratives to create an inspirational story of faithful immigrants, in *Gathering to Nauvoo* (American Fork, UT: Covenant Communications, 2002). Richard L. Jensen, "Transplanted to Zion: The Impact of British Latter-day Saint Immigration upon Nauvoo," *BYU Studies* 31 (Winter 1991): 77-87, lays the groundwork and invites further study of the quarter of Nauvoo's population that was British. Kinship and friendship networks could also be explored for clusterings of Nauvoo immigrants from the upper South, the mid-Atlantic region (especially Pennsylvania), and New England. A nondenominational, comparative approach is advocated in Jay P. Dolan, "The Immigrants and Their Gods: A New Perspective in American Religious History," *Church History* 56 (March 1987): 61-72.

One of the most significant influences on the development of Mormonism was Joseph Smith's introduction of new doctrinal insights during the Nauvoo years. (For a fuller exposition, see David L. Paulsen, "The Search for Cultural Origins of Mormon Doctrine," in this volume.) For specialists in Church history, the article by Larry C. Porter and Milton V. Backman Jr., "Doctrine and the Temple in Nauvoo," *BYU Studies* 32 (Winter/Spring 1992): 41-56, offered the first look at this topic since T. Edgar Lyon's overview eighteen years earlier: "Doctrinal Development of the Church during the Nauvoo Sojourn, 1839-1846," *BYU Studies* 15 (Summer 1975): 435-46. Lyon centered his discussion on free agency, society, and eternal progression. Porter and Backman elaborate on teachings related to temple ordinances, including premortal life, the materiality of the spirit, the nature of God, and the plurality of gods. Larry E. Dahl, "Doctrinal Teachings in Nauvoo: A Two-edged Sword," in *Regional Studies . . . . : Illinois,* 125-38, uses Nauvoo examples to show that doctrine can separate the faithful from the unfaithful. The famous sermon delivered at King Follett's funeral has received significant attention because of its importance to temple theology and doctrines of deity. Articles in *BYU Studies* 18 (Winter 1978) by Donald Q. Cannon, "The King Follett Discourse: Joseph Smith's Greatest Sermon in Historical Perspective,"178-92; Stan Larson, "The King Follett Discourse: A Newly Amalgamated Text," 193-208, and Van Hale, "The Doctrinal Impact of the King Follett Discourse," 209-25, establish the benchmark for Follett studies. More recently Jacob Neusner explored the sermon from a Jewish perspective in "Conversation in Nauvoo about the Corporeality of God," *BYU Studies* 36, no. 1 (1996-97): 7-30. Andrew F. Ehat and Lyndon W. Cook, comps. and eds., *The Words of Joseph Smith: The Contemporary Accounts of the Nauvoo Discourses of the Prophet Joseph* (Provo, UT: Religious Studies Center, Brigham Young University, 1980), offers much potential for understanding the religious mind of Joseph Smith and the doctrinal world of Nauvoo's religious community. A general study of preaching during the Nauvoo years is one intriguing possibility. An exemplary study is Harry S. Stout, *The New England Soul: Preaching and Religious Culture in Colonial New England* (New York: Oxford University Press, 1986).

The story of the Nauvoo Temple's construction was introduced early by Stanley B. Kimball, "The Nauvoo Temple," *Improvement Era* 66 (November 1963): 974-84, and Joseph Earl Arrington, "William Weeks: Architect of the Nauvoo Temple," *BYU Studies* 19 (Spring 1979): 337-59; and his "Destruction of the Mormon Temple at Nauvoo," *Journal of the Illinois State Historical Society* 40 (December 1947): 414-25. Adding details more recently are Dennis Rowley, "The Mormon Experience in the Wisconsin Pineries, 1841-1845," *BYU*

Studies 32 (Winter/Spring 1992): 199-48; and Richard O. Cowan, "The Pivotal Nauvoo Temple," in *Regional Studies . . . : Illinois,* 113-23. The need for a thorough history of the temple has recently been filled by Don F. Colvin, who reworked and expanded his 1962 master's thesis for publication as *Nauvoo Temple: A Story of Faith* (American Fork, UT: Covenant Communications, 2002).

Recent looks at neglected details include David R. Crockett, "The Nauvoo Temple: 'A Monument of the Saints,'" *Nauvoo Journal* 11 (Fall 1999): 5-30; Lisle G. Brown, "'A Perfect Estopel': Selling the Nauvoo Temple," *Mormon Historical Studies* 3 (Spring 2002): 61-86; his "Nauvoo's Temple Square [1841-1999]," *BYU Studies* 41, no. 4 (2002): 4-45; and Jill C. Major, "Artworks in the Celestial Room of the First Nauvoo Temple," *BYU Studies* 41, no. 2 (2002): 47-69, which includes full-color illustrations.

To help tourists find historic places in the Nauvoo area, Richard N. Holzapfel and T. Jeffery Cottle published a guide for the Nauvoo Sesquicentennial, *Old Mormon Nauvoo, 1839-1846: Historic Photographs and Guide* (Provo, UT: Grandin Book, 1990). More thoroughly researched building and site histories are found in LaMar C. Berrett, general editor, *Sacred Places: A Comprehensive Guide to Early LDS Historical Sites,* 6 vols. (Salt Lake City: Deseret Book, 1999-), Vol. 3, *Ohio and Illinois* (2002), by Berrett, Keith W. Perkins, and Donald Q. Cannon. A handsome souvenir book is Susan Easton Black and Kim C. Averett, *Nauvoo* (Salt Lake City: Deseret Book, 1997), which includes colored photographs of the city's restored buildings (exterior and interiors) by John Telford. The reconstructed Nauvoo Temple greatly boosted tourism and encouraged such publications as Becky Cardon Smith, *The LDS Family Travel Guide: Independence to Nauvoo* (Orem, UT: LDS Family Travels, 2001); George Givens and Sylvia Givens, *Nauvoo Fact Book: Questions and Answers for Nauvoo Enthusiasts* (Lynchburg, VA: Parley Street Publishers, 2000), which offers a chronology and answers 569 questions, but is flawed by many inaccuracies; John Telford, *Nauvoo: The City Beautiful* (Salt Lake City: Eagle Gate, 2002), includes many photographs not used in the earlier book, including shots of the rebuilt temple; and Heidi S. Swinton, *Sacred Stone: The Temple at Nauvoo* (American Fork, UT: Covenant Communications, 2002). She wrote the Lee Groberg documentary film of the same name to tell the stories of the original temple and its modern replacement, with personal reflections of the people involved. A useful short history of Nauvoo that grew out of the Brigham Young University Semester Program in Nauvoo is Milton V. Backman Jr., *People and Power of Nauvoo: Themes from the Nauvoo Experience* (Salt Lake City: Greg Kofford Books, 2002).

Temple ordinances have been treated only peripherally in most general histories. Three specific probes are M. Guy Bishop, "'What Has Become of Our Fathers?': Baptism for the Dead at Nauvoo," *Dialogue* 23 (Summer 1990): 84-98; Lisle G. Brown, "The Sacred Departments for Temple Work in Nauvoo: The Assembly Room and the Council Chamber," *BYU Studies* 19 (Spring 1979): 361-74; and Alexander L. Baugh, "'For This Ordinance Belongeth to My House': The Practice of Baptism for the Dead Outside the Nauvoo Temple," *Mormon Historical Studies* 3 (Spring 2002): 47-58. Broader in chronological coverage but detailed for the Nauvoo period as well is David John Buerger, "The Development of the Mormon Temple Endowment Ceremony," *Dialogue* 20 (Winter 1987): 33-76; and his *The Mysteries of Godliness: A History of Mormon Temple Worship* (San Francisco: Smith Research Associates, 1994). A more detailed and comparative study is Michael W. Homer, "'Similarity of Priesthood in Masonry,': The Relationship between Freemasonry and Mormonism," *Dialogue* 27 (Fall 1994): 1-116. The administration of temple ordinances before the Prophet's death is discussed in Devery S. Anderson, "The Anointed Quorum in Nauvoo, 1842-45," *Journal of Mormon History* 29 (Fall 2003): 137-57. Some aspects of temple marriage are also discussed in descriptions of early polygamy. (See Martha Sonntag Bradley, "Our of the Closet and into the Fire: The New Mormon Historians' Take on Polygamy," in this volume).

Studies of ecclesiastical development have been part of the widening interest in Nauvoo's history. The women's Relief Society had its beginning in Nauvoo, as did the ward as an administrative unit. These changes involved Joseph Smith. In addition, as president

PEOPLE AND POWER OF NAUVOO: THEMES FROM THE NAUVOO EXPERIENCE

BY

MILTON V. BACKMAN, JR.

Greg Kofford Books
Salt Lake City 2002

of the Quorum of the Twelve Apostles, Brigham Young built upon existing precedent to expand and alter the roles of his own and other Melchizedek Priesthood quorums. All of these Nauvoo topics have been explored in recent years as part of broader inquiries. (See also Todd Compton, "The New Mormon Women's History," in this volume.) Relief Society received attention from Jill Mulvay Derr, Janath Russell Cannon, and Maureen Ursenbach Beecher, *Women of Covenant: The Story of Relief Society* (Salt Lake City: Deseret Book, 1992). William G. Hartley explored the "Nauvoo Stake, Priesthood Quorums, and the Church's First Wards," *BYU Studies* 32 (Winter-Spring 1992): 57-80; and D. Michael Quinn examined the development of a hierarchical Church government, the political Kingdom of God, and a ministerial theocracy in Nauvoo, in *Mormon Hierarchy: Origins of Power*, chaps. 1-4. These examinations of Church organizations and how they functioned at Nauvoo do not exhaust the options. Among possibilities for further work are studies of the priesthood quorums and ecclesiastical organization outside of Nauvoo during the early 1840s.

The process by which Brigham Young and the Twelve won majority acceptance in Nauvoo as Joseph Smith's successors has brought forth contrasting interpretations. Michael Quinn has challenged the traditional view of its inevitability in *Mormon Hierarchy: Origins of Power*, chaps. 5-7. Defending the traditional perspective is Ronald K. Esplin, "Joseph, Brigham, and the Twelve: A Succession of Continuity," *BYU Studies* 21 (Summer 1980): 300-310. Two articles examine an episode in the transfer of power: Reid L. Harper, "The Mantle of Joseph: Creation of Mormon Miracle," *Journal of Mormon History* 22 (Fall 1996): 35-71; and Lynne Watkins Jorgensen and *BYU Studies* staff, "The Mantle of the Prophet Joseph Passes to Brother Brigham: A Collective Spiritual Witness," *BYU Studies* 36, no. 4 (1996-97): 125-204. In addition, E. Gary Smith has explored succession in the patriarchal office, in "The Patriarchal Crisis of 1845," *Dialogue* 16 (Summer 1983): 24-35. The story of Joseph Smith III's gradual acceptance of his role as Joseph the Martyr's ecclesiastical heir in the Community of Christ has been examined in W. Grant McMurray, "'True Son of a True Father': Joseph Smith III and the Succession Question," *Restoration Studies* 1 (1980): 131-45; and Roger D. Launius, "Joseph Smith III and the Mormon Succession Crisis, 1844-46," *Western Illinois Regional Studies* 6 (1983): 5-22; and his *Joseph Smith III: Pragmatic Prophet* (Urbana: University of Illinois Press, 1988).

A New Synthesis

When T. Edgar Lyon began working on a history of the Nauvoo period in 1972, Mormon historical approaches favored a traditional narrative form. Like his contemporaries—especially David Miller—Lyon was steeped in the history of the American West. In addition, his work with Nauvoo Restoration Incorporated gave Lyon a strong sense of Nauvoo as place. His chapter outlines read like a town history, or, perhaps more appropriately, a headquarters history of the Church. When I inherited the project during Lyon's final illness, I used his structure as a skeleton, overlaid with new "flesh" to create a new synthesis that incorporated traditional themes—politics, government, economy, and conflict—with healthy doses of social, community, religious, and Church history. Written for a Utah Mormon audience, my *Nauvoo: A Place of Peace, A People of Promise*, presented thematic and narrative stories set in the context of unfolding revelation and the attempts made by the early Latter-day Saints to understand and accept (or reject) Joseph Smith's expanding vision of the meaning of the Restoration.

While this book was awarded prizes by both the Mormon History Association and the John Whitmer Historical Association, individual historians differed significantly in their assessments of its depiction of the newest Nauvoo. Writers within the Utah Mormon perspective found a "friendly history," "readable and engaging," offering both a "religious history" and "much more." Reviews include Gary James Bergera, *Dialogue* 35 (Fall 2002): 239-42; Audrey M. Godfrey, in *Utah Historical Quarterly* 71 (Summer 2003): 268-69; Dennis Lythgoe, *Deseret News*, June 16, 2002, E1, E3, E4; and Alma R. Blair, *Journal of Mormon History* 30, no. 1 (Spring 2004): 213-19. Those immersed in a Missouri Mormon faith rejected its challenge to the interpretive framework articulated by Midwestern historians.

Excavating Mormon Pasts

The RLDS Church's rejection of Nauvoo is described in Howard, *The Church through the Years,* 1:273-302; his "The Nauvoo Heritage of the Reorganized Church," *Journal of Mormon History* 16 (1990): 41-52; and Hallwas and Launius, eds., *Cultures in Conflict: A Documentary History of the Mormon War in Illinois,* 1-11. Reviews include Launius, "The Nauvoo of the Imaginations: A Book Review Essay," *John Whitmer Historical Association Journal,* 23 (2003): 165-78; and William D. Russell, comments, panel discussion, Sunstone Symposium, Salt Lake City, August 8, 2002, audiocassette SL02-132. Bryon C. Andreasen, a historian at the Abraham Lincoln Presidential Library, reviewed it in *Mormon Historical Studies* 3, no. 1 (2002): 263-72, as a reading of a people of faith on the Illinois frontier, weighed the strengths and weaknesses of Leonard's approach, and compared the book with Flanders's.

These divergent views reflect an increasing distancing of the two churches from each other and an ongoing attempt within each tradition to redefine their differing visions of the past, an awareness discussed earlier in Douglas D. Alder and Paul M. Edwards, "Common Beginnings, Divergent Beliefs," *Dialogue* 11 (Spring 1978): 18-28. Mark A. Scherer, present Community of Christ Historian, "'Answering Questions No Longer Asked': Nauvoo, Its Meaning and Interpretation in the RLDS/Community of Christ Church," *2002 [JWHA] Nauvoo Conference Special Edition,* 73-77; and an earlier version of the paper in *Sunstone,* July 2002, 28-32, summarizes his body's abandonment of its historical roots—motivated in large part by a long-standing rejection of the Nauvoo experience. Jan Shipps, "How Mormon Is the Community of Christ," *2002 [JWHA] Nauvoo Conference Special Edition,* 195-204, with a response by William D. Russell, 205-6, has offered an alternative interpretation—namely, that the Community of Christ has turned to its roots to reenergize a Church struggling to accept change, just as the Utah Mormons did in the early twentieth century..

As the listings in this essay suggest, attempts to define the religious aspects of the original Church of Jesus Christ of Latter-day Saints play a crucial role in today's approach to Mormon history generally, and, in my view, are especially important for understanding the critical Nauvoo years. Because historians necessarily write from different perspectives, it is not reasonable to expect consensus. Readers frustrated by this healthy reality may take consolation in knowing that they are not alone. The historiographical choices between a "new" elaboration of religion on the one hand and a return or revival of an original, "old" religion on the other, is not unique to Mormonism. Edwin Gaustad, "Historical Theology and Theological History," 104-5, told a Mormon History Association audience in 1984 that all of the religions with American beginnings face the same question in understanding their own histories, a point also explored by Martin E. Marty, "Two Integrities: An Address to the Crisis in Mormon Historiography," *Journal of Mormon History* 10 (1983): 3-19; and Lewis W. Spitz, "History: Sacred and Secular," *Church History* 47 (March 1978): 11-22. Those writing about Nauvoo from the perspectives of political/social/economic history, regional history, religious studies, or traditional Church history, will no doubt continue to mine myriad topics in an unending attempt to comprehend the Nauvoo experience for a variety of audiences.[5]

GLEN M. LEONARD is director of the LDS Museum of Church History and Art in Salt Lake City. With James B. Allen, he coauthored the widely used *The Story of the Latter-day Saints* (1976; 2d. ed. rev. and enl. Salt Lake City: Deseret Book, 1992). A leading authority on the Nauvoo Mormon experience, he has authored a number of scholarly articles and *Nauvoo: A Place of Peace, A People of Promise* (Salt Lake City: Deseret Book; Provo, UT: BYU Press, 2002). He is currently collaborating with coauthors Richard E. Turley Jr. and Ronald W. Walker on a history of the Mountain Meadows Massacre.

---

5. Mormon historians may benefit from essays exploring four approaches to religious history in Harry S. Stout and Darryl G. Hart, *New Directions in American Religious History* (New York: Oxford University Press, 1997), namely, places and regions, universal themes, transformative events, and marginal groups and ethnocultural outsiders.

Chapter 6

Mormonism on the Frontier: The Saints of the Great Basin

Craig L. Foster

The time-period between the Mormon emigration from Nauvoo to the Great Basin and the subsequent colonization of Utah and surrounding states is a long and complex one. This is a period which can be described as a "heroic period" in Mormon history because of the intense suffering and sacrifice of the Mormon migration and the subsequent kingdom-building which occurred in the early years of the Utah territory.

Many of the early works concerning the Church in territorial Utah, while full of detailed information, have lacked impartiality and professional analysis.[1] Often polemical in nature, the works generally focused on Mormon triumphs and generally ignored failures. Because of the "us versus them" approach in the majority of these works, the lack of scholarly analysis and impartiality was inevitable.

In sharp contrast to the earlier works was Leonard J. Arrington, *Great Basin Kingdom: An Economic History of the Latter-day Saints: 1830-1900* (Cambridge, MA: Harvard University Press, 1958). Arrington's book, which strove for objectivity and approached the Mormon experience from a complex socioeconomic model, subjected this period to painstaking analysis. While the eventual professionalization of Mormon historiography was inevitable, Arrington's foundational work acted as a catalyst for what eventually became known as the New Mormon History. Arrington's example has encouraged other scholars to approach practically every aspect of Mormon and Utah history as it has related to the Latter-day Saints.

Complex and sometimes uncomfortable issues, such as Mormon economics, political domination, race relations, plural marriage, doctrinal development, and conflicts with the federal government have been tackled and discussed to the enjoyment of some readers and the discomfort of others. While these various historiographical works have not always been readily accepted, they have, nonetheless, opened up new ways of thinking and have encouraged new dialogue about one of the most significant periods in Latter-day Saint history. This historiographical essay will discuss significant works and themes about the Mormon migration and territorial Utah. It will also suggest areas which need further discussion.

General Works

With the great Mormon migration and territorial Utah period encompassing almost a third of the Latter-day Saints' history, it is not surprising that practically every gen-

---

1. A good example of a work which provides an abundant amount of information but is hampered by an obvious bias and defensive posture is Orson F. Whitney, *History of Utah,* 4 vols. (Salt Lake City: George Q. Cannon and Sons, 1892). Ernest H. Taves, *This Is the Place: Brigham Young and the New Zion* (Buffalo, NY:

GREAT BASIN KINGDOM

An Economic History of the Latter-day Saints

1830–1900

LEONARD J. ARRINGTON

HARVARD UNIVERSITY PRESS
Cambridge, Massachusetts
1958

eral history of the Church discusses at least some aspects of this time period. The best general work on this period is James B. Allen and Glen M. Leonard, *The Story of the Latter-day Saints* (1976; 2d ed. rev., Salt Lake City: Deseret Book, 1993) with seven chapters describing the move from Nauvoo to Utah's admission to the Union in 1896.[2]

Another important work is Leonard J. Arrington and Davis Bitton, *The Mormon Experience: A History of the Latter-day Saints* (New York: Alfred A. Knopf, 1979). A fine general history of the earlier territorial period is Eugene E. Campbell's posthumously published *Establishing Zion: The Mormon Church in the American West, 1847-1869* (Salt Lake City: Signature Books, 1988), originally commissioned as part of an official sixteen-volume sesquicentennial history that was eventually scrubbed, leaving the authors who completed their works to seek publication on their own. Richard D. Poll, Thomas G. Alexander, Eugene E. Campbell, and David E. Miller, eds., *Utah's History* (Provo, UT: Brigham Young University Press, 1978) is a well-written volume that brought together the historical talents of a large number of scholars. While giving significant space to Latter-day Saint history and the Mormon influence on Utah, the editors have attempted to take a more sophisticated approach to the diverse aspects of this subject. Celebrating the state centennial in 1996 were Thomas G. Alexander, *Utah: The Right Place. The Official Centennial History* (1995, 2d ed., Salt Lake City: Gibbs Smith Publisher, 1996), and histories on each of the nineteen Utah counties prepared by both local and professional historians and copublished by each county and by the Utah Historical Society under the general editorship of Allan Kent Powell.

An important interpretation of Mormonism's evolution in the nineteenth century, with broad implications for the Church's development in the American West is Jan Shipps, *Mormonism: The Story of a New Religious Tradition* (Urbana: University of Illinois Press, 1985). In this work Shipps argues that Mormonism is not a denomination, sect, or cult. Instead it is a new religious tradition, related to American Protestantism in the same way that early Christianity was related to Judaism. The definition of this new religion was, in large measure, the result of pioneering on the American frontier in the nineteenth century.

Several other general studies of lesser importance have also appeared. A less analytical book than those already mentioned is the second volume of a two-part set: Russell R. Rich, *Ensign to the Nations: A History of the LDS Church from 1846 to 1972* (Provo, UT: Brigham Young University Publications, 1972). Wallace Stegner's *Mormon Country* (1942; reprint ed., Lincoln: University of Nebraska Press, 1981), is an eloquent and sympathetic portrait of Mormonism as a unique culture that grew in isolation in the Rocky Mountain West. A solid, short introduction to Mormonism in the Rocky Mountain West is an older essay by Leonard J. Arrington and D. Michael Quinn, "The Latter-day Saints in the Far West, 1847-1900," in *The Restoration Movement: Essays in Mormon History,* edited by F. Mark McKiernan, Paul M. Edwards, and Alma R. Blair (Lawrence, KS: Coronado Press, 1973), 257-71.

Brigham Young

After the death of Joseph Smith in 1844, the Mormon movement divided into several schismatic factions, the largest of which was presided over by Brigham Young. To Young goes the credit of using the theological innovations of plural marriage and temple ordinances that Joseph Smith had launched in Nauvoo to wield his followers into a cohesive body that managed the arduous trek across the plains and the settlement period in the Intermountain West. This period, which began in the summer of 1845, ended with Young's death in 1877.

Although Young's role and achievement has always been a popular subject, two treatments stand out: Leonard J. Arrington's *Brigham Young: American Moses* (New York:

Prometheus Books, 1991) is a modern example of a book which not only does not contain any decent analysis but is inexcusably incorrect on simple facts such as dates and names.

2. While this essay focuses on works published after *Great Basin Kingdom,* it is important to note several earlier works that were well researched, analytical, and scholarly: Nels Anderson, *Desert Saints: The Mormon Frontier in Utah* (Chicago: University of Chicago Press, 1942); Ray B. West, *Kingdom of the Saints: The Story of Brigham Young and the Mormons* (New York: Viking Press, 1957); and Thomas F. O'Dea, *The Mormons* (Chicago: University of Chicago Press, 1957).

Excavating Mormon Pasts

Alfred A. Knopf, 1985), extensive and well-documented, focuses most clearly on Young's years in the Great Basin where he directed the colonization of Utah and the growth of the Mormon church. However, so much attention is placed on Brigham Young as a church and community leader, that only one side of this complex man is presented to the reader, thus leaving an incomplete and rather dry picture of an individual who was anything but dry and one-dimensional.[3] A good companion work is Newell G. Bringhurst, *Brigham Young and the Expanding American Frontier* (Boston: Little, Brown, 1986). This readable biography, while somewhat weak on administrative history, complements *American Moses* with its intimate portrayal of Brigham Young and his family. Young emerges as a complex man with hopes and fears, strengths and weaknesses.[4]

Several interesting articles discussing aspects of Brigham Young's life and views have also been published. Some of the more memorable are Gordon Irving, "Encouraging the Saints: Brigham Young's Annual Tours of the Mormon Settlements," *Utah Historical Quarterly* 45 (Summer 1977): 233-51, a fascinating look at Young's purposeful travels among his people and, even more interesting, their reaction to these visits. A solid overview of Young's administration can be found in Leonard J. Arrington and Ronald K. Esplin, "Building a Commonwealth: The Secular Leadership of Brigham Young," *Utah Historical Quarterly* 45 (Summer 1977): 216-32. Linda P. Wilcox, "The Imperfect Science: Brigham Young on Medical Doctors," *Dialogue: A Journal of Mormon Thought* 12 (Fall 1979): 26-36, discusses Young's skepticism about the medical profession, while Lester E. Bush, Jr., "Brigham Young in Life and Death: A Medical Overview," *Journal of Mormon History* 5 (1978): 79-103, explores issues of his health. On a more personal note, Dean C. Jessee's "Brigham Young's Family: The Wilderness Years," *BYU Studies* 19 (Summer 1979): 474-500, reviews the interaction between Brigham Young and his large family during the years of the exodus to Utah; while Ronald W. Walker and Ronald K. Esplin, "Brigham Himself: An Autobiographical Recollection," *Journal of Mormon History* 4 (1977): 19-34, discusses his views about himself. That Young had his share of interpersonal difficulties can be seen in his relationship with Emma Hale Smith, the widow of Joseph Smith, in Valeen Tippetts Avery and Linda King Newell, "The Lion and the Lady: Brigham Young and Emma Smith," *Utah Historical Quarterly* 48 (Winter 1980): 81-97. Dean C. Jessee edited the award-winning *Letters of Brigham Young to His Sons* (Salt Lake City: Deseret Book, 1974). This book offers absorbing and often poignant insights into Brigham Young as a concerned and, at times, doting father. Colleen Whitley, ed., *Brigham Young's Homes* (Logan: Utah State University Press, 2002), offers an examination of the domiciles in which Brigham Young housed his large and complicated family, ranging from quickly erected cabins to "Amelia's Palace."

Other Mormons

The Mormons whom Young and his successors led from the 1840s through the rest of the nineteenth century have also received some biographical treatment, although it has been uneven at best. (For a more detailed discussion, see Newell G. Bringhurst, "Mormon Biography: Paradoxes, Progress, and Problems," in this volume.)

Leonard J. Arrington, ed., *Presidents of the Church* (Salt Lake City: Deseret Book, 1986), contains article-length studies of each Mormon prophet, including those of the pioneer period (Brigham Young, John Taylor, Wilford Woodruff, Lorenzo Snow, and Joseph F. Smith). Young's immediate successor, although it took three years before he had consolidated sufficient support within the hierarchy to be ordained to the president, was John Taylor.

---

3. See also Leonard J. Arrington, "The Settlement of the Brigham Young Estate, 1877-1879," *Pacific Historical Review* 21 (February 1952): 1-20.

4. In sharp contrast is Stanley P. Hirshson's lamentable *The Lion of the Lord: A Biography of Brigham Young* (New York: Alfred A. Knopf, 1969), openly biased against Brigham Young and the Latter-day Saints. Many Mormon historians have condemned it as embarrassingly reliant on secondary rather than primary sources and lacking in decent analysis. See also the disappointing Eugene England, *Brother Brigham* (Salt Lake City: Bookcraft, 1980), which devoted four of its seven chapters to the Church in the Great Basin, rather than to Young, and Francis M. Gibbons, *Brigham Young: Modern Moses, Prophet of God* (Salt Lake City: Deseret Book, 1981), an overly simplistic portrait.

Samuel W. Taylor, his grandson and a professional writer, has written an impressionistic, troubling, and at times brilliant biography of Taylor in *The Kingdom or Nothing: The Life of John Taylor, Militant Mormon* (New York: Macmillan, 1976; reprinted under the title of *John Taylor: The Last Pioneer* [Salt Lake City: Signature Books, 1998]). It is not the final word on the subject, however, and Taylor's eventful career deserves further research and reflection.

Such is not the case, at least for the immediate future, when considering Wilford Woodruff, Taylor's successor as president of the Church. Thomas G. Alexander's prize-winning *Things in Heaven and Earth: The Life and Times of Wilford Woodruff, a Mormon Prophet* (Salt Lake City: Signature Books, 1991) fills a major gap in the historiography of the Mormon presidency.[5] There are, sadly, no comparable biographies available about Woodruff's successors in the prophetic office, Lorenzo Snow and Joseph F. Smith, although there is a pressing need for them.[6]

Several members of Mormon leadership quorums, besides Brigham Young, have received acceptable biographical treatment. Young's capable and much-married first counselor is the subject of an outstanding biography: Stanley B. Kimball, *Heber C. Kimball: Mormon Patriarch and Pioneer* (Urbana: University of Illinois Press, 1981). Had Kimball not died in 1868, before Young, he probably would have succeeded to the presidential office and the course of Mormonism might have been far different.[7] Young's other principal advisors—Willard Richards, Jedediah M. Grant, and Daniel H. Wells—are notably lacking in solid biographical treatment.[8]

Only a handful of good biographies of General Authorities in the Great Basin during this period have been published. For instance, Breck England, *The Thought of Orson Pratt* (Salt Lake City: University of Utah Press, 1985), is an excellent intellectual biography, but it fails to deal adequately with the most significant controversy in the apostle's past—his struggle with and then acceptance of plural marriage.[9] Andrew Karl Larson, *Erastus Snow: The Life of a Missionary and Pioneer for the Early Mormon Church* (Salt Lake City: University of Utah Press, 1971), is reasonably detailed and insightful but not particularly stirring, although Snow's career was certainly a colorful one. Howard H. Barron, *Orson Hyde: Missionary, Apostle, Colonizer* (Bountiful, UT: Horizon Publishers, 1977), is a disappointing popular work, while Myrtle Stevens Hyde, *Orson Hyde: The Olive Branch of Israel* (Salt Lake City: Agreka Books, 2000), must be considered a descendant's admiring though detailed biography. Davis Bitton's award-winning *George Q. Cannon: A Biography* (Salt Lake City: Deseret Book, 1999) filled a much-needed gap in understanding the life and work of arguably one of the most important and influential people in LDS Church history. *"Be Kind to the Poor": The Life Story of Robert Taylor Burton* (N.p.: Robert Taylor Burton Family Organization, 1988) by Janet Burton Seegmiller, is a well-written and informative biography of the colorful life and career of a member of the Presiding Bishopric during the 1880s. Amasa Lyman will be treated in a full-length biography by Mormon historian and

---

5. See also Alexander, "Wilford Woodruff and the Changing Nature of Mormon Religious Experience," *Church History* 45 (March 1976): 1-14; and his "The Odyssey of a Latter-day Prophet: Wilford Woodruff and the Manifesto of 1890," *Journal of Mormon History* 17 (1991): 169-206.

6. The only works generally available are Thomas C. Romney, *The Life of Lorenzo Snow* (Salt Lake City: Deseret News Press, 1955); Francis M. Gibbons, *Lorenzo Snow: Spiritual Giant, Prophet of God* (Salt Lake City: Deseret Book, 1982); Joseph Fielding Smith, *The Life of Joseph F. Smith* (Salt Lake City: Deseret News Press, 1938); Hyrum M. Smith III and Scott G. Kenney, eds., *From Prophet to Son: Advice of Joseph F. Smith to his Missionary Sons* (Salt Lake City: Signature Books, 1981); and Leonard J. Arrington, "Joseph F. Smith: From Impulsive Young Man to Patriarchal Prophet," *John Whitmer Historical Association Journal* 4 (1984): 30-40.

7. Indeed, had not the presidency realigned the quorum, Orson Pratt might have been the LDS president. See Gary James Bergera, "Seniority in the Twelve: The 1875 Realignment of Orson Pratt," *Journal of Mormon History* 18 (Spring 1992): 19-58; and his *Conflict in the Quorum: Orson Pratt, Brigham Young, Joseph Smith* (Salt Lake City: Signature Books, 2002).

8. The only works of substance on them are Bryant S. Hinckley, *Daniel Hamner Wells* (Salt Lake City: Deseret News Press, 1942); Mary G. Judd, *Jedediah M. Grant* (Salt Lake City: Deseret News Press, 1969); Gene A. Sessions, *Mormon Thunder: A Documentary History of Jedediah Morgan Grant* (Urbana: University of Illinois Press, 1982); and Ronald W. Walker, "Jedediah and Heber Grant," *Ensign*, July 1979, 48-50.

9. A good article that focuses on Pratt's first wife and her disillusion with polygamy and Mormonism is Richard S. Van Wagoner, "Sarah M. Pratt: The Shaping of an Apostate," *Dialogue* 19 (Summer 1986): 69-99.

Excavating Mormon Pasts

descendant Edward Leo Lyman, while Dennis B. Horne has edited *An Apostle's Record: The Journals of Abraham H. Cannon* (Clearfield, UT: Gnolaum Books, 2004). Still, such notable figures as Cannon himself, Parley P. Pratt, Jedediah M. Grant, George A. Smith, Francis M. Lyman, Moses Thatcher, Brigham Young, Jr., and many others merit careful, analytical treatment.[10]

Below the level of General Authorities, several notable biographies have been written about second-echelon individuals. Leonard J. Arrington and Davis Bitton, *Saints without Halos: The Human Side of Mormon History* (Salt Lake City: Signature Books, 1981), and Donald Q. Cannon and David J. Whittaker, eds., *Supporting Saints: Life Stories of Nineteenth-Century Mormons* (Provo, UT: Religious Studies Center, Brigham Young University, 1985), present essays on lesser-known figures showing both their foibles and their strengths, while Susan Hendricks Swetnam, *Lives of the Saints in Southeastern Idaho: An Introduction to Mormon Pioneer Life Story Writing* (Moscow: University of Idaho Press, 1991), analyzes common themes in family history. Roger D. Launius and Linda Thatcher, eds., *Differing Visions: Dissenters in Mormon History* (Urbana: University of Illinois Press, 1994), presents biographical essays on people who disaffiliated from Mormonism, including several from the pioneer period.

Book-length works on individuals are James B. Allen, *Trials of Discipleship: The Story of William Clayton—a Mormon* (Urbana: University of Illinois Press, 1987); Marjorie Newton, *Hero or Traitor? A Biographical Study of Charles Wesley Wandell* (Independence: John Whitmer Historical Association Monograph Series, 1992); Leonard J. Arrington, *From Quaker to Latter-day Saint Bishop: Edwin D. Woolley* (Salt Lake City: Deseret Book, 1976); William G. Hartley, *"My Best for the Kingdom": History and Autobiography of John Lowe Butler, Mormon Frontiersman* (Salt Lake City: Aspen Books, 1993); Myrtle Stevens Hyde and Everett L. Cooley, *The Life of Andrew Wood Cooley: A Story of Conviction* (Provo, UT: Andrew Wood Cooley Family Association, 1991); and Guy M. Bishop, *Henry William Bigler: Soldier, Gold Miner, Missionary, Chronicler, 1815-1900* (Logan: Utah State University, 1998).

Articles have appeared as well: Charles S. Peterson, "Jacob Hamblin: Apostle to the Lamanites and the Indian Mission," *Journal of Mormon History* 2 (1975): 21-34; Leonard J. Arrington and Richard L. Jensen, "Lorenzo Hill Hatch: Pioneer Bishop of Franklin," *Idaho Yesterdays* 17 (Summer 1973): 2-8; Davis Bitton, "Charley Walker, Dixie Pioneer," in *One Hundred and Fifty Years* (Provo, UT: Harold B. Lee Forum Committee, 1980), 19-26; and Glen M. Leonard, "Truman Leonard: Pioneer Mormon Farmer," *Utah Historical Quarterly* 44 (Summer 1976): 240-60.

Two fascinating and moving biographies are works concerning John D. Lee and Orrin Porter Rockwell, both of whom were Mormon zealots and both of whose biographies were written by nonhistorians who approached the studies as literature. Juanita Brooks, *John Doyle Lee: Zealot, Pioneer Builder, Scapegoat* (Glendale, CA: Arthur H. Clark, 1961), tells in elegant detail and with moving sympathy the story of the man accused of engineering the Mountain Meadows Massacre of 1857. He was abandoned by Brigham Young to be executed twenty years to the day after the event. Just as powerful, but problematic for its sensationalistic tone, is Harold Schindler, *Orrin Porter Rockwell: Man of God, Son of Thunder* (Salt Lake City: University of Utah Press, 1966), which narrates the intriguing story of one of Brigham Young's chief bodyguards and enforcers of Mormonism. Both of these books have deservedly been kept in print by presses interested in Mormon studies.

---

10. Available works include Beatrice Cannon Evans and Janath Russell Cannon, eds., *Cannon Family Historical Treasury* (Salt Lake City: G. Q. Cannon Family Association, 1967); Steven Pratt, "Eleanor McLean and the Murder of Parley P. Pratt," *BYU Studies* 15 (Winter 1975): 225-56; Merlo J. Pusey, *Builders of the Kingdom: George A. Smith, John Henry Smith, George Albert Smith* (Provo, UT: Brigham Young University Press, 1981); Loretta L. Hefner, "Amasa Mason Lyman, the Spiritualist," *Journal of Mormon History* 6 (1979): 75-87; Edward Leo Lyman, "The Alienation of an Apostle from his Quorum: The Moses Thatcher Case," *Dialogue* 18 (Summer 1985): 67-91; Loretta L. Hefner, "From Apostle to Apostate: The Personal Struggle of Amasa Mason Lyman," *Dialogue* 16 (Spring 1983): 90-104; Leonard J. Arrington, *Charles C. Rich: Mormon General and Western Frontiersman* (Provo, UT: Brigham Young University Press, 1974); and Davis Bitton, "The Ordeal of Brigham Young Jr.," in his *The Ritualization of Mormon History and Other Essays* (Urbana: University of Illinois Press, 1994), 115-49.

One of the exciting and liberating aspects of recent historical writing about Mormonism on the frontier has been the emphasis on Mormon women. Several biographical treatments provide useful introductions to this rich subject. For example, Claudia L. Bushman, ed., *Mormon Sisters: Women in Early Utah* (1976; 3rd. ed., Logan: Utah State University Press, 1997); Vicky Burgess-Olson, ed., *Sister Saints* (Provo, UT: Brigham Young University Press, 1978); Lavina Fielding Anderson, ed., *Utah's First Ladies* (Salt Lake City: Utah Women's History Association/Utah Endowment for the Humanities, 1981); and Leonard J. Arrington and Susan Arrington Madsen, *Sunbonnet Sisters: The Stories of Mormon Women and Frontier Life* (Salt Lake City: Bookcraft, 1984), provide excellent introductory sketches to numerous Mormon frontier women. Rebecca Bartholomew, ed., *Audacious Women: Early British Mormon Immigrants* (Salt Lake City: Signature Books, 1995), includes excerpted first-person accounts from this specialized group of Mormon converts.

Studies of several individual women have been completed. Perhaps the most important woman in the region was Eliza R. Snow, whose life has been chronicled in Maureen Ursenbach Beecher, *Eliza and Her Sisters* (Salt Lake City: Aspen Books, 1991); Jill C. Mulvay, "Eliza R. Snow and the Mormon Question," *BYU Studies* 16 (Winter 1976): 250-64; Maureen Ursenbach Beecher, "The Eliza Enigma: The Life and Legend of Eliza R. Snow," *Dialogue* 11 (Spring 1978): 30-43; Jill Mulvay Derr, "Form and Feeling in a Carefully Crafted Life: Eliza R. Snow's 'Poem of Poems,'" *Journal of Mormon History* 26, no. 1 (Spring 2000): 1-39; and her (with Karen Lynn Davidson), A Wary Heart Becomes 'Unalterably Fix'd:' Eliza R. Snow's Conversion to Mormonism," *Journal of Mormon History* 30, no. 2 (Fall 2004): forthcoming. Derr and Davidson are also collaborating on an edition of Snow's poetry. Also forthcoming is a multi-volume biography by Carol Cornwall Madsen of early Mormon feminist and Relief Society general president Emmeline B. Wells. An engaging intergenerational group biography is Martha Sonntag Bradley, *Four Zinas: Mothers and Daughters on the Mormon Frontier* (Salt Lake City: Signature Books, 2000).

A good introductory bibliography for those who want to pursue this subject further is Patricia Lyn Scott and Maureen Ursenbach Beecher, "Mormon Women: A Bibliography in Process, 1977-1985," *Journal of Mormon History* 12 (1985): 113-27. A pathbreaking sketch, pointing up the importance of this subject is Maureen Ursenbach Beecher, "Under the Sunbonnet: Mormon Women with Faces," *BYU Studies* 16 (Summer 1976): 471-85.

Only recently have Mormon historians developed an interest in non-Mormons in the West and their relationship with the Church. As a result a few notable studies have appeared. One of the most significant non-Mormons to come to the Mormon commonwealth during the pioneer period was Patrick Edward Connor, Civil War commander of the First California Volunteers and worthy opponent of Mormonism. Brigham D. Madsen's book, *Glory Hunter: A Biography of Patrick Edward Connor* (Salt Lake City: University of Utah Press, 1990), is a serviceable study that focuses on Connor's activities in opposition to the Mormons, promotion of mining and railroads, and Indian relations. Other friends, rivals, and enemies of the Mormon Church in the West such as Thomas L. Kane, Philip St. George Cook, Phillipe Regis de Trobriand, T. B. H. and Fanny Stenhouse, Albert Cumming, and the like also deserve sustained biographical treatment. Indeed, in spite of the work completed to date, there is a great need for biographical treatments of women, individuals who were not among the top ranks of the church hierarchy, and non-Mormons who interacted with the Saints of the West.

Mormon Migration and Settlement

Without doubt, the pivotal event for the Saints of this era was their migration and colonization of the Great Basin. Because of its significance, there is a plethora of literature concerning almost all aspects of this experience. This already abundant supply of literature was greatly enhanced during the sesquicentennial celebrations which took place in 1997. A good survey of the experience, written by a master of western literature, is Wallace Stegner's sympathetic *The Gathering of Zion: The Story of the Mormon Trail* (New York: McGraw-Hill, 1964). Overviews of the Mormon and other trails are the late Stanley B. Kimball, *Historic*

Excavating Mormon Pasts

Sites and Markers Along the Mormon and Other Great Western Trails (Urbana: University of Illinois Press, 1988);[11] Peter Delafosse, *Trailing the Pioneers: A Guide to Utah's Emigrant Trails, 1829-1869* (Logan: Utah State University Press with Utah Crossroads, Oregon-California Trails Association, 1994); John S. Nealon, "'Morning Fair, Roads Bad:' Geology, Topography, Hydrology, and Weather on the Iowa and Nebraska Mormon Trail, 1846-1847," *Nauvoo Journal* 10 (Spring 1998): 67-95; Glenda Riley, "Sesquicentennial Reflections: A Comparative View of Mormon and Gentile Women on the Westward Trail," *Journal of Mormon History* 24 (Spring 1998): 28-53; and Joseph E. Brown, *The Mormon Trek West: The Journey of American Exiles* (Garden City, NY: Doubleday, 1980). Carol Cornwall Madsen, ed., *Journey to Zion: Voices from the Mormon Trail* (Salt Lake City: Deseret Book, 1997), introduces journal excerpts and reminiscences about Iowa, the wagon-train migration, and the handcart experience with insightful interpretive essays.[12] A significant dissertation that should be published after revision and with a new title is Lewis Clark Christian, "A Study of the Mormon Westward Migration between February 1846 and July 1847, with Emphasis on and Evaluation of the Factors that Led to the Mormons' Choice of Salt Lake Valley as the Site of their Initial Colony" (Ph.D. diss., Brigham Young University, 1976).

One of the fundamental aspects of the Mormon exodus was its magnitude and organization, including its way stations, established under centralized orders to help Latter-day Saints on the trails. The most significant of these was Winter Quarters, on the Missouri River near present-day Council Bluffs, Iowa. A fine study of this locale is Richard E. Bennett, *Mormons at the Missouri. 1846-1852: "And We Should Die . . ."* (Norman: University of Oklahoma Press, 1987). Leland H. Gentry also discusses "The Mormon Way Stations, Garden Grove and Mt. Pisgah," *BYU Studies* 21 (Fall 1981): 445-61. Robert A. Trennert Jr. describes "The Mormons and the Office of Indian Affairs: The Conflict Over Winter Quarters, 1846-1848," *Nebraska History* 53 (Fall 1972): 381-400. Fred R. Gowans and Eugene E. Campbell, *Fort Bridger: Island in the Wilderness* (Provo, UT: Brigham Young University Press, 1975), expertly describes the centrality of that trading post at South Pass to the Mormon migration. Fred R. Gowen, *Fort Supply: Brigham Young's Green River Experiment* (Provo, UT: Brigham Young University. Press, 1976), does much the same for this attempt to create a logistics base for Mormon emigrants.

LeRoy R. and Ann W. Hafen, *Handcarts to Zion: The Story of a Unique Western Migration, 1856-1860* (Glendale, CA: Arthur H. Clark, 1960) tells the story of that unusual four-year experiment; but the most dramatic tale of suffering is unquestionably the ill-fated Willie and Martin handcart companies, highlighted in Rebecca Bartholomew and Leonard J. Arrington, *Rescue of the 1856 Handcart Companies,* Charles Redd Monographs in Western History, No. 11 (Provo, UT: Charles Redd Center for Western History, 1982); and LeRoy R. Hafen, "Handcarts to Utah, 1856-1860," *Utah Historical Quarterly* 24 (October 1956): 309-17.

Continuing the theme of different modes of transportation for the early pioneers, Dean L. May, "Rites of Passage: The Gathering as Cultural Credo," *Journal of Mormon History* 29, no. [1] (Spring 2003): 1-42, explored the little-emphasized sea leg of the pioneer migration. Conway B. Sonne, *Ships, Saints, and Mariners: A Maritime Encyclopedia of Mormon Migration, 1830-1890* (Salt Lake City: University of Utah Press, 1987), while lacking analysis, is of immense importance for tracking the various companies who immigrated to America by ship and for understanding what experiences these people had. Lorin K. Hansen, "The Voyage of the *Brooklyn*," *Dialogue* 21 (Autumn 1988): 47-72, is an interesting and thorough account of Samuel Brannan's company which traveled by sea from New York to California. Other valuable specialized migration stories are P.A.M Taylor, *Expectations Westward: The Mormons and the Emigration of their British Converts in the Nineteenth Century* (Edinburgh, Scotland: Oliver and Boyd, 1965); William Mulder, *Homeward to Zion:*

---

11. See also Kimball, "The Mormon Trail Network in Iowa, 1838-1863: A New Look," *BYU Studies* 21 (Fall 1981): 417-30; and his "The Mormon Trail Network in Nebraska, 1846-1868: A New Look," *BYU Studies* 24 (Summer 1984): 321-36.

12. An older study that still can be read with profit is Preston Nibley, *Exodus to Greatness: The Story of the Mormon Migration* (Salt Lake City: Deseret News Press, 1947).

The Mormon Migration from Scandinavia (Minneapolis: University of Minnesota Press, 1958); and Ronald D. Dennis, *The Call of Zion: The Story of the First Welsh Mormon Migration* (Provo, UT: Religious Studies Center, Brigham Young University, 1987). William G. Hartley discussed the Church's novel transport system in "Down-and-Back Wagon Trains: Travelers on the Mormon Trail in 1861," *Overland Journal: Quarterly Journal of the Oregon-California Trails Association* 11 (Fall 1993): 23-34. Hartley had earlier examined this topic in "The Great Florence Fitout of 1861," *BYU Studies* 24 (Summer 1984): 341-71, and revisited it in "Brigham Young's Overland trails Revolution: The Creation of the 'Down-and-Back' Wagon-Train System, 1860-61," *Journal of Mormon History* 28, no. 1 (Spring 2002): 1-30. John K. Hulmston, "Mormon Migration in the 1860s: The Story of the Church Trains," *Utah Historical Quarterly* 58 (Winter 1990): 32-48, also studies this topic.

Despite these notable achievements, forty years have passed since Wallace Stegner wrote his synthesis of the Mormon trek west, popularly focused though it was, and it is clear that a new analysis of the overall experience is overdue. The basis for such a new synthesis has been laid in the scores of articles about the Mormon exodus. It would be foolhardy to try to list all of them. A representative sample, however, include Richard E. Bennett, "Lamanism, Lymanism, and Cornfields," *Journal of Mormon History* 13 (1986-87): 45-60; Ronald K. Esplin, "'A Place Prepared': Joseph, Brigham, and the Quest for Promised Refuge in the West," *Journal of Mormon History* 9 (1982): 85-111; Orval F. Baldwin II, "A Mormon Bride in the Great Migration," *Nebraska History* 58 (Spring 1977): 53-71; Kenneth N. Owens, "The Mormon Carson Emigrant Trail in Western History," *Montana: The Magazine of Western History* 42 (Winter 1992): 14-25; Steven F. Pratt, "Parley P. Pratt in Winter Quarters and the Trail West," *BYU Studies* 24 (Summer 1984): 373-88; Russell W. Belk, "Moving Possessions: An Analysis Based on Personal Documents from the 1847-1869 Mormon Migration," *Journal of Consumer Research* 19 (December 1992): 339-61; Richard H. Jackson, "The Mormon Experience: The Plains as Sinai, the Great Salt Lake as the Dead Sea, and the Great Basin as Desert-cum-Promised Land," *Journal of Historical Geography* 18 (January 1992): 41-58; Davis Bitton, "American Philanthropy and Mormon Refugees, 1846-1849," *Journal of Mormon History* 7 (1980): 63-82; and William J. Peterson, "The Mormon Trail of 1846," *Palimpsest* 47 (September 1966): 353-67.

During the early Mormon migration, a parallel experience of lasting consequence for the Saints was the Mormon Battalion, a military expedition organized during the Mexican-American War of 1846-48 with the still-standing distinction of having performed the longest march in American military history. Some of the many works on this subject include Daniel Tyler, *A Concise History of the Mormon Battalion in the Mexican War, 1846-1847* (1881; reprint ed., Glorietta, NM: Rio Grande Press, 1964); Dan Talbot, *A Historical Guide to the Mormon Battalion and Butterfield Trail* (Tucson, AZ: Westernlore Press, 1992); and John F. Yurtinus, "A Ram in the Thicket: A History of the Mormon Battalion in the Mexican War" (Ph.D. diss., Brigham Young University, 1975). Probably the most in-depth and comprehensive study of the Mormon Battalion is Norma B. Ricketts, *The Mormon Battalion: U.S. Army of the West, 1846-1848* (Logan: Utah State University, 1996). The Mormon Battalion has been the center of an interesting historical debate about authority and leadership, really a continuation of the struggle within the battalion over secular versus ecclesiastical control. Such studies include Susan Easton Black, "The Mormon Battalion: Conflict Between Religious and Military Authority," *Southern California Quarterly* 74 (Winter 1992): 313-28; Larry D. Christiansen, "The Struggle for Power in the Mormon Battalion," *Dialogue* 26 (Winter 1993): 51-69; Eugene E. Campbell, "Authority Conflicts in the Mormon Battalion," *BYU Studies* 8 (Winter 1968): 127-42; and John F. Yurtinus, "'Here Is One Man Who Will Not Go, Dam'um': Recruiting the Mormon Battalion in Iowa Territory," *BYU Studies* 21 (Fall 1981): 475-98.

Mormon Settlements

There has been considerable interest in documenting the colonization of Mormonism in the Great Basin and throughout the remainder of the Far West.

Excavating Mormon Pasts

Unfortunately, no compelling synthesis has yet been produced. The only work that comes close is the exceptionally important Richard H. Jackson, ed., *The Mormon Role in the Settlement of the West*, Charles Redd Monographs in Western History, No. 9 (Provo, UT: Brigham Young University Press, 1978). It replaced the disappointing Joel E. Ricks, *Forms and Methods of Early Mormon Settlement in Utah and Surrounding Regions: 1847 to 1877* (Logan: Utah State Utah Press, 1964). Although older and dated, more satisfying are Andrew L. Neff, *History of Utah: 1847-1869*, edited by Leland H. Creer (Salt Lake City: Deseret News Press, 1940); Leland H. Creer, *The Founding of an Empire: The Exploration and Colonization of Utah, 1776-1856* (Salt Lake City: Bookcraft, 1947); Milton R. Hunter, *Brigham Young the Colonizer* (Independence: Zion's Printing and Publishing Co., 1945); Gustive O. Larson, *Prelude to the Kingdom: Mormon Desert Conquest—A Chapter in American Cooperative Experience* (Francestown, NH: Marshall Jones, 1947); Lowry Nelson, *The Mormon Village: A Pattern and Technique of Land Settlement* (Salt Lake City: Deseret News Press, 1940); and Dale L. Morgan, "The State of Deseret," *Utah Historical Quarterly* 8 (April, July, October 1940): 65-239. A powerful thesis on Mormon colonization methods is Eugene E. Campbell, "Brigham Young's Outer Cordon: A Reappraisal," *Utah Historical Quarterly* 41 (1973): 220-53.

Most of the work has taken place on the level of local history: the founding of communities and the impact of Mormon colonization in the community's particular area. Many focus exclusively on settlement in the Great Basin, like Morris A. Shirts and Kathryn H. Shirts, *A Trial Furnace: Southern Utah's Iron Mission* (Provo, UT: BYU Studies, [2001]), L. A. Fleming, "The Settlements on the Muddy, 1865-1871: 'A God-forsaken Place,'" *Utah Historical Quarterly* 35 (Spring 1967): 147-172; Kerry William Bates, "Iron City, Mormon Mining Town," *Utah Historical Quarterly* 50 (Winter 1982): 47-58; and Thomas G. Alexander and James B. Allen, *Mormons and Gentiles: A History of Salt Lake City* (Boulder, CO: Pruett Publishing, 1984). However, there is a good sampling of works concerning colonization outside of Utah in such places such as Arizona, Nevada, California, Idaho, Wyoming, Canada, and even Hawaii. These works include James H. McClintock, *Mormon Settlement in Arizona* (Tucson: University of Arizona, 1985); Charles S. Peterson, *Take Up Your Mission: Mormon Colonizing Along the Little Colorado River, 1870-1900* (Tucson: University of Arizona Press, 1973); Andrew Karl Larson, *"I Was Called to Dixie": The Virgin River Basin, Unique Experiences in Mormon Pioneering* (1961; reprint ed., St. George, UT: Dixie College, 1983); his *The Red Hills of November: A Pioneer Biography of Utah's Cotton Town* (Salt Lake City: Deseret News, 1957); Edward Leo Lyman, "The Rise and Decline of Mormon San Diego," *BYU Studies* 29 (Fall 1989): 43-65; his *San Bernardino: The Rise and Fall of a California Community* (Salt Lake City: Signature Books, 1996); Davis Bitton, "The Making of a Community: Blackfoot, Idaho, 1878-1910," *Idaho Yesterdays* 19 (Spring 1975): 2-15; Dean L. May, "Between Two Cultures: The Mormon Settlement of Star Valley, Wyoming," *Journal of Mormon History* 13 (1986-87): 125-140; Lawrence B. Lee, "The Mormons Come to Canada, 1887-1902," *Pacific Northwest Quarterly* 59 (January 1968): 11-22; Brigham Y. Card et al., eds., *The Mormon Presence in Canada* (Logan: Utah State University Press, 1990); R. Lanier Britsch, *Moramona: The Mormons in Hawaii* (Laie, HI: Institute for Polynesian Studies, 1989); Leonard J. Arrington, *The Mormons in Nevada* (Las Vegas: Las Vegas Sun, 1979); William S. Abruzzi, "Ecology, Resource Redistribution, and Mormon Settlement in Northeastern Arizona," *American Anthropologist* 91 (September 1989): 642-55; Clifford L. Stott, *Search for Sanctuary: Brigham Young and the White Mountain Expedition* (Salt Lake City: University of Utah Press, 1984); J. Kenneth Davies, "Mormons and California Gold," *Journal of Mormon History* 7 (1980): 83-99; and Eugene E. Campbell, "The Gold Mining Mission of 1849," *BYU Studies* 1 (Autumn-Winter 1959-1960): 19-31. None of these studies, however, present the kind of compelling analysis that would help to incorporate Mormon studies in the emerging New Western History with its emphasis on regionalism.[13]

---

13. See Patricia Nelson Limerick, et al., eds., *Trails: Toward a New Western History* (Lawrence: University Press of Kansas, 1991); and her Tanner Lecture, "Peace Initiative: Using the Mormons to Rethink Culture and Ethnicity in American History," *Journal of Mormon History* 21 (Fall 1995): 1-29.

Mormons & Gentiles
A History of Salt Lake City

Thomas G. Alexander **James B. Allen**

Volume V
The Western Urban History Series

PRUETT PUBLISHING COMPANY
Boulder, Colorado

Excavating Mormon Pasts

Several studies on the dynamics of community life have delved into a heretofore underdeveloped area of Mormon history. Dean L. May, "The Making of Saints: The Mormon Town as a Setting for the Study of Cultural Change," *Utah Historical Quarterly* 45 (1977): 75-92, as well as his insightful *Three Frontiers: Family, Land, and Society in the American West, 1850-1900* (Cambridge, MA: Cambridge University Press, 1994), Jan Shipps, Cheryll L. May, and Dean L. May, "Sugar House Ward: A Latter-day Saint Congregation," in *Portraits of Twelve Religious Communities,* Vol. 1 of AMERICAN CONGREGATIONS, edited by James P. Wind and James W. Lewis (Chicago: University of Chicago Press, 1994), 293-348, and Ronald W. Walker, "'Going to Meeting' in Salt Lake City's Thirteenth Ward, 1849-1881: A Microanalysis," in *New Views of Mormon History: A Collection of Essays in Honor of Leonard J. Arrington* edited by Davis Bitton and Maureen Ursenbach Beecher (Salt Lake City: University of Utah Press, 1987), 138-61, look at the dynamics of local Mormon communities at both the town and ward level.

An interesting collection of essays concerning various aspects of Mormon pioneers and community life is found in Ronald W. Walker and Doris Dant, eds., *Nearly Everything Imaginable: The Everyday Life of Utah's Mormon Pioneers* (Provo, UT: Brigham Young University Press, 1999). Subjects include the dynamics of Mormon villages, pioneer homemaking, furniture making, dancing, diet, church activity, childhood and young adulthood, schooling, aging, and death and burial in early Utah.

An area that has unfortunately been ignored by most historians is that of family relationships and how they affected settlement and Mormon colonization, among them Dean L. May, "People on the Mormon Frontier: Kanab's Families of 1874," *Journal of Mormon History* 1 (1976): 169-192, and Nancy Jacobus Taniguchi, "Rebels and Relatives: The Mormon Foundation of Spring Glen, 1878-90," *Utah Historical Quarterly* 48 (Fall 1980): 366-78.[14]

In terms of revolutionizing the study of Mormon settlement patterns, perhaps one of the more significant early works to be published was Lowell "Ben" Bennion, "Mormon Country a Century Ago: A Geographer's View," in *The Mormon People: Their Character and Traditions,* edited by Thomas G. Alexander (Provo, UT: Brigham Young University Press), 1-26. In this essay, Bennion proposed a revisionist view to the idea of the Mormon compact settlement pattern which had been generally accepted by most historians. Bennion further developed his revisionist theory in "A Geographer's Discovery of Great Basin Kingdom," in *Great Basin Kingdom Revisited: Contemporary Perspectives,* edited by Thomas G. Alexander (Logan: Utah State University Press, 1991), 109-32. While a number of significant works have been published on Mormon colonization, settlement patterns, and community life, this topic has enormous potential for significant studies in community and family dynamics.

Economics

It was, many observers have concluded, with the publication of Leonard Arrington's *Great Basin Kingdom* that the "New Mormon History" had its beginning. It is, therefore, not surprising that a significant number of articles have been published on such aspects of early Utah industry as agriculture, sugar manufacturing, mining, and the coming of the railroad. They include Charles L. Schmalz, "The Failure of Utah's First Sugar Factory," *Utah Historical Quarterly* 56 (Winter 1988): 36-54; and Leonard J. Arrington, "Utah's Pioneer Beet Sugar Plant: The Lehi Factory of the Utah Sugar Company," *Utah Historical Quarterly* 34 (Spring 1966): 95-120. Both Robert G. Athearn's "Opening the Gates of Zion: Utah and the Coming of the Union Pacific Railroad," *Utah Historical Quarterly* 36 (Fall 1968): 291-314 and his "Contracting for the Union Pacific," *Utah Historical Quarterly* 37 (Winter 1969): 16-40, look at the railroad's social and economic impact on Mormon Utah. Among articles which concern agriculture are Leonard J. Arrington and Dean L. May, "'A Different Mode of Life': Irrigation and Society in Nineteenth-Century Utah," *Agricultural History* 49 (1975): 3-20; Leonard J. Arrington, "The Mormon Cotton Mission in Southern

---

14. See also John W. Van Cott, *Utah Place Names: A Comprehensive Guide to the Origins of Geographic Names: A Compilation* (Salt Lake City: University of Utah Press, 1990).

Utah," *Pacific Historical Review* 25 (August 1956): 221-38; and Charles S. Peterson, "The 'Americanization' of Utah's Agriculture," *Utah Historical Quarterly* 42 (1974): 108-25. An interesting look at labor relations is J. Kenneth Davies, "Utah Labor Before Statehood," *Utah Historical Quarterly* 34 (Summer 1966): 202-17, a topic that could well bear more examination. Useful brief introductions, although now dated, are three articles by Leonard J. Arrington: "Objectives of Mormon Economic Policy," *Western Humanities Review* 10 (Spring 1956): 180-85; "Religion and Economics in Mormon History," *BYU Studies* 3 (Spring-Summer 1961): 15-33; and "Religion and Economic Planning in the Far West: The First Generation of Mormons in Utah," *Economic History Review* 11 (August 1958): 71-86, written with P.A.M. Taylor. Another is Dean L. May, "The Economics of Zion," *Sunstone* 14 (August 1990): 15-23.

Leonard J. Arrington, Feramorz Y. Fox, and Dean L. May, *Building the City of God: Community and Cooperation Among the Mormons* (Salt Lake City: Deseret Book, 1976) placed the Mormon community within a broader social and economic context, while Dean L. May, "Brigham and the Bishops: The United Order in the City," in *New Views of Mormon History*, 115-37, gave a narrower analysis on the economic experience of just one community. Once again, while some excellent work has been done in the field of economic history, much more awaits. Issues of gender, race, and class in relation to economics and the Mormon frontier must be more thoroughly explored to gain a better understanding of Mormon economic history.

When the Mormons settled in the Great Basin they had to begin commerce virtually from scratch, including establishing banks, issuing currency, regularizing property ownership, and establishing legal practices. Leonard J. Arrington, "Coin and Currency in Early Utah," *Utah Historical Quarterly* 20 (January 1952): 56-76; and his "Mormon Finance and the Mormon War," *Utah Historical Quarterly* 20 (July 1952): 219-37, reviewed the money issue; while Lawrence A. Linford, "Establishing and Maintaining Land Ownership in Utah Prior to 1869," *Utah Historical Quarterly* 42 (Spring 1974): 126-43, and Mark P. Leone, *Roots of Modern Mormonism* (Cambridge, MA: Harvard University Press, 1979), analyzed the question of land ownership and property rights to such valuable commodities as water.

The Political Kingdom of God

One of the most interesting fields in Mormon frontier historiography has been competing views of the Mormon attempt to create a commonwealth in the Great Basin. As God's chosen people, Mormons viewed themselves as the bearers of not only theological but political truth. Shortly before his death, Joseph Smith organized the Council of Fifty to act as the Church's political arm. This organization traveled to Utah with the Mormon leadership. Klaus J. Hansen, in his groundbreaking *Quest for Empire: The Political Kingdom of God and the Council of Fifty in Mormon History* (East Lansing: Michigan State University Press, 1967)—a revised edition is forthcoming from Greg Kofford Books—portrayed this little-known council as a powerful group of men who secretly ran early territorial politics as an extension of their ecclesiastical callings. D. Michael Quinn, "The Council of Fifty and Its Members, 1844 to 1945," " *BYU Studies* 20 (Winter 1980): 163-97, critiqued Hansen's treatment, concluding that the council was more symbolic than powerful in territorial politics. An earlier study, anticipating many of Hansen's themes, as well as providing a convincing case for the council's management of secular affairs in Utah Territory, is James R. Clark, "The Kingdom of God, the Council of Fifty, and the State of Deseret," *Utah Historical Quarterly* 26 (April 1958): 130-48. David L. Bigler, *Forgotten Kingdom: The Mormon Theocracy in the American West, 1847-1896*, Vol. 2 of KINGDOM IN THE WEST: THE MORMONS AND THE AMERICAN FRONTIER SERIES, edited by Will Bagley (Spokane, WA: Arthur H. Clark, 1998), is also relevant.

While the Council of Fifty's role remains shadowy, the influence of the Mormon Church on Utah politics is undeniable. James B. Allen, "Ecclesiastical Influence on Local Government in the Territory of Utah," *Arizona and the West* 8 (Spring 1966): 35-48; R. Collin Mangrum, "Furthering the Cause of Zion: An Overview of the Mormon Ecclesiastical

BUILDING THE CITY OF GOD

Community & Cooperation Among the Mormons

Leonard J. Arrington
Feramorz Y. Fox
Dean L. May

Deseret Book Company
Salt Lake City, Utah
1976

Court System in Early Utah," *Journal of Mormon History* 10 (1983): 79-90; P.A.M. Taylor, "Early Mormon Loyalty and the Leadership of Brigham Young," *Utah Historical Quarterly* 30 (Spring 1962): 102-32; Alvin Karl Koritz, "The Development of Municipal Government in the Territory of Utah" (M.A. thesis, Brigham Young University, 1972); and Leland H. Creer, "The Evolution of Government in Early Utah," *Utah Historical Quarterly* 27 (January 1958): 23-42, all demonstrate the Church's powerful influence on local government.

Because of the Mormon political influence, conflicts between Mormons and the federal government were inevitable. Alan E. Haynes, "The Federal Government and Its Policies Regarding the Frontier Era of Utah Territory, 1850-1877" (Ph.D. diss., Catholic University of America, 1968); Ronald C. Jack, "Utah Territorial Politics: 1874-1896" (Ph.D. diss., University of Utah, 1970); J. Keith Melville, *Conflict and Compromise: The Mormons in Mid-Nineteenth Century American Politics* (Provo, UT: Brigham Young University Press, 1975); and Richard D. Draper, "Babylon in Zion: The LDS Concept of Zion as a Cause for Mormon-Gentile Conflict, 1846-1857" (M.A. thesis, Arizona State University, 1974), also survey these conflicts with varying degrees of insight. The topic of Mormons in politics remains one of the most popular subjects in Mormon historiography. Among the numerous works are Michael W. Homer, "The Judiciary and Common Law in Utah, 1850-1861," *Dialogue* 21 (Spring 1988): 97-108; E. B. Long, *The Saints and the Union: Utah Territory during the Civil War* (Urbana: University of Illinois Press, 1981); Glen M. Leonard, "The Mormon Question in the 1849-1850 Statehood Debates," *Journal of Mormon History* 18 (Spring 1992): 114-136; Gwynn W. Barrett, "Dr. John M. Bernhisel, Mormon Elder in Congress," *Utah Historical Quarterly* 36 (Spring 1968): 143-167; and Joseph H. Groberg, "The Mormon Disenfranchisements of 1882 to 1892," *BYU Studies* 16 (Spring 1976): 399-408. Jean Bickmore White, "Women's Place is In the Constitution: The Struggle for Equal Rights in Utah in 1895," *Utah Historical Quarterly* 42 (Fall 1977): 344-69, reports the generally little-known participation of women in the statehood process. Edward Leo Lyman, "The Alienation of an Apostle from His Quorum: The Moses Thatcher Case," *Dialogue* 18 (Summer 1985): 67-91; and his "Mormon Leaders in Politics: The Transition to Statehood in 1896," *Journal of Mormon History* 24 (Fall 1998): 30-54, show the sometimes painful process of achieving statehood which caused conflict and unusual political machinations among the hierarchy.

Realizing that statehood would bring more self-governance and local power, Church leaders tried desperately for four decades to achieve statehood. This topic is covered in Guy M. Bishop, "Mormonism in Transition, 1890-1945," in this volume.

The Mormon Reformation and the Utah War

While tensions between the Mormons and others existed at several levels, concerned about what they perceived to be the Church's "moral and spiritual decay" Mormon leaders commenced what became known as the Reformation of 1856-57. This revival encouraged members to rededicate themselves to living the commandments but also produced an almost hysterical state of fanaticism which culminated with the Utah War and the Mountain Meadows Massacre. The movement's chief spokesman, Jedediah M. Grant, so whipped up the Saints that he is single-handedly (dis)credited with creating the climate of zealousness that led to the Mountain Meadows Massacre. In the process, Grant "literally preached and baptized himself into a frenzy that led him to his deathbed within a period of two months."[15] The first historian to emphasize the connection between the reformation and the Utah War was Gustive O. Larson, "The Mormon Reformation," *Utah Historical Quarterly* 26 (January 1958): 45-68. Other studies are Howard C. Searle, "The Mormon Reformation of 1856-1857" (M.A. thesis, Brigham Young University, 1956); Paul H. Peterson's award-winning essay, "The Mormon Reformation of 1856-1857: The Rhetoric and the Reality," *Journal of Mormon History* 15 (1989): 59-88; his "The Mormon Reformation," (Ph.D. diss., Brigham

---

15. Gene A. Sessions, "The Holding Forth of Jeddy Grant," *Dialogue* 12 (Winter 1979): 62-70, quotation p. 69.

Excavating Mormon Pasts

Young University, 1981); and Thomas G. Alexander, "Wilford Woodruff and the Mormon Reformation, 1855-1857," *Dialogue* 25 (Summer 1992): 25-39.

While the Reformation was under way, federal officials complained, even beyond their normal laments, to U.S. President James Buchanan about Mormon disloyalty in Utah Territory. In reaction to real and perceived problems, Buchanan ordered what amounted to about a third of the U.S. Army to march to Utah and put down a supposed rebellion. Norman F. Furniss, *The Mormon Conflict, 1850-1859* (New Haven, CT: Yale University Press, 1960), describes the context and the expedition itself. A well-done short introduction to this subject that is still remarkably insightful is Richard D. Poll, "The Mormon Question Enters National Politics, 1850-1856," *Utah Historical Quarterly* 25 (April 1957); 117-31. Outstanding is LeRoy R. Hafen and Ann W. Hafen, *The Utah Expedition, 1857-1858: A Documentary Account of the United States Military Movement under Colonel Albert Sidney Johnston and the Resistance by Brigham Young and the Mormon Nauvoo Legion* (1958; reprint ed., Glendale, CA: Arthur H. Clark, 1982).

Among other numerous works concerning the Utah Expedition are Wilford Hill LeCheminant, "A Crisis Averted? General Harney and the Change in Command of the Utah Expedition," *Utah Historical Quarterly* 51 (Winter 1983): 30-45; William P. Mackinnon, "125 Years of Conspiracy Theories: Origins of the Utah Expedition of 1857 58," *Utah Historical Quarterly* (Summer 1984): 212-30; and Richard D. Poll and William P. MacKinnon, "Causes of the Utah War Reconsidered," *Journal of Mormon History* (Fall 1994): 16-44. Arthur H. Clark will soon publish MacKinnon's *At Sword's Point: A Documentary History of the Utah War, 1857-1858*. A non-Mormon woman's perspective of the Utah War is offered in Audrey M. Godfrey, "Housewives, Hussies, and Heroines, or the Women of Johnston's Army," *Utah Historical Quarterly* 54 (Spring 1986): 157-78.[16]

Due in part to delaying tactics by Mormon guerillas, the federal troops made it only as far as Fort Bridger, in present-day southwestern Wyoming, before the winter of 1857-58. The principal Mormon military commander was Lot Smith, whose troops burned several federal supply trains. He has been elegantly profiled by Charles S. Peterson in "'A Mighty Man was Brother Lot': A Portrait of Lot Smith, Mormon Frontiersman," *Western Historical Quarterly* 1 (October 1970): 393-414. Exemplifying the ironies of Utah and Latter-day Saint history was Smith's short service with the Union Army protecting the Wyoming mail routes. A discussion of his and other Utahns' service is Craig L. Foster, "The Men of the Lot Smith Company," *Utah Genealogical Journal* 4, no. 26 (1998): 147-62. Protagonists on the non-Mormon side have been discussed in William F. Mackinnon, "The Buchanan Spoils System and the Utah Expedition: The Careers of W. M. F. Magraw and John M. Hockaday," *Utah Historical Quarterly* 31 (Spring 1963): 127-50. The man most responsible for negotiating a peaceful settlement to the crisis has been discussed in Richard D. Poll, "Thomas L. Kane and the Utah War," *Utah Historical Quarterly* 61 (Spring 1993): 112-35, and in the much older essay by Albert L. Zobell, "Thomas L. Kane: Ambassador to the Mormons," *Utah Humanities Review* 1 (October 1947): 320-46. A fascinating and informative look at the aftermath of the Utah war is William P. MacKinnon, "Epilogue to the Utah War: Impact and Legacy," *Journal of Mormon History* 29, no. 2 (Fall 2003): 186-248.

As part of the settlement process, federal troops were allowed to enter the Salt Lake Valley unmolested in 1858. In preparation for their entrance, however, the Mormons had planned an evacuation, discussed in Richard D. Poll, "The Move South," *BYU Studies* 29 (Fall 1989): 65-88, for fear that the U.S. government would renege on its promises of peace. The army established Camp Floyd west of Utah Lake, where it brought both economic prosperity and conflicts with the Mormons until it was disbanded in 1861. These and other questions have been covered in what is so far the most comprehensive history of Camp Floyd: Donald R. Moorman and Gene A. Sessions, *Camp Floyd and the Mormons:*

---

16. In contrast to the well-equipped army of 1857-58, the Mormons lacked good equipment and used older weaponry. An interesting look at Mormon-owned firearms during the territorial period is Hany W. Gibson, "Frontier Arms of the Mormons," *Utah Historical Quarterly* 42 (Winter 1974): 4-26.

The Utah War (Salt Lake City: University of Utah Press, 1992). Other works concerning the camp are Thomas G. Alexander and Leonard J. Arrington, "Camp in the Sagebrush: Camp Floyd, Utah, 1858-1861," *Utah Historical Quarterly* 34 (1966): 3-21, which provides a general overview. Social historian Audrey M. Godfrey has explored another side of the camp in "Home Hungry Hearts," *Utah Historical Quarterly* 60 (Winter 1992): 47-54; and her excellent "A Social History of Camp Floyd, Utah Territory, 1858-1861" (M.A. thesis, Utah State University, 1989).

While the Utah War was, on the whole, a "bloodless" conflict, the Mountain Meadows Massacre stands out as an irreducible tragedy. At least 120 members of a wagon train headed for California were killed by Mormons and Indians in southern Utah in the fall of 1857. For almost 100 years very little was written or openly spoken about this catastrophic event. The first effort to examine this massacre in a thorough and scholarly fashion was Juanita Brooks's well-researched and erudite *The Mountain Meadows Massacre* (Stanford, CA: Stanford University Press, 1950). While criticized by certain well-meaning Latter-day Saint spokesmen, the book was heralded by historians of all persuasions as an insightful and balanced explanation of a difficult chapter in the church's history. Brooks's approach was straightforward and honest, showing that she was not afraid to face uncomfortable events. Contextual treatments of violence on the Utah frontier include Thomas E. Austin and Robert S. McPherson, "Murder, Mayhem and Mormons: The Evolution of Law Enforcement on the San Juan Frontier, 1880-1900," *Utah Historical Quarterly* 35 (Winter 1987): 36-49; Robert Kent Fielding, *The Unsolicited Chronicler: An Account of the Gunnison Massacre* (Brookline, MA: Paradigm Publications, 1993); and D. Michael Quinn, "National Culture, Personality, and Theocracy in the Early Mormon Culture of Violence," in *John Whitmer Historical Association 2002 Nauvoo Conference Special Edition*, edited by Joni Wilson (N.p.: John Whitmer Historical Association, 2002), 159-86.

Additionally, Roger V. Logan, Jr., "New Light on the Mountain Meadows Caravan," *Utah Historical Quarterly* 60 (Summer 1992): 224-37, explored the stories of the victims of the massacre. William Wise, *Massacre at Mountain Meadow: An American Legend and a Monumental Crime* (New York: Thomas E. Crowell, 1976) was mediocre in comparison to Brooks, and even less satisfactory was Jim Lair, *The Mountain Meadows Massacre: An Outlander's View* (Arkansas: The Carroll County Historical and Genealogical Society, 1986). Lair, in his poorly written and inadequately researched work made no attempt to conceal his contempt for the Mormon Church and its members, warning readers to shun Mormon doctrines and recommending the sensationalist exposé *The God Makers* for further information.

The last few years have seen renewed interest in the massacre. This could be, in part, because of the construction and dedication of a new monument and a burial cairn at the meadow. Whatever the reason, these works include Anna Jean Backus, *Mountain Meadow Witness: The Life and Times of Bishop Philip Klingensmith* (Spokane, WA: Arthur H. Clark, 1995); Will Bagley, *Blood of the Prophets: Brigham Young and the Massacre at Mountain Meadows* (Norman: University of Oklahoma Press, 2002; Sally Denton, *American Massacre: The Tragedy at Mountain Meadows, September 1857* (New York: Knopf, 2003); and Jon Krakauer, *Under the Banner of Heaven: A Story of a Violent Faith* (New York: Doubleday, 2003). Backus's poignant portrayal of Klingensmith's involvement in the massacre and subsequent sad life adds new light from the perspective of the perpetrators of this tragedy. Bagley's book is well-researched, well-written, and well-documented and should certainly be considered an important work. Denton's disappointing work is substandard in scholarship, understanding of the sources, and readability. Krakauer's book touches on the Mountain Meadows Massacre only as context for his main focus on the murderous zealotry of the Lafferty brothers. While Krakauer addresses the interesting and important issue of religious violence, his profound anti-religious bias and ignorance of basic Mormon history hurts what could have otherwise been a real contribution to the study of Mormon history and modern Mormon fundamentalism. A highly anticipated work is Richard E. Turley Jr., Glen M. Leonard, and Ronald W. Walker, *Tragedy at Mountain Meadows* (New York: Oxford University

THE MOUNTAIN MEADOWS MASSACRE

By
JUANITA BROOKS

Stanford University Press
Stanford, California

Press, forthcoming), which will probably be the most thorough and intensively researched book ever written about Mountain Meadows.

Missionary Work and the Mormon Image

Although economics and politics played a major role in the development of what Arrington termed the Great Basin Kingdom, other important events and trends have also attracted the attention of Mormon historians. Without the vigorous efforts of Mormon missionaries and the continuous flow of immigrant members from the eastern United States and Europe, Utah would not have grown as quickly as it did.

Lacking and much-needed is a bold general synthesis of Mormon missionary activity during this important time period. Some contributions to more localized missionary work are Richard Jensen, "Without Purse or Scrip? Financing Latter-day Saint Missionary Work in Europe in the Nineteenth Century," *Journal of Mormon History* 12 (1985): 3-14; Bruce A. Van Orden, "The Decline in Convert Baptisms and Member Emigration from the British Mission after 1870," *BYU Studies* 27 (Spring 1987): 97-105; and, Michael W. Homer, "The Church's Image in Italy from the 1840s to 1946: A Bibliographic Essay," *BYU Studies* 31 (Spring 1991): 83-114. Carol Cornwall Madsen, "Mormon Missionary Wives in Nineteenth Century Polynesia," *Journal of Mormon History* 13 (1986-1987): 61-88, and M. Guy Bishop, "Waging Holy War: Mormon-Congregationalist Conflict in Mid-Nineteenth-Century Hawaii," *Journal of Mormon History* 17 (1991): 110-19, analyze the missionary experience in Hawaii, while Tracey E. Panek, "Life at Iosepa, Utah's Polynesian Colony," *Utah Historical Quarterly* 60 (Winter 1992): 64-77, examines the problems associated with transplanting an ethnic minority into the Great Basin.

Partly in reaction to Mormon missionary work, as well as Mormon doctrines and practices, anti-Mormon tracts and exposés flourished, warning readers and claiming to reveal the religion's sinister practices. While usually polemic and sensational, these works are revealing both for what they do and do not say about Mormonism within the larger sociocultural setting of Victorian society and its values.

Some general overviews of nineteenth-century anti-Mormon literature and its themes are Leonard J. Arrington and Jon Haupt, "Intolerable Zion: The Image of Mormonism in Nineteenth-Century American Literature," *Western Humanities Review* 22 (Summer 1968): 243-60; Craig L. Foster, "Victorian Pornographic Imagery in Anti-Mormon Literature," *Journal of Mormon History* 19 (Spring 1993): 115-32; his *Penny Tracts and Polemics: A Critical Analysis of Anti-Mormon Pamphleteering in Great Britain, 1837-1860* (Salt Lake City: Greg Kofford Books, 2002); Gary L. Bunker and Davis Bitton, "Illustrated Periodical Images of Mormons, 1850-1860," *Dialogue* 10 (Spring 1977): 82-94, and their *The Mormon Graphic Image: 1834-1914. Cartoons, Caricatures, and Illustrations* (Salt Lake City: University of Utah Press, 1983). In addition, Rebecca Foster Cornwall et al., "The Perpetuation of a Myth: Mormon Danites in Five Western Novels, 1840-1890," *BYU Studies* 23 (Spring 1983): 147-65, and Neal E. Lambert, "Saints, Sinners and Scribes: A Look at the Mormons in Fiction," *Utah Historical Quarterly* 36 (Winter 1968): 63-76, mine Mormon images from popular fiction. Lester E. Bush Jr. described nineteenth-century America's preoccupation with Mormon morality and sexuality in his interesting "Mormon Elders' Wafers: Images of Mormon Virility in Patent Medicine Ads," *Dialogue* 10 (Autumn 1976): 89-93.

The theme of national perceptions of the Mormons continued in the important Gary L. Bunker and Davis Bitton, *The Mormon Graphic Image, 1834-1914: Cartoons, Caricatures, and Illustrations* (Salt Lake City: University of Utah Press, 1983); Douglas McKay, "The Puissant Procreator: The Comic Ridicule of Brigham Young," *Sunstone* 7 (November-December 1982): 15-17; and Gary L. Bunker and Davis Bitton, "The Death of Brigham Young: Occasion for Satire," *Utah Historical Quarterly* 54 (Fall 1986): 358-70. Both articles analyzed the graphic image of Brigham Young as examples of the public perception of Mormonism.

Excavating Mormon Pasts

Blood of the Prophets

Brigham Young and the Massacre at Mountain Meadows

WILL BAGLEY

UNIVERSITY OF OKLAHOMA PRESS : NORMAN

Dissenting Movements

As with any religious movement, a number of members disaffiliated from the Mormon Church during its pioneer period. While many left Utah Territory for the East or California, not all left their new home. A. J. Simmonds, *The Gentile Comes to Cache Valley: A Study of the Apostasies of 1874 and the Establishment of Non-Mormon Churches in Cache Valley, 1873-1913* (Logan: Utah State University Press, 1976) studied the influence of other denominations on the Mormon community.

Although other denominations entered Utah as competition for the Mormon Church, several movements were the product of dissenters inside the Church itself. C. LeRoy Anderson, *"For Christ Will Come Tomorrow": The Saga of the Morrisites* (Logan: Utah State University Press, 1981), and C. LeRoy Anderson and Larry J. Halford, "The Mormons and the Morrisite War," *Montana: The Magazine of Western History* 24 (Autumn 1974): 42-53, look at the ill-fated Morrisite movement. The second better-known dissident movement is the subject of Ronald W. Walker, "The Commencement of the Godbeite Protest: Another View," *Utah Historical Quarterly* 42 (Summer 1974): 217-44; his "The Stenhouses and the Making of a Mormon Image," *Journal of Mormon History* 1 (1974): 51-72; and his *Wayward Saints: The Godbeites and Brigham Young* (Urbana: University of Illinois Press, 1998), which surveys the Godbeite protest as a reaction to differing views on doctrine as well as economics.

Biographies of individual dissenters are Lynne Watkins Jorgensen, "John Hyde Jr., Mormon Renegade," *Journal of Mormon History* 17 (1991): 120-44; Ronald W. Walker, "Edward Tullidge: Historian of the Mormon Commonwealth," *Journal of Mormon History* 3 (1976): 55-72; and Craig L. Foster, "From Temple Mormon to Anti-Mormon: The Ambivalence of Increase Van Dusen," *Dialogue* 27 (Fall 1994), all dealing with former Mormons who wrote against their former faith. Davis Bitton, "Mormonism's Encounter with Spiritualism," *Journal of Mormon History* 1 (1974): 39-50, reviews the complex history of the attraction and development of this unusual movement in Utah. Polly Aird, "'You Nasty Apostates, Clear Out': Reasons for Disaffection in the Late 1850s," *Journal of Mormon History* 30, no. 2 (Fall 2004), forthcoming, looks at seven people who disaffiliated from the church in Utah during the Reformation and wrote about it, either in contemporary letters or in memoirs.

The topic of dissent and religious competition offers many additional avenues. For example, the impact of missionary work by the Reorganized Church of Jesus Christ of Latter Day Saints in Utah needs to be explored more fully.[17] Another fruitful field for further inquiry is those who drifted away from Utah's mainstream Mormonism but did not affiliate with other Mormon-rooted groups.

Doctrinal Development and Interpretation

While 1846-96 was not as dynamic in doctrinal development as Joseph Smith's lifetime, it still saw significant developments in the introduction or reinterpretation of doctrines and concepts. T. Edgar Lyon, "Religious Activities and Development in Utah, 1847-1910," *Utah Historical Quarterly* 35 (Fall 1967): 292-306, gives a good general overview of this time period. Larry M. Logue, *A Sermon in the Desert: Belief and Behavior in Early St. George, Utah* (Urbana: University of Illinois Press, 1988), and his "A Time of Marriage: Monogamy and Polygamy in a Utah Town," *Journal of Mormon History* 11 (1984): 3-26, examine not only the doctrinal, but also the social, familial, and economic composition of Utah's Dixie.

Interesting articles on more specific subjects are David John Buerger, "The Adam-God Doctrine," *Dialogue* 15 (Spring 1982): 14-58; Thomas G. Alexander, "The Word of Wisdom: From Principle to Requirement," *Dialogue* 14 (Autumn 1981): 78-88; "The Reconstruction of Mormon Doctrine: From Joseph Smith to Progressive Theology,"

---

17. For some beginning approaches, see Roger D. Launius, *Joseph Smith III: Pragmatic Prophet* (Urbana: University of Illinois Press, 1988); Richard Lyle Shipley, "Voices of Dissent: The History of the Reorganized Church of Jesus Christ of Latter Day Saints in Utah, 1863-1900" (M.A. thesis, Utah State University, 1969); and relevant chapters in Valeen Tippetts Avery, *From Mission to Madness: Last Son of the Mormon Prophet* (Urbana: University of Illinois Press, 1998).

Excavating Mormon Pasts

Sunstone 5 (July/August 1980): 22-34; reprinted in *Sunstone* 10, no. 5 (May 1985): 8-18 and *Line Upon Line: Essays on Mormon Doctrine*, edited by Gary James Bergera (Salt Lake City: Signature Books, 1989), 53-66; D. Michael Quinn, "Latter-day Saint Prayer Circles," *BYU Studies* 19 (Fall 1978): 79-105; Gary James Bergera, "The Orson Pratt-Brigham Young Controversies: Conflict Within the Quorums, 1853-1868," *Dialogue* 13 (Summer 1980): 7-49; and William G. Hartley, "Ward Bishops and the Localizing of LDS Tithing, 1847-1856," in *New Views of Mormon History*, 96-114.

Discussing the development and interpretation of doctrine concerning priesthood authority are D. Michael Quinn, "The Evolution of the Presiding Quorums of the LDS Church," *Journal of Mormon History* 1 (1974):21-38; Gary James Bergera, "Seniority in the Twelve: The 1875 Realignment of Orson Pratt," *Journal of Mormon History* 18 (Spring 1992): 19-58, a topic expanded and deeply contextualized in his *Conflict in the Quorum: Orson Pratt, Brigham Young, Joseph Smith* (Salt Lake City: Signature Books, 2002); William G. Hartley, "The Priesthood Reorganization of 1877: Brigham Young's Last Achievement," *BYU Studies* 20 (Fall 1979): 3-36; and his "The Seventies in the 1880s: Revelations and Reorganizing," *Dialogue* 16 (Spring 1983): 62-88.

Plural Marriage

Probably no doctrine of the Mormon Church caused more negative reaction from non-Mormons than that of plural marriage. Another essay in this volume is devoted to this subject, so I will mention only a few important books as starting points: Lawrence Foster, *Religion and Sexuality: Three American Communal Experiments of the Nineteenth Century* (New York: Oxford University Press, 1981); Richard S. Van Wagoner, *Mormon Polygamy: A History* (1986; 3rd ed., Salt Lake City: Signature Books, 1992); and B. Carmon Hardy, *Solemn Covenant: The Mormon Polygamous Passage* (Urbana: University of Illinois Press, 1992); Lawrence Foster, *Women, Family, and Utopia: Communal Experiments of the Shakers, the Oneida Community, and the Mormons* (Syracuse, NY: Syracuse University Press, 1991); Lee L. Bean, Geraldine P. Mineau, and Douglas L. Anderton, *Fertility Change on the American Frontier: Adaptation and Innovation* (Berkeley: University of California Press, 1990); Kathryn M. Daynes, *More Wives Than One: Transformation of the Mormon Marriage System, 1840-1910* (Urbana: University of Illinois, 2002); Marie Cornwall, Camela Courtright, and Laga Van Beek, "How Common the Principle? Women as Plural Wives in 1860," *Dialogue* 26 (Summer 1993): 139-53; Gary Wyatt, "Mormon Polygyny in the Nineteenth Century: A Theoretical Analysis," *Journal of Comparative Family Studies* 20 (Spring 1989): 13-20. Significant in revising the commonly accepted figure of 2-3 percent frequency of polygamy is Lowell "Ben" Bennion, "The Incidence of Mormon Polygamy in 1880: 'Dixie' versus Davis Stake," *Journal of Mormon History* 11 (1984): 27-46.

While the Mormons defended their marriage system on theological, economical, and social grounds, the American public countered with arguments focusing on its perceived sensuality, its threat to public morality, and its attack on the traditional family. Useful introductions to these arguments are David J. Whittaker, "Early Mormon Polygamy Defenses," *Journal of Mormon History* 11 (1984): 43-64; and Charles A. Cannon, "The Awesome Power of Sex: The Polemical Campaign Against Mormon Polygamy," *Pacific Historical Review* 43 (February 1974): 61-82. Roger D. Launius documents Joseph Smith III's active role in "Politicking Against Polygamy: Joseph Smith III, the Reorganized Church, and the Politics of the Anti-polygamy Crusade, 1860-1890," *John Whitmer Historical Association Journal* 7 (1987): 35-44, and "Methods and Motives: Joseph Smith III's Opposition to Polygamy, 1860-90," *Dialogue* 20 (Winter 1987): 105-20. Interesting articles which look at nineteenth- and early twentieth-century beliefs about polygamy's physical effects are Lester E. Bush Jr., "A Peculiar People: The Physiological Aspects of Mormonism, 1850-1875," *Dialogue* 12 (Fall 1979): 97-106; and Gary L. Bunker and Davis Bitton, "Polygamous Eyes: A Note on Mormon Physiognomy," *Dialogue* 12 (Fall 1979): 114-19.

Ultimately, the reaction of the American public was to clamor for a cessation of this morally repugnant practice. The standard work on this subject is Gustive O. Larson,

The "Americanization" of Utah for Statehood (San Marino, CA: Huntington Library, 1971), which argues that the Mormons had to give up polygamy before Utah was sufficiently "American" to warrant admission to the union. Two important studies by Richard D. Poll, never published, are still valuable works on the subject of the anti-polygamy crusade: "The Twin Relic: A Study of Mormon Polygamy and the Campaign by the Government of the United States for Its Abolition, 1852-1890" (M.A. thesis, Texas Christian University, 1939); and "The Mormon Question, 1850-1865: A Study in Politics and Public Opinion" (Ph.D. diss., University of California, Berkeley, 1948). Additionally, Barbara Hayfield, "Utah's Anti-Polygamy Society, 1878-1884" (M.A. thesis, Brigham Young University, 1980); and Joan Smyth Iverson, *The Antipolygamy Controversy in U.S. Women's Movements, 1880-1925: A Debate on the American Home* (New York: Garland Publishing, 1997), examined movements on the popular level to stop plural marriage.

A number of works analyze the legal aspects of the conflict between the Mormons and the federal government. Some of these works include Mark S. Lee, "Legislating Morality: Reynolds vs. United States," *Sunstone* 10 (April 1985): 8-12; Kenneth D. Driggs, "The Prosecutions Begin: Defining Cohabitation in 1885," *Dialogue* 21 (Spring 1988): 109-25; Edwin Brown Firmage, "The Judicial Campaign Against Polygamy and the Enduring Legal Questions," *BYU Studies* 27 (Summer 1987): 91-118; Edwin B. Firmage and R. Collin Mangrum, *Zion in the Courts: A Legal History of the Church of Jesus Christ of Latter-day Saints, 1830-1900* (Urbana: University of Illinois Press, 1988); Orma Linford, "The Mormons and the Law: The Polygamy Cases," *Utah Law Review* 9 (Winter 1964/Summer 1965): 308-70, 543-91; Joseph H. Groberg, "The Mormon Disfranchisements of 1882-1892," *BYU Studies* 16 (Spring 1976): 399-408; Kenneth D. Driggs, "The Prosecution Begins: Defining Cohabitation in 1885," *Dialogue* 21 (Spring 1988): 109-26; Carol Cornwall Madsen, "'Sisters at the Bar': Utah Women in Law," *Utah Historical Quarterly* 61 (Summer 1993): 208-32; her "'At Their Peril': Utah Law and the Case of Plural Wives, 1850-1900," *Western Historical Quarterly* 21 (November 1990): 425-43; Douglas H. Parker, "Victory in Defeat—Polygamy and the Mormon Legal Encounter with the Federal Government," *Cardozo Law Review* 12 (February-March 1991): 805-19; Edwin B. Firmage, "Free Exercise of Religion in Nineteenth-Century America: The Mormon Cases," *Journal of Law and Religion* 7 (1989): 281-313; and Edwin B. Firmage, "Religion and the Law: The Mormon Experience in the Nineteenth Century," *Cardozo Law Review* 12 (February/March 1991): 765-803. An important work is Sarah Barringer Gordon's prize-winning *The Mormon Question: Polygamy and Constitutional Conflict in Nineteenth-Century America* (Chapel Hill: University of North Carolina Press, 2002).

That the Mormons were not just "free love" advocates can be seen in their efforts to punish extramarital sexual expression. See Kenneth L. Cannon II, "'Mountain Common Law': The Extralegal Punishment of Seducers in Early Utah," *Utah Historical Quarterly* 51 (Fall 1983): 308-27. Two judges active in polygamy prosecutions are featured in Thomas G. Alexander, "Charles S. Zane, Apostle of the New Era," *Utah Historical Quarterly* 34 (Fall 1966): 291-314; C. Peter Magrath, "Chief Justice Waite and the 'Twin Relic': *Reynolds vs. United States*," *Vanderbilt Law Review* 18 (1965): 507-543; and Michael W. Homer, "The Federal Bench and Priesthood Authority: The Rise and Fall of John Fitch Kinney's Early Relationship with the Mormons," *Journal of Mormon History* 13 (1986-87): 89-110.

An extremely important work which provides a comprehensive list of Mormon men who served time in the territorial penitentiary for conscience's sake is Rosa Mae McClellan Evans, "Judicial Prosecution of Prisoners for LDS Plural Marriage: Prison Sentences, 1884-1895" (M.A. thesis, Brigham Young University, 1986). William Mulder, "Prisoners for Conscience Sake," in *Lore of Faith and Folly*, edited by Thomas E. Cheney (Salt Lake City: University of Utah Press, 1971), 135-44; B. Carmon Hardy, "The American Siberia: Mormon Prisoners in Detroit in the 1880s," *Michigan History* 50 (September 1966): 197-210; and Melvin Bashore, "Life Behind Bars: Mormon Cohabs of the 1880s," *Utah Historical Quarterly* 47 (Winter 1979): 22-41, describe the sense of commitment and sacrifice which most of the men felt as they served prison terms for their religion. The articles also look at the suffering which the men and their families experienced. Interestingly, Stephen

Excavating Mormon Pasts

Cresswell, *Mormons and Cowboys, Moonshiners and Klansmen: Federal Law Enforcement in the South and West, 1870-1893* (Tuscaloosa: University of Alabama Press, 1991), chap. 3, explores the commonalities (and there were more than might be expected) and divergences of southern and western justice on the polygamy issue.

However, not all men chose to go to prison for their religion. James B. Allen explains the conflicting teachings that led to conflicting choices about continuing plural marriage in "'Good Guys' vs. 'Good Guys': Rudger Clawson, John Sharp, and Civil Disobedience in Nineteenth-Century Utah," *Utah Historical Quarterly* 48 (Spring 1980): 148-74. Sharp's experience is also addressed in my, "John Sharp and T. B. H. Stenhouse: Two Scottish Converts Who Chose Separate Paths," *John Whitmer Historical Association Journal* 17 (1997): 81-93.

The campaign against Mormon polygamy finally had the desired effect when, in 1890, Wilford Woodruff's manifesto officially withdrew support for new plural marriages, even though it took more than a decade and at least two more manifestos to make it clear that this was the Church's official position. Some of the more significant articles are Henry J. Wolfinger, "A Reexamination of the Woodruff Manifesto in Light of Utah Constitutional History," *Utah Historical Quarterly* 39 (Fall 1971): 328-49; Jan Shipps, "The Principle Revoked: A Closer Look at the Demise of Plural Marriage," *Journal of Mormon History* 11 (1984): 65-77; Thomas G. Alexander, "The Odyssey of a Latter-day Prophet: Wilford Woodruff and the Manifesto of 1890," *Journal of Mormon History* 17 (1991): 169-206; B. Carmon Hardy, "Self-Blame and the Manifesto," *Dialogue* 24 (Fall 1991): 43-57; and E. Leo Lyman, "The Political Background of the Manifesto," *Dialogue* 24 (Fall 1991): 21-39. Also deeply researched standard sources on this transition are D. Michael Quinn, "LDS Church Authority and New Plural Marriages, 1890-1904," *Dialogue* 18 (Spring 1985): 9-105, and B. Carmon Hardy's powerful *Solemn Covenant: Mormon Polygamous Passage* (Urbana: University of Illinois Press, 1992). For discussions of schismatic post-Manifesto polygamy, see Martha Sonntag Bradley, "Out of the Closet and into the Fire: The New Mormon Historians' Take on Polygamy," in this volume.

Women, Children, and Family Structure and Dynamics

Most significantly affected by the introduction of plural marriage was the family unit. Both a winner and a loser in the practice of and long struggle against polygamy, the Mormon family unit did indeed exhibit certain peculiar characteristics. Probably the two best general overviews of family structure and dynamics are Jessie L. Embry, *Mormon Polygamous Families: Life in the Principle* (Salt Lake City: University of Utah Press, 1987) and Vicky Burgess-Olsen, "Family Structure and Dynamics in Early Utah Mormon Families, 1847-1855" (Ph.D. diss., Northwestern University, 1975). Jessie L. Embry, "Effects of Polygamy on Mormon Women," *Frontiers: A Journal of Women's Studies* 7 (1984): 56-61, and Julie Dunfrey, "'Living the Principle of Plural Marriage: Mormon Women, Utopia, and Female Sexuality in the Nineteenth Century," *Feminist Studies* 10 (Fall 1984): 523-36, both look at women's roles in Mormon polygynous marriages. Carol Cornwall Madsen, "'At Their Peril': Utah Law and the Case of Plural Wives, 1850-1900," *Western Historical Quarterly* 21 (November 1990): 425-43, looks at the difficult legal situation of Mormon plural wives.

Lola Van Wagenen has made significant contributions to Mormon women's suffrage in the national context, including "In Their Own Behalf: The Politicization of Mormon Women and the 1870 Franchise," *Dialogue* 24 (Winter 1991): 31-43, and her prize-winning dissertation, "Sister-wives and Suffragists: Polygamy and the Politics of Woman Suffrage, 1870-1896," (Ph.D. diss., New York University, 1994), which has been reprinted by the Joseph Fielding Smith Institute for LDS History and *BYU Studies*, 2003). Joan Smyth Iverson also looked at women's suffrage in "The Mormon Suffrage Relationship: Personal and Political Quandaries," *Frontiers: A Journal of Women's Studies* 11 (1990): 8-16; and her *The Antipolygamy Controversy in U.S. Women's Movements, 1880-1925: A Debate on the American Home* (New York: Garland Publishing, 1997). Additionally, Kathleen Marquis, "'Diamond Cut Diamond': Mormon Women and the Cult of Domesticity in the Nineteenth Century,"

Papers in Women's Studies: University of Michigan 2 (1974): 105-23, analyzes Mormon women's roles in light of society's role for women.

Because of the complexity and peculiarity of the Mormon marriage system, divorce was a necessary recourse for failed marriages. One of the earliest studies was Eugene E. Campbell and Bruce L. Campbell, "Divorce Among Mormon Polygamists: Extent and Explanations," *Utah Historical Quarterly* 46 (Winter 1978): 4-23, followed by Richard I. Aaron, "Mormon Divorce and the Statute of 1852: Questions for Divorce in the 1880s," *Journal of Contemporary Law* 8 (1982): 5-45.

An area in dire need of serious study concerns Mormon children during this time period. Strong beginning examinations of this field include Larry M. Logue, "Modernization Arrested: Child-Naming and the Family in a Utah Town," *Journal of American History* 74 (June 1987): 131-38; Martha Sonntag Bradley, "'Hide and Seek': Children on the Underground," *Utah Historical Quarterly* 51 (Spring 1983): 133-53; Davis Bitton, "Zion's Rowdies: Growing Up on the Mormon Frontier," *Utah Historical Quarterly* 50 (Spring 1982): 182-95; and Elliott West, "Becoming Mormon," *Journal of Mormon History* 28, no. 1 (Spring 2002): 31-51, which examined the different social demands placed on children from Mormonism's earliest years through the 1850s.

Ethnicity and Race

Another area of study which needs more attention is ethnicity and race within Mormonism. A very good overview of the topic focused on Utah, rather than Mormonism per se, is Helen Z. Papanikolis, *The Peoples of Utah* (Salt Lake City: Utah Historical Society, 1976), reinforced by Leslie G. Kelen and Eileen Hallet Stone, eds., *Missing Stories: An Oral History of Ethnic and Minority Groups in Utah* (Logan: Utah State University, 2000). African Americans in territorial Utah are treated in Newell G. Bringhurst, *Saints, Slaves, and Blacks* (Westport, CT: Greenwood Press, 1981); his "The Mormons and Slavery—A Closer Look," *Pacific Historical Review* 50 (August 1991): 329-38; his "The 'Descendants of Ham' in Zion: Discrimination against Blacks Along the Shifting Mormon Frontier, 1830-1920," *Nevada Historical Society Quarterly* 24 (Winter 1981): 298-318; and Dennis L. Lythgoe, "Negro Slavery in Utah," *Utah Historical Quarterly* 39 (Winter 1971): 51-54. For a comparison on LDS and RLDS (Community of Christ) attitudes toward race and ethnicity, see Robert Ben Madison, "'Heirs According to the Promise': Observations on Ethnicity, Race and Identity in Two Factions of Nineteenth-Century Mormonism," *John Whitmer Historical Association Journal* 12 (1992): 66-82; and Roger D. Launius, *Invisible Saints: A History of Black Americans in the Reorganized Church* (Independence: Herald Publishing House, 1988).

An exception to the general neglect of ethnic studies is American Indians, particularly when their presence affected the lives of the Mormon settlers. An excellent review of the literature is David J. Whittaker, "Mormons and Native Americans: A Historical and Bibliographical Introduction," *Dialogue* 18 (Winter 1985): 33-48. Lawrence G. Coates, "Brigham Young and Mormon Indian Policies: The Formative Period, 1836-1851," *BYU Studies* 18 (Spring 1978): 428-52; Ronald W. Walker, "Toward a Reconstruction of Mormon and Indian Relations, 1847-1877," *BYU Studies* 29 (Fall 1989): 23-42; and his "Seeking the 'Remnant': The Native American during the Joseph Smith Period," *Journal of Mormon History* 19 (Spring 1993): 1-33, all examine the history and context of official Mormon policies on peaceful relations between the two peoples.[18] Among works on individual Indians are Scott R. Christensen, *Sagwitch: Shoshoni Chieftain, Mormon Elder, 1822-1884* (Logan: Utah State University, 1999); and Matthew E. Kreitzer, ed., *The Washakie Letters of Willie Ottogary: Northwestern Shoshone Journalist and Leader, 1906-1929* (Logan: Utah State University, 2000). Carole Gates Sorensen is at work on a biography of Chief Kanosh, who played an important diplomatic role in the balance of power during Brigham Young's lifetime.

---

18. Two articles by Lawrence G. Coates examine the pre-Utah period of Mormon-Indian relations: "Refugees Meet: The Mormons and Indians in Iowa," *BYU Studies* 21 (Fall 1981): 492-512; and "Cultural Conflict: Mormons and Indians in Nebraska," *BYU Studies* 24 (Summer 1984): 275-300.

Excavating Mormon Pasts

Exploring Indian wars in Utah are John Alton Peterson, *Utah's Black Hawk War* (Salt Lake City: University of Utah Press, 1999); Howard A. Christy, "The Walker War: Defense and Conciliation as Strategy," *Utah Historical Quarterly* 47 (Fall 1979): 395-420; Albert Winkler, "The Circleville Massacre: A Brutal Incident in Utah's Black Hawk War," *Utah Historical Quarterly* 55 (Winter 1987): 4-21; his prize-winning "The Ute Mode of War in the Conflict of 1865-68," *Utah Historical Quarterly* 60 (Fall 1992): 300-18; his "Justice in the Black Hawk War: The Trial of Thomas Jose," *Utah Historical Quarterly* 60 (Spring 1992): 124-36; Warren Metcalf, "A Precarious Balance: The Northern Utes and the Black Hawk War," *Utah Historical Quarterly* 57 (Winter 1989): 24-35; and Newell Hart, *The Bear River Massacre* (Preston, ID: Cache Valley Newsletter Publishing, 1982); Brigham Madsen, *The Shoshoni Frontier and the Bear River Massacre* (Salt Lake City: University of Utah Press, 1985).

Some of the sprinkling of works concerning other races and ethnic groups are Frederick S. Buchanan, "Scots Among the Mormons," *Utah Historical Quarterly* 36 (Fall 1968): 328-52; his edition of *"A Good Time Coming": Mormon Letters to Scotland* (Salt Lake City: University of Utah Press, 1988); Ronald D. Dennis, *The Call of Zion: The Story of the First Welsh Mormon Emigration* (Provo, UT: Religious Studies Center, Brigham Young University, 1987); William Mulder, *Homeward to Zion: The Mormon Migration from Scandinavia* (Minneapolis: University of Minnesota Press, 1957); P.A.M. Taylor, *Expectations Westward: The Mormons and the Emigration of Their British Converts in the Nineteenth Century* (Ithaca, NY: Cornell University Press, 1966); Douglas F. Tobler, "Heinrich Hug and Jacob Tobler: From Switzerland to Santa Clara, 1854-80," *Dialogue* 26 (Winter 1993): 107-128; and, D. Michael Polson, "The Swedes in Grantsville, Utah, 1860-1900," *Utah Historical Quarterly* 56 (Summer 1988): 208-21.

Jessie L. Embry has made a long-term and major commitment to ethnic Mormon studies with "Little Berlin: Swiss Saints of the Logan Tenth Ward," *Utah Historical Quarterly* 56 (Summer 1988): 222-35; *Black Saints in a White Church: Contemporary African American Mormons* (Salt Lake City: Signature Books, 1994); "Ethnic American Mormons: The Development of a Community," in *Mormon Identities in Transition,* edited by Douglas J. Davies (New York: Cassell, 1996), 63-67; *"In His Own Language": Mormon Spanish Speaking Congregations in the United States* (Salt Lake City: Signature books, 1998); "Separate but Equal?": The Advantages and Challenges of Separate Ethnic Wards and Branches," in (no editor), *For Ye Are All One in Christ Jesus:: The Global Church in a World of Ethnic Diversity,* Proceedings of the Sixth Annual Conference of the International Society, August 21, 1995 (Provo, UT: David M. Kennedy Center for International Studies, BYU, 1996), 41-43; and *Asian American Mormons: Bridging Cultures* (Provo, UT: Charles Redd Center for Western Studies, 1999).

Mormon Architecture

Reflective of the many different nationalities which eventually settled in Utah are the buildings and towns. Many of the early buildings reflected the New England and Atlantic states background of many of the members. Thomas Carter, "North European Horizontal Log Construction in the Sanpete-Sevier Valleys," *Utah Historical Quarterly* 52 (Winter 1984): 50-71, discussed the Scandinavian influence on house building. The unique Mormon marriage and family system also encouraged ingenuity in architecture. Keith Bennett and Thomas Carter, "Houses with Two Fronts: The Evolution of Domestic Architectural Design in a Mormon Community," *Journal of Mormon History* 15 (1989): 47-58, and Joseph Heinerman, "The Mormon Meetinghouse: Reflections on Pioneer Religious and Social Life in Salt Lake City," *Utah Historical Quarterly* 50 (Fall 1982): 340-53, both looked at Mormon architecture. Newly published is Richard W. Jackson, *Places of Worship: 150 Years of LDS Architecture* (Provo, UT: Religious Studies Center, BYU, 2004), a comprehensive history of Mormon meetinghouses illustrated with the author's drawings.

Without question, the most important architectural projects among the Mormons have been their temples. These buildings, which the early Saints imbued with so many hopes and dreams, have been the subject of several interesting historical, architectural, and theological studies. Laurel B. Andrew, *The Early Temples of the Mormons: The Architecture of the Millennial Kingdom in the American West* (Albany: University Press of New York, 1978) focuses on the four nineteenth-century Utah temples at St. George, Logan, Salt Lake City, and Manti. A solid history of the Salt Lake Temple, written in commemoration of its hundredth anniversary is Richard Neitzel Holzapfel, *Every Stone a Sermon: The Magnificent Story of the Construction and Dedication of the Salt Lake Temple* (Salt Lake City: Bookcraft, 1992). Another useful commemorative work is Nelson B. Wadsworth, *Set in Stone, Fixed in Glass: The Great Mormon Temple and Its Photographers* (Salt Lake City: Signature Books, 1992). More specifically architectural is C. Mark Hamilton et al., *The Salt Lake Temple: Monument to a People* (Salt Lake City: University Services, 1982). Other Mormon temples of the western pioneer period have not received the same sustained attention as the Salt Lake edifice.

Education and Communication

In a land where survival was the primary concern, it is remarkable that education received the emphasis that it did. Charles S. Peterson addressed the problems of early education in the territory, "The Limits of Learning in Pioneer Utah," *Journal of Mormon History* 10 (1983): 65-78. The conflict between Mormon and non-Mormon control of the territorial schools and curriculum was analyzed in C. Merrill Hough, "Two School Systems in Conflict: 1867-1890," *Utah Historical Quarterly* 28 (April 1960): 113-30. Questions concerning cultural and religious conflict between the Mormons and non-Mormons, as well as between the various ethnic groups need to be answered. R. Douglas Brackenridge, *Westminster College of Salt Lake City: From Presbyterian Mission School to Independent College* (Logan: Utah State University Press, 1998), probes the early conflicted history between this school and its Mormon host culture.

The need for better communication among the various nationalities arriving as converts in Utah, as well as a desire to create a community apart from the rest of the world was the stimulus for the development of the short-lived Deseret Alphabet described in Douglas D. Alder, Paula J. Goodfellow, and Ronald G. Watt, "Creating a New Alphabet for Zion: The Origin of the Deseret Alphabet," *Utah Historical Quarterly* 52 (Summer 1984): 278-86.

Conclusion

The period between 1846 and 1896 is highly significant for the Church of Jesus Christ of Latter-day Saints. Indeed, in aspects of personal and collective struggle and accomplishments, as well as in non-Mormon perceptions of Mormonism, this period truly was "heroic." Leonard J. Arrington's *Great Basin Kingdom* broke from the traditional apologetic and defensive Mormon accounts in setting a standard of scholarly, thought-provoking history. The books and articles that have taken the same approach have allowed people both inside and outside of the Church to gain a better understanding of Mormon and Utah history.

Many of these works have broken ground, asked important and, sometimes, difficult questions, and proposed new, but not always comfortable, answers. A large body of the available literature has covered the traditional political, economic, doctrinal, and social experience of the Church as a whole, while other publications have focused on individuals and communities as a lens through which to view the larger Mormon experience. Despite this important groundwork, much more needs to be done on the local and individual level to reconstruct life in the early Mormon communities in territorial Utah.

The encouraging trend during the past few decades has been to move away from institutional-oriented history toward a more personal and human history. This more human approach to history can greatly aid our understanding of the lived experience of Mormons during the 1847-96 period by focusing closely on the systems, events, and historical figures and how they interacted with each other. As Russian State Archivist Igor Sahkarov observed: "Every person who has lived is no less of a person than the most important person of the time, in the eyes of God."[19]

While this general trend has been helpful in producing significant, professional publications about the Mormon experience during this time period, much more needs to

---

19. Address to the Genealogical Society of Utah, Salt Lake City, Utah, November 1993; notes in my possession.

be done. Perhaps complacency is one of the greatest enemies to Mormon historiography. New questions must be continuously asked and models of study redefined. Community of Christ historians have been particularly thoughtful in reflecting on larger historiographical questions, as, for example, Roger D. Launius, "The 'New Social History' and the 'New Mormon History': Reflections on Recent Trends," *Dialogue* 27 (Spring 1994): 109-28. Themes of race, ethnicity, class, and gender must be used in addressing questions concerning Mormon history.

For example, what do census, tax, and land records tell us about the economic stability of some of the smaller outlying communities? Could a tragedy like the Mountain Meadows Massacre have occurred in northern Utah or did this event reflect a culture or mind-set limited to southern Utah? What ecclesiastical and social role did non-English speaking people play in early Utah? How were early apostates and "Jack Mormons" treated in smaller Mormon communities and how did this treatment differ from the larger communities like Salt Lake City and Ogden? What economic role did women play in early Utah?

Another area with great potential for illuminating the Mormon experience is that of the family and its involvement in Church and community affairs. What can diaries, ward records, and genealogical data tell us about inter- and intra-familial dynamics in some of the Mormon communities? What role did women play in defining and enforcing morality in the community? Were childhood and youth in Mormon-dominated settlements different from these same developmental stages in non-Mormon communities? How did the family experience differ by nationality and were there any trends that can be followed over several generations?

While Mormon historians have been able to go beyond the defensive "us versus them" approach to history so prevalent in the earlier works on the Mormon Church during the pre-statehood period of Utah history, much remains to be done. By gaining a greater understanding of the common members of the Mormon Church, historians will be able to better understand a significant part of American religious history. However, the potential for understanding does not stop there. Mormon historians need to place Mormon history and events in the context of the larger Western American and American social and historical context. This approach will almost certainly yield a greater understanding of the impact and significance of Mormonism on American history—and vice versa.

CRAIG L. FOSTER is a research archivist at the LDS Family History Library and, with his wife, Suzanne, served as executive secretary for the Mormon History Association for seven years. He is the author of numerous articles dealing with various aspects of nineteenth-century Latter-day Saint history. His *Penny Tracts and Polemics: A Critical Analysis of Anti-Mormon Pamphleteering in Great Britain, 1837-1860* (Salt Lake City: Greg Kofford Books, 2002) is based on his dissertation.

Chapter 7

Mormonism in Transition, 1890-1945

M. Guy Bishop

Anthropologist Mark P. Leone observes that the modern Latter-day Saints have transformed themselves into a "middle class, business oriented and urban" society who has given up their former "agrarian orientation."[1] The historiography enveloping the period 1890-1945 reflects the dynamics of this critical juncture in Mormon history. It was an age characterized by change, transition, and accommodation. A major target of these actions was to achieve acceptance by the larger American society.

On the cutting edge of today's New Mormon History was Leonard J. Arrington, *Great Basin Kingdom: An Economic History of the Latter-day Saints, 1830-1900* (1958; reprint ed., Lincoln: University of Nebraska Press, 1966).[2] Although Arrington ended his study at 1900, many of the topics he addressed are still vital in Mormon studies.

From the Nauvoo years of the 1840s, and carrying over to their settlement in the Great Basin under Brigham Young's leadership in 1847, the Mormons were seen as a "peculiar" or different people because of their distinctive doctrines and disconcerting social and economic customs. This chapter traces the Mormon majority who, after the 1844 murder of the religion's founder, Joseph Smith Jr., followed Young to the isolation of today's Utah. Other chapters in this volume, "Travelers on the New Mormon History Trail: Community of Christ Contributions to the New Mormon History," by Mark A. Scherer, and "Studies of Mormon Fissiparousness: Conflict, Dissent, and Schism in the Early Church," by Danny L. Jorgensen, track developments with other groups rooted in Joseph Smith's teachings.

This essay focuses on the period of transition marked by the Woodruff Manifesto in 1890, which withdrew official approval for new plural marriages, through the end of World War II. It is a period that offers exceptional scope for the talents of the New Mormon historians, one characteristic of whom is an acceptance of multiple causes and influences on events, an effort to understand historical actors in terms of psychological motivations, a serious mastery of original sources, and analyses that, while not excluding spiritual and religious influences, does not rely primarily on them. The best scholarly treatment of this period is Thomas G. Alexander, *Mormonism in Transition: A History of the Latter-day Saints, 1890-1930* (Urbana: University of Illinois Press, 1986). Alexander's closing date, 1930, was the centennial of the Church's organization. This chapter ends with World War II, a national conflict that played a significant function in Mormonism's social and cultural transformation at the end of its first century.

---

1. Mark P. Leone, *Roots of Modern Mormonism* (Cambridge, MA: Harvard University Press, 1979), 1.
2. For more recent views on this foundational book, see *Great Basin Kingdom Revisited: Contemporary Perspectives*, edited by Thomas G. Alexander (Logan: Utah State University Press, 1991).

Mormonism in Transition

A HISTORY OF
THE LATTER-DAY SAINTS,
1890–1930

Thomas G. Alexander

University of Illinois Press
Urbana and Chicago

A thought-provoking investigation of the region's territorial years, is David L. Bigler, *Forgotten Kingdom: The Mormon Theocracy in the American West, 1847-1896* (Spokane, WA: The Arthur H. Clark Company, 1998), chaps. 15-17. Bigler's thesis is: During "the middle of the nineteenth century a theocratic state was established in the American West whose people were governed by inspiration from God to their leaders on earth" (15). Bigler's provocative account looks particularly at Mormon relations with Gentiles and Native Americans, the two groups most likely to rebuff pious LDS visions for the region.

In the course of defending themselves from intrusions into their religious culture by the federal government, anti-polygamy crusaders, and a host of other critics, the Latter-day Saints reluctantly accepted accommodation as the strategy to follow during the last decade of the nineteenth-century. James B. Allen and Glen M. Leonard, *The Story of the Latter-day Saints,* (1976; 2nd ed. rev. and enl., Salt Lake City: Deseret Book, 1992) observe, "the Saints reached a compromise with the federal government that seemed satisfactory to all" (301). In addition to the solid overview and excellent bibliography of this book is a second survey of LDS history, Leonard J. Arrington and Davis Bitton, *The Mormon Experience: A History of the Latter-day Saints* (New York: Alfred A. Knopf, 1979).

LDS Accommodation

The surrender of the Church on issues like polygamy, political control, and economic involvement served to pave the way toward statehood and home rule. These three issues were intricately entwined, since together they constituted the practices drawn from Mormonism's most deeply held beliefs, even though polygamy was the "hot-button" issue that mobilized and focused the nation's wrath. Edward Brown Firmage and Richard Collin Mangrum, *Zion in the Courts: A Legal History of the Church of Jesus Christ of Latter-day Saints, 1830-1900* (Urbana: University of Illinois Press, 1988), devote much of their book to the legal challenges that forced Mormon compliance, hypothesizing that the larger American society found Mormonism inherently intolerable because "Mormonism was devoted to the ideal of Zion, a perfect community of Saints, organized in economic, political and social affairs [in preparation for] the Second Coming" (x).

In 1890 Church President Wilford Woodruff (1807-98), acting to save the Church from legal dismemberment under crushing federal pressure against polygamy, issued a manifesto declaring "my intention to submit to those laws" and further declaring that "my advice to the Latter-day Saints is to refrain from contracting any marriage forbidden by the law of the land" (D&C—Declaration 1). Phrased as "advice" and conspicuously confining itself only to new plural marriages but without commenting on existing unions, this action was still deemed sufficient to relax tensions with the government and pave the way for Utah statehood six years later. For the Latter-day Saints, plural marriage was a deeply theological principle and practice and they confidently expected the Second Coming of Christ to deliver them from federal harassment, as Thomas G. Alexander makes clear in his "Wilford Woodruff and the Changing Nature of Mormon Religious Experience," *Church History* 45 (March 1976): 50-69; *Things in Heaven and on Earth: The Life and Times of Wilford Woodruff, a Mormon Prophet* (Salt Lake City: Signature Books, 1991); and "The Odyssey of a Latter-day Saint Prophet: Wilford Woodruff and the Manifesto of 1890," *Journal of Mormon History* 17 (1991): 169-206.[3] B. Carmon Hardy, *Solemn Covenant: The Mormon Polygamous Passage* (Urbana: University of Illinois Press, 1992), also documents the difficulty of making that reluctant transition for Mormonism's most devout believers.

Bruce Van Orden, *Prisoner for Conscience' Sake: George Reynolds* (Salt Lake City: Deseret Book, 1992), deals with the crucial court case, *Reynolds v. the United States,* decided by the U.S. Supreme Court as the test case of the legality of plural marriage. Reynolds, a

---

3. Wilford Woodruff, *Wilford Woodruff's Journal, 1833-1898,* typescript, edited by Scott G. Kenny, 9 vols. (Midvale, Utah: Signature Books, 1983-85), is an almost-daily diary, an invaluable primary source and intimate insider's perspective on the fight over polygamy and the events leading to the 1890 Manifesto. Scott G. Kenney has done a great service for scholars by making this typescript edition available, in print and also in Smith Research Associates, *New Mormon Studies CD-ROM,* 1998.

young polygamist and a secretary to the First Presidency, cooperated with the prosecution and served his time as a model prisoner in this revealing look at the personal dimensions of polygamy prosecution that affected virtually every community in the Mormon corridor.

Whether they personally practiced the principle, almost all devout Latter-day Saints, supported the principle. Henry Bigler, the Mormon Battalion soldier who discovered gold at Sutter's Mill, never took a plural wife; but as a church missionary to Hawaii during the late 1850s, he zealously defended the practice as the word of God, as recounted in my *Henry William Bigler: Soldier, Gold Miner, Missionary, Chronicler 1815-1900* (Logan: Utah State University Press, 1998), 89, 101, 114.

Kathryn M. Daynes, *More Wives Than One: Transformation of the Mormon Marriage System 1840-1910* (Urbana: University of Illinois Press, 2001), is a household-by-household study of Manti, Utah, that convincingly demonstrates how plural marriage provided upward mobility for many poor young women of the community.

An eye-opening look at the sufferings which polygamy and its demise imposed on at least some Latter-day Saints are Annie Clark Tanner, *A Mormon Mother: An Autobiography* (Salt Lake City: University of Utah Library, 1969), and S. George Ellsworth, ed., *Dear Ellen: Two Mormon Women and Their Letters* (Salt Lake City: University of Utah Press, 1974). The women are Ellen Spencer Clawson of Salt Lake City and Ellen Pratt McGary of San Bernardino, California, both plural wives whose marriages spanned the Manifesto and its inevitable adjustments.

Statehood

The definitive treatment of the polygamy-statehood controversy, which consumed Mormon energies during the last two decades of the nineteenth century is Edward Leo Lyman, *Political Deliverance: The Mormon Quest for Utah Statehood* (Urbana: University of Illinois Press, 1986), supplemented by his "Isaac Trumbo and the Politics of Utah Statehood," *Utah Historical Quarterly* 41 (Spring 1973): 128-49; which documents how Trumbo (1858-1912), a California businessman and mining investor, offered to facilitate statehood in exchange for being named one of Utah's first two U.S. senators. Although Mormon leaders accepted Trumbo's help, they rejected his terms. Lyman explored their role in greater depth in "Mormon Leaders in Politics: The Transition to Statehood in 1896," *Journal of Mormon History* 24 (Fall 1998): 30-54. "As much as some might regret it," he writes, "there is realistically no way for leaders of the Church of Jesus Christ of Latter-day Saints to be completely removed from the realm of political activity" (30).

Earlier works that discuss the process of accommodation are Gustive O. Larson, *The "Americanization" of Utah for Statehood* (San Marino, CA: Huntington Library Press, 1971), an important pioneering work, and Richard D. Poll, "The Americanization of Utah," *Utah Historical Quarterly* 44 (Winter 1976): 76-93. The socio-economic exclusiveness previously fostered by the close-knit Mormon community gave way with the privatization of Church enterprises, like the Zion's Cooperative Mercantile Institution (ZCMI), Zion's Bank, and the Provo Woollen Mills.

Writing a state constitution that would successfully represent the violently competing interests in the state and negotiate successfully past the still-hostile U.S. Congress was a task of some concern for Latter-day Saints and the Gentiles in Utah. Henry J. Wolfinger pioneered this topic in "A Re-examination of the Woodruff Manifesto in Light of Utah Constitutional History," *Utah Historical Quarterly* 39 (Fall 1971): 337-45. More recent is political scientist Jean Bickmore White's study, *Charter for Statehood: The Story of Utah's Constitution* (Salt Lake City: University of Utah Press, 1996), chronicling more than fifty years of Utahns' efforts to formulate an acceptable state constitution. As White makes abundantly clear, Mormons played a major role in drawing up the state's constitution. Howard R. Lamar, "National Perspectives of Utah's Statehood," *Journal of Mormon History* 23 (Spring 1997): 42-65, credits Utah statehood to "the Mormon Church's efforts" (67).

Political Deliverance

The Mormon Quest for Utah Statehood

EDWARD LEO LYMAN

With a Foreword by
Leonard J. Arrington

UNIVERSITY OF ILLINOIS PRESS
Urbana and Chicago

Excavating Mormon Pasts

Part of the larger transition was Utah's passage of woman suffrage in 1870. Misinformed politicos in the East predicted that Mormon women would use it to free themselves from polygamy but seriously misread the spirit of Mormon women, according to Carol Cornwall Madsen, "Schism in the Sisterhood: Mormon Women and Partisan Politics, 1890-1900," in *New Views of Mormon History: Essays in Honor of Leonard J. Arrington,* edited by Davis Bitton and Maureen Ursenbach Beecher (Salt Lake City: University of Utah Press, 1897): 212-41. Women's franchise was cancelled during the polygamy prosecutions; whether it would be reinstated as part of Utah's constitution furnished some of the controversial moments surrounding statehood, but women's advocates prevailed and Utah became the second state/territory to grant women the franchise. (Wyoming was the first; but due to the scheduling of the elections, Utah women were the first to vote.)

In short, the main task of Mormonism at the turn of the twentieth century was to reconcile the spiritual kingdom with the worldly realm. In addition to negotiating a protracted and reluctant withdrawal from polygamy, the Mormons also had to accept economic pluralism, disentangling it from religious motives and means that had been largely responsible for the success of the Mormon settlement period. (See Craig L. Foster, "Mormonism on the Frontier: The Saints of the Great Basin," in this volume.) As Utah sought to become more "American," Leonard J. Arrington writes in *Great Basin Kingdom,* the days of the "proud, isolated, self-sufficient Kingdom was past." Thomas G. Alexander, "To Maintain Harmony: Adjusting to External and Internal Strifes, 1890-1930," *Dialogue* 15 (Winter 1982): 44-58, has clearly identified the problems of this turbulent period, especially how the Church's leading quorums negotiated complex transactions both internally and with non-Church constituencies. Among the most important was the challenge of maintaining group cohesiveness while securing a satisfactory place in larger American society.

Post-Manifesto Polygamy and Fundamentalism

Considering the strength of belief required to accept plural marriage as a divine principle, it is hardly surprising that some Mormons continued the activity long after the Manifesto was issued. Today these groups are known generally as "fundamentalists," and they constitute a genuine subculture within larger Mormon and American society. Both Alexander, *Mormonism in Transition,* and Bigler, *Forgotten Kingdom,* chaps. 15-17, deal with the movement away from plural marriage. Particularly significant was a controversial revelation reportedly received by Woodruff's successor as Church president, John Taylor, in 1877—a visitation of the Savior confirming the righteousness of the practice and committing the Saints to never give it up. Although the account of this revelation appears repeatedly in fundamentalist literature, its existence is also affirmed by Samuel Woolley Taylor, *The Kingdom or Nothing: John Taylor, Militant Mormon* (New York: Macmillan Publishing, 1976), 367-ff. This revelation, filed with the LDS Church Historian's Office by Lorin Woolley in 1912, was never canonized and hence is not recognized as a revelatory document by current Church leaders and members (367 note 10).

A good place to begin inquiries into polygamy, including fundamentalism, is Patricia Lyn Scott, "Mormon Polygamy: A Bibliography 1977-92," *Journal of Mormon History* 19 (Spring 1993): 133-55, and her "Mormon Polygamy: A Bibliography, 1900-1999," in *Wrestling with the Principle: Readings on Polygamy from the Journal of Mormon History* (Salt Lake City: Signature Books, forthcoming). An excellent book-length study of one fundamentalist group and its fight to endure is Martha Sonntag Bradley, *Kidnapped from That Land: The Government Raids on the Short Creek Polygamists* (Salt Lake City: University of Utah Press, 1993), especially Chapter 1, which supplies historical context for the 1950s raids. Bradley has also written a discerning article, "Changed Faces: The Official LDS Position on Polygamy, 1880-1900," *Sunstone* 14 (February 1990): 26-33. Additional examinations of continuing polygamous activity can be found in Richard Van Wagoner, *Mormon Polygamy: A*

Forgotten Kingdom

The Mormon Theocracy
in the American West,
1847–1896

by
David L. Bigler

THE ARTHUR H. CLARK COMPANY
Spokane, Washington
1998

History, 2d ed. (1986; 2d ed. rev., Salt Lake City: Signature Books, 1989) and Hardy, *Solemn Covenant: The Mormon Polygamous Passage.*

Some members of the Church hierarchy promoted polygamy after the Manifesto, often outside the borders of the United States. A path-breaking study is Kenneth L. Cannon II, "Beyond the Manifesto: Polygamous Cohabitation Among LDS General Authorities after 1890," *Utah Historical Quarterly* 46 (Winter 1978): 24-36. However, the most detailed history of the Church hierarchy's complicity in new post-Manifesto polygamous marriages is D. Michael Quinn, "LDS Church Authority and New Plural Marriages," *Dialogue: A Journal of Mormon Thought* 18 (Spring 1985): 9-105, an exhaustive study, and his "Plural Marriage and Mormon Fundamentalism," in *Fundamentalism and American Society,* edited by Martin E. Marty and R. Scott Appleby (Chicago: University of Chicago Press, 1993); 240-93.

Valuable complementary studies include Ken Driggs, "After the Manifesto: Mormon Polygamy and Fundamentalist Mormons," *Journal of Church and State* 32 (Spring 1990): 367-89; and his "Twentieth-Century Polygamy and Fundamentalism in Southern Utah," *Dialogue* 24 (Winter 1991): 44-58.

Accommodation in the Early Twentieth-Century

Allen and Leonard observe in *The Story of the Latter-day Saints:* "The turn of the century was a time of transition [for the Mormons]; the pioneering past [was] gone, new challenges lay ahead" (441). Among them are the six themes they identify as challenges for a "new generation": political challenges occasioned largely by recurring charges of polygamy, the need to create a new public image, economic problems, family life and education, missionary work, and significant organizational reforms (441-42). Leadership passed from Wilford Woodruff to Lorenzo Snow to Joseph F. Smith, the first Church president to have been born a Mormon. (For biographies of these and other key figures, see Newell G. Bringhurst, "Mormon Biography: Paradoxes, Problems, and Progress" in this volume.) A convenient work for tracking the counselors in the First Presidency is Michael K. Winder, comp., *Counselors to the Prophets* (Roy; UT: Eborn Books, 2001).

While statehood represented the external sign of acceptance into the larger society, perhaps the parallel marker of the internal transition was the dedication of the Salt Lake Temple in 1893 under Wilford Woodruff. This event not only culminated forty years of effort, with all of the spiritual significance involved in that symbol, but it also served as a transition toward a new, more image-conscious church. For the first time in LDS history, a temple dedication served a public relations purpose as recounted in M. Guy Bishop and Richard Neitzel Holzapfel, "'The St. Peter's of the New World': The Salt Lake Temple and a New Public Image for Utah," *Utah Historical Quarterly* 61 (Spring 1993): 136-49.

Mormons saw the Spanish-American War of 1898 as a test of their citizenship, a transition recounted in a superb study by D. Michael Quinn, "The Mormon Church and the Spanish-American War: An End to Selective Pacifism," *Pacific Historical Review* 53 (August 1974): 342-66. Their patriotic enthusiasm stood in sharp contrast to the deliberate aloofness with which the Saints had regarded the American Civil War three decades earlier. Another evidence of Mormon outreach and participation in the larger nation's interests is William G. Hartley, "The Saints and the San Francisco Earthquake [1906]," *BYU Studies* 23 (Fall 1983): 430-59.

Gordon Irving, "Coming of Age in a Western Farm Community: Union, Utah, 1900-1910," in *New Views of Mormon History,* 162-96, is a fine social history of growing up in a rural Mormon town at the turn of the twentieth-century. Providing a larger context are studies of the Progressive Era, the period between the late 1890s and World War I marked by political and social reform movements, in which the Church engaged with considerable energy. These developments are insightfully documented in Thomas G. Alexander, "Between Revivalism and the Social Gospel: The Latter-day Saint Advisory Committee, 1916-1922," *BYU Studies* 23 (Winter 1983): 19-39; and David Hall, "Anxiously Engaged: Amy Lyman Brown and Relief Society Charity Work, 1917-45," *Dialogue* 27 (Summer 1994): 73-92. Brown was general secretary of the Relief Society under president Clarissa Smith

Williams, then became its general president (1940-45). She was named a member of the State Council on Defense in 1917, and the local ward Relief Societies were also organized during this national crisis, as chapters of the Red Cross. Lyman provided steady leadership as the Church's traditional charitable organization acquired new professionalism with its emphasis on social work. Among other studies of their contributions is Miriam Murphy, "Utah Women in World War I," *Utah Historical Quarterly* 58 (Fall 1990): 335-50.

Because of the Word of Wisdom, announced by Joseph Smith in Kirtland, Ohio, Mormons had an additional reason for joining with other American citizens in the movement to prohibit the consumption of alcohol. This topic is explored in Brent G. Thompson, "Standing Between Two Fires: Mormons and Prohibition, 1908-1917," *Journal of Mormon History* 10 (1983): 35-52; and Helen Zeese Papanikolas, "Bootlegging in Zion: Making and Selling the 'Good Stuff,'" *Utah Historical Quarterly* 53 (Summer 1982): 268-91. Prohibition exposed a surprising rift in the Latter-day Saint hierarchy—not over the desirability of abstinence, but over the political ramifications of prohibition. Some senior members of the Twelve, such as Heber J. Grant and Francis M. Lyman, supported prohibition while John Henry Smith and Church President Joseph F. Smith opposed it..

During the tenure of Joseph F. Smith (1901-1918), LDS Apostle Reed Smoot was elected to serve as U.S. Senator in 1901, launching a heated clash with opponents of the Church who charged that Smoot, even though he was a monogamist, must advocate plural marriage. He was seated, but a subcommittee held four years of heated hearings on whether he should retain it. He was finally confirmed, thanks at least in part to support from U.S. President Theodore Roosevelt; and until he was swept out of office in the Democratic landslide of 1932, he championed protective tariffs and land issues. Solid considerations of his positions are Thomas G. Alexander, "Senator Reed Smoot and Western Land Policy," *Arizona and the West* 13 (Autumn 1971): 245-64; his "Reed Smoot, the LDS Church, and Progressive Legislation, 1903-1933," *Dialogue* 7 (Spring 1972); 47-56; Jan Shipps, "The Public Image of Senator Reed Smoot, 1902-1932," *Utah Historical Quarterly* 45 (Fall 1977): 380-400; and Milton R. Merrill, *Reed Smoot: Apostle in Politics* (Logan: Utah State University Press, 1990). Harvard Heath, ed., *In the World: The Diaries of Reed Smoot* (Salt Lake City: Signature Books, 1997) provide a readily accessible primary account of Smoot's involvement in the events of the early twentieth-century.

Like his successor, Joseph F. Smith, Heber J. Grant (1856-1945), the next Church president, has yet to receive a definitive biography, although Francis M. Gibbons, *Heber J. Grant: Man of Steel, Prophet of God* (Salt Lake City: Deseret Book, 1979), provides a popular outline of his life. Ronald W. Walker's anticipated biography is still pending, but he has published a number of scholarly essays on Grant, including "Crisis in Zion: Heber J. Grant and the Panic of 1893," *Arizona and the West* 21 (1979): 257-78; "Heber J. Grant and the Utah Loan and Trust Company," *Journal of Mormon History* 8 (1981): 21-36; "Heber J. Grant's European Mission, 1903-1906," *Journal of Mormon History* 14 (1988): 16-33; "Strangers in a Strange Land: Heber J. Grant and the Opening of the Japanese Mission," *Journal of Mormon History* 13 (1986/87): 20-43; "Young Heber J. Grant and His Call to the Apostleship," *BYU Studies* 18 (Fall 1977): 121-26; and biographical articles on Grant in *Encyclopedia of Mormonism*, 4 vols. (New York: Macmillan Publishing, 1992), 2:564-68; *Utah History Encyclopedia* (Salt Lake City: University of Utah Press, 1994), 230-31; and *The Presidents of the Church*, edited by Leonard J. Arrington (Salt Lake City: Deseret Book, 1986), 211-50. Grant served as church president for twenty-seven years (1918-45); and perhaps one of his most significant influences on twentieth-century Church administration was the fact that he called the long-lived conservative J. Reuben Clark Jr. and future Church president David O. McKay as his counselors, both of whom served during the entire tenure of his own successor, George Albert Smith (1945-51).

War, Depression, and Dissent

On the heels of prohibition came World War I. In 1917, the United States joined the bloodbath in eastern France. Despite strong isolationist tendencies, Mormons also saw the war as an opportunity to showcase their patriotism. Although Latter-day Saint historians have treated this conflict only marginally, Utah historians have demonstrated much greater interest, in the process shedding light on the involvement of Mormons in this international conflict. The *Utah Historical Quarterly* devoted its fall 1990 issue to the topic, including Richard C. Roberts, "The Utah National Guard in the Great War, 1917-18," 312-34, which prominently features Colonel Richard W. Young, a grandson of Brigham Young, as commander of the 145th Field Artillery unit and B. H. Roberts of the First Council of the Seventy as its chaplain. Roberts devoted two chapters of his *Comprehensive History of the Church*, 6 vols. (1930; Provo, UT: BYU Press, 1968 printing), to this unit's achievements. According to Roberts, "One unique thing about the Utah regiment was that it was recruited from one religious body, and LDS traits and values contributed greatly to their performance. (6:460). One of these soldiers' experiences is chronicled in the engagingly written Lynne Watkins Jorgensen, "'Begging to Be in the Battle: A Mormon Boy in World War I," *Journal of Mormon History* 29, no. 1 (Spring 1993): 101-34. Miriam B. Murphy, "'If Only I Shall Have the Right Stuff': Utah Women in World War I," *Utah Historical Quarterly* 58 (Fall 1990), 335-50, describes "a number of war-related activities under the State Council of Defense" that Utah women undertook (335), including citizenship classes for alien residents, domestic relief, and intensified production and storage of food.

The next national crisis—the Great Depression—fell even more heavily on Utah, as described in Wayne Hinton, "Some Historical Perspectives on the Mormon Response to the Great Depression," " *Journal of the West* 24 (October 1985): 19-26, and his "The Economics of Ambivalence: Utah's Depression Experience," *Utah Historical Quarterly* 54 (Summer 1986); 268-85. The Great Depression is also featured as Chapter 7 of Garth L. Mangum and Bruce D. Blumell, *The Mormons' War on Poverty: A History of LDS Welfare 1830-1990* (Salt Lake City: University of Utah Press, 1993). A compassionate view of the human suffering caused by the Depression is James R. Swensen, "Dorothea Lange's Portrait of Utah's Great Depression," *Utah Historical Quarterly* 70 (Winter 2002): 39-62. In 1936, Lange recorded her acclaimed "Migrant Mother" in the mining district of Carbon County, then traveled to the "isolated" Mormon towns of Escalante and Widtsoe, just north of Bryce Canyon. According to Swensen, she documented a town "already on the edge of decay" (51). Ironically Mormon apostle Melvin J. Ballard had, in 1917, buoyed its Mormon settlers with the "promise that the valley would become a Garden of Eden if its inhabitants kept God's commandments and stayed out of debt" (Swensen, 51).

Mormon women provided stellar service during the Great Depression, their selfless service chronicled in Jill Mulvay Derr, Janath Russell Cannon, and Maureen Ursenbach Beecher, *Women of Covenant: The Story of the Relief Society* (Salt Lake City: Deseret Book, 1992). Louise Yates Robinson, the seventh general president of the Relief Society (1928-45), a native of Scipio, urged the women to "get the spirit of the pioneers" (255) and encouraged cooperative gardening, sewing, and canning projects.

Also required reading for understanding official Church efforts to counter the effects of depression is Richard D. Poll, *Working the Divine Miracle: The Life of Apostle Henry D. Moyle,* edited by Stan Larson (Salt Lake City: Signature Books, 1999). As the president of the LDS Cottonwood Stake during the early 1930s, Moyle fulfilled his calling so "effectively" that he was soon asked to "help shape" the Churchwide response to the Depression (vii). According to Poll, helping people to "cope with economic adversity" characterized Henry Moyle's apostolic career (82).

Jessie L. Embry, "The Relief Society Grain Storage Program, 1876-1940" (M.A. thesis, Brigham Young University, 1974), adds a valuable dimension in describing this program, carried over from pioneer times until the Church sold the Relief Society's wheat to the government during World War I.

Thousands of Utah Mormons enlisted in that next national crisis, and some 3,500 died in the conflict. A consummate collection of personal experiences is Robert C. Freeman and Dennis A. Wright, *Saints at War: Experiences of Latter-day Saints in World War II* (American Fork, UT: Covenant Communications, 2001), drawn from oral histories in the

SAINTS AT WAR

KOREA AND VIETNAM

ROBERT C. FREEMAN AND DENNIS A. WRIGHT

Excavating Mormon Pasts

Saints at War Collection, L. Tom Perry Special Collections, Harold B. Lee Library, BYU, Provo, Utah. This collection preserves "the personal histories, journals, letters, photographs and other documents [of] the veterans" (2).

James B. Allen and Richard O. Cowan have also treated LDS involvement in World War II in their *Mormonism in the Twentieth Century* (Provo, UT: Brigham Young University Press, 1967), with additional attention in Cowan, *The Church in the Twentieth Century* (Salt Lake City: Bookcraft, 1985), chap. 10. Allan Kent Powell, who has published voluminously on Utah history during this period, includes Mormons in *Utah Remembers World War II* (Logan: Utah State University Press, 1991); and his *Splinters of a Nation: German Prisoners of War in Utah* (Salt Lake City: University of Utah, Press, 1989), which includes the recollection of German POW Josef Becker, a prisoner/farm laborer in Tooele County, that the local Mormons were compassionate and friendly. Two informative, although obscure, accounts of Latter-day Saints directly involved in World War II are Terry Buhle Montague, "... *Mine Angels Round About": Mormon Missionary Evacuation from Western Europe, 1939* (Murray, UT: Roylance Publishing, 1989); and Gordon Richard Bradford, *Discovering the Face of the Sky: The World War II Experiences of Gordon Richard Bradford,* edited by Sondra Bradford Packard (N.p.: privately published, n.d.). A Latter-day Saint from Spanish Fork, Bradford served in the military from 1942-45. Boyd Jay Petersen, *Hugh Nibley: A Consecrated Life* (Salt Lake City: Greg Kofford Books, 2003), included three chapters (12-14) on that eminent scholar's front-line experience in France in the U.S. Army and its impact on his Book of Mormon studies about warfare.

An internal Church organizational conundrum with lengthy antecedents before this period is skillfully treated in Irene M. Bates and E. Gary Smith, *The Lost Legacy: The Mormon Office of Presiding Patriarch* (Urbana: University of Illinois Press, 1996). Joseph Smith had established this office and bestowed it first upon his father. It passed successively to his brother Hyrum, who died with him, then briefly to his maverick brother William, until he fell afoul of Brigham Young. Thereafter, it descended through the Hyrum Smith line with a couple of nonlineal interim office holders until Church President Spencer W. Kimball rather dramatically terminated the office in October 1979, although the Patriarch Emeritus, Eldred G. Smith, as of this writing, is still alive and functioning in his calling. The seventh Church patriarch, Joseph F. Smith (not to be confused with either the Church president by that name nor with President Joseph Fielding Smith), served only four years (1942-46) and was released for "health" reasons. According to Bates and Smith, "Disquieting allegations of some involvement in homosexual activity had early reached the office of the First Presidency," who disregarded it until the spring of 1946 (195). A more detailed account in D. Michael Quinn, *Same-Sex Dynamics Among Nineteenth-Century Americans: A Mormon Example* (Urbana: University of Illinois Press, 1996), suggests that Smith was involved in a long-running homosexual relationship, which "probably began in the fall of 1926" (369). Although no formal action was taken against Smith, he was not given another calling for a decade until informal restrictions were lifted at the request of his stake president in Hawaii where he had moved his family. At the time of his death, he was serving as a high councilor.

The decades immediately preceding and during World War II also saw the flowering of what may be called a proto-New Mormon History, although such studies frequently took an almost aggressively naturalistic stance, sometimes spelling out explicit rejections of traditional Mormon positions in ways that alienated and polarized readers. Three indispensable historians with Mormon roots during this period were Dale L. Morgan, Fawn Brodie, and Juanita Brooks, all three of whom are insightfully treated in Gary Topping, *Utah Historians and the Reconstruction of Western History* (Norman: University of Oklahoma Press, 2003). John Phillip Walker, ed., *Dale Morgan on Early Mormonism: Correspondence and a New History* (Salt Lake City: Signature Books, 1986); and Charles S. Peterson, "Dale L. Morgan," in *Utah History Encyclopedia,* 376, provide overviews of Morgan's life (1914-71). Deafened in youth by illness, he was a prodigious researcher and writer on western topics, including the fur trade, but never finished his long-planned study of Mormon history.

Fawn McKay Brodie (1915-81) published what was likely Mormonism's most detested book of her generation: *No Man Knows My History: The Life of Joseph Smith* (1945; 2d. ed. rev., New York: Alfred A. Knopf, 1971). A niece of Church President David O. McKay, she went to the University of Chicago, married out of the faith, and produced a biography that, though admiring of Joseph Smith's creativity, frankly portrayed him as a fraud and a philanderer. Important studies of her life are Newell G. Bringhurst, *Fawn McKay Brodie: A Biographer's Life* (Norman: University of Oklahoma Press, 1999); his "Fawn McKay Brodie: Dissident Historian and Quintessential Critic of Mormondom," *Differing Visions: Dissenters in Mormon History*, edited by Roger D. Launius and Linda Thatcher (Urbana: University of Illinois Press, 1994), 279-300.

Juanita Brooks (1898-1989), a native of Bunkerville, Nevada, lived and worked in Utah's Dixie all her life. Unlike Morgan and Brodie, she remained a committed Mormon even while producing two studies of Mormonism's darkest hour and its architect: *Mountain Meadows Massacre* (1950; 2d ed., Norman: University of Oklahoma Press, 1962); and *John Doyle Lee: Zealot, Pioneer Builder, Scapegoat* (1961; reprint ed., Logan: Utah State University, 1992). Juanita Brooks's legacy to the New Mormon History is one of sound research and unmitigated historical honesty. When a critic called *The Mountain Meadows Massacre* "the most vicious thing published against the Church since the days of Nauvoo apostates John C. Benned [*sic*] and William Law," Brooks responded: "You think I've done an evil thing, I believe sincerely that I have done a wholesome thing and done the church I love, a service."[4] In what could have been a manifesto for New Mormon historians who retained profound attachments to the faith, Brooks sympathetically advised a BYU professor working on Oliver Cowdery in 1986: "I realize your dilemma, employed at BYU and writing for a Church publication, you are forced to look at only what will build to the point you set out to prove, and carefully bury or ignore anything that will raise questions in the minds of the readers."[5]

The International Church

Although missionary work, including in overseas locales, had been part of Mormonism since its earliest decades, by the 1940s, Mormonism began to take on a more international look, the first flowering of spectacular post-war growth outside North America. Thus, as Allen and Leonard observe, *The Story of the Latter-day Saints*, "The story of the Church between 1939 and 1976 was characterized by two things: growth and internationalization" (537). In the 1940s, the chronological termination of this chapter, the Church had 862,000 members. "Growth and Internationalization: The LDS Church Since 1945," by Kahlile Mehr, Mark L. Grover, Reid L. Neilson, Donald Q. Cannon and Grant Underwood in this volume carries on this rich and complex story.

However, for background and context to that flourishing, a readily accessible starting point for the study of this internationalization is Richard O. Cowan, *The Church in the Twentieth Century* (Salt Lake City: Bookcraft, 1985), 231-56. With the exception of Great Britain (and, to a lesser degree, Scandinavia) during the mid-nineteenth century, LDS proselyting and expansion accelerated during the first half of the twentieth-century. Bruce A. Orden, *Building Zion: The Latter-day Saints in Europe* (Salt Lake City: Deseret Book, 1996), provides an overview of the history and contemporary status of the Church in Europe. The analytical reader, however, should probably also weigh the appraisal of Wilfred Decoo, a Belgian Latter-day Saint, reviewing this work in the *Journal of Mormon History* 23 (Spring 1997): 140-76. Decoo "found praiseworthy aspects" in this book but concluded, "My honest appraisal is that it embodies many of the limitations that have more than once disturbed me about Utah-produced stories of the Church and its members in 'foreign' countries" (140). These limitations

---

4. Quoted in Levi S. Peterson, *Juanita Brooks: Mormon Woman Historian* (Salt Lake City: University of Utah Press. 1988), 209-10. This biography is both a sympathetic and careful analysis.

5. The scholar, Richard L. Anderson, angrily rejected the implication that his "independence of mind" and dedication to objective history" might be compromised. According to Peterson, the two reached a kind of reconciliation and did not continue their correspondence (333).

include the concentration on Utah-generated Church sources, historical inaccuracies, and stereotypes. Some methodological problems in Van Orden's work received separate attention in the *Journal of Mormon History* 24, no. 1 (Spring 1998): v-lvii.

An important episode in changing Scandinavian hostility to Mormon missionaries is John C. Thomas, "Apostolic Diplomacy: The 1923 European Mission of Senator Reed Smoot and Professor John A. Widtsoe," *Journal of Mormon History* 28 (Spring 2002): 130-65. Once again, a major contribution was dismantling stereotypes of Mormon polygamy. As early as 1895, Assistant Secretary of State Edwin Uhl had informed the U.S. consul in Tahiti that "repressive action" should not be applied to the Mormons "because polygamy is no longer announced as a chief tenet of Mormonism," although the author notes: "That said, the views of governments and societal elites often lagged behind the shift in official U.S. policy" (133).

Another area of impressive missionary success beginning in the late nineteenth-century was in Mexico. F. LaMond Tullis, *Mormons in Mexico: The Dynamics of Faith and Culture* (Logan: Utah State University Press, 1987) chronicles the story of Mexican Mormonism beginning in 1895. The Saints' early interest in Mexico was principally motivated by hopeful plans of proselyting among the descendants of Book of Mormon Lamanites and seeking potential areas for colonization. The mission was shut down in 1888, largely due to pressures of federal legislation over polygamy. In August 1901, Ammon M. Tenney, an early missionary to Mexico, reopened the mission, in at least one area finding the members "resentful and rebellious" due to their earlier "abandonment" (196).

As these examples show, the internationalization of Mormonism is one of the most exhilarating areas of the New Mormon History, especially by drawing on primary in-language sources, oral histories, and participant observations. However, the 1890-1945 period also offers other exciting topics that remain to be explored. Several of its leading figures are in dire need of scholarly biographies. Polygamy not only has an enduring appeal as a historical topic (which is certainly also true of the Mountain Meadows Massacre), but it seems to be gaining adherents despite almost uniformly negative publicity and regular schisms. David L. Bigler's emphasis in *Forgotten Kingdom* on the Church's attempt to develop a theocratic state in the Mountain West should prompt deeper, more specialized studies. The landscape first mapped in Leonard J. Arrington's *Great Basin Kingdom* and Thomas G. Alexander's *Mormonism in Transition* suggests many rewarding investigations of how Mormonism's socio-religious culture as well as its economic practices sought an accommodation with accepted national practices.

Mormon participation in both World War I and World War II await the kind of incisive political and social analysis that Quinn gave to Latter-day Saints and the Spanish-American War. Mormon women have received attention primarily in the context of polygamy (although see Todd Compton, "The New Mormon Women's History," in this volume), but even so, we know more about their lives and experiences than we do about second-echelon Mormon men.

Thomas G. Alexander must be recognized as the dean of Mormon historians for this period, particularly the early decades of the twentieth century. Nevertheless, younger scholars face a tempting array of topics, especially if they employ such tools from the new social history like demography, quantitative analysis, and class, sex, and race studies. The fields of local history and family history have long attracted talented amateurs; providing them with professional tools will benefit the entire field as well as individual works.

M. GUY BISHOP is an independent scholar and the author of two books, *Henry William Bigler: Soldier, Gold Miner, Missionary, Chronicler, 1815-1900* (Logan: Utah State University Press, 1998) and *A History of Sevier County* (Salt Lake City: Utah State Historical Society, 1997), and more than twenty articles published in various scholarly periodicals. His biography of Stephen Post is forthcoming from Greg Kofford Books.

Chapter 8

The LDS Church in the United States since 1945

Jessie L. Embry

On June 9, 1978, LDS Church President Spencer W. Kimball announced a revelation that allowed black men to receive the Church's lay priesthood and black men and women to receive ordinances only performed in the temples. At a symposium on the tenth anniversary of this revelation, Dallin H. Oaks, one of the Church's Quorum of Twelve Apostles, explained the impact of the announcement on members of the Church: "There are some events that claim a place in almost everyone's memory. If you were an adult at the time of the attack on Pearl Harbor, you remember where you were and what you were doing when you heard the announcement. The same is true of the assassination of President John F. Kennedy. For most adult Latter-day Saints the revelation on the priesthood ten years ago was an event of such magnitude that it is also etched in memory."[1]

The impact of Kimball's announcement was felt throughout the United States. Presses stopped to include the story. *Time Magazine* initially planned to run a cover story. Journalists rushed to collect the reactions of black Mormons, scholars of Mormonism, leaders of other religious groups, and black leaders. Sterling McMurrin, a University of Utah professor who had publicly spoken against the policy, called "it the most important day for the Church of the century."[2]

The timing of Kimball's announcement shocked Mormons and non-Mormons alike. The change in policy did not come during the 1960s when the civil rights leaders, universities, and some Latter-day Saints tried to pressure the Mormon Church into changing its policy. Yet as non-Mormon historian Jan Shipps interpreted the event, the revelation's timing had more to do with the Church than with outside pressure. In an interview with the *Christian Century,* she explained, "The June 9 revelation will never be fully understood if it is regarded simply as a pragmatic doctrinal shift ultimately designed to bring Latter-day Saints into congruence with mainstream America. . . . This revelation came in the context of worldwide evangelism rather than . . . American social and cultural circumstances."[3]

---

1. Dallin H. Oaks, "For the Blessings of All of His Children," keynote address, LDS Afro-American Symposium, June 8, 1988, videotape, Charles Redd Center for Western Studies, Manuscript Division, Harold B. Lee Library, Brigham Young University, Provo, Utah.
2. *Deseret News,* June 10, 1978, A-3.
3. Jan Shipps, "The Mormons: Looking Forward and Outward," *Christian Century,* August 16-23, 1978, 762.

Excavating Mormon Pasts

Most changes in the Mormon Church since 1945, like the 1978 priesthood revelation, have come for the same reason. As the LDS Church has grown throughout the United States and the world, its leaders have faced new challenges.

Growth

The Church of Jesus Christ of Latter-day Saints experienced its greatest growth in the last half of the twentieth century. From being an essentially western American sect centered in Utah, it became a worldwide church of over 11 million. In 1940 there were only 862,600 Latter-day Saints worldwide; by 1975 that number expanded to 3.5 million; by 1990 there were over 8 million Mormons; and membership topped 11 million in 2000. In 1984 sociologist Rodney Stark, "The Rise of a New World Faith," *Review of Religious Research* 26 (September 1984): 23, predicted: "If growth during the next century is like that of the past, the Mormons will become a major world faith. If, for example, we assume they will grow by 30 percent per decade, then in 2080 there will be more than 60 million Mormons." He pointed out, however, that since World War II, the LDS Church had grown at a rate of 50 percent per decade so by 2080 there could be 265 million Mormons. Lowell C. "Ben" Bennion, "The Geographic Dynamics of Mormonism, 1965-1995," *Sunstone* 18 (December 1995): 21-32, has examined locales of differential growth. S. Kent Brown, et al., eds., *The Historical Atlas of Mormonism* (New York: Simon & Schuster, 1994) includes maps on the growth of the Church.

Why has the Mormon Church grown so rapidly especially when "mainline" churches have lost members? According to sociologist Andrew M. Greeley, *Religious Change in America* (Cambridge, MA: Harvard University Press, 1989), 68, people historically selected their religion based on the "old lines of class, race, ethnicity, region" and family. According to Dean R. Hoge and David A. Roozen, "Some Sociological Conclusions about Church Trends," *Understanding Church Growth and Decline, 1950-1978,* edited by Hoge and Roozen (New York: Pilgrim Press, 1970), 323, as these factors waned in strength, membership in mainline religions dropped while churches that "strongly emphasized local evangelism, maintained a distinctive life-style and morality apart from mainstream culture, maintained a unitary set of beliefs, and de-emphasized social action and ecumenism . . . grew." These characteristics were also true of the LDS Church. Hoge "A Test of Theories of Denominational Growth and Decline," in ibid., 192, found, in his 1978 study of seventeen denominations, that the LDS Church rated first in lack of ecumenism, first in central authority, first in distinctive lifestyle, third in emphasis on evangelism (the Southern Baptist Convention and the Seventh-day Adventists rated higher), and third in unwillingness to allow different beliefs among its members (Seventh-day Adventists and the Lutheran Church-Missouri Synod rated higher).

Once the Mormons abandoned polygamy, political separatism, and economic communal lifestyles (see "Mormonism in Transition, 1890-1945," by M. Guy Bishop in this volume), they adapted their beliefs to those of mainstream America. During most of the twentieth century, Mormons' belief in the Protestant work ethic and strong moral convictions made them the nineteenth-century Victorian ideal. They became "super" Americans. Shipps referred to the LDS Church as the American "Reader's Digest" Church and Harold Bloom characterized it as the best example of an "American religion."[4]

---

4. Jan Shipps quoted in Martin E. Marty, *American Religious Values and the Future of America*

At the same time, American society became more accepting of the Mormon Church. Sociologists Wade Clark Roof and William McKinney, *American Mainline Religion: Its Changing Shape and Future* (New Brunswick, NJ: Rutgers University Press, 1987), described Mormons as having risen from the lowest position on the bottom rank of the "status hierarchy of the denominations" (110) in 1945 to the highest position of the middle rank by 1987. This classification is based on income, education, profession, and social class. Historian Mario S. De Pillis, "Viewing Mormonism as Mainline," *Dialogue: A Journal of Mormon Thought* 24 (Winter 1991): 59-68, concluded that Mormons are now part of the higher socio-economic class in the United States, acquiring in the process, "a new Mormon status that goes with being mainline" (67). Sociologists have tried to determine why. Mark Leone, *Roots of Modern Mormonism* (Cambridge, MA: Harvard University Press, 1979), pointed to the Church's ability to adapt to change. Gordon and Gary Shepherd, "Mormonism in Secular Society: Changing Patterns in Official Ecclesiastical Rhetoric," *Review of Religious Research* 26 (September 1984): 28-41, however, perceived that the Church's reinforcement of traditional moral and family values provides "an alternative to the confusing diversity and moral ambiguity of modern secular life" (40). O. Kendall White, Jr., *Mormon Neo-Orthodoxy: A Crisis Theology* (Salt Lake City: Signature Books, 1987), 109-110, also finds that part of Mormonism's appeal lies in its conservatism.

Two closely related concerns—rapid growth and development as an international Church—have dominated the history of the LDS Church in the last half of the twentieth century. (See also "Growth and Internationalization: The LDS Church since 1945," by Kahlile Mehr, Mark L. Grover, Reid L. Neilson, Donald Q. Cannon, and Grant Underwood, in this volume.) Historians James B. Allen and Glen M. Leonard, , *The Story of the Latter-day Saints* (1976; 2d ed., Salt Lake City: Deseret Books, 1992), contend that while the years since World War II have been "marked by" attempts to deal with internal problems and changes and to work with new social and political concerns, "All this seemed transitory compared with the continuing challenge of administering a rapidly growing organization, accommodating programs to suit diverse cultures, and carrying out a determination to expand even further" (537). In fact, however, all of these concerns are interrelated. The tremendous growth has meant that the Church has developed a bureaucracy which has led to internal strife; the development of an international church has forced the institution to interact with other cultures. And growth means more visibility so that members and nonmembers are more keenly aware of the Church's stand on social and political concerns.

While the Mormon Church has changed significantly since 1945, documenting that transformation is difficult. Allen's and Leonard's bibliography for those years consists of articles and primary sources. Because so little has been published about the Church's development in the last half of the twentieth century, they had to rely on their own research to paint its broad outlines, a marked contrast with earlier time periods, especially the Church's first fourteen years between its founding in 1830 and Joseph Smith's death in 1844. Susan Easton Black, et al., "The Times and Seasons of the Doctrine and Covenants," *Ensign,* January 1993, 38-43, an article to supplement the adult Sunday School course of

---

(Philadelphia: Fortress Press, 1978), 40-41; Harold Bloom, *The American Religion: The Emergence of the Post-Christian Nation* (New York: Simon and Schuster, 1992).

Roots of Modern Mormonism

Mark P. Leone

HARVARD UNIVERSITY PRESS
Cambridge, Massachusetts,
and London, England
1979

study that year, naturally concentrated on Joseph Smith's lifetime. However, of its six pages of Church history, events from 1951 to 1992 were given only half a page. Most items were listing the administrations of successive Church presidents.

Why have historians paid so little attention to the time when the Church has experienced its most rapid growth? Why is the focus still on the early years of the Church? Jan Shipps, "In the Presence of the Past: Continuity and Change in Twentieth-Century Mormonism," in *After 150 Years: The Latter-day Saints in Sesquicentennial Perspective*, edited by Thomas G. Alexander and Jessie L. Embry (Provo, UT: Charles Redd Center for Western Studies, 1983), 1-35, has argued that Mormonism is more than simply another Protestant sect; it is a "new religious tradition." While she describes in detail the changes that have taken place in the Mormon Church since Joseph Smith, she explains that the essence of Mormonism lies in the early years. Mormonism, according to Shipps, has a "usable past" which enables it to develop its future, a point she also argues in her "The Mormons: Looking Forward and Outward," in *Where the Spirit Leads: American Denominations Today*, edited by Martin E. Marty (Atlanta, GA: John Knox Press, 1980), 25-40.

Another way to explain the general absorption with the LDS Church's first fourteen years is that many Mormons—including historians—are caught up in what Roger D. Launius refers to as the "mystique of the prophet." Joseph Smith is the center of these years. His visions and translation of the Book of Mormon created the Church; his charisma kept the Church together. His presidency is, with reason, seen as most consequential because the Church's basic beliefs were developed during his presidency. To Mormons, Smith was God's spokesman to prepare for the second coming of the Savior. In addition, many Mormon leaders and members seem to look back with nostalgia at the glorious days when the Church was persecuted for Christ's sake in contrast to the arduous but unglamorous challenges of dealing with contemporary but mundane problems.

Yet to say that historians have focused on the early Church only because of its significance in developing a new religious tradition or because of the Prophet's "mystique" is only part of the problem. The study of the American West is also caught up in a romance of the nineteenth century. Even the new western historians who are displacing Frederick Jackson Turner's frontier thesis with a broader interpretation of the interactions of cultures, classes, genders, and ethnicities, have spent most of their time looking at the early time period. They argue that these events shaped the present and the future. But the preoccupation with the nineteenth century may also be pseudoadventures without any real risks of everyday life, as Ralph Keyes has observed in *Chancing It: Why We Take Risks* (Boston: Little, Brown and Company, 1985), 257.

Other problems include a lack of sources. The Mormon Church has cut back on paper trails. The last complete Church census by the Presiding Bishopric was conducted in 1950, but only selected results were published.[5] While the Church has continued to survey its members to identify demographic and belief patterns, nearly all of these studies have been restricted to headquarters use. The relatively rare exceptions include Marie Cornwall,

---

5. John A. Widtsoe, "How Is Church Membership Divided as to Ages?" *Improvement Era* 55 (February 1952): 78-79; Widtsoe, "What Are the Occupations of Latter-day Saints?" ibid. (March 1952): 142-43, 167; Widtsoe, "Are Latter-day Saints Homeowners?" ibid. (April 1952): 222-23; and "What Are the Educational Attainments of the Latter-day Saints?" ibid. (May 1952): 310-11.

Excavating Mormon Pasts

Tim B. Heaton, and Lawrence A. Young, *Contemporary Mormonism: Social Science Perspectives* (Urbana: University of Illinois Press, 1994); Stan L. Albrecht and Tim B. Heaton, "Secularization, Higher Education, and Religiosity," *Review of Religious Research* 26 (September 1984): 43-58; Stan L. Albrecht, "The Consequential Dimension of Mormon Religiosity," *BYU Studies* 29 (Spring 1989): 57-108; and Marie Cornwall et al., "The Dimensions of Religiosity: A Conceptual Model with an Empirical Test," *Review of Religious Research* 27 (March 1986): 233. In at least one case, Brent L. Top and Bruce A. Chadwick, "Helping Teens Stay Strong," *Ensign,* March 1999, 27-34, selected results have been published to help members. Helping to fill such gaps are Gilbert W. Fellingham et al., "Statistics on Suicide and LDS Church Involvement," BYU Studies 39, no. 2 (2000): 173-80; and James T. Duke, ed., *Latter-day Saint Social Life: Social Research on the LDS Church and Its Members* (Provo, UT: Religious Studies Center, Brigham Young University, 1998).

Similarly, the Church has not published its finance statements since 1958. The auditor's report at the LDS Church's general conference is simply a statement that the financial records are kept, examined, and balanced. Another gap in documentation is a lack of official ward and stake records. Since 1983 wards and stakes have not been required to submit minutes and quarterly reports to the Church headquarters. All of this information is neatly summarized in annual histories which lack detail. While this is a very recent development, the minutes that my father took as a ward clerk in the 1960s and 1970s were very different from some of the minutes that I have read for the nineteenth century. My father was required only to list those who spoke, the hymns sung, and the men who presided. While some of the nineteenth-century minutes were also brief, many included more information about what was said in the meetings and what happened in the wards and branches. Twentieth-century Church records will not answer hard questions about how the Church operated.

Even more damaging to the effort of reconstructing the Church's historical workings are records that remain closed in the LDS Church Archives because they are "sacred, private, or confidential." Briefly, during the 1970s when Leonard J. Arrington was Church historian, researchers had unparalleled access to archival records, a period sometimes referred to as "Camelot." He describes his tenure in *Adventures of a Church Historian* (Urbana: University of Illinois Press, 1998). In the early 1980s, however, many nineteenth-century and newly created twentieth-century manuscripts were closed. For example, although the Historical Department has conducted interviews with General Authorities and Church members, they are not available to researchers. Scholars may also shy away from more recent history because they fear disapproval from present Church leaders.

There is also the definitional question of "Is this recent event really history?" Such a question assumes that closeness to events impacts on the historian's ability to interpret them—which indeed it does, but distance from events also impacts, sometimes in ways just as serious, on the historian's interpretive ability. Much of the writing that has been done about the LDS Church since 1945 has been written by people who lived through the events. As scholars look back on a round table about the Vietnam War published in *Dialogue,* for example, it will become a primary source to better understand that time period. Even when the focus of the articles are not a contemporary problem, the authors often add their own memories, thus adding an element of the personal essay to what is intended as a historical study. A history of Oakland, California, written in 1935 addressed this concern of writing

Adventures of a Church Historian

Leonard J. Arrington

UNIVERSITY OF ILLINOIS PRESS

URBANA AND CHICAGO

recent history: "It is difficult to present a strictly up-to-the-minute history of any city. We lack perspective. We cannot easily stand off and look at ourselves. Too many details crowd the picture and only time can determine those of lasting value."[6]

Because so little has been done about LDS Church history since 1945, this chapter cannot provide a neat summary of books and even articles that have been written on the subject. Rather, it can point to general studies that have attempted to deal with the time period as part of their overall agenda, identify some of the problems that have been raised, and point to some useful articles. Additional research needs to be done in all the fields. While only future historians can tell whether, in fact, we stood too close to the subject to understand all of its ramifications, historians need to study this time of colossal change to see where the LDS Church is going. For example, the LDS Church's stand on the Equal Rights Amendment in the 1970s has clearly had more impact on my life as an LDS woman than the revelation recorded by Joseph Smith in the 1830s to his wife Emma calling her "an elect lady."

General Studies

Because they were willing to go beyond the written sources and do primary research, Allen and Leonard's *The Story of the Latter-day Saints* is the most comprehensive study of the LDS Church since 1945. The authors do a good job of summarizing the major concerns facing Mormonism and then give brief illustrations. Their invaluable bibliography lists articles and primary sources of more information. Allen, who began work on a history of the Church since World War II as part of the projected sixteen-volume sesquicentennial history that was cancelled with the new archival restrictions, has continued his research and plans to begin writing soon.

Another general study is Richard O. Cowan, *The Church in the Twentieth Century* (Salt Lake City: Bookcraft, 1985). While it looks mainly at the Church from a chronological point of view and focuses on presidents on the Church, it does raise some of the significant social problems that have confronted the Mormon Church during this time period—for example, its stand on the Equal Rights Amendment and the MX missile controversy. It was published too soon, however, to deal with the 1978 revelation extending the lay priesthood to blacks and other recent changes. More than Allen and Leonard, Cowan tells the story factually and straightforwardly with little interpretation..

Armand L. Mauss, a sociologist, has conceptualized the last half of the twentieth century in *The Angel and the Beehive: The Mormon Struggle for Assimilation* (Urbana: University of Illinois Press, 1994), a concept he first developed in "Assimilation and Ambivalence: The Mormon Reaction to Americanization," *Dialogue* 22 (Spring 1989): 30-67, and returned to later in "The Mormon Struggle with Assimilation and Identity: Trends and Developments Since Midcentury," *Dialogue* 27 (Spring 1994): 129-49. Mauss contends that the Mormon Church is in a "retrenchment" mode, trying to return to a nineteenth-century Victorian ideal which probably never existed. As a result, although the Church began at midcentury in harmony with much of American society, it is now moving away from that

---

6. C. A. Cummings and E. S. Pladwell, *Oakland . . . A History* (Oakland: Grant D. Miller Mortuaries, 1942), 113.

center. Yet its conservative bent also puts it, on some issues, in the same camp as the evangelical churches that have been among the most rapidly growing in the United States.

A final general study which looks at the changing face of Mormonism is Catholic sociologist Thomas F. O'Dea, *The Mormons* (Chicago: University of Chicago Press, 1957). Although it was written toward the beginning of the study period, it still provides remarkable insight into Mormon life. From a perspective thirty-five years later, his chapter on "Sources of Strain and Conflict" clearly identifies concerns still facing Mormonism: the emphasis on education with the resulting friction between the scholarly community, the conservative Church leadership, and the secular society; "rationality versus charisma," "authority and obedience versus democracy and individualism," "consent versus coercion," "family ideals versus equality of women," "progress versus agrarianism," "political conservativism versus social idealism," "patriotism versus particularism," and "belief versus environment" (222-57).

Although these concerns continue to challenge Mormonism, to find the information about them requires patiently examining and synthesizing many articles that deal with single and restricted topics. Much of what has been written about Mormon Church history until the development of the New Mormon History has simply "told what happened" with few attempts to analyze why it happened or how it was influenced by the larger world. The result, by and large, has been a faithful history which has not asked crucial "why" questions. For example, the book- and article-length biographies of Church presidents who have served since 1945 are nearly all sedate chronicles of when the man was born, his faith-promoting life, the miraculous events that led to his becoming president, and his "mission" as leader of the Church. A sterling exception is Edward L. Kimball and Andrew E. Kimball Jr., *Spencer W. Kimball: Twelfth President of the Church of Jesus Christ of Latter-day Saints* (Salt Lake City: Bookcraft, 1977). While still a blow-by-blow account of Kimball's life, this significant biography makes a greater attempt to understand his life in a larger perceptive. Edward Kimball has continued to research his father's presidency and has an administrative history of his presidency forthcoming. Other excellent studies of Church leaders include D. Michael Quinn, *J. Reuben Clark: The Church Years* (Provo, UT: Brigham Young University Press, 1983), updated and revised as *Elder Statesman: A Biography of J. Reuben Clark* (Salt Lake City: Signature Books, 1999), and Richard D. Poll and Eugene E. Campbell, *Hugh B. Brown: His Life and Thought* (Salt Lake City: Bookcraft, 1975).

Multiculturalism

With an international membership, Church leaders must deal in ever-changing ways with a variety of cultures. According to Allen and Leonard, the 1970s saw a crucial change: "Mormonism was still an American religion as far as most of the population was concerned, but the ratio of Americans was decreasing and the Church's cultural perspective was clearly beginning to change" (537). James B. Allen addresses some of the concerns raised by this worldwide growth in "On Becoming a Universal Church: Some Historical Perspectives," *Dialogue* 25 (March 1992): 13-36. An important question, however, is just how much has the Church's "cultural perspective" has changed? To what extent has the Mormon Church adjusted to meet the needs of its new members or have converts modified their culture to American Mormonism? According to Jan Shipps, "The Mormons:

Excavating Mormon Pasts

Looking Forward and Outward," 39, "Notwithstanding the rosy picture of a world filled with Mormons which is being projected by the *Church News* and the official *Ensign,* the power of the LDS gospel to sustain communities of Saints throughout the world without requiring them to adopt peculiarly American attitudes and stereotyped life styles has not yet been fully proven."

The question Shipps raises is a concern even within the United States. Just as multicultural studies show that America has not been the melting pot that was presented in earlier history books, the Mormon Church has not been uniformly successful in assimilating people from throughout the world. While during the nineteenth-century the LDS Church was able to include immigrants from northern Europe quite well, it has been less successful in the twentieth century, especially with people of color. And a continuing separate ward for German-speaking members in Salt Lake City, Utah, in the heartland of the Church, shows that the need to assimilate even northern Europeans continues.

An introduction to these concerns is Richard L. Jensen, "Mother Tongue: Use of Non-English Languages in the Church of Jesus Christ of Latter-day Saints in the United States," in *New Views of Mormon History: Essays in Honor of Leonard J. Arrington,* edited by Davis Bitton and Maureen Ursenbach Beecher (Salt Lake City: University of Utah, 1987), 273-303. Chad M. Orton also addresses these concerns in *More Faith than Fear: The Los Angeles Stake Story* (Salt Lake City: Bookcraft, 1987), an area where the Church has experienced rapid growth, especially among Latino Americans. Robert G. Larsen and Sharyn H. Larsen, "Refugee Converts: One Stake's Experience," *Dialogue* 20 (Fall 1987): 37-55, focuses directly on the problems of multiculturalism in Oakland, California. Mario S. De Pillis puts the study of ethnic groups into the larger context of the role of community in "The Persistence of Mormon Community into the 1990s," *Sunstone* 15 (October 1991): 28-49.

The LDS Ethnic Groups Oral History Project at the Charles Redd Center for Western Studies at Brigham Young University has been looking at the experiences of ethnic members in the United States. I have published three books, *Black Saints in a White Church: Contemporary African American Mormons* (Salt Lake City: Signature Books, 1995), *"In His Own Language": Mormon Spanish Speaking Congregations in the United States* (Provo, UT: Charles Redd Center for Western Studies, 1997), and *Asian American Mormons: Bridging Cultures* (Provo, UT: Charles Redd Center for Western Studies, 1999). My article "Ethnic Groups and the LDS Church," *Dialogue* 25 (Winter 1993): 81-97, surveys some of the persistent issues regarding ethnic members. Other articles include my "Speaking for Themselves: LDS Ethnic Groups Oral History Project" (99-110), "Living Histories: Selected Biographies from the Manhattan First Ward" (58-78), and several "Personal Voices" by ethnic members in the United States and Canada. All these studies show that the Mormon Church has a mixed record in terms of adapting the Church's practices to meet the needs of other ethnic groups.

How successful is Mormonism in adapting to new cultures? How well do such cultural items export as celebrating July 24th, a Utah holiday honoring the arrival of Brigham Young into the Salt Lake Valley, considering white shirts and ties as standard male attire for meetings, and using only organ or piano music for worship services? Converts from throughout the world are pioneers in their own right, not with the usual connotation of traveling and settling on the frontier; but in 1997 the LDS Church celebrated the 150th anniversary of Brigham Young's entrance into the Salt Lake Valley. While the theme "Faith in Every Footstep" was chosen to show that pioneers can be found in the Church worldwide, the major emphasis was on the Mormon pioneers crossing the Great Plains, and members in many countries picked up on that theme. For example, Mormons in Siberia made a handcart, now in the Museum of Church History and Art in Salt Lake City.[7] Other Mormons, however, complained that *pioneer* is an Anglo concept that does not translate well into other cultures. Anecdotal reports I have heard when the subject of Mormon "culture" comes up include the fact that white shirts and ties are not a standard dress for natives in Bolivia and are, in fact, an unnecessary expense. And in some parts of Africa, the story goes, organs are played only in brothels. Relief Society and Melchizedek Priesthood lessons about kissing a spouse goodbye before leaving for work create consternation in Japan where the custom is unknown. Even something as simple as telling a story about snow can be confusing for Mormons in the South Pacific. Several articles in *Dialogue* address the problems of determining what is part of the "gospel" and what is "Mormon culture." For example, Lee Copeland wrote "From Calcutta to Kaysville: Is Righteousness Color-Coded?" 21 (Autumn 1988): 89-99; Jiro Numano looked at "How International Is the Church in Japan?" 13 (Spring 1980: 85-91). Garth N. Jones saw problems in "Spreading the Gospel in Indonesia: Organizational Obstacles and Opportunities," 15 (Winter 1982): 79-90. Even when the language and some cultural elements were similar, Marjorie Newton pointed out American insensitivities in "'Almost Like Us': The American Socialization of Australian Converts," 24 (Fall 1991): 9-20.

Furthermore, the image of the Church as a rich American Church with direct connections with the U.S. government has led to acts of terrorism against chapels and physical attacks on Mormon missionaries abroad. Examinations of the "Americanism" in Mormonism include F. LaMond Tullis, "The Church Moves Outside the United States: Some Observations from Latin America," *Dialogue* 13 (Spring 1980): 63-73; David C. Knowlton, "Missionaries and Terror: The Assassination of Two Elders in Bolivia," *Sunstone* 13 (August 1989): 10-15; and his "Thoughts on Mormonism in Latin America," *Dialogue* 25 (Summer 1992): 41-53. Mark Grover, "Relief Society and Church Welfare: The Brazilian Experience," *Dialogue* 27 (Winter 1994): 29-38, provides an insightful comparison of Church welfare in Brazil and Utah.

Secularism

One of the major concerns for the Mormon Church since 1945 has been how to deal with modernity. As this article has already explained, part of the attraction to Mormonism has been the conservative, return-to-fundamental beliefs regarding family and moral issues. In *Mormon Neo-Orthodoxy*, O. Kendall White argues that, in reaction to modernity, recent Mormon theologians "have embraced some fundamental doctrine of Protestant neo-orthodoxy" including the "sovereignty of God, the depravity of human nature, and the necessity of salvation by grace." While the Mormon Church has adapted to secularization on the institutional level by following corporate patterns, "its efforts at resisting secular society in other respects remain a hallmark." For example, while Protestant churches "accommodated" the "sexual revolution" of the 1960s, the Mormons reenforced traditional sexual norms (159). Mormons also questioned secular concerns about the population explosion and continued to have large families through the last half of the twenti-

---

7. "A Demonstration of Faith," *Church News,* March 8, 1997, 8-10.

eth century. In addition, White notes, Church leaders resisted redefining gender roles (109-10). For example, while American women (including Mormon women) entered the work force, Church President Ezra Taft Benson strenuously encouraged Mormon women to remain at home.

Other topics that could benefit from scholarly exploration include official directions to engage in only "appropriate" entertainment (leading to endless debates about the use of the movie rating system), and to closely regulate internet use to avoid pornography. Hugo Olaiz, "One Lord, One Faith, Many Chat Rooms: Mormons, the Internet, and the Complexities of Open Spaces," *Sunstone,* December 2002, 26-46, explores some dimensions of this dynamic. The Church's public relations triumph during the Winter Olympics, documented in "This Was the Place: Utah and Mormons on an Olympic-sized Stage," *Sunstone,* April 2002, 18-23, could obviously merit professional analysis.

Other scholars predicted the Mormons' conflict with secularism long before it happened. E. E. Ericksen, *The Psychological and Ethical Aspects of Mormon Group Life* (Chicago: University of Chicago Press, 1922) and O'Dea's 1957 study recognized possible friction between the changing world and the Mormon's traditional values. According to O'Dea, "Mormonism's greatest and most significant problem is its encounter with modern secular thought" (244).

Education

One of the reasons that O'Dea predicted internal conflict was because of the Church's simultaneous emphasis on education and conservative values. In an introduction to a republished edition of Nels Anderson's *Desert Saints,* O'Dea wrote, "Utah has three universities which confront young Mormon minds with modern thought. Impersonalization of life, religious crisis and drought, and a search of new values and new identities can be found."[8]

On the surface O'Dea's concerns might seem ill-founded. The Mormon Church has always promoted education with the result that its members are more educated than most Americans. Despite the contemporary trend that mainline churches lose educated members, Mormonism has been dramatically successful at retaining its educated members. While the LDS Church no longer sponsors its own U.S. academies (high schools) and colleges (except for Brigham Young University, Brigham Young University—Idaho (formerly Ricks College), and Brigham Young University—Hawaii), it still encourages its members to obtain a secular education and has even expanded its program of providing seminaries on the high school level and institutes near university campuses to give religious training—undaunted by the fact that high school students in Utah can no longer receive credit for attending its Old and New Testament classes. Frederick S. Buchanan documents this development in "Masons and Mormons: Released-Time Politics in Salt Lake City, 1930-56," *Journal of Mormon History* 19 (Spring 1993): 67-114. Linda Sillitoe describes a similar struggle in Logan in *Friendly Fire: The ACLU in Utah* (Salt Lake City: Signature Books, 1996). Gary James Bergera, "Ernest L. Wilkinson and the Office of Church Commissioner of Education," *Journal of Mormon History* 22 (Spring 1996): 137-73, looks at the internal administrative struggle within the Mormon educational system; and Frederick S. Buchanan,

---

8. Quoted in White, *Mormon Neo-Orthodoxy,* 111.

Culture Clash and Accommodation: Public Schooling in Salt Lake City, 1890-1994 (San Francisco: Smith Research Associates, 1996) examines other Mormon and public school issues.

Yet accompanying the Church's encouragement of education has been a anti-intellectual counterbalance. This tension between the scholarly community and the Mormon Church came to a head in August 1991 when the First Presidency and Quorum of the Twelve issued a statement warning members to be cautious about attending unauthorized symposia. Although the carefully worded statement did not name one group, it mentioned topics that had been discussed at a well-publicized Sunstone Symposium, a conference sponsored by an independent magazine dealing with Mormon issues and often seen by some leaders as critical of the Church. The tension continued with the preparation of an academic freedom statement at BYU and discussions between scholars and their Church leaders. Articles providing background on these tensions appeared in *Dialogue* 26 (Spring 1993), including Lavina Fielding Anderson, "The LDS Intellectual Community and Church Leadership: A Contemporary Chronology," 7-64; Richard D. Poll, "Dialogue Toward Forgiveness: A Supporting View—A Response to 'The LDS Intellectual Community and Church Leadership: A Contemporary Chronology,'" 67-75; Paul James Toscano, "A Plea to the Leadership of the Church: Choose Love Not Power," 95-106; and Elbert Eugene Peck, "A Response to Paul Toscano's 'A Plea to the Leadership of the Church: Choose Love Not Power,'" 95-106.

However, six months later in September 1993, five outspoken intellectuals and feminists, including Anderson and Toscano, were excommunicated, and another was disfellowshipped. About half a dozen other excommunications followed between 1993 and 2000. This may be one area where the situation is too close to be history. Personal statements from five of the September Six were published in "Spiritual Paths after September 1993," *Sunstone* Issue no. 130 (December 2003). Gary James Bergera and Ronald Priddis, *Brigham Young University: A House of Faith* (Salt Lake City: Signature Books, 1985), points out that these types of problems are not new to the intellectual community; they recur periodically, and then die down, a historical perspective also reinforced by my discussion with longtime BYU professor James B. Allen. Bryan Waterman and Brian Kagel, *The Lord's University: Freedom and Authority at BYU* (Salt Lake City: Signature Books, 1998), goes into detail on both the historical context and the specific problems at BYU between 1993 and 1998.

Political Affairs

Since Utah's statehood in 1896, the Mormon Church has not directly controlled politics, although, in cases where the Church felt that there was a moral issue at stake, it has taken a public stand with various degrees of success. For most of the time period under consideration here, Church leaders have presented a united front when they have taken stands on political matters. Exceptions are mostly confined to the early part of this period. For example, after World War II, conservative Republican J. Reuben Clark Jr. spoke out against the United States's involvement in the United Nations while the more liberal Democrat Hugh B. Brown spoke in favor of U.S. participation. Both were counselors to Church President David O. McKay. In reaction to statements that the Church favored the Republican Party, McKay issued a statement that the Church did not take stands on political issues. These topic are explored in D. Michael Quinn, *The Mormon Hierarchy: Extensions of Power* (Salt Lake City: Signature Books, 1997); Gary James Bergera, "'A Strange Phenomena': Ernest L. Wilkinson, the LDS Church, and Utah Politics," *Dialogue* 26 (Summer 1993): 89-115; and Jeffery E. Sells, ed., *God and Country: Politics in Utah* (Salt Lake City: Signature Books, 2004). This anthology, which grew out of widespread community dissatisfaction with the Salt Lake City council's sale of a block of Main Street to the Church for a plaza, includes such authors as former Utah governor Calvin L. Rampton, former Utah Supreme Court chief justice Michael D. Zimmerman, Third District Court judge Judith S. Hanson Atherton, former ACLU legal director Stephen C. Clark, and other authors, both Mormon and non-Mormon.

During the 1950s Apostle Ezra Taft Benson served as Secretary of Agriculture in the cabinet of U.S. President Dwight D. Eisenhower. In addition to Benson's autobiography, *Crossfire: The Eight Years with Eisenhower* (Garden City, NY: Doubleday, 1962), is Edward L. Schapsmeier and Frederick H. Schapsmeier, *Ezra Taft Benson and the Politics of Agriculture: The Eisenhower Years, 1953-1961* (Danville, IL: Interstate Printers and Publishers, 1975). Benson's relationship with the John Birch Society and conservative American thought, a chapter in Quinn's book, earlier appeared as "Ezra Taft Benson and Mormon Political Conflicts," *Dialogue* 26 (Summer 1993): 1-87. Daniel Combs, a BYU graduate student, is examining anti-Communism in the Church during the 1950s and 1960s as his doctoral dissertation.

The 1960s civil rights movement also had an impact on the Church. Jeffery O. Johnson, "Change and Growth: The Mormon Church in the 1960s," *Sunstone* 17 (June 1994): 25-29, looks at the overall effect of the 1960s on the Church. Conservative Church leaders such as Benson feared African Americans, efforts to gain civil rights, claiming they were "fomented almost entirely by the communists" (ibid., 169). For the most part, though, the LDS Church tried with limited success to separate its priesthood exclusion from the civil rights movement. This history is documented in Armand L. Mauss and Lester Bush, *Neither Black Nor White* (Midvale, UT: Signature Books, 1984) and Newell G. Bringhurst, *Saints, Slaves, and Blacks: The Changing Place of Black People within Mormonism* (Westport, CT: Greenwood Press, 1981). Quinn also deals with the struggle among the Church leaders in how to respond to African Americans in *Mormon Hierarchy: Extensions of Power*. Mauss's second book, *All Abraham's Children: Changing Mormon Conceptions of Race and Lineage* (Urbana: University of Illinois Press, 2003), is also rooted in the Church's nineteenth-century history but brings the theme up to the present in his penetrating examination of the place of African Americans, American Indians, and other ethnic groups over time. "Twenty-five Years: A Quarter Century after the Priesthood Revelation: Where Are We Now?" *Sunstone*, Issue no. 126 (March 2003); and Newell G. Bringhurst and Darron Smith, eds. *Black and Mormon: Reflections on Latter-day Saint African-Americans since 1978* (Urbana: University of Illinois Press, 2004), make it clear that the race issue is not of historical interest only.

The General Authorities encouraged its members to oppose legislation which they felt involved moral issues. In 1968 the Church opposed liquor by the drink, supported Sunday closing laws, and favored right to work laws. BYU professor Brian Cannon is researching Sunday closing laws. The Mormon Church also took a stand in opposition to the Equal Rights Amendment in the 1970s. While LDS women were divided in their support, Barbara B. Smith, the Relief Society general president, came out in opposition to the amendment, reinforced in October 1976 by a First Presidency statement of opposition.

The Church's stand, its mobilization of thousands of women lobbyists, and its fund-raising efforts influenced the vote in Utah, Florida, Virginia, and Illinois, and impacted states such as Idaho which rescinded their earlier ratification of the amendment. The LDS Church's viewpoints were presented in Rex D. Lee, *A Lawyer Looks at the Equal Rights Amendment* (Provo, UT: Brigham Young University Press, 1980) and Barbara B. Smith, *A Fruitful Season: Reflections on the Challenging Years of the Relief Society, 1974-1984* (Salt Lake City: Bookcraft, 1988). More analytical studies include O. Kendall White Jr., "'A Feminist Challenge': Mormons for ERA as an Internal Social Movement," *Journal of Ethnic Studies* 13 (Spring 1985): 29-50; his "Overt and Covert Politics: The Mormon Church's Anti-ERA Campaign in Virginia," *Virginia Social Science Journal* 18 (Winter 1980); his "Mormonism and the Equal Rights Amendment," *Journal of Church and State* 31 (Spring 1989): 249-67; and Quinn, *The Mormon Hierarchy: Extensions of Power,* chap. 6, much of which was earlier published as "The LDS Church's Campaign Against the Equal Rights Amendment," *Journal of Mormon History* 20 (Fall 1994): 85-155.

In addition to opposing the ERA, Mormons attended activities for the International Women's Year held in each state throughout the United States. Articles reporting these experiences include Dixie Snow Huefner, "Church and Politics and the IWY Conference," *Dialogue* 11 (Spring 1978): 58-75 and Linda Sillitoe, "Women Scorned: Inside Utah's IWY Conference," *Utah Holiday* 6 (August 1977): 26. The Mormon Church also made national news by excommunicating an outspoken supporter of the ERA, Sonia Johnson, discussed in Sillitoe, "Church Politics and Sonia Johnson: The Central Conundrum," *Sunstone* 5 (January-February 1980): 35-42, and in Johnson's autobiography, *From Housewife to Heretic* (Garden City, NY: Doubleday, 1981). Using oral history interviews, Martha Sonntag Bradley, "The Mormon Relief Society and the International Women's Year," *Journal of Mormon History* 21 (Spring 1995):105-167 looks at the same experience. She has also given booklength treatment to the topic in a book forthcoming in 2005 from Signature Books. Jenny Lynn Harris, a BYU graduate student, is completing a thesis on the Utah IWY meetings.

Marilyn Warenski, *Patriarchs and Politics: The Plight of the Mormon Woman* (New York: McGraw-Hill, 1978), probed the role of the LDS Church in these meetings and its opposition to the ERA. She saw a pattern of repressing women within the Church. The Mormon Women's Forum, a contemporary feminist organization, continues to study the Church's influence on women and examines such issues as the ordination of women to the priesthood. Dorice Williams Elliott, "Women, the Mormon Family, and Class Mobility: Nineteenth-Century Victorian Ideology in a Twentieth-Century Church," *Sunstone* 15 (December 1991): 19-26, argues that the LDS model for women fits the Victorian era better than that created after the women's movement of the 1970s. In reaction to the negative press, BYU started a women's conference, now cosponsored by the Relief Society, that attracts thousands of women annually and produces an annual volume of inspirational readings. Gale Lewis, a BYU graduate student, is researching this topic for her thesis. The Joseph Fielding Smith Institute for Latter-day Saint History sponsored a strong academic seminar in March 2004 to commemorate the bicentennial of Eliza R. Snow's birth: "New Scholarship on Latter-day Saint Women in the Twentieth Century." Several papers focused on issues involving Mormons in the last half of the twentieth century.

Excavating Mormon Pasts

In another current issue, the First Presidency also spoke out against placing the MX missile system in Utah in 1981: "Our fathers came to this western area to establish a base from which to carry the gospel of peace to the peoples of the earth. . . . It is ironic, and a denial of the very essense of that gospel, that in this same general area there should be a mammoth weapons system potentially capable of destroying much of civilization." Plans for the MX were then moved to Wyoming and later abandoned. Steven A. Hildreth wrote two articles about the statement: "The First Presidency Statement on MX in Perspective," *BYU Studies* 22 (Spring 1982): 215-25, and "Mormon Concern over MX: Parochialism or Enduring Moral Theology," *Journal of Church and State* 26 (1984): 255-72. Jacob W. Olmstead, a BYU graduate student is writing his thesis on the MX crisis. The Church has been careful not to align itself too conspicuously with U.S. foreign policy, leaving Church members free to vigorously debate such issues as the Bush administration's conduct of the Iraqi war. Articles in the spring 2004 issue of *Dialogue* are an example.

While ERA and MX were widely published examples of the LDS Church's involvement in public affairs, they were not the only ones. Examples of published articles include Eugene England, "Hanging by a Thread: Mormons and Watergate," *Dialogue* 9 (Summer 1974): 9-18. Ronald W. Walker, "Sheaves, Bucklers, and the State: Mormon Leaders Respond to the Dilemmas of War," *Sunstone* 7 (July-August 1982): 43-56, looks at the Mormon views of all wars and includes a discussion of Vietnam. Other articles looked at just the Vietnam situation and include Edwin Brown Firmage, "Allegiance and Stewardship: Holy War, Just War, and the Mormon Tradition in the Nuclear Age," *Dialogue* 16 (Spring 1983): 47-61; and D. Michael Quinn, "Christian Soldiers or Conscientious Objectors?" *Sunstone* 10 (March 1985): 14-23. *Dialogue* 2 (Winter 1967): 65-100, also published a roundtable about Vietnam.

Mormons have also come out strongly against abortion, and Utah passed one of the strongest pro-life laws in the United States in 1991. While the issue has become more pressing in the late 1980s and 1990s, it was already a concern when *Sunstone* published Richard Sherlock, "Abortion, Politics, and Policy: A Deafening Silence in the Church," *Sunstone* 6 (July-August 1981): 17-19; and Donald G. Hill Jr., "Abortion, Politics, and Policy: The Beginning of Actual Human Life," ibid., 25-27.

In 1992 the LDS Church came out against a parimutuel betting proposal in the state of Utah; several of the General Authorities mentioned this subject in the October general conference just prior to the election. The measure was soundly defended. In the 1990s, the Church has also come out in favor of traditional family values, issuing a proclamation on the subject and actively resisting and funding anti-gay rights proposals in several states.

Correlation

The growing Church has required a developing bureaucracy and more supervision of programs. This project had started around the turn of the century when Joseph F. Smith had attempted to reorganize the Church under priesthood authority, but its greatest effects have been felt since 1960 when Harold B. Lee started a correlation program which eventually required all auxiliaries to clear anything sent to the general Church membership through a correlation committee. In addition, programs run by the Relief Society, such as its social services, became a separate Church department, the consolidation of the Church magazines, and the transfer of individual auxiliaries' funds into the central coffers. Tina Hatch, "'Changing Times Bring Changing Conditions': Relief Society, 1960 to the Present," *Dialogue* 38, no. 3 (Fall 2004): forthcoming, puts the organization's "losses" in the larger perspectives of greater unity in and benefits to the worldwide membership.

In 1971 the Church hired two consulting firms, Cresap, McCormack, and Paget of New York, and Safeway Stores, Inc., of Oakland, California, to look at the Church's policies. The Cresap report showed that General Authorities were too heavily involved with administrative responsibilities and suggested that General Authorities concentrate on policy formation while transferring day-to-day operations to full-time managing directors. The reports also suggested creating a Public Communications and Internal Communications department. The LDS Church leaders adapted many of these suggestions, creating an even larger Church bureaucracy. Sociologist Marie Cornwall discusses the question of how successful such measures are in "Mormonism and the Challenge of the Mainline," *Dialogue* 24, no. 2 (Winter 1991): 68-71. She concludes: "Centralized control versus local management and administration will continue to be an issue within Mormonism over the next several decades." Other studies are James B. Allen, "'Course Corrections': Some Personal Reflections," *Sunstone* 14 (October 1990): 34-40; D. Michael Quinn, "From Sacred Grove to Sacral Power Structure," *Dialogue* 17 (Summer 1984): 9-34; J. Lynn England, "The Importance of Programs in Our Religious Community," *Sunstone* 14 (October 1990): 41-43; Marie Cornwall, "The Paradox of Organization," *Sunstone* 14 (October 1990): 44-47; Jill Mulvay Derr, Janath Cannon, and Maureen Ursenbach Beecher, *Women of Covenant* (Salt Lake City: Deseret Books, 1992); and William G. Hartley, "From Men to Boys: LDS Aaronic Priesthood Offices, 1829-1996," *Journal of Mormon History* 22 (Spring 1996): 80-136.

Finances

The LDS Church has been called one of the richest Churches in the United States. Doing research on the finances of the Church is difficult, however, since it has not published its financial statements since 1958. Some of its business activities are matters of public record. Following World War II, for example, the Church established what eventually became a chain of fifteen hospitals throughout the intermountain West. In 1975, it sold the hospitals to a separate corporation, arguing that it needed to attend to health needs for its international membership.

Other changes in finance showed that the Church was doing well. In 1982 instead of requiring local congregations to put up much of the money for new construction, that figure was cut to 4 percent. Later the Church absorbed the entire costs. In 1990 Church leaders announced that all ward and branch operating costs would come from tithes and offerings. As a result, Church members no longer needed to pay ward budget, a contribution on top of tithing which paid for the upkeep of meetinghouses and the congregation's activities. And in 1991 the costs for missionaries were equalized around with world at $350 US and $400 Canadian; missionaries and their parents now make contributions to their wards to comply with IRS regulations, while the funds are distributed through the central Church office to the missions. Quinn explores the topic of finances in *The Mormon Hierarchy: Extensions of Power*, and "LDS Church Finances from the 1803 to the 1990s," *Sunstone* 19 (June 1996): 17-29. The topic of Mormon wealth and power has also fascinated journalists, forming a major element in their attempts to capture this successful American-based religion. While they have seldom provided new material, such studies have brought the Church into the public eye: Robert Gottlieb and Peter Wiley, *America's Saints: The Rise of Mormon Power* (New York: Putnam's, 1984); John Heinerman and Anson Shupe, *The Mormon Corporate Empire* (Boston: Beacon Press, 1985); and Richard N. Ostling and Joan Ostling, *Mormon America: The Power and the Promise* (New York: HarperSanFrancisco, 1999).

Further Research

Many other topics concerning Mormon history need additional research, among them missionary work and community life. While missionary work has been an important part of the LDS Church since 1830, some major changes have taken place since 1945. Before World War II, missionaries distributed pamphlets and held cottage meetings, but there were no formal lessons and language training. In the 1950s, the Church introduced the first standard missionary discussions and then in 1969 established a Language Training Mission. In the 1970s Missionary Training Centers throughout the world trained missionaries in languages, contacting and teaching techniques, and some cultural specifics. Some examinations are: Richard L. Cowan, *Every Man Shall Hear the Gospel in His Own Tongue: A History of the Missionary Training Center and Its Predecessors* (Provo, UT: Missionary Training Center, 1984); James B. Allen and John B. Harris, "What Are You Doing Looking Up Here: Graffiti Mormon Style [at the MTC]," *Sunstone* 6 (March/April 1981): 27-40; and my "Without Purse or Scrip," *Dialogue* 29 (Fall 1996): 77-93. Gary and Gordon Shepherd, *Mormon Passage: A Missionary Chronicle* (Urbana: University of Illinois Press, 1998), uses their personal experiences as missionaries in Mexico in the 1960s as the basis for analyzing not only the functioning of the highly Americanized church in that country but also the role of LDS missions in indoctrinating young Mormon men. But many other topics should be explored, such as the increased use of salesmanship and positive thinking methods in missionary techniques and the increased use of women and couples as missionaries. Articles on sister missionaries include my "LDS Sister Missionaries: An Oral History Response," *Journal of Mormon History* 23 (Spring 1997): 100-139; and Tania Rands Lyon and Mary Ann Shumway McFarland, "Not Invited but Welcome: The History and Impact on Church Policy on Sister Missionaries," *Dialogue* 36, no. 3 (Fall 2003): 71-101.

Another area that has been under-researched for the last half of the twentieth century is the role of community. Lowry Nelson, *The Mormon Village: A Pattern and Technique of Land Settlement* (Salt Lake City: University of Utah Press, 1952) looked at Mormon village development, providing a solid foundation for a study that examines how these villages have changed during the rest of the twentieth century. What provides a sense of belonging for Mormons who do not live in small towns? Douglas D. Alder explored this question in his Mormon History Association presidential address "The Mormon Ward: Congregation or Community?", *Journal of Mormon History* 5 (1979): 61-78; while additional insights come from Jan Shipps, Dean L. May, and Cheryll L. May, "Sugar House Ward: A Latter-day Saint Congregation," in *American Congregations,* edited by James P. Wind and James W. Lewis (Chicago: University of Chicago Press, 1994), 294-348. While there are many ward histories, most are chronological celebrations and do not address the ward as community. Susan Buhler Taber, *Mormon Lives: A Year in the Elkton Ward* (Urbana: University of Illinois Press, 1993), is an unique portrait based on oral histories of members in a Maryland ward. My

Mormon Lives

A Year in the Elkton Ward

Susan Buhler Taber

University of Illinois Press
Urbana and Chicago

Excavating Mormon Pasts

Mormon Wards as Community (Binghamton, NY: Global Academic Publishing, 2001), uses my experiences to explore what makes up a community.

Conclusion

Mormonism was started by a young man with a vision; those who joined the early Church were viewed as radicals. The Mormon Church is now run by leaders who match the Victorian ideal more than the Mormons who lived in the early nineteenth century. As radical as the early Mormon Church may have appeared, by the end of the twentieth century it had swung completely to the other side and was viewed as extremely traditional. Even though the LDS Church seems out of step with the post-modern world, it continues to grow—not in spite of—but because of its conservativism. Yet the mushrooming growth throughout the world, with its increasing bureaucracy, symbolizes both the successes and the problems of the Mormon Church. More thorough study would be of value, not only for the Church, but also for understanding twentieth-century society. Fortunately, young scholars are asking these questions.

JESSIE L. EMBRY is associate director of the Charles Redd Center for Western Studies and an instructor of history at Brigham Young University. She is the author of seven books and over eighty articles dealing with Mormon, western, and Utah history. Her specialty is oral history.

Chapter 9

Growth and Internationalization: The LDS Church Since 1945

*Kahlile B. Mehr, Mark L. Grover,
Reid L. Neilson, Donald Q. Cannon, and Grant Underwood*

Even though the history of the LDS Church experience in the international arena has appeared in print only sparsely, it is the scene of the Church's greatest growth and challenges. In some cases, this situation exists because much of this history is in the recent past and the documentation is not yet available to develop a comprehensive perspective. Except for Europe, Australasia, and a few countries scattered on other continents, the Church cannot be said to have had a major international presence until after World War II. At the end of the twentieth century, it was still largely a western hemisphere church, rather than a global one. In other cases, the history goes back for decades but has been largely ignored because the American experience dominates Church historiography. Likewise, it sometimes takes decades or centuries for watershed events to come into focus.

This article will identify the landscape of international Church historiography for the last half of the twentieth century. Only after World War II, did the Church begin to fulfill a destiny envisioned by earliest prophet, Joseph Smith, when he spoke in a small log schoolhouse in Kirtland, Ohio: "It is only a little handful of Priesthood you see here tonight, but His Church will fill North and South America—it will fill the world." Those writing the history of the international Church live mostly in the United States and are either observers in academia or those who participated in Church events abroad, usually while serving as missionaries. Another group is employees of Church publications sent abroad to interview and report progress. Members native to areas outside the borders of the United States, such as in Latin America and Europe, have begun to craft their history from their perspective, ensuring a richer tapestry of how the past is portrayed in print. (See also "The LDS Church in the United States Since 1945" by Jessie L. Embry in this volume.)

Whereas in 1901, five out of six members lived in the Intermountain West, by 1996 more members were living outside than inside the borders of the United States.[1] At mid-century, that trend was still nascent when newly appointed Church president George Albert Smith said at October general conference in 1945, "We must preach the gospel to the South American countries which we have scarcely touched. We must preach the gospel to every African section that we haven't been in yet. We must preach the gospel to Asia. And I might go one step further and say in all parts of the world where we have not yet been permitted to go. I look upon Russia as one of the fruitful fields for the teaching of

---

1. (No author), *Out of Obscurity: The LDS Church in the Twentieth Century* (Salt Lake City: Deseret Book, 2000), vii.

the gospel."[2] World War II had just ended, and the prospects envisioned by President Smith all unfolded before century's end and continue to flower.

While a physical relocation of many foreign converts to the United States characterized the nineteenth-century Church, the message of the new century was for converts to strengthen the stakes of the Church wherever they were established. Two great events of the David O. McKay administration that symbolized this shift of philosophy were two important "firsts": the erection in 1955 of a temple in Zollikofen, Switzerland, and the creation in 1958 of a stake in Auckland, New Zealand. (Hawaii had both a temple and stakes earlier, but it was part of the United States and was also in the western hemisphere.) Two decades later, Spencer W. Kimball repeatedly emphasized the obligation of young men to serve missions, the result being a doubling of the missionary force between 1974 and 1978—but still not enough, in Kimball's opinion, for the task at hand. Thus, he stated at the Regional Representative Seminar in September, "It is still a big world so far as numbers of people are concerned when we think of nations like China, the Soviet Union, India, the whole continent of Africa, and our Arab brothers and sisters."[3]

Two classics of international Church history, both published in 1978, heralded this new age of expansion. Spencer J. Palmer, ed., *The Expanding Church* (Salt Lake City: Deseret Book, 1978), describes Church programs intended to open the spiritual doors of the nations and then provides case studies of expansion into Western Europe, Latin America, Asia, and the Pacific. Particularly significant are David M. Kennedy, "More Nations than One," 69-79, on his efforts as a special representative of the First Presidency to the nations and Bruce R. McConkie, "To the Koreans, and All the People of Asia," 137-52, detailing the challenges facing the Church in the international realm. F. LaMond Tullis, ed., *Mormonism: A Faith for All Cultures* (Provo, UT: BYU Press, 1978), is a compilation of presentations from a Brigham Young University symposium on the "Expanding Church," held in honor of the U.S. Bicentennial in 1976. It presents a comprehensive status report of the international Church nearing its 150th anniversary, including many first-hand accounts of foreign Church leaders, and analyzes how the Church might adapt its program to accommodate the diversity of world cultures, without modifying the essential truths of its message. (Some chapters are noted in the regional summaries later on.) This symposium received wide attention within the English-speaking Church through an excellent summary, Lavina Fielding, "The Expanding Church," *Ensign,* December 1976, 7-13. Less well-known is James R. Moss, R. Lanier Britsch, James R. Christensen, and Richard O. Cowan, *The International Church* (Provo, UT: BYU Press, 1982), a comprehensive summary of Church history in each world region and discussion of a few general topics such as patterns of international growth. This book was updated and substantially reworked: Donald Q. Cannon, Richard O. Cowan, R. Lanier Britsch, David F. Boone, and Fred E. Woods, *Unto Every Nation: Gospel Light Reaches Every Land* (Salt Lake City: Deseret Book, 2003).

Two more volumes appeared, focused on the Church's growth and internationalization, both the results of symposia at Brigham Young University. The same issues discussed in 1978 were still current. Elder Spencer J. Condie gave the keynote speech, "Christian Values and Ethnic Diversity: How Much of a Country's Culture Can a Christian Convert Keep?" for the Sixth Annual Conference of the International Society, held at Brigham Young University in 1995. The proceedings were published as (no author or editor), *"For Ye Are All One in Christ Jesus": The Global Church in a World of Ethnic Diversity* (Provo, UT: David M. Kennedy Center for International Studies, BYU, 1996). The essays in the section titled "Challenges Abroad" concerned the challenge of accommodating ethnic and cultural diversity. About half of the second volume, proceedings of the twenty-ninth annual Sidney B. Sperry Symposium, (no author), *Out of Obscurity: The LDS Church in the Twentieth Century* (Salt Lake City: Deseret Book, 2000), pertain to internationalization. For example, Victor L. Ludlow, "The Internationalization of the Church," 204-26, presented a variety of statistics other than membership, such as Book of Mormon sales,

---

2. Quoted in Spencer J. Palmer, ed., *The Expanding Church* (Salt Lake City: Deseret Book, 1978), 4.
3. Quoted in ibid., 7.

Church Education System enrollment, numbers of foreign-born General Authorities and missionaries, and numbers of international stakes and temples to define the extent to which the Church has become international. Other specific articles will be noted hereafter.

Two general Church histories include chapters summarizing the Church's international experience in the second half of the twentieth century. Richard O. Cowan, *The Latter-day Saint Century* (Salt Lake City: Deseret Book, 1999), devotes considerable attention to the international Church and the impact of the Church worldwide. This work revises and updates his *The Church in the Twentieth Century* (Salt Lake City: Bookcraft, 1985). The other history treating this subject is James B. Allen and Glen M. Leonard, *The Story of the Latter-day Saints* (1976; 2d ed. rev. and enl., Salt Lake City: Deseret Book, 1992). Francis M. Gibbons, *The Expanding Church: Three Decades of Remarkable Growth among the Latter-day Saints, 1970-1999* (Bountiful, UT: Horizon Books, 1999), contains two statistical chapters, one on the "global" and the other on the "growing" Church. Another indicator of Church internationalization is the spread of temples documented in Richard O. Cowan, *Temples to Dot the Earth* (Springville, UT: Cedar Fort, 1997).

Accounts of foreign-born General Authorities appear in Derin Head Rodriguez, *From Every Nation* (Salt Lake City: Deseret Book, 1990). A wide-ranging compilation of stories about early Church leaders in many foreign countries is Bruce A. Van Orden, D. Brent Smith, and Everett Smith Jr., eds., *Pioneers in Every Land: Inspirational Stories of International Pioneers Past and Present* (Salt Lake City: Bookcraft, 1997). The individual chapters of this book are noted in the regional summaries later on.

In 1997, the Church published an excellent video, *An Ensign to the Nations,* that recounts the experiences of Church pioneers worldwide along with the commentary of Church leaders.

While the international Church is much too broad for academic theses or dissertations, two of them treat important aspects. L. Grant Shields, "Language Challenges Facing the Church of Jesus Christ of Latter-day Saints in Preaching the Gospel to 'Every Nation'" (Ph.D. diss., Brigham Young University, 1976), recounts the history of translating modern scripture, including the unheralded efforts of many foreign converts. Samuel M. Otterstrom, "International Diffusion of the Mormon Church" (M.A. thesis, Brigham Young University, 1994), identifies the general growth patterns of Church internationally from early contacts to governmental recognition, from the establishment of missions to the growth of local leadership sufficient to permit the creation of stakes, and from establishing centers in cities to moving outward into the countryside.

An extensive number of articles have been published on the nature and challenges of the Church's growth and internationalization, but this list identifies some of the more significant: three articles in the proceedings of the Eighth Annual Sidney B. Sperry Symposium, *A Sesquicentennial Look at Church History* (Provo, UT: Religious Education, Brigham Young University, 1980): Richard O. Cowan, "Meeting the Needs of the Worldwide Church: Significance of Recent Developments"; Spencer J. Palmer, "The Long Promised Day Has Come: Vital Signs of Prophetic Leadership"; James R. Moss, "The Patterns and Process of Growth"; Garth N. Jones, "Expanding LDS Church Abroad: Old Realities Compounded," *Dialogue: A Journal of Mormon Thought* 8 (Spring 1980): 8-22; and his "Spiritual Searching: The Church on Its International Mission," *Dialogue* 20 (Summer 1987): 58-74; and Rodney Stark, "The Rise of a New World Faith," *Review of Religious Research* 26 (September 1984): 18-27.

Other significant articles include James B. Allen, "On Becoming a Universal Church: Some Historical Perspectives," *Dialogue* 25, no. 1 (March 1992): 13-16; Lawrence A. Young, "Confronting Turbulent Environments: Issues in the Organizational Growth and Globalization of Mormonism," in *Contemporary Mormonism: Social Science Perspectives,* edited by Marie Cornwall, Tim B. Heaton, and Lawrence A. Young (Urbana: University of Illinois Press, 1994), 43-63; and Eugene England, "Becoming a World Religion: Blacks, the Poor—All of Us," *Sunstone,* issue 110 (June 1998), 49-60.

THE LATTER DAY SAINT CENTURY
1901–2000

RICHARD O. COWAN

Revised and updated edition of
The Church in the Twentieth Century

BOOKCRAFT
SALT LAKE CITY, UTAH

Anson D. Shupe and John Heinerman, "State-within-a-State Diplomacy: Mormon Missionary Efforts in Communist and Islamic Countries," *The Politics of Religion and Social Change,* edited by Anson Shupe and Jeffrey K. Hadden (New York: Paragon House, 1988), summarized BYU cultural programs that sought to improve the image of the Church preceding attempts to obtaining recognition and sending in missionaries. Armand L. Mauss, "Identity and Boundary Maintenance: International Prospects for Mormonism at the Dawn of the Twenty-first Century," in *Mormon Identities in Transition,* edited by Douglas J. Davies (New York: Cassell, 1996), 9-19, stated that a Mormon identity in each country permits the Church to transcend cultural boundaries.

Dialogue 29 (Spring 1996) was devoted to the international Church, not only its history but the future of expanding the Church into the international realm. Significant articles here included: Armand L. Mauss, "Mormonism in the Twenty-first Century: Marketing for Miracles," 236-49; Lowell C. "Ben" Bennion and Lawrence A. Young, "The Uncertain Dynamics of LDS Expansion, 1950-2020," 8-32; and Gordon and Gary Shepherd, "Membership Growth, Church Activity, and Missionary Recruitment," 33-57. Other articles from this issue of *Dialogue* will be noted hereafter.

Kahlile B. Mehr wrote three articles, all published in the *Journal of Mormon History* on behind-the-scenes activities that molded the growth of the Church internationally. "An LDS International Trio, 1974-1997," 25 (Fall 1999): 101-20, describes the work of David M. Kennedy, the International Mission, and the International Affairs Office in opening up new countries to missionary work. "Area Supervision: Administration for a Worldwide Church, 1960-2000," 27 (Spring 2001): 192-214, describes how the administrative backbone of the international Church evolved at the end of the century. "Missionary Couples in Eastern Europe," 29 (Spring 2003): 179-99, discusses the innovative ways in which senior couples have been integrated into the missionary work of the Church based on examples of that effort in eastern Europe.

Numerous articles in Church publications deal with the growth and internationalization of Church in general, in specific countries, and the contributions of its pioneer members worldwide. Some of the more significant from the *Ensign* are: Dean L. Larsen, "The Challenges of Administering a Worldwide Church," July 1974, 18-22; Justus Ernst, "Every Man . . . in His Own Language," July 1974, 23-27; Howard W. Hunter, "All Are Alike unto God," June 1979, 72-74; Spencer W. Kimball, "The Uttermost Parts of the Earth," July 1979, 2-9; Lavina Fielding Anderson, "The Church's Cross-Cultural Encounters," April 1980, 44-50; and Richard O. Cowan, "From Footholds: Spreading the Gospel Worldwide," June 1993, 56-61. These and articles yet to be mentioned in this chapter are but a fraction of the available material.

Mehr analyzed a compilation by Mark Davies at Illinois State University (used courtesy of Davies) and found that 2,632 articles appeared on the international Church between 1986 and 2000 in the *Ensign* (741), *New Era* (131), *Friend* (108), and *Church News* (1,652). The regional distribution of this wealth of material pertains to Europe (34 percent), Asia and the Pacific (27 percent), Latin America (26 percent), and Africa and the Middle East (13 percent).

Another important source for information on the international Church is the firsthand accounts found among the five thousand interviews of the James H. Moyle Oral History Program, Archives, Family and Church History Department, Church of Jesus Christ of Latter-day Saints, Salt Lake City (hereafter LDS Church Archives). Staff member Matthew K. Heiss has conducted nearly a thousand interviews over the last fifteen years, a majority of which pertain to the former countries of the Soviet Bloc (100 in Russia alone) and to Africa. Another staff member, Gordon Irving, has conducted hundreds of interviews in Latin America over the last thirty years. Various other staff members in the last few years have conducted approximately six hundred interviews in Asia, Europe, and Africa.

Excavating Mormon Pasts

The Pacific and Australasia

When missionaries debarked at Tahiti in 1844, they initiated the first systematic proselytizing effort abroad in a language other than English. Now, nine of the ten countries worldwide where the highest proportion of the population is Church members are in the Pacific. The Church has built more temples per capita in that region than elsewhere in the world; and among the 400,000 Pacific Islands members are some who are sixth-generation members, equal to any Church lineage in the United States. Living remote from Church headquarters, their faith is legendary.

For a number of years, the sole academic practitioner of writing Pacific history, and the most prolific over time, is R. Lanier Britsch. His early efforts to explore the modern Church in the Pacific Islands include, "The Church in the South Pacific," *Ensign*, February 1976, 19-27; "On the Pacific Frontier: The Church in the Gilbert Islands," *Ensign*, October 1981, 28-31; and "Fiji, Micronesia-Guam, and Other Non-Polynesian Areas," in *Proceedings, Fifth Annual Conference, Mormon History in the Pacific, March 3, 1984* (Laie, HI: BYU—Hawaii Campus, 1984), 2-11, which discusses Church growth in Fiji, New Caledonia, New Hebrides, the Solomon Islands, the Gilbert Islands, Guam, and New Guinea. Britsch's Pacific studies culminated in *Unto the Islands of the Sea: A History of the Latter-day Saints in the Pacific* (Salt Lake City: Deseret Book, 1986), the single most important volume on the subject. Its path-breaking narrative depth on most locales and its solid academic foundation make it the standard work on the subject.

Beyond Britsch's work are two important volumes that include coverage of the Church in the Pacific during the latter half of the twentieth century. Grant Underwood, *Voyages of Faith: Explorations in Mormon Pacific History* (Provo, UT: BYU Press, 2000), is a selection of polished papers from the annual meetings of the Mormon Pacific History Society (MPHS). MPHS blends the efforts of both scholars and lay people. Its proceedings total nearly two hundred presentations since 1980 but were difficult to come by except for photocopied proceedings distributed to members. Another volume of overall significance is Russell T. Clement, *Mormons in the Pacific: A Bibliography* (Laie, HI: Institute for Polynesian Studies, 1981), containing 2,877 entries on the topic.

The Hawaiian Islands is the major island group of the North Pacific, while the South Pacific is traditionally divided into three regions: Polynesia, Melanesia, and Micronesia. What follows is a region-by-region review of significant publications for these areas for the period after World War II.

The second island group to be visited by missionaries (in 1850), Hawaii became the center of Church activity in the Pacific. As a result, its history has been studied far more extensively than other island groups, with the nineteenth century receiving most of the attention. R. Lanier Britsch, *Moramona: The Mormons in Hawaii* (Laie, HI: Institute for Polynesia Studies, BYU—Hawaii, 1989), is the most comprehensive history. Lance D. Chase, *Temple, Town, Tradition: The Collected Historical Essays of Lance D. Chase* (Salt Lake City: Publishers Press for The Institute for Polynesian Studies, 2000), includes numerous topics of Hawaiian history. Another resource is Richard C. Harvey, "The Development of The Church of Jesus Christ of Latter-day Saints in Hawaii," (M.A. thesis, Brigham Young University, 1974).

The Church's Polynesian Cultural Center (PCC), created in the 1960s, has also drawn considerable attention, including: Vernice Wineera and Rubina Rivers Forester, "The Polynesian Cultural Center: Reflections and Recollections," *Voyages of Faith*, 209-38; and James Whitehurst, "Mormons and the Hula: The Polynesian Cultural Center in Hawaii," *Journal of American Culture* 12 (1989): 1-5. Full-length studies include Robert O'Brian, *Hands across the Water: The Story of the Polynesian Cultural Center* (Laie, HI: Polynesian Cultural Center, 1983) and several graduate works: Craig Ferre, "A History of the Polynesian Cultural Center's Night Show, 1963-1983" (Ph.D. diss., Brigham Young University, 1988); Ann Marie Robinson, "The Polynesian Cultural Center: A Study of Authenticity" (M.A. thesis, California State University—Chico 1991); and Vernice Wineera, "Selves and Others: A Study of Reflexivity and the Presentation of Culture in Touristic Display at the

Polynesian Cultural Center" (Ph.D. diss., University of Hawaii at Manoa, 2000). R. Lanier Britsch is scheduled to write an official fortieth anniversary history of the center.

The history of the Church College of Hawaii is recounted by its inaugural president, Reuben D. Law, in *The Founding and Early Development of the Church College of Hawaii* (St. George, UT: Dixie College, 1972) and continued by a subsequent president, Alton Wade, "BYU—Hawaii: A Promise in the Pacific," *Brigham Young Magazine,* 48 (1994): 34-39. Kenneth Baldridge recorded a behind-the-scenes glimpse of deliberations in "Search for a Site: Selection of the Church College of Hawaii Campus," in *Voyages of Faith,* 191-208. Baldridge, in the closing years of his service on the faculty of BYU—Hawaii, prepared a full-length history of the college based on an extensive oral history project with present and past participants. P. Alfred Pratte is completing the history and preparing it for publication.

Two fine studies probe the variety of ethnic experience in Hawaii: Max E. Stanton, "Samoan Saints: Samoans in the Mormon Village of Laie, Hawaii" (Ph.D. diss., University of Oregon, 1973); and Russell T. Clement and Shen-Luen Tsai, "East Wind to Hawaii: History and Contributions of Chinese and Japanese Latter-day Saints in Hawaii," in *Voyages of Faith,* 89-106.

Polynesia, where the first Mormon missionaries in the Pacific began their labors, includes American Samoa, the Cook Islands, Easter Island, French Polynesia, Niue, Pitcairn Island, Western Samoa, Tokelau, Tonga, Tuvalu, and Wallis and Futuna. Norman Douglas, "Latter-day Saint Missions and Missionaries in Polynesia, 1844-1960" (Ph.D. diss., Australian National University, Canberra, 1974), provided scholars with an overview of Church development from the beginning until fifteen years after World War II. A history of the first island group to be visited by missionaries appears in S. George Ellsworth and Kathleen C. Perrin, *Seasons of Faith and Courage: The Church of Jesus Christ of Latter-day Saints in French Polynesia, A Sesquicentennial History 1843-1993* (Sandy, UT: Yves R. Perrin, 1994), with Ellsworth covering the early period while Perrin provides excellent information about the post-World War II years. Kathleen's husband, former Tahitian Mission President Yves A. Perrin, wrote *L'histoire de l'Eglise Mormone en Polynesie Francaise de 1844 à 1982 [The History of the Mormon Church in French Polynesia 1844-1982]* (Papeete: Tahiti Imprimerie CES-STP, 1982). In May 1966 the *Improvement Era* ran historical articles on the major islands groups of French Polynesia, Samoa, Tonga, Rarotonga (Cook Islands), while later Church publications followed up with additional coverage.

Mormon missionaries entered Samoa in the 1860s and established a enclave that survived, despite its isolation, for a quarter century until formal missionary work began again in 1888. According to the *2003 Deseret News Church Almanac,* by 2001, Mormons constituted 60,000 out of a population just over 159,000 (405). The only book-length history of the Samoan Church is R. Carl Harris et al., *Samoa Apia Mission History, 1888-1983* (Pesega, Western Samoa: Samoa Apia Mission, 1983). Harris, like Perrin, is a former mission president. A little-known autobiography of the first Samoan stake president and regional representative is Jennie Hart, ed., *Autobiography of Percy John Rivers* (Downey, ID: Ati's Samoan Printshop, 1996). Eugene England, "Mission to Paradise," *BYU Studies* 38, no. 1 (1999): 171-85, is an account of the service he and his wife, Charlotte, rendered in 1954-56, teaching school, training leaders, and proselytizing. The December 1974 *Ensign* carried Janice Clark, "The Saints in Samoa," 21-24.

Nearly one out of every two Tongans is Mormon, the highest percentage of Church membership of any nation in the world (*2003 Church Almanac,* 405). Ermel J. Morton, the founding principal of Liahona High School in Tonga and translator of Mormon scriptures into Tongan, prepared a *Brief History of the Tongan Mission of the Church of Jesus Christ of Latter-day Saints* (Suva: Fiji times Print, 1968) for the mission's jubilee anniversary. John H. Groberg wrote fascinating and spiritually uplifting accounts about his experiences in Tonga as a missionary in *In the Eye of the Storm* (Salt Lake City: Bookcraft, 1993, later reissued under the title *The Other Side of Heaven*). He chronicled his later experiences as a Church leader in Tonga and the Pacific Area in *The Fire of Faith* (Salt Lake City:

SOUTHERN CROSS SAINTS

THE MORMONS IN AUSTRALIA

Marjorie Newton

MORMONS IN THE PACIFIC SERIES

Published by
The Institute for Polynesian Studies
Laie, Hawaii

Funded by
Polynesian Cultural Center
Brigham Young University–Hawaii

Deseret Book, 1996). Eric B. Shumway, an acknowledged authority on Tongan language and culture and one of few nonislanders to be honored with a chiefly title, translated and edited biographical sketches of Tongan Church members in *Tongan Saints: Legacy of Faith* (Salt Lake City: Publishers Press for The Institute for Polynesian Studies, 1991). Two topically focused graduate theses of the value are the provocative dissertation of Tamar Gordon, "Inventing Mormon Identity in Tonga" (University of California, Berkeley, 1988), and Sosaih H. Naulu, "Incidental Effects of Church Activity on Development, Landscapes and Culture: An Example from Tonga" (M.A. thesis, Brigham Young University, 1990). An account of the Liahona High School, which played a significant role in the expansion of the Church in Tonga after its completion in 1952, is Delworth Keith Young, "Liahona High School, Its Prologue and Development to 1965" (M.A. thesis, Utah State University, 1967). More recently, the *Ensign* published "Tonga: A Land of Believing People," September 2001, 42-47, by staff writer LaRene Porter Gaunt.

The island nations of Fiji, New Caledonia, Papua New Guinea, the Solomon Islands, and Vanuatu, situated northeast of Australia, comprise Melanesia. Because the people resemble Africans, the Church stayed away from these islands until the mid-twentieth century because of the priesthood issue. In 1955, after a stopover in Fiji, President David O. McKay decided that Fijian men did not fall under the priesthood ban and ordered missionary work to commence. The first Melanesian Church congregations were established in Fiji and New Caledonia soon thereafter. Two decades later the Church entered Vanuatu. The first serious missionary efforts in Papua New Guinea occurred in 1979. Missionaries entered the Solomon Islands in 1994. *Ensign* articles on the Church in Melanesia include Janet Brigham and Herbert F. Murray, "The Saints in Fiji," November 1973, 27-29; Shirleen Meek, "Fiji: Islands of Faith," December 1990, 32-37; Michael R. Morris, "'One Talk' in Papua New Guinea," February 1995, 22-29; R. Val Johnson, "Islands of Light" [New Caledonia], March 2000, 31-35; and Connie and Ralph Andersen, "Vanuatu: Gospel Growth in the Islands of the Sea," October 2001, 73.

Micronesia includes Belau (Palau), Federated States of Micronesia, Guam, Kiribati, Northern Marianas, Marshall Islands, and Nauru and is situated roughly between the Philippines and Hawaii. Missionaries served in Guam beginning in 1955. Other areas were not opened until the middle 1970s. An important book discussing the proselyting efforts of Mormon missionaries who served on the heels of World War II campaigns that liberated the area is William W. Cannon, *Beachheads in Micronesia* (Salt Lake City: W. W. Cannon, 1997), while a later period is the topic of David M. Walden, "An Exploration of Recent Religious Conversion on Guam" (M.A. thesis, University of Guam, 1978). *Ensign* features include Alf Pratte, "News of the Church—The Gospel Moves to Micronesia," February 1978, 76; R. Val Johnson, "Charting a New Course in Micronesia," July 1996, 38-42; and his "The Seabirds of Kiribati," December 2000, 40-44.

A few Pacific-wide articles surpass regional boundaries. One is R. Lanier Britsch, "Latter-day Saint Education in the Pacific Islands," in *New Views of Mormon History: A Collection of Essays in Honor of Leonard J. Arrington,* edited by Davis Bitton and Maureen Ursenbach Beecher (Salt Lake City: University of Utah Press, 1987), 197-211. The labor mission program which involved many young Polynesian men during the 1950s and 1960s is recounted in David W. Cummings, *Mighty Missionary of the Pacific: The Building Program of The Church of Jesus Christ of Latter-day Saints, Its History, Scope, and Significance* (Salt Lake City: Bookcraft, 1961). A valuable study that includes comments about the Church is Manfred Ernst, *Winds of Change: Rapidly Growing Religious Groups in the Pacific Islands* (Suva, Fiji: Pacific Conference of Churches, 1994). Finally, a forthcoming volume to be published by the Religious Studies Center, BYU, will contain highlights from the 1997 Pioneers in the Pacific Sesquicentennial Conference held in Laie, Hawaii.

As with the Pacific islands, Australia and New Zealand were first visited by early Church missionaries in 1851 and 1854 respectively. Marjorie Newton, an Australian Church member, has written extensively on Church growth and the social challenges of implementing Church programs in Australasia. Her most important works on Australia include

Excavating Mormon Pasts

Southern Cross Saints: The Mormons in Australia (Laie, HI: The Institute for Polynesia Studies, 1991), and *Dialogue* articles "'Almost Like Us:' The American Socialization of Australian Converts," 24 (Fall 1991): 9-20; and "Toward 2000: Mormonism in Australia," 29 (Spring 1996): 193-206. Ross Geddes describes the maturing Church in "Before Stakehood: The Mission Years in Brisbane, Australia," *Journal of Mormon History* 22 (Fall 1996): 92-119. Christopher K. Bigelow highlights Church outreach efforts in "Australia: Coming Out of Obscurity Down Under," *Ensign,* December 1998, 34-40.

Australia's near neighbor is treated in Brian W. Hunt, *Zion in New Zealand: A History of the Church of Jesus Christ of Latter-day Saints in New Zealand, 1854-1977* (Temple View, NZ: Church College of New Zealand, 1977). Marjorie Newton contributed significantly with her historically detailed revisionist "Mormonism in New Zealand: A Historical Appraisal" (Ph.D. diss., University of Sidney, 1998) and "From Tolerance to 'House Cleaning:' LDS Leadership Response to Maori Marriage Customs, 1890-1990," *Journal of Mormon History* 22 (Fall 1996): 72-91. Henry A. Smith, *Matthew Cowley, Man of Faith* (Salt Lake City: Bookcraft, 1954), recounts the contributions of a well-loved and influential apostle in the Pacific during and just after World War II. The multiethnic character of Auckland, New Zealand, occasioned by a large influx of diverse peoples from all over the South Pacific during the last half-century is described in Ruby Welch, "Ethnicity Amongst Auckland Mormons" (M.A. thesis, University of Auckland, 1989); while other scholarly contributions are Eric G. Schwimmer, "Mormonism in a Maori Village: A Study in Social Change" (M.A. thesis, University of British Columbia, 1965); Ian G. Barber, "Between Biculturalism and Assimilation: The Changing Place of Maori Culture in the Twentieth Century New Zealand Mormon Church," *New Zealand Journal of History* 29 (October 1995): 142-69; and Grant Underwood, "Mormonism, the Maori, and Cultural Authenticity," *Journal of Pacific History* 35 (September 2000): 133-46.

Much remains to be done in pursuing such topics as adapting missionary techniques and Church programs to meet local needs, biographies of leaders, a comparison of the Mormon experience with that of other Christian movements, the impact of World War II, the significance of the labor missionary program, and the doctrine of gathering in "island zions" instead of gathering to the United States. Auguring well for this future is that the historians of the Pacific and Australasia include not only North American but local scholars, providing an essential perspective to the historiography of the region.

The British Isles

In a majority of countries around the world, the period of most rapid growth in Church membership has been the time since World War II. For the British Isles and western Europe, however, the period of greatest growth began in the 1830s in Britain and in the 1850s in western Europe. The story of the LDS Church in these two areas since 1945 is simply a continuation of the historical process which began much earlier.

While several general studies of the Church in the British Isles since 1837 are available, very few such studies cover the period since 1945. The only book-length study was written by Elder Derek A. Cuthbert of the Seventy, *The Second Century: Latter-day Saints in Great Britain, Volume I, 1937-1987* Cambridge, UK: Cambridge University Press, 1987), is well-written and gives excellent personal insights into the Church in this era. Two chapters in V. Ben Bloxham, James R. Moss, and Larry C. Porter, *Truth Will Prevail: The Rise of the Church of Jesus Christ of Latter-day Saints, 1837-1987* Cambridge, UK: Church of Jesus Christ of Latter-day Saints, 1987), also contain general studies of the period since 1945: James R. Moss, "The Great Awakening," 394-423; and Anne S. Perry, "The Contemporary Church," 424-41. Perry's essay describes changes in the 1970s and 1980s. It was written with enthusiasm but is not overdone.

Only a few scholarly articles have been written on the post-World War II period, several of them the publications of a BYU symposium celebrating British Church's sesquicentennial. Derek A. Cuthbert, "Church Growth in the British Isles, 1937-1987," *BYU Studies* 27 (Spring 1987): 13-26, essentially summarizes his book. Also in the same issue of

Pioneers
in Every Land

Edited by
Bruce A. Van Orden,
D. Brent Smith, and
Everett Smith, Jr.

BOOKCRAFT
Salt Lake City, Utah

Excavating Mormon Pasts

BYU Studies are two other articles. Madison H. Thomas, "The Influence of Traditional British Social Patterns on LDS Growth in Southwest Britain," 107-17, analyzes the conflict between American missionaries and native members in England. This physician-mission president claims that the conflict resulted from vestiges of feudalism and colonialism. To resolve this conflict, he encouraged sharing leadership with local members. "The Making of British Saints in Historical Perspective," 119-35, is a sophisticated sociological analysis by Tim B. Heaton, Stan L. Albrecht, and J. Randall Johnson. They conclude that growth occurred in Britain because of greater financial resources, changes in the missionary lessons, and secularization.

Two articles in *Sunstone* deal with the rapid increase in numbers of young converts attracted to the Church through the missionaries' baseball programs of the 1950s and 1960s: D. Michael Quinn, "I-Thou-vs.-I-It Conversions: The Mormon Baseball Era," 16 (December 1993): 30-44; and Richard Mavin "The Woodbury Years: An Insider's Look at Baseball Baptisms in Britain," 19 (March 1996): 56-60.

An example of the dearth of studies on recent history is Donald Q. Cannon, ed., *Regional Studies in Latter-day Saint History: British Isles* (Provo, UT: BYU Department of Church History and Doctrine, 1990). Of its ten articles, only one is on the period since 1945. Richard O. Cowan, "The Church Comes of Age in Britain," 193-214, is a solid analysis of recent trends in the British Isles, including the genesis of the London Temple area conferences, and the creation of stakes. Claudia W. Harris, "Mormons on the Warfront: The Protestant Mormons and Catholic Mormons of Northern Ireland," *BYU Studies* 30 (Fall 1990): 7-19, is a thoughtful analysis of how the Church has helped bridge the gap between opposite sides in this bitterly divided country.

Ensign articles on the British Isles since 1945 include Muriel Cuthbert, "The Saints Around the World: Strong Saints in Scotland," October 1978, 34-38; Derek A. Cuthbert, "Breakthrough in Britain: The 1950s, '60s, and '70s Brought Great Growth and Stability to the Church," July 1987, 28-32; Orson Scott Card, "The Mormons in Ireland," February 1978, 45-48; and Don L. Searle, "The Church in the United Kingdom and Ireland," June 1978, 40-44.

Theses and dissertations follow the familiar pattern, with most being devoted to the nineteenth century. Brent Barlow, "History of the Church in Ireland since 1840" (M.A. thesis, Brigham Young University, 1968) includes a solid study of the Church in modern-day Ireland.

Western Europe

Some reviewers have faulted Bruce A. Van Orden, *Building Zion: The Latter-day Saints in Europe* (Salt Lake City: Deseret Book, 1996) for its dependence on secondary sources that were not always correctly noted; nevertheless, it remains the only book on this topic and, furthermore, is a highly useful research tool. A briefer treatment of the subject by Van Orden is "Europe: From First to Last, But Still 'Mighty' Important," *Mormon Heritage Magazine,* March/April, 23-27, and May/June 1995, 16-19. Douglas F. Tobler, contributed a general essay, "The Church in Europe," *Encyclopedia of Mormonism,* 4 vols. (New York: Macmillan Publishing, 1992), 2:467-75, that contains useful information on recent events.

Books on the Church in the late twentieth century are extremely scarce. In fact, only four have been published, two on Germany and two on Finland. Gilbert W. Scharffs, *Mormonism in Germany: A History of the Church of Jesus Christ of Latter-day Saints in Germany Between 1840 and 1970* (Salt Lake City: Deseret Book, 1970), grew out of his Brigham Young University dissertation on the same subject. It contains a useful amount of material on the twentieth century. Wolfgang Zander and Ulrich Ruckauer, *Die Mormonen im Suedwesten Deutschland: Auf den Spuren Ihres Lebens und Ihrer Geschichte* [*The Mormons in Southwest Germany: As Seen in the Marks of Their Lives and History*] (Stuttgart, Germany: Pfahl Stuttgart, 1986) is one of the few works by European members. Alvin S. Anderson, Udell E. Poulsen, and Philemon B. Robinson Jr., *Sumoi Calls* (Salt Lake City: Finnish Mission Society, 1957), is an early work on the Church in Finland. (No author or editor), *Muistamme, 1947-1997* (Salt Lake City: Artistic Printing for Henry A. Mathis Family Society, 1997), contains the memoirs of mission presidents and others who served in the Finnish Mission, published to commemorate the first fifty years of its existence.

Tullis, ed., *Mormonism: A Faith for All Cultures* (1978) contains some useful chapters on modern Europe: Douglas F. Tobler, "Challenges of the Second Century," 37-43; Charles A. Didier, "The Church in French-Speaking Europe," 44-47; F. Enzio Busche, "The Church in Germany, Austria, and Switzerland," 48-50; Bo G. Wennerlund, "The Church in Scandinavia and Finland," 51-56; and Dan Jorgensen, "The Church in Italy," 64-65. All of these chapters contain solid information but are very brief. Two chapters in Van Orden, Smith, and Smith, eds., *Pioneers in Every Land: Inspirational Stories of International Pioneers Past and Present* are useful and inspirational studies: Hermann Moessner, "Mormon Pioneers in Southern Germany," 74-93; and Wolfgang Zander, "In God's Hands in Divided Germany," 148-62, the latter dealing with information on both East and West Germany.

Scholarly articles on the Church in modern Western Europe are quite numerous. Michael Homer, a Utah lawyer, historian, and former missionary to Italy, has written several excellent articles on the Church in that country. His "LDS Prospects in Italy in the Twenty-first Century," *Dialogue* 29 (Spring 1996): 139-58, contains a realistic assessment of problems facing Church members living in Italy today. Wilfried Decoo has written about the Church in Belgium and France and also the conditions of Church members in Europe, in general. His article "Feeding the Fleeing Flock: Reflections on the Struggle to Retain Church Members in Europe," *Dialogue* 29 (Spring 1996): 97-118, analyzes the problem of retention. Written from the perspective of a native Belgium member, this article calls attention to such problems as isolation from the surrounding society and alienation from friends and family. In this same issue of *Dialogue,* Dutch-Mormon anthropologist Walter E. A. Van Beek, "Ethnization and Accommodation: Dutch Mormons in Twenty-first Century Europe," 119-38, calls for the Church to pay attention to real problems facing Dutch members.

Mark Grover is best known for his work on Latin America, but he has also written insightfully about refugees from Angola who joined the Church in the 1970s in "Migration, Social Change and Mormonism in Portugal," *Journal of Mormon History* 21 (Spring 1995): 65-79. Kahlile B. Mehr, "Trial of the French Mission," *Dialogue* 21 (Autumn 1988): 27-46, known for his work on the Church in Eastern Europe, explored a troubled period in 1958 when some missionaries in France began preaching false doctrine and were subsequently excommunicated. C. Brooklyn Derr published a fascinating comparison, "Messages from Two Cultures: Mormon Leaders in France, 1985," *Dialogue* 21 (Summer 1988): 98-112, showing that the Church is far from being "the same" everywhere. His study used techniques from his human resource research at the University of Utah.

The *Ensign* has published a number of articles about the Church since 1945 in Western Europe, although space precludes mentioning more than Douglas F. Tobler, "Update on Western Europe," August 1976, 30-34; Laurie J. Wilson, "The Saints in France," January 1976, 77-81; and LaRene Porter Gaunt, "A Blooming France," March 1995. The magazine's annual index or a search of the magazines on the Church's website <www.lds.org>, will lead readers to other articles on Germany, Spain, Portugal, Italy, Belgium, the Netherlands, Switzerland, Austria, and the Scandinavian countries.

Church Educational System personnel have produced a number of masters' theses on the Church in postwar Europe: Curtis B. Hunsaker, "A History of the Norwegian Mission from 1851-1960" (Brigham Young University, 1965), Marius A. Christensen, "A History of the Danish Mission . . . 1850-1964" (Brigham Young University, 1966), Gary Ray Chard, "A History of the French Mission . . . 1850-1960" (Utah State University, 1965), Keith C. Warner, "A History of the Netherlands Mission . . . 1861-1966" (Brigham Young University, 1967); Dale Z. Kirby, "History of the Church of Jesus Christ of Latter-day Saints in Switzerland" (Brigham Young University, 1971); Carl-Erik Johansson, "History of the Swedish Mission . . . 1905-1973" (Brigham Young University 1973); and Kaija H.

Excavating Mormon Pasts

Penley, "Leadership of Mormon Missionary Efforts in Finland and Its Influence on Conversion Rates in the Finnish Mission, 1947-1969" (Utah State University, 1994). These historical narratives provide useful general histories.

John C. Jarvis, "Mormonism in France: A Study of Cultural Exchange and Institutional Adaptation" (Ph.D. diss., Washington State University, 1991), discusses the creation of authentic cultural identity for the Church in France. He developed this theme further in "Mormonism in France: The Family as a Universal Value in a Globalizing Religion," in *Family, Religion, and Social Change in Diverse Societies* (New York: Oxford University Press, 2000), 237-66. He concludes that the family ideal of Mormonism transcends cultural barriers and gives French members a key to dealing with the uncertainties of the present.

Efforts are underway to fill in some of the gaps on the recent history of Church in the British Isles and western Europe. The most recent is Donald Q. Cannon and Brent L. Top, eds., *Regional Studies in Latter-day Saint History: Europe* (Provo, UT: BYU Department of Church Doctrine and History, 2003), which contains ten articles, eight of them on the twentieth century, four of them on the post-World War II period.

Latin America, General

In contrast to the Pacific and Western Europe, the Church in Latin America is the product of twentieth-century missionary work. Growth was minimal and limited until the 1960s. In 1961, Elder A. Theodore Tuttle met with President Henry D. Moyle of the First Presidency and was given an assignment, unusual for a General Authority at that time, to move with his family overseas. In his case, he was sent to Uruguay to supervise the South American missions, a daunting task since he spoke no Spanish and had limited experience in Latin America. Although General Authorities had earlier presided over the European Mission, it was an unprecedented assignment for South America and surprising because membership there constituted less than one percent of the Church total.[4] But the 1926 prediction of Apostle Melvin J. Ballard that the Church growth in Latin America would be small at first, then meteoric, was about to be fulfilled.[5] Apostles Harold B. Lee, Spencer W. Kimball, and Henry D. Moyle who visited during the 1960s, all returned to Salt Lake City convinced that the Church could experience significant growth in Latin America. According to Mark L. Grover, "The Maturing of the Oak: The Dynamics of Latter-day Saint Growth in Latin America," *International Forum Series, Winter 2003* (Provo, UT: David M. Kennedy Center for International Studies, BYU, March 19, 2003), their impressions were correct. By the end of 2001, the Church in South America numbered more than 4 million members. Of the ten nations in the world with largest number of Church members, six were in Latin America. Significantly, the Church in Latin America was 37 percent of the entire Church population, with the potential of comprising half of the Church membership within twenty years, given the same growth rate manifest through 2001.

Yet to be written is a general book-length summary history on the Church in Latin America. F. LaMond Tullis planned a volume on this topic as part of a multi-volume series to commemorate the Church's 1980 sesquicentennial; the series was canceled and the book was never finished. Nevertheless, Tullis was the most eloquent scholar to seriously focus the attention of the academic community on the Church in Latin America. Most of his early articles were written for the U.S. membership, attempting to underscore problems of perception they and Church leaders had of Latin America. Most important of several articles were, "The Church Moves Outside the United States: Some Observations from Latin America," *Dialogue* 8 (Spring 1980): 63-73; and "Church Development Issues Among Latin Americans," in *Mormonism: A Faith for All Cultures,* 85-105. His works on specific countries

---

4. Lowell C. "Ben" Bennion and Lawrence A. Young, "The Uncertain Dynamics of LDS Expansion, 1950-2020," *Dialogue* 29 (Summer 1996): 18.

5. Bryant S. Hinckley, *Sermons and Missionary Service of Melvin Joseph Ballard* (Salt Lake City: Deseret Book, 1949), 100.

will be noted later. Because of his research, influence, and mentoring, Tullis's influence on the study of Latin America is important and long lasting.

An article-length general summary of the evolution about the Church through the 1970s is Gordon Irving, "Mormonism in Latin America: A Preliminary Historical Survey," *Task Papers in LDS History, No. 10* (Salt Lake City: History Division, Historical Department, Church of Jesus Christ of Latter-day Saints, 1976). Several articles focus on Latin American Mormonism, even though they are not completely historical. They include Wesley W. Craig Jr., "The Church in Latin America: Progress and Challenge," *Dialogue* 5 (Autumn 1970): 66-74; David C. Knowlton, "Thoughts on Mormonism in Latin America," *Dialogue* 25 (Summer 1992): 41-53; and his "Mormonism in Latin America: Towards the Twenty-first Century," *Dialogue* 29 (Spring 1996): 159-76. An anthropologist, he has a keen understanding of how culture and politics interact throughout Latin America, especially in the Andean countries. Like Tullis, he has helped focus attention of the academic community and the Church on concerns over cultural insensitivity, growth versus retention, leadership development, and the limited recognition of Latin American contributions to the Church. In a presentation designed for general readership, Mark L. Grover, examines the Church's Latin American growth and its potential impact in "Miracle of the Rose and the Oak in Latin America," in *Out of Obscurity: The LDS Church in the Twentieth Century*, 138-50. Other specific articles will be noted later.

Mexico and Central America

By far the most developed historiography of the Church in Latin America is that of the Mormon colonies in northern Mexico, even though they are more closely connected to the western United States than to Latin America. This essay will not describe works focused on pre-World War II history. Nelle Spilsbury Hatch, *Colonia Juárez: An Intimate Account of a Mormon Village* (Salt Lake City: Deseret Book, 1954); Hannah S. Call, *The History of Colonia Dublán* (Mexico: n.pub., 1985); Evelyn K. Jones, *Henry Lunt: Biography and History of the Development of Southern Utah and Settling of Colonia Pacheco, Mexico* (Cedar City, UT: E. K. Jones, 1996); and Annie R. Johnson, *Heartbeats of Colonia Diaz* (Salt Lake City: Publishers Press, 1972) present the history of the individual colonies. Hatch, the most prominent of these local historians, published extensively on the colonies. Her most significant work is a large collection about the early colonists, organized by B. Carmon Hardy and published posthumously as *Stalwarts South of the Border* (N.p., CA: E. Hatch, 1985).

The history of the Church among native Mexicans has received more attention than other countries of Latin America. Tullis, *Mormons in Mexico: The Dynamics of Faith and Culture* (Logan: Utah State University Press, 1987), is not only important to Church history in Mexico but is the most significant study on the Church in Latin America. The book combines a detailed historical treatment of early missions and Church history through the 1950s with a second part analyzing the challenges of growth, leadership, and culture differences facing the Church in Mexico. Tullis's book is supplemented by Agrícol Lozano Herrera, *Historia del Mormonismo en México* [*History of Mormonism in Mexico*] (Mexico D.F.: Editorial Zarahemla, 1983). The author was a prominent member and part-time lawyer for the Church. Additional publications on post World War II Church history in Mexico are: David L. Clawson, "Religion and Change in a Mexican Village" (Ph.D. diss., University of Florida, 1976); Clark V. Johnson, "Mormon Education in Mexico: The Rise of the 'Sociedad Educativa y Cultural'" (Ph.d. diss., Brigham Young University, 1977); Byron J. McNeil, "The History of the Church of Jesus Christ of Latter-day Saints in Mexico" (M.A. thesis, San Jose State University, 1990)—he concludes that leadership development is the most inhibiting factor on Church growth in Mexico; and Thomas W. Murphy, "Other Mormon Histories: Lamanite Subjectivity in Mexico," *Journal of Mormon History* 26 (Fall 2000): 179-214.

The Church entered Central America much later than Mexico—beginning with Guatemala in 1947. An early status report on Church progress in that region is Terrence L. Hansen, "The Church in Central America," *Ensign*, September 1972, 40-42. Marvin K.

MORMONS IN MEXICO

The Dynamics of Faith and Culture

F. LaMond Tullis

UTAH STATE UNIVERSITY PRESS
1987

Gardner, "Taking the Gospel to their Own People," *Ensign,* October 1988, 12-16, describes local missionaries. Henri Gooren, "De Expanderende Mormoonse Kerk in Latijns Amerika: Schetsen Uit Een Wijk in San José, Costa Rica," ["The Expansion of the Mormon Church in Latin America: Sketch of a District in San José, Costa Rica"] (M.A. thesis, University of Utrecht, 1991), is an interesting work in Dutch which can, hopefully, be translated into English and Spanish. Gooren, *Rich Among the Poor: Church, Firm, and Household Among Small-Scale Entrepreneurs in Guatemala* (Amsterdam: Thelathesis, 1999), expands his work on Mormonism into Guatemala. His "Analyzing LDS Growth in Guatemala: Report from a Barrio," *Dialogue* 33 (Summer 2000), 97-117, focuses on one ward in Guatemala City.

The expansion of the Church into Guatemala in 1947 was primarily due to the influence of John Forres O'Donnal, an American working for the U.S. government. His autobiography, *Pioneer in Guatemala* (Yorba Linda, CA: Shumway Family History Services, 1997), describes the Church's introduction and evolution in Guatemala from the perspective of an American who spent most of his life there. His story is told briefly in Keith J. Wilson, "A Nation in a Day: The Church in Guatemala," in *Out of Obscurity: The LDS Church in the Twentieth Century,* 363-78. Also of interest for Guatemala are the two articles by anthropologist Thomas W. Murphy, examining cultural conflict and development in "Guatemalan Hot/Cold Medicine and Mormon Words of Wisdom: Intercultural Negotiation of Meaning," *Journal for the Scientific Study of Religion* 36 (June 1997): 297-308; and "Reinventing Mormonism: Guatemala as Harbinger of the Future?" *Dialogue* 29 (Spring 1996): 177-92.

South America

After Mexico, the second Latin American area to receive Mormon missionaries was Argentina in 1925. A work covering the early post-World War II period is Joel Alva Flake, "The History of the Church of Jesus Christ of Latter-Saints in South America: 1945-1960" (M.A. thesis, Brigham Young University, 1975). The most significant study of the foundation of the Church in Argentina and South America is that of Frederick S. Williams and Frederick G. Williams, *From Acorn to Oak Tree: A Personal History of the Establishment and First Quarter Development of the South American Missions* (Fullerton, CA: Etcetera, 1987). The book is an extensive memoir of Frederick S. Williams's mission in Argentina, his later service as mission president in both Argentina (1938-42) and Uruguay (1947-51), and his professional experience in other parts of Latin America. Consequently, it provides a detailed description of Church beginnings in much of South America. Michael B. Smurthwaite has studied "Socio-Political Factors Affecting the Growth of the Mormon Church in Argentina since 1925" (M.A. thesis, Brigham Young University, 1970).

Other important publications on Argentina are those of Nestor Curbelo, head of the Buenos Aires LDS Institute and local amateur historian, documentary maker, and photographer. *Historia de los Mormones en Argentina: Relatos de Pioneros [History of the Mormons in Argentina: Accounts of Pioneers]* (Buenos Aires: Author, 2000) includes a brief and somewhat spotty history of major events, told by pioneer members, but reinforced by a detailed chronology. Curbelo has produced similar volumes on Uruguay and Paraguay: *Historia de los Santos de los Últimos Días en Uruguay: Relatos de Pioneros [History of the Latter-day Saints in Uruguay: Accounts of Pioneers]* (Buenos Aires: Author, 2001) and *Historia de los Santos de los Últimos Días en Paraguay: Relatos de Pioneros [History of the Latter-day Saints in Paraguay: Accounts of Pioneers]* (Buenos Aires: Author, 2003). English translations of these titles are forthcoming from Greg Kofford Books. Over the past twenty years, Curbelo, a dedicated amateur historian, has amassed in Buenos Aires a significant archive of documents, photographs, and oral histories.

In 1928, missionaries from Argentina established the Church in the German colonies of southern Brazil. Mark L. Grover has produced most of the published research on Brazil. "Mormonism in Brazil: Religion and Dependency in Latin America" (Ph.D. diss, Indiana University, 1985), covers through the 1970s. His "Religious Accommodation in the

Land of Racial Democracy: Mormon Priesthood and Black Brazilians," *Dialogue* 17 (Autumn 1984): 23-24, and "The Mormon Priesthood Revelation and the São Paulo, Brazil Temple," *Dialogue* 23 (Spring 1990): 39-53, deal with racial issues. His "Milton and Irene Soares: Mormon Pioneers of Northeastern Brazil," in *Pioneers in Every Land,* 88-112, is a biographical sketch of the first members in that region. An anthropological look at racial issues in northeast Brazil from a Marxist perspective is Nádia Fernanda Maia de Amorim, *Os Mormons em Alagoas: Religião e Relações Raciais [The Mormons in Alagoas: Religion and Racial Relations]* (São Paulo: FFLCH/USP, 1986). An interesting commentary on the need for missionaries to be sensitive to southern Brazil's culture is G. Benson Whittle, "From the Mission Field—Brazil," *Dialogue* 1 (Winter 1966): 135-140; Marcus Helvécio Martins, "The Oak Tree Revisited: Brazilian LDS Leaders' Insights on the Growth of the Church in Brazil" (Ph.D. diss., Brigham Young University, 1996), analyzes the effect of Church growth on leadership development.

The first major study of the Church in Chile is A. Delbert Palmer, "Establishing the L.D.S. Church in Chile" (M.A. thesis, Brigham Young University, 1979). Palmer was president of the country's first mission in 1961, so the thesis is part memoir but also includes significant historical research. Rodolfo Acevedo A. wrote a master's thesis, published as *Los Mormones en Chile [The Mormons in Chile]* (Santiago, Chile: Impresos y Publicaciones Cumora, 1990). It provides a chronological history, then focuses on the development in specific regions. Although the analysis is limited, it is an adequate beginning. An important analysis of the phenomenal Church growth in Chile is David C. Knowlton, "Mormonism in Chile," in *Mormon Identities in Transition,* 68-79.

The only other country in Latin America to receive significant study is Bolivia, again from David Knowlton: "Conversion to Protestantism and Social Change in a Bolivian Aymara Community" (M.A. thesis, University of Texas, 1982), and "Searching Minds and Questioning Hearts: Protestantism and Social Context in Bolivia" (Ph.D. diss., University of Texas, 1988). Both works examine the evolution of the Church in the context of Bolivia's culture and social change. Also significant is his "Missionary, Native, and General Authority Accounts of a Bolivian Conversion: The Creation of Sacred Mormon Myth," *Sunstone* 13 (January 1989): 14-20, exploring variants of a faith-promoting story about the wholesale conversion of the village of Huacuyo. He has also explored "'Gringo Jeringo': Anglo Mormon Missionary Culture in Bolivia," in *Contemporary Mormonism: Social Science Perspectives,* 218-36. Knowlton's contribution to understanding the Church, not only in Bolivian but also in Latin American culture, is important. Carlos Pedraja, an early member and director of the Institutes in Cochabamba, Bolivia, has written *Historia de la Iglesia en Bolivia [History of the Church in Bolivia]* (Bochabamba, Bolivia: Sistema Educativo de la Iglesia de Jususcristo de los Santos de los Ultimas Dias, 2001), written for Institute of Religion classes.

It parallels (no author), *Historia de la Iglesia en Colombia: Suplemento para el Curso de Historia de la Iglesia [History of the Church in Colombia: Supplement for a History Course of the Church]* (Bogata: Sistema Educativo . . . , 1986) and *Un Bosquejo de la Historia de la Iglesia en Venezuela [An Account of the History of the Church in Venezuela]* (Caracas: Sistema Educativo . . ., 1986).

The *Improvement Era,* May 1963, focused on Latin America's then-five missions: Argentine, Andes (Bolivia, Peru, and Ecuador), Chilean, Uruguaian, and Brazilian. Some *Ensign* articles contain historical material: Marvin K. Gardner, "Pioneers in Paraguay," March 1994, 39-45; Allen Litster, "Pioneering in the Andes," January 1997, 16-22; and Don L. Searle, "Tudo Bem in Brazil," March 1997, 40-49. Space limitations preclude citing the numerous historical sketches and historic biographies in Church publications, but they should not be overlooked.

Constructing an understanding and history of the Church in Latin America is a complicated and challenging task, but a start seems to have been made through the combined attention of professionally trained academic specialists and local faith-promoting amateur historians. As the Church grows and local members receive academic training, more locally produced histories will appear. Understanding the Church in Latin America is an interesting, exciting, and important facet to the evolution of the Church in general.

Asia: General Works

The next continent after Latin America to see dramatic Church growth in the twentieth century was Asia, where congregations began to burgeon in the 1960s. Though Church history on that continent reaches back to the early 1850s, when President Brigham Young called missionaries to proselyte in India, Burma (Myanmar), Siam (Thailand), and China; Church activity faltered and these missions closed within a decade. Today, these areas are normally divided into East Asia (China, Hong Kong, Japan, Korea, Mongolia, and Taiwan), Southeast Asia (Burma, Cambodia, Indonesia, Laos, Malaysia, the Philippines, Singapore, Thailand, and Vietnam), and South Asia (Bangladesh, Bhutan, India, the Maldives, Nepal, Pakistan, and Sri Lanka).

In addition to his well-respected writings on Church history in Hawaii and the Pacific, R. Lanier Britsch has also written about Asia. While much of his history pertains to the nineteenth century, he brought in the twentieth century with the publication of *From the East: The History of the Latter-day Saints in Asia, 1851-1996* (Salt Lake City: Deseret Book, 1998), the most comprehensive and important volume on the Church in Asia. Among his most significant articles for the post World War II period is "From Bhutan to Wangts'ang: Taking the Gospel to Asia," *Ensign*, June 1980, 7-10, with Richard C. Holloman Jr., a discussion of the Church's missionary challenges in Asia.

Spencer J. Palmer, one of Britsch's mentors, also contributed to the historiography of the Church in Asia, particularly Korea, where he served as a military chaplain, as president of the Korean Mission, and as president of the Korean Temple. After receiving his doctorate in history, emphasizing Korean studies and world religions, from the University of California at Berkeley, Palmer published *The Church Encounters Asia* (Salt Lake City: Deseret Book, 1970), *The Expanding Church,* containing a section on Asia, 135-210; and *Brigham Young University and the People's Republic of China: The First Five Years* (Provo, UT: David M. Kennedy Center for International Studies, BYU, 1984). His other contributions for specific regions will be noted later.

A number of other Church leaders and scholars have explored the opportunities and challenges of the Asian mission field. *Improvement Era* articles written by Church leaders covering the last five decades of the Mormon experience in Asia include Harold B. Lee, "Report on the Orient," December 1954, 926-30; Gordon B. Hinckley, "The Church in the Far East," June 1962, 440-43, and his "The Church in the Orient," March 1964, 166-92. The March 1970 issue of the *Improvement Era* is devoted to Asia. Individual articles will be noted later. Don Hicken, "The Church in Asia," *Dialogue* 3 (Spring 1968): 134-42, suggests how to improve the Church image in Asia. R. Lanier Britsch, Paul S. Rose, H. Grant Heaton, Adney Y. Komatsu, and Spencer J. Palmer contributed to "A Symposium of Former Mission Presidents" in "Problems and Opportunities of Missionary Work in Asia," *BYU Studies* 7 (Autumn 1971): 85-106. Paul V. Hyer, "Revolution and Mormonism in Asia: What the Church Might Offer a Changing Society," *Dialogue* 7 (Spring 1972): 88-93, offers his insights as former president of the Taiwan Mission. Sheri L. Dew, *Go Forward with Faith: The Biography of Gordon B. Hinckley* (Salt Lake City: Deseret Book, 1996), refers throughout the book to President Hinckley's long-term association with the Asian people.

East Asia

In 1901, the First Presidency appointed Elder Heber J. Grant to initiate missionary work in Japan, the first East Asian nation to be dedicated for preaching the gospel in the twentieth century. The mission closed in 1924, due to limited success. American LDS servicemen reestablished the Church in postwar Japan. Sources on this renewal include Hilton A. Robertson, *Conference Report,* April 1947, 53-56; Terry G. Nelson, "A History of The Church of Jesus Christ of Latter-day Saints in Japan from 1948 to 1980" (M.A. thesis, Brigham Young University, 1986); Shinji Takagi, "The Eagle and the Scattered Flock:

Church Beginnings in Occupied Japan, 1945-48," *Journal of Mormon History* 28 (Fall 2002): 104-39, and his "Riding on the Eagle's Wings: The Japanese Mission under American Occupation, 1948-52," ibid., 29 (Spring 2003): 200-32.

The LDS pavilion at Expo '70, Osaka, Japan, marked a new era of Church visibility and respect in Japan as described in Bernard P. Brockbank, "The Mormon Pavilion at Expo '70," *Improvement Era,* December 1970, 120-22; and Gerald Joseph Peterson, "History of Mormon Exhibits in World Expositions" (M.A. thesis, Brigham Young University, 1974). The first Asian temple was built in Tokyo, an event commemorated in several articles in the October 1980 *Tambuli.*

Several observers have written about Church development in Japan beginning with Hugh B. Brown, "Prophecies Regarding Japan," *BYU Studies* 10 (Winter 1970): 159-60. Seiji Katanuma, "The Church in Japan," *BYU Studies* 14 (Autumn 1973): 16-28, is a fine historical overview. Two theses are Richard E. Durfee, "Modernity and Conversion: Mormonism in Twentieth Century Japan" (M.A. thesis, Arizona State University, 1988); and Tomoko Aizawa, "The LDS Church as a New Religious Movement in Japan" (M.A. thesis, Brigham Young University, 1995). Jiro Numano, a Japanese professor of English and editor of *Mormon Forum,* an independent journal for Japanese Church members, debated the success of the Church among the Japanese in "How International Is the Church in Japan?" *Dialogue* 8 (Spring 1980): 85-92, and in his "Mormonism in Modern Japan," *Dialogue* 29 (Spring 1996): 223-35.

The *Improvement Era* carried an article on Japan by Eleanor Knowles, "The History of the Chuch in Japan," March 1970, 23-26. Historically important *Ensign* articles concerning Japan include Kan Watanabe et al., "Japan: Land of the Rising Sun," August 1975, 36-43; R. Lanier Britsch, "The Blossoming of the Church in Japan," October 1992, 32-39; and Don L. Searle, "Japan: Growing Light in the East," September 2000, 44-50.

In August 1955, Elder Joseph Fielding Smith dedicated Korea for the preaching of the gospel. Its history is explored in Dong S. Choi, "Marks of Success in American Mission Policies in Korea" (M.A. thesis, Brigham Young University, 1984); his "A History of the Church of Jesus Christ of Latter-day Saints in Korea, 1950-1985" (Ph.D. diss., Brigham Young University, 1990); Rhee Ho Nam (first stake president in Korea and president of the Korea Pusan Mission), "Korea: Land of Morning Calm," *Ensign,* August 1975, 44-46; his "The Church in Korea," in *Mormonism: A Faith for All Cultures,* 163-69; his "The Korean War and the Gospel," in *Out of Obscurity: The LDS Church in the Twentieth Century,* 286-96; Spencer J. Palmer, "Rhee Honam: Hallmarks of a Korean Pioneer," in *Pioneers in Every Land,* 57-73; his "Pioneering in South Korea," October 1997, 26-31; and with his wife, Shirley, *The Korean Saints: Personal Stories of Trial and Triumph, 1950-1980* (Provo, UT: Religious Education, BYU, 1995); In Sang Han, "Encounter: The Korean Mind and the Gospel," *Ensign,* August 1975, 47-50; and Kellene Ricks, "Korea: Land of the Morning Calm," *Ensign,* July 1992, 32-37.

Elder Matthew Cowley dedicated Hong Kong for missionary work in 1949, and Elder Mark E. Petersen dedicated Taiwan in 1959. Scholarly studies include Gary G. Y. Chu, "A Q-Sort Comparison between Cultural Expectations of Chinese and Cultural Perceptions of Returned Latter-day Saint Missionaries from the United States Who had Been Assigned to Chinese Missions" (M.A. thesis, Brigham Young University, 1974); Candace Sheila Gutzman Hsiao, "Factors Influencing the Use of Health Services for Four Wards in the Taipei Taiwan Relief Society of the Church of Jesus Christ of Latter-day Saints" (M.S. thesis, Brigham Young University, 1977); Bruce J. M. Dean, "Chinese Christianity Since 1849: Implications for the Church of Jesus Christ of Latter-day Saints" (M.A. thesis, Brigham Young University, 1981); and Feng Xi, "A History of Mormon-Chinese Relations: 1849-1993" (Ph.D. diss., Brigham Young University, 1994).

Robert J. Morris, a former missionary in Asia and a member of BYU's Asian Studies Department, describes challenges facing missionaries in Asia, especially in Taiwan, in "Middle Buddha," *Dialogue* 4 (Spring 1969): 41-50, and "Some Problems in Translating Mormon Thought into Chinese," *BYU Studies* 10 (Winter 1970): 173-85. Bill Heaton, then a Senior Research Fellow at the National Defense University, wrote "Mormonism and Maoism: The Church and People's China," *Dialogue* 13 (Spring 1980): 40-52. Also of interest is Caroline Pluss, "Chinese Participation in the Church of Jesus Christ of Latter-day Saints (Mormon) in Hong Kong," *Journal of Contemporary Religion* 14 (January 1999): 63-76; and Richard B. Stamps, "The Cultural Impact of Mormon Missionaries on Taiwan," *BYU Studies* 41 (2002): 103-14. Most noteworthy of the *Ensign* articles on the Church in Hong Kong and Taiwan include William Heaton, "China and the Restored Church," August 1972, 14-18; Jay A. Parry, "Hong Kong: Pearl of the Orient," August 1975, 51-54; and in the same issue, Janice Clark, "Taiwan: Steep Peaks and Towering Faith," 55-57; (no author), "A Dream Come True in Hong Kong," June 1996, 44-51; and Christopher K. Bigelow, "Taiwan: Four Decades of Faith," September 1998, 38-46.

Mongolia was officially opened as a mission field in 1993. Kenneth H. Beesley discusses Church educational assistance in "The LDS Church and Higher Education in Mongolia," in the proceedings of the Fifth Annual Conference of the International Society: *"I Was An Hungered and Ye Gave Me Meat": Development and Relief Efforts of the LDS Church in a Troubled World* (Provo, UT: David M. Kennedy Center for International Studies, BYU, 1995), 32-34. Charlotte D. Lofgreen, "Mongolia: The Morning Breaks," *Cameo: Latter-day Women in Profile* 2 (February 1994): 26. Mary Nielsen Cook, "A Mighty Change in Mongolia," *Liahona,* February 1997, 10-14, profile Latter-day pioneers in Mongolia, while Steven C. Harper, summarizes the Mongolian experience in "'Nothing More Miraculous:' The First Decade of Mormonism in Mongolia," *BYU Studies* 42, no. 1 (2003): 19-49.

Southeast and South Asia

Successful missionary work began in Southeast Asia after World War II—the Philippines were the first to be dedicated for missionary work—and in most cases, after the Vietnam War. Lowell E. Call, "Latter-day Saint Servicemen in the Philippine Islands: A Historical Study of Their Religious Activities and Influences Resulting in the Official Organization of the Church of Jesus Christ of Latter-day Saints in the Philippines" (M.A. thesis, Brigham Young University, 1955), followed by Joseph P. Gray, "Ecclesiastical Conversion as a Social Process: A Case Study from the Philippines" (Ph.d. diss., University of Colorado, 1976). *Ensign* articles with a significant historical component are (no author), "Philippines: The Land of Joyous Service," August 1975, 58-65; and Augusto A. Lim, "Missionary Work in the Philippines," November 1992, 82-83.

Elder Gordon B. Hinckley dedicated Vietnam for missionary work during the war in 1966. Relevant articles include Desmond L. Anderson (special assistant to the president of the Southeast Asia Mission), "Meeting the Challenges of the Latter-day Saints in Vietnam," *BYU Studies* 10 (Winter 1970): 186-96; William R. Heaton Jr., "Vietnam and the Restored Church," *Ensign,* June 1973, 34-39; David L. Hughes, "The Saints in Saigon: An End, a Beginning," *This People,* April 1985, 46-63; and (no author), "Giving New Meaning to Military 'Service,'" *Ensign,* June 1992, 62-63, which describes efforts of the Veterans Association for Service Activities Abroad to help member families trapped by the fall of Saigon.

Elder Hinckley dedicated Thailand two years after Vietnam. Historical sources include Manoth Suksabjarern, "Roman Catholic, Protestant and Latter-day Saint Missions in Thailand: An Historical Survey" (M.A. thesis, Brigham Young University, 1977); Craig G. Christensen, "The Beginnings of the Church in Thailand," *Improvement Era,* March 1970, 32-34; and Joan Porter Ford and LaRene Porter Gaunt, "The Gospel Dawning in Thailand," *Ensign,* September 1995, 48-55; while David Mitchell published a series of Thai conversion stories in *Tambuli,* 1992-94: Wisit Kharakham, May 1992, 32-35; Poinchair Juntrratip, February 1993, 43-48; and Ruchirawan Phonphongrat, June 1994, 10-17.

In April 1969, Elder Ezra Taft Benson dedicated Singapore and Indonesia. Two fine sources are J. Talmage Jones, *In Singapore and Other Asian Cities* (Salt Lake City: Printers Press, 1984); and Beng L. Pang, *A History of the Church of Jesus Christ of Latter-day Saints in Singapore: Journey to Stakehood, 1964-1997* (Singapore: Singapore Stake, Church of Jesus

Excavating Mormon Pasts

Christ of Latter-day Saints, 1997). G. Carlos Smith, former president of the Southeast Asia Mission, described the Church's status in Singapore, Thailand, Vietnam, and Indonesia in "The Saints in Southeast Asia," *Ensign,* September 1973, 16-26. Richard Tice emphasized the diversity and harmony of "Singapore Saints," *Ensign,* April 1990, 24-29.

Indonesian sources include an account of the Book of Mormon's translation into Bahasa Indonesian in "The Saints in Indonesia," *Ensign,* January 1977; 86-90; and Garth N. Jones, "Spreading the Gospel in Indonesia: Organizational Obstacles and Opportunities," *Dialogue* 15 (Winter 1982): 79-91.

Cambodia is the most recent Southeast Asian nation to be dedicated for missionary work—by President Hinckley in May 1996. Leland D. White and his wife Joyce B. White relate their experiences presiding over the newly formed Cambodia Phnom Penh Mission in "The Gospel Takes Hold in Cambodia," *Liahona,* October 1997, 40-46.

Elder Benson dedicated India, the largest nation in South Asia, in April 1969. Resources of interest concerning South Asia include Roger R. Keller, "India: A Synopsis of Cultural Challenges," in *Mormon Identities in Transition,* 87-90; Alma Heaton and Marie Heaton, missionaries, *Behind the Taj Mahal: Spiritual Adventures in India* (Provo, UT: A. & M. Heaton, 1992); Michael R. Morris, "India: A Season of Sowing," *Ensign,* July 1995, 40-48; G. F. Hilton, "A Mini-Mission to India: A Year Teaching Eye Surgery," *Journal of Collegium Aesculapium,* Winter 1998, 14-17. The *Tambuli* editors interviewed Elder Monte J. Brough of the Seventy, Asia Area President, and his counselors, Elders John K. Carmack and Tai Kwok Yuen of the Seventy, for "The Church in India, Pakistan, Bangladesh, and Sri Lanka," *Tambuli,* October 1993, 22-24.

With the passing of Spencer Palmer and the retirement of R. Lanier Britsch, the two most prolific specialists on Asia, the need is apparent for a new generation of scholars and members on both sides of the Pacific to continue their work. The history of Mormonism in South and Southeast Asia since 1945 needs the most attention. Furthermore, LDS historians need to provide better contextualization in local religious, economic, and social history.

Africa and the Middle East

Church history among white Africans began in 1853 in South Africa, but proselytizing black Africans did not begin until after the 1978 revelation extended the priesthood to all worthy males. In contrast to the 8,000 members on the continent before 1978, by 2001, there were 150,000 with 54 percent sacrament meeting attendance, second only to the Utah South Area.[6] Humbled by their social, political, and economic circumstances, Africans have a spiritual sensitivity that disposes them to listen to and believe the missionaries. While Church growth has been impressive, the Church proceeds in an orderly fashion, baptising fewer converts than would be possible to permit leadership to keep up with growth, according to James O. Mason, "The Kingdom Progresses in Africa," *Ensign,* November 1994, 30.

The historiography of the Church in Africa is surprisingly robust given how recent most of the events are. The story of these beginnings has been documented, possibly better than any other segment of the international Church, through the monumental work of E. Dale LeBaron, professor emeritus of the Brigham Young University Religion Department and former president of the South African Mission. Upon his return from that service the year after the priesthood revelation, he began a twenty-plus year project to document though 700 oral histories the story of Church beginnings in Africa. His project is documented in three oral history interviews conducted by Matthew K. Heiss, Salt Lake City, 1989, 1992, 1998, James H. Moyle Oral History Project. LeBaron, *All Are Alike Unto God: Fascinating Conversion Stories of Africa Saints* (Salt Lake City: Bookcraft, 1990), draws from this collection, as does his "Gospel Pioneers in Africa," *Ensign,* August 1990, 40-43;

---

6. E. Dale LeBaron, devotional speech, Ricks College, Idaho, April 5, 2001, Ricks College News Release.

"Revelation on the Priesthood: The Dawning of a New Day in Africa," in the proceedings of the seventeenth Sperry Symposium, *Doctrines for Exaltation,* edited by Susan Easton Black et al. (Salt Lake City: Deseret Book, 1989), 127-38; and "Official Declaration 2: Revelation on the Priesthood," in *The Heavens are Open: The 1992 Sperry Symposium on the Doctrine and Covenants and Church History,* edited by Byron R. Merrill et al. (Salt Lake City: Deseret Book, 1993), 194-207.

South Africa was the only place on the continent where missionaries served before 1978. Histories include Farrell Ray Monson, "History of the South African Mission of the Church of Jesus Christ of Latter-day Saints: 1853-1970" (M.A. thesis, Brigham Young University, 1971); Evan P. Wright (mission president, 1948-53), *A History of the South African Mission, Period 3, 1944-1970* (N.p.: Author, 1987), with earlier volumes covering 1852-1944. Though this history is primarily descriptive, it includes a wealth of information, including copies of primary source materials.

Although the priesthood ban prevented proselytizing among blacks in Africa before 1978, many who learned a little about the Church in many different ways sought additional information, sometimes establishing congregations in anticipation of a "brighter day." Spencer J. Palmer, *Mormons in West Africa: New Terrain for the Sesquicentennial* (Provo, UT: BYU Press, 1979), gives an excellent assessment of the situation in West Africa, especially Nigeria and Ghana, when President Spencer W. Kimball sent him to observe the situation there in 1979. Other accounts of pre-1978 activities are James B. Allen, "Would-Be Saints: West Africa before the 1978 Priesthood Revelation," *Journal of Mormon History* 17 (1991): 207-47; E. Dale LeBaron, "Black Africa: Prepared and Waiting for the Glorious Day," *Mormon Heritage Magazine,* March/April 1994, 18-27; and his *Glen G. Fisher: A Man to Match the Mountains* (Edmonton, Alberta: Fisher House Publishing, 1992). President McKay sent Fisher as the Church's first representative to West Africa in 1960.

Academic explorations of culture, race, and traditional Mormon missionary work are M. Neff Smart, "The Challenge of Africa," *Dialogue* 7 (Summer 1979), 54-57; Newell G. Bringhurst, "Mormonism in Black Africa: Changing Attitudes and Practices, 1830-1981," *Sunstone* 6, no. 3 (May-June 1981): 51-21; and William Lye, "From Burundi to Zaire: Taking the Gospel to Africa," *Ensign,* March 1980, 10-15; Lye, a longtime African expert, contextualized the history of Africa and discussed characteristics of Africa that would affect the Church's development.

The premier volume on the cultural, social, and economic challenges is Alexander B. Morrison, *The Dawning of a Brighter Day: The Church in Black Africa* (Salt Lake City: Deseret Book, 1990). Briefer introductions to the subject are LeBaron, "Mormonism in Black Africa," in *Mormon Identities in Transition,* 80-86; and his "The Church in Africa," in *Out of Obscurity: The LDS Church in the Twentieth Century,* 177-89.

The early missionaries to blacks in West Africa were senior couples. The experiences of Rendell and Rachel Mabey are *Brother to Brother: The Story of the Latter-day Saint Members Who Took the Gospel to Black Africa* (Salt Lake City: Bookcraft, 1984) by Rendell N. Mabey and Gordon T. Allred. Mabey updated this volume in *An African Legacy: Brother to Brother Revisited, Twenty Years of Glory* (Salt Lake City: Artistic Printing, 1998). The story of the second couple, Edwin and Janath Cannon, is Janath R. Cannon, *Together: A Love Story* (Salt Lake City: Desktop Publishing, 1999). Other accounts by missionary couples include Marjorie Wall Folsom, *Golden Harvest in Ghana: Gospel Beginnings in West Africa* (Bountiful, UT: Horizon, 1989); Hermine B. Horman, *African Dragons* (Salt Lake City: Hawkes, 1994) (about the Ivory Coast); and Ray Caldwell, *A Mission to Mozambique: Impressions of the First Senior Missionaries Serving in Maputo* (N.p.: R&S Caldwell, 2001), compiled from the correspondence to their children, 1999-2000. These memoirs are important sources for these African beginnings from the perspective of American missionaries.

"Emmanuel Abu Kissi: A Gospel Pioneer from Ghana," has been profiled by LeBaron in *Pioneers in Every Land,* 210-20; and in the Church-produced video, *Lives of Service* (1991). His autobiography, *Walking in the Sand* is forthcoming from the Joseph Fielding Smith Institute for LDS History, BYU, 2004.

Mormon Identities in Transition
Edited by Douglas J. Davies

CASSELL

A personal account is Julia Mavimbela, "I Speak from My Heart: The Story of a Black South African Woman," in *Women of Wisdom and Knowledge: Talks Selected from the BYU Women's Conferences,* edited by Marie Cornwall and Susan Howe (Salt Lake City: Deseret Book, 1990), 61-72; with a biography forthcoming, written by Laura Harper, and excerpted in "Serving Where She Stands: Julia Mavimbela in Soweto," *This People,* Winter 1998, 27-32. She is also featured in the Church video, *Lives of Service* (1991).

The young Church in East Africa is growing more slowly than in West Africa. In addition to LeBaron, "Pioneers in East Africa," *Ensign,* October 1994, 20-25, his "Pioneering in Chyulu, Kenya," *Liahona,* November 2001, 33-38, includes accounts of members in Uganda and Tanzania. Also relevant is Larry Brown, "Developing Sustainable Long-Term Relief Efforts in the Church in Africa: The Chyulu Project," in *"I Was An Hungered and Ye Gave Me Meat,"* 29-31.

Members of African area presidencies have authored important historical accounts for the *Ensign:* Alexander B. Morrison, "The Dawning of a New Day in Africa," November 1987, 25-26; James O. Mason, "The Kingdom Progresses in Africa," November 1994, 30-31; Glenn L. Pace, "A Temple for West Africa," *Ensign,* May 2000, 25-26. Numerous other *Ensign* and *Liahona* on West and South Africa have been published, among them Janet Brigham, "Nigeria and Ghana: A Miracle Precedes the Messengers," *Tambuli,* September 1980, 51-56; and Robert L. Mercer, "Pioneers in Ivory Coast, *Liahona,* March 1999, 16-24. Peggy Fletcher Stack, "LDS in Africa: Growing Membership Sees American Church with Unique Vision" *Sunstone* 21, no. 2 (June 1998): 71-74, is a reprint of her twenty-year anniversary articles from the *Salt Lake Tribune.*

Among academic analyses are Newell G. Bringhurst, "The Image of Blacks within Mormonism as Presented in the *Church News* (1978-1988)," *American Periodicals: A Journal of History, Criticism, and Bibliography* 2 (Fall 1992): 113-23. Bringhurst suggests that Church public relations used Africa and blacks as a key image to highlight the Church's international growth. He also perceives a change of racial attitudes within the Church in part because of the Church's success in Africa. Cardell K. Jacobson et al., "Black Mormon Converts in the United States and Africa: Social Characteristics and Perceived Acceptance," in *Contemporary Mormonism: Social Science Perspectives,* 326-47, uses LeBaron's data to show that African converts have significantly higher educational and social status than the general population and suggest that Mormon converts are upwardly mobile and educated.

Dennis L. Thomson, "African Religion & Mormon Doctrine: Comparisons & Commonalities," in *Religion in Africa,* edited by Thomas D. Blakely et al. (Portsmouth, NH: Neinemann, 1994), 89-99, suggests that some Mormon doctrines that differ from traditional Christianity compare favorably with traditional African religious beliefs. Murray Boren, "Worship through Music Nigerian Style," *Sunstone* 5, no. 6 (November/December 1980): 41-43, examines African musical styles and Mormon traditional music.

Located at the nexus of Europe, Africa, and Asia, the Middle East is largely untouched by the Church. Missionary activity in the Middle East was curtailed with the demise of the Near East Mission in 1950. Since then, the only Church presence in most countries is expatriate members living there on business, in the military, or as students. Proselyting missionaries served in Lebanon during the 1960s and 1970s; and senior couples serve in Dubai, Qatar, Bahrain, Jordan, Syria, Turkey, Lebanon, and Syria. Arabic-speaking branches exist in Jordan and Lebanon.

An important account about expatriates in Israel and Palestine is Steven W. Baldridge, comp., *Grafting In: A History of the Latter-day Saints in the Holy Land* (Murray, UT: Jerusalem Branch, 1989). A microfilmer for the Genealogical Society of Utah living in the Middle East during 1986-88, Baldridge compiled a history Jerusalem Branch and district records, 1969-89. Daniel C. Peterson, *Abraham Divided: An LDS Perspective on the Middle East* (Salt Lake City: Aspen Books, 1992), 343-53, describes opposition to the construction of the Jerusalem Center. A more decorous account by David B. Galbraith, D. Kelly Ogden, and Andrew C. Skinner, *Jerusalem: The Eternal City* (Salt Lake City: Deseret Book, 1996), chap. 26, quotes official statements on both sides. Ogden has also written an engaging, personal account of the Church in Israel (1972-90), Pioneering the East (Provo, UT:Brigham Young University: 2002). H. Donl Peterson wrote *All the Jews Don't Live in New York City* (Provo, UT: H. D. Peterson, 1993) for the twenty-year reunion of participants in the 1973 Brigham Young University Semester Abroad in Jerusalem when he served as program director. A comprehensive history on Mormon activities in Israel by LaMar C. Berrett is forthcoming.

Two histories record the experience of Church expatriates in Egypt: Arthur Wallace, *LDS Roots in Egypt* (Los Angeles: L. L. Company, 1981); and Edwin O. Haroldsen, *History of the Cairo Branch, Egypt, 1974-1985* (Cairo: E. Haroldsen, 1985). For most of the countries and regions in the Middle East, the only summaries of the Church presence are individual entries in the *Encyclopedia of Mormonism* and the *Encyclopedia of Latter-day Saint History,* edited by Arnold K. Garr, Donald Q. Cannon, and Richard O. Cowan (Salt Lake City: Deseret Book, 2000), many of them authored by James A. Toronto, a professor of Asian and Near Eastern languages at BYU, who is establishing himself as an authority on this region of the world.

The embryonic historiography of the Church in Africa and the Middle East, primarily the work of participants, has laid a foundation for more analytical and synthetic appraisals in the future.

Eastern Europe

Although East Germany had significant LDS congregations before World War II, that conflict and the Cold War curtailed missionary efforts in Eastern Europe until the collapse of international Communism in 1989. When the Berlin Wall was breached, persevering members in the German Federal Republic embraced a new contingent of missionaries. Rapidly, missionaries continued eastward to realms previously untouched by the gospel message. Kahlile B. Mehr, *Mormon Missionaries Enter Eastern Europe* (Provo, UT: Brigham Young University, 2002), is a comprehensive survey, country by country, of the century that preceded the evaporation of seemingly impermeable barriers almost overnight. Its strength is its participant accounts, but much relevant documentation is not yet readily available and some of the events are too close to allow for a judicious historical assessment of the period. An earlier account about missionary work in Central and Eastern Europe is a chapter in Bruce A. Van Orden, *Building Zion: The Latter-day Saints in Europe,* 267-311.

Elder Ezra Taft Benson spent a postwar year in Europe surveying the plight of Church members. His traveling companion, returned German missionary Frederick W. Babbel, wrote *On Wings of Faith* (Salt Lake City: Bookcraft, 1972), which supplements Benson, *A Labor of Love: The 1946 European Mission of Ezra Taft Benson* (Salt Lake City: Deseret Book, 1989), compiled from Benson's journals, correspondence with his wife, Flora, and unpublished reports in the Church archives.

Poland became the first Soviet satellite to grant legal status to the Church in 1977. It was a crowning success of David M. Kennedy's efforts in Eastern Europe as the First Presidency's special representative, documented in Martin B. Hickman, *David Matthew Kennedy: Banker, Statesman, Churchman* (Provo, UT: David M. Kennedy Center for International Studies, Center, BYU, 1987).

Articles in Church publications provide brief but comprehensive portrayals of events in Eastern Europe. Jay M. Todd, "An Encore of the Spirit," *Ensign,* October 1991, 32-53, recounts the Tabernacle Choir's public relations success in Europe, giving the Church some legitimacy where it was previously not known or regarded with suspicion. Elder Russell M. Nelson, "Drama on the European Stage" *Ensign,* December 1991, 7-17, records many dramatic incidents from his five-year responsibility for Eastern Europe that had not been previously publicized because of Church concern about delicate negotiations in the Soviet realm. Elder Dennis B. Neuenschwander, "Reflections on Establishing the Gospel in Eastern Europe," *Liahona,* October 1998, 38-48, summarizes his responsibility in moving young missionaries into the rapidly developing missions of Eastern Europe.

Leo A. Jardine and Judith C. N. Jardine, *Out of Obscurity, Out of Captivity, Out of Darkness: The Church and Humanitarian Services in Former Yugoslavia and the Russian Empire* (Salt

Lake City: L. & J. Jardine, 1998), recounts their experiences as humanitarian service missionaries (1995-96), including the activities of General Authorities not normally made public and statistics rarely available from official Church sources on the extent of the aid rendered.

Seven books deal with specific countries of the former Soviet bloc. In *A Cherry Tree Behind the Iron Curtain: The Autobiography of Martha Toronto Anderson* (Salt Lake City: Author, 1977), Anderson offers a compelling story of her experiences as a mission president's wife in Czechoslovakia and eyewitness to the German occupation in 1939 and the Communist takeover in 1950. Olga Kovarova Campora, *Saint Behind Enemy Lines* (Salt Lake City: Deseret Book, 1997) bookends the conclusion of the Communist epoch in Czechoslovakia with an account of her conversion as the first young person to join the Church there in three decades and her subsequent efforts to teach gospel principles indirectly. An enthralling view of Communism from the inside out, it is, so far, the lone autobiography from an Eastern Europe member. She is also the subject of Carri P. Jenkins, "After the Revolution," *BYU Today,* March 1991, 30-34. Gary Browning, *Russia and the Restored Gospel* (Salt Lake City: Deseret Book, 1997) is a combination of his journal and members' conversion accounts. It provides a wealth of information and will be an important source of primary material for histories yet to be written. In a similar vein, Garold N. and Norma S. Davis, serving with the first wave of missionaries into East Germany in 1989-90, compiled the stories of East German members, faithful throughout their forty-year isolation from the rest of the Church in *Behind the Iron Curtain: Recollections of Latter-day Saints in East Germany, 1945-1989* (Provo, UT: BYU Studies, 1995). They drew on this material for an article with the same title, *BYU Studies* 35, no. 1 (1995): 47-78; and two *Ensign* articles, "Behind the Wall," April 1991, 22-27; and "The Wall Comes Down," June 1991, 32-36. Meditations on personal experiences appear in Thomas F. Rogers, *A Call to Russia: Glimpses of Missionary Life from the Journal of a Mission President in the Russia St. Petersburg Mission* (Provo, UT: BYU Studies, 1999).

Howard L. Biddulph, *The Morning Breaks: Stories of Conversion and Faith in the Former Soviet Union* (Salt Lake City: Deseret Book, 1996), focuses on early missionary work in the Ukraine with lesser treatments of Belarus and Russia. A political scientist, he analyzes the social and political environment that the Church encountered during the transition out of the Communist era. Carmin Clifton, *Come, Lord, Come: A History of the Church of Jesus Christ of Latter-day Saints in Romania* (San Jose, CA: Writer's Club Press, 2002), is an excellent comprehensive history of events not documented elsewhere, based on primary sources, interviews with participants, and first-hand accounts.

Of particular interest are Elder Thomas S. Monson, who oversaw work in Eastern Europe (1968-85), *Faith Rewarded: A Personal Account of Prophetic Promises to the East German Saints* (Salt Lake City: Deseret Book, 1996), and six chapters of Spencer J. Condie, *Russell M. Nelson: Father, Surgeon, Apostle* (Salt Lake City: Deseret Book, 2003). Elder Nelson was apostolic first contact to central and eastern Europe during the tumultuous demise of Communism, providing glimpses of his hidden ministry to leaders of the Soviet bloc during the careful negotiations to obtain recognition for the Church.

Kresimir Cosic, BYU basketball star and later Croatian political leader, is featured in Carri P. Jenkins, "Kresimir Cosic Moves from Basketball to Diplomatic Courts," *BYU Today,* November 1992, 10-12; and Kahlile B. Mehr, "Kresimir Cosic of Yugoslavia," in *Pioneers in Every Land,* 22-38, a more comprehensive biographical sketch.

Most articles concerning Eastern Europe were published after 1990 when the same political sensitivities no longer prevailed. Two exceptions are *Ensign* articles in 1971: Gilbert W. Scharffs, "The Branch that Wouldn't Die" (the Selbongen Branch, 1929-71, in territory that belonged first to Germany, then to Poland), *Ensign,* April 1971, 31-38; and Edwin O. Haroldsen, "To Be Free," *Ensign,* October 1971, 10-11, the story the Kiriakov family who escaped from Communist Bulgaria. Twenty years later, the father served as the first president of the Bulgaria Sofia Mission.

Excavating Mormon Pasts

Kahlile B. Mehr has authored a number of articles on the missionary work in Eastern Europe, many of them incorporated into *Mormon Missionaries Enter Eastern Europe*. Two traced Church history in Hungary and Czechoslovakia, covering from pre-World War II to the fall of Communism: "The Eastern Edge: LDS Missionary Work in Hungarian Lands," *Dialogue* 24 (Summer 1991): 27-46; and "Enduring Believers: Czechoslovakia and the LDS Church, 1884-1990," *Journal of Mormon History* 18 (Fall 1992): 111-54; both later condensed in the *Ensign*. His "1989-90: The Curtain Opens," *Ensign*, December 1993, 36-37, resulted from the chance opportunity to interview two of the first missionaries to serve in Russia. His most complete article on the post-Communist period is "Keeping Promises: The LDS Church Enters Bulgaria, 1990-1994," *BYU Studies* 36, no. 4 (1996-97): 69-106.

Academic treatments were Gary Browning (a mission president), "Out of Obscurity: The Emergence of the Church of Jesus Christ of Latter-day Saints in 'That Vast Empire' of Russia," *BYU Studies* 33, no. 4 (1993): 674-88; "Pioneering in Russia," *Ensign*, June 1997, 25-30; and "Russia and the Restoration," his most analytical piece, in *Out of Obscurity: The LDS Church in the Twentieth Century*, 63-75; and Douglas F. Tobler, "Before the Wall Fell: The Experience of the Mormons in the German Democratic Republic, 1945-1989," *Dialogue* 25 (Winter 1992): 11-31.

Staff writers for the *Ensign*, but even more for the Church's international magazine (known first as *Tambuli* and later as *Liahona*), have contributed human interest accounts on pioneer members in Eastern Europe: Richard Daniels, "Getting Things Started [in Hungary]," *Tambuli*, May 1990, 38-41; Giles H. Florence, "The Gospel in the Soviet Union," *Tambuli*, October 1991, 10-17; Marvin K. Gardner, "Jiri and Olga Snederfler: A Closer Look at Two Czech Pioneers," *Liahona*, September 1997, 16-24; and "Witnesses Through Trial and Triumph," *Ensign*, December 1999. Numerous stories of lesser historical import have also been published in the *Liahona* and *Ensign* and can be accessed on the Church's website (www.lds.org).

Missionary Charone H. Smith wrote "Albania, a Labor of Love," in *To Rejoice as Women: Talks from the 1994 Brigham Young University Women's Conference*, edited by Susette Fletcher Green and Dawn Hall Anderson (Salt Lake City: Deseret Book, 1995), while her husband, Thales Smith, wrote, "Balkan Adventure: Humanitarian Missionaries in Albania," *Journal of Collegium Aesculapium*, Fall 1994, 26-33. A lone published account by a young missionary is Timothy J. Kuta, "Apostles to the Slavs," *Latter-Day Digest* 3, no. 8 (August 1994): 10-32.

Greece, somewhat isolated for much of the twentieth century by Communist countries to the north, has traditionally been as inimical to missionary work as any country in the Eastern Bloc, a mood captured in LeGrande W. Smith, "Trial and Triumph in Thessaloniki: The Challenges of Opening Greece for the Preaching of the Gospel," *Latter-Day Digest* 3, no. 7 (July 1994): 20-34.

A final development in the historiography of Eastern Europe is its academic study. Stephen Van Orden, "Spit-Shined Shoes, Clear Decisions, and West German Mission Horror Stories" (M.A. thesis, Brigham Young University, 1996), discusses the reasons for missionary lore that ennobled the Dresden Mission in East Germany as compared to "fallen" missions elsewhere in Germany. Significant work by Bruce W. Hall includes "Gemeindegeschichte als Vergleichende Geschichte: The Church of Jesus Christ of Latter-day Saints in East Germany, 1945-1989" (M.A. thesis, Brigham Young University, 1998); "'And the Last Shall be First': The Church of Jesus Christ of Latter-day Saints in the Former East Germany," *Journal of Church and State* 42, no. 3 (Summer 2000): 485-505; and "'Render unto Caesar': State, Identity and Minority Religion in the German Democratic Republic, 1945-1989" (Ph.D. diss., State University of New York at Buffalo, 2003). Both draw upon local member sources available only in German and files of the Stasi, East German secret police, from newly opened German archives. Hall concludes that, after forty years of scrutiny, the secret police eventually saw Mormons as model citizens. This favorable regard translated to a temple in Freiberg and to missionaries crossing the border before the Berlin Wall fell. The first event is documented in Raymond M. Kuehne, "The

Freiberg Temple: An Unexpected Legacy of a Communist State and a Faithful People," *Dialogue* 37 (Summer 2004): 97-133.

In summary, the outsider perspective on Church history in Eastern Europe is represented in histories and narratives now available. Much more remains to be done, particularly as in-country sources become available.

Historiography of Growth and Internationalization

The Church's expansion into realms extremely different from its traditional homeland in the Intermountain West poses significant historiographical questions. Some trends indicate that while growth in numbers and nations where the Church now has a presence has been extraordinary during the last half of the twentieth century, that growth has now plateaued in most countries. The number of convert baptisms leveled off in the 1990s and, in 2002, was at the lowest level in a decade. The number of stakes actually declined in 2002 as units were consolidated.[7] Leadership growth and retention apparently failed to match baptismal rates. Perhaps in response, Apostle Dallin H. Oaks and Jeffrey R. Holland were dispatched to the Philippines and Chile respectively to train leaders and improve convert retention. President Hinckley and other General Authorities have issued calls for better missionary preparation, more senior couples, and more strenuous efforts at convert retention. Outside factors may also have played a role. Perhaps the Church needs to understand better how to make the gospel message apply to cultures in which values and mores differ significantly from those of the historic Church population. At the same time, the growth of secularism worldwide combined with sluggish global economies could well be focusing people's attentions on financial worries and pushing spiritual concerns to the background.

Most of the histories described in this chapter were written by faithful members of the Church who tend to emphasize the positive. Only a few analyze the problematic and controversial; yet even optimistic historians must be willing to make their appraisals of the Church's past reflect reality, even when it is not complimentary. Indeed, a major purpose of knowing the past is to guide the Church on the path its future course.

The history of the international Church is mostly in the future. Eleven million believers, many of them only nominal in their devotion, are charged to preach the restored gospel to the billions that constitute every nation, kindred, tongue, and people. As time passes, historians will be able to better interpret the meaning of the Church's growth and internationalization in the last half of the twentieth century.

KAHLILE B. MEHR has worked for twenty-five years in the LDS Family History Library, Salt Lake City, as a cataloger, supervisor, collection development specialist for Eastern Europe, and manager. A graduate of Brigham Young University with an M.A. in family and community history, M.L.S. in librarianship, and B.A. in the Russian language, he has been authoring articles and books on the international Church for over twenty years. His book on this topic is *Mormon Missionaries Enter Eastern Europe* (Provo, UT: BYU Studies, 2002). He has been honored by the Mormon History Association with T. Edgar Lyon awards in 1989, 1993, and 2000.

MARK L. GROVER has been, for the past thirty years, on the faculty at Brigham Young University where he is the Latin American Studies bibliographer in the Harold B. Lee Library. He received both a master's degree and Ph.D. in history from Indiana University. His research has focused on Brazil, Portugal, and Argentina. His publications include books and articles on librarianship, history, and religion in Latin America and Portugal, most recently the "Miracle of the Rose and the Oak in Latin America," in *Out of Obscurity: The Church in the Twentieth Century* (Salt Lake City: Deseret Book, 2000). He is

---

7. David Stewart, "LDS Church Growth Today," April 14, 2003, p. 2, retrieved May 2003 from http://www.cumorah.com/report.html.

presently finishing a book on the history of the LDS Church in South America in the 1960s and working on a history of Latin American library collections and librarianship in the United States.

REID L. NEILSON is a Ph.D candidate in religious studies at the University of North Carolina at Chapel Hill with graduate degrees in American history and business administration from Brigham Young University. He is the author and coeditor of several books, chapters, and articles on Mormonism, including *Believing History: Latter-day Saint Essays of Richard Lyman Bushman* (New York: Columbia University Press, 2004). He is currently writing his dissertation on Mormonism in Asia.

DONALD Q. CANNON received B.A. and M.A. degrees in history from the University Utah and his Ph.D. in history from Clark University, Massachusetts. He taught U.S. history at the University of Maine and, since 1973, has taught LDS Church history at Brigham Young University. His most recent publication is *Unto Every Nation: Gospel Light Reaches Every Land* (Salt Lake City: Deseret Book, 2003), a history of the international expansion of the LDS Church. He will serve as the 2004-2005 president of the Mormon History Association. He and his wife, JoAnn McGinnis Cannon, are the parents of six children.

GRANT UNDERWOOD is a professor of history at Brigham Young University and research historian at the Joseph Fielding Smith Institute for Latter-day Saint History. He is author of the prize-winning *Millenarian World of Early Mormonism* (Urbana: University of Illinois Press, 1993) and editor of *Voyages of Faith: Explorations in Mormon Pacific History* (Provo, UT: BYU Studies, 2000). He recently helped complete a 900-page manuscript that will be the first volume of the Documents Series in the new *Joseph Smith Papers*. While teaching at BYU-Hawaii for eight years, he conducted research in New Zealand, Papua New Guinea, the Solomon Islands, Vanuatu, and Fiji, and is a past president of the Mormon Pacific Historical Society. He and his wife Sheree are the parents of seven children, among them two sets of twin girls.

Chapter 10

Studies of Mormon Fissiparousness: Conflict, Dissent, and Schism in the Early Church

Danny L. Jorgensen

Mormonism, the new American religion formally organized by Joseph Smith Jr. and a few followers on April 6, 1830, has produced more than a hundred independent organizations in its brief history. Dissension, sedition, and tergiversation were common during the Mormon prophet's lifetime; and between 1830 and 1844, there were at least ten breaches in the church's organization. Smith's martyrdom in 1844 effected a leadership crisis, fragmentation of the church at Nauvoo, Illinois, and at least twelve more distinctive groups over the next decade. Most Latter Day Saint factions have continued to generate additional fissures.

In spite of the proliferation of Latter Day Saint associations, studies of Mormonism have focused almost exclusive attention on its one or sometimes two largest, most auspicious representatives. While its other assemblies are small and less successful by comparison, they are not insignificant. The various Latter Day Saint factions warrant scholarly study in and of themselves as collective efforts to deal with the ultimate, sacred meaning of human existence. Different versions and associations of a common religious tradition, even (and sometimes especially) when they have not flourished, provide invaluable opportunities for comparative study. Scrutinizing the ways in which different collectivities emerged and developed is crucial for an understanding of Latter Day Saint doctrines, practices, and activities. The formation of independent assemblages of Mormonism indicates unequivocally that it is exceedingly complex and diverse. Scholarly interpretations that completely ignore its variations and the social processes whereby they emerged and developed overlook one of its utterly essential and intriguing features. An adequate scholarly understanding of this new American religion in all of its heterogeneity and vicissitudes consequently necessitates explicit recognition that there are a variety of Mormonisms.

Fissiparousness (or schism), the division of an organization into two or more separate collectivities or groups, transpires through a complex social process.[1] It fundamentally involves conflict and dissent over ideology (values, beliefs, norms), practices, activities, and especially authority, frequently resulting in struggles for power and control of an organization. Conflict is inevitably expressed symbolically by competing ideologies, and it may center predominantly on collective values and beliefs, or practices and means of goal attainment. Disharmony may extend over a lengthy time before separation. Opponents generally proceed by defining one another as significantly different and then deviant, com-

---

1. Nancy T. Ammerman, "Schism: An Overview," in *The Encyclopedia of Religion,* edited by Mircea Eliade (New York: Macmillan, 1987), 13:98-102.

monly eventuating in charges of heresy or apostasy.[2] Through labeling, the parent group, the seceding faction, or both may define the other as straying from or perverting the truth.[3] Disputes about authority and battles for power and control are routine when an organization splinters.

Scholarly thinking about religious schism reflects a cultural tendency to evaluate harmony and order positively, and conflict and change negatively. Americans have traditionally subscribed to social theories emphasizing voluntarism, order, and equilibrium, as well as gradual, evolutionary change.[4] Religious fissiparousness is customarily attributed to disruptive changes in culture and society. Modernity, especially in the form of industrialization, urbanization, and rationalization, it is widely thought, has induced radical sociocultural and historical transformations. More specifically, cultural pluralism, structural differentiation, and individualism have been directly linked to certain forms of religious organization—churches, denominations, sects, and cults—as well as their propensity for schism.[5] While religious fragmentation frequently has been evaluated negatively and treated fortuitously, it is directly relevant to intellectual problems of the utmost gravity for the current historical epoch, particularly debates over modernity and especially its secularizing influences.[6]

Scholarly investigations of religious schism have not resulted in the uniform articulation of definitive theories. It is nevertheless possible to identify certain more or less discrete theoretical perspectives and a few cogent hypotheses. Rejecting the intuitively pleasing idea that schism is caused by doctrinal disputes, scholars conventionally have focused on social differentiation. The hypothesis that social class, ethnic, or regional differences galvanize ideological conflict and, in turn, promote fissiparousness along these lines of cleav-

---

2. Whether an idea, act, or person is deviant depends on the definition applied through a social interactional process. The label results from evaluating something or someone in concrete situations. See Howard S. Becker, *Outsiders* (New York: Free Press, 1963); and Kai T. Erikson, *Wayward Puritans* (New York: Wiley, 1966).

3. By examining who does the defining, Ammerman, "Schism," 99, identified three types of schism. One form results when those in power define perceive innovations as deviant. If the reputed changes are seen as intolerable, those defined as heretics or apostates may be forced out. Schism consequently may be unintentional (or accidental) in the sense that the reformers did not deliberately seek independence. Another type develops when protesters label the parent organization illegitimate and depart. In such cases, the parent organization frequently tried to retain the schismatics, as illustrated by disputes over local autonomy. In the third case, the completing factions mutually define each other as deviants and may pursue reconciliation before concluding that their differences preclude unity. Since schism generally results in sectarian organizations, various sect typologies may suggest additional forms. See, for instance, Bryan Wilson, *Religious Sects: A Sociological Study* (New York: McGraw-Hill, 1970).

4. See Roscoe C. Hinkle, *Founding Theory of American Sociology, 1881-1915* (Boston, MA: Routledge and Kegan Paul, 1980); Hinkle, *Developments in American Sociological Theory, 1915-1950* (Albany, New York: State University of New York Press, 1994); and Peter Kovick, *That Noble Dream: The Objectivity Question and the American Historical Profession* (Cambridge, MA: Cambridge University Press, 1988).

5. See Max Weber, *The Sociology of Religion,* translated by Ephraim Fischoff, (1922; reprint ed., Boston, MA: Beacon, 1963); Weber, *The Theory of Social and Economic Organizations,* translated by A. M. Henderson and Talcott Parsons (1925; reprint ed., New York: Oxford University Press, 1947); and H. H. Gert and C. Wright Mills, trans. and eds., *From Max Weber: Essays in Sociology* (New York: Oxford University Press, 1946). The Weberian church-sect dichotomy was developed by Ernst Troeltsch, *The Social Teachings of the Christian Churches,* 2 vols. (1931; reprint ed., New York: Harper and Row, 1960). Since it did not apply well to the United States, H. Richard Niebuhr added denomination as a third category in *The Social Sources of Denominationalism* (New York: Meridian, 1929). In clarification, Howard P. Becker added a fourth type, the cult, in *Systematic Sociology on the Basis of the Beziehungslehre and Gebildelehre of Leopold Van Wiese* (New York: Wiley, 1932). This category was developed further by J. Milton Yinger, *The Scientific Study of Religion* (New York: Macmillan, 1970), 266-73; and especially Colin Campbell, "Clarifying the Cult," *British Journal of Sociology* 28, no. 3 (1977): 375-88. An outstanding discussion of the relationship between religious organizations and forms of society is Steve Bruce, *Religion in the Modern World: From Cathedrals to Cults* (New York: Oxford University Press, 1996), esp. chap. 4. For a sound discussion of continuing disputes over the typology, see Meredith B. McGuire, *Religion: The Social Context* (Belmont, CA: Wadsworth, 1992), 133-247.

6. See Olivier Tschannen, "The Secularization Paradigm: A Systematization," *Journal for the Scientific Study of Religion* 30, no. 4 (December 1991): 395-415; and R. Stephen Warner, "Work in Progress Toward a New Paradigm for the Sociological Study of Religion in the United States," *American Journal of Sociology* 98, no. 5 (March 1993): 1044-93.

age has been highly influential.[7] This hypothesis has been largely incorporated into the structural-functional theory that schism is caused by social changes that produce stresses and strains in the structure of society and the corresponding psychosocial deprivation or relative deprivation of its members.[8] Viewed in this way, schism is a consequence of people's efforts to address grievances effected by perceived deprivation and resolve the resulting uncertainties within an organization.[9]

Revisions of the theory have deemphasized stress-strain and deprivation by concentrating on the mobilization and deployment of scarce resources (time, money, members, rewards, and so on) by a social movement organization in relationship with its environment.[10] Conflict and schism sometimes are functional as well as dysfunctional, according to an application of the reformulated theory.[11] The resource-mobilization theory of social movements has netted a few specific hypotheses. Higher probabilities of schism are predicted as organizational size and diversity increase, while lower probabilities are anticipated as authority becomes more centralized.[12] Another popular hypothesis is that schism is exacerbated by different styles of leadership, interpersonal conflicts, and personality differences.[13]

Sociology of knowledge contentions about how human "realities" are socially constructed have shown considerable promise for explaining religious schism.[14] They have

---

7. H. Richard Niebuhr, *The Social Sources of Denominationalism* (New York: Meridian, 1929); James S. Coleman, "Social Cleavage and Religious Conflict," *Journal of Social Issues* 12 (1956): 44-56; and Andrew M. Greeley, *The Denominational Society: A Sociological Approach to Religion in America* (Glenview, IL: Scott, Foresman, 1972). For supporting studies, see Liston Pope, *Millhands and Preachers: A Study of Gastonia* (New Haven, CT: Yale University Press, 1942); Will Herberg, *Protestant, Catholic, Jew: An Essay in American Religious Sociology* (New York: Doubleday, 1955); Christopher Dawson, "What About Heretics? An Analysis of the Causes of Schism," *Commonweal*, September 18, 1942, 513-17; Gus Tuberville, "Religious Schism in the Methodist Church: A Sociological Analysis of the Pine Grove Case," *Rural Sociology* 14 (1949): 29-39; S. L. Greenslade, *Schism in the Early Church* (London: SCM Press, 1953); and Robert Doherty, *The Hicksite Separation: A Sociological Analysis of Religious Schism in Early Nineteenth Century America* (New Brunswick, NJ: Rutgers University Press, 1967).

8. See Talcott Parsons: *The Structure of Social Action* (New York: McGraw-Hill, 1937), *Toward a General Theory of Action* (New York: Harper and Row, 1951), and *The Social System* (New York: Free Press, 1951); Robert Merton, *Social Theory and Social Structure* (New York: Free Press, 1949); and Charles Y. Glock and Rodney Stark, "On the Origin and Evolution of Religious Groups," in Charles Y. Glock and Rodney Stark, eds., *Religion and Society in Tension* (Chicago: Rand McNally, 1965), 242-59.

9. In a derivative model, modified by a theory of collective behavior, John Wilson, "The Sociology of Schism," *A Sociological Yearbook of Religion in Britain* (London: SCM Press, 1971), 4:1-21, specified that successive conditions—a conducive environment, a sense of grievance and crisis, precipitating events, conflict, and struggles for power—must accumulate to produce schism. For an application see Mary Lou Steed, "Church Schism and Secession: A Necessary Sequence?," *Review of Religious Research* 27, no. 4 (June 1986): 344-55.

10. K. Peter Takayama, "Formal Polity and Change of Structures, Denominational Assemblies," *Sociological Analysis* 37 (1976): 83-84, and his "Strains, Conflicts and Schism in Protestant Denominations," in *American Denominational Organization*, edited by Ross P. Scherer (Pasadena, CA: William Carey Library, 1980), 298-329.

11. Bryan V. Hillis, *Can Two Walk Together Unless They be Agreed? American Religious Schisms in the 1970s* (Brooklyn, NY: Carlson, 1991).

12. Mayer N. Zald and Roberta Ash, "Social Movement Organizations: Growth, Decay and Change," *Social Forces* 44 (1966): 327-40; Mayer N. Zald, "Theological Crucibles: Social Movements in and of Religion," *Review of Religious Research* 23, no. 4 (June 1982): 317-36; Robert C. Liebman, John R. Sutton, and Robert Wuthnow, "Exploring the Social Sources of Denominationalism: Schisms in American Protestant Denominations, 1890-1980," *American Sociological Review* 53 (June 1988): 343-52; and William Gamson, *The Strategy of Social Protest* (Homewood, IL: Dorsey, 1975). Propositions about social differentiation, stress-strain and deprivation, and organizational dynamics, as well as the idea that religion sometimes is an expression of psychopathology, have been subordinated and reduced to behavioristic mechanisms of exchange in a formal deductive theory of religion by Rodney Stark and William Sims Bainbridge, *The Future of Religion: Secularization, Revival and Cult Formation* (Berkeley: University of California Press, 1985), esp. 99-125, and their *A Theory of Religion* (New York: Peter Lang, 1987), 121-53. Schism, in this rational choice model, is reduced to the analysis of an individual's motives, defined by a hedonistic reward-seeking, cost-avoiding calculus.

13. Steed, "Church Schism and Secession," 344-55; Malcolm J. C. Calley, *God's People: West Indian Pentecostal Sects in England* (London: Oxford University Press, 1965); and Bryan Wilson, *Religious Sects*.

14. Peter L. Berger and Thomas Luckmann, *The Social Construction of Reality: A Treatise in the Sociology of Knowledge* (New York: Doubleday, 1966). Also see Harold Garfinkel, *Studies in Ethnomethodology* (Englewood

focused on claims to knowledge and their legitimation through charismatic, traditional, rational, and/or legal authority. The ability of potential leaders to secure authority for legitimating separation has been identified as a crucial feature of fissiparousness. "The propensity to schism," Roy Wallis has hypothesized, "increases directly with the availability of means of legitimating authority." In other words: "The more bases of legitimation there are, or the more widely available they are, the greater the likelihood of schism."[15]

This chapter focuses on conflict, dissent, and schism in the early Mormon church. Why did Mormonism promulgate more than twenty different collectivities in less than twenty-five years? I critically review the manner in which Latter Day Saint fissiparousness has been addressed by scholars, especially from the perspective of the New Mormon History. The New Mormon History, as I use the term, is an intellectual movement committed to ordinary, professional standards of scholarship. That professionalism would require a separate definition will probably be perplexing to those unfamiliar with this subculture. The issues involved are complex, however, and not unlike those faced by other scholars of religion. For faithful Mormon scholars, the matter, at least in part, concerns what to do when secular history conflicts with and contradicts sacred history and faith. The complexity of this potential dilemma is compounded greatly by the current epistemological crisis in Western thought. Mormon historians, however, generally subscribe to more conventional epistemological and methodological viewpoints and have been reluctant to enter these debates.

I limit my discussion primarily to published secondary literature on the organization founded by Joseph Smith and its derivations, excluding the two largest representatives—the Church of Jesus Christ of Latter-day Saints (or LDS), the Community of Christ (formerly the Reorganized Church of Jesus Christ of Latter Day Saints or RLDS)—and schisms from them. Roger D. Launius, the original editor of this volume, suggested these basic parameters because Mark D. Scherer's essay in this volume discusses RLDS contributions, and most of the other essays focus either on the Joseph Smith period or are written primarily from the LDS perspective. There are difficulties associated with unambiguously distinguishing the schisms of Nauvoo Mormonism from splinters of the organizations headed by Brigham Young and other leaders. I have included the literature on the fissiparous groups led by Lyman Wight, James Emmett, and Alpheus Cutler because they were a result of the post-1844 dispersion of the Nauvoo Saints and, technically, were therefore schisms of Brigham Young's movement. Other cases, such as the disaffected collectivities involving William Smith, David Whitmer, James Colin Brewster, and Granville Hedrick, are even more difficult to classify unequivocally. On a variety of grounds, all of the inclusive cases may be seen, perhaps arguably, as deriving from early Mormonism or its schisms other than those of the LDS and RLDS. I do not review the archival materials or the literature issued by the various factional groups, since they appear abundantly in the secondary literature which is my focus. I also ignore a large body of literature on Mormon schisms written from a clearly partisan viewpoint since it violates cardinal principles of scholarship, even (and especially) when it was produced by people with scholarly credentials.

I proceed by examining different approaches to and perspectives on conflict, dissent, and schism in early Mormonism. Then I survey and critically assess the literature on

---

Cliffs, NJ: Prentice-Hall, 1967; Stanford M. Lyman and Marvin B. Scott, *A Sociology of the Absurd* (New York: Appleton-Century-Crofts, 1970); and Jack D. Douglas and John M. Johnson, eds., *Existential Sociology* (New York: Cambridge University Press, 1977). See Danny L. Jorgensen, "Dissent and Schism in the Early Church: Explaining Mormon Fissiparousness," *Dialogue: A Journal of Mormon Thought* 28 (3, Fall 1995): 15-39, for a critical evaluation of these different sociological perspectives and an application of a sociology of knowledge viewpoint to early Mormonism.

15. Roy Wallis, *Salvation and Protest: Studies of Social and Religious Movements* (New York: St. Martin's, 1979), esp. 174-192, quotations p. 186. Also see Roy Wallis (ed.), *Sectarianism: Analyses of Religious and Non-Religious Sects* (New York: Halsted, 1976); Wallis, *The Road to Total Freedom: A Sociological Analysis of Scientology* (New York: Columbia University Press, 1977); and Steve Bruce, *A House Divided: Protestantism, Schism, and Secularization* (New York: Routledge, 1990).

particular schismatic movements. In conclusion, I provide suggestions for revising current images of Mormon fissiparousness and highlight consequential topics and questions in need of further study.

Perspectives on Mormon Fissiparousness

Mormon scholars, like believers, traditionally have found it difficult to think about schism apart from theological, faith-based contentions about how particular groups are related to the original Latter Day Saint church. Dale Morgan's modest survey of writings by and on early Mormon dissidents and schismatics, "A Bibliography of the Churches of the Dispersion," *Western Humanities Review* 7 (Summer 1953): 255-66, probably is the earliest attempt to treat the issue from a nonsectarian standpoint. "Instructive studies could be made of all" Mormon factions, Morgan argued, "and a book to discuss them comprehensively is one of the imperative needs of Mormon scholarship" (255). Identifying one of the greatest sources of difficulty for such an undertaking, he astutely observed: "The death of the Prophet totally changed the picture for Mormonism's dissenting churches. Henceforth individual churches could and did claim to be not only the one true church but the legitimate inheritor of the Prophet's mantle" (258).

The Utah (LDS) church has generally taken the view that other Latter Day Saint organizations are impostors and have largely ignored them or, less commonly, treated them as insignificant curiosities. Serviceable information about various Mormon groups appears in E. Cecil McGavin, "Apostate Factions Following the Martyrdom of Joseph Smith," published in the *Improvement Era* (serialized in 1944); Russell R. Rich, *Those Who Would Be Leaders* (Provo, UT: BYU Press, 1958); his *Little Known Schisms of the Restoration* (Provo, UT: BYU Press, 1962); Kate B. Carter, *Denominations that Base their Beliefs on the Teachings of Joseph Smith, the Mormon Prophet* (Salt Lake City: Daughters of Utah Pioneers, 1969); and a series of essays on particular factions published in 1976 (and thereabouts) by William Y. Beasley in the *Gospel Anchor*. All of them, however, reflect a partisan viewpoint. While it has been impossible for other Latter Day Saints to disregard the largest Mormon church, they frequently have responded to it as an abomination and aberration.[16] Labeling one another deviant is a conventional and extremely useful Latter Day Saint strategy for accentuating exclusive claims to truth and moral superiority, thereby generating in-group solidarity, yet it has seriously inhibited scholarly thinking about schism.[17]

Traditional faith-based approaches to Mormon studies generally have treated nonconformity, dissension, conflict, and especially schism as abnormal, dysfunctional, and thereby bad in ways that mirror and reinforce key values of the Mormon subculture. Labels such as *heretic, apostate,* and *defector* have been presented simply as descriptions of actions by a person or group. All of them, however, are emotionally loaded evaluations that presuppose a particular frame of reference. Even when a writer specifies the grounds for these judgments, they contain such ambiguities that it is extremely difficult, if not impossible, to form an independent assessment. These evaluative labels therefore are useful for scholarly purposes only when the foundation for them has been clearly specified. Even then it may not be possible to unambiguously say anything more than that someone was perceived to be or labeled a heretic, apostate, or defector from a certain standpoint. By labeling dissenters as deviants, traditional histories also have transformed them into enemies of the Church. Once dissent and conflict have been placed outside of the Mormon Church, these reactions become "persecution." This strategy means that the writer has affirmed and

---

16. The identities of almost all other Mormon groups were fashioned from their opposition to Utah Mormonism, as their primary literature illustrates. Excellent discussions of how the RLDS movement proceeded are Roger D. Launius, *Joseph Smith III: Pragmatic Prophet* (Urbana: University of Illinois Press, 1988); Roger D. Launius and W. B. "Pat" Spillman, eds., *"Let Contention Cease": The Dynamics of Dissent in the Reorganized Church of Jesus Christ of Latter Day Saints* (Independence: Graceland/Park Press, 1991); and Richard P. Howard, *The Church through the Years*, 2 vols. (Independence: Herald House, 1992-93).

17. For an interesting discussion of the messages strategically advanced by schismatic factions following the 1844 leadership crisis see Douglas W. Larche, "The Mantle of the Prophet: A Rhetorical Analysis of the Quest for Mormon Post-Martyrdom Leadership, 1844-1860" (Ph.D. diss., Indiana University, 1977).

emphasized unity and continuity, rather than conflict and discontinuity as Mormonism's dominant features.

Over the years, however, histories grounded in faith have increasingly described with greater candor principal episodes of conflict, dissent, and schism in the early Church. In *The Story of the Latter-day Saints* (1976; 2d ed. rev. and enl., Salt Lake City: Deseret, 1992), James B. Allen and Glen M. Leonard adequately narrated the conflicts at Kirtland, the origin of the Danites as agents of dissident control in Missouri, and the activities of John C. Bennett and other Nauvoo dissidents and schismatics. However, the authors called dissenters "apostates," and their interpretation conformed closely to the Mormons' sacred story. The "Exodus to a New Zion" (217-56), for instance, barely mentioned the Nauvoo church's fragmentation, as if its development was one of continuous, uninterrupted evolution. Paul M. Edwards, *Our Legacy of Faith: A Brief History of the Reorganized Church of Jesus Christ of Latter Day Saints* (Independence: Herald House, 1991) neglected conflict except for a standard treatment of the post-martyrdom crisis of leadership. He also briefly discussed the major schism leaders and movements (113-26). In *The Church Through the Years,* 2 vols. (Independence: Herald House, 1992, 1993), former RLDS Church Historian Richard P. Howard employed professional scholarship to reconstruct a sacred story. However, he attributed schism in the early Latter Day Saint Church to sociocultural diversity and authoritarian beliefs without adequate supporting evidence or arguments (1:303-25). Howard also relied on Steven Shields, *Divergent Paths of the Restoration* (1975, reprint ed., Los Angeles: Restoration Research, 1990), for his summary of early dissenters and schisms without taking advantage of more recent scholarship.

A more balanced approach is evident in professional scholarship, including the New Mormon History; yet conflict, fragmentation, discontinuity, and schism have not appeared in the major works as central problems in need of analysis and interpretation. In spite of Mark P. Leone's preoccupation with authoritarianism, his anthropological study, *Roots of Modern Mormonism* (Cambridge, MA: Harvard University Press, 1979), for example, dealt exclusively with Utah Mormonism and said almost nothing about social conflict, dissent, or schism. Klaus J. Hansen, *Mormonism and the American Experience* (Chicago: University of Chicago Press, 1981) very briefly acknowledged schismatic propensities. However, his complex and penetrating interpretation of the interrelationships between Mormonism and American culture construed Mormonism as a single highly monolithic religion. The provocative thesis that Mormonism is a distinctively new religious tradition, not merely another variant of Christianity, defended by Jan Shipps in *Mormonism: The Story of a New Religious Tradition* (Urbana: University of Chicago Press, 1985) depends heavily on continuity. It therefore glossed over the problem of fissiparousness. However, recognizing that the RLDS experience represented a potentially damaging exception to the argument, she strained to include that group.

Joseph Smith's unsympathetic biographer, Fawn M. Brodie, dealt with conflict more explicitly in *No Man Knows My History: The Life of Joseph Smith The Mormon Prophet* (1945; 2d ed. rev. New York: Alfred A. Knopf, 1990). She devoted entire chapters to narrating the "Disaster in Kirtland" (194-207), the Danites and their treatment of dissenters (208-24), and the Nauvoo dissidents and their schism (367-79). She also mentioned several post-martyrdom schismatic leaders in the "Epilogue" (396). Brodie's psychological approach might illuminate the role of personality dynamics in religious splintering but demonstrated little interest in the social organization of Mormonism. Brodie, therefore, did not contribute substantially to the problem of fragmentation or schism.

Leonard J. Arrington and Davis Bitton, *The Mormon Experience: A History of the Latter-day Saints* (1979; reprint ed., Urbana: University of Illinois Press, 1992), an outstanding synthesis of the New Mormon History, devoted an entire chapter to external conflict and persecution. They candidly acknowledged that "the same principles that united the church also contained seeds that threatened disunion" (66). Furthermore, they briefly but more than adequately summarized what little is known about the earliest dissenters and schisms, and reviewed the principal incidents of discord within the Church through the

DIVERGENT PATHS OF THE RESTORATION

A History of the Latter Day Saint Movement

Third Edition, Revised and Enlarged

STEVEN L. SHIELDS

post-martyrdom period (66-79, 89-94). The doctrines of the gathering and prophetic revelation, they argued, "precipitated a condition of dissent" (66). They also cited resistance to changing doctrines as a source of disharmony in the Nauvoo church, attributing its fragmentation after 1844 to personality cults, unfamiliarity with, or rejection of doctrinal innovations, and questions about succession legitimacy.

Differing Visions: Dissenters in Mormon History (Urbana: University of Illinois Press, 1994), edited by Roger D. Launius and Linda Thatcher, is one of a very few scholarly works on Mormonism to take dissent and schism seriously as a principal issue. Their inclusive essay, "Introduction: Mormonism and the Dynamics of Dissent" (1-22), provided useful hints pertinent to scholarly thinking about schism, but not a fully developed theoretical framework or interpretation. The seventeen essays contained in this collection selectively discuss particular dissenters in Mormon history. (I mention the chapters relevant to my own topic below.)

One of the most significant scholarly histories of conflict, dissent, and schism in the Mormon organization from 1830 to 1844 is Marvin S. Hill, *Quest for Refuge: The Mormon Flight from American Pluralism* (Salt Lake City: Signature Books, 1989). He skillfully advanced a variant of the change, stress-strain, and deprivation theory while avoiding many of the limitations of a functionalist perspective. Mormonism was for Hill a product of modernity and a profoundly conservative reaction to pluralism, perceived changes in the basic fabric of American life, and socioeconomic deprivation. His richly detailed, extremely sensitive, subtle, and sophisticated historical interpretation attended to order and change, as well as conflict and discontinuity. It reflected a balanced approach to conflict with the larger society and within this new religion; and it narrated and interpreted most of the known incidents of early Mormon fissiparousness. Hill's nuanced analysis of conflict, dissent, and schism in the Ohio and Missouri churches, as will be discussed in more detail below, represented a fresh and highly promising perspective on early Mormonism.

Thomas F. O'Dea, *The Mormons* (Chicago: University of Chicago Press, 1957), remains one of the most significant scholarly treatments of Mormon social organization. Based on his doctoral dissertation, it reflected O'Dea's training in sociology at Harvard under Talcott Parsons, the progenitor of the once dominant structural-functional paradigm. His personal commitments to Catholicism were not represented as anti-Mormon sentiments, and his work did not suffer from an attempt to balance faith and scholarship. His participant observational familiarity with the Mormon subculture, unlike the sometimes clumsy efforts of outsiders, represented a shining example of a *verstehen Religionssoziologie*. He viewed Mormonism, at least implicitly, from the standpoint of a social change, structural stress-strain, psychosocial deprivation perspective. But his interpretation, like the general theory, is not compelling as an explanation. O'Dea, like Hill, may have appreciated the problems associated with specifying deprivations and linking them functionally or causally with structural conditions without resorting to ad hoc interpretation, circular reasoning, and tautology. Appropriately, his concern was to understand how the Mormon social system was produced and shaped by concrete social and cultural circumstances. This approach may be helpful for identifying conditions of organizational stability; but since these conditions are not necessary or sufficient causes, they are unnecessary for a sociological explanation of schism.

O'Dea's chapter on Mormonism's organization and institutionalization derived from Max Weber's typology of authority filtered through Talcott Parsons's social systems theory. "The problem of authority," he noticed, "is one that every human community must solve in some way, for the co-ordination of social life and its stability depend upon the solution" (155). Although charisma is uniquely suited for legitimating religious innovations, it does not contribute to social cohesion. By definition, it is individualistic; almost anyone can claim the gift of prophecy; and it strongly resists refutation. Because charisma has a strong democratic impulse, this form of authority is easily dispersed; it is insufficient for legitimating organizational structure; and any collectivity founded on it is very susceptible to fragmentation. If an organization is to acquire stability and durability, charisma must be constrained.

The potential for fission remains great, O'Dea maintained, even when charisma is restricted to a few people, since rival claims provoke conflict that requires authority for its adjudication. He argued that early Mormonism faced a choice between two paths of development: "It could permit unrestrained prophecy and thereby splinter into smaller and smaller groups, finally breaking into a Babel of private revelation"; or "it could restrain prophetic gifts, restricting revelation and prophecy to one man, and develop a centrally directed organization about that one leader" (156). The Book of Mormon, O'Dea demonstrated perspicaciously, served as an organizational model (chap. 2). Regrettably, he failed to explain why Mormonism developed into a more authoritarian, sect-like organization. He simply jumped over this crucial issue in pointing to its empirical advantages.

In other observable instances, such as spiritualism and pentecostalism, charisma remains less restrained. Why, then, did Mormonism take one path rather than the other? If O'Dea had approached the problem from a sociology of knowledge perspective, he might have discovered a solution in Mormon epistemology. Monopolistic truth claims necessarily contain a hierarchical principle: If truth is absolute, then not all claims are equal, and there must be a way of deciding among them. In the cases of spiritualism and pentecostalism, charisma has almost exclusive priority, thereby dissolving the inherent principle of hierarchy. For early Mormonism, however, epistemological authoritarianism (the claim to be the one absolutely true religion) was at least as important as the claim to prophetic revelation. In fact, the two claims were interrelated and interdependent. O'Dea claimed that Joseph Smith introduced a hierarchical principle in 1829, even before the church was formally organized, by titling himself as first elder and Oliver Cowdery as second (157). Furthermore, because Oliver Cowdery dissented within the decade and was excommunicated in 1838, the hierarchical principle grew stronger. Serviceable biographies of the "second elder" are Stanley R. Gunn, *Oliver Cowdery: Second Elder and Scribe* (Salt Lake City: Bookcraft, 1962); and Phillip R. Legg, *Oliver Cowdery: The Elusive Second Elder of the Restoration* (Independence: Herald Publishing House, 1989). Charismatic authority thereby was subordinated to the rational authority of the Church's emergent organizational structure.

O'Dea's thesis, then, is that charismatic authority was constrained by rationally binding and routinizing it within an increasingly centralized organizational hierarchy. He sketches how this organization principle pertains to schism but not in sufficient historical detail. However, he implies a highly suggestive periodization of Mormonism's organizational development: the exclusive concentration of charisma in Smith's role as prophet (1829-32); the introduction of rational, hierarchical structures (1833-37); their elaboration (1838-40); and greater centralization of authority (1841-44). In each period, he argued, dissent, conflict, and schism evoked responses that promoted these particular organizational developments.

Inexplicably, O'Dea provided only a transitory analysis of the post-martyrdom crisis of authority and the transition from prophetic to priestly leadership (described by Max Weber's theory) as charismatic authority became routinized and institutionalized in Utah Mormonism. He concluded: "Charisma had been successfully contained within the organized structure of the church and identified with the functions of church office. It had, in fact, to some extent been routinized, and organizational procedures under the direction of a strong authoritarian leader largely replaced visions and revelations, a process that had already started in the last days of Joseph's rule in Nauvoo" (160).

Other significant issues, such as "hierarchical structure versus congregationalism" (160-65), church-state and political relations (165-73), and the subsequent development of the LDS Church's organization (174-85), receive more attention. In his concluding chapter, O'Dea analyzed stresses and strains within the Utah Mormon social system. He specifically identified "education versus apostasy," "rationality versus charisma," "authority and obedience versus democracy and individualism," "consent versus coercion," changing doctrines and views on marriage, "family ideals versus equality of women," industrialism ("progress") versus "agrarianism," "political conservatism versus social idealism," and "patriotism versus particularism" as probable sources of future conflict, dissent, and schism.

O'Dea's interpretation of Mormon social organization is supplemented by more recent studies of its hierarchical development. D. Michael Quinn, "The Evolution of the Presiding Quorums of the LDS Church," *Journal of Mormon History* 1 (1974): 21-38, presented the basic chronology of the emergent hierarchy. It thereby provided a beneficial point of departure, but his analysis contains serious defects. While Quinn skillfully employed a standard historical methodology, his theoretical interpretation, like other examples of the New Mormon History, rests on faith-based presuppositions that resulted in an inappropriate theory of social order and change. While acknowledging O'Dea's work, he disregarded its basic insight that the Mormon hierarchy rationally constrained charismatic authority and the conflict deriving from its irrationality and instability. The plausibility of Quinn's static, consensus theory of the hierarchy's evolution implicitly presupposed that God acted rationally in creating the priesthood through the Mormon prophet. By taking rationality, rather than irrationality, as the basic intellectual problem to be explained, his interpretation became a version of the rationalization process: a part of the ongoing theology and institutionalization of rationality, rather than a historical account of it.

Gregory A. Prince, *"Having Authority": The Origins and Development of Priesthood during the Ministry of Joseph Smith* (Independence: John Whitmer Monograph Series, 1992), is a profitable analysis of authority and how it developed in the early Mormon Church. Although Prince, too, employed the notion of social evolution, he clearly did not envision any gradual unfolding of the hierarchical organization. According to Prince, organizational innovations were followed by periods of evolutionary implementation, punctuated by further additions and then their execution. The interpretation was not theoretically ambitious; it completely ignored relevant sociological thinking; and it is not connected adequately to the existing literature. Prince, however, provided a detailed scholarly account of how structures of authority emerged and subsequently were routinized and legitimated. In his more recent *Power from On High: The Development of the Mormon Priesthood* (Salt Lake City: Signature Books, 1995), Prince addressed many of the same issues in somewhat more systematic detail, although without treating or correcting the deficiencies of his previous work.

The single best treatment of the development of Mormonism's early social organization and leadership authority is D. Michael Quinn, *The Mormon Hierarchy: Origins of Power* (Salt Lake City: Signature Books, 1994).[18] Adding new information and drawing together his many previous writings on this topic and related issues, Quinn provides a comprehensive and skillful scholarly description of the organizational development of Mormonism through the apostolic succession of Brigham Young and the remaining Nauvoo Twelve. His discussion of the post-martyrdom organizational crisis is especially strong. (See discussion below.) Quinn's description has become more critical, less faith promoting, and thereby more appropriately scholarly; yet he remains surprisingly sympathetic to the LDS Church. While providing a much more candid and critical perspective on early Mormonism's development, Quinn continues to see it as a matter of evolution; he does not take advantage of O'Dea's sociological insights or more recent thinking. Rather, he withdraws just when a new theoretical interpretation of Mormonism's leadership and organization seems to be emerging from the data.

Early Mormon Schisms

Several helpful guides to Latter Day Saint churches and some of the related archival materials, documents issued by the various groups, and writings about them that avoid sectarianism have been published in recent years. Wayne Ham, "Center Place Saints:

---

18. Although it lies outside the focus of this essay, his second volume, *The Mormon Hierarchy: Extensions of Power* (Salt Lake City: Signature Books, 1997), describes the organizational development of Mormon leadership in Utah as it reshaped itself after Joseph Smith's death.

The Mormon Hierarchy

ORIGINS OF POWER

D. Michael Quinn

Signature Books
in association with Smith Research Associates
Salt Lake City
1994

Excavating Mormon Pasts

A Survey of Restoration Fragmentation in Zion," *Restoration* 1 (January 1982): 3-8, briefly describes nine "restoration churches," including the LDS and RLDS, with congregations in the Independence, Missouri, area. He summarizes major points of difference in a useful chart. Albert J. Van Nest, *A Directory to the "Restored Gospel" Churches* (Evanston, IL: Institute for the Study of American Religion, 1983, now located at the University of California, Santa Barbara) lists many of the independent organizations. Steven L. Shields, *Divergent Paths of the Restoration,* draws on previous works, especially those by Dale Morgan and Kate Carter, in providing a comprehensive list of about three hundred Mormon dissenters and schisms as well as brief summaries. His *The Latter Day Saint Churches: An Annotated Bibliography* (New York: Garland, 1987), while far from being comprehensive, is the most adequate single guide to the primary and secondary literature on these Mormon dissenters and organizations.

The Earliest Dissenters and Schisms

Study of dissent and schism within the earliest Mormon church has been hampered by a lack of detailed information. The treatments that O'Dea and Quinn give this organizational period (1829-31) probably are the best available sources. What is known about dissidents Hiram Page, John Noah, those who tarred and feathered Joseph Smith and Sidney Rigdon, as well as Wycam Clark, Northrop Sweet, and the others who in 1831 formed the Pure Church of Christ has been summarized adequately by Steven Shields and discussed by Leonard Arrington and Davis Bitton, Richard Howard, Marvin Hill, and others. Almost nothing is known about three other early schisms that Shields catalogs: The Independent Church formed by a man named Hoton in 1832; the Church of Christ founded by Ezra Booth around 1836; and the Church of Christ founded by William Chubby sometime in the 1830s or 1840s to minister to African Americans. No one, to the best of my knowledge, has analyzed the conflict between the Colesville (New York) Saints and the new Ohio converts as a case of socioeconomic differences among the early Mormons.

Dissent and Schism in Ohio and Missouri

Between about 1835 and 1840, conflict and dissent resulted in three breaches in the Mormon Church. Warren Parrish organized the dissident Church of Christ at Kirtland, Ohio, in 1837, including such prominent Mormons and church leaders as apostles Luke S. Johnson, John F. Boynton, and Lyman E. Johnson, as well as Leonard Rich, Stephen Burnett, Sylvester Smith, Cyrus P. Smalling, and Joseph Coe. The Alston Church, a schism of the Mormon organization in Missouri, was founded in 1839 by Isaac Russell. George M. Hinkle established The Church of Jesus Christ, The Bride The Lamb's Wife in Missouri on June 24, 1840. Shields also cataloged and briefly discusses them in his two compilations.

Two important studies have examined conflict among the Mormons in Ohio and Missouri in considerable detail, revising the traditional view that such conflict was a reflection of "apostate mobocracy" but rather focused on ideological differences.[19] Marvin Hill, "Cultural Crisis in the Mormon Kingdom: A Reconsideration of the Causes of Kirtland Dissent," *Church History* 49 (September 1980): 286-97, argued that sociocultural differences among these early Mormons resulted in ideological conflict and dissent over images of the Church and especially its organization. The dissenters favored greater individual freedom and local autonomy as well as a more open relationship with the larger society modeled after evangelical Protestantism. The Mormon prophet and his supporters promoted a more radical image of the kingdom based on a "higher law" and a more authoritarian organization created in opposition to the surrounding culture and society.

In *Exiles in a Land of Liberty: Mormons in America, 1830-1846* (Chapel Hill: University of North Carolina Press, 1989), Kenneth Winn implicitly advanced a version of

---

19. For an overview of histories of this early Mormon period, see Roger D. Launius, "The Church in New York and Ohio: Writing the History of Mormonism's Early Period," and Steven C. LeSueur, "The Mormon Experience in Missouri, 1830-39," in this volume.

the stress-strain and deprivation theory to explain discord and schism in the Kirtland church. He argued that the basic conditions for schism emerged from the Panic of 1837 in the United States which the Saints experienced as uncertainty and conflict over economic means and goals (106-28). Some of them felt that the Church should reject conventional, materialistic norms and values, while others thought that kingdom-building required them to employ traditional economic norms. Economic uncertainty was compounded by the "debacle of Zion's Camp." Collapse of the United States economy, Winn argued, resulted in the Mormon bank fiasco, and it, in turn, "triggered sharp and bitter dissent within the church" (111).

The Mormons' experience of deprivation deriving from economic stress and strain was manifest as ideological conflict. Following Hill's interpretation, Winn then elaborated on O'Dea's contention that the Book of Mormon's republican ideology served as the fundamental model for the organizational development of early Mormonism. The seeds of ideological conflict, he maintained, were planted when the Church was first organized but did not mature until triggered by the events beginning in about 1834 at Kirtland. According to Winn, the dissidents "retained a deep affinity for mainstream American values, particularly those of republican individualism." They perceived "specific actions on the part of the church leadership, especially those of Joseph Smith . . . as a departure from the democratic elements inspired by the Christian primitivism of early Mormonism, and the subsequent growth of the church's tyranny over its membership" (106). The Mormon prophet and a majority of his followers, Winn maintained, "completely rejected this charge of antirepublicanism. The dissenters had mistaken libertarianism for republicanism, and libertarianism would not help build the kingdom of God. Obedience to the Lord through His prophet was necessary for that" (106). Joseph Smith and the loyal core around him labeled the dissenters as "morally flawed men, weak in the faith, whose efforts threatened to subvert the Kingdom" (107). Since the factionalism could not be resolved by compromise, "peace only came finally when, in the summer of 1838, the last leading dissenters were sent, in Sidney Rigdon's words, 'bounding over the prairies' of Missouri; and the doubters who remained were intimidated into silence with strong-arm tactics" (107).

Other important scholarly essays pertinent to dissent and schism during this early period of Mormonism's development include the following essays from Launius and Thatcher, *Differing Visions*: Ronald E. Romig, "David Whitmer: Faithful Dissenter, Witness Apart," 23-44; Kenneth H. Winn, "'Such Republicanism as This': John Corrill's Rejection of Prophetic Rule," 45-75; Richard P. Howard, "William E. McLellin: 'Mormonism's Stormy Petrel,'" 76-101; and Dan Vogel, "James Colin Brewster: The Boy Prophet Who Challenged Mormon Authority," 120-39.

Schisms of the Nauvoo Church

From 1839 until 1844, a rapidly growing Mormon membership gathered at Nauvoo, creating the second largest city in Illinois; Mormonism's social organization was elaborated greatly, thereby becoming increasingly hierarchical, formal, and authoritarian; and the founding prophet introduced exceedingly ambitious new plans for building the Kingdom of God as well as radically innovative doctrines and practices. He publicly presented portions of the new Mormon theology, such as baptism for the dead, temple-building, and concepts about the nature of God and humanity. But many of its more revolutionary elements (like plural marriage), he taught only in private to a highly select circle of his most trusted friends and associates. His innermost circle, "The Holy Order" (or "Quorum of the Anointed," among other names), was organized in May 1842. Similarly, Smith entrusted designs for the parapolitical Kingdom of God on earth to the secretive Council of Fifty, formally established in the spring of 1844.

There is a substantial literature pertinent to Nauvoo Mormonism, which Glen M. Leonard reviews in "The Nauvoo Experience" in this volume. However, the best contemporary scholarship dates from the publication of Robert B. Flanders, *Nauvoo: Kingdom on the Mississippi* (Urbana: University of Illinois Press, 1965), an undeniable classic. He defended

Differing Visions
Dissenters in Mormon History

Edited by
Roger D. Launius and Linda Thatcher

Foreword by
Leonard J. Arrington

UNIVERSITY OF ILLINOIS PRESS
Urbana and Chicago

the thesis that conflict and dissent within Nauvoo Mormonism, although exceptionally complex, revolved around a "simple dichotomy" between "those who favored . . . a 'political' Mormonism as it was expressed in the building of Nauvoo" and "those who came to oppose what Nauvoo stood for and who wished for a simpler, more orthodox manifestation of the faith" (v-vi). Flanders devoted separate chapters to analyzing and interpreting the emergent temple theology (chap. 7), internal conflicts (chap. 9), the political kingdom (chaps. 8, 10), and "the fall of the Kingdom" (chap. 11), all of them directly pertinent to dissent and schism within Nauvoo Mormon. Roger D. Launius and John E. Hallwas, eds., *Kingdom on the Mississippi Revisited* (Urbana: University of Illinois Press, 1996), in fourteen separate essays pursued many of the issues that Flanders raised. In *Cultures in Conflict: A Documentary History of the Mormon War in Illinois* (Logan: Utah State University Press, 1995), John Hallwas and Roger Launius provided scholarly balance to previous studies of the Nauvoo church by describing and presenting important documents representing the views of non-Mormon and anti-Mormon contemporaries. Glen M. Leonard's long-awaited *Nauvoo: A Place of Peace, a People of Promise* (Salt Lake City: Deseret Book, 2002), while rich in details and context, uses a predictably traditional interpretative framework.

The influence of folk magic and the Western occult tradition, particularly hermeticism, is essential for any scholarly understanding of development of Mormon doctrines, especially the Nauvoo temple theology. D. Michael Quinn, *Early Mormonism and the Magic World View* (1987; 2d ed. rev., Salt Lake City: Signature Books, 1998) remains the single best work on this topic. Other useful studies of this issue include Max Nolan, "Joseph Smith and Mysticism," *Journal of Mormon History* 10 (1983): 105-16; Richard L. Bushman, *Joseph Smith and the Beginnings of Mormonism* (Urbana: University of Illinois Press, 1984); and Lance S. Owens, "Joseph Smith and Kabbalah: The Occult Connection," *Dialogue* 27 (Fall 1994):117-94. In *The American Religion: The Emergence of the Post-Christian Nation* (New York: Simon and Schuster, 1992), Harold Bloom speculated wildly about the influence of Western occultism on Mormonism but he otherwise contributed little to this important scholarly issue. John L. Brooke's prize-winning, *The Refiner's Fire: The Making of Mormon Cosmology, 1644-1844* (New York: Cambridge University Press, 1994), contained some very useful information on this topic; but his interpretation was needlessly speculative and seriously flawed in numerous ways. Unfortunately, Brooke failed to exhibit much of an understanding of either hermeticism or Mormonism.

Several other studies of related doctrines and practices are essential for a scholarly understanding of Nauvoo Mormon dissent. Sound summaries of the development of the temple doctrines and rituals have been provided by T. Edgar Lyon, "Doctrinal Development of the Church During the Nauvoo Sojourn, 1839-1846," *BYU Studies* 15, no. 4 (Summer 1974): 435-46; and Michael W. Homer, "'Similarity of Priesthood in Masonry': The Relationship between Freemasonry and Mormonism," *Dialogue* 27, no. 3 (Fall 1994): 1-113. David John Buerger's several essays and book also have made important contributions to this topic: "The Adam-God Doctrine," *Dialogue* 15 (Spring 1982):14-58; "'The Fullness of the Priesthood': The Second Anointing in Latter-day Saint Theology and Practice," *Dialogue* 16 (Spring 1983): 10-44; "The Development of the Mormon Temple Endowment Ceremony," *Dialogue* 20 (Winter 1987): 33-76; and *The Mysteries of Godliness: A History of Mormon Temple Worship* (San Francisco: Smith Research Associates, 1994). In "The Law of Adoption: One Phase of the Development of the Mormon Concept of Salvation," *BYU Studies* 14, no. 3 (Spring 1974): 291-314, Gordon Irving discussed a little-known, yet important Nauvoo Mormon doctrine, while Rex E. Cooper, *Promises Made to the Fathers: Mormon Covenant Organization* (Salt Lake City: University of Utah Press, 1990), takes a social anthropology approach to these fast-developing doctrines.

Much of the scholarly literature on early Mormon polygamy also is relevant. Instructive studies include Linda King Newell and Valeen Tippetts Avery, *Mormon Enigma: Emma Hale Smith, Prophet's Wife, "Elect Lady," Polygamy's Foe, 1804-1879* (New York: Doubleday, 1984); Richard S. Van Wagoner, *Mormon Polygamy: A History* (1986; 3rd ed., Salt Lake City: Signature Books, 1992); Lawrence Foster, *Religion and Sexuality: Three American*

Excavating Mormon Pasts

Communal Experiments of the Nineteenth Century (New York: Oxford University Press, 1981); Jessie L. Embry, *Mormon Polygamous Families: Life in the Principle* (Salt Lake City: University of Utah Press, 1987); George D. Smith, "Nauvoo Roots of Mormon Polygamy, 1841-46: A Preliminary Demographic Report, *Dialogue* 27, no. 1 (Spring 1994): 1-72; and Todd Compton, *In Sacred Loneliness: The Plural Wives of Joseph Smith* (Salt Lake City: Signature Books, 1997).

D. Michael Quinn detailed the emergence, development, and activities of the Anointed Quorum in "Latter-day Saint Prayer Circles," *BYU Studies* 19, no. 1 (Fall 1978): 79-105. Andrew F. Ehat's "Joseph Smith's Introduction of Temple Ordinances and the 1844 Succession Question," (Provo, UT: M.A. thesis, Brigham Young University, 1982) revealed significant information about the Prophet's private teachings to the inner circle in relationship to subsequent events. Consequential scholarly studies of the Council of Fifty include Klaus J. Hansen, *Quest for Empire: The Political Kingdom of God and the Council of Fifty in Mormon History* (1967; Salt Lake City: Greg Kofford Books, forthcoming), presented partly as a polemic with Flanders; D. Michael Quinn, "The Council of Fifty and Its Members, 1844 to 1945," *BYU Studies* 20 no. 2 (Winter 1980): 163-97; and Andrew F. Ehat, "'It Seems Like Heaven Began on Earth': Joseph Smith and the Constitution of the Kingdom of God," *BYU Studies* 21, no. 3 (Spring 1980): 253-79.

Copious dissent within Nauvoo Mormonism notwithstanding, the protesters—whether they were expelled or simply left—generally did not form dissenting churches during Joseph Smith's lifetime. This situation, as interpreted by O'Dea, probably is explained best by the Prophet's success in limiting charismatic authority for the movement exclusively to himself and otherwise constraining it within the Church's formal, hierarchical organization. Steven Shields briefly describes the three known schisms of the Nauvoo church. Long-time dissident Hyrum Page formed a Church of Christ in 1842. Francis Gladden Bishop, who was excommunicated in 1835, restored to membership, but expelled again in 1842, established the Church of Jesus Christ of Latter Day Saints at Little Sioux, Iowa. Richard L. Saunders, "The Fruit of the Branch: Francis Gladden Bishop and His Culture of Dissent" (Launius and Thatcher, *Differing Visions,* 102-19), and his "Francis Gladden Bishop and Gladdenism: A Study in the Culture of a Mormon Dissenter and His Movement" (M.S. thesis, Utah State University, Logan, 1989), are valuable discussions of this dissident. Some of the literature on Nauvoo Mormonism also provides information about these people and events.

Opposition to Nauvoo Mormonism's political kingdom and emergent temple theology, especially the covert practice of plural marriage by the leadership, produced one highly significant schism before the Prophet's death. The True Church of Jesus Christ of Latter Day Saints was founded in the spring of 1844 by William and Wilson Law, Robert D. and Charles A. Foster, Francis M. and Chauncey L. Higbee, Charles Ivins, and Austin Cowles. All of these dissenters were prominent Nauvoo Mormons and a few of them had been participants in the Prophet's inner circle and/or high ranking public officials. Their publication of an opposition newspaper, the *Nauvoo Expositor,* and its destruction by Mormon leaders, ignited a series of events that within weeks resulted in the murders of Joseph and Hyrum Smith by an anti-Mormon mob. Although this schismatic organization was very short-lived, it marked a substantial break within the Church, the consequences of which contributed to the emergence of numerous dissenting factions over the next ten years.

The conflict and dissent leading to Smith's martyrdom, as Dale Morgan noted, have rarely been treated dispassionately. Viewed from the standpoint of particular factions of the Nauvoo church, the dissidents usually have been regarded as either "enemies" or as righteous opponents of a fallen prophet. Flanders provided one of the first genuinely scholarly treatments of these events. Other noteworthy studies include Lyndon W. Cook, "William Law: Nauvoo Dissenter," *BYU Studies* 22, no. 1 (Winter 1982): 47-72; and his "'Brother Joseph Is Truly a Wonderful Man, He Is All We Could Wish a Prophet to Be': Pre-1844 Letters of William Law," *BYU Studies* 20, no. 2 (Winter 1980): 207-18; Dallin H.

Oaks, "The Suppression of the Nauvoo *Expositor*," *Utah Law Review* 9 (Winter 1965): 862-903; and Michael Quinn's *The Mormon Hierarchy: Origins of Power* (esp. chaps. 4, 5).

Nauvoo Mormon dissent has been of special interest in histories of the RLDS Church (now Community of Christ) since it eventually incorporated many of the smaller dissident factions. A thorough review of this literature is beyond the scope of this chapter. However, the more crucial, scholarly works include Robert B. Flanders, "Mormons Who Did Not Go West: A Study of the Emergence of the Reorganized Church of Jesus Christ of Latter Day Saints" (M.A. thesis, University of Wisconsin, Madison, 1954); Alma R. Blair, "The Reorganized Church of Jesus Christ of Latter Day Saints, Moderate Mormons," in F. Mark McKiernan, Alma R. Blair, and Paul M. Edwards, eds., *The Restoration Movement: Essays in Mormon History* (Lawrence, KS: Coronado Press, 1973), 207-30; Richard P. Howard, "The Reorganized Church in Illinois, 1852-82: Search for Identity," *Dialogue* 5, no. 1 (1970): 63-75; his "The Nauvoo Heritage of the Reorganized Church," *Journal of Mormon History* 16 (1990): 41-52; and Roger D. Launius, *Joseph Smith III: Pragmatic Prophet* (Urbana: University of Illinois Press, 1988), esp. 77-96.

Fragmentation of the Nauvoo Church

Following Joseph Smith's martyrdom on June 27, 1844, Nauvoo Mormonism fragmented into rival organizational factions. Most of these groups and related leaders have been catalogued by Steven Shields and the other sources discussed above. Nine of the twelve apostles, headed by Brigham Young, gained control of the largest single Nauvoo Mormon faction. The only serious challenges to the apostles' leadership at this time came from Sidney Rigdon and James J. Strang.

Dissent from Nauvoo Mormon innovations, combined with uncertainty over the question of leadership succession left much of the membership organized by local congregations but unaffiliated with any particular leader or faction. Over about the next ten years, many Mormon congregations located outside Nauvoo declared their independence, and other rival leaders emerged and formed alternative organizations. Noteworthy leaders of alternative organizations of the post-martyrdom period included George J. Adams, Alpheus Cutler, James Emmett, Peter Haws, George Miller, John E. Page, and Lyman Wight, along with a host of followers. Other dissenters and factional leaders of this period included James Colin Brewster, Zodac Brooks, Samuel C. Brown, James Bump, Martin Harris, George M. Hinkle, Samuel James, William E. McLellin, Reuben Miller, Lorenzo D. Oatman, Leonard Rich, Elijah Schwackhammer, Aaron Smith, S. B. Stoddard, Jacob Syfritt, Charles B. Thompson, Increase M. Van Dusen, and David Whitmer, along with assorted followers.

Those Mormons who did not accept (or subsequently rejected) the apostles' leadership added to the complexity and instability of this situation by sometimes changing group affiliations. Many of the dissenting organizations were unable to sustain themselves. Beginning in the early 1850s a substantial number of dissenters and factional organizations came together in the form of a "new organization." Headed by Joseph Smith III after 1860, this collectivity eventually became the RLDS Church, and the second largest Mormon organization.

The most important discussion of Nauvoo Mormonism's fragmentation following the martyrdom of Joseph Smith is D. Michael Quinn, "The Mormon Succession Crisis of 1844," *BYU Studies* 16, no. 2 (1976): 187-234. He argued that the Mormon prophet established eight possible methods for succession between 1834 and 1844. Most of them derived from rational, organizational principles: counselor in the First Presidency (Sidney Rigdon); special appointment (James J. Strang, Lyman Wight, Alpheus Cutler, Joseph Smith III); office of Associate President (Oliver Cowdery, Hyrum Smith); Presiding Patriarch (Hyrum Smith, William B. Smith); Council of Fifty (Lyman Wight, Alpheus Cutler, Peter Haws, George J. Adams, George Miller, John E. Page); Quorum of the Twelve Apostles (Brigham Young); and the three priesthood councils—Twelve Apostles, Quorum of the Seventy, and the Nauvoo high council (William Marks). The eighth method of succession, by a family member or descendant of Joseph Smith Jr. (Hyrum Smith, William B. Smith, Joseph Smith III, David H. Smith), was based on a form of traditional authority, birthright.[20] He also noted that the principle of democratic assent was important in early Mormonism. Quinn correctly observed, however, that Joseph Smith frequently suspended (or ignored) common consent for collective decisions as mandated by Doctrine and Covenants 20; alternatively it was used to ratify actions later, sometimes a considerable time after such actions were effected (193).

Quinn's essay is exceptionally important because it demonstrated that within early Mormonism there were multiple possible means of claiming succession and, thereby, legitimating authority for the organization. The existence of multiple methods of succession suggests that the question of legitimate leadership was ambiguous—that is to say, there were more ways than one of legitimating claims to leadership. Therefore, rather than spending time on the scholarly impossibility of adjudicating the exclusive, sectarian claims of particular factions, Quinn did a nonsectarian analysis and interpretation of the various versions of Mormonism that emerged subsequently. Unfortunately, Quinn did not pursue this argument until much later. Instead, he concluded that: "In time, all but one of the major claimants [the Quorum of Twelve Apostles] were invalidated by their personal circumstances or the insufficiency of their claims" (187). His interpretation, seemingly based on a nonsectarian perspective, therefore supported the theologically based claims of Utah Mormonism.

There are several flaws in Quinn's interpretation. He contended that the succession became a crisis because Smith's public instructions were ambiguous and his unambiguous private directives were communicated only to a privileged elite, not to the general Church membership. Quinn thereby employed a distinction between the Prophet's public and private teachings to eliminate most of the succession claims, particularly those based on rational, publicly recognized organizational principles. Why and how this argument does not also apply to the claims of the Quorum of the Twelve Apostles, a public, formal organizational unit of the Church, is entirely unclear.

The Prophet, presumably based on charisma (his direct relationship with God), frequently directed the activities of individual members, introduced new doctrines, and initiated practices to assorted individuals without much regard for the Church's official hierarchy or formal organization. He also created two momentous, secret bodies—the Quorum of the Anointed and the Council of Fifty—in private. While all of the Apostles were members of the Anointed and the Fifty, these bodies also included other Church members, and even nonmembers, in the case of the Fifty. If, as Quinn argued, the Prophet's private teachings had priority over public policies, then the claims of the Apostles derived from their membership in the Anointed Quorum and/or the Council of Fifty rather than the Quorum of Twelve. This, in fact, seems to have been the position of at least one of the Apostles, Lyman Wight, as well as other members of the Anointed Quorum and the Council of Fifty, such as Alpheus Cutler, James Emmett, Peter Haws, and George Miller.

It consequently does not follow, as Quinn concluded, that the claims of all but the apostolic quorum were rendered invalid or insufficient. His argument seems to hinge on the implicit assumption that God acted rationally in creating the Mormon priesthood and, through His prophet, acted to ensure the continuity of the Church by entrusting its development exclusively to one group, the Quorum of the Twelve headed by Brigham Young. Otherwise, about all that can be said from a scholarly standpoint, based on the available evidence, is that there were multiple possible ways of claiming succession; the succession question was ambiguous; and, as a result of this situation, Mormonism splintered into rival factions. Depending on particular understandings deriving from inside Nauvoo Mormonism, most of the rival, factional leaders had more or less legitimate and persuasive grounds for their claims to succession.

---

20. It seems to me that this is a form of traditional authority, as defined by Max Weber, because its implicit rationale was biblical and therefore derived from folkways and customs appropriated by Mormonism.

Interestingly, this position is essentially the one Quinn took in his more recent reinterpretation of the succession period in *The Mormon Hierarchy: Origins of Power*. This work also provided an outstanding updated summary of the related literature, including discussions of pertinent factions and leaders, such as Sidney Rigdon, Lyman Wight, Alpheus Cutler, James J. Strang, William Smith, and the Prophet's sons.

Many different features of the post-martyrdom situation, largely unrelated to the character of succession claims, influenced the relative success of the various factions. James J. Strang, whose claims were among the weakest, initially was one of the most successful rivals to the leadership of the apostles. Lyman Wight and Alpheus Cutler, both of whose claims derived from the same source as the apostles, were largely unsuccessful in attracting substantial followings, although Cutler's church still exists today. The faction headed by the apostles became the largest and most successful version of Mormonism, in large measure because it was the most visible, public remnant of the founding Prophet's elite inner circle and because this group proved to be the most skilled in transforming and mobilizing the fractured movement's scarce resources, both material and nonmaterial, into a vital religious organization.

Ronald K. Esplin, "Joseph, Brigham and the Twelve: A Succession of Continuity," *BYU Studies* 21, no. 3 (Summer 1981): 301-41, disputed Quinn's contention that succession produced a crisis of authority or leadership: "This was not a succession crisis," argued Esplin, "for most of the dissenters were less concerned about the ability or authority of the Apostles than about the propriety and inspiration of measures that had, in fact, originated with Joseph" (331). Straining to defend the continuity thesis, he failed to examine adequately certain contradictory evidence, particularly in the cases of the Wightites, Millerites, and Cutlerites. Even so, Esplin contributed several significant insights by carefully examining how the apostles acted to secure recognition, by linking succession disputes to previous dissent, by noting that dissent was both functional and dysfunctional for the subsequent development of Utah Mormonism, and by estimating the proportion of the Nauvoo Mormon membership who followed Brigham Young west.

Steven L. Shields, "The Latter Day Saint Movement: A Study in Survival," in *When Prophets Die: The Postcharismatic Fate of New Religious Movements*, edited by Timothy Miller (Albany: State University of New York Press, 1991), 59-77, claimed that more than fifty Mormon organizations still function. He provided useful information about six: the RLDS (Community of Christ), as well as the churches headed by Young, Strang, Cutler, Hedrick, and Bickerton. Shields raised the question of Mormon succession but failed to provide adequate scholarly grounds for analyzing the question, thus unfortunately confusing history with theology.

Scholarly concern for the period from the Nauvoo Mormon exodus to the establishment of the apostles' church in the Salt Lake Valley has focused predominantly on the principal features of the migration and its ultimate success. Very few scholarly studies, except for Richard E. Bennett, have described the Saints' existential situation and critically examined the achievement of transplanting Mormonism organizationally in the face of ongoing conflict and dissent. In "Finalizing Plans for the Trek West: Deliberations at Winter Quarters, 1846-1847," *BYU Studies* 24, no. 3 (1984): 301-21, Bennett documented many of the organizational problems that the apostles encountered involving conflicts over authority, giving particularly attention to those who thought that the Council of Fifty held supreme authority over temporal and political affairs. His interpretation of these events contributed significantly to a scholarly understanding of such dissidents as Alpheus Cutler, James Emmett, Peter Haws, George Miller, and Lyman Wight.

Bennett's "Lamanism, Lymanism, and Cornfields," *Journal of Mormon History* 13, (1986-87): 45-59, focused even more specifically on conflict, dissent, and schism within Brigham Young's organization during the exodus period. He furnished important information about the precariousness of the apostles' leadership and critical insights into the schisms formed by Alpheus Cutler, George Miller, and Lyman Wight. The most adequate scholarly study of George Miller as well as people and events connected with him is

Excavating Mormon Pasts

Richard E. Bennett, "'A Samaritan Had Passed By': George Miller—Mormon Bishop, Trailblazer, and Brigham Young Antagonist," *Illinois Historical Journal* 82, no. 1 (Spring 1989): 2-16. In "Mormon Renegade: James Emmett at the Vermillion, 1846," *South Dakota History* 15, no. 3 (1985): 217-33, he chronicled the activities of another Council of Fifty member who dissented from Brigham Young's Mormon leadership. Bennett's consequential work on this period is elaborated and summarized in his *Mormons at the Missouri, 1846-1852: "And Should We Die . . . "* (Norman: University of Oklahoma Press, 1987). His *We'll Find the Place: The Mormon Exodus, 1846-1848* (Salt Lake City: Deseret Book, 1997), deals with Brigham Young's consolidation of leadership by reconstituting the First Presidency at Kanesville in 1847, an event also dealt with most revealingly in Gary James Bergera, *Conflict in the Quorum: Orson Pratt, Brigham Young, Joseph Smith* (Salt Lake City: Signature Books, 2002), which includes the minutes of those intense Kanesville meetings.

Sidney Rigdon's claims to Mormon leadership following the death of Joseph Smith have been examined thoroughly by much of the literature on Nauvoo Mormonism and related studies of the succession crisis reviewed above. On October 15, 1844, Rigdon organized the Church of Jesus Christ of the Children of Zion. Mormons affiliated with him included Samuel James and George M. Hinkle. Fred C. Collier ed., "The Trial of Sidney Rigdon: First Counselor to the Prophet Joseph Smith," *Doctrine of the Priesthood* 7, no. 12 (December 1990): 2-70, provided important information, but little interpretation, about to Rigdon's claims and excommunication by the apostles. Other noteworthy works on Rigdon and this schism include Thomas J. Gregory, "Sidney Rigdon: Post Nauvoo," *BYU Studies* 21 (Winter 1981): 51-54; and M. Guy Bishop, "Stephen Post: From Believer to Dissenter to Heretic," in *Differing Visions*, 180-95. Bishop's full-length biography on Stephen Post is forthcoming from Greg Kofford Books. Until recently, the only scholarly biography of this important Mormon leader was F. Mark McKiernan, *The Voice of One Crying in the Wilderness: Sidney Rigdon, Religious Reformer, 1793-1876* (Lawrence, KS: Coronado Press, 1971). Richard S. Van Wagoner's *Sidney Rigdon: A Portrait in Religious Excess* (Salt Lake City: Signature Books, 1994) provided a fresh study of this important early Mormon leader.

James J. Strang's life and schismatic organization have attracted inordinate attention, apparently because of its peculiar improbability and initial success. Dale L. Morgan's "A Bibliography of the Church of Jesus Christ of Latter Day Saints (Strangite)," *Western Humanities Review* 5 (Winter 1950-51): 42-114, provided an invaluable guide to the primary and secondary literature on this schism. The best early biography, Milo M. Quaife, *The Kingdom of Saint James: A Narrative of James J. Strang, the Beaver Island Mormon King* (New Haven, CT: Yale University Press, 1930), remains a standard scholarly source. Roger Van Noord, *King of Beaver Island: The Life and Assassination of James Jesse Strang* (Urbana: University of Illinois Press, 1988) is the most recent and comprehensive scholarly work on this Mormon schism and its leader. Vickie Cleverley Speek has completed a booklength social history, "For the Good of the Kingdom: A Narrative of the Strangite Mormons," in manuscript.

Other noteworthy scholarship pertinent to the Strangites includes Klaus J. Hansen, "The Making of King Strang: A Reexamination," *Michigan History* 46 (September 1962): 209-29; William D. Russell, "King James Strang: Joseph Smith's Successor?," in *The Restoration Movement*, 231-56; Russell, "'Printed by Command of the King': James J. Strang's Book of the Law of the Lord," *Restoration* 3 (April 1984): 19-21; Lawrence Foster, "James J. Strang: The Prophet Who Failed," *Church History* 50 (June 1981): 182-92; David Rich Lewis, "'For Life, the Resurrection, and the Life Everlasting': James J. Strang and Strangite Mormon Polygamy, 1849-1856," *Wisconsin Magazine of History* 66 (Summer 1983): 274-91; and John Quist, "Polygamy among James Strang and His Followers," *John Whitmer Historical Association Journal* 9 (1989): 31-48. A recent essay by Craig L. Foster, "From Temple Mormon to Anti-Mormon: The Ambivalent Odyssey of Increase Van Dusen," *Dialogue* 27, no. 3 (Fall 1994): 275-286, provided helpful information about several early Strangites, particularly the Van Dusens.

Charles B. Thompson, a Nauvoo Mormon dissenter and initial follower of Strang's formed an independent organization, the Congregation of Jehovah's Presbytery of Zion, in 1847. His life and activities have been examined in two essays by Newell G. Bringhurst, "Forgotten Mormon Perspectives: Slavery, Race, and the Black Man as Issues Among Non-Utah Latter-day Saints, 1844-1873," *Michigan History* 61, no. 4 (Winter 1977): 353-70," and "Charles B. Thompson and the Issues of Slavery and Race," *Journal of Mormon History* 8 (1981): 37-47. The first essay also contains a scholarly discussion of James J. Strang.

Lyman Wight, a dissident apostle who pursued a Council of Fifty assignment in Texas, has been discussed in much of the literature on the succession crisis. Other members of the Fifty involved with this venture were George Miller and Lucien Woodworth. C. Stanley Banks, "The Mormon Migration into Texas," *Southwestern Historical Quarterly* 49 (October 1945): 233-44, describes the Wight colony in Texas. Philip C. Wightman's "The Life and Contributions of Lyman Wight" (Provo: M.A. thesis, Brigham Young University, 1971) furnished a biography. Davis Bitton, "Mormons in Texas: The Ill-Fated Lyman Wight Colony, 1844-1858," *Arizona and the West* 11, no. 2 (Spring 1969): 5-26, and Bitton ed., *Lamoni Wight: Life in a Mormon Splinter Colony on the Texas Frontier* (Salt Lake City: University of Utah Press, 1970), contain the most comprehensive interpretation of this schism and its intriguing leader.

The dissenting activities of William B. Smith, the only surviving brother of the founding Prophet, have been treated by much of the scholarship on early Mormonism. His life, claims to leadership, and involvements with several post-martyrdom schisms have been examined by Irene M. Bates, "William Smith, 1811-1893: Problematic Patriarch," *Dialogue* 16, no. 2 (Summer 1983): 11-23; Paul M. Edwards, "William B. Smith: The Persistent Pretender," *Dialogue* 18 (Summer 1985): 128-39; Edwards, "William B. Smith: 'A Wart on the Ecclesiastical Tree,'" in *Differing Visions*, 140-57; E. Gary Smith, "The Patriarchal Crisis of 1845," *Dialogue* 16, no. 2 (Summer 1983): 24-39; and Irene M. Bates and E. Gary Smith, *Lost Legacy: The Mormon Office of Presiding Patriarch* (Urbana: University of Illinois Press, 1996).

I have reported extensively on the faction headed by Alpheus Cutler, the Church of Jesus Christ (Cutlerite). In "The Social Backgrounds and Characteristics of Those People Who Founded the Church of Jesus Christ (Cutlerite)," paper presented to Mormon History Association, Quincy, Illinois, May 1989, I examined and rejected the hypothesis that this schism was a product of underlying sociocultural differences between its founders and other early Mormon converts. "The Old Fox: Alpheus Cutler," in *Differing Visions*, 312-58 provided an overview of Cutler's career in Mormonism and generally described the formation of his schism. My "The Fiery Darts of the Adversary: An Interpretation of Early Cutlerism," *John Whitmer Historical Association Journal* 10 (1990): 67-83, demonstrated that Cutlerite beliefs and practices derived from and endeavored to preserve an image of Nauvoo Mormonism. I examined the activities resulting from Cutler's conviction that Joseph Smith gave him a Council of Fifty assignment to pursue Lamanite ministries in "Building the Kingdom of God: Alpheus Cutler and the Second Mormon Mission to the Indians, 1847-1853," *Kansas History* 15, no. 3 (1992): 192-209. My "Conflict in the Camps of Israel: The Emergence of the 1853 Cutlerite Schism," *Journal of Mormon History* 21, no. 1 (Spring 1995): 24-62, argued that the Cutlerite schism was largely an accidental product of conflict over goals and authority within Brigham Young's westward bound movement. Another essay, "Cutler's Camp at the Big Grove on Silver Creek: A Mormon Settlement in Iowa, 1847-1853," *Nauvoo Journal* 9, no. 2 (Fall 1997): 39-51, endeavors to capture a sense of this place. The history of this schism in Iowa was summarized in "The Cutlerites of Southwestern Iowa: A Latter-day Saint Schism, 1846-1865," *Annals of Iowa* 58, no. 2 (Spring 1999): 131-61. In "The Scattered Saints of Southwestern Iowa: Cutlerite-Josephite Conflict and Rivalry, 1855-1865," *John Whitmer Historical Association Journal* 13 (1993): 80-97, I described the establishment of Cutler's organization in southwestern Iowa during the early 1850s, the Cutlerites' relationships with the "new organization" (RLDS), and that about half of Cutler's followers had converted to the Reorganization by 1865. After Cutler's death

The Reminiscences and Civil War Letters of Levi Lamoni Wight

LIFE IN A MORMON SPLINTER COLONY ON THE TEXAS FRONTIER

DAVIS BITTON
Editor

University of Utah Press
Salt Lake City

in 1864, the remnants of his church migrated to Minnesota, established the first permanent white settlement in Otter Tail County, and subsequently endeavored to preserve their image of Nauvoo Mormonism against the corrosive intrusion of modernity as described in my "North from Zion: The Minnesota Cutlerites, 1864-1964," paper presented to the Mormon History Association, St. George, Utah, May 1992.

Biloine W. Young's "Minnesota Mormons: The Cutlerites," *Courage* 3, 2-3 (1973): 117-37, overviewed the Cutlerite church, focusing specifically on its development in Minnesota. In "The Ecclesiastical Position of Women in Two Mormon Trajectories," *Journal of Mormon History* 14 (1988): 63-79, Ian G. Barber mistakenly construed the Cutlerites' Nauvoo Mormon belief in women's priesthood through the endowment as an instance of feminism. Biloine Whiting Young provided a popular summary of this schism in *Obscure Believers: The Mormon Schism of Alpheus Cutler* (St. Paul, MN: Pogo Press, 2002). Other literature, including the several essays and books by D. Michael Quinn and Richard E. Bennett discussed above also contributed important information about Cutler and his church.

What little is known about the other Mormon leaders and organizations of the period from June 1844 through the early 1850s is contained in the general studies of Mormonism and its schisms reviewed above or scattered among other possible sources. To the best of my knowledge, there have been no concerted scholarly efforts to examine them specifically.

Conclusions

Efforts to interpret or explain early Mormonism's propensity to schism have been hampered by the strong cultural tendency of American scholars to envision social order and harmony positively and social change and conflict negatively. New Mormon historians have also experienced difficulty in analyzing and interpreting dissension and organizational fissiparousness independently of the monopolistic claims of early Mormon organizations to truth and authority. While dramatic sociocultural changes resulting in the relative psychosocial deprivation of societal members may be necessary conditions, they are not sufficient causes of religious schism. The reformulated theory that focuses, more specifically, on how religious movements mobilize scarce resources in relationship to the larger sociocultural environment provides significant scholarly insights into why and how some organizational factions are more or less successful. However, it does not provide a comprehensive model or explanation of religious schism.

A more promising scholarly perspective on religious schism is a sociology of knowledge approach that focuses on claims to truth and authority in relationship to their organizational consequences. While much more research and analysis will be required, this theory seems to explain early Mormonism's propensity for schism. Viewed in this way, conflict, dissent, and organizational fragmentation in Mormonism is one of its most basic, interesting, and significant features. Studies of the schismatic process and its results, particularly those factions that largely have been neglected because they have been seen as trivial curiosities, thereby become imperative. Too little has changed since 1953 when Dale Morgan called the problem of schism to scholarly attention and recommended that: "Historically, many of these bodies [Mormon schisms] deserve extended individual treatment. Instructive studies could be made of all, and a book to discuss them comprehensively is one of the imperative needs of Mormon scholarship" (255). Treating this long-standing neglect will require that scholars of Mormonism reorient their thinking to multiple versions of the faith and devote greater attention to the comparative study of the different varieties of Mormonism. Thinking in terms of many different Mormonisms will result in a reassessment of this new religion, thereby directing scholars to work more comparatively and less provincially to understand it, to probe what it has to say about American religion, and to explore its significance for the study of religion generally.

Excavating Mormon Pasts

DANNY L. JORGENSEN is professor of religion at the Center for Interdisciplinary Studies in Culture and Society at the University of South Florida, St. Petersburg, past president of the John Whitmer Historical Society, and author of numerous articles dealing with various aspects of Latter Day Saint dissent and schism. He is working on a comprehensive sociological history of the Church of Jesus Christ (Cutlerite), enjoys spending time with his wife, June Hansen Jorgensen, and riding his Belgian stallion, Prance, with his sixteen-month-old granddaughter, Isa Jorgensen.

Chapter 11

"Travelers on the New Mormon History Trail": Community of Christ Contributions to the New Mormon History Movement

Mark A. Scherer

The writings in Latter Day Saint history by those affiliated with the Community of Christ[1] from the early 1960s to the present reflect the general characteristics of the New Mormon History movement. The New Mormon History movement emerged in response to the desire of many historians to break away from the old debating paradigm of either attacking or defending the legitimacy of Mormonism. Going beyond the tired argument of which church, LDS or RLDS, was the true successor to the early church of Joseph Smith Jr., participants in the movement chose topics that focused on the lives of grassroots members, both male and female, leaders and followers. Movement historians also applied modern critical research methodologies in their attempts to understand Latter Day Saintism. No longer would their studies be constructed as battering rams or immovable defenses of decisions made by historical figures. Paul M. Edwards explains this approach in "The New Mormon History," *Saints Herald,* 133 (November 1986): 12-14, 20.

In this chapter, I describe how the Community of Christ history community, including both baptized members and those closely associated with the Church, pursued with professionalism previously unavailable historical materials, using a wide variety of techniques and research methodologies. These scholars manifested a penchant for grassroots topics while they emphasized a holistic approach in their quest for authentic accounts of the Latter Day Saint movement. Because of the vast quantity of scholarship from this community of history scholars—another characteristic of the New Mormon History movement—this essay highlights only certain foundational books, periodicals, journal articles, and academic capstone projects, within the historical field of research on the Restoration movement, as well as selected key works in progress. Finally, I discuss briefly the important contributions of the John Whitmer Historical Association to the corpus of literature focusing on the church story.

Community of Christ Trail-Blazers

Robert Bruce Flanders blazed the trail into the New Mormon History movement for those within the Community of Christ in his *Nauvoo: Kingdom on the Mississippi* (Urbana:

---

1. I will use this name interchangeably with its former name, the Reorganized Church of Jesus Christ of Latter Day Saints.

Excavating Mormon Pasts

University of Illinois Press, 1965), which was based on his University of Wisconsin doctoral dissertation. Flanders offered a critical account of Joseph Smith's attempts to build a Mormon economic and political city-state on the Illinois banks of the Mississippi River (v-vi). The book's longevity may well be the best testament to its enormous contribution. Though written four decades ago, *Nauvoo* is still the single most important political, social, and economic work on the topic.

Many historians associated with the Community of Christ followed Flanders's lead by looking critically at topics ranging from the historical context of early nineteenth-century American society to significant events in the landscape of Latter Day Saintism in the opening decade of the twenty-first century. Perhaps the most important Community of Christ official to travel the New Mormon History trail was Richard P. Howard, Church historian from 1965 to 1994. His role in modernizing the Church's historical processes cannot be overstated. Assisted by able staff in the Church's Library-Archives and by W. Grant McMurray, then Assistant History Commissioner and now Church president, Howard introduced professional standards of collection, preservation, and the cataloging of Church historical materials that became the grist for the mills of serious historians. Under Howard's direction, this fertile institutional repository opened new vistas to scholars, thus generating a vast array of historical interpretations about the origins and development of the religious movement.

Early in Howard's thirty-year career, he focused on the evolution of Church scriptures. The result of his exploration was *Restoration Scriptures: A Study of Their Textual Development* (1969; rev. ed. Independence: Herald House, 1995). This important work consists of three parts: the Book of Mormon, Joseph Smith's "New Translation" of the Bible, and the Doctrine and Covenants. Howard provided the reader with almost a hundred pages of appendices (220-314) that included photographic facsimiles of manuscripts pivotal to the development of Latter Day Saint scripture.

Of particular interest to Community of Christ readers is Richard Howard's careful analysis of the Book of Abraham, written by Joseph Smith Jr. between 1835 and 1842 (chap. 12). Since the early Reorganized Church did not canonize the Book of Abraham, most Community of Christ members know very little of the writing. Thus, Howard's careful study, assisted the reader to understand the book as a product of the first Mormon prophet's "theological reflection, aided by his intuitive powers of mental imagery." Howard summarized his analysis by stating: "Whatever the early Saints felt about the Book of Abraham, it seems not to have been either an inspired or scholarly translation. Joseph Smith referred to himself as a revelator and translator. He often used those term interchangeably. His work as translator, however, did not equip him as a linguist of Egyptian language symbols" (204).

A significant early contribution to the New Mormon History movement is Wayne Ham, *"Publish Glad Tidings": Readings in Early Latter Day Saint Sources* (Independence: Herald House, 1970). This intellectual history was based on the accurate assumption that valuable insights can be gleaned from a close inspection of the original literature of the times. Ham crafted brief historical explanations of the *Evening and Morning Star* (1832-34), the *Latter Day Saints' Messenger and Advocate* (1834-37), the *Elders' Journal* (1837-38), and the *Times and Seasons* (1839-44). Then, by highlighting selected portions of these early writings, Ham identified the pressing issues, emotional responses, and decisions by Church leaders which drove the religious movement in the early years.

Edward A. Warner, in "Mormon Theodemocracy: Theocratic and Democratic Elements in Early Latter-Day Saint Ideology, 1827-1844" (Ph.D. diss., Iowa University, 1973), dispelled the popular notion that Mormonism was completely theocratic in its views of church-state relations. To construct his persuasive argument, Warner drew upon extensive research to discuss a necessary tension between theocratic characteristics of the Mormon Church institution (centralized in the prophetic office and hierarchialized in a graded system of priesthood offices) and the democratic characteristics (decentralized prerogatives among the Mormon membership). Critical of historical

RESTORATION SCRIPTURES

A STUDY OF THEIR TEXTUAL DEVELOPMENT

BY RICHARD P. HOWARD

Department of Religious Education
Reorganized CHURCH OF JESUS CHRIST of Latter Day Saints

PUBLISH GLAD TIDINGS

READINGS IN EARLY LATTER DAY SAINT SOURCES

SELECTED AND EDITED BY WAYNE HAM

HERALD PUBLISHING HOUSE

orthodoxy, Warner concluded that these characteristics were neither oppositional nor mutually exclusive, for early Mormons saw them conjoined into one theodemocratic system (10, 44-45).

Graceland College, Lamoni, Iowa

The New Mormon History movement gained strong support among the faculty at Graceland College (now Graceland University), the Church-sponsored institution of higher education located in Lamoni, Iowa. Leading support came from Paul M. Edwards, professor of history and philosophy, who wrote *The Hilltop Where: An Informal History of Graceland College* (Lamoni, IA: Venture Foundation, 1972). This book is more than a nostalgic look at the first seventy-five years of the Graceland story since Edwards outlined the difficult decisions involved in setting directions for the denominational college, its physical construction and educational offerings, and the achievements of its faculty members and students. In his concluding chapter, Edwards gave a philosophical commentary, challenging the reader to look critically at society and appreciate the important role that higher education played in shaping it (140-43).

In the Community of Christ history community, few have made a greater contribution to serious historical inquiry than Graceland history professor Alma R. Blair. "The Reorganized Church of Jesus Christ of Latter Day Saints: Moderate Mormons," in *The Restoration Movement: Essays in Mormon History* edited by F. Mark McKiernan, Alma R. Blair, and Paul M. Edwards (1972, rev. ed., Independence: Herald House, 1992), may be his most significant writing in terms of defining foundational identity issues. Blair was the first modern professional historian to observe that those who joined the Reorganization did so for reasons ranging far beyond lineal succession (203). Although the Community of Christ is rooted in the fourteen years of common history it shares with the Salt Lake church, it attracted those who stood against Brigham Young and the doctrine of polygamy, the belief in a plurality of gods, theological speculations about preexistence and exaltation, and the practice of baptism for the dead. Blair concluded that the Reorganized Church earned its reputation as moderate Mormons (219).

Larry E. Hunt, also of Graceland's history faculty, forged from his doctoral dissertation his two-volume biography *F. M. Smith: Saint as Reformer*, 2 vols. (Independence: Herald House, 1982). By placing the second prophet of the Reorganized Church in the historical context of the Mugwump political movement during America's Gilded Age at the turn of the twentieth century, Hunt brilliantly demonstrated that Smith's institutional reforms were in alignment with the larger social reform movement and concluded that the RLDS prophet, though more comfortable among his Church followers and in the pulpit, would also have fit well in secular political circles advocating similar social reforms (1:17).

Perhaps the most provocative professor of history at Graceland University is William D. Russell. Representative of Russell's insightful questioning is "The Historicity of the Book of Mormon and the Use of the Sermon on the Mount in III Nephi," in *Restoration Studies II: A Collection of Essays about the History, Beliefs, and Practices of the Reorganized Church of Jesus Christ of Latter Day Saints*, edited by Maurice L. Draper (Independence: Herald House, 1982). Joining others in a thoughtful critique of the Book of Mormon's historical veracity, Russell interrogated the organizational format, language, cultural characteristics, and authors' biases evident in the III Nephi account. Russell concluded that "the Book of Mormon should not be regarded as a historical account of ancient people who inhabited the Americas" (197).

Following the Trail Blazers

Motivated by the belief that much can be learned from the literary works of the man who led the Reorganized Church through two world wars and the nation's greatest economic depression, Norman D. Ruoff compiled *The Writings of President Frederick M. Smith*, 3 vols. (Independence: Herald House, 1978-81). Drawing articles from the movement's primary publication, the *Saints' Herald*, radio and pulpit sermons, and talks to civic groups to reveal the priorities of Smith's presidential leadership, Ruoff's three volumes identified the three major themes of F. M. Smith's presidency: Zion, stewardship, and education. This important research tool, absent of specific interpretive insights, required readers to draw their own conclusions about F. M. Smith's intellectual and spiritual leadership.

F. Mark McKiernan was a leader in the Community of Christ history community from the 1960s until his untimely passing in 1997. His most significant contribution, *The Voice of One Crying in the Wilderness: Sidney Rigdon, Religious Reformer, 1793-1876* (1971; 2d ed., Independence: Herald House, 1986), reflected New Mormon History themes. Reprinted eight times by two publishers, *Rigdon* became the definitive early work on the great Mormon orator until Richard Van Wagoner's *Sidney Rigdon: A Portrait in Religious Excess* (Salt Lake City: Signature Books, 1994) emerged more than two decades later. McKiernan found in Rigdon's life many of the great religious themes of the era introducing him as "a man with a vision, a quest, and a mission" (11) and "a refraction of the religious tendencies held by millions of early nineteenth century Americans who were greatly concerned about the fate of their eternal souls and joined one religious denomination after another" (12). McKiernan concludes that Rigdon's obituary should have quoted Mark 1:3—that Rigdon was truly "the voice of one crying in the wilderness, Prepare ye the way of the Lord" (145).

McKiernan made a second important contribution by editing, with Roger D. Launius, *An Early Latter Day Saint History: The Book of John Whitmer Kept by Commandment* (Independence: Herald House, 1980). The editors introduced Whitmer as an individual who "stood at the very thresholds of great power and authority within the restored church but never attained the authority nor the recognition that [he] probably deserved" (9). Less than a year after the Church's organization, Joseph Smith Jr., through a revelation dated March 8, 1831, called Whitmer to "write and keep a regular history" (D&C 47:1a, Community of Christ edition), thus replacing Oliver Cowdery who was on a mission to the West. The RLDS Church acquired the John Whitmer manuscript history from the Whitmer family in 1903. Five years later, Church Historian Heman C. Smith published parts of the history in the RLDS *Journal of History* but the full version was not available except in manuscript until McKiernan and Launius completed their edition. A wealth of explanatory footnotes contextualized this nineteenth-century document.

F. Mark McKiernan joined Graceland faculty members Alma R. Blair and Paul M. Edwards in editing a significant collection of thirteen essays on Latter Day Saint history in *The Restoration Movement: Essays in Mormon History*. Leading historians, both inside and outside Reorganized Latter Day Saintism, contributed essays on crucial topics. In addition to the high quality of the content and skillful interpretation, *Restoration Movement* demonstrated the collegiality of New Mormon History scholars by spanning the theological divide between the two churches. After its original publication by Coronado Press in Lawrence, Kansas, Herald House in Independence acquired the copyright and has added two printings to the five earlier printings.

The Writings of Roger D. Launius

Any essay on RLDS contributions to Mormon historiography must include the works of historian Roger D. Launius who first became interested in Church history as a baccalaureate student at Graceland College. His experiences as a summer intern at the Community of Christ historic properties in Nauvoo, Independence, and Kirtland solidified his career as a professional historian and a prolific researcher of Restoration history topics. In *Zion's Camp: Expedition to Missouri, 1834* (Independence: Herald House, 1984), Launius transformed his master's thesis from Louisiana State University into a book-length narrative documenting that the march was an attempt by Church leaders to regain lost land in Jackson County, boost the morale of the victimized Saints, and provide them with money and supplies. In addition to these purposes, Launius also noted how Zion's Camp assisted the Mormon prophet in creating an ecclesiastical structure and finding appropriate candidates to fill the positions. Because the participants assumed positions in the developing Church hierarchy, Launius observed that "Zion's Camp—either intentionally or by acci-

An Early Latter Day Saint History:

The Book of John Whitmer
Kept by Commandment

Edited by
F. Mark McKiernan and Roger D. Launius

---

dent—served as a crucible out of which the prophet forged a more powerful and efficient Church organization. [Smith's] contact with the most committed and talented men of the Church during the expedition greatly aided in the development of Church administration" (8). Launius did not intend to levy judgments by fixing blame for failure of the march (and failure, it was, in terms of restoring the Saints to their Jackson County lands) but gave a fair accounting of the doomed efforts of liberation.

Following the narrative format in *Zion's Camp,* Launius produced a historical account of the first Mormon temple in *The Kirtland Temple: A Historical Narrative* (Independence: Herald House, 1986). After discussing the conceptualization of a temple, Launius identified the temple as a dream of the membership through its beginning, realization, and shattering. The author also discussed "The Kirtland Temple Suit" (chap. 5), calling the legal action brought by the RLDS Church "the most spectacular event bearing on the history of the Kirtland Temple, save its dedication" (100). Six informative appendices provide a list of those who received a special blessing for assisting in the temple construction, elements of the dedication service on March 27, 1836, accounts by those who reported visitations of Jesus Christ in the weeks following the dedication, the Church's petition in the Kirtland Temple suit, and the court's opinion (171-98). Unfortunately, this volume is not illustrated, a deficiency Launius remedied with informative historic photographs in a thirty-one-page *Illustrated History of the Kirtland Temple* (Independence: Herald House, 1986), that included explanatory essays.

Roger Launius's most significant early contribution to the New Mormon History was his research on Joseph Smith III, founder of the Reorganized Church. This project began as his doctoral dissertation at Louisiana State University, again expanded to a book-length work. *Joseph Smith III: Pragmatic Prophet* (Urbana: University of Illinois Press, 1988) became the first modern biography of Joseph the Seer's eldest son. Launius characterized Joseph Smith III as a consensus builder whose priorities were "unity and commonality, steadfastness of purpose, and rightness of action" (x). Because Joseph Smith III was a second-generation Latter Day Saint, the author observed that the young Smith "was not as overcome by the awe of the spiritual vision as those who had gone before; he was able to take aspects of the grandiose dreams of his father, separate the logical from the impractical, and build on them" (xi). Launius concluded that Joseph III's "career represents an important case study in the union of principle and pragmatism in American religious history" (369). For this important work, Launius received the 1989 Evans Biography Award from the Center for Regional Studies at Utah State University.

A prolific researcher and writer, Launius was also the first to produce a book-length social history exploring the experiences of black Americans in the Reorganized Church. Echoing Ralph Ellison's influential 1953 novel, *The Invisible Man,* Launius titled his work *Invisible Saints: A History of Black Americans in the Reorganized Church* (Independence: Herald House, 1988) because, as Ellison had described society's overall neglect of the needs of blacks, the RLDS Church had "left its small black membership out of the mainstream of the movement" (9). Launius admitted the difficulty of performing this work—a white man trying to adequately, even accurately, portray the black person's experience within the Church. Hearteningly, he concluded that the Community of Christ stood in the national mainstream because of its response to the social needs of black Americans and, therefore, reflected American egalitarianism (12). Other writings by Launius will be discussed below.

The Administrative Biography Series

In the mid-1980s, historian Paul M. Edwards observed that an intense focus on the first fourteen years of the Restoration movement limited the horizons of historical understanding of the Reorganized Church. To broaden the view, he pursued a project with the cooperation of Herald Publishing House to promote investigations into the growth of the Reorganized Church as an institution. Thus, the Administrative Biography Series was designed to advance the historical understanding of the work of the Reorganized Church

Joseph Smith III

PRAGMATIC PROPHET

Roger D. Launius

University of Illinois Press
Urbana and Chicago

presidents, with Edwards agreeing to be the series editor. As of this writing, four works have been completed.

Edwards launched the series with *The Chief: An Administrative Biography of Fred M. Smith* (Independence: Herald House, 1988), very much an insider's history as the nicknames in the title indicate. Frederick Madison Smith, oldest son of Joseph Smith III, presided over the Church for nearly a third of the twentieth century. Edwards portrayed him as a figure of controversy and paradox, presiding over an institution in transition. F. Henry Edwards, the author's father, served in the Quorum of Twelve Apostles for more than twenty-three years and was married to Fred M.'s daughter, Alice. Paul Edwards's writings reflect his affection for his grandfather; indeed, many stories are first-person accounts. In addition to serving at times as a participant-observer, he astutely analyzes and interprets Fred M.'s sometimes controversial efforts to make his religious institution into a modern church (272).

Roger D. Launius contributed the second volume to the ADMINISTRATIVE BIOGRAPHY SERIES. With a tighter focus, Launius retraced his steps from his earlier works on the subject and produced *Father Figure: Joseph Smith III and the Creation of the Reorganized Church* (Independence: Herald House, 1990). Here Launius argued that "by background, temperament, training, and, in some instances, clairvoyance, [Joseph Smith III] charted a cautious, practical, and basically moderate course for a people" (12). He analyzed the success of young Smith's leadership style in forging a new religious institution and in shepherding the Reorganized Church for fifty-four years.

Norma Derry Hiles produced the third work in the ADMINISTRATIVE BIOGRAPHY SERIES. With Fred M.'s successor, Israel Alexander Smith, as her subject in *Gentle Monarch: The Presidency of Israel A. Smith* (Independence: Herald House, 1991), Hiles offered a warm biography of the least-researched and least well-known president of the Reorganized Church. Unfortunately, only three of the eight chapters explored the uncharted terrain of Israel Smith's presidential administration lasting from 1946 to 1958. An epilogue of five memory tributes concluded *Gentle Monarch*, with a statement from his half-brother and presidential successor W. Wallace Smith, who "looked to my big brother with respect and admiration" (197). Although Hiles charted a narrow path, serious historical analysis of the crucial years of Israel A. Smith and his contribution to Reorganized Latter Day Saintism still remains.

Maurice L. Draper contributed the fourth book to the series with his *The Founding Prophet: An Administrative Biography of Joseph Smith, Jr.* (Independence: Herald House, 1991). In it, he mapped out the origins and development of Latter Day Saintism by examining Joseph the Seer's role in major aspects of life in the early Church. Draper's credentials as a former member of the Quorum of Twelve Apostles and counselor in the First Presidency added to his writing the interesting dimension of someone who had wrestled with similar administrative issues. His twelfth chapter highlighting the missionary fervor of the early Saints was particularly effective. Draper wrote with a seasoned understanding of the historical and theological issues inherent with his subject and exemplified principles of the New Mormon History by articulating his personal biases at various points so that the reader could evaluate their impact. For example, when introducing the theological issue of premortal existence, a significant Nauvoo doctrine that went west with Brigham Young but did not thrive in the Reorganization, Draper stated: "I personally find such ideas to be theologically unsound and irrational" (188). Written in an engaging style, *The Founding Prophet* is an excellent addition to the ADMINISTRATIVE BIOGRAPHY SERIES.

General Surveys

Responding to the influences of the New Mormon History movement, general agreement arose on the need to replace Inez Smith Davis's well-loved but quite outdated *The Story of the Church: A History of the Church of Jesus Christ of Latter Day Saints, and of Its Legal Successor, the Reorganized Church* (Independence: Herald House, 1934), still in print as late as 1985. Historians Paul M. Edwards and Richard P. Howard responded to the need for a general survey of Church history that could reinterpret the Reorganized Church story using modern historical methodology. In the popular *Our Legacy of Faith: A Brief History of the Reorganized Church of Jesus Christ of Latter Day Saints* (Independence: Herald House, 1991), Edwards surveyed the church story from its historical setting in post-revolutionary America to the 1980s. He also included a valuable appendix of important events in Church history and a list of World Church leaders.

As a capstone to his career as church historian, Richard Howard produced his *The Church through the Years*, 2 vols. (Independence: Herald House, 1992, 1993). Howard's first volume began with an insightful explanation of the contribution that the discipline of history makes in the reader's life. Eloquently, Howard explained his purpose: "The capacity to be thankful for our heritage rests in the power of memory. A central purpose of these pages is to help the Church remember the lives, struggles, hopes, and joys of those who make up our history. Let us be glad for the faith and the good works of those who sacrificed, toiled, and rejoiced in one another to create and keep alive this household of faith" (1:20).

Howard began Volume 2 with the search of first-generation "Josephites" for Restoration members lost in the decade and a half after the Martyr's death, and concluded with an exploration of issues surrounding the construction of the Independence Temple. An appendix included the five sections of the Doctrine and Covenants that appeared in a separate historical appendix in the 1970 edition but were removed by action of the Church's 1990 World Conference. Howard also added W. Wallace Smith's letter of instruction related to his resignation as prophet-president of the Reorganized Church. Finally, Howard's selected readings section is thorough and comprehensive. Perhaps the greatest weakness of Howard's two-volume work is found in its limited index. Nevertheless, *The Church Through the Years* remains the best general work that focuses on the Reorganized Church story.

The Reorganized Church and the Theme of Dissent

Clare D. Vlahos, in "The Challenge to Centralized Power: Zenas H. Gurley, Jr., and The Prophetic Office," *Courage: Journal of History, Thought, and Action* 1, no. 3 (March 1971): 141-58, laid the groundwork for discussing the recurring theme of dissension. Vlahos used Gurley's challenge to Joseph III's authority in the early 1880s to demonstrate the controversial nature of prophetic power in leading the Church.

Tensions surrounding the exercise of prophetic authority became the focus of attention for Reorganized Church members a decade later. The 1980s were the most turbulent period in the history of the Community of Christ, not even excepting Fred M.'s controversial drive for "supreme directional control." That the Reorganized Church history community should reflect this theme of dissent in their scholarship is not surprising. Mormonism suffered shattering schisms after the death of the Prophet Joseph Smith in June 1844. During these difficult times, many individuals in various leadership positions testified of being divinely ordained or prophetically appointed to lead the Restoration movement. These movements emphasized different aspects of the institutional structure and theology that evolved from Palmyra, New York. Historian Steven L. Shields skillfully charted the histories and theologies of these various churches in *Divergent Paths of the Restoration*, 4th rev. ed. (Los Angeles: Restoration Research, 1990).

Other historians also recognized the 1980s as a decade of disruption. Roger D. Launius and W. B. "Pat" Spillman coedited *Let Contention Cease: The Dynamics of Dissent in the Reorganized Church of Jesus Christ of Latter Day Saints* (Independence: Graceland/Park Press, 1991.) The nine essays in this book analyzed various aspects of religious dissent, particularly in the context of the Reorganized Church. To inform the reader of the long-standing tradition of dissent within the movement that officially reorganized in Amboy, Illinois, on April 6, 1860, Spillman observed, "The Reorganized Church of Jesus Christ of Latter Day Saints began as an organization of dissenters—those who disagreed with others who claimed to inherit the prophetic mantle after the assassination of Joseph Smith, Jr. Since its earliest days, members of the church have cherished their independence of thought and freedom of expression" (10). Launius and Spillman successfully represented the broad spectrum of opinions on the controversial issue of dissent.

Roger D. Launius expanded his 1991 project on RLDS dissent to the larger history of the Mormon movement in *Differing Visions: Dissenters in Mormon History* (Urbana: University of Illinois Press, 1994) with coeditor Linda Thatcher. They solicited essays from scholars within RLDS, LDS, and unaffiliated history communities, who mined numerous research repositories for little-known information about the leaders of separatist movements. In his foreword to *Differing Visions,* Leonard J. Arrington introduced the reader to common themes such as the various interpretations of Joseph Smith's life and death, the range of motivations for separation (usually not self-serving), and the phenomenon that those who had once associated with the Restoration movement, even as dissenters could seldom fully reject it (x-xi). *Differing Visions* is a crucial work in understanding the historical context of dissent as a key characteristic of Latter Day Saintism.

Conflict between Mormonism and the "old settler" culture surrounding Nauvoo in the early 1840s became the focus of *Cultures in Conflict: A Documentary History of the Mormon War in Illinois* edited by John E. Hallwas and Roger D. Launius (Logan: Utah State University Press, 1995). The editors used nearly a hundred historical documents to reveal dimensions of the clash between these two divergent cultures in western Hancock County, Illinois. Arranged in chronological order, the documents were divided into six periods within the era: the coming of the Mormons, the origins of the conflict, the trouble in Nauvoo, the murders in Carthage, the trial of the accused assassins and vigilante violence against outlying settlements, and the exodus in February 1846 and the battle of Nauvoo in September 1846. Hallwas and Launius explored regional archives and personal papers of contemporary individuals, some of which had never been published before, to present a well-balanced contemporary understanding by and about Illinois's mid-nineteenth-century Mormons who lived within their separatist community. A valuable historical and interpretive headnote prefaces each document. In their introduction, Hallwas and Launius criticized leading Mormon scholars for their orthodox approach to the Mormon dilemma at Nauvoo, stating that the standard religious persecution theme only partially explained the murders of Joseph and Hyrum Smith. Rather, "conflict between these groups arose because of their strikingly different cultural values. The experience of people in Hancock County during the 1840s demonstrates the inevitable conflict between theocratic and democratic government, the danger of demonizing other people, and the self-deceptions fostered by the myths of innocence and political righteousness" (8).

The same two historians again joined forces to collect previously published essays in *Kingdom on the Mississippi Revisited: Nauvoo in Mormon History* (Urbana: University of Illinois Press, 1996). Launius and Hallwas selected fourteen essays representing the best scholarship on the Mormons of the Mississippi River town. Because the Reorganized Church holds the "elect lady" in such high esteem, many in the RLDS history community may see "The Lion and the Lady: Brigham Young and Emma Smith" by Valeen Tippetts Avery and Linda King Newell (198-213) as the best essay in the collection (originally printed in the *Utah Historical Quarterly* 48 [Winter 1980]: 81-97.) Avery and Newell recounted the struggle, courage, and persistence that Emma Hale Smith Bidamon exhibited in the difficult years after the murder of her husband. An exhaustive bibliographic essay on secondary sources at the end of the book (251-67) provided added value to the work.

Makers of Church Thought Series

The Makers of Church Thought Series is a collection of extended essays about five men who brought leadership skills to the Reorganization in very important ways. Series editor Paul M. Edwards again launched this series and modeled the collection of works with *F. Henry Edwards: Articulator for the Church* (Independence: Herald House, 1995). Edwards, this time writing about his father, introduces his topic by describing how he searched for the proper appellation. He looked past "theologian," "doctrinaire," "historian," and "apologist," and chose "articulator," because F. Henry Edwards gave "words to the strongly held but hazily understood beliefs of his generation of Church members" (10). Paul Edwards included a thirty-five-page list of books and articles written by his father to document the powerful influence F. Henry had on the evolution of church thought. The author concluded: "[F. Henry Edwards's] writings and addresses cover the intellectual history of the movement for half a century. The impact of his contribution is observable today both in the doctrine of the movement and in the lives of those people for whom he was a significant aid in the formation of their own beliefs" (125).

Alan D. Tyree wrote *Evan Fry: Proclaimer of Good News* (Independence: Herald House, 1995), the second volume in the MAKERS OF CHURCH THOUGHT series. Evan Fry was a prominent radio minister for the RLDS Church from 1938 until just before his death in 1958. A contemporary of F. Henry Edwards, Fry offered the Church his gift of "presenting complex ideas in simple language and through illustrations that endeared him to his audience" (7). Tyree argued that Fry, though blazing no new theological paths for the Reorganized Church, became "the Church's best-known proclaimer of the gospel" (9).

Henry K. Inouye, *Roy A. Cheville: Explorer of Spiritual Frontiers* (Independence: Herald House, 1996), the third volume in the MAKERS OF CHURCH THOUGHT series, offered more than just a monographic biography of a Reorganized Church leader. Inouye placed Cheville in the context of twentieth-century Latter Day Saint history. Far more theoretical than the other series authors, Inouye demonstrated his training in religious philosophy in his analysis of Cheville's theology. However, at times, the focus on Cheville got lost in Inouye's discussions of process theology, existentialism, rationalism, and personal relations with the Cosmic Personality (81).

The fourth volume of the MAKERS OF CHURCH THOUGHT series, *Arthur A. Oakman: An Artist with Words* (Independence: Herald House, 1997) by Maurice L. Draper, added significantly to an understanding of the architects of modern church beliefs. Consistent with other series authors' approaches to their subjects, Draper argued that the greatest contribution that this long-serving apostle made to the Reorganization was in his ability to communicate with the membership. Draper wrote: "Oakman's verbal artistry was best demonstrated in his oral expressions, as in preaching, lecturing, and prophetic utterances. Voice inflections, posture and gestures, and facial expressions accompanying his choice of words added to the motivational power of delivery. His persuasive public address style stimulated his hearers to share his faith commitments long after the specific content of his message might have been forgotten" (17).

Instead of using a chronological format in his exploration of Oakman's ministry, Draper presented Oakman's views on a variety of theological subjects, including the nature of the deity, incarnation, revelation, and foundations of the faith, just to name a few. Although claiming this approach as Oakman's preference (21), Draper thereby sacrificed the valuable historical contextualization of his subject.

Wayne Ham's study, *Geoffrey F. Spencer: Advocate for an Enlightened Faith* (Independence: Herald House, 1998), focused on the significant contribution of one of the Reorganized Church's leading thinkers. Ham acknowledged Spencer's preference to avoid being considered a trained theologian. Instead Spencer "endeavored to discern the significant elements in the contemporary experience of the church and to state these in each situation with sufficient reasonableness and clarity that they could provide the basis for a consensus among church leaders" (10). This work is the fifth, and most recent, book of the MAKERS OF CHURCH THOUGHT series.

General Interest Works

The significant contribution by Community of Christ to the New Mormon History movement can be seen throughout the historical landscape. The scholarship of L. Madelon Brunson, Barbara Hands Bernauer, Isleta L. Pement, Paul M. Edwards, and Roger D. Launius is representative of this contribution. These intellectuals have produced a number of leading studies.

Excavating Mormon Pasts

Madelon Brunson's excellent study of the role of women in the early years of Mormonism and the Reorganization in *Bonds of Sisterhood: A History of the RLDS Women's Organization, 1842-1893* (Independence: Herald House, 1985) was very timely. Brunson, then RLDS Church archivist, published her work at the time of the first ordination of women into the RLDS priesthood. In *Bonds of Sisterhood,* she identified the female experience in the Reorganization as a paradox—women were integrated into the organization and essential aspects of the church, yet they were excluded from decision making (9). Brunson argued that, as women determined their own participation in the church, some responded with the fear that their actions threatened the Church structure. In her research, Brunson found, "The sisters did not intend damage to the institution or infringement of the priesthood system. Some of the women, however, believed exclusion of half the membership from substantial activities paralyzed the church as the body of Christ" (12-13). In *Bonds of Sisterhood,* Brunson provided the best historical treatment on women's participation in early Mormonism and the Reorganized Church.

Barbara Hands Bernauer, assistant archivist in the Community of Christ Library-Archives, investigated the mystery and discovery of the actual burial location of Joseph the Seer, and his brother, Hyrum. Appropriately titled, "Still 'Side by Side': The Final Burial of Joseph and Hyrum Smith," *John Whitmer Historical Association Journal* 11 (1991): 17-33, Bernauer received acclaim for this superior research and writing when her article won the John Whitmer Historical Association's Best Article award in 1992. Two years later, she published her extensive essay in booklet format, and it remains the definitive work on this topic. An added personal dimension guided her research since Bernauer is the granddaughter of W. O. Hands who supervised the 1928 archaeological dig in Nauvoo.

Any discussion of Community of Christ historians traveling the New Mormon History trail must include a statement on the Church's official publisher. Although its name has changed somewhat over the decades and is now Herald House, its historic name is Herald Publishing House. Isleta L. Pement and Paul M. Edwards coauthored *A Herald to the Saints: History of Herald Publishing House* (Independence: Herald House, 1992), in which they argued that, beginning with the day when Joseph Smith Jr. and Oliver Cowdery first carried the Book of Mormon manuscript into the printing establishment of Egbert B. Grandin in Palmyra, New York, every generation of Latter Day Saintism has realized the communicative value of the written word. From their extensive research, Pement and Edwards concluded that, although publishing technology has gone through dramatic changes, the original purpose of the Herald Publishing House—to serve as a natural viaduct to the people—has changed very little (10-11). The authors showed that Herald Publishing House has played an indispensable role for the history-minded in the Community of Christ since the vast majority of the New Mormon History scholarship emerged from its presses.

Roger D. Launius, *Alexander William Doniphan: Portrait of a Missouri Moderate* (Columbia: University of Missouri Press, 1997), offered a fresh look at one of the most important figures in Missouri's pre-Civil War history. Doniphan was a "household name" after the 1846 war with Mexico that paved the way for annexing the territory that eventually became New Mexico and Arizona. Launius argued that Doniphan charted a path of moderation in the face of the social extremism that surrounded him (xii-xiii). Those who have studied the history of Latter Day Saintism know well that Doniphan's moderation saved Joseph Smith from execution at Far West in 1838; but Launius showed how this important event was but one demonstration of a lifelong pursuit of accommodation without compromise of personal principles. Launius's best example of this characteristic was Doniphan's effort to mediate compromise between unionists and slave owners at the state and national levels. Launius described Doniphan's dejection as the Civil War broke out during the spring and summer of 1861:

> [Doniphan] had worked . . . to preserve peace and to secure the rights of all sides in the sectional conflict. This effort had come to very little. Missouri did not secede,

and he believed that was the right decision, but it brought no serenity to his soul. With a foot in both camps, passionately in favor of the Union and believing in its highest ideals while maintaining his proslavery leanings, Doniphan wrestled with his conscience over the crisis and his response to it. [A]ll he could do was to declare neutrality, work for justice as he understood it, and long for peace. (254)

With this scholarly treatise, Launius reminded the reader of the importance of seeing the history of Latter Day Saintism in the larger context of American history.

Scholarly Historical Journals and Articles

It is impossible to review adequately over thirty years of journal scholarship by historians associated with the Reorganized Church. The panorama of topics is simply too vast. This section provides a small, but representative, sample of pivotal journal articles on historical topics. The criteria for this selection centered on interpretations that either initiated or accompanied shifts in the understanding of historic events. Not surprisingly, these articles generated initial controversy but gained general acceptance over time. This is not to suggest a complete agreement among the membership of the Reorganized Church on these interpretations, but it does acknowledge each author's significant contribution to his or her specific field of inquiry.

Courage: A Journal of History, Thought, and Action

Coinciding with the New Mormon History movement, three important journals served as venues for innovative interpretations. The first journal, *Courage: A Journal of History, Thought, and Action,* published its pilot issue in April 1970 as a means of expression for independent thought. *Courage* had no official connection with either the RLDS Church or Graceland College even though it was published in Lamoni, Iowa. *Courage* was edited, however, by individuals associated with the RLDS Church who were convinced that a free discussion of issues was necessary for the well-being of the Church and its members.
The editorial committee of *Courage* announced these intentions in "Critical Function of Courage," *Courage: A Journal of History, Thought, and Action*, pilot issue (April 1970): 49-52. Financial deficits ended the venture in 1973. Still, *Courage* was the crucible in which future intellectual journals associated with the Reorganized Church would be forged.

Courage hosted several leading articles in Church history during its three-year lifespan. For example, Richard P. Howard in "The 'Book of Abraham' in the Light of History and Egyptology," *Courage,* pilot issue (April 1970): 33-47, suggested that the interesting work "represents simply the product of Joseph Smith, Jr.'s imagination, wrought out in the midst of what to him must have been a very crucial and demanding and complex set of circumstances" (45). Howard concluded by encouraging scholars to recognize the integrity of the Book of Abraham as a historical fact, while at the same time purging its associations of historicity.

Richard Howard, "Latter Day Saint Scriptures and the Doctrine of Propositional Revelation," *Courage* 1, no. 4 (June 1971): 209-25, was a second crucial article, appearing when professional standards of analysis were being applied to Church history and theology. Howard, as both the Church's historian and leading scriptorian, highlighted the inherent problems of scriptural inerrancy and provided a primary voice in a Churchwide discussion on the issue.

Wayne Ham, "Problems in Interpreting the Book of Mormon as History," *Courage* 1, no. 2 (September 1970): 15-22, challenged readers to openly espouse a nonhistorical view of the Book of Mormon. In presenting nine specific criticisms in such areas as the story of the book's coming forth, narrative, propensity to reflect in detail the religious concerns of the American frontier, the developed Christological perspectives, ethical implications as binding upon all, use of biblical passages, specific use of Isaiah, anachronisms, and changes in later editions, Ham demonstrated the difficulties of considering the Book of Mormon as literal history. In his conclusion, Ham called for liberating the Book of Mormon from traditional problems associated with accepting it unquestioningly as a pure and undefiled history. Instead, Ham observed that seeing the Book of Mormon as "a product of the American frontier" to be honored as "an interesting artifact of the Restoration movement in the nineteenth century" allowed it to be enjoyed as a "fascinating piece of literature for the very first time" (21).

W. B. "Pat" Spillman, "On Conceptualization of Zion," *Courage* 3, no. 1 (Fall 1972): 37-43, contributed new understandings about the meaning of "Zion" in both its theological and historical contexts. Spillman identified three distinct conceptions of Zion within Reorganized Latter Day Saintism: a city, a condition in the hearts and minds of the people, and a process of becoming. He did not argue any specific viewpoint but called for constant reinterpretation in the context of Zion's meaning to each generation.

Restoration Studies

Since 1980, historians associated with the Community of Christ have used *Restoration Studies: A Collection of Essays about the History, Beliefs, and Practices of the Reorganized Church of Jesus Christ of Latter Day Saints* to publish their research and findings. This publication has served for almost twenty years as a valuable forum to express, as well as to challenge, orthodoxy over the range of matters listed in the journal's subtitle. Various scholars have served on the editorial board that supervised production of its eight volumes, published as occasional papers rather than on a fixed schedule. From the first volume produced in association with the 1980 sesquicentennial celebration of the movement, articles were selected on the basis of their contribution to "pursue of truth 'wherever it may lead,'" as Maurice L. Draper, editor of the first volume, expressed it (9).

Several significant *Restoration Studies* articles have had lasting impact on the journey taken by Church history community. Richard P. Howard, "Joseph Smith's First Vision: An Analysis of Six Contemporary Accounts," *Restoration Studies I* (1980): 95-117, set the tone in the Community of Christ for reinterpreting events in the early Restoration years. Howard's account added significantly to the work on the same topic by other notable historians such as Fawn M. Brodie and Dean C. Jessee. After weighing six different portrayals of Joseph Smith Jr.'s experience in the grove by using a rubric of fourteen criteria, Howard noted the specific differences in each account. Then, he cautioned against oversimplification and directly denied the validity of using his research as ammunition for either attack or defense. Instead, he concluded that the varying explanations point out the complexities associated with "interpreting events that are beyond history" (116-17).

One *Restoration Studies* article, written for the sesquicentennial edition, made history itself in addition to providing an authoritative account of presidential succession in the Reorganized Church. D. Michael Quinn, "The Mormon Succession Crisis of 1844," *BYU Studies* 16 (Winter 1976): 187-233, had earlier identified eight succession concepts that Joseph the Seer had at least partially implemented during his lifetime. W. Grant McMurray, "'True Son of a True Father': Joseph Smith III and the Succession Question," *Restoration Studies I* (1980): 131-145, summarized relevant points from Quinn's article. Then, McMurray described the pivotal revelatory experiences of Jason W. Briggs and Zenas H. Gurley Sr. in southern Wisconsin during the fall of 1851, that led to the creation of the "New Organization," a small gathering of saints yearning for a president who would be a lineal descendant of Joseph the Seer. The most obvious candidate was Joseph III, his oldest son. After a description of "Young Joseph's" hesitation to assume the prophetic mantle, McMurray, who was Richard Howard's Assistant History Commissioner, described key events that led to Joseph III's ordination, the issues Smith saw as central to succession, and the role of lineage in RLDS succession. The title comes from Joseph III's August 1861 "First General Epistle of the President," *True Latter Day Saints' Herald* 2 (August 1861): 121-24. The twenty-eight-year-old prophet referred to himself as "a true son of a true father" as he launched his fifty-four-year tenure as the first prophet-president of the Reorganized Church. Sixteen years after this article's publication, McMurray made history in his own right by beginning his tenure as the sixth prophet-president of the Reorganization, the first non-Smith to hold that office.

John Whitmer Historical Association

Since its beginning in 1972, the John Whitmer Historical Association (JWHA) has provided Community of Christ historians, and those affiliated with other religious movements, a forum for sharing the fruits of their research in an annual conference. JWHA's independent status from any religious institution has allowed for free scholarly exploration of historical issues. Numerous papers from these conferences have been published in its annual *Journal,* which first appeared in 1981. Over the years, many controversial issues have been aired here, still a lively tradition. Again, space limitations allow the mention of only a few benchmark essays that have strongly impacted historical thought among those affiliated with the Reorganization.

Richard P. Howard, "The Changing RLDS Response to Mormon Polygamy: A Preliminary Analysis," *John Whitmer Historical Association Journal* 3 (1983): 14-29, was a history-making article since it courageously moved away from the traditional RLDS position that Joseph the Martyr was not the author of Nauvoo polygamy. Howard, as Church historian, revealed the diversity of responses to polygamy in the early Reorganization, then explained the factors influencing the development of polygamy in Nauvoo. After a brief discussion of responses from both the gentile and Mormon communities, Howard provided a nine-point summary. He referred to strong evidence that the entrance of polygamy into the Mormon community at Nauvoo was "accidental" because the situation of deceased spouses had not been foreseen in the development of temple "sealing" rituals in either Kirtland or Far West. Howard concluded: "Once Joseph Smith, Jr., came to see the harm being done to the church, he sought the help of [William] Marks to use all their combined power to put down polygamy in the church. However, by that time things had gone too far" (25). Even though Howard concluded that extant evidence only indirectly connected Joseph the Seer to the actual initiation of Nauvoo polygamy, such a conclusion caused much controversy among some RLDS members, especially when, three years later, his article was reprinted under the same title in *Restoration Studies III* (Independence: Herald House, 1986): 145-62.

Don H. Compier, "The Faith of Emma Smith," *John Whitmer Historical Association Journal* 6 (1986): 64-72, was part of the JWHA spring lecture series in 1986; but his work assumed increased importance because of the ordination of women, accepted by RLDS World Conference action in 1984 with the first ordinations occurring a year later. Compier highlighted Emma Smith's strong influence in the evolution of Mormonism particularly during the difficult Nauvoo years and the emergence of the Reorganization. The first half of the article focused on the powerful presence of Methodism in Emma's early life and how Emma expressed that religious influence in the development of the Word of Wisdom, charitable and quasi-political activities through the Female Relief Society of Nauvoo, and especially in the Elect Lady's demand for marital loyalty. According to Compier, Emma expressed her commitment to Latter Day Saintism after the martyrdom by affirming the validity of the Book of Mormon, her love for Joseph Jr., and her strenuous efforts to publish the New Translation of the Bible (66-67).

Also, Community of Christ president W. Grant McMurray chose the *JWHA Journal* to respond to critiques of the historical enterprise that impinged on identity issues for the Church that had been made earlier by historian Roger D. Launius, "The Reorganized Church, the Decade of Decision, and the Abilene Paradox," *Dialogue: A Journal of Mormon Thought* 31 (Spring 1998): 47-65, philosopher Paul M. Edwards, "Christ-Centered Boredom: History and Historians," *JWHA Journal* 18 (1998): 21-37), and sociologist Danny L. Jorgensen, "Beyond Modernity: The Future of the RLDS Church," *JWHA Journal* 18 (1998): 5-20. In "History and Mission in Tension: A View from Both Sides," *JWHA Journal* 20 (2000): 34-47, McMurray charted the interaction between his years of service as Assistant Church Historian, World Church Secretary, and then as a member of the First Presidency with his training in historical methodology and noted a distinctive tension. McMurray exposed the inherent problems of incorporating history and mission into scholarly writings and acknowledged a point "where the work of the historian ends and the work of the theologian begins." In addressing his critics, McMurray counseled historians to be "acutely aware of motivations and predilections" to confuse history and theology, particularly in the examination of the relationship between faith, history, and mission.

The closing session of Thirtieth Annual Meeting of the John Whitmer Historical Association at Nauvoo, Illinois, in late September 2002, was titled, "The Singing Saints: A Festival of Hymns and Hymnody." Conference attendees participated in a hymnfest led by Richard Clothier, Junia Braby, and Brett Jagger. Participants representing a variety of Latter Day Saint traditions gave background readings to specially selected historical hymns. Where possible, original music scores were used. In a historic first, the program was preserved on a CD and inserted into the back cover of the special conference edition.

A highlight of JWHA conferences is the Sterling M. McMurrin Lecture Series delivered in commemoration of an amazing LDS scholar and educator, who divided his academic career between the philosophy and history departments at the University of Utah, served as U.S. Commissioner of Education in John F. Kennedy's administration, and wrote two influential and so far unreplaced treatises, *The Philosophical Foundations of Mormon Theology* (Salt Lake City: University of Utah Press, 1959), and *The Theological Foundations of the Mormon Religion* (Salt Lake City: University of Utah Press, 1965). Paul M. Edwards, in "Christ-Centered Boredom: History and Historians," launched this plenary session presentation as an endowed lecture in the 1997 annual meeting. Since then Richard P. Howard, Mario S. De Pillis, Stephen C. LeSueur, and D. Michael Quinn have used the McMurrin Lecture as a forum to challenge thinking and to blaze trails into new fields of study. Most memorable was the sixth annual lecture presented by Robert Bruce Flanders, "Nauvoo on My Mind," *JWHA Journal* 23 (2003): 13-20. Given in Nauvoo, Illinois, on the thirtieth anniversary of the history association, Flanders reflected on his own career since his tenure as the first president of the association in 1972. He encouraged listeners to see the history of Nauvoo as more than just a controversial episode in the Church story; rather, Nauvoo was a "genetic marker" of Church identity to be continually explored for new understandings.

John Whitmer Historical Association Monograph Series

Another valuable literary source sponsored by the John Whitmer Historical Association is its Monograph Series. JWHA provided this forum for historical research projects that range between article and book length. Only two monographs have been published so far in this series, both by LDS historians. First, Marjorie Newton, *Hero or Traitor?: A Biographical Study of Charles Wesley Wandell* (Independence: Independence Press, 1992) focused on the missionary most responsible for founding both the LDS and RLDS churches in Australia. Second, Gregory A. Prince, *Having Authority: The Origins and Development of Priesthood During the Ministry of Joseph Smith* (Independence: Independence Press, 1993), is the best treatment on the Mormon bicameral priesthood in its historical setting. A third monograph by Matthew Bolton, *Charles Neff: Missionary and Humanitarian* (John Whitmer Historical Association) is in progress. Bolton's biography will chronicle the late RLDS apostle's early life, conversion to the Church, rise to Church leadership, and pivotal role in the Church's worldwide expansion in the 1960s and 1970s. The author will also show how Neff's experience as a naval officer in World War II and his missionary work among the poor in the developing world fostered a deep social conscience, leading him to found several humanitarian organizations, like the Community of Christ-sponsored Outreach International, and to challenge the causes of human suffering throughout the world.

Academic Capstone Projects

Several capstone academic works make worthy contributions to Community of Christ historical scholarship—three are representative. In 2003 Kimberly L. Loving completed his Master of Arts in Religion degree through Graceland University, Lamoni, Iowa, by authoring "Ownership of the Kirtland Temple: Legends, Lies, and Misunderstandings." This scholarly study delved into the context of the events by which the Reorganized Church of Jesus Christ of Latter Day Saints legally acquired title to House of the Lord in Kirtland, Ohio. Loving combined his legal skills with historical methodology to provide a unique view of the litigation. This study of the actual judicial findings dispelled a long-established myth that emerged after the litigation by claiming that the legitimacy of ownership rests solely on principles of property abandonment, and for no other reason. Thus, this historical analysis of the Kirtland Temple litigation of 1879 and 1880 substantiated neither the traditional claim of the legitimacy of Joseph Smith III's presidential succession, nor the assertion that Reorganized Church of Jesus Christ of Latter Day Saints wrested ownership from the Church of Jesus Christ of Latter Day Saints. This article is forthcoming in the *Journal of Mormon History* 30, no. 2 (Fall 2004).

In 1995 Richard A. Waugh completed his doctor of philosophy degree in geography at the University of Wisconsin—Madison. His dissertation, "Sacred Space and the Persistence of Identity: The Evolution and Meaning of an American Religious Utopia," examined the development of sacred space within the RLDS Church. In this fascinating study, Waugh assessed such concepts as Zion and the construction and placement of temples using postmodern criteria.

A third academic capstone project is my "A Material Cultural Analysis of the Foundational History of Latter Day Saintism, 1827-1844" (Ph.D. diss., University of Missouri at Kansas City, 1998). This work is a qualitative, interdisciplinary exploration of early nineteenth-century material culture and educational practices. It documents that early Church members practiced a "language of Latter Day Saintism" in their choice of architectural styles as well as in their educational institutions and practices and argues that Joseph Smith Jr. launched his movement by observing an important principle of material culture studies when he included the testimonies of witnesses who "saw and touched" the Book of Mormon plates: "seeing is believing, but feeling is truth." Three fields of inquiry in the study of material culture—structuralism, symbolism, and functionalism—provide a framework for this analysis.

Works in Progress

New Mormon History frontiers are still being explored by those associated with Community of Christ history community. Three manuscripts are forthcoming from Graceland University history professor William D. Russell. The first, tentatively titled *"Repent or Be Destroyed": The 1989 Cult Murders in Kirtland, Ohio,* explores how cult leader Jeffrey Lundgren gathered a small but devout group of followers, the religious sources he used to persuade others of his beliefs, his mounting extremism, and how more than a dozen adults eventually participated in, or acquiesced to, Lundgren's murder of five people. Russell's second work focuses on schism in the RLDS Church from 1958 to the present. This book seeks to explain how the RLDS Church has moved from sect to denomination in the period since the 1958 ordination of W. Wallace Smith, grandson of Joseph Smith Jr., and some of the groups who have resisted that movement. The third, tentatively titled *Homosexual Saints: The Community of Christ Experience* begins with a historical introduction to more than thirty personal experiences contributed by members of the Community of Christ who have negotiated a broad range of solutions to their sexual orientation within their faith movement.

In addition to his work on the Far West period of LDS history, Michael S. Riggs—though not a baptized member of the Community of Christ, certainly a kindred spirit—is researching in two unrelated fields of historical Latter Day Saintism. His first focus is on the disaffection of Jason W. Briggs and Zenas H. Gurley Jr. Riggs offers the term "emerging second-generational RLDS theology" to describe Joseph III's strategy of "outliving his opposition." He first broached this topic in "'His Word Was as Good as His Note': The Impact of Justus Morse's Mormonism(s) on His Families," " *JWHA Journal* 17 (1997): 49-80. Riggs's second interest is the influence of folk magic in the Cutlerite movement. Strongly persuaded by sociologist Danny L. Jorgensen about the importance of the Cutlerite movement to the history of Latter Day Saintism, Riggs found influential the magisterial work, D. Michael Quinn, *Early Mormonism and the Magical World View* (1987; rev. ed., Salt Lake City: Signature Books, 1998) establishing a folk magic milieu for earlier Mormonism. However, to his mind, John L. Brooke, *The Refiner's Fire: The Making of Mormon Cosmology, 1644-1844* (New York: Cambridge University Press, 1994), pushed Mormonism's occult connections beyond credibility by denying that the early Mormons were not influenced theologically by Puritanism. Against this background, Riggs is studying the mystical dimensions of the Cutlerite worldview and its impact on the RLDS Church. Since early Reorganized Church missionaries had great success among the Cutlerites, these new converts brought with them their hermetic beliefs. Thus, Riggs is dealing with the question: To what extent did this Cutlerite folk magic influence the Josephite Church?

Also, Ronald E. Romig, Community of Christ Church archivist, continues to explore and publish on early Church experiences relating to the Missouri period, mapping early Church sites, stewardship, and early Church visual materials. In her work in progress "Gathering the Remnants: Establishing the RLDS Church in Southwestern Iowa," Community of Christ Church Assistant Archivist Barbara H. Bernauer is researching the beginnings of the RLDS Church in southwestern Iowa, 1859-70. Because of the large concentration of LDS members who either did not go to Utah or who "backtrailed," early RLDS missionaries had great success in "gathering the remnants." Christin Craft Mackay and Lachlan Mackay, "The Kirtland Temple: A Time of Transition, 1838-1880," *John Whitmer Historical Association Journal* 18 (1998): 133-48, focuses on the Kirtland Temple after the general Mormon exodus from Kirtland.

Conclusion

Bibliographic essays, like the stream of time, are without beginning and without end. A flood of scholarship occurred before and after the scope of this writing. It is a daunting task to attempt historiographical coverage of over thirty years of scholarship in such a brief essay. Just as sculptors reveal much about themselves as about their subject, this essay portrays some of the stronger influences on my personal exploration of the Latter Day Saint story from the perspective of historians associated with the Community of Christ. I caution readers against concluding that, because a certain article or book is not mentioned, the work is neither influential nor meritorious. Rather, this chapter reveals the need for further comprehensive and unbiased studies of historical literature on Latter Day Saintism, especially those that provide a more in-depth focus on the history of the Reorganized Church now called the Community of Christ. In important ways, and through resources such as these, this Church history community has made a significant contributions by blazing trails across the New Mormon History field of inquiry.

MARK A. SCHERER is Church Historian for the Community of Christ, is completing his service on the council of the Mormon History Association, and is president of the John Whitmer Historical Association. His published articles have appeared in the *Herald* (official organ of the Community of Christ), *Journal of Mormon History, Sunstone,* and the *John Whitmer Historical Journal.*

Chapter 12

The New Mormon Women's History

Todd Compton

An important aspect of the New Mormon History has always been its interest in women's history. In fact, many of its practitioners have been and are women. In the "old Mormon history" (before such "new history" pioneers as Brooks and Arrington), one is hard pressed to name one woman historian who wrote using professional standards of research, writing, and scholarship, though many women wrote memoirs, diaries, and character sketches that are historical and literary jewels. However, in the New Mormon History women and women's history play a prominent part.[1] When Leonard Arrington, perhaps the central figure in the New Mormon History, described the limitations of the former Mormon history, the second of five major biases he identified was "the male bias."[2] He wrote, "Anyone who spends a substantial amount of time going through the materials in church archives must gain a new appreciation of the important and indispensable role of women in the history of the LDS church—not to mention new insights into church history resulting from viewing it through the eyes of women." The "male bias" may be especially marked in Mormon culture, in which the main structure of an authoritarian church leadership is exclusively male and in which male priesthood authority is a basic Church doctrine. (In modern mainstream Mormonism, priesthood is still viewed as an exclusively male prerogative.)

Mormon women's history thus is closely connected with the woman's movement in Mormonism, and Mormon women's history has been one of the most controversial strands of the New Mormon History. Since a basic axiom of feminism is that women should have rights and opportunities that are equal with men's, the women's movement—which would expect that women should have full equality within the Church, and thus priesthood opportunities—has been viewed with suspicion by the Church hierarchy. Women's history in the New Mormon History has given support to those women who see the need for women to hold expanded opportunities and rights—including, for some,

---

1. Roger D. Launius, "The 'New Social History' and the 'New Mormon History': Reflections on Recent Trends," *Dialogue: A Journal of Mormon Thought* 27 (Spring 1994): 109-27, 122-26; Thomas G. Alexander, "Toward the New Mormon History: An Examination of the Literature on the Latter-day Saints in the Far West," in *Historians and the American West*, edited by Michael P. Malone (Lincoln: University of Nebraska Press, 1983), 344-68, 357.

2. Leonard J. Arrington, "The Search for Truth and Meaning in Mormon History," *Dialogue* 3 (Summer 1968): 56-66, reprinted in *The New Mormon History: Revisionist Essays on the Past*, edited by D. Michael Quinn (Salt Lake City: Signature Books, 1992), 1-11, quotation p. 7. Quinn makes a similar statement in his introduction. The "new history" (Mormon or American) "examines the experiences of 'common people' and reverses the lack of emphasis on women, children, families, and ethnic minorities" (vii). The other four biases that Arrington listed were the theological marionette bias, the solid achievement bias, the centrifugal bias, and the unanimity bias.

priesthood. Their precedents are directly historical: Women in the nineteenth-century Church often gave each other and their children and husbands formal blessings, healings, and anointings that in the contemporary Church are associated only with male priesthood. Joseph Smith included women in his innermost priesthood circle, the Anointed Quorum, and encouraged women's organizational expression and service in the Relief Society.

In addition, polygamy is an important theme in the New Mormon History; and since the study of the Mormon polygamous family is largely a history of women and since many women and men perceive polygamy as inherently causing inequities for women, polygamy is an important part of the new Mormon women's history. The Mormon hierarchy, which withdrew public support for new plural marriages in 1890 and more fully renounced the practice in 1904, has deep-seated feelings of ambivalence toward polygamy. On the one hand, it was introduced, practiced, and praised as an eternal doctrine. The most important nineteenth-century Church leaders fought for it, beginning with Joseph Smith, Brigham Young, and John Taylor. On the other hand, polygamy does not fit the image of middle-American mainstream normalcy that the modern Church has striven to achieve, so some Church leaders would prefer that it be mentioned as little as possible. However, some feminist historians have found positive value in polygamy in that it caused women to develop independence and close feelings of sisterhood. Paradoxically, these positive values were caused by the frequent absence of men from the plural families, which can be interpreted ambiguously as an advantage or disadvantage.

My article is selective, rather than exhaustive; I have also limited my survey mostly to printed sources since these are the works that form the ongoing historiographical dialogue on the topic.[3] I will begin with two important Mormon historians who were women, Juanita Brooks and Fawn Brodie, will then consider Leonard Arrington's role in encouraging Mormon women's history, and then explore the burgeoning literature on Mormon women's written in significant part by Mormon women.

Brooks, Brodie, and Arrington

Scholars have selected different books as the landmark text marking the beginning of the New Mormon History. I concur with Maureen Ursenbach Beecher, Davis Bitton, James B. Allen, and D. Michael Quinn, in viewing Juanita Brooks, *The Mountain Meadows Massacre* (Stanford, CA: Stanford University Press, 1950) as a good candidate for the beginning of the movement.[4] However, other scholars have opted for Fawn Brodie's *No Man Knows My History: The Life of Joseph Smith the Mormon Prophet* (1945; 2d ed. rev. New York: Alfred A. Knopf, 1985)[5] or Leonard Arrington's *Great Basin Kingdom: An Economic History of the Latter-day Saints* (Cambridge: Harvard University Press, 1958).[6] Whatever one's individual selection, it is significant that two of these authors were women. Although they were not professionally trained historians and both were raising children as they wrote their major books, they learned the historian's craft well enough to write significant, brilliant his-

---

3. I would like to thank Lorie Winder Stromberg, Valeen Tippetts Avery, Jill Mulvay Derr, Lavina Fielding Anderson, and D. Michael Quinn for background conversations related to this paper.

4. See Davis Bitton and Maureen Ursenbach [Beecher], "Riding Herd: A Conversation with Juanita Brooks," *Dialogue* 9 (Spring 1974): 11; James B. Allen, "Since 1950: Creators and Creations of Mormon History," in *New Views of Mormon History: A Collection of Essays in Honor of Leonard J. Arrington,* edited by Davis Bitton and Maureen Ursenbach Beecher (Salt Lake City: University of Utah Press, 1987), 407-38, 411; Michael Quinn, "Editor's Introduction," in his *The New Mormon History,* viii.

5. See Robert B. Flanders, "Some Reflections on the New Mormon History," *Dialogue* 9 (Spring 1974): 34-41, 35, reprinted in George D. Smith, *Faithful History: Essays on Writing Mormon History* (Salt Lake City: Signature Books, 1992), 35-46, 37; Roger D. Launius, "From Old to New Mormon History: Fawn Brodie and the Legacy of Scholarly Analysis of Mormonism," in *Reconsidering No Man Knows My History: Fawn M. Brodie and Joseph Smith in Retrospect,* edited by Newell G. Bringhurst (Logan: Utah State University Press, 1996), 195-233, 195-96.

6. Thomas G. Alexander, "Toward The New Mormon History," 353-54, 353, viewed *Mountain Meadows Massacre* as "the first example of New Mormon History" but found it a "rather narrow" study lacking systematic analysis; he therefore identified Leonard J. Arrington's *Great Basin Kingdom* as "the single most significant bellwether of the New Mormon History."

tory. Both *Mountain Meadows Massacre* and *No Man Knows My History* were published by major non-Mormon presses.

However, it is also significant that neither Brooks nor Brodie took women as their central subjects, so they must be seen as transitional feminist writers. This is not meant as a criticism; in the New Mormon (and American) History, women should not be confined to writing about women, and men should not be confined to men. I consider Brooks's masterpiece to be a woman's view of the Mountain Meadows Massacre. However, Brooks wrote biographies of men, most significantly *John Doyle Lee: Zealot, Pioneer Builder, Scapegoat* (1961, rev. ed. Logan: Utah State University, 1992). She also edited or coedited numerous extremely important documents written by Mormon men, such as "Diary of the Mormon Battalion Mission: John D. Lee," *New Mexico Historical Review* 42 (July-October 1967):165-209, 281-332; Robert Cleland, and Juanita Brooks, *A Mormon Chronicle: The Diaries of John D. Lee*, 2 vols.(San Marino, CA: Huntington Library, 1955); and *On the Mormon Frontier: The Diary of Hosea Stout [1844-1861]*, 2 vols. (Salt Lake City: University of Utah Press/Utah State Historical Society, 1964). However, she also wrote a biography of one of Lee's wives, *Emma Lee* (Logan: Utah State University Press, 1975), slender and informal as it may be, and she later edited *Not By Bread Alone: The Journal of Martha Spencer Heywood, 1850-1856* (Salt Lake City: Utah State Historical Society, 1978). In addition, in Brooks's biographies of men, the reader can discern a steady interest in and sympathy for their wives. She also wrote some important articles about women in polygamy and Mormon family life, including her first historical publication, "A Close-Up of Polygamy," *Harper's*, February 1934, 299-307.[7] Finally, her autobiography, *Quicksand and Cactus: A Memoir of the Southern Mormon Frontier* (Salt Lake City: Westwater Press, 1981), is a beautifully written primary portrait of a significant Mormon woman.

No Man Knows My History was the first scholarly study of Joseph Smith and is a landmark, if only for that reason. It is also beautifully written. However, it has remained controversial because of its naturalistic view of Joseph Smith, Mormonism, and religion, and for its reliance on secondary, negative sources rather than on primary documents (many of which were admittedly not available to her before the professionalization of the LDS Church Archives). After *No Man Knows My History*, Brodie went on to write four more biographies, all of men (and none on a Mormon subject). However, *No Man* has a limited feminist component: its interest in polygamy and Joseph Smith's wives. Brodie herself was shocked by the details of Smith's marriages[8] and created an appendix listing the forty-eight women Brodie accepted as plural wives with short biographies. However, she did not seem interested in these women for their own lives and personalities; they were factors in her portrayal of Smith. Nevertheless, these thumbnail sketches are women's history, rudimentary and indirect as they may be.[9]

Leonard Arrington's major books were not directly focused on women's history, but he consistently strove to offset the "male bias" in Mormon history and wrote a number of pioneering articles on women in Mormonism: "The Economic Role of Pioneer Mormon Women," *Western Historical Review* 9 (Spring 1955): 145-64; "Blessed Damozels: Women in Mormon History," *Dialogue* 6 (Summer 1971): 22-31 (this article was his presidential address at the Western Historical Association in 1969); "Persons for All Seasons: Women in Mormon History," *BYU Studies* 20 (Fall 1979): 39-58; "Mormon Lysistratas: Mormon Women in the International Peace Movement," *Journal of Mormon History* 15 (1989): 89-104; and "The Legacy of Early Latter-day Saint Women," *John Whitmer Historical Association Journal* 10 (1990): 3-17.

---

7. See also "I Married a Family," in *Dialogue* 6 (Summer 1971): 15-21. (This is the "pink" *Dialogue*, discussed below.)

8. See Bringhurst, *Fawn McKay Brodie*, 89. This book is discussed more fully below.

9. Brodie, *No Man Knows My History*, 2nd ed., 457-88. Unfortunately, this appendix, though it is an important pioneering effort, has many errors. See my "Fawn Brodie on Joseph Smith's Plural Wives and Polygamy: A Critical View," in *Reconsidering No Man Knows My History*, 154-94, 173-75.

THE JOURNAL OF MARTHA SPENCE HEYWOOD
1850-56
EDITED BY JUANITA BROOKS

Utah State Historical Society
Salt Lake City

He also actively mentored Mormon women, suggested topics, shared sources, and supported Mormon women's history throughout his long and productive career. Maureen Ursenbach Beecher, for instance, ascribes her start in Mormon history (leading to many accomplishments) in large part to Arrington's direction and encouragement.[10] When a group of Boston women turned their research on individual Mormon women for a self-taught Institute of Religion class into a book, *Mormon Sisters: Women in Early Utah* (Cambridge, MA: Emmeline Press, 1976; still in print through USU Press), editor Claudia L. Bushman dedicated it to Leonard: "He took us seriously." One woman in that initial group, Laurel Thatcher Ulrich, went on to become the most highly honored historian who is also a Mormon. She recalled the impact one of Arrington's articles had on these women, who went on to put out a special issue of *Dialogue* and founded *Exponent II*, a Mormon women's paper that is still publishing:

> I will never forget the exhilaration of walking in late to one of the *Dialogue* meetings and hearing Claudia [Bushman] reading the story of Ellis Shipp from Leonard Arrington's newly submitted manuscript on women in church history. When she came to the fateful passage in which Ellis defies her husband to go back to medical school, the whole room cheered. "Yesterday you said that I should not go. I am going, going now!" With Ellis's words Leonard let the pioneer generation of Mormon feminists out of the closet, and there was no putting them back.[11]

Thus, the New Mormon History and the women's movement in Mormonism intertwined. Arrington also wrote "Women As a Force in the History of Utah," which introduced a special edition of *Utah Historical Quarterly* 38 (Winter 1970): 3-6, marking the centennial of women suffrage in Utah. With his daughter, Susan Arrington Madsen, he coauthored two popular books on Mormon women: *Sunbonnet Sisters: True Stories of Mormon Women and Frontier Life* (Salt Lake City: Bookcraft, 1984), and *Mothers of the Prophets* (Salt Lake City: Deseret Book, 1987). The last book he published before his death was *Madelyn Cannon Stewart Silver: Poet, Teacher, Homemaker* (Salt Lake City: Publishers Press, 1998). In "Blessed Damozels," Arrington saw how the history of women in Mormon history could increase the independence of modern women: he pointed out that the Mormon "tradition of womanly independence and distinction should inspire a later generation of women who are seeking their rightful place in the world" (31).

A Mormon Mother

Although Brooks, Arrington, and Brodie all made contributions to women's history, perhaps the New Mormon History's first full-fledged classic written by a woman and devoted to a woman's experience is Annie Clark Tanner, *A Mormon Mother: An Autobiography* (1941, limited edition; reprint ed., Salt Lake City: Tanner Trust Fund/University of Utah Press, 1969). It tells the tragic story of a woman's painful experience with an emotionally distant polygamous husband. As a young woman, Annie looked on polygamy as the highest religious ideal, despite problems in her own father's polygamous family. When she married a charismatic Brigham Young University professor, Joseph Tanner, as his second wife, however, he immediately failed to give her emotional support. Only a few months later, he married a third wife without warning. Annie spent the 1880s on the underground with her babies, penning a haunting recollection of painful rootlessness as she traveled, hid, and

---

10. Maureen Ursenbach Beecher, "Leonard J. Arrington: Reflections on a Humble Walk," *Dialogue* 32 (Spring 1999): 1-5; Stanford Cazier, "Honoring Leonard Arrington," *Dialogue* 22, (Winter 1989): 55-56. Beecher came to Arrington's team as an English major, and partially through his encouragement became a historian.

11. Laurel Ulrich, "The Pink *Dialogue* and Beyond," *Dialogue* 14 (Winter 1981): 28-39, quotation p. 33. Ulrich won the Bancroft Prize, the Joan Kelly and John H. Dunning Prizes of the American Historical Association, and the Pulitzer Prize for History for *A Midwife's Tale: The Life of Martha Ballard, Based on Her Diary, 1785-1812* (New York: Knopf, 1991). She then received the $320,000 John D. and Catherine T. MacArthur Foundation Award and became the first tenured woman faculty member at Harvard University.

A Mormon Mother

◻

AN AUTOBIOGRAPHY

By ANNIE CLARK TANNER

◻

THE UNIVERSITY OF UTAH PRESS
Salt Lake City, Utah
1969

concealed her identity under many names. Her husband bought land in Canada and insisted on using Annie's sons as farmhands (ironically, as he was an educator), while Annie insisted that they have a full education. Joseph continued to marry wives after the Manifesto, fell from favor with Church leaders, and eventually abandoned Annie completely, leaving her struggling in poverty to raise and educate her children.

Aside from showing the New Mormon History's concern for primary documents and the book's intrinsic interest as a story of a woman in Mormonism, *A Mormon Mother* also breathes an interest in critical thought and independence of mind. It deals frankly with polygamy and its limitations from a woman's perspective.[12] Perhaps most significantly, it necessarily becomes a critique of the infallibility of those who had preached that polygamy was a central doctrine of Mormonism, necessary for achieving complete salvation. Annie Clark Tanner was not just a "Mormon mother," facing the trials of polygamy and the concomitant struggles for financial survival—she was a new type of liberal Mormon woman, influenced by John Stuart Mill's ideas on liberty and not afraid of critical interpretation of the Bible. Nevertheless, her loyalty to Mormonism remained strong.

In addition, Tanner's book reflects a period of history important to the New Mormon History—the pre- and post-Manifesto period of transition that would result in classic treatments by Thomas Alexander, D. Michael Quinn, and B. Carmon Hardy. While the old Mormon history emphasized the "heroic" period of Mormonism in which the larger-than-life Joseph Smith received revelations, Mormonism was persecuted in the Midwest, then made its biblical exodus to Utah, the New Mormon History was fascinated by this painful and perplexing period of transition. Tanner's narrative captures this feeling of loss and disillusion as polygamy, the crown of Mormon doctrine, for which Mormons (and especially Mormon women) had sacrificed with great heroism, went underground. Their internal negotiations as the practice was publicly discontinued, then came to be viewed with suspicion and contempt are fraught with complicated emotions. Dale Morgan, "Literature in the History of the Church: The Importance of Involvement," *Dialogue* 4 (Autumn 1969): 26-32, commented that Tanner's *A Mormon Mother* might well be "one of the monuments of Mormon literature . . . for the valiance of her spirit and the sensitive reflection of a rare life, rather than for the distinction of the prose that I vividly remember, after almost thirty years" (32).

One of the key technical advances of the New Mormon History was its use of and appreciation for uncensored primary texts, which always reflected a more complex historical reality than idealized secondary history, to produce more nuanced and truthful history. This concern manifested itself in professional editions with care to reproduce the holograph variations, complete with explanatory notes, and without excisions of uncomfortable material.[13]

---

12. Derr, in "'Strength in Our Union'," 165-66 (see below), concludes: "There is no indication that female companionship assuaged the pain of the 'obscure and lonely life' Annie often lived as the second wife of Joseph Marion Tanner."

13. For important publications of primary texts by women in addition to those already mentioned, see Maureen Ursenbach Beecher, "'Tryed and Purified as Gold'" *BYU Studies* 34 (1994): 16-34; S. George Ellsworth, ed., *Dear Ellen: Two Mormon Women and Their Letters* (Salt Lake City: Tanner Trust Fund/University of Utah Library, 1974); Maureen Ursenbach Beecher, "'All Things Move in Order in the City': The Nauvoo Diary of Zina Diantha Huntington Jacobs," *BYU Studies* 19 (Spring 1979): 285-320; *A Fragment: The Autobiography of Mary Jane Mount Tanner* (Salt Lake City: Tanner Trust Fund, 1980); Kenneth W. Godfrey, Audrey M. Godfrey, and Jill Mulvay Derr, eds., *Women's Voices: An Untold History of the Latter-day Saints, 1830-1900* (Salt Lake City: Deseret Book, 1982); Constance L. Lieber and John Sillito, eds., *Letters from Exile: The Correspondence of Martha Hughes Cannon and Angus M. Cannon, 1886-1888* (Salt Lake City: Signature Books/Smith Research Associates, 1989); Jennifer Moulton Hansen, ed., *Letters of Catharine Cottam Romney, Plural Wife* (Urbana: University of Illinois Press, 1992); Maria S. Ellsworth, ed., *Mormon Odyssey: The Story of Ida Hunt Udall, Plural Wife* (Urbana: University of Illinois Press, 1992); Marilyn Higbee, ed., "'A Weary Traveler': The 1848-1850 Diaries of Zina D. H. Young," *Journal of Mormon History* 19 (Fall 1993): 86-125; Ogden Kraut, comp., *Autobiographies of Mormon Pioneer Women*, Vol. 1 (Salt Lake City: Pioneer Press, 1994); Joyce Kinkead, *"A Schoolmarm All My Life": Personal Narratives from Frontier Utah* (Salt Lake City: Signature Books 1996); Jeni Broberg Holzapfel and Richard Neitzel Holzapfel, *A Woman's View: Helen Mar Whitney's Reminiscences of Early Church History* (Provo, UT.: Religious Studies Center, Brigham Young University, 1997); Todd Compton, "'Remember Me in My Affliction': Louisa Beaman Young and Eliza R. Snow Letters, 1849," *Journal of Mormon History* 25 (Fall 1999): 46-69. See also the magnificent LIFE WRITINGS OF FRONTIER WOMEN series published by Utah State University Press, referred to below.

Excavating Mormon Pasts

Two important books on polygamy appeared in the 1950s: Samuel W. Taylor, *Family Kingdom* (New York: McGraw Hill, 1951) and Kimball Young, *Isn't One Wife Enough?* (New York: Henry Holt, 1954). Taylor, a journalist, novelist, and humorist, presented *Family Kingdom* as the biography of his father, John W. Taylor, an apostle who was excommunicated for post-Manifesto polygamy; but the book was based largely on interviews with Samuel Taylor's mother, Janet ("Nettie") Maria Woolley Taylor, and it is as much a biography of her as it is of John Taylor. It is a fascinating story, told by a great storyteller. It is characteristic of the New Mormon History in its willingness to tackle a "taboo" subject, in its interest in the post-Manifesto period, and in its willingness to tell a complex story that is not simply good guys versus bad guys, even though Taylor's standards for research and documentation on this, and other of his Mormon histories, often seem to be those of a novelist or journalist rather than a historian. Young's book is a sociological analysis of polygamy based on interviews with many polygamous women and men and, thus, is an important resource for Mormon women's history.

Women in Camelot: Beecher, Derr, and Madsen

In the 1960s, the woman's movement in America became more influential and began to impact Mormon women. Little of significance was published in the field of Mormon women's history during this decade, but in the early 1970s came a burst of publication and interest—or perhaps, two bursts, localized in Salt Lake City and in Boston.

The Utah cluster of Mormon women's history was part of the Leonard Arrington renaissance. Appointed Church Historian in 1972, he worked in the Church Archives with a team of professionally trained scholars, and encouraged women to participate. Three women historians—Maureen Ursenbach Beecher, Jill Mulvay Derr, and Carol Cornwall Madsen—began writing women's biographies, histories of women's organizations, and analyses of the differing status of nineteenth- and twentieth-century women in Mormonism. Working steadily through the years, they have accomplished an enormous amount. They also brought to Mormon women's history insights from the flourishing field of American women's history outside of Mormonism—for instance, the theoretical perspectives of Barbara Welter and Carroll Smith-Rosenberg.[14]

---

14. Barbara Welter, "The Cult of True Womanhood: 1820-1860," *American Quarterly* 18 (1966): 151-74, reprinted in Welter's *Dimity Convictions: The American Woman in the Nineteenth Century* (Athens: Ohio University Press, 1976). For an application of Welter's perspectives to Mormon women, see Kathleen Marquis, "'Diamond Cut Diamond': Mormon Women and the Cult of Domesticity in the Nineteenth Century," *University of Michigan, Papers in Women's Studies* 2 (1976): 105-24. See also Carroll Smith-Rosenberg, "The Female World of Love and Ritual: Relations Between Women in Nineteenth-Century America," *Signs* 1 (1975): 1-29, collected in Smith-Rosenberg's *Disorderly Conduct: Visions of Gender in Victorian America* (New York: Alfred A. Knopf, 1985). For the historiography of western women, see Sandra L. Myres, "Women in the West," in Malone, *Historians and the American West*, 369-86. See also, for the wider context of American women's history, such books as Eleanor Flexner, *Century of Struggle: The Woman's Rights Movement in the United States* (Cambridge, MA: Belknap Press/Harvard University Press, 1959); Mary S. Hartman and Lois Banner, eds., *Clio's Consciousness Raised: New Perspectives on the History of Women* (New York: Harper, 1974); Berenice A. Carroll, ed., *Liberating Women's History: Theoretical and Critical Essays* (Urbana: University of Illinois Press, 1976); Mabel E. Deutrich and Virginia C. Purdy, eds., *Clio Was a Woman: Studies in the History of American Women* (Washington DC: Howard University Press, 1976); Adrienne Rich, *Of Woman Born* (New York: Bantam Books, 1976); Nancy Cott, *The Bonds of Womanhood: Woman's Sphere in New England, 1780-1835* (1977; 2d rev. ed., New Haven, CT: Yale University Press, 1997); Ann Douglas, *The Feminization of American Culture* (New York: Avon, 1977); Gerda Lerner, *The Majority Finds Its Past: Placing Women in History* (New York: Oxford University Press, 1979); Carl N. Degler, *At Odds: Women and the Family in America from the Revolution to the Present* (New York: Oxford University Press, 1980); Barbara Leslie Epstein, *The Politics of Domesticity: Women, Evangelism, and Temperance in Nineteenth-Century America* (Middletown, CT: Wesleyan University Press, 1981); Mary Ryan, *Womanhood in America* (New York: Franklin Watts, 1983); Ann Firor Scott, *Making The Invisible Woman Visible* (Urbana: University of Illinois, 1984); Joan W. Scott, *Gender and the Politics of History* (New York: Columbia University Press, 1988); Steven Mintz, *Domestic Revolutions: A Social History of American Family Life* (New York: Free Press, 1988); Peter Novick, "Every Group Its Own Historian," chap. 14 of his *That Noble Dream: The 'Objectivity Question' and the American Historical Profession* (New York: Cambridge University Press, 1988); Judith Walkowitz, Myra Jehlen, and Bell Chevigny, "Patrolling the Borders: Feminist Historiography and the New Historicism," *Radical History Review* 43 (1989): 23-43; Kathleen Barry, "The New Historical Synthesis: Women's Biography," *Journal of Women's History* 1, no. 3 (Winter 1990): 75-105; Judith P. Zinsser, *History and Feminism: A Glass Half Full* (New York: Twayne, 1993).

Beecher, a Canadian whose first love had been literature, took Eliza R. Snow and other leading sisters of Zion as her central subject.[15] Many of her essays have become classics, particularly "The Eliza Enigma," in *Essays on the American West, 1974-1975,* edited by Thomas G. Alexander, Charles Redd Monographs in Western History, No. 6 (Provo: BYU Press, 1974-75), 34-39, the beginning of modern scholarly work on Eliza R. Snow; "Under the Sunbonnets: Mormon Women with Faces," *BYU Studies* 16 (Summer 1976): 471-84; "Women's Work on the Mormon Frontier," *Utah Historical Quarterly* 49 (Summer 1981): 276-90, a good Arringtonian title;[16] "The 'Leading Sisters': A Female Hierarchy in Nineteenth-Century Mormon Society," *Journal of Mormon History* 9 (1982): 25-39, which began the study of "feminine prosopography" in Mormonism;[17] and "Women in Winter Quarters," *Sunstone* 8, no. 4 (July-August 1983): 11-19, another collective study which analyzed how Mormon women, separated from men, engaged in ecstatic and ritual actions in Winter Quarters.

Beecher's scholarly work on Eliza R. Snow culminated in two books: *Eliza and Her Sisters,* which collected many of her essays on Snow, and *The Personal Writings of Eliza Roxcy Snow* (1995; reprint ed., Logan: Utah State University Press, 2000). This book published all of Snow's diaries and a long autobiographical sketch, with an insightful introduction and valuable annotations, receiving the well-merited Best Book of the Year award from the Mormon History Association in 1996.

Another major contribution to Mormon women's history was Beecher's coeditorship, with Lavina Fielding Anderson, of *Sisters in Spirit: Mormon Women in Historical and Cultural Perspective* (Urbana: University of Illinois Press, 1987). The book came into being as a result of informal lunches at the Lion House and was a response to the Church's excommunication of ERA activist, Sonia Johnson in December 1979 (xiii). *Sisters in Spirit* tried to express a moderate feminism. Beecher wrote, of the lunch group, "Almost all of us were married, most of us career-oriented, many with children at home. All connected deeply to the church . . . We watched as outsiders accused Mormon culture of chauvinism, sometimes with justification; we observed how insiders defended the faith, sometimes with sophistries we could not

---

15. See Leonard J. Arrington, "Foreword," to Maureen Ursenbach Beecher, *Eliza and Her Sisters* (Salt Lake City: Aspen Books, 1991), vii-ix; Beecher, *Sisters in Spirit,* 269; Leonard J. Arrington, *Adventures of a Church Historian* (Urbana: University of Illinois Press, 1998), 85, 109-10; Bushman, *Mormon Sisters,* 2d ed. (Logan: Utah State University Press, 1997), 283.

16. All of the articles in this issue of the *Utah Historical Quarterly* deal with women, including John R. Sillito, "Women and the Socialist Party in Utah, 1900-1920," 220-38; Carol Ann Lubomurdrov, "A Woman State School Superintendent: Whatever Happened to Mrs. McVicker?" 254-61; and Sherilyn Cox Bennion, "Enterprising Ladies: Utah's Nineteenth-Century Women Editors," 291-304. *Utah Historical Quarterly* 46 (Spring 1978) is also devoted to women, including, for example, Miriam B. Murphy, "The Working Women of Salt Lake City: A Review of the *Utah Gazetteer, 1892-93*," 121-35; Juanita Brooks and Janet G. Butler, "Utah's Peace Advocate, the 'Mormona': Elisa Rurer Musser," 151-67; and Laurence P. James and Sandra C. Taylor, "'Strong Minded Women': Desdemona Stott Beeson and Other Hard Rock Mining Entrepreneurs," 136-50. See also Chris Rigby Arrington, "The Finest of Fabrics: Mormon Women and the Silk Industry in Early Utah," *Utah Historical Quarterly* 46, no. 4 (Fall 1978): 376-96; Jessie L. Embry, "'Separate but Unequal': Schoolmarms of Utah, 1900-1905," in *From Cottage to Marketplace: The Professionalization of Women's Sphere,* edited by John R. Sillito (Salt Lake City: Utah Women's History Association, 1983), 28-46; Christine Croft Waters, "Pioneering Women Physicians, 1847-1900," ibid., 47-61; Leonard Arrington, "Rural Life Among Nineteenth-Century Mormons: The Woman's Experience," *Agricultural History* 58 (1984): 239-46; Michael Vinson, "From Housework to Office Clerk: Utah's Working Women, 1870-1900," *Utah Historical Quarterly* 53 (Fall 1985), 326-35; Carol Cornwall Madsen, "'Sisters at the Bar': Utah Women at Law," *Utah Historical Quarterly* 61 (1993): 208-32; and Thomas C. Jepsen, "Women Telegraph Operators on the Western Frontier," *Journal of the West* 35 (April 1996): 75-76, 78.

17. Reprinted in Quinn, ed., *The New Mormon History,* 153-68. For other collective studies of Mormon women, see D. Gene Pace, "Wives of Nineteenth-century Mormon Bishops: A Quantitative Analysis," *Journal of the West* 21 (1982): 49-57; Linda Thatcher and John R. Sillito, "Sisterhood and Sociability: The Utah Woman's Press Club, 1891-1928," *Utah Historical Quarterly* 53 (Spring 1985): 144-56; Maureen Ursenbach Beecher, Carol Cornwall Madsen, and Lavina Fielding Anderson, "Widowhood Among the Mormons: The Personal Accounts" in *On Their Own: Widows and Widowhood in the American Southwest, 1848-1939,* edited by Arlene Scadron (Urbana: University of Illinois Press, 1988), 117-39; Geraldine Mineau, "Utah Widowhood: A Demographic Profile," ibid., 140-65; Linda Thatcher, "Women Alone: The Economic and Emotional Plight of Early LDS Women," *Dialogue* 25 (Winter 1992): 45-55; and Rebecca Bartholomew, *Audacious Women: Early British Mormon Immigrants* (Salt Lake City: Signature Books, 1995).

ELIZA
AND HER
SISTERS

MAUREEN URSENBACH BEECHER
WITH A FOREWORD BY LEONARD J. ARRINGTON

accept" (xiii). The lunch group felt that they should be building bridges: "sisterhood was too significant to be lost in jangling discord." Marilyn Warenski, *Patriarchs and Politics: The Plight of the Mormon Woman* (New York: McGraw-Hill, 1978), had appeared the year before Johnson's excommunication, and they had seen it as undervaluing the accomplishments of Mormon women in an "irresponsible" and unbalanced attack on Mormon patriarchalism.[18]

Sisters in Spirit dealt with Mormon women's theology and spirituality, but the historical context was everywhere in the book. For instance, Linda P. Wilcox's important essay, "The Mormon Concept of a Mother in Heaven" (originally published in *Sunstone* 5 [September/October 1980]: 9-15) started with historical research into Eliza R. Snow's writing of "O My Father." Devotion to a Mother in Heaven has become a basic tenet of Mormon feminism.[19] Significantly, Wilcox also worked for a time as one of Leonard Arrington's research assistants. Paired with this essay was her equally detailed article "Mormon Motherhood: Official Images," 208-26.

Also in *Sisters in Spirit* was Linda King Newell's "Gifts of the Spirit: Women's Share,"[20] a classic essay which documented nineteenth-century women performing rites such as blessings, healings, washings, and anointings that are now associated exclusively with male priesthood holders, and how these privileges were gradually withdrawn by modern Church leaders.[21]

The longest essay in the book, "'Strength in Our Union': The Making of Mormon Sisterhood," (153-208) was written by the third woman historian in Arrington's Camelot, Jill Mulvay Derr.[22] This is one of many important essays Derr has written, and it shows her interest and expertise in studying Mormon women as a group. Other notable essays authored by Derr are "The Liberal Shall Be Blessed: Sarah M. Kimball," *Utah Historical Quarterly* 44 (Summer 1976): 205-21, a biography of an important Mormon suffragist and feminist, and with C. Brooklyn Derr, her husband, "Outside the Mormon Hierarchy: Alternative Aspects of Institutional Power," *Dialogue* 15 (Winter 1982): 21-43, which showed the power of Mormon women outside of the male organizational structure.[23]

---

18. See also Laurel Thatcher Ulrich, "Out of the Slot," (review of Warenski), *Dialogue* 12 (Summer 1979): 125-28.

19. Modern conservative Church leaders have, in response, made devotion to Mother in Heaven a litmus test for "apostasy," despite the fact that the doctrine had been accepted by many nineteenth-century General Authorities. Gail Turley Houston, for instance, was terminated from Brigham Young University largely because she had described comforting spiritual experiences in which she had felt close to her Mother in Heaven. Bryan Waterman and Brian Kagel, *The Lord's University: Freedom and Authority at BYU* (Salt Lake City: Signature Books, 1998), 302-68. Janice Allred was excommunicated partially for an article written on Mother in Heaven. See her *God the Mother, and Other Theological Essays* (Salt Lake City: Signature Books, 1997). See also John Heeren, Donald B. Lindsey, and Marylee Mason, "The Mormon Concept of a Mother in Heaven: A Sociological Account of Its Origin and Development," *Journal for the Scientific Study of Religion* 23 (1984): 396-411.

20. This was originally published in *Sunstone* 6 (September-October 1981): 16-25, as "A Gift Given, A Gift Taken: Washing, Anointing, and Blessing the Sick Among Mormon Women." It appears, with its original title, in Quinn, *The New Mormon History*, 101-20.

21. Other articles that analyze the connection of women and priesthood are Anthony Hutchinson, "Women and Ordination: Introduction to the Biblical Context," *Dialogue* 14 (Winter 1981): 58-74; Nadine Hansen, "Woman and the Priesthood," ibid., 48-57; Margaret Toscano, "The Missing Rib: The Forgotten Place of Queens and Priestesses in the Establishment of Zion," *Sunstone* 10 (July 1985): 16-22; Melodie Moench Charles, "Scriptural Precedents for Priesthood," *Dialogue* 18 (Fall 1985): 21-32; Linda King Newell, "The Historical Relationship of Women and Priesthood," ibid., 21-32; Kathryn H. Shirts, "Priesthood and Salvation: Is D&C 84 a Revelation for Women Too?" *Sunstone* 15 (September 1991): 20-27; Richard P. Howard, "What Sort of Priesthood for Women at Nauvoo?" *John Whitmer Historical Association Journal* 13 (1993): 18-30; Meg Wheatley-Pesci, "An Expanded Definition: Some Present and Future Consequences," *Dialogue* 18 (Fall 1985): 33-42; Todd Compton, "'Kingdom of Priests': Priesthood, Temple and Women in the Old Testament and in the Restoration," *Dialogue* 36 (Fall 2003): 41-60.

22. Arrington, *Adventures of a Church Historian*, 85, 129, 161, 209; Bushman, *Mormon Sisters*, 285.

23. See also Derr's "Our Foremothers and the 1870 Franchise," *Exponent II* 1 (December 1974): 14; "The Two Miss Cooks: Pioneer Professionals for Utah Schools," *Utah Historical Quarterly* 43 (Fall 1975): 396-409; "Three Mormon Women in the Cultural Arts," *Sunstone* 1 (Spring 1976): 29-39; "Woman's Place in Brigham Young's World," *BYU Studies* 18 (Spring 1978): 377-95; and "Changing Relief Society Charity to Make Way for Welfare, 1930-1944," in *New Views of Mormon History*, 242-72.

Derr, now the director of the Joseph Fielding Smith Institute for Latter-day Saint History at BYU, is working on a biography of Eliza R. Snow, unquestionably the most important Mormon woman of the pioneer period, and, with Karen Lynn Davidson, an edition of Snow's poetry. Foretastes of this work can be found in Derr, "Eliza R. Snow and the Woman Question," *BYU Studies* 16 (Winter 1976): 250-64; "The Significance of 'O My Father' in the Personal Journey of Eliza R. Snow," *BYU Studies* 36, no. 1 (1996-97): 85-126; "Form and Feeling in a Carefully Crafted Life: Eliza R. Snow's 'Poem of Poems,'" *Journal of Mormon History* 26 (Spring 2000): 1-39; and an edition of significant women's documents, including the Nauvoo Relief Society minutes, is also forthcoming in 2004 from the Joseph Fielding Smith Institute under her direction.

Derr's central accomplishment, thus far, is a full, meticulously researched, institutional history of the LDS Church's woman's organization, the Relief Society, coauthored with Janath Russell Cannon and Maureen Ursenbach Beecher—*Women of Covenant: The Story of the Relief Society* (Salt Lake City: Deseret Book, 1992). Some reviewers felt that this history, published by the official LDS press, glossed over problems in the history of Mormon women and men.[24] Certainly, the book is an organizational history and thus surveys many noncontroversial events. In addition, it was commissioned by the Relief Society general presidency in 1979 and reviewed in manuscript by Apostle Dallin H. Oaks, so the expectation was clear that it should tell the organization's "official" story (xi). But it deals straightforwardly with many of the difficult moments in Relief Society history—such as Emmeline B. Wells's unexpected and emotionally devastating release as Relief Society general president by President Heber J. Grant (222-23); and Zina D. Huntington Young's discomfort when the Church hierarchy pushed through the legal incorporation of the Relief Society (144-45). As the first scholarly history of the central LDS woman's organization, it is a landmark.[25]

Carol Cornwall Madsen chose the brilliant Emmeline B. Wells—long-time Relief Society secretary, editor of *Woman's Exponent*, fourth general president of the Relief Society, and plural wife of both Newel K. Whitney and Daniel H. Wells—as her central subject. She began with "Emmeline B. Wells: A Mormon Woman in Victorian America" (Ph.D. diss., University of Utah, 1985), and has published a steady sequence of articles: "Emmeline B. Wells: 'Am I Not a Woman and a Sister?'" *BYU Studies* 22 (Spring 1982): 161-78; "Emmeline B. Wells: A Voice for Mormon Women," *John Whitmer Historical Association Journal* 2 (1982): 11-21; "A Bluestocking in Zion: The Literary Life of Emmeline B. Wells," *Dialogue* 16 (Spring 1983): 126-40; "'The Power of Combination': Emmeline B. Wells and the National and International Councils of Women," *BYU Studies* 33 (1993): 646-73. "Schism in the Sisterhood: Mormon Women and Partisan Politics, 1890-1900," in *New Views of Mormon History*, 212-41, includes Wells as a central character. Madsen's forthcoming multi-volumed biography of Wells should be a milestone in Mormon history, as Wells's personal life is rich, varied, fascinating in its sweep (from the Mormonism of early polygamy to the twentieth-century church), and is full of dramatic and tragic events, such as the breakup of her first marriage to James Harris and the death of her youngest daughter, Louie Wells Cannon, in childbirth. Because Wells kept one of the fullest diaries in Mormon history, when it is published, readers will be able to see her life, from her own perspective, in depth.

---

24. Cheryll Lynn May, "A Diminished Thing?" *Dialogue* 27 (Summer 1994): 235-37; Peggy Pascoe, "A History of Two Stories," ibid., 237-45; and Jessie L. Embry, "Homemaking Meetings," *Sunstone* 16, no. 5 (July 1993): 70-71.

25. See also Jessie L. Embry, "Grain Storage: The Balance of Power Between Priesthood Authority and Relief Society Autonomy," *Dialogue* 15 (Winter 1982): 21-43; Loretta L. Hefner, "The National Women's Relief Society and the U.S. Sheppard-Towner Act," *Utah Historical Quarterly* 50 (1982): 255-67; Maureen Ursenbach Beecher, "Priestess Among the Patriarchs: Eliza R. Snow and the Mormon Female Relief Society, 1842-1877," in Carl Guarneri and David Alvarez, eds., *Religion and Society in the American West: Historical Essays* (Lanham, MD: University Press of America, 1987), 153-70; Carol Cornwall Madsen, "Creating Female Community: Relief Society in Cache Valley, Utah, 1868-1900," *Journal of Mormon History* 21 (1995): 126-54.

WOMEN OF COVENANT
THE STORY OF
RELIEF SOCIETY

Jill Mulvay Derr
Janath Russell Cannon
Maureen Ursenbach Beecher

Deseret Book Company
Salt Lake City, Utah

Excavating Mormon Pasts

In addition, Madsen has published valuable popular scholarly books: with Susan Staker Oman, *Sisters and Little Saints: One Hundred Years of Primary* (Salt Lake City: Deseret Book, 1979), and two edited anthologies of first-person writings, *In Their Own Words: Women and the Story of Nauvoo* (Salt Lake City: Deseret Book, 1994)[26] and *Journey to Zion: Voices from the Mormon Trail* (Salt Lake City: Deseret Book, 1997). Other thoughtful essays include "Mormon Women and the Temple: Toward a New Understanding," *Sisters in Spirit*, 80-110; "Mormon Women and the Struggle for Definition: The Nineteenth Century Church" *Sunstone* 6 (November-December 1981): 7-11; "Mormon Missionary Wives in Nineteenth Century Polynesia," *Journal of Mormon History* 13 (1986-87): 61-88; "'At Their Peril': Utah Law and the Case of Plural Wives, 1850-1900," *Western Political Quarterly* 21 (1990), 425-44; "'Feme Covert': Journey of a Metaphor," *Journal of Mormon History* 17 (1991): 43-61, an important historiographical contribution; and "Decade of Détente: The Mormon-Gentile Female Relationship in Nineteenth-Century Utah," *Utah Historical Quarterly* 63 (1995): 298-319.

Madsen also edited *Battle for the Ballot: Essays on Women Suffrage in Utah, 1870-1896* (Logan: Utah State University Press, 1997), which reprinted important essays: Jean Bickmore White, "Gentle Persuaders: Utah's First Women Legislators," which had appeared in the 1970 women's issue of the *Utah Historical Quarterly*; Joan Smyth Iversen; Beverly Beeton, author of *Women Vote in the West: The Woman Suffrage Movement, 1869-1896* (New York: Garland Publishing, 1986), Thomas Alexander, Madsen, Derr, and Lola Van Wagenen. Van Wagenen's important dissertation, "Sister-Wives and Suffragists: Polygamy and the Politics of Woman Suffrage, 1870-1896" (New York University, 1994), was reprinted in the JFS Institute/BYU Studies series, DISSERTATIONS IN LATTER-DAY SAINT HISTORY (2003). One of the great ironies of Mormon history is that nineteenth-century Mormon women were generally united in their fight for equal voting rights; and as a result, in 1870 Utah became the second territory in the nation to grant women's suffrage (after Wyoming). However, twentieth-century mainstream Church leaders and Mormon women generally opposed the Equal Rights Amendment. The stance of the nineteenth- and twentieth-century Church leaders toward women's rights is only part of the equation in understanding that contrast, though an important part.

Beecher's, Derr's, Madsen's, and Arrington's Camelot was indeed a rich journey of discovery for LDS women's history.

Pink *Dialogue* and *Mormon Sisters*: Bushman and Ulrich

Meanwhile, in Boston, another group of Mormon women began an informal group of meetings that would result in more important contributions to LDS women's history. Ten years later, Laurel Thatcher Ulrich recalled those beginnings:

> Some time in June 1970, I invited a few friends to my house to chat about the then emerging women's movement. If I had known we were about to make history, I would have taken minutes or at least passed a roll around, but of course I didn't. All I have now to document that momentous gathering are memories. I remember Claudia Bushman sitting on a straight oak chair near my fireplace telling us about women's lives in the nineteenth century. Since she had just begun a doctoral program in history, she was our resident scholar. If we had a resident feminist, it was Judy Dushku, who came to that first meeting with a rhymed manifesto she had picked up at the university where she taught. We laughed at the poem's pungent satire, then pondered its attack on "living for others." "Isn't that what we are supposed to do?" someone said. Our potential for disagreement was obvious, yet on that bright morning we were too absorbed in the unfamiliar openness to care. The talk streamed through the room like sunshine. None of us recognized that we were beginning a discussion that would continue for more than a decade. We only knew that it felt good to talk, and that we did not want to stop when it was time to go home. Before

---

26. This work pairs well with Richard Neitzel Holzapfel and Jeni Broberg Holzapfel, *Women of Nauvoo* (Salt Lake City: Bookcraft, 1992).

many weeks had passed, we were not only meeting regularly but had volunteered to put together a special issue of *Dialogue*.

So wrote Laurel Thatcher Ulrich in 1981.[27] This article chronicles the birth pangs of that pink *Dialogue* issue, which appeared in the summer of 1971, and included articles by Juanita Brooks, Leonard Arrington, Ulrich, and Bushman. On its back cover was a quotation from Brigham Young: "We believe that women are useful, not only to sweep houses, wash dishes, make beds, and raise babies, but they should stand behind the counter, study law or physic, or become good bookkeepers and be able to do the business in any counting house, and all this to enlarge their sphere of usefulness for the benefit of society at large. In following these things they but answer the design of their creation."[28] The use of this quotation shows how Mormon feminism and Mormon history were intertwined in this Boston movement.

Ulrich continued:

The pink *Dialogue* was not responsible for this outpouring of women's voices, but it did begin it. In my manic moods, I like to remember that. If I could somehow figure out the exact date of our first meeting, I would propose it for historic recognition. A handsome brass plaque would look nice, set in the front lawn of my old house at 380 Dedham Street in Newton, somewhere between the peach tree and the birch. "Here," the inscription would read, "in this ordinary looking, gambrel-roofed house, the second generation of Mormon feminists was born."[29]

And we might say, another generation of Mormon women historians was born. In spring 1973, the group gave a series of lectures on Mormon women at the Cambridge LDS Institute, then turned them into *Mormon Sisters: Women in Early Utah* (1976), edited by Bushman and published by the group's own "Emmeline Press." This book was the first collection of historical essays on Mormon women since Edward Tullidge's *Women of Mormondom* in 1877. As such, is a benchmark in Mormon women's history and self-conscious Mormon feminism. It benefitted by a cross-pollination from the LDS Church Archives women historians, with essays by Maureen Ursenbach Beecher, Chris Rigby Arrington (who had been Leonard's secretary at Utah State University and later married his son Carl), and Jill Mulvay Derr. Though there were two biographical chapters (on Eliza R. Snow and Susa Young Gates, a daughter of Brigham Young, and a writer and administrator often known as the "Thirteenth Apostle"), most chapters were topical, with intriguing titles. Bushman's "Mystics and Healers" educated modern Mormons on earlier LDS women's spiritual gifts and ritual administrations.[30] Judith Rasmussen Dushku wrote "Feminists" and Carrel Hilton Sheldon examined "Mormon Haters."[31] Two chapters dealt

---

27. Laurel Thatcher Ulrich, "The Pink *Dialogue* and Beyond," *Dialogue* 14 (Winter 1981): 28-40, 28-29. *Dialogue* has continued to publish periodic women's issues. The second appeared in Winter 1981 under the editorship of Mary L. Bradford and included, in addition to poetry, fiction, and personal essays, reminiscences about the previous ten years, women and priesthood, divorce, and Carol Cornwall Madsen's "Mormon Women and the Struggle for Definition," 40-47. The third and most recent appeared in Fall 2003. It included sections on "Women and Priesthood," "Women and Missions," "Scripture and Sexuality," and "The Women's Movement in Mormonism."

28. *Journal of Discourses*, 26 vols. (London: Latter-day Saints' Book Depot, 1855-86), 13:61.

29. Ulrich, "Pink *Dialogue*," 30. Claudia Bushman's memoir of the same events appears in "My Short Happy Life with *Exponent II*," *Dialogue* 36 (Fall 2003): 179-92.

30. See also Elaine J. Lawless, "'I Know If I Don't Bear My Testimony, I'll Lose It': Why Mormon Women Bother to Speak at All," *Kentucky Folklore Record* 20 (1984): 79-96; Margaret K. Brady, "Transformations of Power: Mormon Women's Visionary Narratives," *Journal of American Folklore* 100 (1987): 461-68; John Sillito and Constance L. Lieber, "'In Blessing We Too Were Blessed': Mormon Women and Spiritual Gifts," *Weber Studies* 5 (Spring 1988): 61-73; Martha Sonntag Bradley, "'Seizing Sacred Space': Women's Engagement in Early Mormonism," *Dialogue* 27 (Summer 1994): 57-70.

31. Though non-Mormon women in Utah are technically not a central part of Mormon history, they existed with Mormon women in a close, if oppositional, symbiosis, so are part of the Mormon story. A recent

with Mormon women in polygamy with additional chapters on midwives and schoolmarms. Ulrich contributed a chapter on "Fictional Sisters."

Claudia Bushman went on to become a skilled and productive historian but has not written further on Mormon women although she directed a half-dozen women interns writing on Mormon women in the twentieth century for the JFS Institute's summer program in 2003. Those interested in American women's history, however, will want to read her *"A Good Poor Man's Wife": Being a Chronicle of Harriet Hanson Robinson and Her Family in Nineteenth-century New England* (Hanover, NH: University Press of New England, 1981). She served briefly as the first editor of *Exponent II*, the feminist magazine that looked to the nineteenth-century *Women's Exponent* of Emmeline B. Wells as a model to empower modern Mormon women. Though *Exponent II* was viewed with suspicion by Church conservatives because it was not an official Church publication, Bushman pursued a moderate stance: "The simple truth is that angry females, clamoring for their real or supposed rights, offend the canons of womanliness and femininity. The harder such women fight, the tighter the ranks close against them. . . . In most cases repression is more often imagined than real."[32]

Like Bushman, Laurel Thatcher Ulrich built her spectacular career in fields others than Mormon women's history. After producing the brilliant *Good Wives: Image and Reality in the Lives of Women in Northern New England, 1650-1750* (New York: Alfred A. Knopf, 1982), Ulrich published her much-lauded *A Midwife's Tale,* which also became the basis for a fine PBS documentary. In it, Ulrich published the sparse, cryptic diary of Martha Ballard, an eighteenth-century New Hampshire midwife, bringing the references to life with brilliant, painstaking historical analysis and poetic, incisive, sympathetic prose. It is a great book; but for the lover of Mormon history, one can only regret that she has not yet written a book on a Mormon subject.[33]

Nevertheless, Ulrich has written a number of personal essays on Mormonism, many published in *Exponent II* and *Dialogue,* and this body of material, trenchant, humorous, and insightful, qualifies as "contemporary" Mormon history.[34] Some of these essays are collected in *All God's Critters Got a Place in the Choir,* a collaboration with poet and essayist Emma Lou Thayne (Salt Lake City: Aspen Books, 1995). Because of Ulrich's tremendous contributions, she was proposed as keynote speaker at a Brigham Young University women's conference in 1993, but BYU's Board of Trustees turned down the request at a meeting in which women members of the board were absent—an awkward and embarrassing episode.[35] But it shows how women's history, even non-Mormon women's history, can quickly become a lightning rod for censorship from conservative Church leaders in the modern Mormon culture wars. It is somewhat ironic, because the leadership's chosen targets have usually been moderate feminists, married, with children, active in the Church—

---

article on non-Mormon women in Utah is Jana Kathryn Riess, "'Heathen in Our Fair Land': Presbyterian Women Missionaries in Utah, 1870-90," *Journal of Mormon History* 26 (Spring 2000): 165-95. Polygamy, the "twin relic of barbarism," was the chief bone of contention in the conflict between Mormon and non-Mormon American women. See Joan Smyth Iversen, *The Antipolygamy Controversy in U.S. Women's Movements, 1880-1925: A Debate on the American Home* (New York: Garland Publishing, 1997).

32. Bushman's "A Wider Sisterhood: *Exponent II*," *Dialogue* 11 (Spring 1978): 96-99, 97. Examinations of the original *Woman's Exponent* include Sherilyn Cox Bennion, "The *Woman's Exponent*: Forty-Two Years of Speaking for Women," *Utah Historical Quarterly* 44 (1976): 222-39, her "*The New Northwest* and *Woman's Exponent*: Early Voices for Suffrage," *Journalism Quarterly* 54 (Summer 1977): 286-92, and a chapter in her "*Equal to the Occasion: Women Editors of the Nineteenth-Century West* (Reno: University of Nevada Press, 1990), 72-83.

33. Meanwhile, Donna Toland Smart's sensitive editing and detailed documentation of *Mormon Midwife: The 1846-1888 Diaries of Patty Barlett Sessions* (Logan: Utah State University, 1997), makes a diary of one of Mormonism's most famous midwives available to readers.

34. See, for example, her *Dialogue* articles: "Counseling the Brethren," 9 (Summer 1974): 68-70; "A Little Bit of Heaven," 9 (Autumn 1974): 63-65; "Family Scriptures," 20 (Summer 1987): 119-27; "Border Crossings," 27 (Summer 1994): 1-7; and "The Significance of Trivia," *Journal of Mormon History* 9 (Spring 1993): 52-66.

35. See "BYU Rejects LDS Pulitzer Prize Winner as Speaker," *Sunstone* 16 (March 1993): 69; L. Jackson Newell, "Scapegoats and Scarecrows in Our Town: When the Interests of Church and Community Collide," *Sunstone* 16 (December 1993): 22-28, 23; Waterman and Kagel, *The Lord's University*, 212-13.

whom Church leaders might have welcomed as allies. Ulrich has subsequently received invitations from organizations at BYU, though not from the university itself.

Mormon Sisters was followed by two important anthologies: *Sister Saints,* edited by Vicky Burgess-Olson (Provo, UT: Brigham Young University Press, 1978), and *Women's Voices: An Untold History of the Latter-day Saints 1830-1900,* edited by Kenneth W. Godfrey, Audrey M. Godfrey, and Jill Mulvay Derr (Salt Lake City: Deseret Book, 1982). *Sister Saints,* with contributions from Beecher, Derr, Madsen, Jean Bickmore White, and Rebecca Foster Cornwall, was a book of biographies that created the first scholarly sketches of important Mormon women such as Amy Brown Lyman (social worker and Relief Society general president), Martha Hughes Cannon (the first state senator in American history), and Ellis Reynolds Shipp (a pioneer woman physician). Burgess-Olson had a background in psychology and family therapy, so this book represents the cross-disciplinary tendency of the New Mormon History. Burgess-Olson's doctoral thesis was entitled, "Family Structure and Dynamics in Early Utah Mormon Families, 1847-1885" (Ph.D. diss., Northwestern, 1975). In the same tradition of short biographies of Mormon women are Colleen Whitley's *Worth Their Salt: Notable but Often Unnoted Women of Utah* (Logan: Utah State University Press, 1996); and *Worth Their Salt, Too: More Notable but Often Unnoted Women of Utah* (Logan: Utah State University Press, 2000). Biographical articles about women have appeared steadily in Mormon historical periodicals.[36]

Women's Voices, compiled at Leonard Arrington's request, was the first volume of excerpted primary documents written by Mormon women. Structured chronologically with selections from each era of nineteenth-century Mormon history, it offered further information on women profiled in *Sister Saints* and let them speak in their own words.

Mormon Enigma

The year 1984 saw the appearance of a book by two homemakers whose self-trained research easily met professional standards. Linda King Newell and Valeen Tippetts Avery, *Mormon Enigma: Emma Hale Smith, Prophet's Wife, "Elect Lady," Polygamy's Foe* (Garden City, NY: Doubleday, 1984), became a landmark in the New Mormon History. Surprisingly enough, this was the first scholarly biography of a Mormon woman ever published by a major press. For Utah Mormons, Emma Smith was an inherently controversial topic because of her rejection of her polygamy, her refusal to follow Brigham Young west, and her support of the Reorganized Church of Jesus Christ of Latter Day Saints (now Community of Christ) that, under the leadership of her oldest son, Joseph Smith III, denounced polygamy. Yet simultaneously, Emma was venerated as the Prophet's loyal and self-sacrificing wife who buried baby after baby as she followed him across the United States and also as the founding president of the Relief Society. Simply to write a serious,

---

36. For instance, from *Utah Historical Quarterly:* Chris Rigby, "Ada Dwyer: Bright Lights and Lilacs," 43 (1975): 41-51; Miriam B. Murphy, "Sarah Elizabeth Carmichael: Poetic Genius of Pioneer Utah," ibid., 52-66; Susa Young Gates, "From Impulsive Girl to Patient Wife: Lucy Bigelow Young," 45 (1977): 270-88; David A. Hales, "'There Goes Matilda': Millard County Midwife and Nurse," 55 (1987): 278-93; Martha Sonntag Bradley, "Mary Teasdel, Yet Another American in Paris," 58 (1990): 244-60; Harriet Horne Arrington, "Alice Merrill Horne, Art Promoter and Early Utah Legislator," ibid., 261-76; Catherine M. Johnson, "Emma Lucy Gates Bowen: Singer, Musician, Teacher," 64 (1996): 344-55; Robert S. McPherson and Mary Lou Mueller, "Divine Duty: Hannah Sorenson and Midwifery in Southeastern Utah," 65 (1997): 335-54; Sandra Dawn Brimhall, "Sara Alexander: Pioneer Actress and Dancer," 66 (1998): 320-33. See also Lavina Fielding Anderson, "Mary Fielding Smith: Her Ox Goes Marching On," in *Blueprints for Living: Perspectives for LDS Women,* edited by Maren M. Mouritsen (Provo, UT: BYU Press, 1980), 2:2-13, also in *Dialogue* 14 (Winter 1981): 91-100; Ronald G. Walker, "Rachel R. Grant: The Continuing Legacy of the Feminine Ideal," in *Supporting Saints,* edited by Donald Q. Cannon and David Whittaker (Provo, UT: BYU Religious Studies Center, 1985), 17-42; Henry J. Wolfinger, "A Test of Faith: Jane Elizabeth James and the Origins of the Utah Black Community," in *Social Accommodation in Utah,* edited by Clark Knowlton (Salt Lake City: American West Center, University of Utah, 1975), 130-50; Linda King Newell and Valeen Tippetts Avery, "Jane Manning James: Black Saint, 1847 Pioneer," *Ensign,* August 1979, 26-29; and Donald Godfrey, "Zina Presendia Young Williams Card: Brigham's Daughter, Cardston's First Lady," *Journal of Mormon History* 23 (Fall 1997): 107-27.

Mormon Enigma: Emma Hale Smith

Prophet's Wife, "Elect Lady," Polygamy's Foe, 1804–1879

Linda King Newell
and
Valeen Tippetts Avery

Doubleday & Company, Inc., Garden City, New York
1984

sympathetic treatment of Emma's whole life, including the years after she parted company with Brigham Young and married a non-Mormon, required a certain resolve.

Mormon Enigma faced Joseph Smith's polygamy squarely; it updated Brodie and was based on fuller, more balanced research than *No Man Knows My History*. The authors painstakingly combed through the documents that had become newly accessible under Leonard Arrington in the Church Archives. Moreover, this volume looked at Smith's polygamy from the viewpoint of Emma, the first wife. While Utah Mormons have often viewed Emma as wrongly trying to keep Joseph Smith from divinely mandated polygamous marriages, this book portrayed the complexity of polygamy from a woman's perspective. Particularly unsettling was its documentation of Joseph's marriages to young women (in some cases, very young women) without Emma's knowledge. Nevertheless, Newell and Avery wrote their biography with balance and a deep sympathy for its subject. Leonard Arrington, on the back of the dust jacket, called it "a model of honesty, clarity, and fairness." Mormon readers who had dismissed Brodie's *No Man Knows My History* as biased were faced with the reality of Nauvoo polygamy in this book. Seeing Joseph Smith through a woman's eyes caused an important paradigm shift in *Mormon Enigma's* broad readership.

Mormon Enigma also broke new ground by covering a figure central to both LDS and RLDS history. Although conservatives in both groups were troubled by the book, it was generally warmly received. Paul M. Edwards, a descendant of Emma Smith, reviewed it positively in "An Enigma Resolved: The Emma Smith of Newell and Avery," *Journal of Mormon History* 11 (1984): 119-24. A history instructor at the RLDS Church's Graceland College, William D. Russell, told me that *Mormon Enigma* is always the favorite book of students in his Mormon history class. Avery earned a Ph.D. in history, selecting as her dissertation topic Joseph and Emma's brilliant and troubled youngest son, David Hyrum Smith. Published as *From Mission to Madness: Last Son of the Mormon Prophet* (Urbana: University of Illinois Press, 1998), it won the prestigious Evans Award for Biography. Newell has written or cowritten histories of Garfield, Piute, and (with Edward Leo Lyman) Millard counties as part of Utah's statehood sesquicentennial project.

My own book, *In Sacred Loneliness: The Plural Wives of Joseph Smith* (Salt Lake City: Signature Books, 1997) complements *Mormon Enigma* by providing chapter-length biographies of each of the thirty-three (by my count) women who became Joseph Smith's plural wives, following their lives from birth through Nauvoo to their deaths, often in Utah. Intended as straightforward feminist history, it celebrates the lives of remarkable Mormon women but also analyzes the woman's experience in polygamy, which I concluded was ambiguous. Although it was rich in religious and social prestige, and included an undoubted spiritual dimension as men and women participated in a marriage system restored from the days of patriarchal prophets in the Old Testament, in the daily experience of "practical" polygamy, the woman often endured emotional and financial isolation, since husbands, despite their best efforts, were required to divide their time and resources among many wives. The more elite the man—and those who remarried Joseph Smith's widows were usually apostles—the more wives he was expected to have, since quantity of wives provided higher exaltation after death, in Mormon ideology.

Another important contribution to understanding the women around Joseph Smith is Lavina Fielding Anderson, *Lucy's Book: A Critical Edition of Lucy Mack Smith's Family Memoir* (Salt Lake City: Signature Books, 2001), which tells the story of Joseph Smith from a woman's perspective, in this case, his mother.

RLDS Women

Women's history in the Community of Christ/RLDS branch of the New Mormon History is also a notable story. The liberal-leaning RLDS Church leadership awarded

---

37. Richard P. Howard, *The Church Through the Years. Volume 2: The Reorganization Comes of Age, 1860-1992* (Independence: Herald Publishing House, 1993), 396-406. See also Madelon Brunson, *Bonds of Sisterhood: A History of the RLDS Women's Organization, 1842-1983* (Independence: Herald Publishing House, 1985).

38. See William D. Russell, "The Fundamentalist Schism, 1958-Present," in *Let Contention Cease: The*

women priesthood rights by a revelation in 1984,[37] which was a major factor in causing a substantial schism of conservatives from the central RLDS Church.[38] The first women were ordained to the priesthood on November 17, 1985, and today the RLDS Church has women apostles. Nevertheless, RLDS women have been somewhat neglected by historians. Community of Christ historian Danny L. Jorgensen wrote, in "Sisters' Lives, Sisters' Voices: Neglected Reorganized Latter Day Saint Herstories," *John Whitmer Historical Association Journal* 17 (1997): 25-42: "Today . . . women still have not been substantially written into the RLDS story. . . . Although helpful, the modest literature on Reorganization women contains few scholarly interpretations of their lives and roles in church history. . . . The story of the Reorganized Church consequently is composed predominantly of his-stories to the exclusion of her-stories" (27-28).

Still, one can find the beginnings of an RLDS her-story in RLDS publications, most notably in Madelon Brunson's 1985 *Bonds of Sisterhood: A History of the RLDS Women's Organization, 1842-1983*, a counterpart to the LDS *Women of Covenant*. A number of articles also give great insight into RLDS women: Brunson's "Stranger in a Strange Land: A Personal Response to the 1984 Document," *Dialogue* 17 (Autumn 1984): 11-16, reprinted in *Restoration Studies* 3 (1986): 108-15; Velma Ruch, "To Magnify Our Calling: A Response to Section 156," *Restoration Studies* 3 (1986): 97-107, both reactions to the priesthood revelation; Patricia Struble, "Mite to Bishop: RLDS Women's Financial Relationship to the Church," *John Whitmer Historical Association Journal* 6 (1986): 23-32; Roger Launius, "A Black Woman in a White Man's Church: Amy E. Robbins and the Reorganization," *Journal of Mormon History* 19 (Fall 1993): 65-85;[39] William D. Russell, "Ordaining Women and Transformation from Sect to Denomination," *Dialogue* 36 (Fall 2003): 61-64; and Barbara Higdon, "Present at the Beginning: One Woman's Journey," *Dialogue* 36 (Fall 2003): 65-70.

Women Writing on Men; Men Writing on Women

While *Mormon Enigma* provides us with an example of women writing on women, there has also been frequent "cross-pollination" in the New Mormon History: women writing on men, and men writing on women. Women writers who have made significant accomplishments in Mormon studies, without taking women as their central subjects include Jan Shipps, Mary Lythgoe Bradford, and Irene M. Bates. Shipps, a Methodist, and thus one of Mormon history's "inside-outsiders,"[40] has written a number of significant articles over the year, most notably, "The Prophet Puzzle: Suggestions Leading Toward a More Comprehensive Interpretation of Joseph Smith," published in the first volume of the *Journal of Mormon History* in 1974.[41] Her *Mormonism: The Story of a New Religious Tradition* (Urbana: University of Illinois Press, 1985) is a stimulating and important attempt to put Mormonism into the context of the history of religions. She has published *Sojourner in the Promised Land: Forty Years among the Mormons* (Urbana: University of Illinois Press, 2000), a book of historical essays interleaved with reminiscences.

Mary Lythgoe Bradford is well known as a graceful essayist, a staunch supporter of *Dialogue* from its beginning, and its third editor.[42] She made a permanent contribution in contemporary Mormon history with her superb biography of one of Mormonism's

---

Dynamics of Dissent in the Reorganized Church of Jesus Christ of Latter Day Saints, edited by Roger D. Launius and W. B. "Pat" Spillman (Independence: Graceland/Park Press, 1991), 125-52, 134-37; Howard, *The Church Through the Years*, 2:409-32.

39. See also Launius, "The 'New Social History' and the 'New Mormon History,'" 122-26, a discussion of possible directions for writing on gender issues in Mormon history.

40. See her "An 'Inside-Outsider' in Zion," *Dialogue* 15 (Spring 1982): 139-61.

41. Reprinted in Quinn, *The New Mormon History*, 53-74. See also her "Utah Comes of Age Politically: A Study of the State's Policies in the Early Years of the Twentieth Century," *Utah Historical Quarterly* 35 (Spring, 1967): 91-111; "The Mormon Past: Revealed or Revisited?" *Sunstone* 6 (November-December 1981): 55-58; "The Principle Revoked: A Closer Look at the Demise of Plural Marriage," *Journal of Mormon History* 11 (1984): 67-78. Shipps also wrote the foreword to *Sisters in Spirit*.

42. See Bradford's "Big D/little d: The View from the Basement," *Dialogue* 20 (Fall 1987): 13-22. Her *Leaving Home* (Salt Lake City: Signature Books, 1987), is a book of personal essays that collectively make a sort of autobiography.

most influential teachers, *Lowell L. Bennion: Teacher, Counselor, Humanitarian* (Salt Lake City: Dialogue Foundation, 1995), who, with Leonard Arrington, was one of the great moral leaders of modern Mormonism. She is currently working on a biography of Virginia Sorensen, with coauthors Susan Elizabeth Howe and Sue Saffle.

Irene M. Bates, a convert to the LDS Church from England, authored, with E. Gary Smith, *Lost Legacy: The Mormon Office of Presiding Patriarch* (Urbana: University of Illinois Press, 1996), a fascinating study of the lineal office of presiding patriarch, a General Authority position from Joseph Smith's day. His father was the first to hold that office, but it provides a textbook interpretation of Max Weber's process on the "routinization" of charisma in social groups—the office was retired during the Spencer W. Kimball administration although that last incumbent, Eldred G. Smith (Gary's father) is still alive at this writing and giving patriarchal blessings..

In turn, two men, Levi S. Peterson and Newell G. Bringhurst, wrote significant biographies of two women in the first generation of the New Mormon History: Peterson's *Juanita Brooks: Mormon Woman Historian* (Salt Lake City: University of Utah Press, 1988) and Bringhurst's *Fawn McKay Brodie: A Biographer's Life* (Norman: University of Oklahoma Press, 1999). Both books are fascinating, insightful studies, showing how Brooks and Brodie struggled to balance the demands of raising a family and their talent for writing and research, as well as balancing Church pressures and loyalties with the need for intellectual honesty and freedom.

Polygamy and Women

In the 1980s and 1990s, a wealth of important books on polygamy, which has special relevance to Mormon women, were published. Lawrence Foster, *Religion and Sexuality: Three American Communal Experiences of the Nineteenth Century* (New York: Oxford University Press, 1981) is a solid and stimulating introduction to three alternative marriage systems—the mystical celibacy of Shakerism, with its woman founder-prophet; the "complex marriage" of John Humphrey Noyes; and the plural marriage of Mormonism. This book is especially valuable in placing Mormon polygamy in the broader context of American religion. Foster covers much of this same ground but with a perspective more focused on women in *Women, Family, and Utopia: Communal Experiments of the Shakers, the Oneida Community, and the Mormons* (Syracuse, NY: Syracuse University Press, 1991). The four Mormon chapters are entitled, "Between Two Worlds: Plural Marriage and the Experiences of Mormon Women in Illinois during the Early 1840s"; "James J. Strang: The Prophet Who Failed"; "Polygamy and the Frontier: Mormon Women in Early Utah"; and "From Activism to Domesticity: The Changing Role of Mormon Women in the Nineteenth and Twentieth Centuries."

Louis J. Kern, in his *An Ordered Love: Sex Roles and Sexuality in Victorian Utopias—the Shakers, the Mormons, and the Oneida Community* (Chapel Hill: University of North Carolina Press, 1981), coincidentally also looked at Mormonism, Shakers, and the Oneida movement, though with more of a Freudian and pointed feminist perspective. Kern and Foster reviewed each other's books, mostly favorably, in *Dialogue* 4 (Winter 1981): 204-12.

Two influential articles on polygamy appeared in the mid-1980s. Joan Smyth Iversen, "Feminist Implications of Mormon Polygamy," *Feminist Studies* 10 (Fall 1984): 505-22, argued that polygamy, because the husbands were often absent from their plural families, caused women to become more independent. "Patriarchal" marriage, often seen as sexist and demeaning to women, paradoxically thus developed more capable women and thus furthered the feminist cause. Undoubtedly, there is some truth to this, although there are many other aspects to consider in evaluating whether polygamy was generally beneficial to women, nor is it clear that women always defined this forced autonomy as developing their capabilities rather than imposing a crushing burden upon them.[43] D. Michael Quinn, "LDS Church Authority and New Plural Marriages, 1890-1904," *Dialogue* 18 (Spring 1985): 9-105,

---

43. See also, in the same issue, Julie Dunfrey, "'Living the Principle' of Plural Marriage: Mormon Women, Utopia, and Female Sexuality in the Nineteenth Century," *Feminist Studies* 10 (Fall 1984): 523-36.

one of the classic articles in the New Mormon History, documents how a majority of Mormon General Authorities and second-level leaders continued *sub rosa* polygamy after the Manifesto in 1890, thus creating a "double" reality of conflicting messages in Mormonism whose after-effects remain with us today.

Richard Van Wagoner, *Mormon Polygamy: A History* (1986; 3rd ed., Salt Lake City: Signature Books, 1992) gives a valuable chronological narrative of Mormon polygamy, often quoting from the diaries and autobiographies of Mormon women. Jessie L. Embry, a specialist in oral histories at Brigham Young University, used that expertise and the interviews she conducted in the mid-1980s with the children and grandchildren of polygamists to examine *Mormon Polygamous Families: Life in the Principle* (Salt Lake City: University of Utah Press, 1987), an insightful analysis of Mormon polygamy in the tradition of Kimball Young's *Isn't One Wife Enough?*

B. Carmon Hardy, *Solemn Covenant: The Mormon Polygamous Passage* (Urbana: University of Illinois Press 1992) follows Quinn in exploring the story of post-Manifesto polygamy. It is a haunting book, expressing the tragedy that resulted from the double messages and contradictory teachings and practices accepted as necessary by men, women, and children alike during Mormonism's painful and ambiguous passage to monogamy. Though *Solemn Covenant* focuses primarily on men, the plight of plural wives married during this period, who could not live in the freedom and security of an avowed marriage, is sometimes retold with striking poignancy. An example is his thumbnail sketch of Eliza Avery Clark Woodruff, who became a plural wife of Apostle Abraham O. Woodruff in 1901: "It has been said that Avery, living with her family in Wyoming, was already engaged to a young man when approached by Woodruff. He and Matthias F. Cowley [another apostle] spoke to her of the blessings she would receive by marrying the apostle. Avery was persuaded. She broke her engagement and married Woodruff, the ceremony being performed by Cowley in Preston, Idaho. Avery then moved to a Mormon community in Mexico, where her relationship with Woodruff was less likely to be discovered" (208-9). Abraham, and his first wife then died of smallpox in 1904.

Another woman, Margaret Cullen, married William Geddes polygamously in 1884, then, after his death in 1891, married David Eccles polygamously and secretly in 1898 and bore a son the following year. Her local Church leaders, supposing the child illegitimate, threatened her with excommunication, until General Authorities secretly instructed them to drop the case. Margaret was subpoenaed to testify in Washington, D.C., during the Senate investigation of post-Manifesto polygamy as part of deciding whether to deprive monogamous Apostle and Senator Reed Smoot of his seat. She made the long trip alone, then testified humiliatingly (and untruthfully) in December 1904 that she was not a plural wife and that her son was illegitimate. Eight years later when David Eccles died, she discovered that he had left nothing from his extensive estate to her or her son; and as a polygamous wife, she had no claim on it. This was the final straw for Margaret. During the legal battle that followed, she told the story of her post-Manifesto marriage openly and succeeded in having her son recognized as a legal heir (184-85).

Three books in the 1990s looked at modern "fundamentalism"—the schismatic breakoffs from Mormonism whose members felt (and feel) that they were called by God to continue living polygamously, a position that becomes more understandable in light of the "double messages" about post-Manifesto polygamy that came from General Authorities. Martha Sonntag Bradley, *Kidnapped from That Land: The Government Raids on the Short Creek Polygamists* (Salt Lake City: University of Utah Press, 1993) focused primarily on one incident. In 1953, Utah and Arizona police, supported by LDS leaders, "raided" the polygamous colony of Short Creek (now Colorado City) on the Utah-Arizona border and separated a number of children from their parents. The nation's shocked reaction turned the raid into a public relations fiasco for both states. Bradley offered a very humanizing portrait of the women participating in polygamy. Bradley, coeditor of *Dialogue* during the 1990s, left a position in BYU's History Department in the wake of the September Six actions in 1993 (see discussion below), and now teaches architectural history at the

University of Utah, directs the university's Honors Program, and served as president of MHA in 2003-04. With Mary Brown Firmage Woodward, she published *4 Zinas: A Story of Mothers and Daughters on the Mormon Frontier* (Salt Lake City: Signature Books, 2000). This important collective biography focuses on Zina Diantha Huntington Jacobs Smith Young (the third general president of the Relief Society); her mother (Zina Baker Huntington), her daughter by Brigham Young (Zina Young Williams Card, a prominent Mormon women leader in Canada and a plural wife of Charles O. Card), and her granddaughter (Zina Card Brown, wife of liberal Mormon apostle and First Presidency member, Hugh B. Brown). Zina Diantha was still married to and living with her first husband, Henry Jacobs, when she was married polygamously and polyandrously in succession to Joseph Smith and Brigham Young. Every treatment of Joseph Smith's polygamy has attempted to unravel the enigmatic complexity of Zina's marriages. Though one of the great nineteenth-century Mormon women, she had received less than her due of scholarly attention before this biography.[44]

Polygamous Families in Contemporary Society (New York: Cambridge University Press, 1996) was written by Irwin Altman, professor of psychology and family and consumer studies at University of Utah, and Joseph Ginat, professor of social and culture anthropology at the University of Haifa, Israel. It is rich in portraits of contemporary polygamous wives—many content in their "alternative" life style, others struggling with it. Often these women are intelligent and educated, though living in a very conservative, patriarchal social environment. For example, in the Colorado City milieu, women, often at a young age, are required to enter into marriages arranged by the male "prophet" of the community, though sometimes they or their parents are allowed to have input in the decision (105-7). This book also exemplifies the New Mormon History's interest in fresh perspectives, as Altman and Ginat bring anthropological theory to bear on Mormon polygamy, analyzing how polygamists balance dyadic and communal relationships to try to make polygamy work.

Women's historians have at times viewed polygamous and Mormon women as passive victims of male patriarchy, but this view is often contrasted by views of plural women as vigorous, intelligent, and independent, despite living in less than ideal social situations.[45] Janet Bennion, *Women of Principle: Female Networking in Contemporary Mormon Polygamy* (New York: Oxford University Press, 1998) focuses entirely on women in plural families. These families are often very patriarchal and authoritarian, though still imposing a major share of the economic burden on the women. Bennion concludes, "In spite of the presence of formal subordination to male authority, the Allred group [the largest polygamous group, near Salt Lake City] is a place where women have a significant degree of influence in the household and the community." Though women are sometimes marginalized, their networking allows them "a degree of freedom and solidarity" (150-53).

Articles on polygamy which have special relevance to women's history are Eugene E. Campbell and Bruce L. Campbell, "Divorce among Mormon Polygamists: Extent and Explanation," *Utah Historical Quarterly* 46 (Winter 1978): 4-23 (reprinted in Quinn, *New Mormon History*, 181-98), which showed that divorce rates were higher among polygamous marriage than in monogamous unions; Julie Roy Jeffrey, "'If Polygamy Is the Lord's Order, We Must Carry It Out,'" a chapter in her *Frontier Women: Trans-Mississippi West, 1840-1880* (New York: Hill and Wang, 1979), 147-78; Kimberly Jensen James, "'Between Two Fires': Women on the 'Underground' of Mormon Polygamy," *Journal of Mormon History* 8 (1981): 49-61, telling the story of what women endured while hiding from federal marshals during the 1880s; Kahlile Mehr, "Women's Response to Plural Marriage," *Dialogue* 18 (Fall 1985): 84-98; Richard Van Wagoner, "Sarah M. Pratt: The Shaping of an Apostate," *Dialogue* 19 (Summer 1986): 67-99; Jeffery Ogden Johnson, "Determining and Defining 'Wife': the Brigham Young Households," *Dialogue* 20 (Fall 1987): 57-70, the definitive list of Brigham Young's wives, with occasional thumbnail sketches of their lives; Martha Sonntag Bradley,

---

44. See also Maureen Ursenbach Beecher, "Each in Her Own Time: Four Zinas," *Dialogue* 26 (1993): 119-38; and my chapter on Zina Diantha in *In Sacred Loneliness*, 71-113.

45. For a broader comparison, see Myres, "Women in the West," 376-77.

Excavating Mormon Pasts

"The Women of Fundamentalism: Short Creek, 1953," *Dialogue* 23 (Summer 1990):14-37; and Jessie L. Embry, "Ultimate Taboos: Incest and Mormon Polygamy," *Journal of Mormon History* 18 (Spring 1992): 93-113, which concludes that, by modern definition, incest was rare in the history of Mormon polygamy.

Recent important articles on polygamy and women are Marie Cornwall, Camela Courtright, and Laga Van Beek's statistical analysis, "How Common the Principle? Women as Plural Wives in 1860," *Dialogue* 26 (1993): 139-53; Paula Kelly Harline, "Polygamous Yet Monogamous: Cultural Conflict in the Writings of Mormon Polygamous Wives," in *Old West-New West: Centennial Essays,* edited by Barbara Howard Meldrum (Moscow, Ida.: University of Idaho Press, 1993), 115-32, which analyzes the contrast between women's public pronouncements on polygamy and their private struggle with it; B. Carmon Hardy, "Lords of Creation: Polygamy, the Abrahamic Household, and Mormon Patriarchy," *Journal of Mormon History* 20 (Spring 1994): 119-52, which argues that the doctrine of polygamy had, as its subtext, an ideology of female inferiority; and John Bennion, "Mary Bennion Powell: Polygamy and Silence," *Journal of Mormon History* 24 (Fall 1998): 85-128, which focuses on the trauma experienced by Mary when she discovered at age twelve that her father was a post-Manifesto polygamist and which underscores the differences in male/female perceptions of polygamy.[46]

Kathryn M. Daynes, *More Wives Than One: Transformation of the Mormon Marriage System* (Urbana: University of Illinois Press, 2001), is a superb every-household treatment of Mormon plural marriage in the small Mormon town of Manti that deservedly won the Mormon History Association's Best Book of the Year Award. It is typical of the New Mormon History in two ways. First, it is interdisciplinary in its application of American family studies theory to Mormonism. Second, it looks at nonelite Mormons far from Salt Lake City. Though it includes extensive summaries of the history of polygamy, it is strongest in its treatment of Manti and American family law. Its sociological interpretation of polygamy as the Mormon culture's method of supporting single women economically, while partially valid, arguably underplays the enormous religious significance plural marriage had in LDS belief and practice.[47]

Sarah Barringer Gordon's excellent *The Mormon Question: Polygamy and Constitution Conflict in Nineteenth-Century America* (Chapel Hill: University of North Carolina Press, 2002), another Mormon History best book winner, is typical of the New Mormon History in its interdisciplinary marriage of Mormon and legal history.

The woman's experience in Mormon polygamy will continue to fascinate historians, as they wrestle with its feminist and anti-feminist aspects. Many LDS women will simply be glad that polygamy is no longer a requirement for achieving the highest form of salvation, as it was for their nineteenth-century foremothers. Other women, taking nineteenth-century Church leaders at their word, will continue to enter into schismatic fundamentalist polygamy in Utah.

"Contemporary" Women's History

History tells the story of and analyzes the past. Mainstream Mormon history often looks back to the nineteenth century, beginning with the "heroic" eras of New York, Kirtland, Missouri, and Nauvoo, with the charismatic and enigmatic founder Joseph Smith looming over events, followed by the transcontinental exodus and the settlement of Utah under Brigham Young. The New Mormon History has also explored less "heroic" eras: the painful, complex realities of the 1890s as Mormons reluctantly relinquished their political, economic, and marital practices and entered the mainstream of American life in the 1900s.

---

46. See also Davis Bitton, "Mormon Polygamy," *Journal of Mormon History* 4 (1977): 101-18; Patricia Lyn Scott, "Mormon Polygamy: A Bibliography, 1977-92," in *Journal of Mormon History* 19 (Spring 1993): 133-55; and her "Mormon Polygamy: A Bibliography, 1900-2004," forthcoming in a joint publication from the *Journal of Mormon History* and Signature Books with the working title *Wrestling with the Principle: Readings on Polygamy*.

47. See my review in *Dialogue* 35 (Winter 2002): 161-64.

In general, the twentieth century brought acceptance, monogamy, political conservatism, financial stability, and enormous growth, particularly internationally. (See "Growth and Internationalization: The LDS Church Since 1945" by Kahlile B. Mehr, Mark L. Grover, Reid L. Neilson, Donald Q. Cannon, and Grant Underwood in this volume.) Two key books here are Thomas G. Alexander, *Mormonism in Transition: A History of the Latter-day Saints, 1890-1930* (Urbana: University of Illinois Press, 1986) and D. Michael Quinn, *The Mormon Hierarchy: Extensions of Power* (Salt Lake City: Signature Books, 1997). In fact, "history" begins with each passing second, so there is such a thing as "contemporary" history: history that attempts to give a balanced, scholarly account of contemporary or near contemporary events. There are obvious disadvantages to writing contemporary history. Often key diaries and autobiographies are not available for many years; in addition, it sometimes takes time and the patient accumulation of many interlocking pieces of information to achieve perspective on events. But there are also advantages to "contemporary" history: The historian can actually interview the principals in a story, while the events that transpired are still fresh in their minds. Important documents have not been lost or destroyed. (In fact, the problem may be too *many* documents.) In addition, sometimes the historian becomes part of the story, and so has the benefit of her or his narrow but valuable perspective, although this advantage comes with the ever-present danger of personal bias.

A limited amount has been written on the history of contemporary Mormon women. However, four memoirs by women show the range of contemporary Mormon women's history.[48] Terry Tempest Williams, *Refuge: An Unnatural History of Family and Place* (New York: Pantheon Books, 1991) is a memoir of mother-daughter relationships and both the science and the mysticism of land, water, animal, bird, and the environment. (Williams is a naturalist.) She also documents how the United States's testing of nuclear weapons in the Nevada desert near Utah from 1951 to 1962 caused numerous cases of cancer, including possibly the death by cancer of Williams's mother that is the central drama of *Refuge*. At times Williams depicts her Mormon background sympathetically, as in her account of the LDS Church's response to the 1983 floods (45-46) and her description of family rituals (34, 158). At other times, she views the Church critically.[49] This personal memoir is not only Mormon women's contemporary history but also, enriched by its environmental perspective, is a contribution to ecobiography.[50]

---

48. In addition to these memoirs, see Marie Cornwall, "The Institutional Role of Mormon Women," in *Contemporary Mormonism: Social Science Perspectives,* edited by Marie Cornwall, Tim B. Heaton, and Lawrence A. Young (Urbana: University of Illinois Press, 1994), 239-64, which argued that modern Mormon women are identified chiefly with the family, which has made them much less visible in their contributions to the church; Marie Cornwall, "Women: Changing Ideas and Institutions," *Sunstone* 14 (June 1990): 53-55; and her "Beyond Fertility: What We Don't Know about Utah Women," in *Utah in the 1990s: A Demographic Perspective,* edited by Tim B. Heaton, Thomas A. Hirschl, and Bruce A. Chadwick (Salt Lake City: Signature Books, 1996), 193-211. Cornwall headed the BYU Women's Research Institute for a number of years. See also Maureen Ursenbach Beecher and Kathryn L. MacKay, "Women in Twentieth-Century Utah," in *Utah's History,* edited by Richard D. Poll, Thomas G. Alexander, Eugene E. Campbell, and David E. Miller, (Provo, UT: BYU Press, 1978), 563-86; the final Mormon chapter in Foster, *Women, Family and Utopia;* Laurence R. Iannaccone and Carrie A. Miles, "Dealing with Social Change: The Mormon Church's Response to Change in Women's Roles," in Cornwall, Heaton, and Young, *Contemporary Mormonism,* 265-86; Lavina Fielding Anderson, "Ministering Angels: Single Women in Mormon Society," *Dialogue* 16 (Autumn 1983): 59-72; Linda W. Harris, "The Legend of Jessie Evans Smith," *Utah Historical Quarterly* 44 (1976): 351-64; and Miriam Murphy, "'If Only I Shall Have the Right Stuff': Utah Women in World War I," *Utah Historical Quarterly* 58 (1990): 334-50. One can also focus on women in such books as Susan Buhler Taber, *Mormon Lives: A Year in the Elkton Ward* (Urbana: University of Illinois Press, 1993); James W. Ure, *Leaving the Fold: Candid Conversations with Inactive Mormons* (Salt Lake City: Signature Books, 1999).

49. Laura Bush, "Terry Tempest Williams's *Refuge*: Sentimentality and Separation," *Dialogue* 28 (Fall 1995): 147-60, complained that Williams portrayed Mormon women stereotypically as "frequently mindless victims."

50. Cecilia Konchar Farr and Phillip A. Snyder, "From Walden Pond to the Great Salt Lake: Ecobiography and Engendered Species Acts in *Walden* and *Refuge,*" in *Tending the Garden: Essays on Mormon Literature,* edited by Eugene England and Lavina Fielding Anderson (Salt Lake City: Signature Books, 1996), 197-209.

Excavating Mormon Pasts

Mormonism, and conservative religion in general, have had difficulty facing the challenges of homosexuality. At their worst, Mormons have regarded gays with a reactionary homophobia, reinforced by the Church's explicit funding of and political support for anti-gay rights measures. A memoir that confronts the human reality of homosexuals and the holocaust of AIDS is Carol Lynn Pearson, *Good-bye, I Love You* (New York: Random House, 1986). Pearson, a popular poet and dramatist, earlier published an important anthology of first-person accounts by Mormon women of spiritual experiences, *Daughters of Light* (1973; reprint ed., Salt Lake City: Bookcraft, 1986). She also used nineteenth-century Orderville as the setting for one of her musicals, *The Order Is Love*. *Good-bye, I Love You*, which became a national bestseller, gives a moving account of her husband's death by AIDS and encouraged Mormons to look at homosexuality with more understanding and compassion.[51]

Dorothy Allred Solomon, *In My Father's House* (New York: Franklin Watts, 1984) gives a first-hand view of modern polygamy. She grew up as one of the many children of Rulon Allred, leader of one of the two main branches of Mormon fundamentalists, the more assimilationist "urban" branch in contrast to the separatist branch in Short Creek/Colorado City. This memoir offers a sympathetic but pointed account of the polygamist life style, showing the real humanity of polygamous men and women, their character and culture flaws balanced by deep sincerity and warmth. The injustice of polygamy seen from the viewpoint of the woman is movingly expressed: "They [the polygamous leaders] said the Principle gave women greater freedom—a half-true statement, for polygamous women had more time and support for individual pursuits than their monogamous counterparts. But men and women both seemed blind to the unrest and suffering born of constant comparison and subtle competition" (55). Solomon followed this memoir with *Predators, Prey and Other Kinfolk: Growing Up in Polygamy* (New York: W. W. Norton, 2003), an even more critical view of polygamy and its culture. Mary Batchelor, Marianne Watson, and Anne Wilde, eds., *Voices in Harmony: Contemporary Women Celebrate Plural Marriage* (Salt Lake City: Principle Voices, 2000), in contrast, is a volume of memoirs and testimonies written by contemporary polygamous women who portray plural marriage in a positive light.

Sonia Johnson, *From Housewife to Heretic* (New York: Doubleday, 1981) tells the story of her enthusiastic support of the Equal Rights Amendment and her presidency of Mormons for ERA. Congress passed this amendment in 1972. In 1976, the LDS Church declared the ERA a "moral issue" and waged a secret campaign using Church resources (and especially Mormon women) to oppose it. Johnson was excommunicated in December 1979.[52] While this excommunication caused little fallout among most Mormons, many LDS intellectuals and feminists were troubled by its anti-feminist message and also felt that it implicitly denied the right of free thought and speech among Mormons.[53] Johnson's tone

---

51. For the history of female homosexuality in Mormonism, see Ron Schow, Wayne Schow, and Marybeth Raynes, eds., *Peculiar People: Mormons and Same-Sex Orientation* (Salt Lake City: Signature Books, 1991), see "lesbian(ism)" in index, 371; D. Michael Quinn, *Same-Sex Dynamics among Nineteenth-Century Americans: A Mormon Example* (Urbana: University of Illinois Press, 1996), 462; Rocky O'Donovan, "'The Abominable and Detestable Crime Against Nature': A Brief History of Homosexuality and Mormonism, 1840-1980," in *Multiply and Replenish: Mormon Essays on Sex and Family*, edited by Brent Corcoran (Salt Lake City: Signature Books, 1994), 123-63, esp. 125-32.

52. See Dixie Snow Huefner, "Church and Politics at the Utah IWY Conference," *Dialogue* 15 (1978): 58-75; Lorie Winder, "LDS Position on the ERA: An Historical View," *Exponent II* (Winter 1980): 6-7; O. Kendall White Jr., "A Feminist Challenge: 'Mormons for ERA' as an Internal Social Movement," *Journal of Ethnic Studies* 13 (Spring 1985): 29-50; Armand L. Mauss, *The Angel and the Beehive: The Mormon Struggle with Assimilation* (Urbana: University of Illinois Press, 1994), 117-18; Linda Sillitoe, "Off the Record: Telling the Rest of the Truth," *Sunstone* 14 (1990): 12-26; Martha Sonntag Bradley, "The Mormon Relief Society and the International Women's Year," *Journal of Mormon History* 21 (1995): 105-67; Quinn, *The Mormon Hierarchy: Extensions of Power*, 373-406. Bradley has written a full-length book on the IWY and ERA that is scheduled for publication in 2005 by Signature Books.

53. See also Mary L. Bradford, "The Odyssey of Sonia Johnson," *Dialogue* 14 (Summer 1981): 14-26; and "All on Fire: An Interview with Sonia Johnson," ibid., 27-47; Alice Allred Pottmyer, "Sonia Johnson: Mormonism's Feminist Heretic," in *Differing Visions: Dissenters in Mormon History*, edited by Roger D. Launius and Linda Thatcher (Urbana: University of Illinois Press, 1994), 366-90; and Heather M. Kellogg, "Shades of Gray: Sonia Johnson's Life through Letters and Autobiography," *Dialogue* 29 (Summer 1996): 77-86.

in *From Housewife to Heretic* is politicized and angry; but it is hard not to admire her sincere struggle for women's rights and sympathize with her experiences during the excommunication. The book also describes the breakup of Johnson's marriage at about the same time and her feelings of personal betrayal during this ordeal. Her engagement with radical feminism distanced her, however, from sympathizers who still maintained ties to Mormonism.

Mormon Women's History and the Institutional Church

LDS leaders sometimes describe themselves as human and fallible; but often they are regarded by the orthodox as speaking directly and absolutely for God, meaning that disagreement with them is rebellion against God. This doctrine of practical infallibility (often applied to the Twelve Apostles, as well as to the Church President and First Presidency) has gained increasing prominence in recent years. Such excommunications as Johnson's show that some Church leaders will not allow disagreement or criticism from Church members and will use ecclesiastical pressures, including excommunication, to limit criticism from Church members and to curtail historical treatments of sensitive historical subjects. Women have often been the target for this kind of action, as activist conservative Church leaders entrench to ward off any attempts to enlarge women's role in the Church.[54]

The LDS Church's increasing commitment to the American political and religious right is striking when compared to the Community of Christ. The Community of Christ has two women in its Council of the Twelve Apostles; in the LDS Church, if a person speaks favorably about giving women equal ecclesiastical rights, priesthood (or giving them equal political rights, as in the case of Sonia Johnson), she or he runs the risk of facing a Church court and expulsion from the Church. Since Mormon women's history, which is rich in its portrayals of devotion to a Mother in Heaven and women performing ordinances that are priesthood ordinances by modern standards, provide precedent for women being given priesthood (or, according to some positions, to recognizing their dormant priesthood), Church leaders have often taken ecclesiastical action against Mormon historians and feminists.

This tradition began with the excommunication of Fawn Brodie in May 1946. Brodie certainly did not believe literally in Mormon miracle claims. Nevertheless, she had family, cultural, and emotional ties to Mormonism and was deeply hurt by the action.[55] As she was pregnant and did not live near the court's location, she declined to attend and was excommunicated in absentia by a mission president and a few young missionaries. Her uncle, Church President David O. McKay, may have helped effect the excommunication.

When Juanita Brooks's *Mountain Meadows Massacre* was published in 1950, she was not formally disciplined but felt that she and her husband were subsequently ostracized in the small community of St. George. General Church leaders had refused to give her access to important documents relating to the massacre and impugned her motives for doing her research.[56]

In 1985, priesthood leaders in Utah and Arizona were instructed, through a telephone tree, not to allow Linda King Newell and Valeen Tippetts Avery, the authors of

---

54. For the LDS Church's movement to the right, see Mauss, *The Angel and the Beehive*, 149; Waterman and Kagel, *The Lord's University*, 415-54. This issue is complex, as Mauss's full analysis shows; the Church's most powerful leaders are by definition those who have been in the hierarchy the longest. Apostle and First Presidency Counselor Hugh B. Brown described himself as almost a minority of one as a Democrat among LDS General Authorities. Edward B. Firmage, ed., *An Abundant Life: The Memoirs of Hugh B. Brown* (Salt Lake City: Signature Books, 1988), 18. See also, Davis Bitton, "Anti-Intellectualism in Mormon History," *Dialogue* 1 (Autumn 1966): 111-34. Arrington's principle of the "bias of unanimity" should be invoked here: I believe some moderate Church leaders disagree with the actions of "activist conservative" leaders, and have worked behind the scenes to temper them. One could argue, however, that the "activist conservatives" have set the agenda.

55. Bringhurst, *Fawn McKay Brodie*, 107-15.

56. Bitton and [Beecher], "Riding Herd," 11-33, 21-22, 29; Peterson, *Juanita Brooks*, 218-19, 415.

57. Lavina Fielding Anderson, "The LDS Intellectual Community and Church Leadership: A Contemporary Chronology," *Dialogue* 26 (Spring 1993): 7-64, 22, 25, 28.

Mormon Enigma, to speak on history topics in Church meetings, and Newell and Avery were subjected to ecclesiastical investigation.[57]

As the New Mormon History developed, Elder Boyd K. Packer, a conservative apostle who saw feminists as a special threat to Mormonism,[58] gained more seniority in the Twelve and combined this seniority with an aggressive administrative style that has made him one of the most influential Church leaders of our generation. In September 1993, five feminists, theologians, and historians were excommunicated and a sixth was disfellowshipped by local Church courts, an act that Packer reportedly encouraged during the final illness of Church President Ezra Taft Benson. Any one of these excommunications alone would have been major news; coming all at the same time, they attracted enormous attention, both within and outside of Utah, including front-page stories in the *New York Times.*[59]

Lynne Kanavel Whitesides, the first to be disciplined, was president of the feminist Mormon Women's Forum. She was disfellowshipped by her bishop, the only one of the September Six not to be excommunicated. Avraham Gileadi, whom many regarded as hyper-conservative, was an Old Testament scholar specializing in Isaiah. Paul James Toscano, who had recently given a Sunstone talk critical of General Authorities, had coauthored with his wife, Margaret Merrill Toscano, *Strangers in Paradox* (Salt Lake City: Signature Books, 1987), a collection of theological essays that included feminist themes strongly supportive of priesthood for women. Margaret often spoke on the theme of Mother in Heaven.[60] In this case, the bishop had initially begun proceedings against Margaret, but the action almost immediately switched to Paul under the stake president's direction. Maxine Hanks had edited an anthology of feminist writings, *Women and Authority: Re-emerging Mormon Feminism* (Salt Lake City: Signature Books, 1992), containing some essays that explicitly advocated priesthood for Mormon women. Lavina Fielding Anderson had just published an article in *Dialogue,* "The LDS Intellectual Community and Church Leadership: A Contemporary Chronology," which documented 133 examples of what she saw as an increasingly tense and unhealthy relationship between the institutional Church and its scholars (primarily historians and feminists).[61] D. Michael Quinn, a former professor of history at Brigham Young University, had published a lengthy article in *Women and Authority* entitled "Mormon Women Have Had the Priesthood Since 1843."

Five of these excommunications were thus related to women's issues. Three of them were related to women's history (Hanks, Anderson, and Quinn). Thus, the ecclesiastical action against the September Six can be seen partially as some Church leaders' attempt to curtail the study of Mormon feminism and women's history. Other liberals have been excommunicated since the September Six. Two were feminists: Janice Allred, author of *God*

---

58. Waterman and Kagel, *The Lord's University,* 272.

59. See "Six Intellectuals Disciplined for Apostasy," *Sunstone* 16 (November 1993): 65-70; Jan Shipps, "Knowledge and Understanding," ibid., 11-12; Lavina Fielding Anderson, "The September Six," in *Religion, Feminism, & Freedom of Conscience: A Mormon/Humanist Dialogue,* edited by George D. Smith (Salt Lake City: Signature Books, 1994): 3-8; Waterman and Kagel, *The Lord's University,* 275-88.

60. See Margaret Merrill Toscano: "Peripheral Visions of the Mormon Mother God: Making the Invisible Visible," *Mormon Women's Forum* 8, nos. 3-4 (Fall/Winter 1997): 3-9.

61. The original version of this paper, written before Lavina became a coeditor of this book, included a section on Lavina. However, Lavina felt that including it would be inappropriate, given her editorial oversight. However, see her "Landmarks for LDS Woman: A Contemporary Chronology," *Mormon Women's Forum* 3, #3,4 (December 1992): 1-20; an update in Lorie Winder Stromberg, "Taking Stock: The 10th Anniversary of the *Mormon Women's Forum,*" *Mormon Women Forum Quarterly* 9 no. 1 (Spring 1998): 1-4; Levi S. Peterson, "Lavina Fielding Anderson and the Power of a Church in Exile," *Dialogue* 29 (Winter 1996): 169-78; and Karen Marguerite Moloney, "Saints for All Seasons: Lavina Fielding Anderson and Bernard Shaw's Joan of Arc," *Dialogue* 36 (Fall 2003): 27-40. Anderson has continued to edit the *Journal of Mormon History*; she also coedits with Janice Merrill Allred, *Case Reports of the Mormon Alliance,* vols. 1-3 (Salt Lake City: Mormon Alliance, 1995-97), which have looked in depth at sexual abuse in the LDS Church, the LDS Church's treatment of homosexuals, types of abusive situations in the LDS mission program, and specific repressive incidents.

62. For subsequent excommunications, see *Case Reports of the Mormon Alliance: Volume 2, 1996* (Salt Lake City: Mormon Alliance, 1997), 117-323; *Case Reports of the Mormon Alliance: Volume 3, 1997* (Salt Lake City: Mormon Alliance, 1998), 291-358. The Toscanos had founded the Mormon Alliance in 1992, in part to document and publish cases of ecclesiastical and spiritual abuse. Allred and Anderson were trustees at the time of

the Mother and Other Theological Essays (Salt Lake City: Signature Books 1997), and a trustee of the Mormon Alliance.[62] In addition, Margaret Merrill Toscano, after being passed over in 1996, was excommunicated in 2000 by a new stake president for advocating recognizing women's priesthood and devotion to Mother in Heaven. Michael Barrett, counsel for the CIA and, ironically, Sonia Johnson's former home teacher, was excommunicated for writing letters to newspapers correcting journalistic errors about Church history, especially about the priesthood ban for blacks and the "cessation" of polygamy.[63]

D. Michael Quinn is a central figure in the New Mormon History in his willingness to examine difficult subjects and in the care and thoroughness of his research and documentation of these issues. He was employed as a historical assistant in Arrington's History Division, received his Ph.D. from Yale University, then accepted a position in BYU's History Department at Brigham Young University. While his earlier writings, a Church-sponsored biography of J. Reuben Clark, an analysis of magic in early Mormonism, and his post-Manifesto polygamy article had reportedly angered Packer, attempts by apostles to silence Quinn had been warded off by a sympathetic stake president, who had intended to call Quinn as a bishop.[64] Facing increasing restrictions in research and publishing, Quinn left BYU. When he returned to Salt Lake City in the summer of 1992, his new stake president began a series of actions against him, resulting in his excommunication in September 1993. The reason for the trial, he was told, was his apostasy as evidenced by "Mormon Women Have Had the Priesthood Since 1843," published in Hanks's *Women and Authority*, "150 Years of Truth and Consequences about Mormon History," *Sunstone* 16 (February 1992): 12-14, and statements he had made to press stating that the Church did not allow a loyal opposition. Quinn was incredulous: "In my wildest fears, I never thought I would be excommunicated for publicizing an article on the status of Mormon women and the priesthood."[65] While Packer's earlier history of antagonism to Quinn certainly was a factor in Quinn's excommunication, it is striking that the main article used to justify the action dealt with Mormon women's history.

Since then, Quinn has published *Same-Sex Dynamics among Nineteenth-Century Americans: A Mormon Example* (Urbana: University of Illinois Press, 1996), the first book of Mormon history to win a national prize (the Herbert Feis Award from the American Historical Association),[66] and his two-part magnum opus, *The Mormon Hierarchy: Origins of Power* and *The Mormon Hierarchy: Extensions of Power*. The last chapter in the second volume is a chapter on the LDS Church's opposition to the Equal Rights Amendment.

Diaries and Autobiographies: Critical Editions

A prime characteristic of the New Mormon History is an increased emphasis on primary sources; and a wealth of women's diaries, memoirs, and autobiographies have been published in recent years. The Utah State University Press has led the way with its series, LIFE WRITINGS OF FRONTIER WOMEN, with Maureen Ursenbach Beecher as general editor. To date, the series includes Maureen Ursenbach Beecher, ed., *The Personal Writings of Eliza Roxcy Snow* (1995, 2000); Maurine Carr Ward, ed., *Winter Quarters: The 1846-1848 Life Writings of Mary Haskin Parker Richards* (1996); Donna Toland Smart, ed., *Mormon Midwife: The 1846-1888 Diaries of Patty Bartlett Sessions* (1997); S. George Ellsworth, ed., *The History of Louisa Barnes Pratt: The Autobiography of a Mormon Missionary Widow and Pioneer* (1998); Noel A. Carmack and Karen Lynn Davidson, eds., *Out of the Black Patch: The Autobiography of Effie*

---

their excommunications.

63. Margaret Merrill Toscano, "Tidying Up Loose Ends?" The November 2000 Excommunication of Margaret Toscano," Sunstone Symposium, August 2001, audiocassette SL01-272.

64. Quinn, "On Being a Mormon Historian (and Its Aftermath)," in *Faithful History: Essays on Writing Mormon History*, edited by George D. Smith, ed. (Salt Lake City: Signature Books, 1992), 69-112; Lavina Fielding Anderson, "DNA Mormon: D. Michael Quinn," in *Mormon Mavericks: Essays on Dissenters*, edited by John Sillito and Susan Staker (Salt Lake City: Signature Books, 2002), 329-64.

65. Quoted in "Six Intellectuals Disciplined," 70.

66. This book also contributes to women's history in its coverage of female homosexuality. See above.

Excavating Mormon Pasts

Marquess Carmack, Folk Musician, Artist, and Writer (1999); and Todd Compton and Charles M. Hatch, *A Widow's Tale: The 1884-1896 Diary of Helen Mar Kimball Whitney* (2003), with more slated to follow. All of these are jewel-like in their spiritual, literary, and historical value. The Carmack and Richards volumes are delightfully readable accounts of nonelite Mormon women, while the edition of Helen Mar Kimball Smith Whitney's 1884-96 diaries, combined with Jeni and Richard Holzapfel's *A Woman's View: Helen Mar Whitney's Reminiscences of Early Church History,* presents the fullest, most revealing record of a Mormon woman that has yet appeared in print.

Women's History and the New Mormon History

Mormon women's history has been firmly launched with women authors producing classics like *Mountain Meadows Massacre, A Mormon Mother, Mormon Enigma,* and *Women of Covenant,* supplemented by biographical anthologies, and critical editions of life writings. The *Utah Historical Quarterly, Journal of Mormon History, Dialogue, BYU Studies, John Whitmer Historical Association Journal, Exponent II,* and the *Mormon Woman's Forum Quarterly* have published a rich profusion of articles on Mormon and Utah women. The various periods of Mormon polygamy have received valuable treatments, with special attention given to women. Innovative *types* of Mormon women's history have been attempted, such as ecobiography, institutional history, economic history, political history, family and community history, and anthropological and sociological examinations. Scholarly bibliographies also aid researchers.[67]

Nevertheless, much remains to be done in Mormon women's history. Hundreds of worthy diaries, letters, and autobiographies still await publication. More work also needs to be done in positioning Mormon women's history in the theoretical frameworks developed in the wider field of American, western, and women's history, and feminist critical theory. The good books in the New Mormon History could and should be reaching a wider audience, and coming to grips with a wider context will help in this goal.

It is striking that contemporary fundamentalist (polygamist) women have received a substantial amount of scholarly attention, while contemporary "mainstream" Mormon women (much more numerous) have been comparatively ignored. More work needs to be done on gender, feminism, and "conservative," and "liberal" women in contemporary Mormonism, both LDS and RLDS.

Finally, a good survey on the history of Mormon women does not yet exist. The closest candidate is *Women of Covenant,* which is limited as an institutional Relief Society history, or Warenski's *Patriarchs and Politics,* which lacks sympathy and balance. A balanced, well-written, scholarly history of women in Mormonism, in the best tradition of the New Mormon History, will be an enormous contribution.

TODD COMPTON, an independent researcher, received his Ph.D. in classics from the University of California, Los Angeles, and has held appointments as a lecturer in various universities in the Los Angeles area. His *In Sacred Loneliness: The Plural Wives of Joseph Smith* (Salt Lake City: Signature Books, 1997) is widely recognized as the definitive work on this topic. In addition to numerous articles that have appeared in a variety of scholarly publications, he is the coauthor with Leland Gentry of *Fire and Sword: A History of the Latter-day Saints in Northern Missouri From 1836 to 1839* (working title) (Salt Lake City: Greg Kofford Books, 2004).

67. See Carol Cornwall Madsen and David J. Whittaker, "History's Sequel: A Source Essay on Women in Mormon History," *Journal of Mormon History* 6 (1979): 123-45; Patricia Lyn Scott and Maureen Ursenbach Beecher, "Mormon Women: A Bibliography in Process, 1977-1985," *Journal of Mormon History* 12 (1985): 113-28; Karen Purser Frazier, *Bibliography of Social Scientific, Historical, and Popular Writings about Mormon Women* (Provo, UT: Women's Research Institute, Brigham Young University, 1990); Patricia Lyn Scott, "Writing Women's Lives: A Bibliography on Writing Biographies on Women," *Genealogical Journal* 27 (1999): 3?23; Foster, *Women, Family and Utopia,* 325-43; Quinn, *Extensions of Power,* 602-3, 623-27; Bushman, *Mormon Sisters,* 2d ed. (1997), 267-81; and relevant entries in James B. Allen, Ronald W. Walker, and David J. Whittaker, eds., *Studies in Mormon History, 1830-1897* (Urbana: University of Illinois Press, 2000) and Ronald W. Walker, David J. Whittaker, James B. Allen, *Mormon History* (Urbana: University of Illinois Press, 2001).

Chapter 13

Out of the Closet and into the Fire: The New Mormon Historians' Take on Polygamy

Martha Sonntag Bradley

The whole subject of the marriage relationship is not within my reach or in any other man's reach on this earth. It is without the beginning of days or the end of years; it is a hard matter to reach. We can feel some things with regard to it; it lays the foundation for worlds, for angels, and for Gods; for intelligent beings to be crowned with glory, immortality, and eternal lives. In fact, it is the thread which runs from the beginning to the end of the holy Gospel of the Son of God; it is from eternity to eternity. —Brigham Young[1]

The doctrine of plural marriage was so central to the nineteenth-century Latter-day Saint Church that it permeated Mormonism like a dye in water. It was the test of the most faithful, the boundary that distinguished those in the faith from those outside it. It was the key to celestial glory. Although the 1890 Manifesto was ineffective in ending official plural marriages, it did end public discourse on "the Principle," as the practice of plural marriage was called by the Saints. At that point, the Church began a process of separating itself from both the doctrine and the story of polygamy—breaking a thread that had been woven through Mormon history from its first generation to the present.

During the last few decades, Mormon historians have again taken up this fabric, finding the story of Mormon polygamy to have a rich and compelling design. Applying the methodologies of a variety of disciplines—legal history, demographics, and social history—the Principle[2] has received careful scrutiny. Furthermore, in a very real sense, the study of Mormon polygamy is vintage New Mormon History. For decades, it was a subject that was considered off limits, embarrassing, perhaps even threatening to the Church,

---

1. John A. Widstsoe, ed., *Discourses of Brigham Young* (Salt Lake City: Deseret Book, 1954), 194.
2. Because of its centrality to the Mormon concept of the plan of salvation, almost from its inception, Mormons referred to the concept of plurality as "the Principle." The principle of plural marriage represented the pinnacle of Mormon marriage, not only for all eternity, but as part of patriarchal order with almost unlimited potential for increase.

certainly counterproductive to missionary work and for that reason deleted from official Church publications.

Nevertheless, the story of how Mormon men and women struggled to restructure their lives, their relationships, and their thinking to adjust to the doctrine of plural marriage and thereby be obedient to what they considered to be the will of the Lord is perhaps the clearest test case of Mormonism's enduring power. Here, the validity of theology was challenged in a stringent test of the Saints' application of ideology. Though left largely unexamined for decades, it proved to be far too fertile research soil for to be left untilled for long.

Precursors

Before midcentury the subject was not discussed in Mormon circles and not usually seriously addressed elsewhere, although two pre-1950s exceptions are Charles E. Shook, *The True Origin of Mormon Polygamy* (Cincinnati, OH: Standard Publishing, 1914) and Fawn M. Brodie, *No Man Knows My History: The Life of Joseph Smith* (1945; rev. ed., New York: Alfred A. Knopf, 1971). It is perhaps fitting that the first serious statistical study of plural marriage was conducted by the son of Apostle Anthony W. Ivins, who had been deeply immersed in post-Manifesto polygamy. Stanley H. Ivins, described by the *Utah Historical Quarterly* as a "quiet, unassuming man, schooled in animal-husbandry, but reared in a home where philosophy, religion, and politics were common fare,"[3] published "Notes on Mormon Polygamy" in the *Western Humanities Review* 10 (Summer 1956): 229-39; reprinted in *Utah Historical Quarterly* 35 (Fall 1967): 309-21. His central thesis was that the extent of polygamy had always been misrepresented according to the self-interests of the speaker and that the essential nature of plural marriages had not, consequently, been accurately understood. Ivins challenged the Church's claim that no more than 3 percent of the Church ever practiced a plurality of wives. Instead, based on his data of about 2,500 marriages, he suggested a figure of between 15 and 20 percent, marked by "sporadic outbursts of enthusiasm, followed by relapses, with the proportion of the Saints living in polygamy steadily falling" (313). In other words, the incidence of polygamous marriage increased in times of crisis—after the death of Joseph Smith, during the 1857 Mormon Reformation, and in response to the passage of the Edmunds Act of 1882. It declined in times of relative calm.

Ivins also disputed the mythic proportions of polygamous families, documenting instead that 66.3 percent of male polygamists married only one extra wife, 21.2 percent had three wives, and 6.7 percent took four wives. Fewer than 6 percent married five or more women. Although polygamy certainly increased the total number of children per male, the number of children per woman was an average of eight for monogamous wives but only 5.9 per plural wife.

Kimball Young fleshed out the story of plurality of wives in his path-breaking book, *Isn't One Wife Enough: The Story of Mormon Polygamy* (New York: Henry Holt, 1954). Based on oral interviews conducted by Young's research associate, James Hulett, as well as primary research in contemporary literature, for decades this book was the definitive word on plural marriage despite its lack of documentation and its unsatisfying use of pseudonyms for the key subjects of the narrative.

---

3. "Tribute to Stanley S. Ivins," *Utah Historical Quarterly* 35 (Fall 1967): 307. Ivins died July 5, 1967.

The Role of the LDS Church Historical Department

It became clear during the administration of Church historian Leonard J. Arrington, who served from 1972 through 1979, that polygamy was no longer an off-limits subject but one essential to a proper understanding of nineteenth-century Mormon culture and society. Arrington himself set the standard for candor in his foundational work, *Great Basin Kingdom: An Economic History of the Latter-day Saints* (1958; reprint ed., Lincoln: University of Nebraska Press, 1966), presenting polygamy as part of a larger Mormon complex in its socio-economic religious context. For instance, Arrington wrote in a characteristic matter-of-fact way, "The effect of the institution was to create somewhat larger family units than was typical on the frontier. This permitted a high degree of specialization among family members, and, at the same time, a high degree of family specialization" (238). Rather than centering his analysis on the highly sensational aspects of the story of plurality, Arrington analyzed its economic impact on family life patterns.

Throughout the 1970s, a series of books and articles appeared from members of the LDS Historical Department that described the polygamous lives of nineteenth-century Mormons including Leonard Arrington, Feramorz Fox, and Dean L. May, *Building the City of God: Community and Cooperation among the Mormons* (1976; 2d ed., Urbana: University of Illinois Press, 1992); Leonard J. Arrington and Davis Bitton, *The Mormon Experience: A History of the Latter-day Saints* (New York: Alfred A. Knopf, 1979); and James B. Allen and Glen Leonard, *The Story of the Latter-day Saints* (1976; 2d ed. rev., Salt Lake City, Utah: Deseret Book, 1992). Unlike Joseph Fielding Smith's classic, *Essentials of Church History* (1973; 26th ed., Salt Lake City: Deseret Book, 1992), these books and articles took a much more matter-of-fact approach to this delicate subject, assuming frankly that polygamy was a fact of nineteenth-century life that needed to be more carefully examined.

Under Arrington's gentle tutelage, three Mormon women spearheaded research projects that examined the lives of nineteenth-century polygamous women. Interestingly, Maureen Ursenbach Beecher, Jill Mulvay Derr, and Carol Cornwall Madsen all came to history with backgrounds in English. Nevertheless, they seemed intuitively suited to the work of unraveling the female story of the early Church. During the early 1970s, concurrent with the resurgence of national interest in women's history, these three women explored literally hundreds of women's diaries, letters, and other materials left virtually untouched by scholars, often implicitly and sometimes explicitly centering their investigations on Mormon polygamy. Beecher illuminated the differences between nineteenth- and twentieth-century women through her writings on Eliza R. Snow, a powerful intellectual and leader of women in pioneer Utah who was also the plural wife of both Joseph Smith and Brigham Young. According to Beecher, Snow, as well as other women of plurality, met the challenges presented by this unusual marriage situation courageously and, in fact, became empowered by the unique opportunities it provided them. As a female leader, and indisputable member of the elite, Snow was one of the Church's most outspoken proponents of the Principle. It seemed, according to Beecher, that polygamy created a situation that allowed women a certain amount of independence, facilitating their involvement in the suffrage movement, the production of their own newspaper (the *Woman's Exponent*), and active engagement in the community. Beecher, Madsen, and Derr portrayed polygamous women as active participants in kingdom building, empowered by their relationships to righteous men and their own personal fortitude. The presentation of their stories, of course, reflected the feminist stance of the writers.

Among significant works are Maureen Ursenbach Beecher, "A Feminist among the Mormons: Charlotte Ives Cobb Godbe Kirby," *Utah Historical Quarterly* 59 (Winter 1991): 22-31; her "Inadvertent Disclosure: Autobiography in the Poetry of Eliza R. Snow," *Dialogue* 23 (Spring 1990): 54-107; and *Eliza and Her Friends* (Salt Lake City: Aspen Books, 1992); Jill Mulvay Derr, "Women's Place in Brigham Young's World," *BYU Studies* 18 (Spring 1978): 377-95; Kenneth Godfrey, Audrey M. Godfrey, and Jill Mulvay Derr, eds., *Women's Voices: An Untold History of the Latter-day Saints, 1830-1900* (Salt Lake City: Deseret Book, 1982); and Carol Cornwall Madsen, "Emmeline B. Wells: A Voice for Mormon Women," *John Whitmer Historical Association Journal* 2 (1982): 11-21. Beecher and Lavina Fielding Anderson edited a collection of essays exploring a series of topics historically important to Mormon women, including polygamy, in *Sisters in Spirit: Mormon Women in Historical and Cultural Perspective* (Urbana: University of Illinois, 1987).

Martha Sonntag Bradley and Mary Firmage Woodward, "Plurality, Patriarchy, and the Priestess: Zina D. H. Young's Nauvoo Marriage," *Journal of Mormon History* 20 (Spring 1994): 84-118; and B. Carmon Hardy, "Lords of Creation: Polygamy, the Abrahamic Household, and Mormon Patriarchy," *Journal of Mormon History* 20 (Spring 1994): 119-52, both challenged this optimistic view of polygamy as empowering by arguing that polygamy limited female access to power and permanently relegated women to a secondary, subordinate role.

A group of Relief Society sisters in the Cambridge Massachusetts Ward, after discovering copies of the *Woman's Exponent* at Harvard, launched an Institute of Religion class, based on scholarly research into the lives of Mormon women. They published their findings in a special issue of *Dialogue: A Journal of Mormon Thought* 6, no. 2 (Summer 1971); and a book of essays, *Mormon Sisters* edited by Claudia L. Bushman, first on their own press (Cambridge, MA: Emmeline Press, 1976; reprint ed., Logan, Utah: Utah State University Press, 1997, with introduction by Anne Firor Scott). It was followed by *Sister Saints*, edited by Vicky Burgess-Olson (Provo, UT: Brigham Young University Press, 1978), a collection of biographical essays. Together these books informed a generation about plural marriage, female blessings, and the role women played in settlement of the Great Basin. Their existence stimulated further research and analysis. Polygamy was at the heart of both books—an unbreakable link between nineteenth-century Mormon women and the larger Church. Again, both books treated polygamy as an interesting facet of Mormon life, addressing the topic head on and usually not defensively.

The Origins of Mormon Polygamy

After forty years of serious historical examination, the Principle's origins are still being debated. Many observers have long been fascinated by the violation of sexual norms that it represents. As a result, the possibility of multiple sexual partners represented by Joseph Smith has received much attention, but the early forms of the discussion were usually melodramatic and judgmental. Fawn M. Brodie, for instance, called her first chapter on the subject, "If a Man Entice a Maid," a title that said much about her attitude. She concluded, in the words of Marvin Hill's disapproving review, "Secular or Sectarian History? A Critique of *No Man Knows My History*," *Church History* 43 (March 1974): 93, that Smith was "a sensualist and a libertine who hid his excessive sexual needs behind the protective cloak of religion." A sense of moral indignation permeates her discussion of polygamy, which was, of course, a sexual institution just as surely as it was a religious, political, economic, and social one. From the "dirty nasty, filthy affair"—the terms in which Oliver Cowdery reported Smith's affair with Fanny Alger in 1835[4]—to his marriage to perhaps three dozen women in the two and a half years preceding his death in 1844, Brodie almost gleefully recounted what she never let the reader forget was sexual misconduct by a man who exercised almost total power and influence over his followers.

The origins of plural marriage in the Mormon Church have continued to be an important topic of discussion among New Mormon Historians. It has also been one of the most contentious. Assigning the origins of polygamy to Brigham Young, rather than Joseph Smith, was the chief point of difference between the LDS and RLDS churches for a century, a topic that triggered defensive reactions over implications of sexual impropriety, loyalty, family feeling, and, especially, religious authority. From the time that Joseph Smith III took the leadership of the Reorganized Church of Jesus Christ of Latter Day Saints (now Community of Christ) in 1860, even though his congregation contained former polygamists, he firmly denied that Joseph Smith had been the author of plural marriage. In fact, in his inaugural address at the organizational conference of the Reorganized Church at Amboy, Illinois, he said: "There is but one principle by the leaders of any faction of this people that I hold in utter abhorrence; that is a principle taught by Brigham Young and those believing in him. I have been told that my father taught such doctrines. I have never believed it and never can believe it. If such things were done, then I believe they never were done by divine authority. I believe my father was a good man, and a good man never could have promulgated such doctrines."[5]

As a matter of official belief, polygamy was considered to be both the creation of Brigham Young and evidence of the Utah church's apostasy. Works by RLDS defenders embodying this orientation include Elbert A. Smith, *Differences that Persist: Between the Reorganized Church of Jesus Christ of Latter Day Saints and the Utah Mormon Church* (Independence: Herald Publishing House, 1943); Roy A. Cheville, *Joseph and Emma: Companions for Seventeen and a Half Years, 1827-1844* (Independence: Herald Publishing House, 1977); Maurice L. Draper, *Marriage in the Restoration* (Independence: Herald Publishing House, 1969); Russell A. Ralston, *Fundamental Differences* (Independence: Herald Publishing House, 1963); George Njeim, "Joseph Smith: Prophet and Theologian," *Saints' Herald* 117 (January 1970): 18-19, 48; (February 1970): 24-26; (March 1970): 34-36, 66; Francis W. Holm Sr., *The Mormon Churches: A Comparison from Within* (Independence: Midwest Press, 1970); and Aleah J. Koury, *The Truth and the Evidence* (Independence: Herald Publishing House, 1965). Adherence to this belief was so staunch, in fact, that Robert B. Flanders, a Community of Christ historian, was virtually shunned within the Reorganization after he published *Nauvoo: Kingdom on the Mississippi* (Urbana: University of Illinois Press, 1965), because he accepted that Smith was responsible for the controversial doctrine and practice (264-74).

---

4. Oliver Cowdery, Letter to Warren A. Cowdery, January 21, 1838, Oliver Cowdery Papers, Huntington Library, San Marino, CA.

5. Quoted in Roger D. Launius, "Politicking against Polygamy: Joseph Smith III, the Reorganized Church, and the Politics of the Antipolygamy Crusade, 1860-1890," *John Whitmer Historical Association Journal* 17 (1987): 35.

This attitude began to shift significantly at the official level only when Reorganized Church historian Richard P. Howard published "The Changing RLDS Response to Mormon Polygamy: A Preliminary Analysis," *John Whitmer Historical Association Journal* 3 (1983): 14-29, which proposed a gentler interpretation. Yes, he conceded, plural marriage arose in Nauvoo (not Kirtland), but it was something of a historical accident, a result of expansive and comforting discussions about the Mormon concept of family and celestial marriage—"a consequence of Mormon history filled with eclectic, speculative theological ferment; unrelenting persecution; strong emphasis on authoritarian control through a hierarchical power elite; an intricate temple cultus designed to guarantee the perpetuity of the Mormon kingdom in this life and the next; [and] a considered rejection of societal strictures and mores in the light of what Mormons felt to be divinely revealed principles transcending 'manmade' laws" (25). Howard's interpretation was too conservative and failed to deal with Smith's earlier sexual history, but it bespoke a serious commitment to careful and scholarly treatment of the Reorganized Church's past. In suggesting questions that still begged to be answered, it opened the door of acceptance for more critical appraisals among the members and historians of the Reorganized Church.

Since that point, Community of Christ historians who have dealt professionally yet compassionately with this transition in historical awareness include Alma R. Blair, "RLDS Views of Polygamy: Some Historiographical Notes," *John Whitmer Historical Association Journal* 5 (1985): 16-28; Paul M. Edwards, "William B. Smith: The Persistent 'Pretender,'" *Dialogue* 18 (Summer 1985): 128-39, his "William B. Smith: 'A Wart on the Ecclesiastical Tree,'" in *Differing Visions: Dissenters in Mormon History*, edited by Roger D. Launius and Linda Thatcher (Urbana University of Illinois Press, 1994), 140-57; Don H. Compier, "The Faith of Emma Smith," *John Whitmer Historical Association Journal* 6 (1986): 64-72; Roger D. Launius, *Joseph Smith III, Pragmatic Prophet* (Urbana: University of Illinois Press, 1988), 190-217; his "Methods and Motives: Joseph Smith III's Opposition to Polygamy, 1860-90," *Dialogue* 20 (Winter 1987): 105-21; and his "Politicking Against Polygamy: Joseph Smith III, the Reorganized Church, and the Politics of the Anti-Polygamy Crusade, 1860-1890," *John Whitmer Historical Association Journal* 7 (1987): 35-44.

Davis Bitton's excellent bibliographic essay, "Mormon Polygamy," *Journal of Mormon History* 4 (1977): 1-118, provided an introductory survey and listed 110 articles and books published on the topic between 1907 and 1977. Patricia Lyn Scott's sequel, also published in the *Journal of Mormon History* 12 (1985): 113-39, extended the bibliography to 1985, a time of steadily increasing interest. According to Scott, an average of 2.5 articles were published per month on the subject. A cursory examination of Mormon History Association annual meeting programs also indicates a healthy and enduring interest in the subject. In a third follow-up, Scott, "Mormon Polygamy: A Bibliography, 1977-1992," *Journal of Mormon History* 11 (1993): 134, noted that the most common types of research were biographical and autobiographical studies, comparative studies, theological studies, and more recently, studies of the significance of family and gender. She consolidated and updated these bibliographies in a comprehensive listing covering from 1900 to 1999 forthcoming in *Wrestling with the Principle: Readings on Polygamy from the Journal of Mormon History* (working title) (Salt Lake City: Signature Books/Journal of Mormon History).

In marked contrast to the Reorganized Church's experience, Latter-day Saint historians never denied Smith's responsibility for originating plural marriage but have had stumbling blocks of their own, most frequently manifested in emphasizing the pious dimension of plural marriage and, in the process, downplaying the sexual aspects of the doctrine. Examples of mixed forthrightness yet reticence are John A. Widstoe, *Joseph Smith: Seeker after Truth, Prophet of God* (Salt Lake City: Deseret Book, 1951); Ivan J. Barrett, *Joseph Smith and the Restoration: A History of the Church to 1846* (1968; 2d ed., Provo, UT: Brigham Young University Press, 1973); Hyrum L. Andrus, *Joseph Smith: The Man and the Seer* (Salt Lake City: Deseret Book, 1976); Francis M. Gibbons, *Joseph Smith: Martyr, Prophet of God* (Salt Lake City: Deseret Book, 1977); Lyndon W. Cook, *The Revelations of the Prophet Joseph Smith* (Provo, UT: Seventy's Mission Bookstore, 1981), 293-95; Thomas G. Alexander, "'A New and Everlasting Covenant': An Approach to the Theology of Joseph Smith," in *New Views of Mormon History,* edited by Davis Bitton and Maureen Ursenbach Beecher (Salt Lake City: University of Utah, 1987), 43-62; and Larry C. Porter and Susan Easton Black, eds., *The Prophet Joseph Smith: Essays on the Life and Mission of Joseph Smith* (Salt Lake City: Deseret Book, 1988).

Because of the Mormon emphasis on the reproductive potential of the plural union and the Gentile emphasis on the lasciviousness of the polygamous male, plurality was, at least, rhetorically about sexuality; and studies of nineteenth-century polygamy have generally been left incomplete by sidestepping the sexual implications of polygamy, both by its opponents and the Mormons themselves. As another example, Brigham Young, Heber C. Kimball, and Wilford Woodruff were all prolific polygamists. Their biographers—Leonard J. Arrington, *Brigham Young: American Moses* (New York: Alfred A. Knopf, 1985), 5-6, 100-102, 117-18; Stanley B. Kimball, *Heber C. Kimball: Mormon Patriarch and Pioneer* (Urbana: University of Illinois Press, 1981), 93-103, 122-23, 227-41, 245-56, 290-98; and Thomas G. Alexander, *Things in Heaven and Earth: The Life and Times of Wilford Woodruff, a Mormon Prophet* (Salt Lake City: Signature Books, 1991), 128, 167, 186, 234-56, 308-26—tended to stress the challenges of the practice, the obedience to spiritual imperatives of these apostles, and, by implication, that they took additional wives not because of any drive of the libido but solely because of their commitment to Mormonism.

Marvin S. Hill, "Secular or Sectarian History?" explicitly explored the sexual motivation explanation for plural marriage and concluded that it probably resulted from Smith's own seriousness about his prophetic role. Those who emphasized the libertine aspects of Smith's life, wrote Hill, "failed to appreciate the degree to which the prophetic role liberated Smith from the social restraints which customarily control sexual behavior." He noted that Smith was not charged with any sexual misconduct until 1832, well after his emergence as a prophetic leader, but that if he had been an ordinary libertine, such behavior should have been noticeable in the 1820s. Hill also commented that Smith seemed to have been greatly influenced in his thinking about plural marriage by his reading of the Old Testament, providing "further proof of Smith's early and complete absorption in his prophetic role." Smith also, according to Hill, did not have sexual relations with many of his wives, which he interpreted as evidence that Smith's sexual drive was not the reason for the practice of polygamy. In short, Hill argued that Smith emerges as a more authentic and legitimate religious leader than Brodie makes him out to be (94-95).

One aspect of the effort to clothe the origins of plural marriage in religious meaning resulted in redating revelatory authorization of the practice back to 1831. The official date on which the revelation about plural marriage was recorded (LDS D&C 132) is July

12, 1843, but the authorization of plural marriage dated from at least 1836, and perhaps even earlier. Danel W. Bachman, "New Light on an Old Hypothesis: The Ohio Origins of the Revelation on Eternal Marriage," *Journal of Mormon History* 5 (1978): 19-31, made the case that on July 17, 1831, Smith had pronounced a revelation in Jackson County, Missouri: "It is my will, that in time, ye should take unto you wives of the Lamanites and Nephites, that their posterity may become white, delightsome and just." Phelps, present at the event, later asked Joseph Smith how the men could fulfill this revelation since they already had wives. Smith had told him that it would be done as it was in the Old Testament with Abraham and Jacob, "by Revelation. Accordingly, the practice was commanded as early as 1831," summarized Bachman, "and Joseph began the systematic process of marrying a series of women in 1841, with the formal recording of an earlier revelation completing the process only in 1843." However, this 1861 recollection of W. W. Phelps is at best a questionable source since polygamy had been firmly established in Utah by then and was under attack both by the federal government and the Reorganized Church as an illegitimate practice.

Still, Danel W. Bachman, "A Study of the Mormon Practice of Plural Marriage before the Death of Joseph Smith" (M.A. thesis, Purdue University, 1975), was a groundbreaking study. Richard S. Van Wagoner, *Mormon Polygamy: A History* (Salt Lake City: Signature Books, 1986), 3-69, likewise examined and accepted the same claims for an 1831 beginning, at least in theory, for polygamy.

Post-Manifesto Polygamy

Besides the work done under the auspices of the LDS Church Historian, independent scholars were responsible for further reconstruction of the controversial practice, opening up what must have seemed like Pandora's box to some Church leaders. Once the subject had been broached, it seemed that each new story proved more challenging and disturbing. Perhaps the most troubling disclosures concerned the extent of post-Manifesto polygamy.

It was a senior history student, Kenneth L. Cannon II, who produced the first important study of post-Manifesto polygamy in "Beyond the Manifesto: Polygamous Cohabitation among LDS General Authorities after 1890," *Utah Historical Quarterly* 46 (Winter 1978): 24-36. He sought to unravel the complexities of what he called the "transitional period" between 1890 and 1905 as Mormon General Authorities continued their own polygamous relationships. His paper, which won the Brigham Young University History Department's best article award for 1978, presented data about the children born to the plural wives of these men in the fifteen years following the Manifesto. He found that eleven (61 percent) General Authorities at the time of the Manifesto continued to illegally cohabit with their plural wives. Twenty-seven of these women give birth to seventy-six children, a figure that, in Cannon's view, indicated a high disregard for the antibigamy legislation (31). Cannon concluded that, because of the Manifesto's vague and ambiguous language, Church leaders were confused about what course to take. As a result each made a personal decision, a situation that caused even greater confusion for the Church at large.

D. Michael Quinn's impressive ninety-four-page article, "LDS Church Authority and New Plural Marriages, 1890-1904," *Dialogue* 18 (Spring 1985): 9-105, tackled the topic of new plural marriages contracted between 1890 and 1904. Quinn's article won the

Mormon History Association's Best Article Award for 1985. In it, he convincingly documents that leaders of the LDS Church continued to approve and perform plural marriages during the fourteen years following the Manifesto. Portrayed as a period of "ambiguity," this era was one of subterfuge and confusion as Church leaders falsely represented how they were conducting their private lives and the Mormon Church's business, uncertain about what the Manifesto meant for the institution and its membership.

The way the LDS Church then treated Quinn was proof positive that some Church leaders still felt that part of the polygamy story should not be told. Three months after the publication of Quinn's polygamy article, his stake president received orders from three apostles to confiscate his temple recommend on the grounds that Quinn was "speaking evil of the Lord's anointed," a violation of a temple covenant. Stake President Hugh West was instructed to take further action if this punishment did not prevent Quinn from publishing controversial material in the future. James M. Paramore, the Seventy and area president who communicated these orders, further instructed West to tell Quinn that this was a "local" matter and reflected the stake's assessment of Quinn's righteousness. West refused to lie to Quinn. "I told the stake president," Quinn later wrote, "that this was an obvious effort to intimidate me from doing history that might offend the Brethren. The stake president also saw this as a back-door effort to have me fired from BYU. He told me to tell BYU officials that I had a temple recommend and not to volunteer that it was in his desk drawer." During the spring of 1986, Quinn met with his dean at BYU, Martin Hickman, who told him that the Board of Trustees had prepared a list of faculty members and research topics for which no research monies would be allowed. Quinn and plural marriage were both on the list. The institutional message was discouragingly clear. Under continued pressure and discrimination, Quinn resigned from BYU in 1988.[6]

Gustive O. Larson's *The "Americanization" of Utah for Statehood* (San Marino, CA: Huntington Library, 1971) traced the LDS Church's exhaustive efforts in the latter part of the nineteenth century to resist accommodation while seeking admittance into the Union. Edward Leo Lyman, *Political Deliverance: The Mormon Quest for Utah Statehood* (Urbana: University of Illinois Press, 1986), is a meticulously researched reconstruction of the negotiations—including bribing leading newspapers—that finally led to Utah statehood. These negotiations were infinitely complicated by plural marriage—its practice, its rumors, and its resistances. Thomas G. Alexander, *Mormonism in Transition: A History of the Latter-day Saints, 1890-1930* (Urbana: University of Illinois Press, 1986) recounts the painful passage that Mormonism traversed to finally find an acceptable place in larger U.S. society. These books position Cannon's and Quinn's research in a richer historiographical context.

Richard Van Wagoner, *Mormon Polygamy: A History* (1986; 3rd ed., Salt Lake City: Signature Books, 1992) was the first book-length comprehensive narrative history of plural marriage. Van Wagoner focused on the administrative and institutional history of the practice, touching briefly on its theology and sociology (what polygamous households were

---

6. D. Michael Quinn, "On Being a Mormon Historian (and Its Aftermath)," in *Faithful History: Essays on Writing Mormon History,* edited by George D. Smith (Salt Lake City: Signature Books, 1992), 69-111, quotations from 91-92. Quinn in this essay more fully tells the story of the pressure leveled against him by Church leaders, particularly Boyd K. Packer because of his research on controversial subjects like plural marriage. He was excommunicated in September 1993 for publishing on another topic the Church strenuously discourages: "Mormon Women Have Had the Priesthood since 1843," in *Women and Authority Re-Emerging Mormon Feminism,* edited by Maxine Hanks (Salt Lake City: Signature Books, 1992), 365-409. Hanks was also excommunicated.

In Sacred Loneliness
The Plural Wives of Joseph Smith

TODD COMPTON

SIGNATURE BOOKS • SALT LAKE CITY

like) as well as pulling together research done on the origins of plural marriage in Kirtland, Church-sanctioned polygamy in the Great Basin, and modern-day fundamentalism.

Although B. Carmon Hardy's *Solemn Covenant: The Mormon Polygamous Passage* (Urbana; University of Illinois Press, 1992), instructed the reader about the sweep of the history of plural marriage among the Mormons, it is really something more than history. Insightfully interpretive and richly informed in the literature of plurality, it provided intelligent analysis of what polygamy meant to the Mormons. In particular Hardy examined what he calls the "polygamous passage" a period between the initial private introduction of the Principle in the 1830s and the point in the 1920s by which the Church, which had wrenched itself free of the religious and social implications of the practice, had reshaped Mormonism's domestic ideal.

Hardy tackled head-on several topics left unexamined by earlier scholars of polygamy. His concluding essay—"Lying for the Lord"—probed the disquieting question of Mormons' willingness to ignore the laws of the land for what they considered the "higher law" of the gospel. The implications of those ethical ambiguities still resonate for the contemporary Church. Hardy made another major contribution in his chapter "The Blessings of the Abrahamic Household," a preliminary attempt to broach the sensitive but intriguing subject of how the relationships of men and women were impacted by the institution of plural marriage.

Additional efforts to explore the domestic life of plural marriage, including some attention to reproductive issues, are Kathleen Marquis, "'Diamond Cut Diamond': Mormon Women and the Cult of Domesticity in the Nineteenth Century," *Papers in Women's Studies, University of Michigan* 2 (1974): 105-23; Julie Dunfrey, "'Living the Principle' of Plural Marriage: Mormon Women, Utopia, and Female Sexuality in the Nineteenth Century," *Feminist Studies* 10 (Fall 1984): 523-36; Jessie L. Embry in her "Effects of Polygamy on Mormon Women," *Frontiers: A Journal of Women's Studies* 7 (1984): 56-61; and her "Ultimate Taboos: Incest and Mormon Polygamy," *Journal of Mormon History* 18 (Spring 1992): 93-113, which analyzed an anti-Mormon article by Theodore Schroeder about Mormon incest. Embry probed the complicated moral and ethical questions raised by marriages to the same man of sisters, mothers and daughters, and first cousins.

Craig L. Foster, "Victorian Pornography Imagery in Anti-Mormon Literature," *Journal of Mormon History* 19 (Spring 1993): 115-32, pointed to the relativity of moral issues and the divergent vantage points of outsiders versus insiders, how interpretations of moral questions depended largely on where one stood in relation to church doctrine. This same theme was explored in perhaps the best social history of insider/outsider views of polygamy: Jeffrey Nichols, *Prostitution, Polygamy, and Power: Salt Lake City, 1847-1918* (Urbana: University of Illinois Press, 2002). He documents how the rhetoric of morality was a weapon wielded by both sides in the contest for power in Utah. Gentiles scandalized by the lasciviousness of plural marriage and Mormons outraged by the commodification of prostitution mutually discredited each other until they gradually found common ground.

Biography as a Lens on Polygamy

By far the most popular genre of history dealing with plural marriage is biography. Without parallel is Linda King Newell and Valeen Tippetts Avery, *Mormon Enigma: Emma Hale Smith—Prophet's Wife, "Elect Lady," Polygamy's Foee* (Garden City, N.Y.: Doubleday,

KATHRYN M. DAYNES

More Wives Than One

TRANSFORMATION OF THE MORMON

MARRIAGE SYSTEM, 1840–1910

UNIVERSITY OF ILLINOIS PRESS
URBANA AND CHICAGO

1984). The result of nine years of collaborative research and writing, *Mormon Enigma* addresses truly difficult questions about the relationship between Joseph and Emma, Emma and the Principle, and the Principle's role in the Nauvoo history. The book was professionally researched and written, responsibly interpreted, and exhaustively documented. Nevertheless, again, similar to the pressure placed upon D. Michael Quinn, both authors were temporarily banned from speaking about Emma Smith in Church settings, primarily because of their critical views on the origins of plural marriage, an action that caused them and their families enormous personal pain.

Todd Compton, *In Sacred Loneliness: The Plural Wives of Joseph Smith* (Salt Lake City: Signature Books, 1997), expands on the more traditional biography which focuses on a single individual to study the network of plural wives who moved in orbit around Joseph Smith. This study contributed to our understanding of plurality by contextualizing it in the lives of men and women, the particular strength of the book. Compton took his readers through the lives of each of the thirty-three women he identifies as wives of Joseph Smith quoting from their diaries, journals, letters, family reminiscences, and legal affidavits to bring each "vividly to life," as he says. The book's important prologue provided an overview of Smith's polygamy, including the timing of each marriage, how many women he married (the actual number may never be known), Compton's criteria for accepting a marriage as verified, and possible motives behind such marriages.

Martha Sonntag Bradley and Mary Brown Firmage Woodward, *Four Zinas: Mothers and Daughters on the Mormon Frontier* (Salt Lake City: Signature Books, 2000), took a generational approach to studying the lives of four Mormon women, two of whom were polygamists and married to leaders of the Church. Again, demonstrating the value of biography as a lens for understanding the ways Church doctrine impacted the lives of real individuals, *Four Zinas* fleshes out plurality through the stories of mothers and daughters profoundly shaped by its unique demands.

These three books are a mere sampler of scores of family histories and biographies written about nineteenth-century Mormon pioneers, who lived the Principle with varying degrees of success. This vast literature is best accessed through the bibliographies cited above and Newell G. Bringhurst, "Mormon Biography: Paradoxes, Problems, and Progress," in this volume.

Regional, Demographic, and Social History

Several regional studies track the incidence of polygamy throughout Mormon territory. F. LaMond Tullis, *Mormons in Mexico: The Dynamics of Faith and Culture* (Logan: Utah State University Press, 1987), is an informed and sophisticated study of the Church's confrontation with another country's culture. Although not the central subject of the book, polygamy provided the impetus for the Mormon colonization of northern settlements in Mexico with resulting complicated relations between the Mormons and the Mexican government.

Polygamy in Canada formed part of the context for several essays in Brigham Y. Card, Herbert C. Northcott, John E. Foster, Howard Palmer, and George K. Jarvis, eds., *The Mormon Presence in Canada* (Logan: Utah State University Press, 1990). Of particular relevance in this volume are Brigham Y. Card, "Charles Ora Card and the Founding of the Mormon Settlements in Southwestern Alberta, North-West Territories," 77-107; Howard

Excavating Mormon Pasts

Palmer, "Polygamy and Progress: The Reaction to Mormons in Canada, 1887-1923," 108-35; Jessie L. Embry, "'Two Legal Wives': Mormon Polygamy in Canada, the United States, and Mexico," 170-85; B. Carmon Hardy, "Mormon Polygamy in Mexico and Canada: A Legal and Historiographical Review," 186-210; and Maureen Ursenbach Beecher, "Mormon Women in Southern Alberta: The Pioneer Years," 211-30.

Demographic Studies

Much more than a regional history, Kathryn M. Daynes, *More Wives Than One: Transformation of the Mormon Marriage System, 1840-1910* (Urbana: University of Illinois Press, 2001), is grounded in solid data reconstructing the demographic profile of plurality in Sanpete County. It then insightfully interprets its theological, economic, social and cultural ramifications. This area, inhabited largely by immigrants from Scandinavia and Great Britain after 1847, came alive through the lens of personal narratives and statistical analyses. Daynes recommended that we move beyond the traditional justification for polygamy on the basis of religious motivation to consider the complicated web of relationships and motives created between economic push-pull factors, familial relationships or situations, and churchwide religious fervor that in infinitely complex ways caused women to decide to enter plural unions. Although scholarship has traditionally concluded that plural marriage was driven by conviction and religious belief, Daynes expands that motivation to include "economic circumstances, concern for status, views about what constitutes marital bliss," and a response to the particular challenges posed by the world outside to the Mormon community wherever it was found. Among the population of plural men and women in Sanpete County, the majority of plural wives were found, according to Daynes among the "fatherless, the widowed, and the divorced, groups with compelling economic reasons to marry in a male-dominated frontier society."

George D. Smith's important and tireless tracking of Nauvoo polygamy is laid out in a series of tables which accompany his article, "Nauvoo Roots of Mormon Polygamy, 1841-46: A Preliminary Demographic Report," *Dialogue* 27, no. 1 (Spring 1994): 1-72. He studied plural marriages between April 5, 1841 (Louisa Beaman's Nauvoo marriage to Joseph Smith) and 1846 when the Mormons moved west. "By the end of the Nauvoo period in 1846," he summarized, "the 153 polygamous husbands had married 587 women and produced 734 children. About 80 percent of Nauvoo plural marriages occurred after Smith's death" (30).

Lowell C. "Ben" Bennion, "The Incidence of Mormon Polygamy in 1880: "Dixie" versus Davis Stake," *Journal of Mormon History* 11 (1984): 27-42, is an exciting demographic analysis of the geographical incidence of polygamy that more concretely identifies regional variations in the practice and definitively demolishes the Church's official attempt to minimize the prevalence of polygamy as merely 2-3 percent. Taking a spatial rather than periodic approach to the analysis of census data and family group sheets, Bennion tracked variation in the occurrence of polygamy and found that larger towns had a higher percentage of polygamous adults (roughly 40 percent or higher) than rural areas. He suggested that smaller towns exhibited a wider range of percentages because of their relative economic instability or "smallness." Polygamy percentages were also higher among southern settlements, Bennion hypothesized, because of an "atmosphere conducive to the acceptance of polygamy as the marital norm" (36). "Historians have always underestimated both the occurrence of plurality and the significance of the practice in the lives of the Saints," Bennion maintained, because of three factors: (1) the Church exercised great diligence in hiding the practice from public view even during its most open years between 1852 and 1882; (2) because it was relatively secret and illegal, records of these marriages are irregular or unavailable altogether; and (3) most studies have focused only on the men involved and have not factored in women. Also a significant demographic contribution is his "Patterns of Mormon Polygamy in 1880," unpublished paper presented at the annual meeting of the Mormon History Association, Provo, Utah, May 11, 1984.

In *A Sermon in the Desert: Belief and Behavior in Early St. George, Utah* (Urbana: University of Illinois Press, 1988), Larry M. Logue convincingly demonstrated that it is possible to reconstruct a clear picture of Mormon marital patterns. Through demographic data and methodologies, he found that the incidence of plural marriage in St. George and the surrounding environs was much more extensive than had been previously believed. Logue found that most monogamist men in St George waited a decade to marry their first plural wife. Twenty percent of all eventual polygamists married a plural wife by age thirty; 75 percent had completed all their marriages (whether three or fewer) by age forty-six. Although only two in five men took plural wives (31.4 percent of men and 62 percent of women), 49 percent of all children lived in polygamous households. Logue's figures thus suggested that plurality was the community norm, a conclusion he probed further in his "Tabernacles for Waiting Spirits: Monogamous and Polygamous Fertility in a Mormon Town," *Journal of Family History* 10 (Spring 1985): 60-74; and "Time of Marriage: Monogamy and Polygamy in a Utah Town," *Journal of Mormon History* 11 (1984): 3-26. But until similar studies are conducted for each Mormon rural community, the actual prevalence of polygamy among the Mormons cannot be charted.

Legal History

Numerous authors have explored the judicial crusade against polygamy, beginning forty years ago with law professor Orma Linford, "The Mormons and the Law: The Polygamy Cases," *Utah Law Review* 9 (Winter 1964): 308-70, and (Summer 1965): 543-91. This article analyzed the anti-polygamy prosecutions and civil disabilities imposed on Church members during the 1870s and 1880s. Focusing on how the federal and territorial courts interpreted the First Amendment while prosecuting cases under the various federal anti-polygamy acts, Linford argued that these cases were the Supreme Court's initial confrontations with questions presented by the First Amendment's guarantee of freedom of religion.

Edwin Brown Firmage and Richard Collin Mangrum, *Zion in the Courts: A Legal History of the Church of Jesus Christ of Latter-day Saints, 1830-1900* (Urbana: University of Illinois Press, 1988), provided more deeply researched explorations of the legal issues presented by the practice of plural marriage. Ken Driggs wrote a series of significant articles using modern fundamentalist cases to scrutinize the legal confrontation between the government and those continuing in the Principle, including "After the Manifesto: Modern Polygamy and Fundamentalist Mormons," *Journal of Church and State* 32 (Spring 1990): 367-89; "Twentieth-Century Polygamy and Fundamentalist Mormons in Southern Utah," *Dialogue* 24 (Winter 1991): 44-58; "Utah Supreme Court Decides Polygamist Adoption Case," *Sunstone* 15 (September 1991): 67-68; and "Who Shall Raise the Children?: Vera

KIDNAPPED FROM THAT LAND

THE GOVERNMENT RAIDS ON THE SHORT CREEK POLYGAMISTS

Martha Sonntag Bradley

University of Utah Press
Salt Lake City

Black and the Rights of Polygamous Utah Parents," *Utah Historical Quarterly* 60 (Winter 1992): 27-46.

A blockbuster and MHA Best Book prize winner is Sarah Barringer Gordon, *The Mormon Question: Polygamy and Constitutional Conflict in Nineteenth-Century America* (Chapel Hill: University of North Carolina Press, 2002). She examined the complicated contest between the federal government, states' rights, the concept of "freedom of religion," emancipation, woman suffrage, and the anti-polygamy movement which played out in the last three decades of the nineteenth century. All of these social and political issues were freighted with moral weight, which Gordon analyzed in terms of the tensions between religious and temporal authorities. For Gordon, the fight was more than a discursive one fought over law and interpretations of faith, but one which challenged the limits of democracy and federalism.

Theological and Social History

Only a few studies have addressed the theological implications of plurality. An important exception is Rex Eugene Cooper, *Promises Made to the Fathers: Mormon Covenant Organization* (Salt Lake City: University of Utah Press, 1990), which focused on covenantal networks established by plural marriage. He interpreted plural marriage as Joseph Smith's "mechanism for maintaining Mormon group identity and solidarity" through a kinship-based system (132). The practice, therefore, defined the boundaries of the "religiously qualified" community characterized by a sealing network of interlocked hierarchies.

Lawrence Foster, *Religion and Sexuality: Three American Communal Experiments of the Nineteenth Century* (New York: Oxford University Press, 1981), and his collection of essays, *Women, Family, and Utopia: Communal Experiments of the Shakers, the Oneida Community, and the Mormons* (Syracuse, NY: Syracuse University Press, 1991), both consider the implications of Mormon polygamy for Mormon communitarianism. In producing this fine body of work, Foster was motivated by the desire to understand the broad spectrum of marital experimentation in antebellum America. He interpreted Joseph Smith as only one of several highly creative and restless souls who were seeking a more perfect relationship of individuals in the 1830s and 1840s and not, consequently, as the licentious womanizer that so many critics perceived. But as a result, Smith also was not, to Foster, the chosen prophet of the living God who restored the true gospel in its ancient purity to the Earth, a corollary that seems to have been largely missed by most Mormons who embraced Foster's work. Foster's admiration for Smith's achievement facilitated the acceptance of *Religion and Sexuality* by Mormon readers, who, for the most part, rejected Louis J. Kern, *An Ordered Love: Sex Roles and Sexuality in Victorian Utopias—the Shakers, the Mormons, and the Oneida Communityy* (Chapel Hill: University of North Carolina Press, 1981). This book, published in the same year as Foster's, chided Smith's sexual misconduct and saw his religious claims as basically dishonest and self-serving. Foster proposed an alternative explanation for Smith's creativity in "The Psychology of Religious Genius: Joseph Smith and the Origins of New Religious Movements," *Dialogue* 26 (Winter 1993): 1-22.

In a general sense, these approaches fall under the historiographical umbrella of social history. Using new methodologies and approaching the topic from significantly different points of view, historians now study men and women largely ignored in traditional historical methodologies. Jessie L. Embry, *Mormon Polygamous Families: Life in the Principle*

Religion and Sexuality

THREE AMERICAN COMMUNAL EXPERIMENTS
OF THE NINETEENTH CENTURY

LAWRENCE FOSTER

New York / Oxford
OXFORD UNIVERSITY PRESS
1981

(Salt Lake City: University of Utah Press, 1987) considered the lives of literally hundreds of nineteenth-century men and women, the precious stock of which history is made. Based primarily on oral interviews conducted under the auspices of the Charles Redd Center for Western Studies at Brigham Young University, Embry's study described what polygamy was like in the common Mormon family as reported by the children and grandchildren of those unions. Embry allowed the personal voice to ring clear, helping the reader to hear what polygamy felt like, how the participants themselves understood what it was.

My *Kidnapped from That Land: The Government Raids on the Short Creek Polygamists* (Salt Lake City: University of Utah Press, 1993), a study of the Mormon fundamentalists of Short Creek, Arizona (now Colorado City), was similarly based on oral interviews and primary literature. It examined both family life and the communal aspects of this fundamentalist community located on the Utah/Arizona border, as well as the federal raids conducted on the community during the 1930s-50s.

Jeffery Ogden Johnson, "Determining and Defining 'Wife': The Brigham Young Households," *Dialogue* 20 (Fall 1987): 57-70, focused on the complex interrelationships, intimacies, and distances in one huge and prominent plural family. Family historian Kathryn M. Daynes similarly focused on the unique dynamics of the polygamous household in her article: "Family Ties: Belief and Practice in Nauvoo," *John Whitmer Historical Association Journal* 8 (1988): 63-75.

Conclusion

For many, the debate over traditional history and the New Mormon History centers on the issue of trust in their institutional church and its story.[7] Ironically, what might be called "faithful history," which screens out Mormonism's difficult and controversial episodes, frequently tries the faith of uninformed Saints who hear problematic stories from other sources. Those who chose not to confront the issues raised by plural marriage consider this story dangerous to religious faith.

However, ignoring plural marriage will not make the story disappear. In fact, as the journalists who flooded Salt Lake City for the 2002 Winter Olympics demonstrated, it is still one of the few concepts associated with Mormonism around the world, even more than a century after the Manifesto. Nor are Mormons bored with the topic or more casual about its acceptance, as the experience of Shane L. Whelan in the fall of 2002 demonstrated. He published a selection of positive statements by nineteenth-century practitioners, *More than One: Plural Marriage, a Sacred Heritage, a Promise for Tomorrow* (Bountiful, Utah: Zion Publishers, 2002), which also listed possible benefits from the Principle's reinstatement. However, he took the orthodox position that only the current prophet could reestablish the practice and then only by revelation and only after the U.S. Supreme Court had declared it legal. He was promptly excommunicated when he refused to stop advertising and selling the book.

Flannery O'Conner, a Catholic novelist who grappled with the fact that some of her writing made her audience uncomfortable, commented insightfully: "The [writer] with

---

7. Martha Sonntag Bradley, "Changed Faces: The Official LDS Position on Polygamy, 1890-1990," *Sunstone* 14 (February 1990): 26-33; and "Joseph W. Musser: Dissenter or Fearless Crusader of Truth?" in *Differing Visions*, 262-78. For information about the fundamentalists claims to priesthood authority, see Max Anderson, *The Polygamy Story: Fiction and Fact* (Salt Lake City: Publishers Press, 1979), or Bradley, *Kidnapped from That Land*.

Excavating Mormon Pasts

Christian concerns will find in modern life distortions which are repugnant to him, and his problem to an audience which is used to seeing them as natural. . . . When you can assume that your audience holds the same beliefs you do, you can relax a little and use more normal means of talking to it; when you have to assume that it does not, then you have to make your vision apparent by shock—to the hard of hearing.'"[8]

Interestingly enough, John Taylor, the Church president whose life ended while he was in hiding to avoid prosecution for the Principle, advocated honesty and full disclosure on the issue. "Some people will say 'Oh, don't talk about it,'" Taylor said in a general conference address. "I think a full, free talk is frequently of great use; we want nothing secret nor underhanded, and for one, I want no association with things that cannot be talked about and will not bear investigation."[9] New Mormon historians have accepted this charge and applied the professional tools of their trade to refine the search.

MARTHA SONNTAG BRADLEY is professor of architectural history and director of the Honors Program at the University of Utah. Current (2003-04) president of the Mormon History Association, she wrote with Mary Brown Firmage Woodward, *Four Zinas: Mothers and Daughters on the Mormon Frontier* (Salt Lake City: Signature Books, 2000), which received the 2001 Best Biography Award from the Mormon History Association. She is also the author of *Kidnapped from That Land: The Government Raids on the Short Creek Polygamists* (Salt Lake City: University of Utah Press, 1993). She has also authored numerous scholarly articles along with two additional book-length studies, *Sandy City: The First Hundred Years* (Sandy, UT: Sandy City, 1993), and *ZCMI: America's First Department Store* (Salt Lake City: ZCMI, 1991).

---

8. Flannery O'Conner, quoted in *Books and Religion* 14 (May/June 1986): 6.
9. John Taylor, *Journal of Discourses,* 26 vols. (London and Liverpool: LDS Booksellers Depot, 1855-86), 20:264.

Chapter 14

Mormon Biography:
Paradoxes, Progress, and Continuing Problems

Newell G. Bringhurst

It could be argued that the essence of Mormon history is biography, the prime example being the life and times of Mormonism's founder, Joseph Smith Jr. This fact is underscored by the classic seven-volume *History of the Church of Jesus Christ of Latter-day Saints,* edited into its final form by Brigham H. Roberts. The first six volumes of this work subtitled "History of Joseph Smith, the Prophet" draw from the personal diaries of Mormonism's founder along with various documents generated by the Church over which he presided. David J. Whittaker has succinctly characterized this epic work as "a marriage of biography and [Church] history."[1] This "blend of biography and institutional history," he says, has influenced the basic form and format of Mormon biography from the Church's earliest days down to the present. This essential feature, in turn, has assured Mormon biography of its continuing, widespread popularity.

Also enhancing the appeal of Mormon biography is that such works serve as "living parables to be studied and understood in the contexts of heaven and earth; [and as] spiritual primers in the school of life," according to BYU English professor and critic Richard H. Cracroft. He asserts that Latter-day Saints "relish the biographer's attempts to clarify this Saint-making process in others' lives," and summarizes, "It's no wonder, then, that most Mormons prefer biography over fiction."[2]

Yet, despite its popularity, Mormon biography has often been judged as lacking by critics, from both within and outside the Latter-day Saint community. Strong criticism emerged, particularly during the late 1970s and early 1980s. Non-Mormon anthropologist Mark Leone, in his foundational *Roots of Modern Mormonism* (Cambridge, MA: Harvard University Press, 1979), lambasted Mormon biography as "amateur history, basically chronicle and vignette, not interpretation" and "unreservedly uncritical" (194). Noted LDS historians James B. Allen and Glen M. Leonard, *The Story of the Latter-day Saints* (1976; 2d ed. rev., Salt Lake City: Deseret Book, 1992), agreed that while "biographical studies of Latter-day Saints are numerous, few are professionally done and many give only a selective look at the life of the individual" (686).

Similarly, Davis Bitton, former Assistant LDS Church Historian and award-winning biographer, observed in 1981; "While the inherent interest and quantity of records for

---

1. David J. Whittaker, "The Heritage and Tasks of Mormon Biography," in *Supporting Saints: Life Stories of Nineteenth-Century Mormons,* edited by Donald J. Cannon and David J. Whittaker, (Provo, UT: BYU Religious Studies Center, 1882), 3.
2. Richard H. Cracroft, "Mormon Biography: Tracking the (Well-Written) LDS Life," *Brigham Young Magazine,* May 1994, 62.

writing Mormon biography are great, the results to date have been mediocre."[3] Likewise, another award-winning Mormon biographer, Ronald W. Walker, compared the collective craft of Mormon biography to "a valley full of dry and lifeless forms, but with the promise of becoming." Walker then quoted Ezekiel 37:3: "And he said unto me, son of man, can these bones live? And I answered, O Lord God, Thou knowest."[4] David J. Whittaker lamented in 1985 that Mormon biographies "read more like eulogies than biographies" seldom moving beyond chronological summary with "almost all of the portraits flat [and] one-dimensional."[5]

Such criticisms raise two fundamental questions: First, what progress, if any, has been made in refining the craft of Mormon biography concurrent with the New Mormon History? Second, what deficiencies and/or gaps remain?

Even though all of the critics, writing in the last quarter century, were surveying the same biographical landscape as I, I would respond to the first question by saying that progress is evident in the number of carefully researched and well-written biographies, some of which were produced as long ago as forty or fifty years. Cracroft noted in 1994 that "Mormon biography has begun to emerge from its traditional defensive, didactic, and hagiographic posturings" (62).

Because space will not allow a comprehensive discussion of all works worthy of consideration, I here focus on a representative sampling of biographies ranging from prominent leaders to the faithful rank-and-file, women, dissidents, and individuals associated with various groups outside of the Utah-based LDS Church.[6]

Biographies of Mormon Presidents

The most important figure, by far, that Mormon biographers have tackled is Joseph Smith, Jr. Appropriately and with some irony, Fawn M. Brodie's controversial *No Man Knows My History: The Life of Joseph Smith* (1945; 2d ed. rev., New York: Alfred A Knopf, 1971) marks the beginning point of modern Mormon biography produced within the context of the New Mormon History. Brodie's foundational study encapsulates the progress along the paradoxes and problems inherit in the writing of Mormon biography. *No Man Knows My History* was, in the words of Mormon historian, David J. Whittaker "something of a watershed in Mormon biography" setting "the agenda for a new generation of studies on Mormons" ("Heritage and Tasks," 10). "Gracefully written, with a compelling momentum" which set it apart from earlier accounts of Mormonism's founder, "Brodie's Joseph Smith is interesting, a flesh-and-blood person with whom one can have sympathy," concedes Bitton (4-5). Brodie, moreover, placed her subject within an analytical framework, one which was "explicitly psychoanalytical" framework, distinguishing it from earlier biographies.[7] But at the same time, Brodie's work betrayed a fundamental paradox, and indeed, problem: This work, in Whittaker's words, "represented the biographical craft at its worst: a secular portrait of a religious man," because Brodie discounted, ignored, and/or simply rationalized the religious strivings and mystic experiences of Joseph Smith (10). This tendency was reenforced by Brodie's heavy, often uncritical, reliance on non-Mormon and anti-Mormon writings. Brodie's study, moreover, was limited by the unavailability of certain crucial primary materials written by Smith and individuals close to him.

Marvin S. Hill has pointed out these and other problems in two detailed review essays written after Brodie's second edition: "Secular or Sectarian History? A Critique of

---

3. Davis Bitton, "Mormon Biography," *Biography: An Interdisciplinary Quarterly* 4 (Winter 1981): 4.
4. Ronald W. Walker, "The Challenge and Craft of Mormon Biography," *BYU Studies* 22 (Spring 1982): 179.
5. Whittaker, "The Heritage and Tasks of Mormon Biography," 8.
6. Two important recent works evaluating the state of Mormon biography are: Ronald W. Walker, David J. Whittaker, and James B. Allen, "The Challenge of Mormon Biography" in their *Mormon History*, edited by (Urbana: University of Illinois Press, 2001), 113-52; and Jill Mulvay Derr, ed., *Lives of the Saints: Writing Mormon Biography and Autobiography* (Proceedings of the 2001 Symposium of the Joseph Smith Institute for Latter-day Saint History) (Provo, UT: BYU Press, 2002).
7. Walker, "The Challenge and Craft of Mormon Biography," 189.

JOSEPH SMITH
The First Mormon

by

Donna Hill

DOUBLEDAY & COMPANY, INC.
GARDEN CITY, NEW YORK
1977

Excavating Mormon Pasts

No Man Knows My History," Church History 43 (March 1974): 78-96; and "Brodie Revisited: A Reappraisal," *Dialogue: A Journal of Mormon Thought* 7 (Winter 1972): 72-85. Other analyses are my "Applause, Attack, and Ambivalence—Varied Responses to Fawn M. Brodie's *No Man Knows My History,* Utah Historical Quarterly 57 (Winter 1989): 46-63; and my "Fawn M. Brodie: Her Biographies as Autobiography," *Pacific Historical Review* 59 (May 1990): 203-29. Other essays critiquing Brodie's work have been collected in *Reconsidering No Man Knows My History: Fawn Brodie and Joseph Smith in Retrospect,* edited by Newell G. Bringhurst (Logan: Utah State University Press, 1996).

A second significant biography examining the life of Joseph Smith within the framework of the New Mormon History is Donna Hill, *Joseph Smith: The First Mormon* (New York: Doubleday, 1977). Writing as a believing Mormon whose "sympathies lie with the Saints," Hill challenged Brodie's naturalistic view of Smith as a "conscious imposter" (x). She had access to important, newly available primary documents, used up-to-date methodologies, and crafted "a more positive yet frank portrait of Smith" that disclosed his often-elusive "human side."[8]

Yet Hill's biography is deficient in several respects. Her narrative is bland and tedious in contrast to Brodie's engaging liveliness. Hill's work also suffers from the lack of a clear, analytical framework. In places, the narrative abandons Smith completely to recount a general history of the Mormon Church. Hill also gets bogged down in a morass of factual information, failing to differentiate between Smith the man and the church he led. As a result, her biography falls short in conveying the drama of a "life being lived."

Four more recent book-length studies also examine Joseph Smith, although from different perspectives. Richard L. Bushman, *Joseph Smith and the Beginnings of Mormonism* (Urbana: University of Illinois Press, 1984), examines Smith's life only to 1831. Nevertheless, Bushman's account offers information and a perspective on Smith not available elsewhere. Bushman, like Hill, writes as a devout Latter-day Saint, affirming his belief in the literal reality of Smith's early religious experiences. In Bushman's account, various divine visitations to young Joseph, the revelations he received, and translation of the Book of Mormon from the golden plates took place pretty much as Mormonism's founder described them to his followers.

But at the same time, Bushman acknowledges Smith as a man with flaws who made mistakes—this helping to "humanize" the Mormon leader. The author also admits that Smith was intrigued with folk magic and sought to make money by hiring himself out as a treasure hunter or so-called "money-digger" prior to becoming a Mormon prophet. While conceding such activities, Bushman asserts that "Joseph Smith is best understood as a person who outgrew his [or this] culture" (7). Carefully and empathetically, Bushman places Smith within the cultural milieu of his time while attributing basic religious motivation to his actions. Consider the following::

> Joseph Smith stood on the line that divided the yearning for the supernatural from the humanism of rational Christianity—one of the many boundaries between the traditional and modern world passing through American culture in the early nineteenth century. Culturally Joseph looked backward toward traditional society's faith in the immediate presence of divine power, communicating through stones, visions, dreams, and angels. On the other hand, Joseph repudiated the superstitions of the past, particularly the Palmyra money diggers' exploitation of supernatural power for base purposes. In the end he satisfied neither religionists nor the local magicians. Joseph Smith, Sr. said at the trial [of Joseph, Jr.] in 1826 that the family believed "that the son of Righteousness would some day illumine the heart of the boy, and enable him to see His will concerning him." (79-80)

Standing in sharp contrast to Bushman's book is Robert D. Anderson's *Inside the Mind of Joseph Smith: Psychobiography and The Book of Mormon* (Salt Lake City: Signature Books,

---

8. Bitton, "Mormon Biography," 5.

Utah, 1999). Extremely provocative in his approach, Anderson wrote from a naturalistic perspective, specifically as a one-time practicing Latter-day Saint turned nonbeliever. Thus, Anderson's interpretation is reminiscent of Brodie's. But in contrast to Brodie's *No Man Knows My History,* Anderson's narrative is highly clinical, more speculative, and much less literary in style. As Anderson explained in his preface, "the primary purposes" of his work was to "investigate the psychology of Joseph Smith, demonstrate the benefits of psychobiography, expand awareness of psychological processes, provide an alternative explanation for at least some supernatural claims, and expand scientific knowledge" (xiii). Anderson, moreover, was candid concerning both his interpretive focus and conclusions: "By using the framework of traditional science and that of the academic historian in this work, I therefore exclude "the hand of God" from consideration. I assume that Joseph Smith composed the Book of Mormon and I read it to understand Smith psychologically. Some may find this approach unacceptable, others might allow it as an hypothesis to be explored" (xxvi).

Anderson further asserted: "Joseph Smith, both knowingly and unknowingly, interjected his own personality, conflicts, and solutions into" the Book of Mormon. This work "can be understood as Smith's autobiography" from which one "can discern repeated psychological patterns in Smith's transformation of his childhood and youth before 1829 into Book of Mormon stories. . . . These observations can contribute to a psychological understanding of Smith" (xxvii-xxviii).

According to Anderson, "The Book of Mormon is not a book of love, but of terror, hatred, and destruction." Indeed, "until historical evidence is presented for the Nephite-Lamanite civilizations, these terrible stories can possibly best be seen as reflecting Joseph's emotions and mental images—filled with violence and hatred—dating from the developmental period when the basic units of his personality were being laid down" (204). Anderson saw Smith as the product of a traumatic childhood and a dysfunctional family. Not surprisingly, his "psychoanalytic profile" of the Mormon founder was less than flattering. He concluded that Smith developed a "narcissistic personality" with tendencies toward grandiose fantasies and excessive, reckless behavior, all culminating in his violent death.

Anderson has produced a provocative portrait with some stimulating ideas. His work has generated debate about Joseph Smith's personality and basic motives, a good thing in and of itself. William D. Morain, *The Sword of Laban: Joseph Smith and the Dissociated Mind* (Washington, DC: American Psychiatric Press, 1998), had earlier made a case that the agonizing triple surgeries on Joseph's leg to relieve typhoid-caused osteomyelitis when he was about seven had traumatic effects on his psyche that also showed up in the Book of Mormon. But Anderson's analysis goes further and ultimately fails to convince. Not only is it highly speculative, but it is excessively reductionist, over-simplifying both Smith's personality and his motives. Most fundamentally, Anderson's work came up short in much the same way as Brodie's—that is, in presenting essentially "a secular portrait of a religious man," as Whittaker stated.

In a third recent work, non-Mormon biographer Robert V. Remini, a distinguished Jacksonian scholar and winner of the National Book Award, has weighed in with his own interpretation in *Joseph Smith* (New York: Viking, 2002). Just 190 pages long, Remini's biography is a part of the prestigious "Penguin Lives" series. Remini skillfully placed Smith within the context of Jacksonian American society and presented him in an even-handed, empathic, and, indeed, sympathetic manner. He explained: "After considerable thought, I decided to present his [Smith's] religious experiences just as he described them in his writings and let readers decide for themselves to what extent they would give credence to them. I am not out to prove or disprove any of his claims. As a historian I have tried to be as objective as possible in narrating his life and work" (x).

Remini effectively discusses Smith's background, specifically, his family's strong religiosity, their economic difficulties, and other adversities during Smith's early life. He provides keen insights into young Joseph's behavior and complex personality. He attributes

Excavating Mormon Pasts

Smith's success as a religious leader to his charisma and "administrative skills" (96). At the same time, he also weighs the varied reasons why "Joseph and his Mormon brethren [were] hated with such intensity as to provoke mob violence and murder" (175).

Strengths notwithstanding, Remini's biography suffered from a number of shortcomings. Among the most significant were its superficiality of analysis and, most disturbing, its numerous errors of fact. Such problems stem from the apparent haste in which Remini researched and wrote his book, without consulting crucial primary archival sources by Joseph Smith and his associates. Remini also seemed unaware of much of the recent scholarship examining various aspects of Joseph Smith's life and career—evident in the incomplete nature of his bibliography.

A more extensively researched work is Dan Vogel's *Joseph Smith: The Making of a Prophet* (Salt Lake City: Signature Books, 2004). Evocative and carefully written, Vogel's biography examines Smith's early life and activities, also seeing the Book of Mormon as autobiographical. Through careful historical analysis, this work traces Smith's early religious-intellectual development, using multi-disciplinary tools, including psychology, sociology, literary analysis, and family systems theory. Woven into the Book of Mormon, according to Vogel, were Smith's "beliefs, struggles, thoughts, dreams, and future plans."

Although Vogel characterizes Smith as a "pious fraud," he goes significantly further than the naturalistic interpretations of Brodie and others, producing a portrait of a complex, elusive personality with inner conflicts and inconsistent motives. Smith emerges in this work as a charismatic religious leader who truly "believed he was called of God to preach repentance to a sinful world but at the same time felt justified in using deception to accomplish this mission more fully."

Vogel ends his study in 1831, thus leaving unexamined most of Joseph Smith's most productive years. Vogel also tends to overstates his case in asserting the Book of Mormon to be a product of nineteenth-century American society. Particularly strained are the parallels Vogel attempts to draw between incidents and characters in the Book of Mormon and contemporary individuals, including Joseph Smith himself and other family members. Vogel is often unconvincing as well in asserting parallels between certain Book of Mormon events and those occurring in the larger nineteenth-century American society. Also while Vogel carefully develops the interpersonal relationships between Smith and other members of his immediate family, he does not adequately explore Smith's complex, often-changing relationships with other important individuals such as Martin Harris, Oliver Cowdery, Newel Knight, and various members of the Whitmer family.

Indeed, the problems evident in each of the above four works underscores the fact that the truly definitive biography on Joseph Smith remains to be written. Such a biography, in my opinion, would be analytical, carefully combining frankness with empathy and sympathy. It would be written in an engaging style within a clear interpretive framework, using in a careful, comprehensive manner the myriad of historical sources, both primary and secondary, currently available. This biography, moreover, would use up-to-date tools of analysis and interpretation—not just those of the historian but also of various other social and behavioral sciences. Most important, it would seek to capture the essence of Smith's elusive, multifaceted personality through a careful consideration of his varied, complex motives. Hopefully, the four books in process on Joseph Smith by Richard L. Bushman, Scott Kenney, Richard Van Wagoner, and Martha Sonntag Bradley will capitalize on such possibilities.[9] Then, perhaps, at long last we will move toward solving what Jan Shipps sagaciously characterized "The Prophet Puzzle: Suggestions Leading toward a More Comprehensive Interpretation of Joseph Smith," in her 1974 essay, reprinted in Bryan Waterman, ed., *The Prophet Puzzle: Interpretive Essays on Joseph Smith* (Salt Lake City: Signature

---

9. An important work containing essays on Joseph Smith by Richard L. Bushman and Dan Vogel, thereby indicating the nature of their forthcoming book-length biographies is Bryan Waterman, ed., *The Prophet Puzzle: Interpretive Essays on Joseph Smith* (Salt Lake City: Signature Books, 1999). This volume also includes essays by a number of other scholars, including my "Joseph Smith, the Mormons, and Antebellum Reform: A Closer Look," 113-40.

Books, 1999) According to Shipps the essential task remains "to integrate "the many facets" of Smith's "complex career." While not achieving the "perfect harmony" hoped for by certain idealists, such an effort might allow a future Smith biographer "to reconcile enough of the inconsistency to reveal, not a split personality but a splendid, gifted—pressured, sometimes opportunistic, often troubled—yet, for all of that, a larger-than-life man" (44).

Turning to Joseph Smith's successor, Brigham Young, the most important biography to appear in the past twenty-five years is, without question, Leonard J. Arrington, *Brigham Young: American Moses* (New York: Alfred A. Knopf, 1985). Extensively researched and carefully written, *American Moses* comes closest to a definitive biography on the Utah Mormon leader. This widely acclaimed biography presents the Mormon leader in a generally favorable light while noting with candor his difficulties and conflicts. Particularly illuminating is Arrington's discussion of sometimes contentious debate within the ruling councils of the Church since Church leaders then, as now, carefully cultivated a public image of unanimity and harmony. Arrington outlines clashes between Young and Apostle Orson Pratt, including Pratt's opposition to Young's 1847 decision to reorganize the First Presidency with himself as president. (Gary J. Bergera has explored this and other Pratt-Young collisions in *Conflict in the Quorum: Orson Pratt, Brigham Young, Joseph Smith* [Salt Lake City: Signature Books, 2003].)

Arrington's Brigham Young emerges as a multifaceted, complex personality. For example, Young chewed tobacco at the very time he was publicly chastising his followers for this same habit. But Arrington explains that Young consumed tobacco not as an indulgence but to relieve the pain caused by his bad teeth and gums. Arrington used Young's papers, previously closed to most scholars, to present a portrait with a richness in texture and tone lacking in earlier biographies (311-12, 207-9, 407).

Arrington's biography is not without its shortcomings, however. He tended to avoid or downplay certain controversial topics, specifically Young's response to and handling of certain conflicts and divisions within Mormonism. The author also glossed over complex relationships and interactions within Young's own large family, causing eminent Western historian Martin Ridge to remark: "One would like to know more about [Young's] home, children, family tensions, divorce, and other matters."[10] Also problematic is the switch from a chronological format to a topical one after the arrival into the Great Basin. From that point, separate chapters deal with Young's multiple roles as Utah territorial governor, Church president, spiritual counselor, family man, Superintendent of Indian Affairs, Western colonizer, etc. Laura Kalpakian, [Review of] "*Brigham Young: American Moses*," *Los Angeles Times Book Review*, July 14, 1985, concedes that this "fragmented approach" was "doubtlessly necessary given the scope of Young's activities but the man we meet in the latter pages . . . loses much of his approachable humanity and becomes a figure exhorting from the mountain tops" (10).

The problem is, in fact, more fundamental: Arrington's difficulty in capturing his subject's inner life, leading David Brion Davis, "Secrets of the Mormons," *New York Review of Books*, August 15, 1985, 18-19, to lament that "we seldom glimpse [Young's] interior motives." Martin E. Marty, [Review of] *Brigham Young: American Moses*, *American Historical Review* 90 (December 1985), also agreed that "something about Young's inner life eludes us." Marty wishes that Arrington "had slowed" the pace of his "old-fashioned, brisk, eloquent narrative prose" and "played ever so cautiously with psychologically informed history" in examining the "inner man" (1271).

Despite its deficiencies, Arrington's *magnum opus* clearly supersedes all earlier book-length studies, most notably Stanley P. Hirshson's superficially researched and sloppily writ-

---

10. Martin Ridge, "Joseph Smith, Brigham Young, and a Religious Tradition," *Reviews in American History*, March 1986, 30. For other insights into Brigham Young's family, see Dean L. Jessee, *Letters of Brigham Young to his Sons* (Salt Lake City: Deseret Book, 1974); his "Brigham Young's Family," *BYU Studies* 18 (Spring 1978): 311-27; and his "Brigham Young's Family: The Wilderness Years," *BYU Studies* 19 (Summer 1979): 474-99.

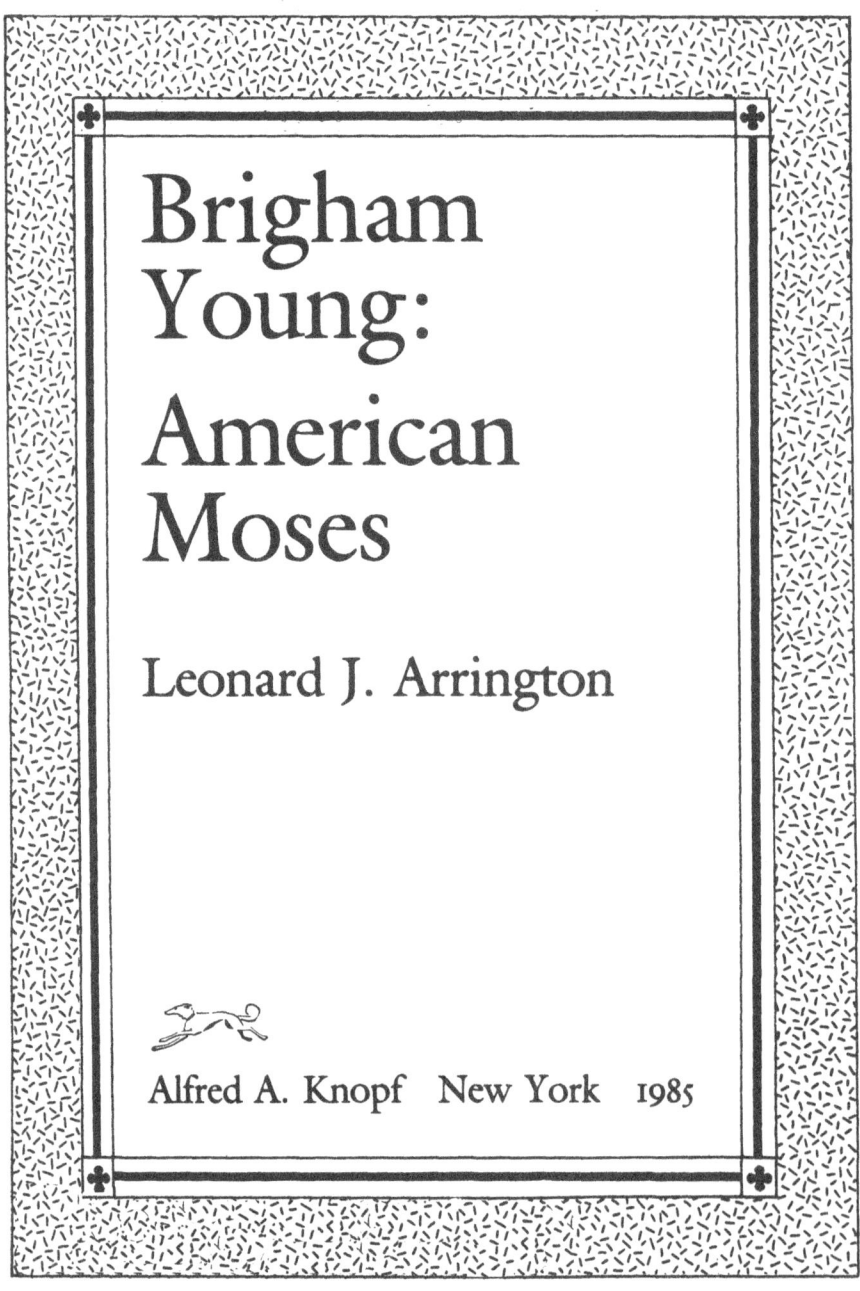

ten *The Lion of the Lord: A Biography of Brigham Young* (New York: Alfred A. Knopf, 1969), a hack work given undeserved scholarly legitimacy through its publisher, who, ironically, published Arrington's biography.[11]

Recent examinations of subsequent presidents of the Utah-based LDS Church have yielded mixed results. Still lacking is a scholarly biography on Young's successor, John Taylor (1880-87). Samuel W. Taylor, *The Kingdom or Nothing: The Life of John Taylor, Militant Mormon* (New York: Macmillan, 1976); reprinted as *The Last Pioneer: John Taylor, a Mormon Prophet* (Salt Lake City: Signature Books, 1999), is a spritely narrative by the president's grandson, also a novelist and journalist. His controversial conclusions and interpretations were, however, based on speculation and limited historical evidence. According to Ronald W. Walker, "Challenge and Craft of Mormon Biography," Taylor's work "exhibits the cares and techniques of the novelist" despite efforts to be history-minded" (184).[12]

In contrast, Taylor's successor, Wilford Woodruff (1889-98) received able treatment in Thomas G. Alexander, *Things in Heaven and Earth: The Life and Times of Wilford Woodruff, a Mormon Prophet* (Salt Lake City: Signature Books, 1991). According to Allen and Leonard, *Story of the Latter-day Saints,* 690, it "offers the most complete examination and only interpretation of Woodruff's life." Alexander, using Woodruff's voluminous journals and other primary sources, presented him as both talented and versatile, competent in his various roles as Church leader, business leader, civic leader, and scholar, and patriarch of nine wives and thirty-three children. While sympathetic, Alexander's biography is no hagiography. This work stands as a definitive standard against which to measure subsequent studies of Woodruff and his contemporaries.

Unfortunately, there are no satisfactory biographies of Woodruff's two immediate successors, Lorenzo Snow (1899-1901) and Joseph F. Smith (1901-18). Francis M. Gibbons, emeritus member of the Seventy, has written biographies of all LDS Church presidents, including these two: *Lorenzo Snow: Spiritual Giant, Prophet of God* (Salt Lake City: Deseret Book, 1982) and *Joseph F. Smith: Patriarch and Preacher, Prophet of God* (Salt Lake City: Deseret Book, 1984). However, his unrelenting focus on shaping his biographies as faith-promoting narratives makes them traditional biographies rather than part of the New Mormon History. Heber J. Grant, Church president from 1918 to 1945, also lacks a full biography, although Ronald W. Walker has written *Qualities That Count: Heber J. Grant as Businessman, Missionary and Apostle* (Provo, UT: BYU Studies, 2004) published as a special issue of that quarterly: 43, no. 1 (2004). It contains twelve articles, including "Young Heber J. Grant's Years of Passage," *BYU Studies* 24 (Spring 1984): 131-49; "Young Heber J. Grant and His Call to the Apostleship," *BYU Studies* 18 (Fall 1977) 121-26; "Strangers in a Strange Land: Heber J. Grant and the Opening of the Japanese Mission," *Journal of Mormon History* 13 (1987): 21-44; "Heber J. Grant and the Utah Loan and Trust Company," *Journal of Mormon History* 8 (1981): 21-36; and "Young Heber J. Grant: Entrepreneur Extraordinary," in *Twentieth Century American West*, edited by Thomas G. Alexander, Howard A. Christy, and Edward Colonna (Provo, UT: Charles Redd Center for Western Studies/BYU Press, 1983), 85-119.

George Albert Smith, Church president from 1945 to 1951, appears in a very competent three-generation study, *Builders of the Kingdom: George A. Smith, John Henry Smith, and George Albert Smith* (Provo, Utah: Brigham Young University Press, 1981), by Merlo Pusey, a prize-winning journalist and biographer. His three successors—David O. McKay (1951-70), Joseph Fielding Smith (1970-72), and Harold B. Lee (1972-73)—also lack scholarly, well-written biographies, although traditional biographies by admiring relatives have appeared for all three: David Lawrence McKay, *My Father, David O. McKay* (Salt Lake City: Deseret Book, 1989); Joseph Fielding Smith Jr. and John J. Stewart, *The Life of Joseph Fielding Smith: Tenth President of the Church* (Salt Lake City: Deseret Book, 1972); and L. Brent

---

11. For a somewhat different effort to deal with the controversial aspects of Brigham Young's life, see my own *Brigham Young and the Expanding American Frontier* (Boston: Little, Brown, and Co., 1986).

12. A careful though limited reconsideration of John Taylor is G. St John Stott, "John Taylor's Religious Preparation," *Dialogue: A Journal of Mormon Thought* 19 (Spring 1986): 123-28.

The Kingdom or Nothing

THE LIFE OF
JOHN TAYLOR,
MILITANT MORMON

by Samuel W. Taylor

MACMILLAN PUBLISHING CO., INC.
New York

COLLIER MACMILLAN PUBLISHERS
London

Goates, *Harold B. Lee: Prophet and Seer* (Salt Lake City: Bookcraft, 1985). Gregory A. Prince is preparing a full-scale biography of David O. McKay, preceded by some tantalizing articles: "The Red Peril, the Candy Maker, and the Apostle: David O. McKay's Confrontation with Communism," *Dialogue* 37, no. 2 (Summer 2004): 37-95; and (with Gary Topping) "A Turbulent Coexistence: Duane Hunt, David O. McKay, and a Quarter-Century of Catholic-Mormon Relations," *Journal of Mormon History* 30, no. 2 (Fall 2004): forthcoming. An oral-history-based essay is my "The Private versus the Public David O. McKay: Profile of a Complex Personality," *Dialogue* 31, no. 3 (Fall 1998): 11-32.

Spencer W. Kimball, Church president from 1973 to 1985, had the good fortune of being treated in a first-rate biography. *Spencer W. Kimball: Twelfth President of the Church of Jesus Christ of Latter-day Saints* (Salt Lake City: Bookcraft, 1977), by Edward L. Kimball and Andrew Kimball Jr., his son and grandson. It quickly established itself as the scholarly model for all future biographies of Church presidents. Not only was Kimball's life "unusually varied and interesting" but he also had kept a voluminous daily diary for years. Most important, the authors were not only frank and analytical in their presentation but could "put together a well-paced biography that convinces by recounting numerous specific experiences," according to Bitton, "Mormon Biography," 7. Walker, "Challenge and Craft of Mormon Biography," 187, added: "Here [is a] struggling personality, the depiction of genuine emotion, and homely details which are at times stark." Edward Kimball, in affirming the virtues of his open approach, stated that "the best people," including his father, "had flaws. . . . If we ignore them completely, that deprives the biography of credibility."[13] Or as he stated more vividly on another occasion: "The whitewash of ancestors, even if they were church leaders, will run in the rain. It lacks credibility and no amount of documentation of that person's good side can persuade an intelligent reader that there is not more to the story."[14] Edward Kimball is currently at work on a history focused on his father's administrative years.

It is regrettable that Spencer W. Kimball's three successors as Church president have not attracted biographers of similar ability. Sorely lacking are candid, analytical biographies on Ezra Taft Benson (1985-94), Howard W. Hunter (1994-95), and Gordon B. Hinckley (1995-present). Sheri L. Dew, vice president of Deseret Book and former second counselor in the LDS Relief Society General Presidency, has written official and rather plodding biographies: *Ezra Taft Benson: A Biography* (Salt Lake City: Deseret Book, 1987), and her *Go Forward with Faith: The Biography of Gordon B. Hinckley* (Salt Lake City: Deseret Book, 1996). The first work, characterized as a "sympathetic overview" by Allen and Leonard, *Story of the Latter-day Saints,* 691, fails to mention such controversial activities as Benson's involvement with the John Birch Society. Robert M. Hogge, Review, *BYU Studies* 36, no. 4 (1996-97): 240, noted that the second was an "authorized biography" whose "early drafts" Hinckley reviewed. Writing with greater forthrightness was Eleanor Knowles, *Howard W. Hunter* (Salt Lake City: Deseret Book, 1994), but the book was limited to Hunter's prepresidential activities. Article-length brief biographies of LDS presidents through Benson appear in Leonard J. Arrington, ed., *The Presidents of the Church* (Salt Lake City: Deseret Book, 1986); but most Mormon Church presidents are still waiting for serious scholarly attention.

Biographies of Other Church Leaders

Outstanding book-length biographies on high Mormon Church leaders below the level of president are also limited. Some early associates of Joseph Smith have received scholarly treatment: Phillip R. Legg, *Oliver Cowdery: The Elusive Second Elder of the Restoration* (Independence: Herald Publishing House, 1989); David J. Whittaker, "East of Nauvoo: Benjamin Winchester and the Early Mormon Church," *Journal of Mormon History* 21 (Fall

---

13. Edward L. Kimball, "Writing Mormon Biography," 5; paper presented at the First Annual LDS Writers' Conference, June 5, 1993; photocopy in my possession; quoted by permission.

14. Edward L. Kimball, "Writing Mormon Biography,"7, panel presentation, Sunstone Symposium, August 8, 1992; photocopy in my possession; quoted by permission.

1995): 31-83; and Richard S. Van Wagoner, *Sidney Rigdon: A Portrait of Religious Excess* (Salt Lake City: Signature Books, 1994). The third is the best—a vivid portrait of this one-time counselor in the First Presidency and later rival to Brigham Young. Unfortunately, Rigdon's wife destroyed most of his personal papers; still, Van Wagoner has crafted a biography that David J. Whittaker, [Review of] *Sidney Rigdon: A Portrait of Religious Excess, Journal of Mormon History* 23, no. 1 (Spring 1997): 189-95, has praised as "comprehensive" and "most ambitious" but also criticized as too naturalistic and marred by Van Wagoner's "pejorative language, his secular descriptions of religious beliefs, and his description of religious faith" as "delusions, silliness, a cover for corruption, or mental illness." Similarly, RLDS scholar Edward A. Warner, [Review of] Van Wagoner, *Sidney Rigdon: A Portrait of Religious Excess, John Whitmer Historical Association Journal* 17 (1997): 146-50, while praising Van Wagoner's presentation of Rigdon as a "very human figure . . . with virtues and vices, gifts and flaws, achievements and disgraces, high callings, and petty temptations" critiques the work as "too normative and unfair" in dismissing "Rigdon's religion . . . as 'pathological,' 'excessive,' 'maladaptive,' ineffective, or a failure."

The lives of other individuals close to Joseph Smith, have been examined with varying degrees of success. Jeffrey S. O'Driscoll, *Hyrum Smith: A Life of Integrity* (Salt Lake City: Deseret Book, 2003), has used numerous primary sources that were unavailable when Pearson H. Corbett, wrote *Hyrum Smith: Patriarch* (Salt Lake City: Deseret Book, 1963). Irene M. Bates and E. Gary Smith, *Lost Legacy: The Mormon Office of Presiding Patriarch* (Urbana: University of Illinois Press, 1996), treat Hyrum in this collective biography that begins with Joseph Smith Sr., and continue to Eldred G. Smith, Gary Smith's father. These patriarchs are, for the most part, Hyrum Smith's descendants. Despite the focus, which is limited to his role as Presiding Patriarch, this work is very competent, providing fascinating analytical insights into the multi-generational dynamics within the Smith family. In a similar fashion, Merlo Pusey's *Builders of the Kingdom: George A. Smith, John Henry Smith, and George Albert Smith* carefully chronicles and analyzes the relationships among George A. Smith (Joseph and Hyrum's first cousin), his son, John Henry Smith, and grandson, George Albert Smith, all of them LDS apostles (and, in the latter's case, Church president).

The lives of two close Brigham Young counselors have each been chronicled in carefully crafted biographies. Heber C. Kimball and George Q. Cannon each served in the Council of the Twelve and First Presidency. Close to the centers of power, they were not hesitant about exercising it themselves. The essence of the earthy, plain-spoken Kimball has been captured in Stanley B. Kimball, *Heber C. Kimball: Mormon Patriarch and Pioneer* (Urbana: University of Illinois Press, 1981). The politically and intellectually sophisticated George Q. Cannon found an able biographer in Davis Bitton. His *George Q. Cannon: A Biography* (Salt Lake City: Deseret Book, 1999), presents Cannon as an energetic, multifaceted personality, patriarch of six wives and forty-two children, a prolific writer, newspaper editor, entrepreneur, and political lobbyist. Particularly compelling is Bitton's treatment of Cannon's political skills. As Utah's territorial delegate to Congress for twelve years, he skillfully defended the Mormons in the teeth of increasing federal anti-polygamy prosecutions. Also effective is Bitton's depiction of Cannon's critical role in achieving the Mormons' long-sought goal of Utah statehood, which eluded them until 1896.

Other scholarly book-length biographies on high-level Church officers include Leonard J. Arrington, *Charles C. Rich: Mormon General and Western Frontiersman* (Provo, UT: Brigham Young University Press, 1974); and Andrew Karl Larson, *Erastus Snow: The Life of a Missionary and Pioneer for the Early Mormon Church* (Salt Lake City: University of Utah Press, 1971), both apostles and noted colonizers. Gene Sessions, *Mormon Thunder: A Documentary History of Jedediah Morgan Grant* (Urbana: University of Illinois Press, 1982), deals with the fiery preacher and counselor in the First Presidency who spearheaded the Mormon Reformation of 1856. Breck England, *The Life and Thought of Orson Pratt* (Salt Lake City: University of Utah Press, 1985), studies nineteenth-century Mormonism's most important theologian.

George Q. Cannon

A Biography

Davis Bitton

Deseret Book Company

Excavating Mormon Pasts

Setting the standard for biographies of more recent Mormon General Authorities are two well-written, thoroughly researched biographies on the noted conservative J. Reuben Clark Jr., whose eventful, controversial career both in public life and as a member of the First Presidency spanned the first half of the twentieth century: Frank Fox, *J. Reuben Clark: The Public Years* (Provo, UT: Brigham Young University Press, 1980); and D. Michael Quinn, *J. Reuben Clark: The Church Years* (Provo, UT: Brigham Young University Press, 1983), which he updated and expanded as *Elder Statesman: A Biography of J. Reuben Clark* (Salt Lake City: Signature Books, 2001). Another counselor in the First Presidency, Anthon H. Lund, a Dane, lacks a full-scale biography although Jennifer L. Lund, "Out of the Swan's Nest: The Ministry of Anthon H. Lund, Scandinavian Apostle," *Journal of Mormon History* 29, no. 2 (Fall 2003): 77-105, provides an analytic overview of his life; and John P. Hatch, ed., *Danish Apostle: The Diaries of Anthon H. Lund* (Salt Lake City: Signature Books, 2004), makes available his interesting and detailed journal.

Apostle Reed Smoot, a conservative Republican, like Clark, served for three decades as an influential U.S. Senator (1903-1933). Milton R. Merrill's 1950 dissertation at Columbia University finally appeared in print as *Reed Smoot: Apostle in Politics* (Logan: Utah State University Press, 1990). At the other end of the political spectrum a generation later was Hugh B. Brown, a Democrat and counselor in the First Presidency, treated in Richard D. Poll and Eugene E. Campbell, *Hugh B. Brown: His Life and Thought* (Salt Lake City: Bookcraft, 1975); and Edwin B. Firmage, ed., *An Abundant Life: The Memoirs of Hugh B. Brown* (Salt Lake City: Signature Books, 1988).

Brigham Henry Roberts, whose career as a Democrat and General Authority spanned both the late nineteenth and early twentieth centuries, is best known as a leading Mormon theologian and one of Mormonism's greatest historians. Truman Madsen, *Defender of the Faith: The B. H. Roberts Story*, treats him with mixed success. Although not a biography, John R. Sillito, ed., *History's Apprentice: The Diaries of B. H. Roberts* (Salt Lake City: Signature Books, 2004) promises long-awaited insights into this pivotal figure. David S. Hoopes and Roy Hoopes, *The Making of a Mormon Apostle: The Story of Rudger Clawson* (Lanham, Md.: Madison Books, 1990), is a scholarly, carefully written study.

The life and career of S. Dilworth Young, a colorful twentieth-century General Authority and direct descendent of both Brigham Young and his brother Joseph Young have been examined in a frank, highly readable narrative by grandson Benson Young Parkinson, *S. Dilworth Young: General Authority, Scouter, Poet* (Salt Lake City: Covenant Communications, 1994). J. Golden Kimball, a colorful, sometimes outspoken cowboy-cum-General Authority, appears in Thomas E. Cheney's engaging *The Golden Legacy: A Folk History of J. Golden Kimball* (Santa Barbara, CA: Peregrine Smith, 1973). James N. Kimball, a grandnephew, has a scholarly biography in progress, and has already published the sympathetic yet analytical "J. Golden Kimball: Private Life of a Public Figure," *Journal of Mormon History* 24, no. 2 (Fall 1998): 55-84.

Henry D. Moyle was a controversial, confrontational General Authority during the 1950s and 1960s whose life has been forthrightly presented by Richard D. Poll in *Working the Divine Miracle: The Life of Henry D. Moyle,* edited by Stan Larson (Salt Lake City: Signature Books, 1999). Although completed in 1983, the biography was held back from publication until 1999 by Moyle family members concerned about the Poll's candor in presenting Moyle as, in the words of reviewer C. Brooklyn Derr, *Journal of Mormon History* 26, no. 1 (Spring 2000): 256-62, "the hard-driving wheeler-dealer [that] he was." Moyle's fall from official Mormon favor occurred because President David O. McKay came to see Moyle as "a 'loose cannon' who was using his authority illegitimately."

More superficial, and less scholarly are G. Homer Durham, *N. Eldon Tanner: His Life and Service* (Salt Lake City: Deseret Book, 1982); F. Burton Howard, *Marion G. Romney: His Life and Faith* (Salt Lake City: Bookcraft, 1988); and Peggy Petersen Barton, *Mark E. Petersen: A Biography* (Salt Lake City: Deseret Book, 1985). Also written for popular audiences are James P. Bell, *In the Strength of the Lord: The Life and Teachings of James E. Faust* (Salt Lake City: Deseret Book, 1999); Dennis B. Horne, *Bruce R. McConkie: Highlights from His Life*

Hugh Nibley:

A Consecrated Life

Boyd Jay Petersen

Greg Kofford Books
Salt Lake City 2002

and Teachings (Roy, UT: Eborn Books, 2000); Michael K. Winder, *John R. Winder: Member of the First Presidency, Pioneer, Temple Builder, Dairyman* (Bountiful, UT: Horizon Publishers, 1999); Spencer J. Condie, *Russell M. Nelson: Father, Surgeon, Apostle* (Salt Lake City: Deseret Book, 2003); Bruce C. Hafen, *A Disciple's Life: The Biography of Neal A. Maxwell* (Salt Lake City: Deseret Book, 2002); and three apostolic biographies by Lucille A. Tate, *LeGrand Richards: Beloved Apostle* (Salt Lake City: Bookcraft, 1982); *David B. Haight: The Life Story of a Disciple* (Salt Lake City: Bookcraft, 1987); and *Boyd K. Packer: A Watchman on the Tower* (Salt Lake City: Deseret Book, 1995). Other biographies on twentieth-century General Authorities have generally been more in the realm of hagiography then biography.

Lesser Leaders and Rank-and-File Latter-day Saints

Also attracting the attention of biographers have been various so-called second, third, and fourth echelon Mormons, albeit with mixed results. On the plus side is James B. Allen, *Trials of Discipleship: The Story of William Clayton, a Mormon* (Urbana: University of Illinois Press, 1987), a model biography, revised and reissued as *No Toil nor Labor Fear: The Story of William Clayton* (Provo, UT: Brigham Young University Press, 2002). While generally sympathetic to this secretary and confidante of Joseph Smith, Allen frankly discusses Clayton's problems with alcohol and his disappointments and his declining status under Brigham Young. Hardbitten and faithful long-time bishop Edwin D. Woolley appears in a skillful portrait: Leonard J. Arrington, *From Quaker to Latter-day Saint: Bishop Edwin D. Woolley* (Salt Lake City: Deseret Book, 1976).

In a class by itself is Harold Schindler's classic *Orrin Porter Rockwell: Man of God, Son of Thunder* (Salt Lake City: University of Utah Press, 1966), which absorbingly reconstructs the colorful Rockwell, a close associate of both Joseph Smith and Brigham Young with a well-deserved reputation for violence on the Mormon frontier. William G. Hartley, *My Best For the Kingdom: History and Autobiography of John Lowe Butler* (Salt Lake City: Aspen Books, 1993), considers the "virtually unknown and unheralded" Butler, whom Cracroft has characterized as "a kind of settled-down Porter Rockwell" "Mormon Biography," 63. A devout convert, Butler was a Danite during the 1838 Mormon War in Missouri and a long-time bishop in Spanish Fork, Utah. Anna Jean Backus, *Mountain Meadows Witness: The Life and Times of Bishop Phillip Klingensmith* (Spokane, WA: Arthur H. Clark, 1995), portrays another devout Mormon caught up in Mormon violence. In contrast, Bill Hickman, an even more colorful vigilante figure, has yet to be interpreted in a competent, scholarly fashion, despite the well-meaning, but flawed *"Wild Bill" Hickman and the Mormon Frontier* (Salt Lake City: Signature Books, 1988) by descendant Hope L. Hilton.

Less colorful but equally important Latter-day Saints who excelled in business, education, the arts, and politics have also received the attention of scholars. Mormon entrepreneur David J. Eccles characterized as "one of the most creative and resourceful businessmen in the history of the Mountain West"[15] has been appraised by Leonard J. Arrington in *David Eccles: Pioneer Western Industrialist* (Logan: Utah State University Press, 1975). Arrington also chronicled the life of another important Mormon entrepreneur, Charles Redd, after whom BYU's western history center was named, in *Utah's Audacious Stockman: Charlie Redd*, (Logan: Utah State University Press/Provo, UT: Charles Redd Center for Western Studies/Brigham Young University Press, 1995). In collaboration with John R. Alley, Arrington also traced the career of *Harold F. Silver: Western Inventor, Businessman, and Civic Leader* (Logan: Utah State University Press, 1992). Richard D. Poll produced a frank biography on Mormon financier *Howard J. Stoddard: Founder, Michigan National Bank* (East Lansing: Michigan State University Press, 1980). Donald G. Godfrey has written a biography of *Philo T. Farnsworth: The Father of Television* (Salt Lake City: University of Utah Press, 2001). An engaging essay perhaps portending a book-length biography, is Edward A. Geary, "Reuben G. Miller: Turn of the Century Rancher, Entrepreneur, and Civic Leader," *Utah Historical Quarterly* 67, no, 2 (Spring 1999): 123-47. Other prominent

---

15. Leonard J. Arrington, "David Eccles: A Man for His Time," *Journal of Mormon History* 25 no. 2 (Fall 1999): 1.

Mormon entrepreneurs are also deserving of scholarly attention, especially Marriner Eccles, one-time chair of the Federal Reserve System and J. Willard Marriott, world-renown hotelier.

Latter-day Saints have long been deeply involved in education, and probably more deserve book-length studies than have received them. Lowell L. Bennion, twentieth-century educator and premier Mormon humanitarian has been sensitively portrayed by Mary Lythgoe Bradford in her award-winning biography, *Lowell L. Bennion: Teacher, Counselor, Humanitarian* (Salt Lake City: Dialogue Foundation, 1995). The career of Sterling M. McMurrin, Mormon theologian, philosopher, teacher, and U.S. Commissioner of Education under John F. Kennedy has been captured in an interesting conversational format combined with excellent scholarship by L. Jackson Newell, *Matters of Conscience: Conversations with Sterling M. McMurrin on Philosophy, Education, and Religion* (Salt Lake City: Signature Books, 1996), and Newell's "Sterling Moss McMurrin: A Philosopher in Action," *Dialogue* 28 (Spring 1995): 1-17.

Also addressed in well-written scholarly biographies are two other important Mormon educators who also had reputations outside the Mormon community. Son-in-law Boyd Jay Petersen, *Hugh Nibley: A Consecrated Life* (Salt Lake City: Greg Kofford Books, 2002), considers the long-time BYU professor, scholar of ancient languages, and prolific author in a remarkably frank, forthright manner. Alan K. Parrish, *John A. Widtsoe: A Biography* (Salt Lake City: Deseret Books, 2003), interprets the life of this educator, international expert on dry farming and irrigation, author of numerous foundational works on Church doctrine, and apostle.

Gary J. Bergera has returned in several articles to Ernest L. Wilkinson, long-time president of Brigham Young University: "Ernest L. Wilkinson's Appointment as Seventh President of Brigham Young University," *Journal of Mormon History* 23, no. 2 (Fall 1997): 128-54; and his "Building Wilkinson's University," *Dialogue* 30, no. 3 (Fall 1997): 105-35. Roger D. Launius, "A Western Mormon in Washington, D.C.: James C. Fletcher, NASA, and the Final Frontier," *Pacific Historical Review* 64 (May 1995): 217-41, examines the career of this former University of Utah president who was twice director of the National Aeronautical and Space Administration.

As for Mormon artists and writers, the number of book-length biographies is limited. Artist Mahonri Macintosh Young, best known for his sculptures of This Is the Place Monument and the Seagull Monument has been treated in Thomas E. Toone, *Mahonri Young: His Life and Art* (Salt Lake City: Signature Books, 1997); and Norma S. Davis, *A Song of Joys: The Biography of Mahonri Macintosh Young: Sculptor, Painter, Etcher* (Provo, UT: Brigham Young University Museum of Art, 1999). Marian Robertson Wilson, *LeRoy Robertson: Music Giant from the Rockies* (Salt Lake City: Blue Ribbon Publications, 1996), describes the contributions of this Mormon composer.

Perhaps surprisingly, Mormon writers have generally been neglected by biographers—those producing fiction as well as nonfiction. Edward A. Geary, "Mormondom's Lost Generation: The Novelists of the 1940s," *BYU Studies* 18 (Fall 1977): 88-99; reprinted in *Tending the Garden: Essays on Mormon Literature*, edited by Eugene England and Lavina Fielding Anderson (Salt Lake City: Signature Books, 1996), reclaims several writers from the neglect of later generations. Leonard J. Arrington and John Haupt probe "The Mormon Heritage of Vardis Fisher," *BYU Studies* 18 (Fall 1977): 27-47. Mary Lythgoe Bradford is writing a biography of Virginia Sorenson with Susan Elizabeth Howe and Sue Simmons Saffle; and Veda Tebbs Hale is at work on a biography of Maurine Whipple. But much remains to be done.

Historians have been keenly interested in other histories as witness Leonard J. Arrington and Davis Bitton, *Mormons and Their Historians* (Salt Lake City: University of Utah Press, 1988); Richard Saunders, "'The Strange Mixture of Intellect': A Social History of Dale L. Morgan, 1933-42," *Dialogue* 28 (Winter 1995): 39-58; Craig L. Foster, "Madeline McQuown, Dale Morgan, and the Great Unfinished Brigham Young Biography," *Dialogue* 31 (Summer 1998): 111-23; and John Phillip Walker, ed., *Dale Morgan on Early Mormonism:*

Excavating Mormon Pasts

Correspondence and a New Mormon History (Salt Lake City: Signature Books, 1986). Gary Topping has critiqued the life and work of Dale L. Morgan in his insightful *Utah Historians and the Reconstruction of Western History* (Norman: University of Oklahoma Press, 2003): 113-73, and also critically examines the life and work of Fawn Brodie, Juanita Brooks, Bernard DeVoto, and Wallace Stegner, noting the influence of Mormonism on the scholarship of each. Leonard Arrington, founding father of the Mormon History Association and prime mover behind the New Mormon History, has set an excellent example for other historians with his frank and vivid *Adventures of a Church Historian* (Urbana: University of Illinois Press, 1998). Lavina Fielding Anderson is working on his biography as well.

Journalist Lee Roderick has written about Utah's long-term Republican Senator and 2000 presidential candidate Orrin Hatch, in *Leading the Charge: Orrin Hatch and 20 Years of America* (Carson City, NV: Gold Leaf Press, 1994); reissued as *Gentleman of the Senate: Orrin Hatch, a Portrait of Character* (Salt Lake City: Evans Books, 2000). F. Ross Peterson is at work on a scholarly biography of Stewart Udall, Secretary of the Interior in the John F. Kennedy and Lyndon B. Johnson administrations. A foretaste of his work is "'Do Not Lecture the Brethren': Stewart L. Udall's Pro-Civil Rights Stance, 1967," *Journal of Mormon History* 25 (Spring 1999): 272-87.

A number of other Latter-day Saints who left their mark in politics have, unaccountably, failed to receive scholarly attention. The best work on George Romney, former Michigan governor and 1968 presidential contender, is still Dennis L. Lythgoe, "The 1968 Presidential Decline of George Romney: Mormonism or Politics," *BYU Studies* 11 (Spring 1971: 214-40. But Romney merits a full-scale biography as do long-time Arizona Congressman Morris Udall who, in 1976, sought the presidency; Esther Peterson, a one-time Assistant Secretary of Labor under John F. Kennedy; Paula Hawkins, United States Senator from Florida—the first and only LDS women to serve in that body; and Lieutenant General Brent Scowcroft who served as National Security Advisor to Presidents Gerald Ford and George Bush. Brief descriptions of these individuals and their connections with Mormonism are in Richard N. and Joan K. Ostling, *Mormon America: The Power and the Promise* (San Francisco: HarperSan Francisco, 1999). *Restless: Memoirs of Labor and Consumer Activist Esther Peterson* by Esther Peterson and Winifred Conkling (Washington, D.C.: Caring Publishers, 1995), is an engaging first-person account that would be a good beginning place for a biographer.

Woefully lacking are careful scholarly biographies on "ordinary" Latter-day Saints—those whom Mormon scholar M. Guy Bishop has labeled "Invisible Saints" and whom David J. Whittaker and Donald Q. Cannon call "supporting Saints."[16] Paradoxically, considering the strong LDS interest in "family history" that results naturally from the unremitting emphasis on genealogical research, the outpouring of accompanying biographies has seldom reflected scholarly standards in either research or analysis. An exception is Jessie L. Embry's carefully researched *Mormon Polygamous Families: Life in the Principle* (Salt Lake City: University of Utah Press, 1987), which suggests some directions that the future family history might take.

While filo-pietism is understandable, it is regrettable since "ordinary" Latter-day Saints of middle to lower socio-economic status reflect the "norm" of the average Mormon life and their biographies would provide a more valid picture of the typical grassroots Mormon experience than the biographies of prominent Latter-day Saints. Clyde A. Milner, former director of the Mountain West Center at Utah State University, has argued for a more inclusive approach: "The daily lives and personal struggles of 'ordinary people' can produce significant historical insights about the human condition."[17] Likewise, Guy Bishop perceptively suggests in "The Invisible Saint," "A solid collection of biographies of

---

16. M. Guy Bishop, "The Invisible Saint: Biography and Lesser Known Mormons," paper presented at the annual meeting of the Western History Association, Tacoma, Washington, October 14, 1989; photocopy in my possession; quoted by permission; David J. Whittaker and Donald Q. Cannon, eds., *Supporting Saints: Life Stories of Nineteenth-Century Mormons* (Provo, UT: Religious Studies Center, Brigham Young University, 1983).

17. Clyde A. Milner II, "[Review of] Lillian Schlissel, Byrd Gibbens, and Elizabeth Hampsten, *Far from Home: Families of the Westward Journey* (New York, 1989) *History Book Club Review*, July 1989, 5.

lesser known [Latter-day] Saints might well raise a whole new set of questions for the historians of Mormonism to ask" (8).

Bishop has produced a model biography of an ordinary Latter-day Saint, *Henry William Bigler: Solder, Gold Miner, Missionary, Chronicler* (Logan: Utah State University Press, 1998). Bigler, whom Bishop characterizes as a "foot soldier for his faith" led a generally unremarkable life, except for his presence at the historic discovery of gold in California which he recorded in his diary. Bigler's life history of unglamorous and faithful consistency, Bishop asserts, "offers a window through which it is possible to understand the experiences of many of his contemporaries" although few "left records as detailed and consistent as Bigler's" (xi-xii).

It might seem that economics drives the biography decision: that the potential audience for biographies of ordinary Saints is too limited. But the appeal of family biographies improves if the stories are deeply researched and skillfully crafted within the context of engaging family history. This is certainly the case with the model family histories produced by William G. Hartley, whose already mentioned award-winning *"My Best for the Kingdom": History and Autobiography of John Lowe Butler* originated as a history of and for the Butler family. Other fine family histories by Hartley include *Kindred Saints: The Mormon Immigrant Heritage of Alvin and Kathryn Christensen* (Salt Lake City: Eden Hill Publishing, 1982); *To Build, To Create, To Produce: Ephraim P. Ellison's Life and Enterprises, 1850-1939* (N.p: Ellison Family Organization, 1997); and *They Are My Friends: A History of the Joseph Knight Family, 1825-1850* (Provo, UT: Grandin Book, 1986), thoroughly revised and enlarged as *Stand by My Servant Joseph: The Story of the Joseph Knight Family and the Restoration* (Provo, UT: Joseph Fielding Smith Institute for LDS History/Salt Lake City: Deseret Book, 2004).

Likewise, Ronald O. Barney's finely crafted *One Side by Himself: The Life and Times of Lewis Barney, 1808-1894* (Logan: Utah State University Press, 2001), explores an ancestor's hardscrabble life as, in Will Bagley's words, a vivid "view of Mormonism's first six decades of controversy, hardship, and triumph . . . from the bottom of the social heap" (back cover). Other well-written family histories, are Davis Bitton, *The Redoubtable John Pack: Pioneer, Proselyter, Patriarch* (N.p.: John Pack Family Association, 1982); S. George Ellsworth, *Samuel Claridge: Pioneering the Outposts of Zion* (Logan: S. George Ellsworth, 1987), his *The Journals of Addison Pratt* (Salt Lake City: University of Utah Press, 1990), and *The History of Louisa Barnes Pratt* (Logan: Utah State University Press, 1998).

Better-done rank-and-file biographies would appeal to the inherent interest in learning about one's ancestors and seeking one's roots—with works about other families serving as mirrors and even analogues of one's own. Clear evidence of this phenomenon was the unusually large number of family history papers presented at the 2000 Mormon History Association annual meeting in Denmark.[18]

Looking into one's own family background brings special rewards and pleasures, deeper understandings of the difficulties and obstacles one's ancestors overcame, and, in the case of Latter-day Saint converts, their commitment to faith and beliefs, often tested

---

18. They include Alexander L. Baugh, "Andrew Jenson's Danish-Norwegian Mission Presidency, 1909-12"; Jennifer L. Lund, "The Ministry of Anthon H. Lund, Scandinavian Apostle"; Alan K. Parrish, "Four European Missions of John A. Widtsoe"; Gary Layne Hatch, "C.C.A. Christensen as Editor, Poet, and Apologist"; Mary Lythgoe Bradford, "'O What a Good Big World!': Virginia Sorensen's Letters from Denmark"; William Mulder, "History and Memory in Virginia Sorensen's Danish Convert-Emigrant Novel, Kingdom Come"; Sue Simmons Saffle, "Danish Family Influences in the Adult Fiction of Virginia Sorensen Waugh"; Susan Elizabeth Howe, "The Danish Genesis of Virginia Sorensen's Novel *Lotte's Locket*"; Kenneth W. Godfrey, "The 1850 Mission of George Parker Dykes: A Study of Conflict, Discord, and Differences in Proselyting Styles, Yet the White Field Was Harvested"; David Dale Coy, "An Aalborger en Route: Regette Marie Nielsen's 1863 Emigration Journey"; Rolf Torgesen, "Christopher S. Winge: Norwegian Missionary and His Long-Lost 1859 Diary"; Jean B. Ohai, "Hans J. Zobell: Danish Seaman, Mormon Emigrant"; Roseland Bergeson Thornton, "Niels Bergeson: A Saint Among Kings"; Tina Mather, "The Forgotten Woman: My 1852 Danish Emigrant Ancestor"; Gregory Christofferson, "The Warnicke Family: A Prototype of Mormon Emigration from Scandinavia in the 1860s"; Richard Forsberg Haglund, "From Dalarna to Zion: The Odyssey of the J. E. Forsberg Family"; and Danny L. Jorgensen, "Eva and Richard Jorgensen: Danish/American Converts to the Reorganization."

against opposition from family, friends, and neighbors. Elderly family members are particularly grateful when children and/or grandchildren express an interest in the activities and significant events of their lives. I found this very much the case in interviewing my own father, George S. Bringhurst, when he was about eighty.

Examining the historical dynamics of one's family can also increase individual self-awareness, specifically in defining the origins of certain personality/family traits and idiosyncracies. A compelling example of a Mormon family history produced as a result of one scholar's pursuit of both self-awareness and sense of time and place was Linda King Newell, "A Web of Trails: Bringing History Home," *Journal of Mormon History* 24 (Spring 1998): 1-27, first delivered as her 1997 Mormon History Association presidential address. In it, Newell described her ancestors' experiences as "a microcosm of the different motivations, beliefs, hopes, hardships, and failing of western Mormons and non-Mormons in the middle of the nineteenth century" (1).

But doing family history has its frustrations and carries risks, as Davis Bitton has pointed out in "Family History: Therapy or Scholarship," World Conference on Records, Series 109, August 1980, 1-6. We might find that important family letters or documents have been destroyed either deliberately or accidentally. A family member may refuse to discuss certain painful experiences—particularly those involving hard times, warfare, or family tragedy. Some surprises can be embarrassing, even though most families have at least a few skeletons in their closet, as I found in researching my own family history. When I began researching the siblings of my paternal grandfather, John T. Bringhurst, one brother, Samuel E. Bringhurst, was obviously a sterling character—president of the Swiss-Austrian Mission who helped David O. McKay select the site for the Swiss Temple. But a sister, Mary ("Mayme") Bringhurst became the third wife of Heber Bennion in 1901, well after the Manifesto, and gave birth to eight children. Another brother, William A. Bringhurst, was a bank robber and murderer, executed in 1924 at San Quintin Penitentiary for killing two Los Angeles policemen.[19]

Another group of Mormon biographies that cry out to be written are those of Latter-day Saints from various ethnic-racial backgrounds. This failure, notes Davis Bitton, "Mormon Biography," leaves "the impression of a white Anglo-Saxon, Utah-based existence" as the "norm" or representative of the total Mormon experience. "Where," he pointedly asks, "are the biographies . . . that give a convincing impression of what it is like to be an American Indian Mormon, a Japanese Mormon, a Tongan Mormon, a Nigerian Mormon?" (11). Such neglect is particularly unfortunate, given the Mormon Church's long history of growth outside of the United States; and more recently, its evolution into a truly international and increasingly ethnically diverse organization. Suggestions for possible future projects appear in Spencer J. Palmer, *The Expanding Church* (Salt Lake City: Deseret Book, 1978); Helen Z. Papanikolas, ed., *The Peoples of Utah* (Salt Lake City: Utah State Historical Society, 1976) (although not focused on Mormons); and Jessie L. Embry, "Ethnic Groups and the LDS Church" *Dialogue* 25, no. 4 (Winter 1992): 81-97.

Exceptions to such neglect are promising studies of Mormon Indians, including Scott R. Christensen, *Sagwitch: Shoshone Chieftain, Mormon Elder, 1822-1887* (Logan: Utah State University Press, 1999); John Alton Peterson, *Utah's Black Hawk War* (Salt Lake City: University of Utah Press, 1999); Lacee Harris, "To Be Native American—and Mormon," *Dialogue* 18, no. 4 (Winter 1985): 143-52; George P. Lee, *Silent Courage, An Indian Story: The Autobiography of George P. Lee, a Navajo* (Salt Lake City: Deseret Book, 1987); and Matthew E. Kreitzer, ed., *The Washakie Letters of Willie Ottogary: Northwestern Shoshone Journalist and Leader, 1906-1929* (Logan: Utah State University Press, 2000), presenting the life of this convert to Mormonism after the 1863 Bear River Massacre.

---

19. For more on Great-Aunt Mayme, see John Bennion, "Mary Bennion Powell: Polygamy and Silence," *Journal of Mormon History* 24 (Fall 1998): 85-128. Great-Uncle William appears in Hartley, *To Build, to Create, to Produce*, while I reported my own investigation in "William A. Bringhurst: From Devout Latter-day Saint to Condemned California Killer, A Personal Confrontation with the Past," paper presented at Mormon History Association Meeting, May 13, 1991, Claremont, California.

Additional ethnic studies include Jessie L. Embry, *Black Saints in a White Church: Contemporary African-American Mormons* (Salt Lake City: Signature Books, 1994); E. Dale LeBaron, ed., *All Are Alike Unto God* (Salt Lake City: Bookcraft, 1990), recounting the conversion experiences of African Mormons; Helvécio Martins with Mark Grover, *The Autobiography of Elder Helvécio Martins* (Salt Lake City: Aspen Books, 1994); and Newell G. Bringhurst, "Elijah Abel and the Changing Status of Blacks within Mormonism," *Dialogue* 12, no. 2 (Summer 1979): 22-36. Biddy Mason, an African American slave and one-time Latter-day Saint, is the focus of DeEtta Demaratus, *The Force of a Feather: The Search for a Lost Story of Slavery and Freedom* (Salt Lake City: University of Utah Press, 2002), a somewhat unorthodox book-length study, part memoir and part historical narrative.

Eric B. Shumway, ed., *Tongan Saints: Legacy of Faith* (Laie, HI: Institute for Polynesian Studies/BYU-Hawaii, 1991), compiles personal narratives. Mark L. Grover, "Execution in Mexico: The Deaths of Rafael Monroy and Vicente Morales, *BYU Studies* 35, no. 3 (1996): 7-28, recounts the tragic endings of two Mexican Mormons.

Latter-day Saint Women

Also in short supply are scholarly, well-written biographies of Latter-day Saint women. (See also Todd Compton, "The New Mormon Women's History," in this volume.) But here as Davis Bitton optimistically prophesied in "Mormon Biography" more than twenty years ago, prospects for the future appear "fairly bright" (9). A benchmark work is Linda King Newell and Valeen Tippetts Avery, *Mormon Enigma: Emma Hale Smith, Prophet's Wife, "Elect Lady," Polygamy's Foe* (1984; rev. ed., Urbana: University of Illinois Press, 1994). Engagingly written, *Mormon Enigma* is a compelling work that presents Joseph Smith's first wife as a fascinating and assertive individual in her own right and not as a bland appendage of her husband. James B. Allen and Glen M. Leonard in *The Story of the Latter-day Saints,* characterize this work as "a much needed balanced treatment" because of its handling of significant controversies during the lifetime of Joseph Smith and following his death (691).

Complementing *Mormon Enigma* is Todd Compton, *In Sacred Loneliness: The Plural Wives of Joseph Smith* (Salt Lake City: Signature Books, 1997), a meticulously researched and carefully written tour de force. Given the intense secrecy about polygamy during Joseph Smith's lifetime, a major achievement is Compton's careful work in identifying the women most probably married to the Mormon prophet (thirty-three) and in providing taut, gripping accounts of their lives. Particularly enthralling is his discussion of the tangled relationships between the Mormon prophet and these various women.[20]

Next to Emma Hale Smith, Eliza R. Snow is undoubtedly the best known of Joseph Smith's plural wives and even the best known of the many plural wives of her second husband, Brigham Young. Pending Jill Mulvay Derr's book-length biography on Eliza R. Snow, historians may rely on her "Form and Feeling in a Carefully Crafted Life: Eliza R. Snow's 'Poem of Poems,'" *Journal of Mormon History* 26, no. 1 (Spring 2000): 1-39; and (with Karen Lynn Davidson), her "A Wary Heart Becomes 'Unalterably Fix'd': Eliza R. Snow's Conversion to Mormonism," *Journal of Mormon History* 30 no. 2 (Fall 2004): forthcoming; Maureen Ursenbach Beecher, *Eliza and Her Sisters* (Salt Lake City: Aspen Books, 1991) and her edition of *The Personal Writings of Eliza Roxy Snow* (Salt Lake City: University of Utah Press, 1995).

In contrast, the plural wives of other nineteenth-century Latter-day Saint leaders have yet to be considered in careful, scholarly detail. Stanley B. Kimball, *Heber C. Kimball: Mormon Patriarch and Pioneer* (Urbana: University of Illinois Press, 1981), includes an appendix listing Kimball's wives and children, but without full biographical entries. The fifty-five

---

20. Compton's list is the most restricted. Brodie, *No Man Knows My History,* 457-88, puts the total at forty-eight, a figure followed by Danel C. Bachman, "A Study of the Mormon Practice of Plural Marriage before the Death of Joseph Smith" (M.A. Thesis, Purdue University, 1975), Appendix C, 333-36, and Newell and Avery, *Mormon Enigma,* 333 note 51. George D. Smith, "Nauvoo Roots of Mormon Polygamy, 1841-46," *Dialogue,* 27, no. 1 (Spring 1994): 1-72, identifies forty-three. See also B. Carmon Hardy, [Review of] Todd Compton, *In Sacred Loneliness: The Plural Wives of Joseph Smith,*" *Journal of Mormon History* 25, no. 2 (Fall 1999): 222-27.

plural wives of the even-more married Brigham Young have received minimal attention. The only, but definitive, identification of these women is Jeffery Ogden Johnson,"Determining and Defining 'Wife': The Brigham Young Households," *Dialogue* 20, no. 3 (Fall 1987): 57-70, to be updated when he completes his book on the topic.

Virtually nothing has been done on the numerous wives of Young's successors as Church presidents who were also polygamists: John Taylor, Wilford Woodruff, Lorenzo Snow, Joseph F. Smith, and Heber J. Grant. Nor has much effort been made to document the lives of plural wives married to other officials in the Church hierarchy.

Some attention has been given to other nineteenth-century Mormon women. Maria S. Ellsworth, *Mormon Odyssey: The Story of Ida Hunt Udall, Plural Wife* (Urbana: University of Illinois Press, 1992), contains both the text of Udall's original diary and Ellsworth's accompanying and bridging narrative. Juanita Brooks, *Emma Lee* (Logan: Utah State University Press, 1975), one of the plural wives of John D. Lee is, according to Brooks's biographer, a sensitive work written in a "lean, prosaic style."[21] Margaret K. Brady, *Mormon Healer and Folk Poet: Mary Susannah Fowler's Life of "Unselfish Usefulness"* (Logan: Utah State University Press, 2002), is an eclectic, interdisciplinary biography.

Additional nineteenth-century Mormon women are represented by their edited journals or by scholarly articles. Carol Cornwall Madsen has published several articles in preparation for her biography of Emmeline B. Wells, editor of the feminist Mormon newspaper *Woman's Exponent* and general president of the Relief Society: "Emmeline B. Wells: 'Am I Not a Woman and a Sister,'" *BYU Studies* 22 (Spring 1982): 161-78; "A Fine Soul Who Served Us: The Life of Emmeline B. Wells," *John Whitmer Historical Association Journal* 2 (1982): 11-21, and "A Bluestocking in Zion: The Literary Life of Emmeline B. Wells," *Dialogue* 16, no. 1 (Spring 1983): 126-40.

Other offerings on women well worth perusing include Jill C. Mulvay, "The Liberal Shall Be Blessed": [Sarah M. Granger Kimball], *Utah Historical Quarterly* 44, no. 3 (Summer 1976): 204-21; Annie Clark Tanner, *A Mormon Mother: An Autobiography* (1941; rev. ed., Salt Lake City: Tanner Trust Fund, University of Utah Library, 1973); Margery W. Ward, ed., *A Fragment: The Autobiography of Mary Jane Mount Tanner* (Salt Lake City: Tanner Trust Fund, University of Utah Library, 1980); "Ellis Reynolds Shipp" in Leonard J. Arrington and Susan Arrington Madsen, *Sunbonnet Sisters: True Stories of Mormon Women and Frontier Life* (Salt Lake City: Bookcraft, 1984); Henry J. Wolfinger, "A Test of Faith: Jane Elizabeth James and the Origins of Utah's Black Community," in *Social Accommodation in Utah,* edited by Clark S. Knowlton; American West Occasional Papers (Salt Lake City: University of Utah Press, 1975); Linda King Newell and Valeen Tippetts Avery, "Jane Manning James: Black Saint, 1847 Pioneer," *Ensign,* August 1979, 26-29; and Harriet Horne Arrington, "Alice Merrill Horne, Art Promoter and Early Utah Legislator," *Utah Historical Quarterly* 58, no. 3 (Summer 1990): 261-76. Two important early compilations of biographical essays are Claudia L. Bushman, ed., *Mormon Sisters* (1976; reprint ed., Logan, Utah: Utah State University Press, 1997); Vicky Burgess-Olson, ed., *Sister Saints* (Provo, UT: Brigham Young University Press, 1978).

Similarly, relatively few twentieth-century Mormon women have found their place in scholarly book-length studies. Outstanding is Levi S. Peterson, *Juanita Brooks: Mormon Woman Historian* (Salt Lake City: University of Utah Press, 1988), a compelling, carefully written account of the "dean of Utah historians," whose life spanned most of the twentieth century. Caroline Eyring Miner and Edward L. Kimball, *Camilla: A Biography of Camilla Eyring Kimball* (Salt Lake City: Deseret Book, 1980), is an warm but professional study of the wife of Mormon Church president, Spencer W. Kimball by her sister and son. Leonard J. Arrington, *Madelyn Cannon Stewart Silver: Poet, Teacher, Homemaker* (Salt Lake City: Publishers Press for Silver Publishers, 1998), deals with this twentieth-century "Mormon princess," a daughter of Angus Cannon and wife of inventor and industrialist Harold Silver.

---

21. Levi S. Peterson, *Juanita Brooks: Mormon Woman Historian* (Salt Lake City: University of Utah Press, 1988): 398-400.

Treated in articles are numerous twentieth-century Mormon women: Linda W. Harris, "The Legend of Jessie Evans Smith," *Utah Historical Quarterly* 44 (Fall 1976): 351-64, the third monogamous wife of Church President Joseph Fielding Smith; Kenneth W. Godfrey, "Warmth, Friendship, and Scholarship: The Life and Times of Virginia Hanson," *Utah Historical Quarterly* 60 (Fall 1992): 335-52, a Cache County, Utah, librarian and literary figure; and David A. Hales, "'There Goes Matilda': Millard County Midwife and Nurse," *Utah Historical Quarterly* 55 (Summer 1987): 278-93; David Hall, "Anxiously Engaged: Amy Brown Lyman and Relief Society Charity Work, 1917-45," *Dialogue* 27 (Summer 1994): 73-91; Massimo Introvigne, "Embraced by the Church? Betty Eadie, Near-Death Experiences, and Mormonism," *Dialogue* 29 (Fall 1996): 99-119; and John Bennion, "Mary Bennion Powell: Polygamy and Silence," *Journal of Mormon History* 24 (Fall 1998): 85-138. Coleen Whitley has edited *Worth Their Salt: Notable But Often Unnoted Women of Utah* (Logan: Utah State University Press, 1996), with a second volume, *Worth Their Salt Too* (Logan: Utah State University, 2000), containing essays on such LDS women as Patty Bartlett Sessions, Jane Manning James, Sarah Elizabeth Carmichael, Elizabeth Ann Claridge McCune, Maud May Babcock, Alice Merrill Horne, Sarah Ann Sutton Cooke, Romania B. Pratt Penrose, Camillia Clara Mieth Cobb, Ella Peacock, Alta Miller, Verla Gean Mill FarmanFarmaian (a Persian name), Esther Eggertsen Peterson, Virginia Eggertsen Sorensen Waugh, and Emma Lou Warner Thayne. Donna Toland Smart has edited *Mormon Midwife: The 1846-1888 Diaries of Patty Bartlett Sessions* (Logan: Utah State University Press, 1998).

An important, pathbreaking work that sets a standard for multi-generational mother-daughter studies is Martha Sonntag Bradley and Mary Brown Firmage Woodward *Four Zinas: A Story of Mothers and Daughters on the Mormon Frontier* (Salt Lake City: Signature Books, 2000). The lives of Zina Baker Huntington, Zina Huntington Young, Zina Young Card, and Zina Card Brown spanned most of the nineteenth and twentieth centuries and dramatized change along the expanding Mormon frontier.

RLDS Historical Figures

The Reorganized Church of Jesus Christ of Latter Day Saints (now Community of Christ) has produced a number of noteworthy biographies. (See also Mark A. Scherer, "Travelers on the New Mormon History Trail: Community of Christ Contributions to the New Mormon History," in this volume.) This church became the major denomination that emerged in the Midwest within the decade after the martyrdom of Joseph Smith Jr., was formally organized in 1860, and has been led, until the current presidency of W. Grant McMurray, by the descendants of Mormonism's founder.

Setting the standard for RLDS biographies is Roger D. Launius, *Joseph Smith III: Pragmatic Prophet* (Urbana: University of Illinois Press, 1988), which insightfully examines the challenges and successes of lineal and prophetic successor. Launius also followed up with an administrative history, *Father Figure: Joseph Smith III and the Creation of the Reorganized Church* (Independence: Herald Publishing House, 1990). Two other volumes in the administrative biographies series examine the succeeding presidents, both of them sons of Joseph III: Paul M. Edwards, *The Chief: An Administrative Biography of Fred M. Smith* (Independence: Herald House, 1988); and Norma Derry Hales, *Gentle Monarch: The Presidency of Israel A. Smith* (Independence: Herald House, 1991). Still pending are biographies of the third son, W. Wallace Smith (1958-78) and his own successor-son, Wallace B. Smith (1978-98).

Another fine biography, of David Hyrum Smith, Joseph III's youngest brother, is Valeen Tippetts Avery, *From Mission to Madness; Last Son of the Mormon Prophet* (Urbana: University of Illinois Press, 1998), with earlier articles on the same topic: "Sketches of the Sweet Singer: David Hyrum Smith, 1844-1904," *John Whitmer Historical Association Journal* 5 (1985): 3-15; and "David H. Smith's Relationship with the Muse of Mormon History," *Journal of Mormon History* 15 (1989): 3-13. Bright, talented, but deeply troubled, David Hyrum served in his brother's First Presidency but spent the last years of his life in a mental institution. William Shepard is currently researching a biography of William Smith,

Excavating Mormon Pasts

Joseph Smith Jr.'s younger brother—a colorful, controversial, sometimes erratic figure who, after many experiments, cast his lot with the Reorganization. Lyndon Cook has also had a long-term interest in William Smith, although his biography of this figure has not yet appeared. Irene M. Bates, "William Smith: Problematic Patriarch," *Dialogue* 16, no. 2 (Summer 1983): 11-35; and Paul M. Edwards, "William B. Smith: The Persistent Pretender," *Dialogue* 18, no. 2 (Summer 1985): 128-39, have presented fascinating glimpses of this last Smith.

The lives of three important second-level RLDS leaders have been considered in book-length biographies: Paul M. Edwards, *F. Henry Edwards: Articulator for the Church* (Independence: Herald Publishing House, 1995); Wayne Ham, *Geoffrey F. Spencer: Advocate for an Enlightened Faith* (Independence: Herald Publishing House, 1998); Henry K. Inouye, *Ray Cheville: Explorer of Spiritual Frontiers* (Independence: Herald Publishing House, 1996). The Spencer and Cheville biographies are part of the MAKERS OF CHURCH THOUGHT series. Other volumes in this series are Alan Tyree, *Evan Fry: Proclaimer of Good News* (Independence: Herald Publishing House, 1995); and Maurice L. Draper, *Arthur Oakman: An Artist with Words* (Independence: Herald Publishing House, 1997). Articles on important Reorganization figures include Roger D. Launius, "R. C. Evans: Boy Orator of the Reorganization," *John Whitmer Historical Association Journal* 3 (1983): 40-50; W. B. "Pat" Spillman, "Thomas W. Williams: Socialist in the Twelve," *John Whitmer Historical Association Journal* 12 (1992): 31-50; and James R. Bingham, "Elijah Banta: Community Builder of the Early Reorganization," 52-65.

Another compelling figure within the Reorganization is Alice Smith Edwards, the intelligent and sometimes outspoken daughter of Frederick M. Smith. Two articles about her are Nancy Hiles Ishikawa, "Alice Smith Edwards: The Little Princess," *Journal of Mormon History* 6 (1979): 61-74; and Paul M. Edwards, "When Will the Little Lady Come Out of the House?" *John Whitmer Historical Association Journal* 5 (1985): 29-40.

Roger D. Launius, "Joseph Smith III and the Art of Biography in the Reorganization," paper presented at the annual meeting of the Western History Association, October 1989, Tacoma, Washington; photocopy in my possession, directs researchers to several needed but as yet unexplored areas.

Dissidents and Schismatics

Among the most historically interesting subjects for Mormon biography are Mormon dissidents and schismatics; but as in other areas, the number of scholarly biographies on Mormon dissidents and schismatics is limited. An important study, suggesting possible directions for future inquiry, is Roger D. Launius and Linda Thatcher, eds., *Differing Visions: Dissenters in Mormon History* (Urbana: University of Illinois Press, 1994), containing essays on seventeen dissenters spanning the course of Mormon history from the 1830s to the present. The volume begins with an intriguing article by Ronald E. Romig on David Whitmer and concludes with an engaging essay by Alice Allred Pottmyer on Sonia Johnson whom she labels "Mormonism's Feminist Heretic." Launius's introduction, "Mormonism and the Dynamics of Dissent," suggests some broad parameters for further inquiry and investigation.

James Jesse Strang, a rival who established his Mormon movement first in Voree, Wisconsin, and later on Beaver Island, Michigan, holds great inherent interest for researchers. Roger Van Noord's *King of Beaver Island: The Life and Assassination of James Jesse Strang* (Urbana: University of Illinois Press, 1988) is significantly more scholarly than the earlier Milo M. Quaife, *The Kingdom of Saint James: A Narrative of the Mormons* (New Haven, CT: Yale University Press, 1930), or O. W. Riegal, *Crown of Glory: The Life of James J. Strang* (New Haven, CT: Yale University Press, 1935). Still, according to John Quist, Review, *Utah Historical Quarterly* 57, no. 2 (Spring 1989): 192-94, Van Noord "fails to explain adequately why Strang attracted the devotion of several hundred individuals or why Strang's following was so volatile." Vickie Cleverley Speek has completed a manuscript on members of the

Strangite Church, "For the Good of the Kingdom: A Narrative of the Strangite Mormons" with an emphasis on Strang's plural wives and their lives after Strang's assassination.

Biloine Whiting Young has considered the activities of schismatic leader Alpheus Cutler in her *Obscure Believers: The Mormon Schism of Alpheus Cutler* (St. Paul, MN: Pogo Press, 2002). Another view of Cutler is Danny L. Jorgensen, "The Fiery Darts of the Adversary: An Interpretation of Early Cutlerism," *John Whitmer Historical Association Journal* 10 (1990): 67-83.

Other important Mormon schismatics have received scholarly attention generally in relationship to the movements with which they were involved. Examples are Davis Bitton, "Mormons in Texas: The Ill-Fated Lyman Wight Colony 1844-1858," *Arizona and the West* 11 (Spring 1969): 6-26; Newell G. Bringhurst, "Charles B. Thompson and the Issues of Slavery and Race," *Journal of Mormon History* 8 (1981): 37-47; Russell Rich, *Those Who Would Be Leaders (Offshoots of Mormonism)*, 2d ed. (Provo, UT: Brigham Young University Extension Publications, 1967); and Steven L. Shields, *Divergent Paths of the Restoration: A History of the Latter Day Saint Movement*, 4th ed. (Bountiful, UT: Restoration Research, 1990).

Some lower-echelon leaders associated with various schisms include these *John Whitmer Historical Association Journal* articles: Noel A. Carmack, "The Seven Ages of Thomas Lyne: A Tragedian Among the Mormons," 14 (1994): 53-72; R. Ben Madison, "'Something Was Wanting': The Meteoric Career of John Greenhow, Mormon Propagandist," 15 (1995): 63-80; William Shepard, "Wingfield Watson and the Reorganization," 16 (1996): 65-78; M. Guy Bishop, "'Simply Folly': Stephen Post and the Children of Zion," ibid., 79-90; Michael S. Riggs, "'His Word Was as Good as His Note': The Impact of Justus Morse's Mormonism(s) on His Families," 17 (1997): 49-80; and William Shepard, "James Blakeslee, the Old Soldier of Mormonism," 113-32.

Still awaiting critical biographies are the important cluster of Nauvoo dissidents: William and Wilson Law, Robert D. Foster, and Austin Cowles, whose opposition to Joseph Smith's political domination and practice of polygamy triggered the train of events leading to his assassination. Andrew Smith, *The Saintly Scoundrel: The Life and Times of Dr. John Cook Bennett* (Urbana: University of Illinois Press, 1997), chronicles the turbulent life of this onetime high official and confidant of Joseph Smith. Like Bennett, John Hyde, Jr. and Increase Van Dusen also published and took to the lecture circuit to express their hostility toward their abandoned faith: Lynne Watkins Jorgensen, "John Hyde, Jr., Mormon Renegade," *Journal of Mormon History* 17 (1991): 120-144; and Craig L. Foster, "From Temple to Anti-Mormon: The Ambivalent Odyssey of Increase Van Dusen," *Dialogue* 27, no. 3 (Fall 1994): 275-286.

Richard Saunders, "'More a Movement Than an Organization': Utah's First Encounter with Heresy, The Gladdenites, 1851-1854," *The John Whitmer Historical Society Journal* 16 (1996): 91-106, explores the disagreements of Francis Gladden Bishop over Brigham Young's leadership claims. Joseph Morris, a more significant threat to Young during the early 1860s, found his biographer in C. LeRoy Anderson, *For Christ Will Come Tomorrow: The Saga of the Morrisites* (Logan: Utah State University Press, 1981). Ronald W. Walker, *Wayward Saints: The Godbeites and Brigham Young* (Urbana: University of Illinois Press, 1998), is a meticulously researched and thoughtfully analyzed collective biography of leaders of the "New Movement," which strongly opposed Young on economic and doctrinal issues during the late 1860s and early 1870s. It includes William S. Godbe, Edward Tullidge, T. B. H. and Fanny Stenhouse, and Apostle Amasa Lyman, all excommunicated for their espousal of Godbe's ideas. In scholarly articles Walker has also published examinations of some of these individuals: "The Commencement of the Godbeite Protest: Another View," *Utah Historical Quarterly* 42 (Summer 1974): 216-44; "The Stenhouses and the Making of a Mormon Image," *Journal of Mormon History* 1 (1974): 51-72; and "Edward Tullidge: Historian of the Mormon Commonwealth," *Journal of Mormon History* 3 (1976): 55-72. Also relevant is Loretta L. Hefner, "Amasa Mason Lyman, the Spiritualist," *Journal of Mormon History* 6 (1979): 75-87. E. Leo Lyman is currently at work on a book-length biography on Amasa M. Lyman.

Noticeably lacking, however, are book-length studies of the principal leaders of the so-called "fundamentalist" Mormon movement, that emerged following the abandonment of plural marriage by the Utah Mormon Church during the early twentieth century. Possible approaches are suggested in Ken Driggs, "Fundamentalist Attitudes Toward the Church: The Sermons of Leroy S. Johnson," *Dialogue* 23, no. 2 (Summer 1990): 39-60; and Martha Sonntag Bradley, "Joseph W. Musser: Dissenter or Fearless Crusader for Truth?," in *Differing Visions*, 262-78.

In addition, careful biographical studies are needed for dissenters not identified with particular schisms. One of the most noteworthy was Samuel Brannan, a colorful, controversial nineteenth-century Latter-day Saint, who brought a shipload of Mormons to California, broke with Brigham Young, and became "California's first millionaire." *Scoundrel's Tale: The Samuel Brannan Papers* (Spokane, WA: Arthur H. Clark, 1999), edited by Will Bagley, while not a biography, presents an effective overview of the life and times of this fascinating figure. It clearly supersedes four earlier book-length Brannan biographies, all rudimentary in research, slipshod in scholarship, and flawed in analysis.[22] Bagley has also written an outstanding article, "'Every Thing Is Favorable! And God Is On Our Side': Samuel Brannan and the Conquest of California," *Journal of Mormon History* 23, no. 2 (Fall 1997): 185-209. Other article-length treatments should also contribute to a first-rate Brannan biography at last, including my "Samuel Brannan and His Forgotten, Final Years," *Southern California Historical Quarterly* 79 (Summer 1997): 139-60.

Disaffected individuals from prominent Mormon families are particularly interesting. They would include Richard S. Van Wagoner and Mary C. Van Wagoner, "Orson Pratt, Jr.: Gifted Son of an Apostle and an Apostate," *Dialogue* 21, no. 1 (Spring 1988): 84-94; Richard S. Van Wagoner, "Sarah M. Pratt: The Shaping of an Apostate," *Dialogue* 19, no. 2 (Spring 1986): 69-99; Kenneth L. Cannon II, "Brigham Bicknell Young, Musical Christian Scientist," *Utah Historical Quarterly* 50, no. 2 (Spring 1982): 124-38; Kenneth W. Godfrey, "Frank J. Cannon: Declension in the Mormon Kingdom," in *Differing Visions*, 241-61.

Two individuals associated with the David O. McKay family have drawn my personal interest. I have already mentioned the first, Fawn McKay Brodie, treated in my *Fawn McKay Brodie: A Biographer's Life* (Norman: University of Oklahoma Press, 1999). I earlier wrote "Fawn McKay Brodie: Dissident Historian and Quintessential Critic of Mormondom," in *Differing Visions*, 279-300. With Frederick S. Buchanan, I have also written "The Forgotten Odyssey of Obadiah H. Riggs: Early Pioneer for Education Reform," *Utah Historical Quarterly* 66 (Winter 1998): 48-64. Riggs, the father-in-law of David O. McKay, left Mormonism and joined the RLDS Church.

Contemporary Mormon women dissidents Sonia Johnson and Deborah Laake were both excommunicated for their public statements about Mormon policies and practices. Relevant articles are Alice Allred Pottmyer, "Sonia Johnson: Mormonism's Feminist Heretic," in *Differing Visions*, 366-89; Heather M. Kellogg, "Shades of Gray: Sonia Johnson's Life through Letters and Autobiography," *Dialogue* 29 (Summer 1996): 77-86; and Newell G. Bringhurst, "Fawn M. Brodie and Deborah Laake: Two Perspectives on Mormon Feminist Dissent," *John Whitmer Historical Association Journal* 17 (1997): 91-112. But, in general, much more can be done on these and other dissidents.

Also meriting consideration are certain prominent individuals who were born Mormon but did not identify with the Church as adults. Butch Cassidy, notorious western outlaw, and Jack Dempsey, world heavy-weight boxing champion during the 1920s, have both appeared in recent book-length biographies: Richard Patterson, *Butch Cassidy: A Biography* (Lincoln: University of Nebraska Press, 1998); and Roger Kahn, *A Flame of Pure Fire: Jack Dempsey and the Roaring '20s* (New York: Harcourt Brace & Company, 1999). Equally prominent but lacking adequate biographical treatment are Gutzon Borglum and Solon Hannibal Borglum, sons of James Borglum, a Danish woodcarver from Jutland who

---

22. James A. B. Shereer, *The First Forty-Niner and the Story of the Golden Tea-Caddy* (New York: Balch & Co., 1925); Paul Bailey, *Sam Brannan and the California Mormons* (Los Angeles: Westernlore Press, 1943); Reva Scott, *Samuel Brannan and the Golden Fleece* (New York: Macmillan, 1944); and Louis J. Stellman, *Sam Brannan: Builder of San Francisco* (New York: Exposition Press, 1953).

joined the Latter-day Saints, migrated to the United States, disaffiliated from Mormonism, and moved to the Midwest where the sons became known for carving Mount Rushmore. William Mulder gives this overview of the Borglum family in "Scandinavian Saga," 141, in *The Peoples of Utah*. A significant unpublished account is Richard Jensen, "The Mormon Years of the Borglum Family," Task Papers in LDS History, No. 26, February 1979.

A step further removed but still worthy of attention are individuals born to Mormon families but who were never Latter-day Saints themselves. Two such personalities who have attracted competent biographies are J. Bracken Lee, a controversial Utah governor and later Salt Lake City mayor, treated in Dennis L. Lythgoe, *"Let 'Em Holler": A Political Biography of J. Bracken Lee* (Salt Lake City: Utah State Historical Society, 1982); and Gary Gilmore, a notorious murderer executed in 1977 by a Utah firing squad, written about by his brother, Mikal Gilmore, *Shot in the Heart* (New York: Doubleday, 1994).

Another "celebrity" category is that of "briefly Mormon." Eldridge Cleaver, one-time militant Black Panther was baptized Mormon in 1983, as I explain in "Eldridge Cleaver's Passage Through Mormonism," *Journal of Mormon History* 28, no. 1 (Spring 2002): 80-110. Jewish Roseanne Barr, the "rough-edged, Emmy-winning TV personality" was "involved in Mormonism for ten years during childhood . . . after a Mormon's prayer appeared to cure her of childhood palsy," according to Richard and Joan Ostling in *Mormon America: The Power and the Promise*, 143. Gladys Knight, a popular black singer, who converted to Mormonism in 1997, ends her autobiography, *Between Each Line of Pain and Glory: My Life Story* (New York: Hyperion Books, 1997) before that point, leaving the field open for a biographer. Another biographical "celebrity" opportunity is treating Thyrl Bailey, African American sports and entertainment star who also recently became Mormon.

Conclusion

As suggested throughout this essay, the craft of Mormon biography has progressed with the advent of the New Mormon History over the past half century. An increasing number of writers have avoided the polemical tone that had characterized all too many works in the past. The level of competence has risen steadily, and some biographies are first rate. This body of work has, in turn, established a scholarly standard against which to evaluate future Mormon biography.

But much remains to be done. There are many interesting and noteworthy Latter-day Saints who have been ignored and/or overlooked, but whose lives merit careful, scholarly examination. Efforts to fill this void are complicated by three major challenges. The first is what Valeen Tippetts Avery, "Scylla, Charybdis, and Achilles's Heels: Pitfalls in Writing Mormon Biography," paper presented at the Western History Association annual meeting, October 1989, Tacoma, Washington, photocopy in my possession, has labeled the "Scylla and Charybdis of Mormon history." One extreme is the perspective that the "divine hand of God" is in all events; the other extreme is reductionism: utterly ignoring the divine or supernatural and finding only secular causes and motives. As Davis Bitton regretfully points out, much of "Mormon Biography," tends "to be adulatory, sentimental and devotional in intent" on the one hand, while a countervailing tendency results in "iconoclastic, anti-Mormon biographies with an equally polemical purpose—that of maligning the entire movement by portraying individual Mormons as knaves" (4). After identifying these problems, however, Bitton noted "a sign of increasing maturity" and lists "several Mormon biographies that escape the either-or dichotomy." This trend has intensified with the appearance of an ever-increasing number of balanced biographies that carefully consider both the secular and religious motives of their subjects.

Mormon biographical writing, however, continues to be plagued by a second major problem—its generally bland writing and presentation. Ronald Walker attributes this dullness to a "spirit of understatement, harmony, and circumspection" stemming from "the didactic and commemorative tendency" evident in all religious literature and also to Mormonism's own heritage as a persecuted people. These factors come together, Walker asserts, to produce the "heroic biography, with clean lines, strong contrasts, and flattering hues" ("Craft and Challenge," 177). Similarly, non-Mormon critic and historian Gary Topping, "Personality and Motivation in Utah Historiography," *Dialogue* 27, no. 1 (Spring 1994): 73-89, attributes Mormon biography's generally bland quality to its focus "on [the] creation of an accurate factual narrative of events to the neglect of history's less tangible elements such as ideas, psychology, and personality," all rooted in a Mormon compulsion to create "faith promoting legends" (88-89). He advises biographers to probe "beneath the surface" to seek the essence of basic ideas, personality, and motivation including "psychological and spiritual" aspects (88-89).

A third related problem is that Mormon biographies tend to present their subjects as static individuals with unchanging personalities and basic beliefs. The result is a lack of real-life tension, essential humanity, and unfolding drama. Davis Bitton has urged biographers to "let their subjects grow and develop and change over time" and to provide meaningful insights into their "inner life" (12-13). Likewise, Ronald Walker has called for greater sensitivity to "the intimacy of a life in its totality, sensing the interior and sometimes hidden aspects of a career" ("Craft and Challenge," 189).

In attempting to overcome these three problems, biographers of Mormon subjects should strive to achieve "the delicate balance between life as history and life as art," as David J. Whittaker explains in "The Heritage and Tasks of Mormon Biography," 11. Or as Andre Maurois insists: "An honest biographer should sit in front of his model, thinking only: 'what do I see, and which is the best way to convey my vision to others.'"[23] In this same spirit, Whittaker encouraged the biographer to create a "true image" of his subject (11). At its best, Mormon biography can achieve the goal that Paul Murray Kendall set for himself in stating that the ultimate goal of biography should be "to elicit, from the coldness of paper, the warmth of a life being lived."[24]

In conclusion, the possibilities and opportunities in Mormon biography are unlimited for aspiring biographers—both professional and amateur. Biographies on Joseph Smith and other prominent Latter-day Saints will continue to fascinate and intrigue Latter-day Saints of all types. Likewise, biographies chronicling the lives of lesser-known Latter-day Saints, particularly well-written ones, will also find a ready audience. Thus, I am both hopeful and confident that the craft of Mormon biography will continue to flourish, attracting the talents of enterprising individuals interested in researching Mormon lives as well as avid readers, willing to consume well-crafted biographies on all types of Latter-day Saint lives, both prominent and ordinary.

NEWELL G. BRINGHURST, professor of history and political science at College of the Sequoias, is a past president of the Mormon History Association. He is the author of three books, *Saints, Slaves and Blacks: The Changing Place of Black People within Mormonism* (Westport, CT: Greenwood Press, 1981); *Brigham Young and the Expanding American Frontier* (Boston: Little, Brown, 1986) and *Fawn McKay Brodie: A Biographer's Life* (Norman: University of Oklahoma Press, 1999). He also edited *Reconsidering* No Man Knows My History: *Fawn M. Brodie and Joseph Smith in Retrospect* (Logan: Utah State University Press, 1996) and is coeditor with Darron Smith of *Black and Mormon: Reflections on Latter-day Saint African-Americans since 1978* (Urbana: University of Illinois Press, 2004). He thanks the individuals who provided information and suggestions helpful in the research and writing of this essay, including Lois C. Allen, Lavina Fielding Anderson, M. Guy Bishop, Davis Bitton, Craig L. Foster, Roger D. Launius, H. Michael Marquardt, Michael S. Riggs, and David J. Whittaker. An earlier version of this essay appeared as "Telling Latter-day Saint Lives: The Craft and Continuing Challenge of Mormon Biography," *Journal of Mormon History* 27, no. 1 (Spring 2001): 1-41.

---

23. Andre Maurois, "The Ethics of Biography," as quoted in *Biography and Truth*, edited by Stanley Weintrub (Indianapolis: Bobbs-Merrill, 1967), 44-50.

24. Paul Murray Kendall, *The Art of Biography* (New York: W. W. Norton, 1965), 28.

Chapter 15

Mormon Society and Culture

Davis Bitton

The phrase "the New Mormon History" is sometimes carelessly used to refer simply to historical works produced "recently." But "the new social history" and "the new cultural history," as these expressions are more carefully used, have reference not to the fact of being produced recently but to distinctive approaches and questions asked. In this sense, it is quite possible for something published this year to not qualify as the "new" history. Much now being written and published about the Mormon past, as well as other historical subjects, is simply the old history perpetuated or extended. It is not helpful to lump it all together as the New Mormon History.

The new social history, since the 1930s and especially since World War II, has the following characteristics:

1. It has been analytical rather than primarily narrative.
2. Where appropriate, it has been quantitative.
3. Where possible it has been interdisciplinary, meaning that it incorporates terms and questions from such adjacent disciplines as sociology and anthropology.
4. It has tended to focus on populations (demographic history) often in small groups such towns and settlements (community studies), families (family history), or elites (prosopographical history).
5. The new social history has shown a heightened awareness of class, ethnicity, race, and gender.[1]

Let us consider, then, Mormon social-cultural history in relation to these emphases. A complete bibliography of relevant works is not possible within the space allotted. Instead I shall attempt to give an idea of several fronts on which progress is being made, referring to enough specific recent works to indicate what is being done and where serious scholarship is still needed.

Community History

Not until Mormons existed in sufficient numbers to constitute a community could they be studied in terms of social interaction. But this started quite early, in Kirtland, Ohio. (See also "Mormon Origins: The Church in New York and Ohio," by Roger D. Launius, in this volume.) Without attempting to review all of the scholarship for the Kirtland period, roughly 1831 to 1838, we can observe that, in some of it at least, we find some social-cultural history. Milton V. Backman, Jr., *The Heavens Resound: A History of the Latter-day Saints*

---

1. A good introduction to the newer interests as led by French historians is Peter Burke, *The French Historical Revolution: The Annales School, 1929-89* (Cambridge: Polity Press, 1990). I am by no means an unqualified champion of the new social-economic history; here I merely describe and, in the remainder of the essay, attempt to gauge its different manifestations in the writing of Mormon history.

Excavating Mormon Pasts

in Ohio, 1830-1838 (Salt Lake City: Deseret Book, 1983), presents a fundamental picture of the economic basis of the community. His chapter on "Life Among the Saints" deals mainly with education at Kirtland but also discusses meetings, hymns, and recreation.

Other works dealing with social history in Kirtland include Linda King Newell and Valeen Tippets Avery, "Sweet Counsel and a Sea of Tribulation: The Religious Life of the Women in Kirtland," *BYU Studies* 20 (Winter 1980): 151-62. The precarious economic foundation on which Kirtland society rested is the subject of a joint study by a historian, economist, and political scientist: Marvin S. Hill, C. Keith Rooker, and Larry T. Wimmer, *The Kirtland Economy Revisited* (Provo, UT: Brigham Young University Press, 1977). Touching on many aspects of life at Kirtland and valuable for its primary source contents, is Karl R. Anderson, *Joseph Smith's Kirtland: Eyewitness Accounts* (Salt Lake City: Deseret Book, 1989).

The experience in Missouri during the same decade of the 1830s has received much attention, little of it analytical with respect to population and cultural issues. In part, this neglect is due to the nature of the experience itself, for nowhere in Missouri did the Mormons have the leisure to establish a settlement of even Kirtland's seven or eight years. It is not easy to analyze a population that is swirling. Still, work needs to be done on the Missouri settlements. (See also Stephen C. LeSueur, "The Mormon Experience in Missouri, 1830-39," in this volume.)

Then comes Nauvoo, the first Mormon city to attract in-depth historical analysis. Again, we are faced with the difference between standard narratives and genuine social-cultural history. But it can be said that Robert Bruce Flanders included an important discussion of the business and economic developments there in *Nauvoo: Kingdom on the Mississippi* (Urbana: University of Illinois Press, 1965).

Kenneth Godfrey called attention to neglected aspects of Nauvoo's social and cultural history in "The Nauvoo Neighborhood: A Little Philadelphia or a Unique City Set upon a Hill," *Journal of Mormon History* 11 (1984): 79-97. Descriptive cultural history—the parades, the schools, theater, etc.—can be found in George W. Givens, *Old Nauvoo: Everyday Life in the City of Joseph* (Salt Lake City: Deseret Book, 1990); Richard Neitzel Holzapfel and Jeni Broberg Holzapfel, *Women of Nauvoo* (Salt Lake City: Bookcraft, 1992); Carol Cornwall Madsen, *In Their Own Words: Women and the Story of Nauvoo* (Salt Lake City: Deseret Book, 1994). Glen Leonard methodically evaluated previous studies relating to Nauvoo in "Recent Writing on Mormon Nauvoo," *Western Illinois Regional Studies* 11 (Fall 1988): 69-93; and "Selected Nauvoo Bibliography: Work Since 1978," *Mormon History Association Newsletter* 71 (January 1989): 4-8, as preparation for his important synthesis *Nauvoo: A Place of Peace, a People of Promise* (Salt Lake City: Deseret Book/Provo, UT: BYU Press, 2003). (See also his "The Nauvoo Experience." in this volume.)

Guy Bishop treats the ever-fascinating subject of sex roles and marriage at Nauvoo in "Sex Roles, Marriage, and Childrearing at Mormon Nauvoo," *Western Illinois Regional Studies* 11 (Fall 1988): 30-45; and "The Celestial Family: Early Mormon Thought on Life and Death, 1830-1846" (Ph.D. diss., Southern Illinois University, 1981). An important 1989 symposium at Brigham Young University filled in some of the gaps and resulted in a special issue of *BYU Studies* on Nauvoo, which included William Mulder's insightful review of travelers in "Nauvoo Observed," *BYU Studies* 32 (Winter/Spring 1992): 95-118; and Kenneth Godfrey's study of "Crime and Punishment in Mormon Nauvoo, 1839-46," *BYU Studies* 32 (Winter/Spring 1992): 195-227.

As an example of the fact that everything did not happen in the city of Nauvoo, Susan Sessions Rugh has written a fine article on "Conflict in the Countryside: The Mormon Settlements at Macedonia, Illinois," *BYU Studies* 32 (Winter/Spring 1992): 149-74. Her important University of Chicago dissertation was revised and published as *Our Common Country: Family Farming, Culture, and Community in the Nineteenth-century Midwest* (Bloomington: Indiana University Press, 2001. Part 1 on "removing the Mormons" is followed by the development of family farming during the generation of the Civil War, and finally the problems of community and decline of the family farm.

After Nauvoo, Mormon history takes on real mass and increasing complexity. Each of the different western settlements could be the subject of its own history. Many local histories have been produced, but relatively few of them have scholarly value. An exception is Richard E. Bennett, *Mormons at the Missouri: 1846-1852. "And We Should Die"* (Norman: University of Oklahoma Press, 1987), a study of the settlements in the vicinity of Council Bluffs and Kanesville.

Salt Lake City, by all odds the most important urban center in the Mormon West, was the subject of early appreciative political histories. Finally, Thomas G. Alexander and James B. Allen, *Mormons and Gentiles: A History of Salt Lake City* (Boulder, CO: Pruett Publishing, 1984), studied it with the sophistication of modern scholars who are aware of some of the social science theoretical literature. However, only to a limited degree is their book Mormon history, resting squarely as it does upon the literature and questions of the "new urban history," which in part reinterprets the development of cities within the context of social history.

To find what community studies can bring to an understanding of Mormon society and culture, we turn to smaller populations. Examples of the community-studies approach are Larry M. Logue, *A Sermon in the Desert: Belief and Behavior in Early St. George, Utah* (Urbana: University of Illinois Press, 1988); Michael Scott Raber, "Religious Polity and Local Production: The Origins of a Mormon Town" (Ph.D. diss., Yale University, 1978); Cynthia J. Sturgis, "The Mormon Village in Transition: Richfield, Utah, as a Case Study" (M.A. thesis, University of Utah, 1978); and her "Bureaucratization and Social Change in Rural Agricultural Communities: Sevier County, Utah, 1900-1930" (Ph.D. diss., University of Utah, 1983).

As examples of local Utah, Idaho, and Idaho communities, see Dean L. May, "People on the Mormon Frontier: Kanab's Families of 1874," *Journal of Family History* 1 (December 1976): 169-91; May, "Between Two Cultures: The Mormon Settlement of Star Valley, Wyoming," *Journal of Mormon History* 13 (1986-87): 125-40; Leonard J. Arrington, "The Mormon Settlement of Cassia County, Idaho, 1863-1921," *Idaho Yesterdays* 23 (Summer 1979): 36-46; and Davis Bitton, "Peopling the Upper Snake: The Second Wave of Mormon Settlement in Idaho," *Idaho Yesterdays* 23 (Summer 1979): 47-52.

The chapters in Lavina Fielding Anderson, ed., *Chesterfield: Mormon Outpost in Idaho* (Bancroft, ID: Chesterfield Foundation, 1982), prove that significant social-cultural questions can be studied even in a very small settlement. Two other studies of small Mormon towns are J. Kent Tucker, "An Examination of the Mormon Settlement of Syracuse, Utah" (M.A. thesis, Brigham Young University, 1987); and Lorine S. Goodwin, "Concepts in American Local History: Community in Winder, Idaho" (M.A. thesis, Brigham Young University, 1981). Applying quantitative analysis to a small settlement is Gordon Irving, "After the Pioneers: The Experience of Young Men in Union, Utah, 1875-1920" (M.A. thesis, University of Utah, 1987), partially summarized in Irving, "Coming of Age in a Western Farm Community: Union, Utah, 1900-1910," in *New Views of Mormon History: Essays in Honor of Leonard J. Arrington,* edited by Davis Bitton and Maureen Ursenbach Beecher (Salt Lake City: University of Utah Press, 1987).

Especially revealing are comparative studies of Mormon and non-Mormon communities. One example is John L. Sorenson, "Industrialization and Social Change: A Controlled Comparison of Two Utah Communities [American Fork and Santaquin]," (Ph.D. diss., UCLA, 1961). A more recent example is Dean L. May, *Three Frontiers: Family, Land, and Society in the Far West, 1850-1900* (Cambridge, UK: Cambridge University Press, 1994), which compares Alpine, Utah, a Mormon community, with an Idaho and Oregon community. As a probing comparative analysis, May's book has been widely praised.

All of these studies show that, as populations have become more heterogeneous, community histories become less *Mormon* history; rather, religion of all varieties is merely one aspect of the local experience. An important example is E. Leo Lyman, *San Bernardino: The Rise and Fall of a California Community* (Salt Lake City: Signature Books, 1996).

Three frontiers
Family, land, and society in the American West, 1850–1900

DEAN L. MAY
University of Utah

One example of an innovative approach is Arlene H. Eakle, Adelia Baird, and Georgia Weber, *Woods Cross: Patterns and Profiles of a City* (Salt Lake City: Woods Cross City Council, 1976). Another useful, probing local study is Martha Sonntag Bradley, *Sandy City: The First Hundred Years* (Sandy, UT: Sandy City, 1993). Offering historiographical reflections on community studies and suggesting lines of future research are Dean L. May, "The Making of Saints: The Mormon Town as a Setting for the Study of Cultural Change," *Utah Historical Quarterly* 45 (Winter 1977): 75-92; Charles S. Peterson, " A Mormon Town: One Man's West," *Journal of Mormon History* 3 (1976): 3-12; and Peterson, "Life in a Village Society, 1877-1920," *Utah Historical Quarterly* 49 (Winter 1981): 78-96.

Sometimes the unit of study has been larger than the town or community but still limited, as in Joel E. Ricks, ed., *The History of a Valley: Cache Valley, Utah-Idaho* (Logan, UT: Cache Valley Centennial Commission, 1956); and Douglas D. Alder, ed., *Cache Valley: Essays on Her Past and People* (Logan: Utah State University, 1976). Also instructive and exciting are Gary B. Peterson and Lowell C. "Ben" Bennion, *San Pete Scenes: A Guide to Utah's Heart* (Eureka, UT: Basin/Plateau Press, 1987); and Dean L. May, "Utah Writ Small: Challenge and Change in Kane County's Past," *Utah Historical Quarterly* 53 (Spring 1985): 170-83.

Charles S. Peterson has written the nourishing *Take Up Your Mission: Mormon Colonizing Along the Little Colorado River, 1870-1900* (Tucson: University of Arizona Press, 1973). Not to be ignored about the same region is George S. Tanner and J. Morris Richards, *Colonization on the Little Colorado: The Joseph City Region* (Flagstaff, AZ: Northland Press, 1977), with several chapters devoted to social and cultural activities.

The 1980s and 1990s stand out as one of the most fertile periods yet in the production of local histories, partially as a result of state-funded studies coinciding with the centennial of Utah's statehood in 1996. Under the Certified Local Government program, overseen by Roger Roper of the Utah State Historical Society, matching grants were made available to cities or counties for historically oriented projects such as records collecting, oral history, studies of sites, and preservation.

Simultaneously, Allan Kent Powell and Craig Fuller served as general editors for new histories of Utah counties.[2] These counties vary greatly in population density and the extent to which the authors considered social and cultural questions as well as those of politics and economics. All of the county history volumes are worth examining, but I single out the following for special mention in their social-cultural emphasis: F. Ross Peterson, *A History of Cache County* (1997); Ronald G. Watt, *A History of Carbon County* (1997); Janet Burton Seegmiller, *A History of Iron County* (1998); Linda H. Smith, *A History of Morgan County* (1999); Robert E. Parson, *A History of Rich County* (1996); Albert C. T. Antrei and Allen D. Roberts, *A History of Sanpete County;* Douglas D. Alder and Karl F. Brooks, *A History of Washington County* (1996); and Richard C. Roberts and Richard W. Sadler, *A History of Weber County* (1997).

We have done little to study the human dynamics of wards and stakes or their social and cultural ramifications. Part of problem lies in the genre itself, for the temptation is strong to let such histories consist of a series of names of officers, buildings, and meetings. Among the hundreds of Mormon ward and stake histories, a few that stand out as valuable to scholarship are Ronald W. Walker, "'Going to Meeting' in Salt Lake City's Thirteenth Ward: A Microanalysis," in *New Views of Mormon History,* 138-61; Chad M. Orton, *More Faith Than Fear: The Los Angeles Stake Story* (Salt Lake City: Bookcraft, 1987); Lee H. Burke, *History of the Washington D.C LDS Ward: From Beginnings (1839) to Dissolution (1979)* (Logan, UT: Author, 1990); Susan Buhler Taber, *Mormon Lives: A Year in the Elkton Ward* (Urbana: University of Illinois Press, 1993); and Jan Shipps, Cheryll L. May, and Dean L. May, "Sugar House Ward: A Latter-day Saint Congregation," in *American Congregations,* edited by James P. Wind and James W. Lewis (Chicago: University of Chicago Press, 1994), 293-348.

---

2. The extent to which any given community is Mormon is a statistical question. Even now, of course, there are localities in Idaho, Wyoming, and Nevada, not to mention Canada and Mexico, that are effectively Mormon.

A HISTORY OF
Cache County

F. Ross Peterson

1997
Utah State Historical Society
Cache County Council

Demographic History

The rise of demographic history since World War II has not left Mormon history unaffected. Two useful general surveys include Dean L. May, "A Demographic Portrait of the Mormons, 1830-1980," in *After 150 Years: The Latter-day Saints in Sesquicentennial Perspective,* edited by Thomas G. Alexander and Jessie L. Embry (Provo, UT: Charles Redd Center for Western Studies, 1983), 37-69; and Thomas K. Martin, Tim B. Heaton, and Stephen J. Bahr, eds., *Utah in Demographic Perspective* (Salt Lake City: Signature Books, 1986).

All community histories, including ward and stake histories, lend themselves to demographic analysis. Studies of specific populations include Larry W. Draper, "A Demographic Examination of Household Heads in Salt Lake City, Utah, 1850-1870" (M.A. thesis, Brigham Young University, 1988); Jerry N. Harrison, "Demographic Transition in a Frontier Town: Manti, Utah, 1849-1948" (Ph.D. diss., University of Tennessee, 1982); Kooros Mohit Mahmoudi, "A Historical Study of Demographic Aspects of Urbanization in Utah, 1900-1960" (M.A. thesis, Utah State University, 1969); Frank E. Burke, "A Demographic Study of a Singles Branch in the Church of Jesus Christ of Latter-day Saints" (M.S. thesis, University of Utah, 1980); and Russell H. Mouritsen, "A Study of Women at the University of Utah Between 1941 and 1953" (Ph.D. diss., University of Utah, 1980).

Historical longitudinal studies and profiles include Laurence M. Yorgason, "Some Demographic Aspects of 100 Early Mormon Converts, 1830-1837" (M.A. thesis, Brigham Young University, 1974); William E. Hughes, "A Profile of the Missionaries of the Church of Jesus Christ of Latter-day Saints, 1849-1900" (M.A. thesis, Brigham Young University, 1986); Rex Thomas Price, "The Mormon Missionary of the Nineteenth Century" (Ph.D. diss., University of Wisconsin-Madison, 1991); Milton V. Backman Jr., *A Profile of Latter-day Saints of Kirtland, Ohio, and Members of Zion's Camp, 1830-1839* (Provo, UT: BYU Department of Church History and Doctrine, 1982); Mark R. Grandstaff, "The Impact of the Mormon Migration on the Community of Kirtland, Ohio, 1830-1839" (M.A. thesis, Brigham Young University, 1984); and Mark R. Grandstaff and Milton V. Backman Jr., "The Social Origins of Kirtland Mormons," BYU Studies 30 (Spring 1990): 47-66.

Studies of British converts include Susan L. Fales, "The Nonconformists of Leeds in the Early Victorian Era: A Study in Social Composition" (M.A. thesis, Brigham Young University, 1984); Lynne W. Jorgensen, "The First London Mormons, 1840-1845" (M.A. thesis, Brigham Young University, 1988); Jan Harris, "Mormons in Victorian England" (M.A. thesis, Brigham Young University, 1987); and Paul F. Smart, "The History of the Early Members of the Church of Jesus Christ of Latter-day Saints in Preston, Lancashire, England" (M.A. thesis, Brigham Young University, 1989).[3]

A team of University of Utah researchers—Lee L. Bean, Geraldine P. Mineau, and Douglas L. Anderton—has done sophisticated quantitative analyses of Mormon fertility and geographic mobility in n *Fertility Change on the American Frontier: Adaptation and Innovation* (Berkeley: University of California Press, 1990).[4]

Prosopography

It was Sir Lewis Namier who most prominently exemplified the analytical study of elite groups, especially the British Parliament in the eighteenth century. Sometimes called

---

3. Valuable research tools for these kinds of scholarly analysis are Susan Easton Black, comp., *Membership of the Church of Jesus Christ of Latter-day Saints, 1830-1848,* 50 vols. (Provo, UT: Religious Studies Center, Brigham Young University, 1984-88); and Black, *Early Members of the Reorganized Church of Jesus Christ of Latter Day Saints,* 6 vols. (Provo, UT: Religious Studies Center Brigham Young University, 1993).

4. In addition to the published articles listed in this work's bibliography, see also Geraldine Mineau, "Fertility Change on the Frontier: An Analysis of the Nineteenth-Century Utah Population" (Ph.D. diss., University of Utah, 1980); Douglas L. Anderton, "A Quantitative Analysis of Behavioral Change in the Utah Frontier Fertility Transition: Women's Birth Cohorts, 1840-1899" (Ph.D. diss., University of Utah, 1983); and Judith L. C. Spicer, "Fertility Changes in Utah, 1960-1975" (Ph.D. diss., University of Utah, 1982).

group biography, prosopography (analytical study of elites) has been applied all the way from ancient Greece and Rome to late twentieth-century politics. An old but good introduction is Lawrence Stone, "Prosopography," 12 *Daedelus* 100 (Winter 1971): 46-79. In Mormon history, the most obvious subject for prosopography is the General Authorities. D. Michael Quinn wrote "Organizational Development and Social Origins of the Mormon Hierarchy, 1832-1932: A Prosopographical Study" (M.A. thesis, University of Utah, 1973); and "The Mormon Hierarchy, 1832-1932: An American Elite" (Ph.D. diss., Yale University, 1976), on the subject, then expanded his research into two volumes: *The Mormon Hierarchy: Origins of Power* (Salt Lake City: Signature Books, 1994), and *The Mormon Hierarchy: Extensions of Power* (Salt Lake City: Signature Books, 1997). This imposing work, which has received both criticism and praise, is intimidating in its scope, but by no means does it preclude other analytical group studies.

Similar studies are quite possible for any defined population. An example is Sharon G. Pugsley, "The Board of Regents of the University of Utah, 1850-1920: Historical Development and Prosopography" (M.A. thesis, University of Utah, 1984). Regional representatives, stake presidents, bishops and their counselors, Relief Society presidents, mission presidents, missionaries—the possibilities are numerous. For these and other groups, one can imagine useful studies focusing on individual countries, or smaller geographical units, for a specific period of time.

Marriage and Family History

For those adults who married, considering the experience from the respective points of view of husband and wife is valuable. But there is also their experience together, including child-rearing. Polygamy has naturally attracted the most attention, generating at least three useful bibliographies: my "Mormon Polygamy," *Journal of Mormon History* 4 (1977): 101-18; Patricia Lyn Scott, "Mormon Polygamy: A Bibliography, 1977-92," *Journal of Mormon History* 19 (Spring 1993): 133-55; and her "Mormon Polygamy: A Bibliography, 1900-2004," in *Wrestling with the Principle: Readings on Polygamy from the Journal of Mormon History* (working title) (Salt Lake City: Signature Books, forthcoming). Because plural marriage receives separate treatment in this volume, (see Martha Sonntag Bradley's essay "Out of the Closet and into the Fire: The New Mormon Historians' Take on Polygamy"), I will not discuss it here. But however important plural marriage was for a half century or more, we do well to remind ourselves that most Mormon marriages have always been monogamous.

Placing the Mormon experience in a broad context, Klaus J. Hansen devotes a chapter to "Changing Perspectives on Sexuality and Marriage," in his *Mormonism and the American Experience* (Chicago: University of Chicago Press, 1981). In addition to his large studies on early Mormon polygamy, Lawrence Foster has compared Mormon marriage with other perspectives in "Between Heaven and Earth: Mormon Theology of the Family in Comparative Perspective—The Shakers, the Oneida Perfectionists, and the Mormons," *Sunstone* 7 (July-August 1982): 6-13; with response by Marybeth Raynes (14-15). Darwin L. Thomas has written an extensive entry on "Family," in the *Encyclopedia of Mormonism,* 4 vols. (New York: Macmillan, 1992), 2:486-92. Several articles of historical significance are included in Brent D. Corcoran, ed., *Multiply and Replenish: Mormon Essays on Sex and Family* (Salt Lake City: Signature Books, 1994).

A major stream of the new social-cultural history is women's history. Useful overviews are Carol Cornwall Madsen and David J. Whittaker, "History's Sequel: A Source Essay on Women in Mormon History," *Journal of Mormon History* 6 (1979): 123-45, and Todd Compton's essay in this volume, "The New Mormon Women's History."

Histories of specific families have long been popular among Mormons, but only a few of them are sufficiently rich, precise, and related to the larger social-cultural currents to be of value in social-cultural history. Exemplifying what can be done with this genre is William G. Hartley, *Kindred Saints: The Immigrant Heritage of Alvin and Kathryne Christenson* (Salt Lake City: Eden Hill, 1982). Biographies can offer valuable insights into everyday life,

MULTIPLY AND REPLENISH
MORMON ESSAYS ON SEX AND FAMILY

Edited by
Brent Corcoran

Signature Books   Salt Lake City   1994

of course, but are best considered under their own rubric. (See Newell G. Bringhurst, "Mormon Biography: Paradoxes, Problems, and Progress," in this volume.)

High Culture

Cultural history is often narrowly interpreted as "high culture"—literature, art, and music—each of which is a vital aspect of Mormon experience. A basic introductory guide to literary writings by Mormons is Eugene England, "Mormon Literature: Progress and Prospects," in *Mormon Americana: A Guide to Sources and Collections in the United States*, edited by David J. Whitaker (Provo, UT: BYU Studies, 1995), 455-505. (Literature with Mormon history themes is examined by Lavina Fielding Anderson in "Fictional Pasts: Mormon Historical Novels," in this volume.)

For Mormon art of the nineteenth century, one must start with James Haseltine's standard survey in *100 Years of Utah Painting* (Salt Lake City: Salt Lake Art Center, 1965); Robert Olpin's convenient *Dictionary of Utah Art* (Salt Lake City: Salt Lake Art Center, 1980); Vern G. Swanson, Robert S. Olpin, and William C. Seifrit, *Utah Painting and Sculpture* (1991; rev. ed., Salt Lake City: Gibbs Smith Publisher, 1997); and Richard G. Oman and Robert O. Davis, *Images of Faith: Art of the Latter-day Saints* (Salt Lake City: Deseret Book, 1995).

Many specific artists have received scholarly attention. Such studies include Wayne K. Hinton, "Mahonri Young and the Church: A View of Mormonism and Art," *Dialogue* 7 (Winter 1972): 35-43; Thomas E. Toone, *Mahonri Young: His Life and Art* (Salt Lake City: Signature Books, 1997); Norma S. Davis, *A Song of Joys: The Biography of Mahonri Mackintosh Young, Sculptor, Painter, Etcher* (Provo, UT: Brigham Young University Museum of Art, 1999); Linda J. Gibbs, "Enoch Wood Perry Jr.: A Biography and Analysis of His Thematic and Stylistic Development" (M.A. thesis, University of Utah, 1981); Barbara B. Ostler, "Lee Greene Richards: Portrait Painter" (M.A. thesis, University of Utah, 1991); Roxie D. Trimble, "Four Utah Mormon Artists [Dianne Dibb Forbis, Phyllis Luch, Blaine M. Yorgason, and Dennis Smith] as Authors" (M.A. thesis, Brigham Young University, 1982); Eugene F. Fairbanks, *A Sculptor's Testimony in Bronze and Stone: The Sacred Sculpture of Avard T. Fairbanks* (Salt Lake City: Publishers Press, 1994); Marian M. E. Wardle, "Minerva Teichert's Murals: The Motivation for Her Large-Scale Production" (M.A. thesis, Brigham Young University, 1988); and Elaine Cannon and Shirley Teichert, *Minerva!: The Story of an Artist with a Mission* (Salt Lake City: Bookcraft, 1997).

The "art missionaries," who studied in France during the 1890s and returned to do Mormon "impressionism" have been the subject of an exhibit and a monograph: Linda Jones Gibbs, *Harvesting the Light: The Paris Art Mission and the Beginning of Impressionism* (Salt Lake City: Museum of Church History and Art, 1987). Joyce A. Janetski has done "A History, Analysis, and Registry of Architectural Art Glass in Utah" (M.A. thesis, University of Utah, 1981). Richard G. Oman is among those who are especially interested in the cultural diversity of contemporary Mormon art, ranging from Indonesian batik to Haitian paintings and Native American pottery.[5] Broad in its coverage is Hal Cannon, ed., *Utah Folk Art: A Catalogue of Material Culture* (Provo, UT: Brigham Young University Press, 1980). Undoubtedly much remains to be done, especially on twentieth-century and contemporary artists and the use of art in magazines, temples, and visitors centers.

Architectural history has made enormous strides during the present generation. A standard introduction is Thomas Carter and Peter L. Goss, *Utah's Historic Architecture, 1847-1949* (Salt Lake City: University of Utah Press, 1988). Also useful is Allen D. Roberts, *Historic Architecture of the Church of Jesus Christ of Latter-day Saints: A Survey of LDS Architecture in Utah: 1847-1930* (Salt Lake City: Author, 1974), while a very comprehensive

---

5. Richard G. Oman, "Artists, Visual" and "Sculptors" in *Encyclopedia of Mormonism,* 4 vols. (New York: Macmillan, 1992), 1:70-73, 3:1285-86; "Sacred Connections: LDS Pottery in the Native American Southwest," *BYU Studies* 35, no. 1 (1995): 107-28; and "Sources for Mormon Visual Arts," in *Mormon Americana,* edited by David J. Whittaker (Provo, UT: BYU Studies, 1995), 607-66.

approach is Richard Jackson, *Places of Worship: 150 Years of LDS Architecture* (Provo, UT: Religious Studies Center Brigham Young University, 2003).

Studies of individual architects include Linda L. Bonar, "Thomas Frazier: Vernacular Architect in Pioneer Utah" (M.A. thesis, University of Utah, 1980); Paul L. Anderson, "William Harrison Folsom: Pioneer Architect," *Utah Historical Quarterly* 43 (Summer 1975): 240-59; and Paul L. Anderson, "Truman O. Angell: Architect and Saint," in *Supporting Saints,* edited by Donald Q. Cannon and David J. Whittaker (Provo, UT: Religious Studies Center, Brigham Young University, 1985), 133-73.

Some of the famous structures of Mormon history, especially the temples, have been scrutinized by architectural historians. Among these are David S. Andrew and Laurel B. Blank, "The Four Mormon Temples in Utah," *Journal of the Society of Architectural Historians* 30 (March 1971): 51-65; Laurel B. Andrew, *The Early Temples of the Mormons* (Albany: State University of New York Press, 1977); Roger D. Launius, *The Kirtland Temple: A Historical Narrative* (Independence: Herald Publishing House, 1986); Elwin C. Robison, *The First Mormon Temple: Design, Construction, and Historic Context of the Kirtland Temple* (Provo, UT: Brigham Young University Press, 1997); Heidi S. Swinton, *Sacred Stone: The Temple at Nauvoo* (American Fork, UT: Covenant Communications, 2002); Kirk M. Curtis, "History of the St. George Temple" (M.S. thesis, Brigham Young University, 1964); Charles Mark Hamilton, "The Salt Lake Temple: An Architectural Monograph" (Ph.D. diss., Ohio State University, 1978); Matthew K. Heiss, "The Salt Lake Temple and the Metaphors of Transformation" (M.A. thesis, University of Virginia, 1986); Richard N. Holzapfel, *Every Stone a Sermon* [on the construction of the Salt Lake Temple] (Salt Lake City: Bookcraft, 1992); Paul L. Anderson, "The Early Twentieth-century Temples," *Dialogue* 14 (Spring 1981): 9-19; and John M. Bezzant, "The Design of a Temple for the Church of Jesus Christ of Latter-day Saints" (M.A. thesis, University of Utah, 1985), on the Portland Temple. Also historical in its focus is Thomas W. Welch, "Early Mormon Woodworking at Its Best: A Study of the Craftsmanship in the First Temples of Utah" (M.S. thesis, Brigham Young University, 1983).

Folk architecture has received a general analysis in Leon S. Pitman, "A Survey of Nineteenth-Century Folk Architecture in the Mormon Culture Region" (Ph.D. diss., Louisiana State University, 1973); while Thomas R. Carter, "Building Zion: Folk Architecture in the Mormon Settlements of Utah's Sanpete Valley, 1849-1890" (Ph.D. diss., Indiana University, 1984), looks at one specific area. One type of structure is examined in Barry M. Roth, "A Geographic Study of Stone Houses in Selected Utah Communities" (M.S. thesis, Brigham Young University, 1973).

Contemporary chapel architecture has been studied in Martha Sonntag Bradley, "The Church and Colonel Sanders: Mormon Standard Plan Architecture" (M.A. thesis, Brigham Young University, 1981); and Bradley, "The Cloning of Mormon Architecture," *Dialogue* 14 (Spring 1981): 20-31.

Furniture has been studied by Connie Morningstar, *Early Utah Furniture* (Logan, UT: Utah State University Press, 1976); Elaine Thatcher, "Nineteenth Century Cache Valley Folk Furniture: A Study of Form and Function" (M.A. thesis, Utah State University, 1983), and Marilyn C. Barker, *The Legacy of Mormon Furniture* (Salt Lake City: Gibbs Smith Publisher, 1995). Material culture, of enormous relevance to understanding a society, is so multi-faceted that I can here only refer the reader to Carol A. Edison, "Material Culture: An Introduction and Guide to Mormon Vernacular," in *Mormon Americana*, 306-35.

After several theses and dissertations on aspects of the subject, Mormon music finally received the thorough treatment it deserves in Michael Hicks, *Mormonism and Music: A History* (Urbana: University of Illinois Press, 1989). But no single work can possibly cover everything in equal depth. Ray L. Bergman, *The Children Sang: The Life and Music of Evan Stephens* (Salt Lake City: Northwest Publishing, 1992), is a rewarding study of the Tabernacle Choir's dynamic early director. A Mormon musician whose importance almost justifies the long subtitle has been studied in Sterling E. Beesley, *Kind Words: The Beginnings of Mormon Melody: A Historical Biography of the Life and Works of Ebenezer Beesley, Utah Pioneer*

Excavating Mormon Pasts

Musician, Containing an Account from the Emigration of 1859 and the Evolution of Latter-day Saint Psalmody (N.p.: Privately published, 1980). We need comparable studies of other composers, of directors like J. Spencer Cornwall, Richard P. Condie, Jay Welch, Jerold Ottley, and Craig Jessop, and such performers as John J. McLellan, Alexander Schreiner, Frank W. Asper, and Tracy Y. Cannon. In some cases, existing works need to be expanded and improved.[6]

A few years ago Ruth Barrus, a professor from Ricks College, working on the history of Mormon music in southeastern Idaho, interviewed me about the Blackfoot area.[7] Her probing questions caused me to recognize the contributions of my own father as violinist, teacher, and choir director on both the stake and ward levels. How many separate stories like this are there? Certainly many.

Other Social-Cultural Topics

Some effort has been made to get at the life of children and youth in Davis Bitton, "Zion's Rowdies: Growing Up on the Mormon Frontier," *Utah Historical Quarterly* 50 (Spring 1982): 182-95; William G. Hartley, "Childhood in Gunnison, Utah," *Utah Historical Quarterly* 51 (Spring 1983): 108-32; Dorothy G. Y. Willey, "Childhood Experiences in Mormon Polygamous Families at the Turn of the Century" (M.S. thesis, Utah State University, 1983); Martha Sonntag Bradley, "'Protect the Children, Protect the Boys and Girls': Child Welfare Work in Utah, 1888-1920" (Ph.D. diss., University of Utah, 1987); and Susan Arrington Madsen, "Growing Up in Pioneer Utah: Agonies and Ecstasies," in *Nearly Everything Imaginable: The Everyday Life of Utah's Mormon Pioneers*, edited by Ronald W. Walker and Doris R. Dant (Provo, UT: BYU Press, 1999), 316-28.

Adolescence, the transition from teenage years to adulthood, tells much about any society. What have been the specific problems and challenges of Mormon youth? Were they the same as or different from those of the general population? What were the changing pressures and dynamics from generation to generation? Much remains to be done in this area of social-cultural history. In the meantime, some suggestive insights are provided in Leonard J. Arrington and Davis Bitton, "Chauncey West: Nineteenth-Century Teenager," in our *Saints Without Halos: The Human Side of Mormon History* (Salt Lake City: Signature Books, 1981), 96-104; William G. Hartley, "Nauvoo Teenager: Henry Sanderson," *New Era* 19 (October 1989), 44-47; my "'Heigh, Ho! I'm Seventeen': The Diary of a Teenage Girl," in *Nearly Everything Imaginable*, 329-40; and Kenneth W. Godfrey, "Charles S. Whitney: A Nineteenth-Century Salt Lake City Teenager's Life," *Journal of Mormon History* 27, no. 2 (Fall 2001): 215-51.

Widowhood has been studied quantitatively and as personal experience in Maureen Ursenbach Beecher, Carol Cornwall Madsen, and Lavina Fielding Anderson, "Widowhood Among the Mormons: The Personal Accounts," and Geraldine P. Mineau, "Utah Widowhood: A Demographic Profile," in *On Their Own: Widows and Widowhood in the American Southwest, 1848-1949,* edited by Arlene Scadron (Urbana: University of Illinois Press, 1988), 117-39, 140-65.

Although old age among the Mormons is far from adequately studied, activities of the "old folks" have received some attention in Joseph Heinerman, "The Old Folks Day: A Unique Utah Tradition," *Utah Historical Quarterly* 53 (Spring 1985): 157-69; and Brian D. Reeves, "Hoary-Headed Saints: The Aged in Nineteenth-Century Mormon Culture" (M.A. thesis, Brigham Young University, 1987). Studies of other population subsets include Lavina Fielding Anderson and Jeffery O. Johnson, "Endangered Species: Single Men in the Church," *Sunstone* 2 (Summer 1977): 2-7; Jeffery O. Johnson, "On the Edge: Mormonism's Single Men," *Dialogue* 16 (Autumn 1983): 48-58; Lavina Fielding Anderson, "Ministering

---

6. Preliminary studies include Howard H. Putnam, "George Edward Percy Careless: His Contributions to the Musical Culture of Utah and the Significance of His Life and Works" (M.A. thesis, Brigham Young University, 1957); Fern D. Gregory, "J. Spencer Cornwall: The Salt Lake Mormon Tabernacle Choir Years, 1935-1957" (Ph.D. diss., University of Missouri, 1984); Annie Rosella Compton, "John J. McClellan, Tabernacle Organist" (M.A. thesis, Brigham Young University, 1951); and Alexander Schreiner, *Alexander Schreiner Reminisces* (Salt Lake City: Publishers Press, 1984).

7. Ruth Barrus Collection, David O. McKay Library, BYU-Idaho, Rexburg, Idaho.

Angels: Single Women in Mormon Society," *Dialogue* 16 (Autumn 1983): 59-72; Marybeth Raynes and Erin Parson, "Single Cursedness: An Overview of LDS Authorities' Statements about Unmarried People," *Dialogue* 16 (Autumn 1983): 35-47; and Beverly L. Shaw, "Sexual Value-Behavior Congruence or Discrepancy: Coping of the Single Adult Mormon" (Ph.D. diss., United States International University, 1987). Linda Thatcher shows historical awareness in her "Women Alone: The Economic and Emotional Plight of Early LDS Women," *Dialogue* 25 (Winter 1992): 45-55.

Important to the social-cultural history of any people are its medical assumptions and practices. A general introduction is Robert T. Divett, *Medicine and the Mormons: An Introduction to the History of Latter-day Saint Health Care* (Bountiful, UT: Horizon Publishers, 1981). A dozen years later came Lester E. Bush, Jr., *Health and Medicine Among the Mormons: Science, Sense, and Scripture* (New York: Crossroads, 1993), a masterful study, broadly based so as to include attitudes on death and dying, madness, and sexuality.

Other expressions of social history are recreation, dance, and sports. Treatments include Arthur R. Jones, " A Historical Survey of Representative Activities Among the Mormons of Nauvoo, 1838-1845" (M.S. thesis, Southern Illinois University, 1970); Ruth Andrus, "A History of the Recreational Program of the Church of Jesus Christ of Latter-day Saints" (Ph.D. diss., University of Iowa, 1962); Davis Bitton, "'These Licentious Days': Dancing among the Mormons," *Sunstone* 2 (Spring 1977): 16-27; Larry V. Shumway, "Dancing the Buckles off Their Shoes in Pioneer Utah," *BYU Studies* 37 (1997-98), 6-50; Darell L. Parkin, "The Athletic Program of the Mormon Church: Its Growth and Development" (M.A. thesis, University of Illinois, 1964); Dean C. Nielson, "The History of Intercollegiate Basketball, Football, and Wrestling at Ricks College" (M.S. thesis, Brigham Young University, 1968); and Stephen B. Moser, *100 Years of Sports at Ricks College* (Rexburg, ID: Ricks College, 1988). A comprehensive analysis of a fifty-year period is Richard Ian Kimball, *Sports in Zion: Mormon Recreation, 1890-1940* (Urbana: University of Illinois Press, 2003).

Not sponsored by the Church and including both Mormons and non-Mormons, baseball has been studied by Kenneth L. Cannon II, "Deserets, Red Stockings, and Out-of-Towners: Baseball Comes of Age in Salt Lake City," *Utah Historical Quarterly* 52 (Spring 1984): 136-57. A compilation of fourteen article-length studies is Stanford J. Layton, ed., *Red Stockings & Out-Of-Towners: Sports in Utah* (Salt Lake City: Signature Books, 2003).

Two dissertations have been written on clothing: Ruth Vickers Clayton, "Clothing and the Temporal Kingdom" (Ph.D. diss., Purdue University, 1987); and Carma DeJong Anderson, "A Historical Overview of the Mormons and Their Clothing, 1840-1850" (Ph.D. diss., Brigham Young University, 1992).

Other Local Studies

The frequent tendency to focus on Nauvoo and then Salt Lake City, the so-called "centrist" bias, risks ignoring important dimensions of Mormon social and cultural experience in the Uintah Basin, the Mexican colonies, or Wyoming. Wherever they are located, Mormons can be studied, paying particular attention to the challenges of a particular environment. With the expansion of the Church from the end of World War II to the present, the challenge for historians becomes overwhelming—but also wonderfully stimulating.

We have ward and stake histories, but too often they omit the real texture of life. How valuable it would be, for example, to examine marriage patterns for small wards and branches in the different mission fields. What is it like to be a Tongan Mormon? What are the special challenges? What are the familial and neighborhood relationships for first-generation Mormons in Chile, in the Philippines, in Ghana? For social-cultural historians, non-American Mormon populations are indeed a field "white already to harvest."

Although the mundane concerns of social-cultural history are often ignored in order to concentrate on other things, some notable contributions include F. LaMond Tullis, *Mormons in Mexico: The Dynamics of Faith and Culture* (Logan: Utah State University Press, 1987); Rudolfo A. Acevedo, *Los Mormones en Chile, 1956-1986* (Santiago, Chile: Author,

1991); Néstor Curbelo, *History of the Mormons in Argentina* (Salt Lake City: Greg Kofford Books, 2004); Mark L. Grover, "Mormonism in Brazil: Religion and Dependency in Latin America" (Ph.D. diss., Indiana University, 1985); and Gerald Haslam, *Clash of Cultures: The Norwegian Experience with Mormonism, 1842-1920* (New York: Peter Lang, 1984).

A diligent and able historian, Marjorie Newton, has produced *Southern Cross Saints: The Mormon Church in Australia* (Laie, HI: Institute for Polynesian Studies, 1991); and "Mormonism in New Zealand: A Historical Appraisal" (Ph.D. diss., University of Sidney, 1998). A thoughtful evaluation from an anthropological perspective is Peter Lineham, "The Mormon Message in the Context of Maori Culture," *Journal of Mormon History* 17 (1991): 62-93. These are examples. A complete listing of books and articles on every country of the world is beyond the scope of this preliminary survey. (See "Growth and Internationalization: The LDS Church Since 1945," by Kahlile Mehr, Mark L. Grover, Reid L. Neilson, Donald Q. Cannon, and Grant Underwood, in this volume.)

Social Science

For the contemporary Church, including roughly the period since World War II, sociologists tell us much. One of several studies by Philip R. Kunz is "Mormons and Non-Mormon Divorce Patterns," *Journal of Marriage and the Family* 26 (May 1964): 211-13. More recent examples are Kristen L. Goodman and Tim B. Heaton, "LDS Church Members in the U.S. and Canada: A Demographic Profile," *AMCAP Journal* 12, no. 1 (1986): 88-107; Harold T. Christensen, "Mormon Sexuality in Cross-Cultural Perspective," *Dialogue* 10 (Autumn 1976): 62-75 (see other studies by this prolific scholar); Mary J. Banigan, "Adolescent Pregnancy in Utah, 1905-1977" (Ph.D. diss., University of Utah, 1980); David C. Spendlove, "Depression in Mormon Women" (Ph.D. diss., University of Utah, 1982); Marguerite I. Adams, "Family Stress and the Role of the Mormon Bishop's Wife" (M.S. thesis, Brigham Young University, 1991); and Christina Mordock, "The Level and Determinants of Burnout of Mormon Mothers in a Utah Suburban Town" (M.S. thesis, Brigham Young University, 1990).

Compilations include Darwin L. Thomas, ed., *The Religion and Family Connection: Social Science Perspectives* (Provo, UT: Religious Studies Center, Brigham Young University, 1988); Marie Cornwall, Tim B. Heaton, and Lawrence Young, eds., *Contemporary Mormonism: Social Science Perspectives* (Urbana: University of Illinois Press, 1994); and James T. Duke, ed., *Latter-day Saint Social Life: Social Research on the LDS Church and Its Members* (Provo, UT: Religious Studies Center, Brigham Young University, 1998).

Uniquely equipped to study cultures in the large sense are anthropologists. A landmark is Evon Z. Vogt and Ethel M. Albert, eds., *People of Rimrock: A Study of Values in Five Cultures* (Cambridge, MA: Harvard University Press, 1966), which compares Mormons to Navahos, Zunis, Spanish-Americans, and Texans. Mark Leone continued his explorations of Mormonism in *Roots of Modern Mormonism* (Cambridge, MA: Harvard University Press, 1979), and "The Economic Basis for the Evolution of the Mormon Religion," in *Religious Movements in Contemporary America*, edited by Irving I. Zanetsky (Princeton, NJ: Princeton University Press, 1974), 722-66.

Other anthropological-historical studies are Rex E. Cooper, *Promises Made to the Fathers: Mormon Covenant Organization* (Salt Lake City: University of Utah Press, 1990); and Steven L. Olsen, "The Mormon Ideology of Place: Cosmic Symbolism of the City of Zion, 1830-1846" (Ph.D. diss., University of Chicago, 1985). John L. Sorenson, always stimulating in his ability to frame significant questions, has published, in addition to the comparative analysis of American Fork and Santaquin mentioned earlier, a compilation of articles entitled *Mormon Culture: Four Decades of Essays on Mormon Society and Personality* (Salt Lake City: New Sage Books, 1997).

Displaying an interdisciplinary perspective are Dean L. May, "Mormons," in *Harvard Encyclopedia of American Ethnic Groups*, edited by Stephen Thernstrom (Cambridge, MA: Harvard University Press, 1980), 720-31; Douglas J. Davies, *Mormon Spirituality: The Latter-day Saints in Wales* (Logan: Utah State University Press, 1987); and many studies by

Contemporary Mormonism
Social Science Perspectives

Edited by
Marie Cornwall, Tim B. Heaton,
and Lawrence A. Young

University of Illinois Press
Urbana and Chicago

Excavating Mormon Pasts

Jessie L. Embry, including *"In His Own Language": Mormon Spanish Speaking Congregations in the United States* (Provo, UT: Charles Redd Center for Western Studies, Brigham Young University, 1997); *Asian American Mormons: Bridging Cultures* (Provo, UT: Charles Redd Center for Western Studies, Brigham Young University, 1999), Embry, "Ethnic American Mormons: The Development of a Community," in Douglas J. Davies, ed., *Mormon Identities in Transition* (London and New York: Cassell, 1996), 63-67.

Not long ago, after sponsoring a symposium the Joseph Fielding Smith Institute for Latter-day Saint History published its proceedings in Ronald W. Walker and Doris R. Dant, eds., *Nearly Everything Imaginable: The Everyday Life of Utah's Mormon Pioneers* (Provo, UT: Brigham Young University Press, 1999). In addition to considerations of local history and biographical sketches, the volume includes studies of regional furniture, clothing, dancing, diet, childhood, schools, the longevity of pioneer married couples, and pioneer oral narratives. Two of my favorites in this compilation are Richard Bushman's thoughtful essay on "refinement" and William G. Hartley's examination of Church activity during the Brigham Young era.

The "new" social-cultural history, as defined at the beginning of this essay, has obviously affected much of the work being done by students of Mormon history. But room remains for other kinds of exploration. It would be unnecessarily self-limiting to allow labels and arbitrary definitions to govern choices of topic and styles of investigation. We should not be satisfied with a superficial narrative that raises no questions, however, and we can rejoice in the extent to which scholarship about Mormons has been informed by the newer approaches.

I repeat the disclaimer made at the beginning of this article. If your own work or something else you are sure should have been included has been omitted here, chalk it up to my ignorance, or, if you are kind, space limitations. Still, just reflecting on these many works excites me as I contemplate the richness of our Latter-day Saint experience in historical time and the possibilities for significant scholarship that stretch out before us.

Like history in general, social-cultural history is vast. Rather than narrowing, it continues to expand as the years accumulate and the geographic diversity increases. The fact remains that the generation of historians extending from the mid-1960s to the present has been the most productive ever. In such aspects of social and cultural history as communities, demography, high culture (literature, art, and music), and historical studies by social scientists, we are immeasurably better off than we were a generation ago.

DAVIS BITTON is former Assistant LDS Church Historian and emeritus professor of history at the University of Utah, and a past president of the Mormon History Association. His *George Q. Cannon: A Biography* (Salt Lake City: Deseret Book, 1999) won numerous awards, including the Evans Biography Award and Mormon History Association Best Book Award. He coauthored with Leonard J. Arrington *The Mormon Experience and Mormons* (New York: Alfred A. Knopf, 1979) and *Mormons and Their Historians* (Salt Lake City: University of Utah Press, 1988).

Chapter 16

Fictional Pasts: Mormon Historical Novels

Lavina Fielding Anderson

While a survey of Mormon historical fiction may seem like a somewhat farfetched addition to a critical survey of the work of the New Mormon History, most readers of Mormon fiction would not so much as raise an eyebrow, accustomed as they are to getting large doses of Mormon history in much of their fiction and I might add (with the utmost seriousness, although with a certain amount of sorrow) quite a lot of fiction in their history.

When Orson Scott Card's novel, *A Woman of Destiny* (hideously subtitled against his will, "The epic saga of a woman who dared to search the world for love") rolled off the press (New York: Berkley Books, 1984), I got a call from an acquaintance who had just acquired a copy because someone told her it was a "Mormon" story, and who had been thoroughly puzzled when she started to read it.

"Is it true?" she asked me.

I thought she was confused because Card set his narrative in an abbreviated frame story: In a preface, "O. Kirkham," who had read the "brutally frank diary" of Dinah Kirkham, his great-aunt, explains that he has written her story from it. "Well, it's fiction," I started to explain.

"I *know* it's fiction," she interrupted. "But is it *true?*"

It turned out that she meant: "Is Dinah Kirkham really Eliza R. Snow?" I sorted through the plot and gave her a few keys. Something very like the English portion where Dinah is forced to abandon her children actually happened to Elizabeth Francis Yates. Eliza R. Snow married Joseph Smith as a secret plural wife and, yes, Emma probably found out. The "honeymoon" of the elderly Dinah and Brigham actually happened, more or less, to Emmeline B. Wells and her husband, Daniel H. Wells, although they had not had an unconsummated relationship earlier.

My acquaintance hung up satisfied. The mixing, matching, and expansion of elements was not a concern to her. She just wanted to know that these plot elements were really part of the Mormon historical story.

It is difficult to overestimate the effect of the Mormon story (or stories) in shaping Mormon identity (or identities). Thus, Mormon historical fiction occupies a unique transitional zone in Mormon studies. Although fictional Mormon history is unquestionably a genre in its own right and, hence, suffers like historically based fiction in general from predictable plots and stereotyped characters, for the most part, its writers make an earnest, though not always successful, to get the historical facts straight. The better writers are stylistically competent and even proficient, avoiding the more obvious pitfalls of cliché and tendentious writing. For the most part, Mormon historical fiction is serious fiction that merits serious attention.

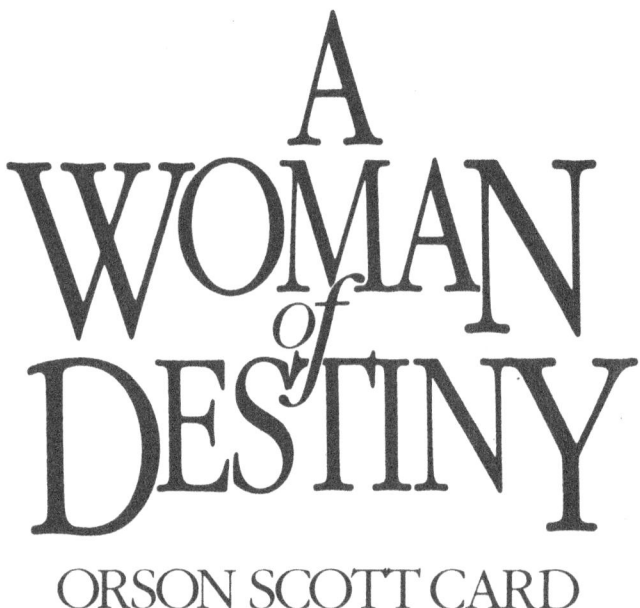

ORSON SCOTT CARD

BERKLEY BOOKS, NEW YORK

But is there such a thing as the *New* Mormon History historical fiction? That is a more difficult question to answer. Historical fiction, by its very nature, is derivative from two fields—history and fiction. To the extent that authors of Mormon fiction draw their research from competent and insightful work by New Mormon historians, some of the insistence on close documentation, quantitative analysis, and better attention to issues of race, class, gender, and culture, then the New Mormon History may have an effect. But since modernist and postmodernist fiction have already gone far beyond historical canons in questions of intent, authorial voice, hidden subtexts, and the unblinking acceptance of the supra-rational that characterizes magical realism, how much influence can be assigned to new currents in fiction and how much to new developments in history?

These questions must be answered only work by work and within a more rigorous framework that establishes precise definitions for much-debated fictional terms. Such an examination, though tempting, is obviously beyond the scope of this brief essay; but I certainly hope someone will tackle it soon. Meanwhile, with only a few exceptions, which I will note in passing, I think it is safe to say that most of the Mormon historical fiction now being written and consumed, still relies on comfortably traditional modes and methods, even when it draws its technical content from the New Mormon History.

Mormon Historical Fictions

Home Literature

It is perhaps more accurate to talk about Mormon historical fiction*s*. Mormon historical fiction developed in tandem with the home literature movement, which was the brainchild of Orson F. Whitney, later an apostle, who published an essay urging Mormons to produce their own literature—mastering all learning but following the Spirit in crafting literary production:

> We must read, and think, and feel, and pray, and then bring forth our thoughts, and polish and preserve them. This will make literature.
>
> Above all things, we must be original. The Holy Ghost is the genius of "Mormon" literature. Not Jupiter, nor Mars, Minerva, nor Mercury. . . . Our literature must live and breathe for itself. Our mission is diverse from all others; our literature must also be. The odes of Anacreon, the satires of Horace and Juvenal, the epics of Homer, Virgil, Dante and Milton; the sublime tragedies of Shakespear [sic]; these are all excellent, all well enough in their way; but we must not attempt to copy them. They cannot be reproduced. We may read, we may gather sweets from all these flowers, but we must build our own hive and honeycomb after God's supreme design.
>
> We will yet have Miltons and Shakespears of our own. God's ammunition is not exhausted.[1]

Enthusiastic disciples of Whitney's position were not wanting, among them B. H. Roberts and Susa Young Gates, daughter of Brigham Young. In 1909, she published what I believe to be the first faith-promoting Mormon historical novel, *John Stevens' Courtship: A Romance of the Echo Canyon War* (Salt Lake City: Deseret News, 1909). It follows the fortunes of a romantically entangled group of young people whose discussions and encounters with Gentiles provide mini-lectures on principles and correct practices during the Utah War. (When one woman succumbs to the charms of a gallant army captain and then is accidentally shot, wise and "placid" Aunt Clara asks, "Is she dead or disgraced?" Answers John Stevens, "Both!" [338]). Gates succeeds in avoiding any mention whatsoever of polygamy, something of a staggering achievement for a novel purporting to describe Mormonism in the 1850s, especially considering that the author was a daughter of Brigham Young.

---

1. Orson F. Whitney, "Home Literature," in *A Believing People: Literature of the Latter-day Saints,* edited by Richard H. Cracroft and Neal E. Lambert (Provo, UT: BYU Press, 1974), 206. This essay was first published in *The Contributor* 9 (June 1888): 297-302.

Excavating Mormon Pasts

Richard H. Cracroft, "Novels," *Encyclopedia of Mormonism*, 4 vols. (New York: Macmillan Publishing, 1992), 2:838, divided Mormon literature into "the 'faithful fiction' of the Home Literature tradition, a didactic and cautionary fiction intended primarily to instruct and inspire the youth of the Church; and [the] 'faithless fiction' of the Lost Generation tradition, generally a more sophisticated fiction in which dissenting or expatriate Latter-day Saints examine church members' lives from a position critical of LDS history and tradition, teachings, leadership, and culture."

Benson Young Parkinson, "Missionary and Deseret Fiction," AML-List, (e-mail list), March 28, 1998, used less emotionally charged terms by proposing the use of "missionary" and "Deseret" fiction, based on the intended audience and the intended effect on that audience. Missionary fiction is designed to create friends and even converts for gospel principles and Mormonism, but its hallmark is that the authors are willing to "go out into the larger world" of letters, fictional techniques, and psychological themes and conflicts that form the larger national literary landscape. In contrast, Deseret fiction is coded for already believing readers. Both languages have their strengths and weaknesses, appeal to different but not mutually exclusive audiences, and require considerable technical craftsmanship on the part of their serious practitioners.

Probably any taxonomic system limited to two terms is excessively limited, especially since, as Cracroft noted, "In recent years, an increasing number of LDS writers have crafted novels that affirm their history and tradition and assert an LDS worldview while achieving artistic sophistication and literary craftsmanship" (838).

Insider/Insider Fiction

I prefer, borrowing a term from Jan Shipps, to talk about insiders and outsiders. Insider/insider fiction is home literature, its whole world encompassed by Mormon myths, premises, and conclusions. For the purposes of quick identification of this genre, I propose Jerilee Eggleston, "Trial of Faith," *Friend*, July 1997, 26-29, a short story of a young pioneer girl in the spring of 1848. She was "hungry. Her bare feet were cracked and bleeding. Her dress was so threadbare that it wouldn't take another washing." Despite strong historical evidence to the contrary, the author locates a killer drought and the infestation of crickets in this year. When seagulls devoured the crickets, "with tears of gratitude, she confessed, 'Oh, Pa, I was so close to losing my faith! I was angry. I thought God had forsaken us. Now I feel ashamed.'" Her father responded, "'Write down what you've been through. . . . Remembering the crickets and seagulls may help you get through other rough times that will surely come.'"

A much more sophisticated insider/insider writer is Gerald N. Lund, whose fabulously successful THE WORK AND THE GLORY series made Mormon history from 1830 to 1847 accessible to a new generation. This series, all published by Bookcraft in Salt Lake City, consists of: Volume 1: *Pillar of Light* (1990) Volume 2: *Like a Fire Is Burning* (1991), Volume 3: *Truth Will Prevail* (1992), Volume 4: *Thy Gold to Refine* (1993), Volume 5: *A Season of Joy* (1994), Volume 6: *Praise to the Man* (1995), Volume 7: *No Unhallowed Hand* (1996), Volume 8: *So Great a Cause* (1997), and Volume 9: *All Is Well* (1998). All of these novels act out their historical scripts through the activities of the fictional Steed family, whose three generations range from unswerving obedience to complete skepticism. A tenth historical novel, though technically not part of this series, is a logical continuation of the history in that it deals with the disaster of the Willie and Martin Handcart companies of 1856: *The Fire of the Covenant: A Novel of the Willie and Martin Handcart Companies* (Salt Lake City: Bookcraft, 1999). The Association for Mormon Letters honored two volumes as best novels of the year in 1991 and 1993; in 1994 the series won both the Frankie and John K. Orton Award for LDS Literature and the LDS Independent Booksellers' Book of the Year Award.

According to Richard H. Cracroft, "Re-Storying the Restoration: Gerald N. Lund's THE WORK AND THE GLORY Saga, and the Historical Novel," *AML Annual*, 1997, 18, "the first volume sold more than 200,000 copies," a phenomenal record for Mormon publishers where print-runs of 5,000 or less for fiction are comparatively standard, "and where

VOLUME 1

THE
WORK
AND THE
GLORY

Pillar of Light
A HISTORICAL NOVEL

Gerald N. Lund

BOOKCRAFT
Salt Lake City, Utah

each succeeding . . . volume has also been a runaway best-seller in Mormon country."[2] Women in my ward who would regard a footnoted article about Joseph Smith with about the same enthusiasm as the news that all of their children had caught chicken pox devoured each of the seven volumes, reread them while waiting for the next volume, stood in line to get each new volume on the day of release, and were plunged into despair when the series ended. They constituted an audience for Mormon historical fiction that did not exist—or at least not to the same degree—before Gerald Lund; and the sheer level of historical information transmitted in his books has helped to fill the gaping void left by the correlated curriculum that basically ends its study of church history with the termination of the Doctrine and Covenants. And even though the Relief Society/Melchezidek curriculum for the past several years (and foreseeable future) is drawn from teachings of Church presidents, they are specifically and purposefully nonhistorical.

Lund, a Church Education System instructor, curriculum writer, and supervisor, was elevated to the Second Quorum of the Seventy in 2002, a calling which terminated his publishing career just as he finished a trilogy named THE KINGDOM AND THE CROWN which reconstructed the life of Christ. While his new calling almost certainly rewards his lengthy career of competent and diligent service, not his fiction, if his fiction had been found blameworthy, it seems unlikely in the extreme that he would have been made a General Authority in spite of it. As a result, his kind of historical fiction (and by extension, other novels) benefit from the halo effect of "approved" status.

This series, responds to the question of readers like the acquaintance who called me about *Woman of Destiny* by including a short but reassuring discussion of sources and "difficult" points for the modern reader at the end of each chapter. Lund's introductions to each volume also reassure the reader that the trials, tribulations, and triumphs of the religiously divided and emotionally intense Steed family during Mormonism's first decade and a half spring from a shared set of orthodox assumptions. In *Praise to the Man,* for instance, the volume dealing with Nauvoo, 1842-44, Lund candidly acknowledges that polygamy may be "troublesome" for some readers, that it was a "major factor" leading to the deaths of Joseph and Hyrum Smith, and that the "hurricane of reaction" led to mutually contradictory documentation. He concludes:

> There are surely some readers who will think I spent far too much time on this subject and will be uncomfortable with what is given and how it is treated. There will surely be others who believe I have deliberately sidestepped far too much and that a fuller treatment was called for. The fundamental issue—for those back then and for us today—comes down to one basic question: Did God reveal this law to Joseph and require him and others to live it, or was it purely the product of Joseph's own mind? . . . Ultimately each reader must answer that fundamental question for himself or herself. Was this of God, or was it of man? (ix)

In the course of the novel, the presentation of "the principle" and both its attack and defense come primarily, not from Joseph himself, but from the vile seducer John C. Bennett, from the faithful and loyal Heber and Vilate Kimball, and from the staunch Brigham Young so that various members of the Steed family act as surrogates for the reader in dealing with shock, bewilderment, repulsion, spiritual struggling, and final acceptance.

In the climactic scene dealing with this theme, Nathan and Lydia meet with Joseph, and Nathan explains the progression of his thinking, from "'Has Joseph fallen? Has he been deceived?'" through "'If God did ask this of Joseph, why would he expect something so difficult?'" to his final position of acceptance: "'What does God want me to do?'"

---

2. Predecessors of Lund's THE WORK AND THE GLORY series included David E. Richardson's self-published *These Were the Valiant* (Salt Lake City: Author, 1980) as the "sesquicentennial" edition of the ROBINSON FAMILY CHRONICLES, with no sequels of which I am aware. The STORM TESTAMENT series of Lee Nelson attracted enough enthusiastic readers to carry it through nine volumes between 1982 and 1994.

"And if I said that God wanted you to take another woman to be your wife?"

There was a long moment of silence as their eyes locked, but finally, Nathan bowed his head. "Then that is what I would do."

Joseph turned. "Lydia?"

. . . But she did not waver from his gaze. "We are ready to do whatever God asks of us, Joseph."

. . . "So no more questions?"

Nathan . . . reached out and took [Lydia's] hand. "Lots of questions, but no more doubts." (476-77)

In a lengthy review essay, Richard H. Cracroft, "Telling the Restoration Story: Gerald N. Lund's THE WORK AND THE GLORY Saga," *Journal of Mormon History* 29 no. 1 (Spring 2003): 233-53, twice declines to evaluate the series for historical accuracy (237, 243), and finds the series' didacticism as accounting in large part for its success. The Steed family is "the Greek chorus of the Restoration," surrogates for the readers whom Lund "subtly prods . . . to confront the series' overriding dramatic question, 'If I had been living back then, how would I have reacted?'" (251). Since the most admirable characters in the novels are also those with the strongest faith, readers are not shocked or offended, even by somewhat difficult historical material. Cracroft observed:

> Lund assumes that his audience traces in the history of their beginnings the moving finger of the Lord, seeing it as a sacred myth, a burning bush that must be approached with shoes removed. The historical novel genre, as rendered by a trusted fellow-believer, enables a luminescence less likely with other forms and earns the confidence of the believing Latter-day Saint reader. Other more psychologically realistic fictional techniques are off-putting to those Latter-day Saints who feel, regardless of the author's literary skill, that their sacred story has been manhandled and violated, and thus profaned. (249)

New Mormon historians have steadfastly taken the position that establishing and confirming faith are religious questions, not historical questions and that history must limit itself to the tasks of reconstructing and interpreting the past that are its proper job. This position has obviously disquieted some General Authorities, as the ecclesiastical punishment of D. Michael Quinn and the removal of Leonard J. Arrington's History Division to Brigham Young University have demonstrated. Quinn recounted his experience in "On Being a Mormon Historian (and Its Aftermath)," in *Faithful History: Essays on Writing Mormon History,* edited by George D. Smith (Salt Lake City: Signature Books, 1992), 69-111, although the sequel to this story, his excommunication, is most accessible in my "DNA Mormon: D. Michael Quinn," in *Mormon Mavericks,* edited by John R. Sillito and Susan Staker (Salt Lake City: Signature Books, 2002), 329-64. Leonard J. Arrington, explains the darkening clouds over his Camelot in *Adventures of a Church Historian* (Urbana: University of Illinois Press, 1998), especially chapters 10, 14.

Lund's didactic purpose, however, is the *raison d'être* of home literature. In hewing to that line, he is harking back to a traditional form of fiction based on more traditional forms of history. According to Cracroft, he is strikingly successful:

> So clearly does Lund advance his players toward their inevitable goals and so clearly does the reader come to understand that God is directing the play, that readers willingly suspend their desire for the Steed family's inwardness and complex psychology to play their roles in God's plan to get the plates translated, the temple dedicated, the mob turned, the conversion of the English affected, the Saints tested, the lame healed, polygamy undertaken, and the Prophet and Hyrum martyred, and the Saints safe at last in the Rocky

Excavating Mormon Pasts

Mountains. The unrolling of divine history makes "the real thing" possible, as the higher reality of God's wonder-working providence eclipses [American novelist Henry] James's earth-bound psychological realism. (252)

The WORK AND THE GLORY series has been available on audiocassette since at least 2002. In 2003, automobile tycoon Larry Miller announced that he was underwriting a movie version of the first volume, *Pillar of Light*, to the tune of $7.4 million with completion expected in late 2004 or early 2005. Deseret Book will market and distribute the soundtrack and editions of the movie in DVD and VHS versions. Lund "will act as a consultant and retains script approval rights," according to "Film," *Irreantum,* Autumn 2003, 88. Millions (more) will know Brother Joseph (or at least director Russ Holt's version of him) again.

Outsider/Outsider Fiction

Outsider/outsider historical fiction occurs when writers experiment with the possibilities of Mormonism's exoticisms. Such use is often, though not always, mere strip-mining. Mark Twain's caricatured description of the Mormons in his nineteenth-century travel narrative *Roughing It* is an example. As a more contemporary example, G. M. Warren's *Destiny's Children* (New York: Pocketbooks, 1979) is fast-moving, violent, and judiciously punctuated with steamy sex scenes. One of the main protagonists, Jubal Dodge, returns from a boyhood in the Rocky Mountains to search for his younger brother in Missouri during the winter of 1838-39. He ends up in Nauvoo, where he runs up against two irresistible forces: the melting eyes of Charity Forsyth and the paralyzing charisma of Joseph Smith. No immovable object he, Jubal succumbs to both, is wounded in attempting to defend Smith from assassination, and recuperates slowly under Charity's devoted care, having somewhere resolved to throw in his lot with the Mormons. Warren, probably prudently, makes no effort to talk about the religious or spiritual aspects of such a decision. Jubal is, in fact, merely baffled by his attraction for Joseph Smith.

Meanwhile, Jubal's long-lost brother, Will, who had previously been engaged to Charity, is conveniently shanghaied in New Orleans on board a ship to China, leaving Annie, a luscious and pregnant widow (not his own) to mourn his disappearance. The arranger of the shanghai, Taylor Reese, is a cold-blooded killer who likes sex and violence, preferably together, and had earlier persuaded Charity that Joseph Smith had sanctioned her "eternal marriage" to him. Jubal and Porter Rockwell both shoot Reese, but not before he gets Charity pregnant. Jubal will marry her anyway, of course, as faces turn west, leaving loose ends crying out for a sequel, a cry that, mercifully, must have been strangled for acute lack of a parallel outcry from readers.

Insider/Outsider Fiction

Insider/outsider writers usually are fluent and skillful, addressing themselves with an insider's knowledge but not with an insider's stance, to audiences both within and outside of Mormonism. At their best, they move with ease and grace across both psychological and technical boundaries in their writing.[3] They publish with both national and regional presses, use the Mormon West as the regional and cultural settings for their stories, and position their characters on a range along the Mormon spectrum, from casual to obsessed. Although the best novels in this genre deal with Mormonism as a faith, it is not only a faith. Rather, it is also a phenomenon like politics or socio-economic status, or the divorces and liaisons that weave through more traditional multi-generational family historical novels.

A literary and artistic example of successful insider/outsider historical fiction is Card's *Woman of Destiny* (which he reissued with a new title, *Saints* [New York: Tom Doherty Associates, 1988]). It received the Association for Mormon Letters' award as best novel in 1985. Card, an active Latter-day Saint, obviously designed this novel for the national market, not primarily the Mormon market. He employs many of the same ele-

---

3. The question of whether the fourth possibility, "outsider/insider" fiction, even exists merits discussion; but no examples come to mind.

ments as a formula historical novel: panoramic scope, meticulously researched period details, and an engrossing central conflict. As in most romances, the English heroine (Dinah Kirkham), trapped in a conflicted marriage, longs for love and receives divine assurance that in America "she would love a man she could not rule, and yet who would not rule her" (284). She and the hero (Joseph Smith) repel each other on sight. However, the obstacles to be overcome for their union, also standard elements in romances, are deeply rooted in an ambitious characterization of Joseph Smith as both erotic male and divinely inspired prophet. The complexity is satisfying, even if the artistic achievement sometimes falls short. For example, when Joseph broaches the subject of plural marriage to Dinah for the first time, he is wearing a shirt she has made (she is earning her living as a seamstress), and she is sensuously aware of his chest beneath the shirt. He tells her:

"It's as a wife I want you, honorably, not like a whore."
"You have a wife," Dinah said.
"If you were the sort of woman who would accept this eagerly, you wouldn't be worthy to be asked."
. . . Desperate to end the conversation, desperate to leave, she challenged him on the very ground where she herself was weakest. Witheringly she said, "And of course you had no lust for me at all."

She waited for him to deny it, for him to protest that he was just doing his duty. But instead his face went pale and his gaze went distant, and he whispered, "I could have answered any other woman truthfully. But I can't think of any answer now that wouldn't be a lie." He looked at his hands. They were trembling. "Emma is my wife and she will be forever. If I have to go hell to fetch her I'll have her with me. I don't want you to take her place. You couldn't do it if you tried."

His tone was so insulting that she was speechless in disbelief. He was the one who had asked for the impossible, and yet now he spoke accusingly, as if she had offended him. But his face immediately softened. "How could I expect you to take this, Sister Dinah? An unmarried man would have courted you, but I can hardly do that. A clever man might have found a way to do this gentler, so you wouldn't be taken by surprise." His eyes glazed with tears. "God has given me no harder commandment to obey. Nothing could be more against my nature. Or against yours, I think. I'm sorry. . . . The Lord has commanded it, and you will marry me. Of your own free will, you'll come to me and tell me that it's time." (402-3)

Clearly, Card's Joseph Smith is more than the heroic icon of a prophet; he is also more than a middle-aged male with wandering eye and a creative way of getting sex. Card thus risks more than Lund in conceptualizing and presenting a believable Joseph Smith explaining polygamy to a prospective wife. Unfortunately for the field of Mormon historical fiction, Card has not followed up this historical novel with others, although he has been prolific and well-recognized in other genres.

However, he tapped Mormon history again, particularly Joseph Smith's biography, for a fascinating fantasy series, THE TALES OF ALVIN MAKER, set in an alternative history of America in which the colonies lost their bid for independence, George Washington was beheaded as a traitor, the Indian tribes formed powerful nations in the West, and spells, hexes, and folk magic were common cultural currency. In this context, Alvin (Joseph) must learn to use his seeric gifts and magical talents to ethically affirm being against nonbeing. Card has published six titles in this series: *Seventh Son* (New York: Guild America Books, 1987), *Red Prophet* (New York: Tom Doherty Associates, 1988), *Prentice Alvin* (New York: Tom Doherty Associates, 1989), *Alvin Journeyman* (New York: Tor Books, 1996), *Heartfire* (New York: Tor Books, 1998), and *The Crystal City* (New York: Tor Books, 2003).

Excavating Mormon Pasts

Another useful example of insider/outsider Mormon historical writing is that of Samuel W. Taylor, grandson of church President John Taylor. A popular, very prolific, and rambunctious writer, he wrote a significant number of Mormon histories, most of them connected to his family. Because he adamantly refused to "clutter" his texts with footnotes, the boundary between his fiction and his history was somewhat blurred, even though he insisted that it was all factually accurate. New Mormon historians, while greatly enjoying his genial and feisty temperament and agreeing with him on the general outlines (a lengthy history of tensions between John Taylor and Brigham Young, for instance) took strong exception to some quirky notions (that Brigham Young's fatal final illness in 1877 was caused by arsenic in the sugar bowl) and dubbed much of his historical writing "faction" to reflect its idiosyncratic blend of fact and fiction.

His most important historical novel was *Nightfall at Nauvoo* (New York: Macmillan, 1971). Richard H. Cracroft, Taylor's most thorough critic, in "Samuel Woolley Taylor: Maverick Mormon Historian," *Journal of Mormon History* 27, no. 2 (Fall 2001): 64-91, called it a "shock-it-to-'em" history, the first in a trilogy that continued with *The Kingdom or Nothing: The Life of John Taylor, Militant Mormon* (1976; reprint, Salt Lake City: Signature Books, 1999 under the title *John Taylor: The Last Pioneer*), and *Rocky Mountain Empire: The Latter-day Saints Today* (1978) (78, 80-81). Apparently Cracroft based his decision to call it history on the presence of a bibliography and Taylor's thesis—that the Mormons "couldn't get along with their neighbors *anywhere*" and had to accept their share of responsibility for mortally offending Gentile neighbors in four states, with Nauvoo's counterfeiting, polygamy, and theocracy as the final affronts (*Nightfall,* 10). I would differ from Cracroft in calling it a novel (although perhaps a more accurate term might be a series of vignettes—a pseudo-docu-drama?) because, despite the thesis, it retells sensational gossip with the same enthusiasm as well-documented events and puts dialogue in the mouths of historical characters for which there is little basis in fact: Emma pushes the pregnant Eliza downstairs, Brigham Young authorizes the murder of dissidents, no known children were born to Joseph Smith's plural wives because John C. Bennett was an abortionist, Porter Rockwell was a psychotic killer held in check only by his doglike devotion to Joseph, and Governor Thomas Ford made himself an easy dupe for anti-Mormon forces led by Thomas Sharp. Unfortunately, this "voices of a city" approach means that no strong single narrator's voice emerges, and four hundred pages of changing narrators fatigues the reader.

Insider Mormons, though they quickly sense that they are not the primary audience of these writers, often respect and enjoy the technical achievement of insider/outsider novelist. In my opinion, this type of fiction represents the trickiest balance, the most demanding standards, and the highest stakes. Mormonism may be the setting, and even the subject, but the author's focus is character and the writing more complex than cautionary. The author writes from inside Mormonism in a way that makes it intelligible to "outsiders" without simultaneously making it seem alien to insider Mormons. As a reader whose consciousness is shaped by my Mormonness, this insider/outsider boundary is one I must cross daily as a reader. I hope I do it skillfully and graciously—not refusing to take seriously or accord full attention to those creative worlds I approach as an outsider, and appreciating the insiders to those worlds who take the trouble to welcome me hospitably and smooth my path.

Connections with the New Mormon History

There are, I believe, three compelling reasons for examining fiction and history in tandem with appraising the work of the New Mormon historians. First, the work of the New Mormon historians has transformed Mormonism's cultural and intellectual landscape, providing a home for creative writers as well. Second, the New Mormon History has provided thematic fields in which Mormon historical fiction also works, though selectively. And third, the boundaries of the two fields, at least in this first generation, are surprisingly permeable, with readers, writers, and historians crossing over with a frequency that will probably dwindle as each develops into more differentiated fields.

The Creation of a Cultural Home

    First, before the New Mormon History, fiction about Mormons, like history about Mormons, could be divided quite easily (though not always fairly) into two types: faith-promoting home literature, and anti-Mormon literature. The New Mormon History literally created the new Mormon historical novel by providing a body of published research that not only provides accurate and painstakingly researched information about the nineteenth-century context but also, by drawing conclusions inductively from the documentary evidence, allows for ambiguity and contradiction among historical figures.

    The absence of the New Mormon History, in my opinion, created Mormonism's "lost generation" of writers. Home literature had dominated Mormon writing from the 1890s until it became a placid trickle of moralistic tales confined to periodicals for women, children, and youth. Edward Geary, who coined the phrase in his influential "Mormondom's Lost Generation: The Novelists of the 1940s," *BYU Studies* 18, no. 1 (Fall 1977): 89-98; reprinted in Eugene England and Lavina Fielding Anderson, eds., *Tending the Garden: Essays on Mormon Literature* (Salt Lake City: Signature Books, 1996), 23-33, to apply to Mormonism's expatriate writers of the 1940s, points out that "there had been very little full-length fiction published on Mormon themes for some thirty years" (24). Among these writers, he identifies Lorene Pearson, Virginia Sorensen, Maurine Whipple, Vardis Fisher, Paul Bailey, Blanche Cannon, Gene Woodman, Richard Scowcroft, Samuel W. Taylor, and George Snell. (He does not mention Ardeth Kennelly, but she should also be included, particularly for her fine novel on polygamy, *The Peaceable Kingdom* [Boston: Houghton Mifflin, 1948], with its strong, salty narrator, Linnea.) Common to these novels is "the author's effort to come to terms with his or her Mormon heritage . . . ambivalen[t] towards a tradition which seems to have failed, yet which still offers the only available spiritual anchor against a tide of meaninglessness." Tellingly, "the central conflict is nearly always between individualism and authority" (26).

    Mormon critic and short story fictionalist Bruce W. Jorgensen, "Digging the Foundation: Making and Reading Mormon Literature," *Dialogue: A Journal of Mormon Thought* 9, no. 4 (Winter 1974): 56, has hypothesized: "Perhaps the literary developments of the 1880s, the 1890s, and especially the 1920s could not be assimilated by Mormon writers still committed to didacticism and to waning literary fashions." In any case, in the absence—perhaps coincidental but I believe causal—of a viable intellectual tradition of history, Mormon fiction in general and Mormon historical fiction in particular dwindled and died for an entire generation during what Jorgensen calls the "Great Gap."

    This gap also meant that the first reaction of the Mormon reading public to expatriate fiction was not appreciation but xenophobia. Although space precludes a discussion comparable to anything like their merits, Virginia Sorensen and Maurine Whipple, two stellar talents who died four months apart (Sorensen in December 1991; Whipple in April 1992), both produced historical fiction of exceptional importance and significance. Sorensen left Mormon country early in her career, divorced her Mormon husband after a long and grueling marriage, then married and lived happily with Alec Waugh, converting to Anglicism. Although presented as short stories, her splendid essays, *Where Nothing Is Long Ago: Memories of a Mormon Childhood* (New York: Harcourt, Brace & World, 1955), are semi-autobiographical. *A Little Lower than the Angels* (New York: Alfred A. Knopf, 1942), is set in the Missouri, Nauvoo, and trek periods as a devoted but sickly first wife sees herself gradually supplanted by a plural wife. In *On This Star* (New York: Reynal and Hitchcock, 1946), Sorensen explores the sensibility of an artistic and unstable son of a second wife, contrasted to the wholesome, hard-working, but boring sons of the first wife in the 1920s in Templeton (Manti). *The Evening and the Morning* (New York: Harcourt, Brace, 1949), with much the same setting, presents the memorable rebel, Kate Alexander, in a thoughtful examination of both the necessity and the limitations of individualism. In *Many Mansions* (New York: Harcourt, Brace, 1954), Sorensen also wrote the first novel I am aware of that deals with post-Manifesto polygamy. In some ways it is a classic triangle: two women, one of them a chronically ill wife, love the same man, a doctor. The second woman is his healthy, compassionate, wholesome nurse. The solution, a post-Manifesto marriage, is proposed by the first wife and is presented, not as the stuff of tragedy, but as a happy and satisfying resolution to the problems of loneliness, fear, and desire. *Kingdom Come* (New York: Harcourt, 1960), featuring the unforgettable Hanne, is an ambitious novel of converts to Mormonism in Denmark and Sweden in 1850-52.

Sorensen's status within Mormonism can be marked by the fact that she has received a steadily swelling amount of critical attention, although most appraisals do not evaluate the historical component of her work.[4] Even more significantly, Signature Books of Salt Lake City has begun reprinting selected works: *A Little Lower than the Angels* appeared in 1997, *Where Nothing Is Long Ago* in 1998.

In contrast, Maurine Whipple wrote a single sunburst of a novel, the still-unsurpassed *Giant Joshua* (Boston: Houghton Mifflin, 1945), which tells the story of the founding of St. George through the eyes of one of the most haunting and enchanting of all Mormon heroines, Clorinda McIntyre. Whipple never married, never converted to another church, and never permanently left St. George; but she also never wrote another novel or published very much besides magazine articles and one tourist guide to Utah. She wrote steadily, even compulsively, but the two volumes which would have made *The Giant Joshua* into a three-generation trilogy remained unfinished at her death, as did two more novels and more than two dozen short stories, nearly all of them unpublished.[5] Her novel, unlike those of Sorensen, has remained permanently in print, accessible to a current generation of readers.

Despite these achievements—and probably because of them—these writers were without an intellectual home in Mormonism during the most productive periods of their working lives, although they never lost their cultural roots. It is an environment that the New Mormon History has changed permanently.

Shared Themes

A second connection between the New Mormon History and the new Mormon historical fiction is that they inevitably work in the same thematic fields. Although the symbols of Mormonism may be shifting in the twenty-first century to temples and an emphasis on the traditional nuclear family, from 1950 to 2000, history *was* identity. Mormons were people with a past, and that past was the same for both historians and novelists. The major themes of Mormonism's historical fiction, despite more than 170 years of history, are concentrated into its first seventy years: the charismatic founding prophet, Joseph Smith, and his experiences; the turbulent hegira of Mormons from New York to Ohio to Missouri to Illinois; the secret teaching and practice of polygamy in Nauvoo; the saga of crossing the plains; creating Mormon settlements in the West; the public practice of polygamy begin-

---

4. In addition to Bruce W. Jorgensen's landmark essay, "'Herself Moving Beside Herself, Out there Alone': The Shape of Mormon Belief in Virginia Sorensen's *The Evening and the Morning*," *Dialogue* 13, no. 3 (Fall 1980): 43-60, a considerable number of critical essays have focused on Sorensen's work. In the 1988-92 of the *AML Annual* appear no fewer than nine: Eugene England, "Virginia Sorensen as the Founding Foremother of the Mormon Personal Essay"; Linda Berlin, "The Strengths and Weaknesses of Virginia Sorensen's *On This Star*"; Edward A. Geary, "Joseph and His Brothers: Rivalry in Virginia Sorensen's *On This Star*"; LuDene Dallimore, "Mercy, Zina, and Kate: Virginia Sorensen's Strong Women in a Man's Society"; Grant T. Smith, "Women Together: Kate Alexander's Search for Self in *The Evening and the Morning*"; Jacqueline C. Barnes, "Sacrifice to the Proper Gods"; Helynne H. Hansen, "In Search of Women's Language and Feminist Expression among Nauvoo Wives in *A Little Lower Than the Angels*"; Susan Elizabeth Howe, "'Little Books' from a Large Soul: The Private Poetry of Virginia Sorensen"; and Mary Lythgoe Bradford, "Virginia Sorensen: Literary Recollections from a Thirty-five Year Friendship." See also Laurie Illions Rodriguez and Joshua P. Rodriguez, "The Example of Virginia Sorensen: Honest Ambivalence and the Mormon Experience," *AML Annual*, 1997, 118-27.

5. Veda Tebbs Hale and I are collaborating on the lost works of Maurine Whipple, and Hale has written Whipple's biography (forthcoming), exploring the causes for the writer's paralysis that seemed to settle over Whipple after 1945. Important critical analyses of *The Giant Joshua* include Bruce W. Jorgensen, "Retrospection: *Giant Joshua*," *Sunstone* 3 (September-October 1978): 6-8; Jessie L. Embry, "Overworked Stereotypes or Accurate Images: Images of Polygamy in *The Giant Joshua*," and Katherine Ashton, "Whatever Happened to Maurine Whipple?" the last two in *AML Annual*, 1988-92, 105-13, 114-19.

ning in 1852 and leading through a series of intensifying crises with the federal government until the Woodruff Manifesto of 1890, statehood in 1896, and the raggedy conclusion of authorized polygamy. Each of these themes has attracted dozens of novelists, and the temptation to turn this overview and analysis into an annotated bibliography is a strong one.

However, perhaps more useful is a comparison and contrast of how three authors spaced over about fifty years have treated Mormonism's founding event, the First Vision of Joseph Smith. Such juxtaposition illustrates both some of the varieties of authorial stances and also some of the literary possibilities inherent in this dramatic epiphany. An intelligent, multi-genred examination of treatments of the First Vision is Richard H. Cracroft, "The Ineffable Made Effable: Rendering Joseph Smith's First Vision as Literature," *AML Annual,* 1997, 96-107.

Vardis Fisher in his *Children of God: An American Epic* (New York: Harper & Row, 1939; reprint, ed., Boise, ID: Opal Laurel Holmes, Publisher, n.d. but after 1969), which received the prestigious Harper Prize, describes Joseph Smith as experiencing a genuine theophany which Fisher recreates, not in the language of faith but in the language of literature:

> For a long moment he hardly realized that he was praying—for he had never prayed aloud before; nor did he quite understand what he said. He was obscurely aware of his trembling body and the strange deep passion of his voice; but his prayer, filled with biblical phrases and archaic terms, seemed not to be his at all. He listened as if to another voice and was moved to deep astonishment. . . . The whole world listened to the anxious humble asking of his voice. . . .
>
> All the meaning of his mind and body was withdrawing to a far and infinite meaning, as if a great power were sucking him dry. . . . He felt sudden and awful terror. . . .
>
> He saw first an intimation of brightness far out in the universe; it grew like the softness of morning, like a gentle flowering out of utter darkness, as if heaven were overflowing the wastelands of night as brilliance spilled from God's robe as He walked. For a long moment the light spread and gathered strength and then suddenly fell downward in a broad beam of terrible splendor, in a great and blinding pillar that touched the earth and lay far out in a white column of eternity. Then, with startling swiftness, two persons appeared in this stupendous shaft of light, the Father and the Son; and they were exactly alike in countenance and in the incandescence of their glory. . . . One called the prostrate lad by name and pointed to his companion and said, "This is my beloved Son. Hear Him!" The Son spoke. He declared in the voice of a great organ that all the creeds of earth were an abomination in His sight. . . . The voice died away in echoes that rolled in solemn music, and the highway of light slowly faded, with Father and Son standing as vanishing silhouettes against the infinite. The light closed like a shutter to a thin wraith of holiness and slowly withdrew to the lone glittering point of a star. (7-8)

A close reading of this passage makes it plain that, although Fisher adds details, none of them contradict Joseph Smith's own version of the First Vision (JS-H 1). Even an orthodox reader would concede that the vision could have occurred like this. However sympathetically the novel may begin, it is not enough. Fisher's portrayal of the sex-obsessed Joseph Smith is distasteful and overly simplistic; his portrayal of the sexually responsive but waspish-tongued virago Emma (the first thing Joseph notices about her is that "her lips were too thin for passionate kissing" [22]) is a demeaning stereotype.

Gerald Lund tells the story in *Pillar of Light* at one remove, not as Joseph Smith experienced it but as Joseph, urged on by a supportive Hyrum Smith, tells it to a skeptical but honest-hearted seeker, Nathan Steed. Lund makes the minimal necessary adaptations

Excavating Mormon Pasts

to Joseph Smith's own language, a reassuring technique for readers long accustomed to hear the account, not as narrative, but as scripture:

> "At the very moment of my deepest despair, as I was about to abandon myself to destruction, at that precise moment, I saw a pillar of light."
>
> Nathan's head snapped up.
>
> Joseph went on steadily now, speaking slowly but with great earnestness. "It was exactly over my head. It was far brighter than the sun at noonday. The light was so intense I thought the very leaves would burst into flame. It descended gradually until it fell upon me. Instantly, the moment the light touched me, I was delivered from the enemy which held me bound.
>
> "When the light rested upon me, I saw two personages—" He stopped, noting the expression on Nathan's face. "I saw two personages," he continued firmly, "whose glory and brightness defy all description. They were standing above me in the air.'"
>
> . . . Nathan's mind was reeling. "Are you saying . . ." He faltered, overwhelmed. "You mean you saw . . ." He could not bring himself to say it.
>
> Joseph nodded with the utmost solemnity. "I saw God and I saw his Son, Jesus Christ." (55-56)

As Lund sketched in his introduction to this volume, the question is not a literary one or even a historical one but a spiritual one: "In the spring of 1820, Joseph Smith went into a grove of trees and emerged bearing witness that he had seen, in a pillar of light, the Father and the Son. To everyone who hears that story, whether at [their] mother's knee or sitting across the table from two young men with short haircuts and missionary name tags, the question is essentially the same as that faced by the Steeds in 1827: *What will be my response to Joseph Smith and his story of a pillar of light?*" (xi)

Franklin Fisher, in his prize-winning novel *Bones* (Salt Lake City: University of Utah, 1990), incorporates the historical Joseph Smith in highly experimental ways that may constitute genuine postmodernist sensibility. His narrator, Lorin Hood, is a Mormon missionary excommunicated for adultery, who slides into psychosis and art simultaneously. His identification with Joseph Smith begins first as an imaginative exercise and then develops into full-blown delusion. One of the last delusions described is the First Vision:

> Out of the corner of his eye he saw that the grass he lay in looked like white flamelets, moving slightly, as though the light had set up a small wind. . . . Directly above him two men in white robes stood looking at him. Bark had been peeled from the dead stump and lay in rags among the wildflowers. The rags were bleached out, too. . . .
>
> The older man pointed to the younger one and said something about a son or the sun. Lorin wondered if he was going to mention any of this when he got home. They were talking about abominations and false prophets, and Lorin reflected that he could no longer feel . . . his back and sides at all, or his feet or hands. He suspected this meant your kinesthetic responses shut off during visions. It meant your nerve endings picked up other signals, your senses fine-tuned to other frequencies. It explained why, now that he thought about it, he was not hearing the chirp of birds or the buzz and click of insects or for that matter the rustling made by the wind in the white flamelets beside his ears. All he could hear was the mild voice of the younger man explaining dreadful things to him, and he worried that he wasn't going to remember them all. He strained to listen very closely, but there were no muscles you could flex to hear better. The most he was able to do was cause a roaring in both ears, and that created interference. Still, he enjoyed watching the shadows ripple across the robes of both men as the wind gently caught the folds. He experienced a mild pang as the younger man's voice began to fade out, and presently he was aware of colors

separating into unstable bands around them both, and he saw the claw of a dead branch through the face and chest of the older man.

He lay for a long time staring at a webwork of twigs in early leaf against a cold blue sky before trying to get up. . . . He heard the frantic scrattle of a key at his lock and opened his eyes in time to see himself stumble through the doorway into the room, holding his head and moaning. He was ready for the interruption but wondered where he had been. (220-21)

It is interesting and significant that Franklin Fisher postulates, with considerable sophistication and success, psychological alternatives to the straightforward simplicity of the orthodox Mormon position on the First Vision: that God the Father and the Son appeared to the young Joseph Smith in a grove in upstate New York—versions that Lund and Vardis Fisher embody in their fiction. While experimentation and alternative explanations certainly have a complexity and intricacy missing from the traditional account and hence may be more interesting and satisfying on that level, at what point do convolutions and subtleties become wearisome and unsubstantial? That point is probably a highly individual one for each reader. And how rewarding is it for writers? Although Fisher's *Bones* was named Best Novel by the Association for Mormon Letters for 1990 and had earlier won first prize in the 1984 Utah Arts Council Original Writing Competition, he has not, to my knowledge, used a Mormon theme again.

There is probably no way of knowing for sure how many Mormon historical novels have been written on a given period or episode in Mormon history. The LDS Historical Department Library aggressively tries to be comprehensive, including acquiring rare and out-of-print novels about Mormonism; and the Harold B. Lee Library maintains an equally vigorous and even broader acquisitions policy (including young adult and children's books), mouthwateringly available in a fully searchable online database that includes biographical information about the authors. (http://MormonLit.lib.byu.edu)

The iconic and dramatic view of Mormon history provided by the unity and myth of the nineteenth century flounders in the twentieth century. Post-Manifesto polygamy continued for fourteen years as secret authorizations from Church leaders to selected individuals. The sensational Reed Smoot hearings resulted in Church President Joseph F. Smith's announcement of the Second Manifesto of 1904, closing loopholes left by the first and ending secret authorizations. Polygamy then went deeper underground as a practice with various forms of private justifications, claims of revelatory guidance, and the development of schisms. Certainly these episodes, the participation of Mormonism in mainstream national life, the experiences of Mormon men and women in two world wars, and the internationalization of the church are not unworthy of fictional treatment.

However, the official histories seem to focus on administrative presidencies (perhaps natural after Brigham Young's thirty-year presidency) and programs (the rise of the auxiliaries, the welfare program, the increase in temples, and the success of missionary work). Twentieth-century history continues the formula in post-hole triumphalism—small beginnings lead in straight-line but usually vaguely described growth to the pinnacle of Mormon success (stakes or even a temple). Here is a typical description: "Just 30 years after the first missionaries arrived here to preach the restored gospel, . . . the 56th temple . . . was dedicated."[6]

In fact, Mormon historical novels exploring twentieth-century themes are surprisingly rare. Dean Hughes broke new ground with his CHILDREN OF THE PROMISE series in five volumes, all published by Deseret Book: *Rumors of War* (1997), *Since You Went Away* (1997), *Far from Home* (1998), *When We Meet Again* (2001), and *As Long As I Have You* (2000). The series begins on the eve of the outbreak of World War II and traces, over the next six years, how that conflict impacted a businessman/stake president in Salt Lake City, his busy and competent wife, and their six children. The oldest son, Alex, who served a mission in

---

6. Gerry Avant, "Temple Dedicated in Madrid, Spain," *Church News,* March 27, 1999, 3, 10.

·CHILDREN OF THE PROMISE·

VOL. I
RUMORS OF WAR

·DEAN HUGHES·

DESERET BOOK COMPANY · SALT LAKE CITY, UTAH

Germany, returned to that theater while the second son, Wally, enlisted after the bombing of Pearl Harbor, served in the Pacific, was taken a prisoner of war in the Philippines, but survived the Bataan death march and a concentration camp to return home. The oldest daughter, Bobbie, becomes a nurse. As their experiences make clear, they are Mormons participating in a national experience, not—like Lund's Steed family—Americans participating in a Mormon experience. This is a crucial difference. However, Lynne Watkins Jorgensen, Review, , *Journal of Mormon History* 28, no. 2 (Fall 2002): 220-24, singled out its historical accuracy for praise: "Hughes's descriptions of the Salt Lake City I knew as a teenager are eerily accurate, and I get the same feeling of authenticity about the details of the war on all fronts" (224). In other words, in its traditional mode of story-telling, Hughes's series relies very much on the same traditional expectations of fiction as Lund and his readers. And presumably the same mode also serves Hughes well in his second series HEARTS OF THE CHILDREN, based on the grandchildren in this same Salt Lake family. So far, titles in this series, also published by Deseret Book, consist of *The Writing on the Wall* (2001), *Troubled Waters* (2002), and *How Many Roads* (2003).

Margaret Blair Young, a writer who also teaches fiction at Brigham Young University, likewise gave one of her novels a World War II setting. *House without Walls* (Salt Lake City: Deseret Book, 1991) is written in an understated style reminiscent of Chaim Potok. Sarah, an unsubmissive and untraditional German Jewish young woman, is spiritually and emotionally tough enough to become a Mormon, then is brutally redefined as Jewish by the Nazis, but survives to bear a son (Isaac) to her rabbi husband (Abraham). Isaac, in a parallel encounter with Mormonism, finds an even deeper faith and returns to Germany as a missionary. It is an emotionally intense novel that asserts, as a nonnegotiable premise, the reality of revelation, grace, and miracles, deals with the Holocaust from a Mormon perspective, and suggests some of the complexities of Mormonism in an international context.

Young, in addition to other fiction, went on to make common cause with Darius Aidan Gray, who is president of the Genesis Group, an official Church auxiliary and support group for ethnic (mostly black) Mormons in Salt Lake City, organized in 1971. Together, they coauthored a remarkable trilogy, STANDING ON THE PROMISES, dealing with the explosive topic of black Mormons who were, between the 1850s and 1978, denied priesthood ordination for their men. These three novels, all published by Bookcraft, are *One More River to Cross* (2000), *Bound for Canaan* (2002), and *The Last Mile of the Way* (2003). The Association for Mormon Letters at its annual meeting in March 2004 announced the creation of a new prize category—historical fiction, for the "unique" place this genre "occupies in our literary tradition," according to the association's president, Melissa Proffit in announcing it. The trilogy received the assocation's first award of this prize.

All three novels are based solidly in historical characters under their own names, and contain chapter endnotes and bibliographies, a device that Gerald Lund had earlier used to help readers answer their running questions, "Did that really happen?" According to Margaret Young, "Young-Gray," aml-list@lists.xmission.com, February 19, 2004, "Mormon historians who generally hate LDS historical fiction have become our greatest fans. But at least one of my English colleagues thought it [the notes] an interruption in the flow of the text."

The first novel begins in Nauvoo where black convert Jane Manning James leads a little group of black believers eight hundred miles on foot and where Elijah Abel was ordained a Seventy in the Melchizedek Priesthood. Louis Gray, a slave in Jackson County, has a poignant cameo role in this novel; he was Darius Gray's great-grandfather. This novel ends in 1848, a year after the arrival in the Salt Lake Valley of the vanguard company, which included three African American slaves. These characters take the position, documented from Lester E. Bush Jr., "Mormonism's Negro Doctrine: An Historical Overview," *Dialogue* 8 (Spring 1973): 11-68, that Joseph Smith had foreseen African Americans as full members of the Mormon community but that exclusionary ideologies accompanied Brigham Young's rise to power:

Book Two

Bound for Canaan

Margaret Blair Young
and Darius Aidan Gray

BOOKCRAFT
SALT LAKE CITY, UTAH

Though Sister Emma opposed it, Jane chose to go with Brigham Young, even moved into his place as a servant. The other Mannings decided not to continue on in Nauvoo, not maybe even with Mormonism. It . . . was a subtle change in attitude—or the subtle revelation of an attitude that had always been lurking. The temple was nearly done, but no Negro was let inside to be endowed. It was the curse of Cain and Canaan, some said, that meant the black man had to stay outside..

In their patriarchal blessings, Hyrum Smith had told the Mannings they were descended from "Cainaan" [a subtle misspelling that blends both biblical names]. That was all right, but none of the Mannings had heard mention how that lineage meant some sort of permanent position on the rough side of the holy gates—leastways, not amongst the Mormons. Of course, most religions talked about lineage some, and "the curse of Cain" was no fresh news. But the Mannings had hoped for better turns of conversation in Zion. (264-65)

Despite this disappointment, Jane and Isaac Manning, and Elijah Abel and their families courageously cross the plains in the second volume, live frugal and hardworking lives in Utah, and endure slow but intensifying exclusion from the Mormon community as time passes. This novel follows the quest for temple blessings that were denied both Jane Manning and Elijah Abel, despite Abel's faithful service as a missionary, describes racial lynchings in Utah, and records John Taylor's grudging consent, delivered through Jane's stake president, to allow her to be baptized in the temple for her kindred dead.

Volume 3 picks up in 1891, soon after Isaac James's death. As an aged woman, Jane is at last allowed into the temple by Joseph F. Smith, but only to be sealed as a "servant" to Joseph Smith's family. The novel then highlights the stories of other twentieth-century blacks including the few descendants of these pioneer families who retained (or gained again) an attachment to Mormonism. A poignant story is that of Len Hope—his real name, so symbolic it would be unbelievable in a novel. He survived Ku Klux Klan threats in the South and made a Mormon home near Philadelphia where he and his family were denied the sacrament at the branch because the other Saints refused to drink out of the common sacramental cup after them. They attended district conference every three month, paid their tithing, and on Fast Sundays held a sacrament meeting in their home with the missionaries, one of whom was future General Authority Marion D. Hanks.

The conclusion of the novel, focused on the Genesis Group, would be unbearably sad were it not for the reader's knowledge of the pending 1978 revelation that would reverse more than a century of exclusion. "Often, it was just Ruffin [Bridgeforth, first president of Genesis] and his wife attending. But they were still there. Ruffin was holding steady, no matter who had left. . . . Who ever would have guessed it'd be so hard to stay united and keep from getting sucked into bitterness? The devil uses a man's weaknesses against him—but we sharpen our own sticks for Satan to stab and bloody us with" (420). Darius Gray appears as a character in this part of the novel under his middle name of Aidan, struggling with all of the ordinary problems of faith but even more exacerbated by racism.

Although this trilogy has a saga-like sweep of multi-generational dynastic historical fiction and begins with a couple of key families, it introduces dozens of characters, at least partly because so many African Americans understandably departed from the Mormon scene. Written with consistently sure emotional touch and superb storytelling skills, these sparingly fictionalized accounts, particularly as they make their way over the next few years, will simultaneously make household names out of Biddy Mason, pioneer Green Flake, that "hard-headed treasure" Lucile Bankhead (Flake's descendant), Paul Howell, Monroe Fleming, and other black Latter-day Saints now obscure to all but specialized historians.

Excavating Mormon Pasts

Also hewing very close to traditional forms and approaches is the very slightly fictionalized R. Lanier Britsch, *Nothing More Heroic* (Salt Lake City: Deseret Book, 1999), described on the cover as "the compelling story of the first Latter-day Saint missionaries in India." It is an interesting and, from my perspective, successful experiment in narrative fiction/history of the seventeen missionaries called to India in 1852. "I have chosen to recount this history in the voice of Amos Milton Musser," Britsch's preface begins (xi). Musser was a twenty-two-year-old youth who not only left a detailed diary but was also assistant Church historian (1902-09). This diary, supplemented by diaries of other missionaries and their letters published in the *Millennial Star* formed the basis for Britsch's version, fictionalized so slightly that it is nowhere referred to as a "novel" but instead is described as a "chronicle," an "amazing story," and an "adventure story" (jacket flaps). In fact, he asserts, "I have not fantasized conversations or created imaginary scenes. Every event is as true to the story as if Amos Milton Musser himself had really written it" (xi).

An evocatively and psychologically challenging Mormon historical novel is Phyllis Barber, *And the Desert Shall Blossom* (Salt Lake City: Signature Books, 1993), based on elements from her own family history. Building Boulder Dam drew the dreamers and the desperate from all over the United States, including Alf and Esther, an economically marginalized Mormon family. Esther's identity lies with her strongly woven, very Mormon clan in Brigham City, "where she [was] the pretty one who sings." Now she is displaced geographically and psychologically. The newly invented city of Boulder grinds away at the family like the hot desert wind with its abrasive, constant grit. It erodes the bonds in their nuclear family, setting the two sons and three daughters adrift from each other and from their parents, stranding Alf somewhere between the orthodox Mormonism that never fit him securely and the possibility of petty power that makes him dip, unsuccessfully, into criminality and adultery.

Although there must be hundreds of novels dealing with nineteenth-century polygamy, traditional Mormon historical authors still see it as a racy topic, difficult to deal with except in the context of self-sacrificing obedience for insider/insider writers or salacious sexual license for outsider/outsider writers. Except for Sorensen's *Many Mansions*, I am aware of only two novels that deal with post-Manifesto polygamy. Insatiable reader and judicious reviewer Jeffrey Needle, commenting on Betty Webb, *Desert Wives* (n.p.: Poisoned Pen Press, 2002) for AML-List, February 6, 2004, summarized the plot. Lena Jones, private detective, poses as the plural wife of a secretly dissident resident of Purity, a small polygamist community on the Arizona/Utah border, so she can to investigate the murder of its prophet. Needle praises the author for keeping the elements of the mystery firmly on track but states that Webb obviously had insider information in providing a setting that include "the horrors of incest, polygamy, spousal abuse and power run amok." Another is Cleo Jones's novel (working title *Talk or Die*), which weaves every nightmare from Utah's polygamist/militia cult past into a single well-written, horrifying story, told from the point of view of a fifteen-year-old on the verge of being married either to her half brother or to a decrepit apostle. Simultaneously she spies nightly on the serial killer who has rented the other half of her mother's duplex as a uninterrupted location for the weeks of raping and torturing his latest victim, who is almost exactly the daughter's age. The novel is a tense race between the killer's movement toward the inevitable orgy of murder and the daughter's innate human decency that urges her to shatter her own years of conditioning toward silence and secrecy.

Intriguingly, two additional mysteries set in contemporary times turn on the significance of potentially destructive historical documents. Paul Edwards, *The Angel Acronym* (Salt Lake City: Signature Books, 2003), hinges on a forged section copied from the Book of Mormon while it was being printed in Palmyra in 1829 but with enough variations that the initial letters of each verse, assembled in reverse, spell "Angel Moroni." The discovery of this document at the Heber C. Kimball home in Nauvoo by the RLDS archivist leads directly to his murder in the Church headquarters building. Bureaucrat-philosopher Toom

Taggart solves the mystery with the aid of a brainy and pretty Church attorney, but not in time to prevent the murderer's suicide, also in the headquarters building.

In John Gates, *Brigham's Day* (New York: Walker & Company, 2000), attorney Brigham Bybee, trying to put his career back on track in Kanab, Utah, as the defense attorney for young man accused of murder, realizes that both of them are being set up, but why? The answer lies in a document more than a hundred years old confessing complicity in the Mountain Meadows Massacre:

> He unfastened the loose knot and pulled out a dried, leather valise. It was scarred, part of it blackened and burned, and the metal snaps and buckles were rusted, some of them broken. He opened it and found an old Bible, a large family edition, bound in black leather with faint gold letters on the bottom that read Josiah Lamb.
>
> "Inside the Bible," Zolene said.
>
> Bybee opened the book and pulled out a folded piece of paper. It was brittle and yellowed, stained by water, . . . and it nearly separated at the creases as he opened it. . . .
>
> "That's what Doug was murdered for," she said. "Watters, too. . . . Mountain Meadows, Brig. . . It will never end." (154-55)

Like the conflict-driven events of pre-1847 Mormonism, Mountain Meadows looms over the landscape of fictional possibilities. Herbert Harker, *Turn Again Home* (New York: Random House, 1977) was, I believe, the first to recast this event from more a contemporary consciousness, in this case a Canadian young man whose father disappeared on his seventy-seventh birthday. The trail led Jared back to the secret that had haunted not only his father but also his father-in-law since their own youth. Marilyn Brown, *The Wine-Dark Sea of Grass* (Springville, UT: Salt Press, 2001), told the story of the massacre, the impact on local families, and John D. Lee's execution twenty years later as straight historical fiction, using as one of her primary point of view characters a young plural wife who is really in love with Lee. Reviewer Terry Jeffries, *Journal of Mormon History* 28, no. 1 (Spring 2002): 266-70, finds that the book gets off to a gripping start with the massacre but the characters thereafter "move about in Lee's shadow and never have any self-motivation. . . . The final 200 pages make tedious reading as they wind down from the tension of the massacre" (269). In contrast, Judith Freeman, *Red Water* (New York: Pantheon Books, 2002) in this, her first Mormon historical novel, experimented boldly with three different narrators, all of them wives of John D. Lee, at different stages of their life. Tough English convert Emma Batchelor takes the trials of polygamy and frontier living in her stride. Thirteen-year-old Ann Gordge is emotionally erratic and romantic, while Rachel is reflecting on her life as an elderly widow in a fictionalized journal. The experiment with narrative voice is an interesting way to approach the many facets of John D. Lee, unquestionably a murderer, undeniably a scapegoat.

Overlapping Practitioners

A third reason for considering Mormon historical fiction in relation to the New Mormon History is its overlapping personnel. Thanks most likely to the extraordinary generosity and personal warmth of Leonard J. Arrington (1917-99), dean of Mormon historians, LDS Church Historian, and historical entrepreneur, the boundary between fiction and history was a remarkable permeable one with amateur scholars being welcomed as colleague-researchers. He set the standard of having broad-based interests rather than a narrow specialty. One of his early papers was on a literary topic: "Intolerable Zion: The Image of Mormonism in Nineteenth Century American Literature," written with Jon Haupt and published in *Western Humanities Review* 22 (Summer 1968): 243-60. It won the Mormon History Association's Prize as best article published in 1968-69.

Gene England, founding coeditor of *Dialogue,* which published many of the earliest manuscripts of the New Mormon History, was a professor of English but was welcomed as a Brigham Young researcher and, in fact, published one of the earliest contemporary histories on Brigham Young: *Brother Brigham* (Salt Lake City: Bookcraft, 1980). England also taught the first course at BYU in Mormon history and helped foster the organization of the Association for Mormon Letters. Maureen Ursenbach Beecher called a group of friends together in the fall of 1976 to discuss the quality and availability of Mormon personal narratives. Maureen was then a member of Leonard J. Arrington's group of historians and holder of a Ph.D. in comparative literature. Eugene England and I were among the eight or ten people who came. Gene tossed out the question, "How could we go about organizing a group focused on the criticism of Mormon literature?" Then he patiently listened as the lively conversation ranged over the "why" and "what" aspects of the question as well for about an hour.

Obviously it was a discussion that could have gone on for years, but Gene glanced at his watch and said abruptly, "I've got to go. Maureen, why don't you chair a steering committee?" Then he walked out. We obediently shifted, on the spot, from academics to activity and organized the steering committee, which Maureen chaired. In that committee's first meeting, the Association for Mormon Letters was formally organized. It was Maureen who persuaded us that the name should be "for Mormon Letters," not "of Mormon Letters," foreseeing, in the words of Linda Brummett, its 1993 president, "the power of the preposition." Steven Sondrup, a member of BYU's Comparative Literature Department, volunteered to be the executive secretary, a position he held until the January 1994 annual meeting, a task which not only included heroically producing mailings, proceedings, and newsletters but also more often than not hosting its officers' meetings.

Orson Scott Card, a prolific and award-winning science fiction author as well as author of *Woman of Destiny,* is the son-in-law of one of Arrington's two Assistant Church Historians, James B. Allen, and author of the script currently used for the Hill Cumorah Pageant. Levi S. Peterson, an English professor at Weber State University until his retirement and now editor of *Dialogue,* wrote *The Backslider* (Salt Lake City: Signature Books, 1986), which is my personal candidate for "the Great Mormon Novel." He also wrote a prize-winning biography *Juanita Brooks: Mormon Woman Historian* (Salt Lake City: University of Utah Press/Tanner Trust Fund, 1958) and is the brother of Charles S. Peterson, himself a noted regional historian and former professor of history at University of Utah. John Sillito, former employee in the LDS Historical Department, now archivist at Weber State University, has employed his historical interests on Martha Hughes Cannon, B. H. Roberts, socialism in Utah, and Richard R. Lyman, while, Linda Sillitoe, has written on-the-edge fiction dealing with women's issues—-*Sideways to the Sun* and *Windows on the Sea and Other Stories* (both Salt Lake City: Signature Books, 1987, 1989)—while also branching out into history: two versions of the Salt Lake County history that is part of the statehood centennial celebration (*A History of Salt Lake County* and *Welcoming the World: A History of Salt Lake County,* both published in 1996 in Salt Lake City by the Utah State Historical Society/Salt Lake County Commission and by the Salt Lake County Commission, respectively), plus *Friendly Fire: A History of the ACLU in Utah* (Salt Lake City: Signature Books, 1996). Especially interesting to Mormon historians is her dual treatment of the Mark Hofmann forgeries and murders: nonfictionally in *Salamander: The Story of the Mormon Forgery Murders* with Allen D. Roberts, which was nominated for the Pulitzer Prize, and fictionally in *Secrets Keep* (both Salt Lake City: Signature Books, 1987, and 1995).

It is true that this network of connections—and dozens more could be traced—may be as much coincidence than causal. Certainly it is possible that I tend to notice first my own friends and neighbors, and that the connections are a result of my own provincialism. Mormonism's intellectual community is still relatively small and new; its participants are likely to be in Utah or to have ties to Utah, are likely to know each other, share similar interests, and have similar skills. The internet has broadened the community, make it simultaneously easier to join in the discussion, and intensifying the bonds by making it so easy to have even daily contacts among participants. . *Dialogue* and *Sunstone* have, since their inception, published both history and fiction. The Sunstone symposiums are hospitable hosts to both writers and historians, although, puzzlingly, there has been little crossovers between the two more specialized organizations—the Mormon History Association and the Association for Mormon Letters.

And third, the Mormon historians who worked in the New Mormon History field were of two generations. The first generation was, for the most part, survivors of World War II, educated by the GI Bill and thus part of the greatest achievement in mass education in American history. The second generation consisted of baby-boomers born immediately after World War II who went on to college as a matter of course in a variety of academic fields. They were graduating with their degrees just as the New Mormon History flowered under Arrington, and it seemed normal and natural for those with intellectual interests to be involved in the heady ferment of Mormon history in the 1970s. As college-trained historians eagerly and confidently applied their professional skills to the task of conceptualizing and constructing Mormon history, so college-trained critical and creative writers employed their trained sensibilities and skills in examining the Mormon experience through fiction.[7] For an appreciation of this period, often called "Camelot" or the "Arrington Spring," see Davis Bitton, "Ten Years in Camelot: A Personal Memoir," *Dialogue* 16 (Autumn 1983): 20-33 and numerous personal expressions in the *Journal of Mormon History* 25, no. 1 (Spring 1999): "In Memoriam: Leonard J. Arrington," 1-10; "Remembering Leonard: Memorial Service, 15 February 1999," 10-33; "The Voices of Memory," 33-103; "Documents and Dusty Tomes: The Adventure of Arrington, Esplin, and Young," by Ronald K. Esplin, 103-12; and "Mormonism's 'Happy Warrior': Appreciating Leonard J. Arrington," by Ronald W. Walker, 113-30.

The Future of Mormon Historical Fiction

The future of Mormon historical fiction raises interesting questions. The enthusiasm and energy with which the New Mormon Historians explored the past, conceptualized their tasks, and established their relationships to a diverse audience did not always protect them from controversy, official punishment, and marginalization. The same fate has not befallen writers of Mormon historical novels, but I suspect that speculative, experimental, and "offensive" works often fail to find publishers and, hence, fail to attract official attention.

An Uneasy Prognosis

Ronald W. Walker, one of Leonard J. Arrington's historians, in his obituary tribute to him, "Mormonism's 'Happy Warrior,'" 127-28, acknowledged the criticism of historian Charles S. Peterson who

> argued that . . . despite [the New Mormon History's] moderate spirit of "acquiescence and well-being," it had failed to gain the support of LDS leaders; it is true that not a single Mormon leader spoke publicly in its favor. Likewise, Peterson believed that it had failed to engage the interest of mainstream American historians. . . . Without the support of the Mormon Church and isolated from its peers, the New Mormon History, Peterson argued, had failed as an important intellectual movement.[8]

Walker admitted:

> The critics have a point. The New Mormon History has not captured a large audience and is not likely to; at the century's end, rank-and-file Mormons prefer historical fiction and popular film to the emotionally aloof history that is being written. Some of the new his-

---

7. Regrettably, space precludes a discussion of Mormon drama, poetry, hymns, and shorter fiction, all equally important genres that have explored historical themes in significant ways.

8. He is quoting Charles S. Peterson, "Beyond the Problems of Exceptionalist History," in *Great Basin Kingdom Revisited: Contemporary Perspectives*, edited by Thomas G. Alexander (Logan: Utah State University Press, 1991), 143, 148.

tory writers, self-absorbed by their quest for roots, produce narrow and lifeless history. (Self-analysis and ennui are usually partners.) Moreover, the practitioners of the New Mormon History are "graying," to use [Roger] Launius's phrase. New and midcareer historians are becoming few as young men and women, warned off by the collapse of the History Division, choose other careers and specialties. Who in the future will bear the historical standard? (129)

The same question must be asked of Mormon historical fiction. To the extent that it came into being as a result of the New Mormon History and rests on the foundation of the New Mormon History, to that extent it may be vulnerable to shifts in official favor and suspicions about the orthodoxy of its practitioners. Historical fiction has so dominated Mormon fiction for two decades that there are relatively few alternatives except for the flourishing contemporary romance/adventure genre (which is not particularly Mormon except in setting and local color) and the Signature Books fiction list—always interesting and high-quality but frequently on the edge in its range of themes and techniques. The whole question of boundaries and audiences is a volatile and controversial one for Mormon fiction. Bruce W. Jorgensen made a powerful and eloquent plea against xenophobia as his AML presidential address, "To Tell and Hear Stories: Let the Stranger Say," *AML Annual: 1988-92,* 19-33, in 1990, urging Mormon readers to be "generous, hospitable" even to "complaining and dissenting voices." The next year's president, Richard H. Cracroft, vigorously countered in "Attuning the Authentic Mormon Voice: Stemming the Sophic Tide in LDS Literature," *AML Annual,* 1994, 1:34-43. He took the position that Mormon writers should instead tailor their productions to the Mormon mainstream. Both essays were reprinted in *Sunstone* (July 1993): 25-35, 36-42. This debate, picked up in later papers at AML and carried on in lively email discussions, has not always resisted the temptation to posture for maximum orthodoxy (and hence greater "spirituality") while casting subtle aspersions on the faithfulness of those deemed less orthodox or, conversely, to see in orthodoxy a safely but deadly dull lack of creativity.[9] Its tensions have been heightened by general unease at Brigham Young University unrelated to the writing of Mormon historical fiction per se but part of a new expectation of heightened orthodoxy; historians D. Michael Quinn, Martha Sonntag Bradley, and Steven Epperson and English faculty Cecilia Konchar Farr, Gail Houston, and Brian Evenson either left voluntarily or were forced out.

Neal Kramer, also of BYU's English faculty and AML president in 1998 and 1999, devoted his first presidential address, "Art and Advocacy: Politics and Mormon Letters," *AML Annual,* 1999, to warning against the postmodernist stance that valorizes dissidence and critiques of power and authority: "Mormon intellectuals, uncritically accepting the current fashion, may fall into the trap of believing that the fundamental attribute of power relationships in all institutions is injustice because all power relationships are unequal," he warned. A "critique is not about to change or reform the institution. It can only attempt to subvert, undermine, oppose, or destroy it. And that will never happen. Because God has made specific promises regarding the survival of the Church and its leaders, the prophets, all attempts at subverting the institution are doomed." He expressed concern for the intellectual who is "disciplined by the Church for writing or [who] write[s] himself out of the Church" because "the writer has so much more to lose" than the church.

He proposed a list of prescriptions for Mormon writers: "Our literature should strive to strengthen faith in Christ. It should reflect and present the common experiences of the faithful. Spiritual gifts and promptings should populate our stories. And we should always be looking for new ways to tell of the infinite mercy and grace of our Savior" (4-5).

---

9. Two responsible returns to the topic are John Bennion, "Renegotiating Scylla and Charybdis: A New Look at Insider and Outsider Stereotypes of Mormonism," and "Undefining 'Faithful Fiction' (The Sophic Stranger Rides Again (With[out] His Evil Twin)," *AML Annual,* 1997, 59-66, and 67-75 respectively. AML-List, a moderated discussion group devoted to Mormon literature, deals with on-going and vigorously debated issues, among others, the relationship between faith and creative writing. Those interested in this list should contact <owner-aml@lists.xmission.com>.

He concluded by suggesting that "the best Mormon literature will advocate, persuade, and invite rather than subvert, shock, and destroy. Mormon literature will seek to edify as it seeks to transform its audience" (6).

Because he cited no examples from Mormon writers, it was not clear which works caused him concern and which he felt were worthy of emulation, but his address communicated a message of distress over at least some Mormon fiction currently being written. It was not possible to tell whether he made an exception for Mormon historical fiction.

History as Myth

History has a strong and secure place in Mormon culture now as myth and ritual. I have deplored this fact for decades, but perhaps I have been unnecessarily hostile and provincial. There is no rule that says bad history necessarily makes bad literature; and certainly literature can be powerfully and skillfully at home in myth and ritual. Whether myth and ritual can foster good historical fiction, however, is still an open question for me. There is no doubt that they *can* foster extremely bad history.

Here are three examples. All depart from Mormon historical novels, but I feel justified in doing so because they *seem* to present Mormon history although they actually do not, thus debasing the already low standards for historical excellence and limiting the forums for its creative expression. First is the Church's public relations film, *Legacy*, shown to thousands of visitors, tourists, and Saints in the Joseph Smith Memorial Building's theater in Salt Lake City until it was replaced by *One Fold and One Shepherd*, and now available on video and DVD. It is a series of vignettes that are less a plot that short-hand evocations of conversion, Haun's Mill, Joseph Smith's charisma (singularly unconvincing since the actor's portrayal is several degrees more wooden than the average cigar-store Indian), suffering, the temple, the exodus, a version of Mary Fielding Smith's ox, wagon trains against the sunset, etc.—but, tellingly, not polygamy. "It was awesome," commented Murray resident and LDS Church member Virgina [sic] Hendrickson. "It was just like being there. It brought to mind again all the terrible things done to the pioneers."[10] In other words, according to this view, the highest product of history is vicarious suffering.

The second example appears in Shirley Sealey's *I Have Chosen You* (Salt Lake City: RIC Publishing, 1982), overtly the journey of self-discovery by a frustrated and neglected wife, Radene, who chaperones a busload of teenagers, including her daughter, on a tour of Church history sites while she decides whether to divorce her husband.

She sees Nauvoo through the bus window: "There it was—the picture she had seen so often on postcards and in books." She "knows" the meaning of Nauvoo before she even gets off the bus: "I used to think it was unfair of Heavenly Father to let them build it all up, even to the last detail of the temple, to sacrifice and give and give when they had so little to give, when He knew it was all going to be destroyed. But now I know the answer. They had to have a picture, a vision of reality in their minds to give them the strength and courage to endure the crossing of the Plains and the ability to see the desert of the Salt Lake Valley as it would look when they built a city of Zion again" (447-48).

This picture-postcard tour of Church history sites comes with a moment of "enlightenment" at each stop, usually tearful awe at the suffering of the Saints. It is therefore inevitable that Radene decides she should stop being selfish and commit herself to the eternal vision of a celestial marriage. Finally, after they have wept over the babies' graves at Winter Quarters, her daughter says, "Oh Mom . . . let's go home. I'm too tired to hurt anymore for these wonderful people" (191).

This novel was written in 1982, long before the reconstruction of the Nauvoo Temple and the heavily touristicized sites and entertainments by "missionary" actors giving agonized renditions of mobs, murder, and crossing the frozen Mississippi. But then and now, the purpose of history for Sealey, as for the Nauvoo missionary-guides, is vicarious suffering. The simplest emotional reaction to Mormon history is to "hurt"; and that pain, achieved by

---

10. Qtd. in Peggy Fletcher Stack, "'Legacy' Puts LDS Past on Wide Screen," *Salt Lake Tribune*, July 9, 1993, E-1, E-2.

piling tragedy on tragedy, persuades the participants (and the reader?) that an emotional *frisson* is equivalent to a spiritual experience and that history is just daytime TV in long dresses.

The third example is an unconsciously sinister comment on the technique of historical fiction writing. Author Montell Seely explained in "Improved Facilities Enhance 15-Year-Old Drama," *Church News,* August 8, 1992, 11, how he wrote his script for the annual pageant of the settlement of Castle Valley: "Each of the settlement stories is basically the same. . . . Only the names are different. Young people fell in love and got married. Babies were born, and loved ones died. They endured the trials of taming a hostile wilderness. With God's help, they won." While this ritual retelling of Mormon history may be comforting and even inspiring, it is hardly creative; nor does the bland assumption that "only the names are different" encourage creativity, diversity, complexity, or ambiguity. In short, the one thing history as ritual cannot deliver is a satisfying *literary* experience.

If more examples of this dreary tendency are needed, and they almost certainly are not, Julie A. Dockstader, "Mormon Values Set in Stone, Bronze," *Church News,* April 4, 1992, 8-10, provided another in her description of the Seagull Monument on Temple Square. The considerably more historically subdued claims for this miracle are readily available; William G. Hartley, "Mormon's Crickets and Gulls: A New Look at an Old Story," was first published in *Utah Historical Quarterly* 38 (Summer 1970): 224-39 and reprinted in *New Mormon History: Revisionist Essays on the Past,* edited by D. Michael Quinn (Salt Lake City: Signature Books, 1992), 137-52. Still, the *Church News* preferred to quote its own 1960s version of the myth:

> "Well-known to Mormons is the story of how seagulls saved the crops of Utah's early settlers from an invading horde of crickets. In the spring of 1848, 4,00 acres of crops had been planted, and a good harvest was expected, according to the Nov. 19, 1960, issue of the Church News.
>
> "Then tragedy struck," continues the article. "Before the month of May had passed the situation changed. . . . Hordes of crickets came into the field. Before the eyes of the pioneers their efforts were being shredded." In desperation, the pioneers turned to God in "fervent prayer." From the sky then came thousands of seagulls, which devoured the crickets and saved the crops.

Exposure to History

The explosion in Church membership during the 1990s means that literally millions of Mormons have not lived through a significant amount of personal history as Mormons nor have they experienced the precorrelation curriculum in which at least some historical material was transmitted. Members of the international Church, who became a numerical majority in February 1996, have virtually no access to Mormon history unless they also read English, have access to histories that are largely published either by Utah presses or by the University of Illinois Press, and, most significantly, have the funds and the interest to do so. (Histories in other languages appear in "Growth and Internationalization: The LDS Church since 1945," by Kahlile Mehr, Mark L. Grover, Reid L. Neilson, Donald Q. Cannon, and Grant Underwood in this volume.)

The sole exception—and it is a crucial one—may be the encounter of members around the world with the history of the Church through the massive national and international publicity in 1997 accompanying the sesquicentennial celebration of the Mormon trek across the plains.[11] The reenactment of this trek proved to be a public relations coup for the Church and an experience so moving to participants and viewers that many referred to it as "sacred" and faltered in efforts to express it in words. Themed "Faith in Every

---

11. Shaun D. Stahle, "Trek Stirs Imagination, Receives Vast Coverage," *Church News,* August 30, 1997, 4, reported that coverage included major articles and sometimes series of articles by Agence France Press, Deutsche Presse Agentur, Associated Press, *Newsweek* (full page spread in May), CBS, *New York Times, Washington Post* (front page coverage on same day), *Atlanta Journal-Constitution,* and television specials in Russia, the Czech Republic, Romania, Italy, France, Belgium, Poland, Hungary, Austria, Ecuador, Philippines, Japan,

Footstep," celebrations were supposed to involve Church units worldwide in local service projects (which they did with marked success), but the most powerful symbol of the trek was the logo of the handcart. On the face of it, this icon seems like a bizarre selection since it commemorates a short-lived (two-year) experiment in moving immigrants that ended, for all practical purposes, when about 150 died—stranded, frozen, and starved in the snows of a Wyoming winter. However, as the sesquicentennial celebrations made clear, these pioneers embodied the three elements that the Church still prizes in its members: steadfastness, sacrifice, and suffering. This message was underscored by the addresses of General Authorities at April 1997 conference who gave a surprising number of examples of the suffering and sacrifice of women and children—individuals who were not included in the planning process conducted by males but who had to deal with the dire results.

Two years after the sesquicentennial, in March 1999, the second page of the *Church News* featured a quotation by novelist George Eliot, "I desire no future that will break the ties of the past," and, on the facing page, Church President Gordon B. Hinckley reiterated the message to be drawn from Church history as he was interviewed in Spain, where he dedicated yet another temple: "We have people who do heroic things in support of the Church. . . . This is a place where there are pioneers and there will continue to be pioneers as they shake off the things of the past and put on the cloak of righteousness in adherence to the principles of the restored gospel."[12] That same issue of the *Church News* reported a reenactment of the organizational meeting of the Relief Society in Nauvoo and quoted Joseph Smith as saying, "I now turn the key in your behalf," phrasing which, it has been reliably shown, was changed from the original wording recorded in Eliza R. Snow's hand on the day of the meeting: "I now turn the key to you."[13] Patient efforts to establish this correct reading have been regarded with official uneasiness as a feminist attempt to increase women's autonomy and decrease priesthood authority.

Meanwhile, Lund's popularity has generated look-alike series and made Mormon publishers more willing to take a risk on them although, as the advertising makes clear, such fiction does not place excessive demands on its readers. The May 1999 Deseret Book Club *Review* included advertisements for Lund's series on tape; two series by Ron Carter, available simultaneously in both audiocassette and print: (1) the SETTLEMENT SERIES, which includes three titles, *Trial of Mary Lou, Blackfoot Moonshine Rebellion,* and *Royal Maccabees* advertised as "set in the old West, this is hilarious LDS fiction for adults", and (2) the PRELUDE TO GLORY series, of which Volume 1, "Our Sacred Honor," entices readers to follow the epic of "the Dunson family as seen against the backdrop of the compelling story of the birth of America. . . . The events that marked America's beginnings were a prelude to the glory that would arise upon the land through the restoration of the gospel" (10). Blaine and Brenton Yorgason's SODERBERG SAGA is described as a "romp through the Old West with the Soderbergs, a family of Latter-day Saint pioneers who encounter outlaws, marshals, Indians, young love, and polygamy problems" in such titles as *In Search of Steenie Bergman, The Bishop's Horse Race, Brother Brigham's Gold,* and *Seven Days for Ruby,* all published by Horizon of Bountiful, Utah (leaflet loose with *Review*). In addition to his CHILDREN OF THE PROMISE and HEARTS OF THE CHILDREN series, Dean Hughes has steadily produced well-crafted stories for juveniles for decades, including a number that use Mormon and Utah history for their settings, and a genuine history: *The Mormon Church: A Basic History* (Salt Lake City: Deseret Book, 1986).

---

and three networks in Germany.

12. Qtd. in Avant, "Temple Dedicated," 3.

13. Elder Loren and Sister Annette Burton, "Relief Society Origin Observed in Nauvoo," *Church News,* March 27, 1999, 12. The wording is given correctly in the Relief Society's sesquicentennial history: Jill Mulvay Derr, Janath Russell Cannon, and Maureen Ursenbach Beecher, *Women of Covenant: The Story of Relief Society* (Salt Lake City: Deseret Book Company, 1992), 47. (Both Derr and Beecher were employed by Arrington's History Division/Joseph Fielding Smith Institute for LDS History.) It was also quoted correctly in Sheri L. Dew, "Something Extraordinary," *Ensign,* March 1992, 52, and by Dallin H. Oaks, "The Relief Society and the Church," *Ensign,* May 1992, 36, a conference talk delivered on April 7. However, he specified, "No priesthood keys were delivered to the Relief Society."

Excavating Mormon Pasts

Time will tell whether the appetite of Mormon readers for historical epics and romances will remain as insatiable as the national fascination with the genre; but the January 2004 issue of the Deseret Book Club catalog had few historical works besides two Heber J. Grant items (his teachings are the Relief Society/Melchizedek Priesthood quorum curriculum), teachings of David O. McKay, a son's biography of Bruce R. McConkie, three single topics extracted from B. H. Roberts (Missouri, the Mormon Battalion, and Nauvoo), and *My Favorite Church History Stories* for children. Fiction, tellingly labeled "Providing Wholesome Entertainment," includes an item from the Blaine M. Yorgason HEARTS AFIRE series, *Fort on the Firing Line* (settling San Juan region in the late nineteenth century), *Saints and Soldiers* by Jeffrey Scott (which "masterfully fictionalizes the story of five men caught behind enemy lines during World War II. Based on Major Motion Picture . . . ." [capitalization in original], and a novel by Dean Hughes with a modern setting. Did this historical skimpiness manifest Deseret Book's disinterest in history and historical fiction, or was that month's catalog simply swamped by an emphasis on keeping New Year's resolutions (twenty-three items on self-improvement and health) and the recommencement of Book of Mormon study in the Sunday School curriculum (twenty-six items)?

Mormon history is so intensely and so ambiguously tied to our sense of Mormonness, to our theological distinctiveness and commitment, that it is a source of pain and pleasure simultaneously, something to be feared and something to be invoked for comfort. Many Mormons avoid Mormon history. Still others find it the reason for the Church's being and find in this or that historical incident "proof" either of cosmic good or of a human guile that taints claims to divinity. Mormon historical fiction is an attempt to assimilate the past, to make it comprehensible, palatable, understandable, usable. Insider/insider Mormon historical fiction is capable of being assimilated easily—even though the essentialness of its Mormon element is problematic. Mormon history as pageant is comfortingly familiar with its assumptions that all events happened as they did as part of some great design and that the future will be as reassuringly simple as this version of the epic past.

The fear of Mormon history is a valid one. Beyond the romance, the pageant, and the genuine power of faith lie the realities of men and women who loved and lost, were born and died, who lived in a world of fresh bread and peaches but also of tears and blood, furious rage, callous disregard of "lesser" human beings, and soul-crushing conformity. How can we assimilate the fact that they included murderers as well as stoic pillars of faithfulness? If we do not know them, we cannot understand them. If we cannot understand them, we cannot forgive them. If we cannot forgive them, we go into the future maimed, rootless, cut off from our past.

Mormon historical novels have no small task before them. Will our versions of the past become rituals and myths that soothe, comfort, instruct, and inflict guilt but fail to teach us about ourselves? Or will they create fictional pasts that do what literature was created to do and what it alone can do best—to reveal the human heart? Will another Great Gap occur until another expatriate generation speaks its truths in farewell to its heritage? Or will the transformation of Mormonism, caused by sheer size and internationalization, open the windows on forms and discourses that will sweep away boundaries and limitations?

Lavina Fielding Anderson, the owner of Editing, Inc., is the editor of the *Journal of Mormon History* (1991-present) and the *AML Annual*, the publication of the Association for Mormon Letters (1988-2002). She is a past president of AML and, with Eugene England, edited *Tending the Garden: Essays on Mormon Literature* (Salt Lake City: Signature Books, 1996). Her *Lucy's Book: A Critical Edition of Lucy Mack Smith's Family Memoir* (Salt Lake City: Signature Books, 2001) was awarded the Mormon History Association's 2002 Steven F. Christensen Award for Best Documentary and the Best Book Award from the John Whitmer Historical Association.

Index

The subjects of biographies are not included unless they are also discussed in the text. For works on a specific individuals, check for the name in both surname-first and first-name-first order. Theses and dissertations later published under the same title are italicized.

A

"Aalborger en Route: Regette Marie Nielsen's 1863 Emigration Journey, An," 341 note 18
Aaron, Richard I., 161
Abel, Elijah, 383, 385
"'Abominable and Detestable Crime against Nature': A Brief History of Homosexuality and Mormonism, 1840-1980, The," 298 note 51
"Abortion, Politics, and Policy: The Beginning of Actual Human Life," 194
"Abortion, Politics, and Policy: A Deafening Silence in the Church," 194
Abraham Divided: An LDS Perspective on the Middle East, 223
Abrams, Jeremiah, 60 note 3
Abruzzi, William S., 146
Abundant Life: The Memoirs of Hugh B. Brown, An, 299 note 54, 336
accommodation (LDS) to national norms, 17, 24, 165-78, 311. *See also* secularization.
Acevedo, Rudolfo A., 216, 363
"Ada Dwyer: Bright Lights and Lilacs," 289 note 36
"Adam-God Doctrine, The," 157, 243
Adams, Dale W., 62, 83
Adams, George J., 245
Adams, Marguerite I., 364
Adamson, Jack, 68
Additional Studies in Mormonism and Masonry, 26
Address to All Believers in Christ, An, 74-75
ADMINISTRATIVE BIOGRAPHY (series), 260-62
"Adolescent Pregnancy in Utah, 1905-1977," 364
Adventures of a Church Historian, 53, 184, 281 note 15, 340, 373
Africa, Mormonism in, 203, 220-23
African Americans, schismatic movement, 240
African Dragons, 221
African Legacy: Brother to Brother Revisited, Twenty Years of Glory, An, 221
"African Religion & Mormon Doctrine: Comparisons & Commonalities," 223
Africans/African Americans, priesthood ban, 161, 179-80, 192, 207, 221, 343, 383
After 150 Years: The Latter-day Saints in Sesquicentennial Perspective, 17 note 20, 18, 183, 357
"After the Manifesto: Mormon Polygamy and Fundamentalist Mormons," 172, 317
"After the Pioneers: The Experience of Young Men in Union, Utah, 1875-1920," 353
"After the Revolution," 225
Ahlstrom, Sydney E., 131
Aird, Polly, 157
Aizawa, Tomoko, 218
"Albania, a Labor of Love," 226
Albert, Ethel M., 364
Albrecht, Stan L., 184, 210
"Alchemist, The," 47 note 9
Alder, Douglas D., 136, 163, 196, 355
Alexander Schreiner Reminisces, 362 note 6
Alexander, Thomas G.
about, 24, 25, 172, 173, 178, 183, 279
quoted, 5, 274 note 6
works by, xii, 1, 5 note 7, 17 and note 20, 18, 62, 119, 127, 139, 141, 146, 148, 152, 153, 157, 159, 160, 165 note 2, 170, 281, 286, 297 and note 48, 311, 309, 331, 353, 357, 389 note 8
"Alexander William Doniphan: Man of Justice," 92
Alexander William Doniphan: Portrait of a Missouri Moderate, 92, 266
Alger, Fanny, 81, 307
"Alice Merrill Horne, Art Promoter and Early Utah Legislator," 289 note 36, 344
"Alice Smith Edwards: The Little Princess," 346
"Alienation of an Apostle from His Quorum: The Moses Thatcher Case, The," 142 note 10, 151
All Abraham's Children: Changing Mormon Conceptions of Race and Lineage, 192
"All Are Alike unto God," 203
All Are Alike Unto God: Fascinating Conversion Stories of African Saints, 203, 220, 343
"All Gnostics Here," 131 note 3
All God's Critters Got a Place in the Choir, 288
All Is Well, 370
"All on Fire: An Interview with Sonia Johnson," 298 note 53
All the Jews Don't Live in New York City, 224
"'All Things Move in Order in the City': The Nauvoo Diary of Zina Diantha Huntington Jacobs," 127, 279 note 13
Allaman, John Lee, 124
Allegiance and Stewardship: Holy War, Just War, and the Mormon Tradition in the Nuclear Age, 194
Allen, C. Leonard, 34, 36, 54, 126
Allen, James B.
about, 274
quoted, 172, 181, 187
works by, x, 1, 16, 20, 24, 53 note 1, 53-54, 58, 63, 64, 66, 68, 79, 83, 88, 113, 120, 132, 139, 142, 146, 149, 160, 167, 176, 177, 186, 191, 195, 196, 201, 221, 234, 274 note 4, 302 note 67, 305, 324 and note 6, 331, 333, 338, 343, 353, 388
Alley, John R., 338
Allred, Gordon T., 221
Allred, Janice Merrill, 283 note 19, 300 and notes 61-62
Allred, Rulon, 298
"'Almost Like Us': The American Socialization of Australian Converts," 189, 208
"'Almost Too Intolerable a Burthen': The Winter Exodus from Missouri, 1838-39," 108
Alpine, Utah, 18

395

Alston Church (1839), 240
Altman, Irwin, 295
Alvarez, David, 284 note 25
Alvin Journeyman, 375
"Amasa Mason Lyman, the Spiritualist," 142 note 10, 347
America's Saints: The Rise of Mormon Power, 196
American Apochrypha: Essays on the Book of Mormon, 22, 61 note 4
American Civil Liberties Union, 191, 192
American Congregations, 148, 196, 355
American Denominational Organization, 231 note 10
American Indians, 161, 167, 192, 249, 342
American Mainline Religion: Its Changing Shape and Future, 181
American Massacre: The Tragedy at Mountain Meadows, September 1857, 153
American Periodicals: A Journal of History, Criticism, and Bibliography, 223
"American Philanthropy and Mormon Refugees, 1846-1849," 145
American Prophet's Record: The Diaries and Journals of Joseph Smith, xi note 3, 58
American Quest for the Primitive Church, The, 34, 36
American Religion: The Emergence of the Post-Christian Nation, The, 21 note 31, 51, 130, 181 note 4, 243
American Religions and the Rise of Mormonism, 21, 64, 79
American Religious Values and the Future of America, 181 note 4
American Samoa, Mormonism in, 205
"American Siberia: Mormon Prisoners in Detroit in the 1880s, The," 159
Americana, 118
Americanization of Religious Minorities: Confronting the Constitutional Order, The, 24
"Americanization" of Utah for Statehood, The, 24, 159, 168, 311
"'Americanization' of Utah's Agriculture, The," 149
AML Annual, 378 notes 4-5
AML-List, 390 note 9
Ammerman, Nancy T., 229 note 1
Anabaptists and Mormons, 21
"Analysis of Six Contemporary Accounts of Joseph Smith's First Vision, An," 64
"Analysis of the Accounts Relating Joseph's Smith's Early Visions, An," 64
"Analyzing LDS Growth in Guatemala: Report from a Barrio," 215
And the Desert Shall Blossom, 386
"'And the Last Shall be First': The Church of Jesus Christ of Latter-day Saints in the Former East Germany," 226
Andersen, Connie and Ralph, 207
Anderson, Alvin S., 210
Anderson, C. LeRoy, 157, 347
Anderson, Carma DeJong, 363
Anderson, Dawn Hall, 226
Anderson, Desmond L., 219
Anderson, Devery S., 133
Anderson, Karl R., 59, 352
Anderson, Kenneth, 47 note 9
Anderson, Lavina Fielding
   about, 191, 274 note 3, 289 note 36, 300 notes 61-62, 340, 394
   works by, xiv, xiii, 49 note 10, 59, 143, 200, 203, 281 and note 17, 291, 297 notes 48 and 50, 299 note 57, 300 and note 59, 301 note 64, 306, 339, 353, 362, 373, 377, 378 note 5
Anderson, Martha Toronto, 225
Anderson, Max, 321 note 7
Anderson, Nels, 18, 139 note 2, 190
Anderson, Paul L., 361
Anderson, Richard Lloyd
   about, 177 note 5
   works by, 61, 64, 66, 68, 69, 71-72, 75, 80, 84, 92, 101, 105, 106
Anderson, Robert D., 3, 27, 61, 326-27
Anderson, Rodger I., 72
Anderton, Douglas L., 158, 357 and note 4
Andreasen, Bryon C., 136
Andrew, David S., 361
"Andrew Jenson's Danish-Norwegian Mission Presidency, 1909-12," 341 note 18
Andrew, Laurel B., 82, 162, 361
Andrus, Hyrum L., 10, 72, 80, 309
Andrus, Ruth, 363
Angel Acronym, The, 386-87
Angel and the Beehive: The Mormon Struggle with Assimilation, The, 17, 186, 298 note 52
Angola, Mormonism in, 211
Anointed Quorum, 243-44, 247, 274
"Anointed Quorum in Nauvoo, 1842-45, The," 133
"Another Side of Early Mormonism," 49
"Answering Questions No Longer Asked: Nauvoo, Its Meaning and Interpretation in the RLDS/Community of Christ Church," 136
"Anthon Transcript: An Evidence for the Truth of the Prophet's Account of the Origin of the Book of Mormon, The," 74
"Anthon Transcript: People, Primary Sources, and Problems, The," 74
anti-Catholicism, 5
anti-intellectualism. *See* New Mormon History, resistance to.
"Anti-Intellectualism in Mormon History," 299 note 54
anti-Mormonism, 108-10, 123
"Anti-Mormonism in Illinois: Thomas C. Sharp's Unfinished History of the Mormon War, 1845," 123
antipluralism. *See* pluralism.
Antipolygamy Controversy in U.S. Women's Movements, 1880-1925: A Debate on the American Home, The, 159, 160, 287 note 31
Antrei, Albert C. T., 355
"Anxious Saints: The Early Mormons, Social Reform, and Status Anxiety," 73, 130
"Anxiously Engaged: Amy Lyman Brown and Relief Society Charity Work, 1917-45," 172, 345
"Apostate Factions Following the Martyrdom of Joseph Smith," 233
Apostle's Record: The Journals of Abraham H. Cannon, An, 142
"Apostles to the Slavs," 226
"Apostolic Diplomacy: The 1923 European Mission of Senator Reed Smoot and Professor John A. Widtsoe," 178
"Appearance of Elijah and Moses in the Kirtland Temple and the Jewish Passover, The," 83
"Applause, Attack, and Ambivalence: Varied Responses to Fawn M. Brodie's *No Man Knows My History,*" 28, 326
Appleby, R. Scott, 172
Appraisal of the So-Called Brodie Book, 31 note 3
Approach to the Book of Mormon, An, 21
architectural history, 162-63, 360-61
"Architecture on the Frontier: The Mormon Experiment," 82
"Are Latter-day Saints Homeowners?," 183 note 5
"Area Supervision: Administration for a Worldwide Church, 1960-2000," 203
Argentina, Mormonism in, 215, 216
"Army of Israel Marches into Missouri, The," 104
Arrington, Carl, 287
Arrington, Chris Rigby, 281 note 16, 287, 289 note 36
Arrington, Harriet Horne, 289 note 36, 344
Arrington, Joseph Earl, 132
Arrington, Leonard J.
   about, x, xi, xiii, 119, 137, 184, 240, 264, 283, 287, 293, 305, 338, 340, 373, 387, 389
   encouragement of women's history, 275, 277, 280, 289
   quoted, 52, 64, 89, 234, 273 and note 2, 291
   works by, xii, 8, 10, 6 note 11, 17, 24, 30, 49, 53, 54, 59, 61, 62, 66, 68, 79, 83, 88, 116, 117, 120, 127, 139, 140, 141 note 6, 142 and note 10, 143, 144, 146, 148, 149, 153, 155, 163,

Index

165, 167, 170, 173, 178, 274-77, 274 note 6, 281 note 15, 305, 309, 329, 333, 334, 338 note 15, 339, 344, 353, 362, 393 note 13
art history, 360
"Art and Advocacy: Politics and Mormon Letters," 390
Art of Biography, The, 350 note 24
Arthur A. Oakman: An Artist with Words, 265, 346
Arthur H. Clark Co., 152
"Artists, Visual," 360 note 5
"Artworks in the Celestial Room of the First Nauvoo Temple," 133
As a Thief in the Night, 39
"'As Historians and Not as Partisans': The Writing of Official History in the RLDS Church," 120
As Long As I Have You, 381
Ash, Roberta, 231 note 12
Ashby, Charles, 108
Ashment, Edward H., 74
Ashton, Katherine, 378 note 5
Ashurst-McGee, Mark, 42
Asia, Mormonism in, 203, 217-20
Asian American Mormons: Bridging Cultures, 162, 188, 366
Asper, Frank W., 362
"Assimilation and Ambivalence: The Mormon Reaction to Americanization," 186
Association for Mormon Letters, 370, 374, 381, 383, 388, 389, 390
At Odds: Women and the Family in American from the Revolution to the Present, 280 note 14
At Sword's Point: A Documentary History of the Utah War, 1857-1858, 152
"'At Their Peril': Utah Law and the Case of Plural Wives, 1850-1900," 159, 160, 286
Atchison, David R., 92-93, 104, 107
"Atchison's Letter and the Causes of Mormon Expulsion from Missouri," 92, 106
Athearn, Robert G., 148
atheists, and Mormons, 14
Atherton, Judith S. Hanson, 192
"Athletic Program of the Mormon Church: Its Growth and Development, The," 363
"Attempted Assassination of Missouri's Ex-Governor Lilburn W. Boggs, The," 92
"Attuning the Authentic Mormon Voice: Stemming the Sophic Tide in LDS Literature," 390
Audacious Women: Early British Mormon Immigrants, 143, 281 note 17
Austin, Thomas E., 153
Australasia, Mormonism in, 204-8
"Australia: Coming Out of Obscurity Down Under," 208
Austria, Mormonism in, 211
"Authority Conflicts in the Mormon Battalion," 145

"Authorship of the History of Joseph Smith: A Review Essay," 59
Autobiographical and Historical Writings, x note 3
Autobiographies of Mormon Pioneer Women, 279 note 13
Autobiography of Elder Helvécio Martins, The, 343
Autobiography of Percy John Rivers, 205
Avant, Gerry, 381 note 6
Avard, Sampson, 98-99, 101, 102, 103
Averett, Kim C., 133
Avery, Valeen Tippets
about, 274 note 3, 299
quoted, 348
works by, 61, 81, 140, 157 note 17, 243, 264, 289 note 36, 289-91, 313, 315, 343, 344, 345, 352
"Awakenings in the Burned-Over District: New Light on the Historical Setting of the First Vision," 66
"Awesome Power of Sex: The Polemical Campaign against Mormon Polygamy, The," 158

B

"B. H. Roberts, Seeker After Truth," 75
"B. H. Roberts and the Book of Mormon," 75
"B. H. Roberts's Studies of the Book of Mormon," 75
Babbel, Frederick W., 224
Babcock, Maud May, 345
"Babylon in Zion: The LDS Concept of Zion as a Cause for Mormon-Gentile Conflict, 1846-1857," 151
Bachman, Danel C., 74, 82, 310, 343 note 20
Backman, Milton V., Jr., 21, 54, 57, 59, 64, 66, 79, 84, 132, 133, 351, 357
Backslider, The, 388
Backus, Anna Jean, 153, 338
Bagley, Will, 149, 153, 341, 348
Bahr, Stephen J., 357
Bahrain, Mormonism in, 223
Bailey, Paul, 348 note 22, 377
Bailey, Thyrl, 348
Bailyn, Bernard, 12
Bainbridge, William Sims, 231 note 12
Baird, Adelia, 355
Baird, Robert, 14
Baldridge, Kenneth, 205
Baldridge, Steven W., 223
Baldwin, Orval F., II, 145
"Balkan Adventure: Humanitarian Missionaries in Albania," 226
Ballard, Martha, 288
Ballard, Melvin J., 174, 212
Bancroft, Hubert Howe, 114, 130, 131
Bangladesh, Mormonism in, 217
Banigan, Mary J., 364
"Bank Born of Revelation: The Kirtland Safety Society Anti-Banking Co.," 83
Bankhead, Lucile, 385
Banks, Stanley, 249
Banner, Lois, 280 note 14
Barber, Ian G., 208, 251
Barber, Phyllis, 386
Barker, Marilyn C., 361
Barlow, Brent, 210
Barlow, Philip L.
quoted, 34, 48-49
works by, 16, 21, 47 note 9, 76, 131 note 3
Barnes, Jacqueline C., 378 note 4
Barnes, Joseph W., 71 note 11
Barney, Kevin L., 76
Barney, Ronald O., 341
Barr, Roseanne, 348
Barrett, Gwynn W., 151
Barrett, Ivan J., 57, 97, 309
Barrett, Michael, 301
Barrois, Bertrand C., 131 note 3
Barron, Howard H., 62, 141
Barrus, Ruth, 362 and note 7
Barry, Kathleen, 280 note 14
Bartholomew, Rebecca, 143, 144, 281 note 17
Barton, Peggy Petersen, 336
Bashore, Melvin, 159
Batchelor, Mary, 298
Bates, Irene M., 62, 176, 249, 292, 293, 334, 346
Bates, Kerry William, 146
Battle for the Ballot: Essays on Women Suffrage in Utah, 1870-1896, 286
"Battle of Nauvoo Revisited, The," 124
Baugh, Alexander L., 92
about, 111
quoted, 106
works by, 92, 97, 99, 102, 106, 108, 111 and note 23, 133, 341 note 18
"Be Kind to the Poor": The Life Story of Robert Taylor Burton, 141
Beachheads in Micronesia, 207
Bean, Lee L., 158, 357
Bear River Massacre, The, 162, 342
Beasley, William Y., 233
Becker, Howard P., 230 notes 2 and 5
Becker, Josef, 176
"Becoming a World Religion: Blacks, the Poor—All of Us," 201
"Becoming Mormon," 161
Becoming Southern: The Evolution of a Way of Life, Warren County and Vicksburg, Mississippi, 1770-1860, 127
Beecher, Maureen Beecher
about, 274, 277 note 10, 280, 283, 287
quoted, 281-82
works by, 10, 28, 42, 53 note 1, 72, 127, 135, 143, 148, 170, 174, 188, 195, 207, 274 note 4, 279 note 13, 280, 281 notes 15 and 17, 283, 284 and note 25, 289, 295 note 44, 297 note 48, 301, 302 note 67, 305, 306,

397

309, 316, 343, 353, 362, 388, 393 note 13
Beesley, Kenneth H., 219
Beesley, Sterling E., 361
Beeton, Beverly, 286
"Before Stakehood: The Mission Years in Brisbane, Australia," 208
"Before the Wall Fell: The Experience of the Mormons in the German Democratic Republic, 1945-1989," 226
"Begging to Be in the Battle: A Mormon Boy in World War I," 174
"Beginnings of the Church in Thailand, The," 219
Behind the Iron Curtain: Recollections of Latter-day Saints in East Germany, 1945-1989, 225
Behind the Taj Mahal: Spiritual Adventures in India, 220
"Behind the Wall," 225
Belarus, Mormonism in, 225
Belau (Palau), Mormonism in, 207
Belgium, Mormonism in, 211
Believing People: Literature of the Latter-day Saints, A, 369 note 1
Belk, Russell W., 145
Bell, James P., 336
Bennett, John C., 234, 372, 376
Bennett, Keith, 162
Bennett, Richard E., 124, 128, 144, 145, 247, 251, 353
Bennion, Heber, 342
Bennion, Janet, 295
Bennion, John, 296, 342 note 19, 345, 390 note 9
Bennion, Lowell C. "Ben," 148, 158, 180, 203, 212 note 4, 316, 339, 355
Bennion, Sherilyn Cox, 281 note 16, 288 note 32
Benson, Ezra Taft
  about, 190, 219, 220, 224, 300, 333
  works by, 192
Benson, Flora, 224
Bentley, Joseph I., 126
Berger, Peter L., 231 note 14
Bergera, Gary James, 78, 111 note 23, 135, 141 note 7, 158, 190, 191, 192, 248, 329, 339
Bergman, Ray L., 361
Berlin, Linda, 378 note 4
Bernauer, Barbara Hands, 123, 265, 266, 272
Berrett, LaMar C., 133, 224
Berrett, William E., 97, 117, 118
Berthoff, Rowland, 85
Best, Karl F., 77
Best Poor Man's Country: A Geographical Study of Early Southeastern Pennsylvania, The, 128
"Between Biculturalism and Assimilation: The Changing Place of Maori Culture in the Twentieth Century New Zealand Mormon Church," 208
Between Each Line of Pain and Glory: My Life Story, 348
"Between Heaven and Earth: Mormon Theology of the Family in Comparative Perspective—The Shakers, the Oneida Perfectionists, and the Mormons," 358
"Between Revivalism and the Social Gospel: The Latter-day Saint Advisory Committee, 1916-1922," 172
"Between Two Cultures: The Mormon Settlement of Star Valley, Wyoming," 146, 353
"'Between Two Fires': Women on the 'Underground' of Mormon Polygamy," 295
"Between Two Worlds: Plural Marriage and the Experiences of Mormon Women in Illinois during the Early 1840s," 293
"Beyond Fertility: What We Don't Know about Utah Women," 297 note 48
"Beyond Modernity: The Future of the RLDS Church," 269
"Beyond the Manifesto: Polygamous Cohabitation among LDS General Authorities after 1890," 172, 310
"Beyond the Problems of Exceptionalist History," 127, 389 note 8
"Beyond the Veil: Two Latter-day Revelations," 78
Bezzant, John M., 361
Bhutan, Mormonism in, 217
Bible
  influence on Mormonism, 28, 33, 39, 49
  Joseph Smith's revision, 76, 269
"Bibliographical Essay," 113
Bibliography of Social Scientific, Historical, and Popular Writings about Mormon Women, 302 note 67
"Bibliography of the Church of Jesus Christ of Latter-day Saints in New York, Ohio, and Missouri, A," 58
"Bibliography of the Churches of the Dispersion, A," 233
"Bibliography of the Church of Jesus Christ of Latter Day Saints (Strangite), A," 248
Bickertonites, 247
Bidamon, Emma Hale Smith. *See* Smith, Emma Hale.
Biddulph, Howard L., 225
"Big D/little d: The View from the Basement," 292 note 42
Bigelow, Christopher K., 208, 219
Bigler, David L., 149, 167, 170, 178
Bigler, Henry, 168
Bilderback, James C., 26
Bingham, James R., 346
Biographical Sketches of Joseph Smith and His Progenitors for Many Generations, 118
Biography and Truth, 350 note 23
biography, challenges in writing, xiv, 348-50
"Birth of Mormon Hymnody, The," 81
birthright Mormons, 20 note 30
Bishop, Francis Gladden, 244, 347
Bishop, Guy M.
  quoted, 340-41
  works by, xiv, 127, 133, 142, 155, 168, 172, 178, 248, 340 note 16, 347, 352
Bishop's Horse Race, The, 393
Bitton, Davis
  about, 240, 274, 362, 366
  quoted, 47, 48-49, 64, 72, 120, 167, 234, 323-24, 333, 342, 343, 348, 350
  works by, x, xiv, ix, 10, 17, 24, 28, 30, 42, 53 note 1, 54, 68, 83, 84, 123, 131 note 3, 139, 141, 142 and note 10, 145, 146, 148, 155, 157, 158, 161, 170, 188, 207, 249, 274 note 4, 296 note 46, 299 note 54, 305, 308, 309, 324 note 3, 334, 339, 341, 342, 347, 353, 358, 362, 363, 389
"Black Africa: Prepared and Waiting for the Glorious Day," 221
Black and Mormon: Reflections on Latter-day Saint African-Americans since 1978, 192
"Black Mormon Converts in the United States and Africa: Social Characteristics and Perceived Acceptance," 223
Black Saints in a White Church: Contemporary African American Mormons, 162, 188, 343
Black, Susan Easton, 44, 88, 127, 128, 133, 145, 181, 221, 309, 357 note 3
"Black Woman in a White Man's Church: Amy E. Robbins and the Reorganization, A," 292
Blackfoot Moonshine Rebellion, 393
blacks. *See also* race *and* African Americans.
Blair, Alma R., 9, 57, 80, 82, 135, 139, 245, 248, 257, 258, 308
Blakely, Thomas D., 223
Blank, Laurel B., 361
Blanke, Gustav H., 88 and note 2
"Blessed Damozels: Women in Mormon History," 275, 277
"Blessings of the Abrahamic Household, The," 313
Blood of the Prophets: Brigham Young and the Massacre at Mountain Meadows, 153
Bloom, Harold
  about, 131 and note 3, 243
  quoted, 21 note 31
  works by, 51, 130, 131, 181 note 4
"Blooming France, A," 211
"Blossoming of the Church in Japan, The," 218
Bloxham, V. Ben, 208
Blueprints for Living: Perspectives for LDS Women, 289 note 36
"Bluestocking in Zion: The Literary Life of Emmeline B. Wells, A," 284, 344

Index

Blumell, Bruce D., 174
Blumin, Stuart, 85
"Board of Regents of the University of Utah, 1850-1920: Historical Development and Prosopography, The," 358
Boggs, Lilburn W., 92, 104, 108, 111
Bohn, David Earl, ix
Bolivia, Mormonism in, 216
Bolton, Matthew, 270
Bonar, Linda L., 361
Bonds of Sisterhood: A History of the RLDS Women's Organization, 1842-1893, 266, 291 note 37, 292
Bonds of Womanhood: Woman's Sphere in New England, 1780-1835, The, 280 note 14
Bones, 380-81
"Book Explores Joseph Smith and Alchemy," 47 note 9
Book of Abraham, 76-77, 254
"'Book of Abraham' in the Light of History and Egyptology, The," 77, 267
Book of Commandments. *See* Doctrine and Covenants.
Book of Mormon. *See also* Alexander Campell *and* Solomon Spaulding.
 as autobiography, 3-4, 327, 328
 as organizational model, 241
 as religious thought, 8
 environmental influences on, 21-22, 30, 32, 42, 43
 historicity of, 61, 63 and note 5, 71-76, 257, 266-68, 269
 twentieth century sales, 201
Book of Mormon: A Reader's Edition, The, 71 note 8
"Book of Mormon and the Anthon Transcript: An Interim Report, The," 74
"Book of Mormon and the American Revolution, The," 21, 72
"Book of Mormon as a Modern Expansion of an Ancient Source, The," 73
Book of Mormon Authorship: New Light on Ancient Origins, 72, 73
"Book of Mormon Goes to Press, The," 73
"Book of Mormon in a Biblical Culture, The," 16, 73
"Book of Mormon Usage in Early LDS Theology," 72, 73
"Book of Mormon in Early Mormon History, The," 42, 72
Boone, David F., 200
Booth, Ezra, 240
Booth, Wayne, 20
"Bootlegging in Zion: Making and Selling the 'Good Stuff,'" 173
"Border Crossings," 288 note 34
Boren, Murray, 223
Borglum, Gutzon, 348
Borglum, James, 348
Borglum, Solon Hannibal, 348

Bosquejo de la Historia de la Iglesia en Venezuela, Un [An Account of the History of the Church in Venezuela], 216
Bound for Canaan, 383
Bowden, Henry Warner, 131
Bowen, Albert E., 31 and note 3
Boyd K. Packer: A Watchman on the Tower, 338
Boynton, John F., 240
Braby, Junia, 270
Brackenridge, R. Douglas, 163
Bradford, Gordon Richard, 176
Bradford, Mary Lythgoe, 287 note 27, 292 and note 42, 298 note 53, 339, 341 note 18, 378 note 4
Bradley, Martha Sonntag
 about, 322, 328, 390
 works by, xiv, 61, 143, 161, 170, 193, 287 note 30, 289 note 36, 294-95, 298 note 52, 306, 315, 321 and note 7, 345, 348, 355, 361, 362
Brady, Margaret K., 287 note 30, 344
"Branch [Selbongen] that Wouldn't Die, The," 225
Brannan, Samuel, 144, 348
"'Brass Plates' and Biblical Scholarship, The," 73
Brazil, Mormonism in, 215, 216
Break, Nancy J., 82
"Breakthrough in Britain: The 1950s, '60s, and '70s Brought Great Growth and Stability to the Church," 210
Brenchley, Julius, 5
Brewster, James Colin, 232, 245
Bridgeforth, Ruffin, 385
Brief History of the Church of Christ of Latter Day Saints, A, 97
Brief History of the Tongan Mission of the Church of Jesus Christ of Latter-day Saints, 205
Briggs, Jason W., 268, 271
Brigham, Janet, 207, 223
"Brigham and the Bishops: The United Order in the City," 149
"Brigham Bicknell Young, Musical Christian Scientist," 348
"Brigham Himself: An Autobiographical Recollection," 140
Brigham Young, 8
Brigham Young: American Moses, 8, 62, 139, 309, 329
"Brigham Young and Mormon Indian Policies: The Formative Period, 1836-1851," 161
Brigham Young and the Expanding American Frontier, 8, 62, 140, 331 note 11
"Brigham Young in Life and Death: A Medical Overview," 140
Brigham Young: Modern Moses, Prophet of God, 140 note 4
Brigham Young the Colonizer, 146
Brigham Young University
 about, 339, 390
 Semester Abroad, 224
 symposia, 200, 208

Brigham Young University: A House of Faith, 191
Brigham Young University and the People's Republic of China: The First Five Years, 217
Brigham Young University—Hawaii, 2055
"Brigham Young's Family: The Wilderness Years," 140, 329 note 10
Brigham Young's Homes, 140
"Brigham Young's Outer Cordon: A Reappraisal," 146
"Brigham Young's Overland Trails Revolution: The Creation of the 'Down-and-Back' Wagon-Train System, 1860-61," 145
Brigham's Day, 387
Brimhall, George H., 6 and note 13
Brimhall, Sandra Dawn, 289 note 36
Bringhurst, George S., 342
Bringhurst, John T., 342
Bringhurst, Mary ("Mayme"), 342
Bringhurst, Newell G.
 quoted, 27, 28
 works by, xiii, 8, 28, 49 note 10, 62, 124, 140, 161, 177, 192, 223, 221, 249, 274 note 5, 275 note 9, 293, 299 note 55, 326, 328 note 9, 331 note 11, 333, 343, 347, 349, 350
Bringhurst, Samuel E., 342
Bringhurst, William, 342 and note 19
Brink, T. L., 3, 27
British Isles, Mormonism in, 208-10, 212
Britsch, R. Lanier
 about, 220
 works by, 146, 200, 204, 205, 207, 217, 218, 386
Brockbank, Bernard P., 218
Brodie, Bernard, 28
Brodie, Fawn McKay
 about, xii, 1, 3, 5-6 note 12, 8 and note 15, 28, 30, 60, 69, 71, 72, 74-75, 130, 176, 177, 268, 299, 306-7, 324-26, 340
 quoted, ix and note 1, 10, 22, 27, 28 and note 1, 71, 63-64
 works by, 3, 49, 63, 74 note 13, 119, 234, 274-75, 291, 304, 327, 343 note 20
"Brodie Revisited: A Reappraisal," 326
Brooke, John L.
 about, 23, 44 and note 8, 45-49, 47 note 9, 69, 131 and note 3
 quoted, 20-21, 48
 works by, xi, 44, 69, 130, 243, 272
Brooks, Juanita
 about, xii, 176, 177, 287, 299, 340
 works by, 142, 153, 274-75, 281 note 16, 344
Brooks, Karl F., 355
Brooks, Zodac, 245
Brother Brigham, 140 note 4, 388
Brother Brigham's Gold, 393
"Brother Joseph Is Truly a Wonder-

399

Excavating Mormon Pasts

ful Man, He Is All We Could Wish a Prophet to Be': Pre-1844 Letters of William Law," 244
Brother to Brother: The Story of the Latter-day Saint Members Who Took the Gospel to Black Africa, 221
Brough, Monte J., 220
Brown, Amy Lyman, 172
Brown, Hugh B.
 about, 191, 299 note 54, 336
 works by, 218, 295
Brown, Joseph E., 144
Brown, Larry, 223
Brown, Lisle G., 133
Brown, Marilyn, 387
Brown, S. Kent, 61 note 4, 180
Brown, Samuel C., 245
Brown, Zina Card, 295, 345
Browning, Gary, 225, 226
Bruce R. McConkie: Highlights from His Life and Teachings, 338
Bruce, Steve, 230 note 5, 232 note 15
Brummett, Linda, 388
Brunson, L. Madelon, 265, 266, 291 note 37, 292
Buchanan, Frederick S., 162, 190, 191, 348
Buchanan, James, 152
"Buchanan Spoils System and the Utah Expedition: The Careers of W. M. F. Magraw and John M. Hockaday, The," 152
Buerger, David John, 78, 133, 157, 243
Builders of the Kingdom: George A. Smith, John Henry Smith, George Albert Smith, 142 note 10, 331, 334
"Building a Commonwealth: The Secular Leadership of Brigham Young," 140
"Building of the Kirtland Temple, The," 82
Building the City of God: Community and Cooperation among the Mormons, 10, 79, 88, 149, 305
"Building the Kingdom of God: Alpheus Cutler and the Second Mormon Mission to the Indians, 1847-1853," 249
"Building Wilkinson's University," 339
"Building Zion: Folk Architecture in the Mormon Settlements of Utah's Sanpete Valley, 1849-1890," 361
Building Zion: The Latter-day Saints in Europe, 177, 210, 224
Bulgaria, Mormonism in, 225
Bullard, Richard, 83
Bullock, Stephen C., 25 note 39
Bump, James, 245
Bunker, Gary L., 155, 158
Burden of Southern History, The, 18 note 21
"Bureaucratization and Social Change in Rural Agricultural Communities: Sevier County, Utah,

1900-1930," 353
Burgess-Olson, Vicky, 143, 160, 289, 306, 344
Burke, Frank E., 357
Burke, Lee H., 355
Burma (Myanmar), Mormonism in, 217
Burned-Over District: The Social and Intellectual History of Enthusiastic Religion in Western New York, 1800-1850, xi, 9, 32, 79, 130
Burnett, Stephen, 240
Burning Bush: Revelation and Scripture in the Life of the Church, The, 73, 76
Burton, Loren and Annette, 393 note 13
Burton, Richard Francis, 5, 6 note 12
Busche, F. Enzio, 211
Bush, Alfred L., 26, 80
Bush, George, 340
Bush, Lester E., Jr., 74, 78, 140, 155, 158, 192, 363, 383
Bush, Laura, 297 note 49
Bushman, Claudia L.
 about, 277
 quoted, 288
 works by, 143, 287 and note 29, 288 note 32, 302 note 67, 306, 344
Bushman, Richard L.
 about, 21, 23, 131, 366
 quoted, 4, 5, 22, 42, 44, 48, 51, 326
 works by, 4 note 3, 4 note 5, 47 note 9, 49, 51, 53, 54, 61, 66, 69, 72, 108, 117, 128-29, 243, 328 note 9
Butch Cassidy: A Biography, 348
Butler, Janet G., 281 note 16
Butler, John Lowe, 101, 338
By His Own Hand Upon Papyrus: A New Look at the Joseph Smith Papyri, 77
By Study and Also by Faith, 63
"By the Gift and Power of God," 74
By the Hand of Mormon: The American Scripture that Launched a New World Religion, 52, 61 note 4
"BYU Rejects LDS Pulitzer Prize Winner as Speaker," 288 note 35
BYU Studies, 66, 69, 302, 352
"BYU—Hawaii: A Promise in the Pacific," 2055

C

Cache Valley: Essays on Her Past and People, 355
Cahoon, Reynolds, 101
Caldwell, Ray, 221
Call, Anson B., 101
Call, Hannah S., 213
Call, Lowell E., 219
Call of Zion: The Story of the First Welsh Mormon Emigration, The, 145, 162
Call to Arms: The 1838 Mormon Defense of Northern Missouri, A, 92, 97, 99, 102, 106, 108, 111
*Call to Russia: Glimpses of Missionary Life from the Journal of a Mission Presi-

dent in the Russia St. Petersburg Mission, A*, 225
Calley, Malcolm J. C., 231 note 13
Cambodia, Mormonism in, 217, 220
Camilla: A Biography of Camilla Eyring Kimball, 344
Camp Floyd and the Mormons: The Utah War, 152-53
"Camp in the Sagebrush: Camp Floyd, Utah, 1858-1861," 153
"Campaign and the Kingdom: The Activities of the Electioneers in Joseph Smith's Presidential Campaign, The," 124
Campbell, Alexander
 about, 3, 4, 5, 8, 73
 quoted, 30 and note 2, 72
 works by, 3 note 2, 4 note 4, 72 note 12
Campbell, Bruce L., 161, 295
Campbell, Colin, 230 note 5
Campbell, Eugene E., 139, 144-46, 161, 187, 295, 297 note 48, 336
Campbellites, 36
Campora, Olga Kovarova, 225
Can Two Walk Together Unless They Be Agreed? American Religious Schisms in the 1970s, 231 note 11
Cannon, Abraham H., 142
Cannon, Angus, 344
Cannon, Blanche, 377
Cannon, Charles A., 158
Cannon, Donald Q.
 about, 228
 quoted, 340
 works by, xiv, 59, 128, 132, 133, 142, 200, 210, 212, 224, 289 note 36, 323 note 1, 340 note 16, 361
Cannon, Edwin, 221
Cannon, Elaine, 360
Cannon Family Historical Treasury, 142 note 10
Cannon, George Q., 334
Cannon, Hal, 360
Cannon, Janath Russell, 135, 142 note 10, 174, 195, 221, 284, 393 note 13
Cannon, Kenneth L., II, 159, 172, 310, 348, 363
Cannon, Louie Wells, 284
Cannon, M. Hamlin, 59
Cannon, Martha Hughes, 289, 388
Cannon, Tracy Y., 362
Cannon, William W., 207
Card, Brigham Y., 146, 315
Card, Charles O., 295
Card, Orson Scott, 210, 374-75, 367, 388
Card, Zina Young Williams, 295, 345
Carmack, John K., 220
Carmack, Noel A., 301, 347
Carmichael, Sarah Elizabeth, 345
Carnes, Mark C., 25 note 39
Carroll, Berenice A., 280 note 14
Carter, Kate, 233, 240
Carter, Ron, 393
Carter, Thomas R., 162, 360, 361

Index

Carthage Conspiracy: The Trial of the Accused Assassins of Joseph Smith, 123
Case Reports of the Mormon Alliance, 300 notes 61-62
Cash, W. J., 18 note 21
Cassidy, Butch, 348
Catholics and Mormons, 14, 16
"Causes of the Utah War Reconsidered," 152
Cavalier and Yankee: The Old South and American National Character, 18 note 21
Cazier, Stanford, 277
"C.C.A. Christensen as Editor, Poet, and Apologist," 341 note 18
"Celestial Family: Early Mormon Thought on Life and Death, 1830-1846, The," 127, 352
"Center Place Saints: A Survey of Restoration Fragmentation in Zion," 238, 240
Central America, Mormonism in, 213-15
Century of Struggle: The Woman's Rights Movement in the United States, 280 note 14
Chadwick, Bruce A., 184, 297 note 48
"Challenge and Craft of Mormon Biography, The," 324 note 4, 333, 350
"Challenge of Africa, The," 221
"Challenge of Historical Consciousness: Mormon History and the Encounter with Secular Modernity, The," 63
"Challenge of Mormon Biography, The," 324 note 6
"Challenge to Centralized Power: Zenas H. Gurley, Jr., and The Prophetic Office, The," 263
"Challenges of Administering a Worldwide Church, The," 203
"Challenges of the Second Century," 211
Chancing It: Why We Take Risks, 183
Chandler, Michael, 77
"Change and Growth: The Mormon Church in the 1960s," 192
"Changed Faces: The Official LDS Position on Polygamy, 1880-1900," 170, 321 note 7
"Changes in the Revelations, 1833 to 1835," 77
"Changing Perspectives on Sexuality and Marriage," 358
"Changing Relief Society Charity to Make Way for Welfare, 1930-1944," 283 note 23
"Changing RLDS Response to Mormon Polygamy: A Preliminary Analysis, The," 81, 82, 269, 308
"'Changing Times Bring Changing Conditions': Relief Society, 1960 to the Present," 195
Changing World of Mormonism, The, 17 note 19
"Character of Joseph Smith: Insights from his Holographs, The," 72
Chard, Gary Ray, 211
"Charles B. Thompson and the Issues of Slavery and Race," 249, 347
Charles C. Rich: Mormon General and Western Frontiersman, 142 note 10, 334
Charles, Melodie Moench, 283, note 21
Charles Neff: Missionary and Humanitarian, 270
"Charles Ora Card and the Founding of the Mormon Settlements in Southwestern Alberta, North-West Territories," 316
"Charles S. Whitney: A Nineteenth-Century Salt Lake City Teenager's Life," 362
"Charles S. Zane, Apostle of the New Era," 159
"Charley Walker, Dixie Pioneer," 142
Charter for Statehood: The Story of Utah's Constitution, 168
"Chartering the Kirtland Bank," 83
"Charting a New Course in Micronesia," 207
Chase, Lance D., 204
"Chauncey West: Nineteenth-Century Teenager," 362
Cheesman, Paul R., 64
Cheney, Thomas E., 159, 336
Cherry Tree behind the Iron Curtain: The Autobiography of Martha Toronto Anderson, A, 225
Chesterfield: Mormon Outpost in Idaho, 353
Chevigny, Bell, 280 note 14
Cheville, Roy A., 307
"Chiasmas in the Book of Mormon," 73
Chief: An Administrative Biography of Fred M. Smith, The, 262, 345
"Chief Justice Waite and the 'Twin Relic': Reynolds vs. United States," 159
"Childhood Experiences in Mormon Polygamous Families at the Turn of the Century," 362
"Childhood in Gunnison, Utah," 362
Children of God: An American Epic, 379
CHILDREN OF THE PROMISE (series), 381-83, 393
Children Sang: The Life and Music of Evan Stephens, The, 361
Chile, Mormonism in, 216, 227
"China and the Restored Church," 219
China, Mormonism in, 217
"Chinese Christianity since 1849: Implications for the Church of Jesus Christ of Latter-day Saints," 218
"Chinese Participation in the Church of Jesus Christ of Latter-day Saints (Mormon) in Hong Kong," 219
Choi, Dong S., 218
"Christ-Centered Boredom: History and Historians," 269, 270
Christensen, Craig G., 219
Christensen, Harold T., 364
Christensen, James R., 200
Christensen, Marius A., 211
Christensen, Scott R., 161, 342
Christian, Lewis Clark, 144
Christian primitivism and Mormonism, 28, 34-39
"Christian Soldiers or Conscientious Objectors?," 194
"Christian Values and Ethnic Diversity: How Much of a Country's Culture Can a Christian Convert Keep?," 200
Christiansen, Larry D., 145
Christofferson, Gregory, 341 note 18
"Christopher S. Winge: Norwegian Missionary and His Long-Lost 1859 Diary," 341 note 18
Christy, Howard A., 162, 331
"Chronology of Danite Meetings in Adam-ondi-Ahman, Missouri, July to September 1838, A," 99
"Chronology of the Ohio Revelations, The," 77
Chu, Gary G. Y., 218
Chubby, William, 240
"Church and Colonel Sanders: Mormon Standard Plan Architecture, The," 361
"Church and Politics and the IWY Conference," 193, 298 note 52
"Church Comes of Age in Britain, The," 210
"Church Development Issues among Latin Americans," 212
Church Education System, 201, 211
Church Encounters Asia, The, 217
"Church Growth in the British Isles, 1937-1987," 208
"Church in Africa, The," 221
"Church in Asia, The," 217
"Church in Central America, The," 213
"Church in Europe, The," 210
"Church in French-Speaking Europe, The," 211
"Church in Germany, Austria, and Switzerland, The," 211
"Church in India, Pakistan, Bangladesh, and Sri Lanka, The," 220
"Church in Italy, The," 211
"Church in Japan, The," 218
"Church in Korea, The," 218
"Church in Latin America: Progress and Challenge, The," 213
"Church in New York and Pennsylvania, 1816-1831, The," 57
"Church in Scandinavia and Finland, The," 211
Church in the Twentieth Century, The, 176, 177, 186, 201

401

"Church in the South Pacific, The," 204
"Church in the United Kingdom and Ireland, The," 210
"Church in the Orient, The," 217
"Church in the Far East, The," 217
"Church Moves Outside the United States: Some Observations from Latin America, The," 189, 212
Church of Christ (founded by Chubby), 240
Church of Christ (1836), 240
Church of Christ (1837), 240
Church of Christ (1842), 244
Church of Jesus Christ (Cutlerite), 249
Church of Jesus Christ of Latter Day Saints (Little Sioux, Iowa), 244
Church of Jesus Christ of the Children of Zion, 248
Church of Jesus Christ, The Bride The Lamb's Wife (1840), 240
"Church Politics and Sonia Johnson: The Central Conundrum," 193
"Church Schism and Secession: A Necessary Sequence?," 231 note 9
Church through the Years, The, 54, 120, 136, 233 note 16, 234, 263, 291 note 37
"Church's Cross-Cultural Encounters, The," 203
"Church's Image in Italy from the 1840s to 1946: A Bibliographic Essay, The," 155
"Churches of the Dispersion," 19 note 27
"Circleville Massacre: A Brutal Incident in Utah's Black Hawk War, The," 162
"Circumstantial Confirmation of the First Vision through Reminiscences," 64, 66
City of Refuge: Quincy, Illinois, A, 128
City of the Saints and across the Rocky Mountains to California, The, 6 note 12
"'City on a Hill': Chartering the City of Nauvoo, A," 124
"Clarifications of Boggs's 'Order' and Joseph Smith's Constitutionalism," 92, 101, 106
"Clarifying the Cult," 230 note 5
Clark, David L., 128
Clark, J. Reuben, Jr., 173, 191, 301, 336
Clark, James R., 149
Clark, Janice, 205, 219
Clark, Stephen C., 192
Clark, Wycam, 240
Clash of Cultures: The Norwegian Experience with Mormonism, 1842-1920, 364
CLASSICS IN MORMON LITERATURE, 118
Clawson, David L., 213
Clawson, Ellen Spencer, 168
Clawson, Mary Ann, 25 note 39
Clawson, Moses, 101

Clay County. *See* Missouri period.
Clayton, Ruth Vickers, 363
Cleaver, Eldridge, 349
Clebsch, William A., 129
Cleland, Robert, 275
Clement, Russell T., 204, 205
Clifton, Carmin, 225
Clio Was a Woman: Studies in the History of American Women, 280 note 14
Clio's Consciousness Raised: New Perspectives on the History of Women, 280 note 14
"Cloning of Mormon Architecture, The," 361
"Close-Up of Polygamy, A," 275
"Clothed with Bonds of Charity: The Law of Consecration and Stewardship in Ohio, 1830-1838," 79
Clothier, Richard, 270
"Clothing and the Temporal Kingdom," 363
Coates, Lawrence G., 161 and note 18
Cobb, Camillia Clara Mieth, 345
Coe, Joseph, 240
Cohen, Charles L., 47 and note 9, 48
Cohn, Norman, 60 note 3
"Coin and Currency in Early Utah," 149
Cole, Abner, 71
Coleman, James S., 231 note 7
"Colesville Branch and the Coming Forth of the Book of Mormon, The," 73
Collier, Fred C., 248
Collins, William, 76
Colonia Juárez: An Intimate Account of a Mormon Village, 213
Colonization on the Little Colorado: The Joseph City Region, 355
colonization. *See* settlement, Utah period.
Colonna, Edward, 331
Colvin, Don F., 133
Combs, Daniel, 192
Come, Lord, Come: A History of the Church of Jesus Christ of Latter-day Saints in Romania, 225
"Coming of Age in a Western Farm Community: Union, Utah, 1900-1910," 172, 353
"Commencement of the Godbeite Protest: Another View, The," 157, 347
"Comment on Joseph Smith's Account of His First Vision and the 1820 Revival, A," 66
"Common Beginnings, Divergent Beliefs," 136
Communism, 224, 225, 226
community and Mormonism, 78-80, 127-29, 146, 148, 196, 351-52
Community of Christ
about, x, xiv, 82, 90, 97, 120, 135-36, 232, 157, 247, 253-72
and Cutlerites, 249
and historiography, 164

attitudes toward race and ethnicity, 161
and cultural accommodation, 19-20
biographies, 345-46
Emma Smith's support of, 289
histories of, 53, 54, 97, 117, 118, 120, 136, 233 note 16, 234, 262-63, 291 note 37. *See also* individual works.
identity and history, 233 note 16, 257
schism in, 232, 245. *See also* dissent.
treatment of polygamy, 307-8
women's ordination, 269, 299
"Comparing Three Approaches to Restorationism: A Response," 37 note 6
Compier, Don H., 269, 308
"Composition and History of the Book of Mormon," 73
Comprehensive History of the Church of Jesus Christ of Latter-day Saints, A, 23, 97, 118, 174
Compton, Annie Rosella, 362 note 6
Compton, Todd
about, 302
works by, xiv, 49 note 10, 82, 92, 121, 244, 275 note 9, 279 note 13, 283 note 21, 291, 295 note 44, 296 note 47, 301, 315, 343
"Concepts in American Local History: Community in Winder, Idaho," 353
Concise History of the Mormon Battalion in the Mexican War, 1846-1847, A, 145
Condie, Richard P., 362
Condie, Spencer J., 200, 225, 338
"Confirming Records of Moroni's Coming," 64
Conflict and Compromise: The Mormons in Mid-Nineteenth Century American Politics, 151
Conflict at Kirtland: The Nature and Causes of Internal and External Conflict of the Mormons in Ohio between 1830 and 1838, 80
"Conflict in the Camps of Israel: The Emergence of the 1853 Cutlerite Schism," 249
"Conflict in the Countryside: The Mormon Settlement at Macedonia, Illinois," 121, 352
Conflict in the Quorum: Orson Pratt, Brigham Young, Joseph Smith, 141 note 7, 158, 248, 329
"Confronting Turbulent Environments: Issues in the Organizational Growth and Globalization of Mormonism," 201
Congregation of Jehovah's Presbytery of Zion, 249
Conkling, J. Christopher, 60
Conkling, Winifred, 340
Connor, Patrick Edward, 143
consecration and stewardship. *See* economics.
"Consequential Dimension of Mor-

Index

mon Religiosity, The," 184
Constructing Brotherhood: Class, Gender, and Fraternalism, 25 note 39
contemporary history, challenges of, 297
"Contemporary Church, The," 208
Contemporary Mormonism: Social Science Perspectives, 184, 201, 216, 223, 297 note 48, 364
Contemporary Views of Mormon Origins (1830), 59
"Contours of the Kingdom: An RLDS Perspective on the Legions of Zion," 105
"Contracting for the Union Pacific," 148
"Conversation in Nauvoo about the Corporeality of God," 132
"Conversion of Sidney Rigdon to Mormonism, The," 62
"Conversion to Protestantism and Social Change in a Bolivian Aymara Community," 216
Cook Islands, Mormonism in, 205
Cook, Lyndon W., x, xi note 3, 59, 76, 79, 88-89, 132, 244, 309, 346
Cook, Mary Nielsen, 219
Cooke, Sarah Ann Sutton, 345
Cooley, Everett L., 142
Cooper, Rex Eugene, 79, 131, 243, 319, 364
Cope, Rachel, 124
Copeland, Lee, 189
Corbett, Pearson H., 61, 334
Corcoran, Brent D., 298 note 51, 358
Cornwall, J. Spencer, 362
Cornwall, Marie, 158, 184, 195, 201, 223, 296, 297 note 48, 364
Cornwall, Rebecca Foster, 155, 289
Correct Account of the Murder of Generals Joseph and Hyrum Smith at Carthage on the 27th Day of June, 1844, A, 123
correlation program, 194-95
Corrill, John, 97-98, 102, 103, 105, 107
Cosic, Kresimir, 225
Cosmos and History: The Myth of the Eternal Return, 130
Cott, Nancy, 280 note 14
Cottle, T. Jeffery, 133
Council of Fifty, 10, 104, 124, 149, 241, 244, 245, 247, 248, 249
"Council of Fifty and Its Members, 1844-1945, The," 10, 149, 244
"Counseling the Brethren," 288 note 34
Counselors to the Prophets, 172
"Counter-Revolution: The Mormon Reaction to the Coming of American Democracy," 54, 68, 72, 109
Courage: A Journal of History, Thought, and Action, x, 267
"'Course Corrections': Some Personal Reflections," 195
Courtright, Camela, 158, 296
Cowan, Richard O., 76, 133, 176, 177, 186, 196, 200, 201, 203, 210, 224
Cowdery, Oliver, 61, 74, 81, 84, 90, 97, 105, 237, 245, 266, 307 and note 4, 328
Cowdery, Warren A., 81, 307 note 4
Cowles, Austin, 244, 347
Cowley, Matthew, 218
Cowley, Matthias F., 294
Coy, David Dale, 341 note 18
Cracroft, Richard H.
 about, 324
 quoted, 338, 370, 373-74, 376, 390
 works by, 64, 323 note 2, 324, 369 and note 1, 379
Craig, Wesley W., Jr., 213
Crawley, Peter, 58, 66, 84, 105
"Creating a Farm Community: Fountain Green Township, 1825-1840," 128
"Creating a New Alphabet for Zion: The Origin of the Deseret Alphabet," 163
"Creating Female Community: Relief Society in Cache Valley, Utah, 1868-1900," 284 note 25
Creer, Leland H., 6, 146, 151
Cresap, McCormack, and Paget, 195
Cresswell, Stephen, 159-60
"Crime and Punishment in Mormon Nauvoo, 1839-1846," 123, 352
"Crisis Averted? General Harney and the Change in Command of the Utah Expedition, A," 152
"Crisis in Zion: Heber J. Grant and the Panic of 1893," 173
"Critical Examination of *No Man Knows My History,* by Fawn M. Brodie," 31-32
"Critical Function of *Courage,*" 267
Croatia, Mormonism in, 225
Crockett, David R., 133
Cronon, William, 79 note 14
Cross, Whitney R., xi, 9, 32, 79, 130
Crossfire: The Eight Years with Eisenhower, 192
Crow, Charles L., 21 note 31
Crowley, Ariel L., 74
Crown of Glory: The Life of James J. Strang, 346
Crystal City, The, 375
Cullen, Margaret, 294
cult, defined, 230 note 5
"Cult of True Womanhood: 1820-1860, The," 280 note 14
Culture Clash and Accommodation: Public Schooling in Salt Lake City, 1890-1994, 191
"Cultural Conflict: Mormons and Indians in Nebraska," 161 note 18, 161
"Cultural Conflicts: History Served on the Half Shell," 121
"Cultural Crisis in the Mormon Kingdom: A Reconsideration of the Causes of Kirtland Dissent," 84, 240
"Cultural Impact of Mormon Missionaries on Taiwan, The," 219
culture, and Mormonism, 1-26, 27-52, 72, 187-89, 203, 221, 223, 227, 351-66
Cultures in Conflict: A Documentary History of the Mormon War in Illinois, 121, 136, 243, 264
Cumming, Albert, 143
Cummings, C. A., 186 note 6
Cummings, David W., 207
Curbelo, Néstor, 215, 364
Curtis, Kirk M., 361
Curtis, William J., 111 note 22
Cuthbert, Derek A., 208, 210
Cuthbert, Muriel, 210
Cutler, Alpheus, 232, 245-47, 249, 347
"Cutler's Camp at the Big Grove on Silver Creek: A Mormon Settlement in Iowa, 1847-1853," 249
Cutlerites, 247, 249, 251
"Cutlerites of Southwestern Iowa: A Latter-day Saint Schism, 1846-1865," 249
Czechoslovakia, Mormonism in, 225, 226

D

Dahl, Curtis, 71 note 9
Dahl, Larry E., 132
"Dale L. Morgan," 176
Dale Morgan on Early Mormonism: Correspondence and a New History, 1 note 1, 8 note 15, 31 note 3, 40, 176, 339
Dallimore, LuDene, 378 note 4
"Dam for Nauvoo: An Attempt to Industrialize the City, A," 126
"Dancing the Buckles off Their Shoes in Pioneer Utah," 363
Daniel Hanmer Wells, 141 note 8
Daniels, Richard, 226
Daniels, William M., 123
Danish Apostle: The Diaries of Anthon H. Lund, 336
"Danish Family Influences in the Adult Fiction of Virginia Sorensen Waugh," 341 note 18
"Danish Genesis of Virginia Sorensen's Novel *Lotte's Locket,* The," 341 note 18
"Danite Band of 1838, The," 99
Danites, 87, 97, 98-104, 107, 111, 234, 338
"Danites Reconsidered: Were They Vigilantes or Just the Mormon Version of the Elks Club?, The," 103
Dant, Doris R., 148, 362, 366
Daughters of Light, 298
David B. Haight: The Life Story of a Disciple, 338
"David Eccles: A Man for His Time," 338 note 15
David Eccles: Pioneer Western Industrialist, 338

403

"David H. Smith's Relationship with the Muse of Mormon History," 235
David Matthew Kennedy: Banker, Statesman, Churchman, 224
"David Whitmer: Faithful Dissenter, Witness Apart," 22-24, 61, 75, 241
"David Whitmer: Unique Missouri Mormon," 75
Davidson, Karen Lynn, 143, 284, 301, 343
Davies, Douglas J., 47 note 9, 162, 203, 364
Davies, J. Kenneth, 146, 149
Davies, Mark, 203
Davis, David Brion
  quoted, 33, 329
  works by, xi, 9-10, 12, 73, 79
Davis, Garold N., and Norma S., 225
Davis, Inez Smith, 97, 117, 118, 262
Davis, James E., 127
Davis, Norma S., 339, 360
Davis, Robert O., 360
Davis, Rodney O., 121
"Dawning of a New Day in Africa, The," 223
Dawning of a Brighter Day: The Church in Black Africa, The, 221
Dawson, Christopher, 231 note 7
Daynes, Kathryn M., 25, 158, 168, 296, 316, 321
de Trobriand, George Phillipe Regis, 143
De Pillis, Mario S.
  about, 33, 119, 270
  quoted, 22, 73
  works by, 9, 17, 22 note 33, 27, 32, 49 note 10, 74 note 13, 79, 85, 128-29, 130, 181, 188
"Dealing with Social Change: The Mormon Church's Response to Change in Women's Roles," 297 note 48
Dean, Bruce J. M., 218
Dear Ellen: Two Mormon Women and Their Letters, 168, 279 note 13
"Death of Brigham Young: Occasion for Satire, The," 155
"Decade of Détente: The Mormon-Gentile Female Relationship in Nineteenth-Century Utah," 286
Decker, Ed, 17 note 19
"Decline in Convert Baptisms and Member Emigration from the British Mission after 1870, The," 155
"Decoding Mormonism," 47 note 9
Decoo, Wilfred, 177-78, 211
"Dedication of Kirtland Temple," 83
Defender of the Faith: The B. H. Roberts Story, 336
Degler, Carl N., 18 note 21, 280 note 14
deists and Mormons, 14
Delafosse, Peter, 144
Delusions: An Analysis of the Book of Mormon, 3 note 2, 72 note 12

Demaratus, DeEtta, 343
Democratization of American Christianity, The, 16, 27
demographic history, 357
"Demographic Examination of Household Heads in Salt Lake City, Utah, 1850-1870, A," 357
"Demographic Portrait of the Mormons, 1830-1980, A," 17 note 10, 357
"Demographic Study of a Singles Branch in the Church of Jesus Christ of Latter-day Saints, A," 357
"Demographic Transition in a Frontier Town: Manti, Utah, 1849-1948," 357
Dempsey, Jack, 348
Dennis, Ronald D., 144, 162
Denominational Society: A Sociological Approach to Religion in America, The, 231 note 7
Denominations that Base their Beliefs on the Teachings of Joseph Smith, the Mormon Prophet, 233
Denton, Sally, 153
"Depression in Mormon Women," 364
Derr, C. Brooklyn, 211, 283, 336
Derr, Jill Mulvay
  about, 274 note 3, 280, 283, 287, 305
  works by, 135, 143, 174, 195, 279 notes 12-13, 283 note 23, 286, 289, 305, 306, 324 note 6, 343, 344, 393 note 13
"'Descendants of Ham' in Zion: Discrimination against Blacks Along the Shifting Mormon Frontier, 1830-1920, The," 161
Deseret Alphabet, 163
Deseret Book, 333, 374, 393
"Deseret Mormons," 18, 20
Deseret News 2003 Church Almanac, 205
"Deserets, Red Stockings, and Out-of-Towners: Baseball Comes of Age in Salt Lake City," 363
Desert Saints: The Mormon Frontier in Utah, 18, 139 note 2, 190
Desert Wives, 386
"Design of a Temple for the Church of Jesus Christ of Latter-day Saints, The," 361
Destiny's Children, 374
"Destruction of the Mormon Temple at Nauvoo," 132
"Determining and Defining 'Wife': The Brigham Young Households," 295, 321, 344
Deutrich, Mabel E., 280 note 14
"Developing Sustainable Long-Term Relief Efforts in the Church in Africa: The Chyulu Project," 223
"Development of Mormon Communitarianism, 1826-1846, The," 79
"Development of Municipal Government in the Territory of Utah, The," 151

"Development of the Doctrine of Preexistence, 1830-1844, The," 78
"Development of the Mormon Temple Endowment Ceremony, The," 78, 133, 243
"Development of The Church of Jesus Christ of Latter-day Saints in Hawaii, The," 204
Developments in American Sociological Theory, 1915-1950, 230 note 4
"Devil Makers: Contemporary Evangelical Fundamentalist Anti-Mormonism, The," 17 note 19
DeVoto, Bernard, xii, 1, 3, 4, 6, 30, 340
Dew, Sheri L., 217, 333, 393 note 13
"Dialogue toward Forgiveness: A Supporting View—A Response to 'The LDS Intellectual Community and Church Leadership: A Contemporary Chronology,'" 191
Dialogue: A Journal of Mormon Thought, x, 44-45, 66, 203, 277, 286-87 and note 27, 287, 288, 292, 293, 294, 302, 306, 387, 388
"'Diamond Cut Diamond': Mormon Women and the Cult of Domesticity in the Nineteenth Century," 160, 280 note 14, 313
"Diary of the Mormon Battalion Mission: John D. Lee," 275
Dick, Thomas, 30, 31-32
Dictionary of Utah Art, 360
Didier, Charles A., 211
Differences That Persist: Between the Reorganized Church of Jesus Christ of Latter Day Saints and the Utah Mormon Church, 307
Differing Visions: Dissenters in Mormon History, 61, 97, 142, 177, 236, 241, 248, 249, 264, 298 note 53, 308, 321 note 7, 346, 348
"'Different Mode of Life': Irrigation and Society in Nineteenth-Century Utah, A," 148
Digging in Cumorah: Reclaiming Book of Mormon Narratives, 61 note 4, 72
"Digging the Foundation: Making and Reading Mormon Literature," 377
"Dimensions of Religiosity: A Conceptual Model with an Empirical Test, The," 184
"Diminished Thing?, A," 284 note 24
Dimity Convictions: The American Woman in the Nineteenth Century, 280 note 14
Directory to the "Restored Gospel" Churches, A, 240
Disciple's Life: The Biography of Neal A. Maxwell, A, 338
Disciples of Christ, 36, 62, 72
Discourses of Brigham Young, 303 note 1
Discovering the Face of the Sky: The World War II Experiences of Gordon Richard Bradford, 176
"Disease and Sickness in Nauvoo,"

127
Disorderly Conduct: Visions of Gender in Victorian America, 280 note 14
dissent, 9-12, 230 note 3, 231 notes 9 and 12, 346-47
   in Community of Christ, 263-64, 271
   LDS, xiv, 87, 120, 157, 229-51
   Kirtland period, 84
   Missouri period, 96-98, 111
   need for research on, 85
"Dissent and Schism in the Early Church: Explaining Mormon Fissiparousness," 120, 231 note 14
"Dissent, Protest, and Reform," 12
DISSERTATIONS IN LATTER-DAY SAINT HISTORY (series), 286
Dissertation on the Coincidence between the Priesthoods of Jesus Christ and Melchisedek, 31
Divergent Paths of the Restoration: A History of the Latter Day Saint Movement, 234, 240, 263, 347
Divett, Robert T., 78, 363
"Divine Duty: Hannah Sorenson and Midwifery in Southeastern Utah," 289 note 36
"Divine Transmutation, The," 47 note 9
"Divorce among Mormon Polygamists: Extent and Explanation," 161, 295
"DNA Mormon: D. Michael Quinn," 301 note 64, 373
"'Do Not Lecture the Brethren': Stewart L. Udall's Pro-Civil Rights Stance, 1967," 340
Dockstader, Julie A., 392
doctrinal development (LDS), 157-58, 254
"Doctrinal Development of the Church during the Nauvoo Sojourn, 1839-1846," 132, 243
"Doctrinal Impact of the King Follett Discourse, The," 132
"Doctrinal Teachings in Nauvoo: A Two-edged Sword," 132
Doctrine and Covenants, 76-77, 81; RLDS, 263
Doctrine and Covenants: Our Modern Scripture, 76
"Doctrine and the Temple in Nauvoo," 132
Doctrines for Exaltation, 221
Document Containing the Correspondence, Orders, &tc. in Relation to the Disturbances with the Mormons; and the Evidence Given before the Hon. Austin A. King, Judge of the Fifth Judicial Circuit of the State of Missouri, 107 note 18, 107
"Documents and Dusty Tomes: The Adventure of Arrington, Esplin, and Young," 389
Dogberry, Obadiah, 71
"Dogberry Papers and the Book of Mormon, The," 71 note 11

Doherty, Robert, 231 note 7
Dolan, Jay P., 132
Domestic Revolutions: A Social History of American Family Life, 280 note 14
Donald, David Herbert, 12
Doniphan, Alexander William, 92-93, 104, 107, 266-67
"Dorothea Lange's Portrait of Utah's Great Depression," 174
Douglas, Ann, 280 note 14
Douglas, Jack D., 231 note 14
Douglas, Norman, 205
"Down-and-Back Wagon Trains: Travelers on the Mormon Trail in 1861," 145
Doyle, Don Harrison, 127
"Dr. John M. Bernhisel, Mormon Elder in Congress," 151
"Drama on the European Stage," 224
Draper, Larry W., 357
Draper, Maurice L., 61, 64, 77, 80, 257, 262, 265, 268, 307, 346
Draper, Richard D., 151
"Dream Come True in Hong Kong, A," 219
"Dream Shattered: The Abandonment of the Kirtland Temple, 1837-1862, The," 82
Driggs, Kenneth D., 80, 159, 172, 317, 319, 348
Dubai, Mormonism in, 223
Dudley, Dean A., 83
Duke, James T., 184, 364
Dumenil, Lynn, 25 note 39
Dunfrey, Julie, 160, 293 note 43, 313
Dunklin, Daniel, 105
Durfee, Richard E., 218
Durham, G. Homer, 10, 336
Durham, Reed C., Jr., 45, 59, 68
Durkheim, Emile, 18
Dushku, Judith Rasmussen, 286, 287
"Duties and Responsibilities of the Apostles of the Church of Jesus Christ of Latter-day Saints, 1835-1945, The," 81
Dykstra, Robert R., 18

E

"Each in Her Own Time: Four Zinas," 295 note 44
"Eagle and the Scattered Flock: Church Beginnings in Occupied Japan, 1945-48, The," 217-18
Eakle, Arlene H., 355
"Early Accounts of Joseph Smith's First Vision, The," 64, 66
"Early Baptist Career of Sidney Rigdon in Warren, Ohio, The," 62, 74 note 13
Early Days of Mormonism: Palmyra, Kirtland, and Nauvoo, 119
Early Independence, Missouri "Mormon" History Tour Guide, 111 note 22
Early Latter Day Saint History: The Book of John Whitmer, An, 59, 258

Early Members of the Reorganized Church of Jesus Christ of Latter Day Saints, 357 note 3
"Early Mormon Communitarianism: The Law of Consecration and Stewardship," 79, 88
Early Mormon Documents (5 vols.), 59
"Early Mormon Historiography: Writing the History of the Mormons, 1830-1858," 1
"Early Mormon Loyalty and the Leadership of Brigham Young," 151
"Early Mormon Polygamy Defenses," 158
"Early Mormon Woodworking at Its Best: A Study of the Craftsmanship in the First Temples of Utah," 361
"Early Mormonism and Early Christianity: Some Parallels and Their Consequences for the Study of New Religions," 28
Early Mormonism and the Magic World View, xi, 21, 41-42, 69, 243, 272
"Early Republic's Supernatural Economy: Treasure Seeking in the American Northeast, 1780-1830, The," 41
Early Temples of the Mormons: The Architecture of the Millennial Kingdom in the American West, The, 82, 162, 361
"Early Twentieth-century Temples, The," 361
Early Utah Furniture, 361
"East of Nauvoo: Benjamin Winchester and the Early Mormon Church," 333
"East Wind to Hawaii: History and Contributions of Chinese and Japanese Latter-day Saints in Hawaii," 205
Easter Island, Mormonism in, 205, 205
"Eastern Edge: LDS Missionary Work in Hungarian Lands, The," 226
Eastern Europe, Mormonism in, 224-27
Eccles, David J., 294, 338
Eccles, Marriner, 339
"Ecclesiastical Conversion as a Social Process: A Case Study from the Philippines," 219
"Ecclesiastical Influence on Local Government in the Territory of Utah," 149
"Ecclesiastical Position of Women in Two Mormon Trajectories, The," 251
"Ecology, Resource Redistribution, and Mormon Settlement in Northeastern Arizona," 146
"Economic Basis for the Evolution of the Mormon Religion, The," 364
"Economic Impact of Fort Leavenworth on Northwestern Missouri 1827-1838. Yet Another Reason for the Mormon War? The," 96, 109

"Economic Role of Pioneer Mormon Women, The," 275
economics
 and Mormonism, 14, 33, 83, 88-90, 148, 168, 195-96, 210
 cooperative, 10
 Kirtland period, 79, 240, 241, 252
 Nauvoo period, 124-26, 254
"Economics of Ambivalence: Utah's Depression Experience, The," 174
"Economics of Zion, The," 149
Ecuador, Mormonism in, 216
Edison, Carol A., 361
"Editing the Revelations for Publication," 77
education, and Mormonism, 163, 190-91, 352
 and Community of Christ, 257
"Edward Tullidge: Historian of the Mormon Commonwealth," 157, 347
Edwards, Alice Smith, 262, 346
Edwards, F. Henry, 76
Edwards, Paul M.
 about, xiii, 262-63, 265
 quoted, 4, 48, 49, 86, 165, 291
 works by, x, xi, 9, 47 note 9, 54, 57, 62, 68, 83, 114, 119, 120, 131 note 3, 136, 139, 234, 245, 248, 249, 253, 257, 258, 260, 262, 264, 266, 269, 270, 308, 345, 346, 386
"Effects of Polygamy on Mormon Women," 160, 313
Eggleston, Jerilee, 370
Egypt, Mormonism in, 224
Ehat, Andrew F., x, xi note 3, 10, 132, 244
"Eight Contemporary Accounts of Joseph Smith's First Vision—What Do We Learn from Them?," 644
"1835 General Assembly and the Doctrine and Covenants, The," 77
1838 Mormon War in Missouri, The, 90, 97, 99, 102, 106, 107, 108, 110, 111
"1850 Mission of George Parker Dykes: A Study of Conflict, Discord, and Differences in Proselyting Styles, Yet the White Field Was Harvested, The," 341 note 18
Eisenhower, Dwight D., 192
Elder Statesman: A Biography of J. Reuben Clark, 187, 336
Elders' Journal (1837-38), 254
"Eldridge Cleaver's Passage through Mormonism," 348
"Eleanor McLean and the Murder of Parley P. Pratt," 142 note 10
Eliade, Mircea, 130, 229 note 1
"Elijah Abel and the Changing Status of Blacks within Mormonism," 343
"Elijah Banta: Community Builder of the Early Reorganization," 346
Eliot, George, 393
Eliza and Her Sisters, 143, 281 and note 15, 306, 343
"Eliza Enigma: The Life and Legend of Eliza R. Snow, The," 143, 281
"Eliza R. Snow and the Mormon Question," 143
"Eliza R. Snow and the Woman Question," 284
"Eliza R. Snow's Nauvoo Journal," 127
Elliott, Dorice Williams, 193
"Ellis Reynolds Shipp," 344
Ellison, Ralph, 260
Ellsworth, Maria S., 279 note 13, 344
Ellsworth, Paul D., 123
Ellsworth, S. George, 9, 168, 205, 279 note 13, 301, 341
"Embraced by the Church? Betty Eadie, Near-Death Experiences, and Mormonism," 345
Embry, Jessie L., xiv, 17 note 20, 18, 160, 162, 174, 183, 196, 198, 244, 281 note 16, 284 notes 24-25, 294, 296, 313, 316, 319, 340, 342, 343, 357, 366, 378 note 5
"Emergence of a Fundamental: The Expanding Role of Joseph Smith's First Vision in Mormon Thought," 63, 64
"Emergence of Brigham Young and the Twelve to Mormon Leadership, 1830-1846, The," 80-81
emigration, 132, 143-45. *See also* trail histories.
Emma Lee, 275, 344
"Emma Lucy Gates Bowen: Singer, Musician, Teacher," 289 note 36
"Emmanuel Abu Kissi: A Gospel Pioneer from Ghana," 221
"Emmeline B. Wells: A Mormon Woman in Victorian America," 284
"Emmeline B. Wells: A Voice for Mormon Women," 284, 306
"Emmeline B. Wells: 'Am I Not a Woman and a Sister?'" 284, 344
Emmeline Press, 287
Emmett, James, 232, 245, 246, 247
"Encore of the Spirit, An," 224
"Encounter: The Korean Mind and the Gospel," 218
"Encouraging the Saints: Brigham Young's Annual Tours of the Mormon Settlements," 140
Encyclopedia of Latter-day Saint History, 224
Encyclopedia of Mormonism, 224, 358, 360 note 5, 369
Encyclopedia of Religion, The, 229 note 1
"Endangered Species: Single Men in the Church," 362
Enders, Donald L., 126, 128
"Ends and Means in Church History," 131
"Enduring Believers: Czechoslovakia and the LDS Church, 1884-1990," 226
England, Breck, 62, 141, 334
England, Charlotte, 205
England, Eugene, 127, 131 note 3, 140 note 4, 194, 201, 205, 297 note 50, 339, 360, 377, 378 note 4, 387-88
England, J. Lynn, 195
"Enigma of Solomon Spaulding, The," 74
"Enigma Resolved: The Emma Smith of Newell and Avery, An," 291
"Enoch Wood Perry Jr.: A Biography and Analysis of His Thematic and Stylistic Development," 360
Ensign, 203, 207, 210, 211, 216, 218, 219, 223, 225, 226
Ensign to the Nations: A History of the LDS Church from 1846 to 1972, 139, 201
"Enterprising Ladies: Utah's Nineteenth-Century Women Editors," 281 note 16
environmental influences on Mormonism. *See* culture.
"Epilogue to the Utah War: Impact and Legacy," 152
Epperson, Steven, 20, 390
Epstein, Barbara Leslie, 280 note 14
Equal Rights Amendment, 186, 192-93, 286, 298 note 52, 299, 301
Equal Rites: Mormonism, Masonry, Gender, and American Culture, 25-26
Equal to the Occasion: Women Editors of the Nineteenth-Century West, 288 note 32
Erastus Snow: The Life of a Missionary and Pioneer for the Early Mormon Church, 141, 334
Erekson, Keith A., 128
Ericksen, Ephraim E., 16, 190
Erickson, Dan, 39
Erikson, Kai T., 230 note 2
"Ernest L. Wilkinson and the Office of Church Commissioner of Education," 190
"Ernest L. Wilkinson's Appointment as Seventh President of Brigham Young University," 339
Ernst, Justus, 203
Ernst, Manfred, 207
Escape from Freedom, 60 note 2
Esplin, Ronald K., 80, 120, 132, 135, 140, 145, 247, 389
Essay in American Religious Sociology, An, 22 note 34
Essays on the American West, 1974-1975, 281
Essentials in Church History, 97, 118, 305
"Establishing and Maintaining Land Ownership in Utah Prior to 1869," 149
"Establishing the L.D.S. Church in Chile," 216
Establishing Zion: The Mormon Church in the American West, 1847-1869, 139
"Ethics of Biography, The," 350 note 23
"Ethnic American Mormons: The

Index

Development of a Community," 162, 366
"Ethnic Groups and the LDS Church," 188, 342
ethnicity and Mormonism, 161, 187-88, 192, 342, 360, 366
"Ethnicity amongst Auckland Mormons," 208
"Ethnization and Accommodation: Dutch Mormons in Twenty-first Century Europe," 211
Europe, Mormonism in, 203, 210-12
"Europe: From First to Last, But Still 'Mighty' Important," 210
"Eva and Richard Jorgensen: Danish/American Converts to the Reorganization," 341 note 18
Evan Fry: Proclaimer of Good News, 265, 346
evangelical protestantism, and Mormonism, 4, 14, 16, 19
"Evangelical America and Early Mormonism," 14, 27
Evanoff, Alexander, 9
Evans, Beatrice Cannon, 142 note 10
Evans, Rosa Mae McClellan, 159
Evening and Morning Star (1832-34), 254
Evening and the Morning, The, 377
Evenson, Brian, 390
"Every Group Its Own Historian," 280 note 14
"Every Man . . . in His Own Language," 203
Every Man Shall Hear the Gospel in His Own Tongue: A History of the Missionary Training Center and Its Predecessors, 196
Every Stone a Sermon: The Magnificent Story of the Construction and Dedication of the Salt Lake Temple, 163, 361
"'Every Thing Is Favorable! And God Is On Our Side': Samuel Brannan and the Conquest of California," 348
"'Everything Is Everything': Was Joseph Smith Influenced by Kabbalah?," 45
"Evolution of Government in Early Utah, The," 151
"Evolution of the Presiding Quorums of the LDS Church, The," 80, 158, 238
"Examination of the Mormon Settlement of Syracuse, Utah, An," 353
"Example of Virginia Sorensen: Honest Ambivalence and the Mormon Experience, The," 378 note 4
"Execution in Mexico: The Deaths of Rafael Monroy and Vicente Morales," 343
Exiles in a Land of Liberty: Mormons in America, 1830-1846, 16, 27, 54, 109, 121, 240
Existential Sociology, 231 note 14
"Exodus to a New Zion," 234

Exodus to Greatness: The Story of the Mormon Migration, 144 note 11
"Expanded Definition: Some Present and Future Consequences, An," 283, note 21
"Expanderende Mormoonse Kerk in Latijns Amerika: Schetsen Uit Een Wijk in San José, Costa Rica, De," ["The Expansion of the Mormon Church in Latin America: Sketch of a District in San José, Costa Rica"], 215
Expanding Church: Three Decades of Remarkable Growth among the Latter-day Saints, 1970-1999, The, 200 and note 2, 201, 217, 342
"Expanding LDS Church Abroad: Old Realities Compounded, The," 201
Expectations Westward: The Mormons and the Emigration of their British Converts in the Nineteenth Century, 144, 162
"Exploration of Recent Religious Conversion on Guam, An," 207
Exploring Mormon Thought: The Attributes of God, 78
"Exploring the Social Sources of Denominationalism: Schisms in American Protestant Denominations, 1890-1980," 231 note 12
Expo '70 (Osaka, Japan), 218
Exponent II, 277, 288, 302
"Expulsion of the Mormons from Jackson County, Missouri, The," 104
"Eyes Single to the Glory: The History of the Heavenly City of Zion," 80
"Ezra Booth Letters, The," 59
Ezra Taft Benson and the Politics of Agriculture: The Eisenhower Years, 1953-1961, 192
"Ezra Taft Benson and Mormon Political Conflicts," 192
Ezra Taft Benson: A Biography, 333

F

F. Henry Edwards: Articulator for the Church, 264, 346
"F. M. Brodie—'The Fasting Hermit and Very Saint of Ignorance': A Biographer and Her Legend," 30, 32
F. M. Smith: Saint as Reformer, 257
"Factors in the Destruction of the Mormon Press in Missouri, 1833," 104
"Factors Influencing the Use of Health Services for Four Wards in the Taipei Taiwan Relief Society of the Church of Jesus Christ of Latter-day Saints," 218
"Failure of the Kirtland Safety Society, The," 83
"Failure of Utah's First Sugar Factory, The," 148
Fairbanks, Eugene F., 360

"Faith of Emma Smith, The," 269, 308
Faith Rewarded: A Personal Account of Prophetic Promises to the East German Saints, 225
"Faithful History," 4 note 5, 53, 69
Faithful History: Essays on Writing Mormon History, 53 note 1, 117, 274 note 5, 301 note 64, 311 note 6, 373
Fales, Susan L., 357
Families and Communities: A New View of American History, 85
family history, 358-59
"Family Formation in an Age of Nascent Capitalism," 85
"Family History: Therapy or Scholarship," 342
Family Kingdom, 280
Family, Religion, and Social Change in Diverse Societies, 212
"Family Scriptures," 288 note 34
"Family Stress and the Role of the Mormon Bishop's Wife," 364
"Family Structure and Dynamics in Early Utah Mormon Families, 1847-1855," 160, 289
"Family Ties: Belief and Practice in Nauvoo," 321
"Family," 358
Far from Home, 381
Far West Record: Minutes of the Church of Jesus Christ of Latter-day Saints, 1830-1844, The, 59
Far West. *See* Missouri period.
Faragher, John Mack, 127
FarmanFarmaian, Verla Gean Mill, 345
FARMS. *See* Foundation for Ancient Research and Mormon Studies.
Farr, Cecilia Konchar, 297 note 50, 390
"Fate and the Persecutors of Joseph Smith: Transmutations of an American Myth," 123
Fate of the Persecutors of the Prophet Joseph Smith, 123
Father Figure: Joseph Smith III and the Creation of the Reorganized Church, 262, 345
Faulring, Scott H., x, xi note 3, 44, 58
"Fawn Brodie on Joseph Smith's Plural Wives and Polygamy: A Critical View," 275 note 7
"Fawn M. Brodie and Deborah Laake: Two Perspectives on Mormon Feminist Dissent," 348
"Fawn Brodie: The Woman and Her History," 30
"Fawn M. Brodie: Her Biographies as Autobiography," 326
Fawn McKay Brodie: A Biographer's Life, 28, 177, 293, 349
"Fawn McKay Brodie: Dissident Historian and Quintessential Critic of Mormondom," 177, 349
"Fawn McKay Brodie's *No Man*

Knows My History: A Fifty-Year Perspective," 49 note 10
"Federal Bench and Priesthood Authority: The Rise and Fall of John Fitch Kinney's Early Relationship with the Mormons, The," 159
"Federal Government and Its Policies Regarding the Frontier Era of Utah Territory, 1850-1877, The," 151
Federated States of Micronesia, Mormonism in, 207
"Feeding the Fleeing Flock: Reflections on the Struggle to Retain Church Members in Europe," 211
Fellingham, Gilbert W., 184
Felt, Nathaniel Henry, 36 note 5
"Female World of Love and Ritual: Relations between Women in Nineteenth-Century America, The," 280 note 14
"'Feme Covert': Journey of a Metaphor," 286
"Feminist among the Mormons: Charlotte Ives Cobb Godbe Kirby, A," 306
"Feminist Challenge: 'Mormons for ERA' as an Internal Social Movement, A," 193, 298 note 52
"Feminist Implications of Mormon Polygamy," 293
"Feminists," 287
Feminization of American Culture, The, 280 note 14
Ferre, Craig, 204
Fertility Change on the American Frontier: Adaptation and Innovation, 158, 357
"Fertility Change on the Frontier: An Analysis of the Nineteenth-Century Utah Population," 357 note 4
"Fertility Changes in Utah, 1960-1975," 357 note 4
"Fictional Sisters," 288
Fielding, Lavina. *See* Anderson, Lavina Fielding.
Fielding, Robert Kent, 83, 153
"Fiery Darts of the Adversary: An Interpretation of Early Cutlerism, The," 249, 347
"Fiji, Micronesia-Guam, and Other Non-Polynesian Areas," 204
"Fiji: Islands of Faith," 207
"Finalizing Plans for the Trek West: Deliberations at Winter Quarters, 1846-1847," 247
finances. *See* economics.
"Fine Soul Who Served Us: The Life of Emmeline B. Wells, A," 344
"Finest of Fabrics: Mormon Women and the Silk Industry in Early Utah, "The," 281 note 16
Finnish Mission, 211
Fire and Sword: The Latter-day Saints in Northern Missouri, 1836-39, 92 note 3, 302
Fire of Faith, The, 205
Fire of the Covenant: A Novel of the Willie and Martin Handcart Companies, The, 370
Firmage, Edward Brown
quoted, 84, 167
works by, 159, 194, 299 note 54, 317, 336
First Forty-Niner and the Story of the Golden Tea-Caddy, The, 348 note 22
"First General Epistle of the President," 268
"First Impressions: The Independence, Missouri, Printing Operation, 1832-33," 90
"First London Mormons, 1840-1845, The," 357
"First Months of Mormonism: A Contemporary View by Rev. Diedrich Willers, The," 59
"First Mormon Mission to the Indians, The," 104
First Mormon Temple: Design, Construction, and Historic Context of the Kirtland Temple, 82, 361
"First Presidency Statement on MX in Perspective, The," 194
First Vision, 40, 63-68, 63 note 5, 268, 379-81
"First Vision Controversy, The," 68
"First Vision Controversy: A Critique and Reconciliation, The," 66
"First Vision Story Revived, The," 66
Fischoff, Ephraim, 230 note 5
Fisher, Franklin, 380-81
Fisher, Glen G., 221
Fisher, Vardis, 377, 379
fissiparousness. *See* dissent.
Flake, Green, 385
Flake, Joel Alva, 215
Flake, Kathleen, 25
Flame of Pure Fire: Jack Dempsey and the Roaring '20s, A, 348
Flanders, Robert B.
about, 9, 30, 119, 136, 244, 307
quoted, xii, 116-17, 130, 243
works by, xi, 19 note 27, 49, 113, 120, 121, 245, 253-54, 270, 274 note 5, 352
Fleming, L. A., 146
Fleming, Monroe, 385
Flexner, Eleanor, 280 note 14
Florence, Giles H., 226
folk magic and Mormonism, 21, 28, 39-50, 68-71, 243, 272, 301
Cutlerite movement, 272
Folsom, Marjorie Wall, 221
"For Christ Will Come Tomorrow": The Saga of the Morrisites, 157, 347
"'For Life, the Resurrection, and the Life Everlasting': James J. Strang and Strangite Mormon Polygamy, 1849-1856," 248
"For the Blessings of All of His Children," 179 note 1
"For the Good of the Kingdom: A Narrative of the Strangite Mormons," 248, 347
"For the Strength of the Hills: Imagining Mormon Country," 18
"'For This Ordinance Belongeth to My House': The Practice of Baptism for the Dead Outside the Nauvoo Temple," 133
"'For Ye Are All One in Christ Jesus': The Global Church in a World of Ethnic Diversity," 162, 200
Force of a Feather: The Search for a Lost Story of Slavery and Freedom, The, 343
Ford, Gerald, 340
Ford, Joan Porter, 219
Ford, Thomas, 121, 123, 376
Forester, Rubina Rivers, 204
Forgotten Kingdom: The Mormon Theocracy in the American West, 1847-1896, 149, 167, 170, 178
"Forgotten Mormon Perspectives: Slavery, Race, and the Black Man as Issues among Non-Utah Latter-day Saints, 1844-1873," 249
"Forgotten Odyssey of Obadiah H. Riggs: Early Pioneer for Education Reform, The," 348
"Forgotten Woman: My 1852 Danish Emigrant Ancestor, The," 341 note 18
"Form and Feeling in a Carefully Crafted Life: Eliza R. Snow's 'Poem of Poems,'" 143, 284, 343
"Formal Polity and Change of Structures, Denominational Assemblies," 231 note 10
Forms and Methods of Early Mormon Settlement in Utah and Surrounding Regions: 1847 to 1877, 146
Forsberg, Clyde R., Jr., 14, 25-26, 47 note 9
Fort Bridger: Island in the Wilderness, 144
Fort on the Firing Line, 394
Fort Supply: Brigham Young's Green River Experiment, 144
Foster, Craig L., xiii, 152, 155, 157, 160, 164, 248, 313, 339, 347
Foster, John E., 315
Foster, Lawrence, xi, 3, 27, 82, 158, 243, 248, 293, 297 note 48, 302 note 67, 319, 358
Foster, Charles A., 244
Foster, Robert D., 244, 347
Foundation for Ancient Research and Mormon Studies, 32, 42, 47
Founder of Mormonism: A Psychological Study of Joseph Smith, Jr., The, 3, 4, 28, 30, 61
Founding and Early Development of the Church College of Hawaii, The, 205
Founding of an Empire: The Exploration and Colonization of Utah, 1776-1856, The, 6, 146
Founding of Utah, The, 6
Founding Prophet: An Administrative Biography of Joseph Smith, Jr., The, 61, 262
Founding Theory of American Sociology,

Index

1881-1915, 230 note 4
"Four European Missions of John A. Widtsoe," 341 note 18
Four Generations: Population, Land, and Family in Colonial Andover, Massachusetts, 85
"Four LDS Views on Harold Bloom: A Roundtable," 131 note 3
"Four Mormon Temples in Utah, The," 361
"Four Utah Mormon Artists [Dianne Dibb Forbis, Phyllis Luch, Blaine M. Yorgason, and Dennis Smith] as Authors," 360
Four Zinas: A Story of Mothers and Daughters on the Mormon Frontier, 143, 295, 315, 345
Fox, Feramorz Y., 10, 79, 88, 89, 149, 305
Fox, Frank, 336
Fragment: The Autobiography of Mary Jane Mount Tanner, A, 279 note 13, 344
France, Mormonism in, 211, 212
"Francis Gladden Bishop and Gladdenism: A Study in the Culture of a Mormon Dissenter and His Movement," 244
"Frank J. Cannon: Declension in the Mormon Kingdom," 348
Frazier, Karen Purser, 302 note 67
"Frederick Granger Williams of the First Presidency of the Church," 62
"Free Exercise of Religion in Nineteenth-Century America: The Mormon Cases," 159
Free Seekers: Religious Culture in Upstate New York, 1790-1835, The, 34
Freedom and Destiny, 60 note 2
Freedom's Ferment: Phases of American Social History to 1860, 6
Freeman, Judith, 387
Freeman, Robert C., 174
Freemasonry and American Culture, 1830-1930, 25 note 39
Freemasonry in Federalist Connecticut, 1789-1835, 25 note 39
Freemasonry. *See* Masonry.
"Freiberg Temple: An Unexpected Legacy of a Communist State and a Faithful People, The," 227
French Polynesia, Mormonism in, 205
Friedman, Rachelle E., 47 note 9
Friend, 203
Friendly Fire: A History of the ACLU in Utah, 190, 388
From Acorn to Oak Tree: A Personal History of the Establishment and First Quarter Development of the South American Missions, 215
"From Activism to Domesticity: The Changing Role of Mormon Women in the Nineteenth and Twentieth Centuries," 293
"From Apostle to Apostate: The Personal Struggle of Amasa Mason Lyman," 142 note 10
"From Assassination to Expulsion: Two Years of Distrust, Hostility, and Violence," 123
"From Bhutan to Wangts'ang: Taking the Gospel to Asia," 217
"From Burundi to Zaire: Taking the Gospel to Africa," 221
"From Calcutta to Kaysville: Is Righteousness Color-Coded?," 189
From Cottage to Marketplace: The Professionalization of Women's Sphere, 281 note 16
"From Dalarna to Zion: The Odyssey of the J. E. Forsberg Family," 341 note 18
From Every Nation, 201
"From Footholds: Spreading the Gospel Worldwide," 203
From Historian to Dissident: The Book of John Whitmer, 59
From Housewife to Heretic, 193, 299, 298
"From Housework to Office Clerk: Utah's Working Women, 1870-1900," 281 note 16
"From Impulsive Girl to Patient Wife: Lucy Bigelow Young," 289 note 36
From Max Weber: Essays in Sociology, 230 note 5
"From Men to Boys: LDS Aaronic Priesthood Offices, 1829-1996," 195
From Mission to Madness: Last Son of the Mormon Prophet, 157 note 17, 291, 345
"From Occult to Cult with Joseph Smith, Jr.," 68
"From Old to New Mormon History: Fawn Brodie and the Legacy of Scholarly Analysis of Mormonism," 274 note 5
From Prophet to Son: Advice of Joseph F. Smith to His Missionary Sons, 141 note 6
From Quaker to Latter-day Saint Bishop: Edwin D. Woolley, 142, 338
"From Sacred Grove to Sacral Power Structure," 80, 195
"From Satyr to Saint: American Attitudes toward the Mormons, 1860-1960," 6 note 14
"From Temple Mormon to Anti-Mormon: The Ambivalence of Increase Van Dusen," 157, 248, 347
From the Dust of Decades: Saga of the Papyri and Mummies, 77
From the East: The History of the Latter-day Saints in Asia, 1851-1996, 217
"From the Mission Field—Brazil," 2166
"From Tolerance to 'House Cleaning:' LDS Leadership Response to Maori Marriage Customs, 1890-1990," 208
"From Walden Pond to the Great Salt Lake: Ecobiography and Engendered Species Acts in *Walden,* and *Refuge,*" 297 note 50
Fromm, Erich, 60 note 2
"Frontier Arms of the Mormons," 152 note 16
Frontier Illinois, 127
Frontier in American History, The, 79 note 14
"Frontier Nauvoo: Building a Picture from Statistics," 127
frontier thesis. *See* Turner, Frederick Jackson.
Frontier Women: Trans-Mississippi West, 1840-1880, 295
Frost, J. W., 47 note 9
"Fruit of the Branch: Francis Gladden Bishop and His Culture of Dissent, The," 244
Fruitful Season: Reflections on the Challenging Years of the Relief Society, 1974-1984, A, 193
Fuller, Craig, 355
"'Fullness of the Priesthood': The Second Anointing in Latter-day Saint Theology and Practice, The," 243
Fundamental Differences, 307
fundamentalism, 170, 294, 302, 311, 321 note 7, 348-49
Fundamentalism and American Society, 172
"Fundamentalist Attitudes toward the Church: The Sermons of Leroy S. Johnson," 348
"Fundamentalist Schism, 1958-Present, The," 291 note 38
Furniss, Norman F., 152
"Furthering the Cause of Zion: An Overview of the Mormon Ecclesiastical Court System in Early Utah," 149-51
"Future of Mormon History, The," 117
Future of Religion: Secularization, Revival and Cult Formation, The, 231 note 12

G

Gager, John G., 28, 130
Galbraith, David B., 223
Galland, Isaac, 51
Gamson, William, 231 note 12
Gardner, Hamilton, 124
Gardner, Marvin K., 213, 215, 216, 226
Garfinkel, Harold, 231 note 14
Garr, Arnold K., 90, 124, 224
Garrett, H. Dean, 112, 124, 127
Gates, John, 387
Gates, Susa Young, 287, 289 note 36, 369
Gathering of Saints: A True Story of Money, Murder, and Deceit, A, 69 note 7
Gathering of Zion: The Story of the Mor-

409

mon Trail, The, 143
"'Gathering Place for the Scandinavian People': Conversion, Retention, and Gathering in Norway, Illinois (1842-1849), A," 128
"Gathering the Remnants: Establishing the RLDS Church in Southwestern Iowa," 272
Gathering to Nauvoo, 132
Gaunt, LaRene Porter, 207, 211, 219
Gause, Jesse, 62
Gaustad, Edwin S., 130, 136
Gayler, George R., 114, 121
Geary, Edward A., 18, 338, 339, 377, 378 note 4
Geddes, Ross, 208
Geddes, William, 294
"Gemeindegeschichte als Vergleichende Geschichte: The Church of Jesus Christ of Latter-day Saints in East Germany, 1945-1989," 226
gender, and Mormonism, 14
Gender and the Politics of History, 280 note 14
General Authorities, international, 201
Genesis Group, 383, 385
"Genesis of Zion and Kirtland and the Concept of Temples, The," 90
"Gentile and Saint at Kirtland," 80
Gentile Comes to Cache Valley: A Study of the Apostasies of 1874 and the Establishment of Non-Mormon Churches in Cache Valley, 1873-1913, The, 157
"Gentiles, Mormons, and the History of the American West," 24
Gentle Monarch: The Presidency of Israel A. Smith, 262, 345
"Gentle Persuaders: Utah's First Women Legislators," 286
Gentleman of the Senate: Orrin Hatch, a Portrait of Character, 340
Gentry, Leland H., 78, 87 note 1, 92, 97, 99, 106, 144
Geoffrey F. Spencer: Advocate for an Enlightened Faith, 265, 346
"Geographer's Discovery of Great Basin Kingdom, A," 148
"Geographic Dynamics of Mormonism, 1965-1995, The," 180
"Geographic Study of Stone Houses in Selected Utah Communities, A," 361
"George Edward Percy Careless: His Contributions to the Musical Culture of Utah and the Significance of His Life and Works," 362 note 6
"George Laub's Nauvoo Journal," 127
George Q. Cannon: A Biography, 141, 334
Germany, Mormonism in, 211, 224, 225, 226
Gert, H. H., 230 note 5
"Getting Things Started [in Hungary]," 226
Ghana, Mormonism in, 221
Giant Joshua, The, 378 and note 5
Gibbons, Francis M., 140 note 4, 141 note 6, 173, 201, 309, 331
Gibbs, Linda Jones, 360
Gibson, Hany W., 152 note 16
"Gift Given, A Gift Taken Away: Washing, Anointing, and Blessing the Sick among Mormon Women, A," 283 note 20
"Gifts of the Spirit: Women's Share," 283
Gilbert Islands, Mormonism in, 204
Gileadi, Avraham, 300
Gilkey, Langdon, 4 and note 4
Gilmore, Gary, 349
Gilmore, Mikal, 349
Ginat, Joseph, 295
Givens, George W., 126, 133, 352
Givens, Sylvia, 133
Givens, Terryl L., 6 note 11, 51-52, 61 note 4
"Giving New Meaning to Military 'Service,'" 219
Glauser, R. Scott, 85
Glen G. Fisher: A Man to Match the Mountains, 221
Glock, Charles Y., 231 note 8
Glory Hunter: A Biography of Patrick Edward Connor, 143
gnosticism, 21 note 31
"Gnosticism Reformed," 131 note 3
Go Forward with Faith: The Biography of Gordon B. Hinckley, 217, 333
Goates, L. Brent, 331, 333
God and County: Politics in Utah, 192
"God and Man in History," 117
God Makers, The, 17 note 19, 153
God the Mother, and Other Theological Essays, 283 note 19, 300
"'God's Base of Operations': Mormon Variation on the American Sense of Mission," 88
God's People: West Indian Pentecostal Sects in England, 231 note 13
Godbe, William S., 347
Godbeites, 19, 69, 157
Godfrey, Audrey M., 135, 152, 153, 279 note 13, 289, 306
Godfrey, Donald G., 121, 289 note 36, 338
Godfrey, Kenneth W., 112, 113, 121, 123, 124, 126, 279 note 13, 289, 306, 341 note 18, 345, 348, 352, 362
"'Going to Meeting' in Salt Lake City's Thirteenth Ward, 1849-1881: A Microanalysis," 148, 355
"Gold Mining Mission of 1849, The," 146
Golden Harvest in Ghana: Gospel Beginnings in West Africa, 221
Golden Legacy: A Folk History of J. Golden Kimball, The, 336
"Golden Pot, The," 42
Goldrup, Lawrence, 5 note 11
"'Good Guys' vs. 'Good Guys':
Rudger Clawson, John Sharp, and Civil Disobedience in Nineteenth-Century Utah," 160
"Good Poor Man's Wife": Being a Chronicle of Harriet Hanson Robinson and Her Family in Nineteenth-Century New England, A, 288
Good Time Coming: Mormon Letters to Scotland, A, 162
Good Wives: Image and Reality in the Lives of Women in Northern New England, 1650-1750, 288
Good-bye, I Love You, 298
Goodfellow, Paula J., 163
"'Goodly Heritage' in a Time of Transformation: History and Identity in the Community of Christ, A," 120
Goodman, Kristen L., 364
Goodman, Paul, 25 note 39
Goodwin, Lorine S., 353
Goodwin, Samuel H., 26
Gooren, Henri, 215
Gordon, Sarah Barringer, 25, 159, 296, 319
Gordon, Tamar, 207
Gospel Anchor, 233
"Gospel Dawning in Thailand, The," 219
"Gospel in the Soviet Union, The," 226
"Gospel Moves to Micronesia, The," 207
"Gospel Pioneers in Africa," 220
"Gospel Takes Hold in Cambodia, The," 220
Goss, Peter L., 360
Gottlieb, Robert, 196
"Government Responses to Mormon Appeals, 1840-1846," 112
"Governor Thomas Ford and the Murderers of Joseph Smith," 123
Gowans, Fred R., 144
Graceland College, 257, 258, 267
Grafting In: A History of the Latter-day Saints in the Holy Land, 223
"Grain Storage: The Balance of Power between Priesthood Authority and Relief Society Autonomy," 284 note 25
Grandin, Egbert B., 266
"Grandison Newell's Obsession," 62
Grandstaff, Mark R., 357
Grant, Heber J., 173, 217, 284, 331, 344, 394
Grant, Jedediah M., 141, 142, 151
Gray, Darius Aidan, 383-85
Gray, James, 31
Gray, Joseph P., 219
Gray, Louis, 383
"Great Awakening, The," 208
Great Basin Kingdom: An Economic History of the Latter-day Saints, 1830-1900, xii, xiii, 10, 49, 52, 116, 127, 137, 148, 163, 165, 170, 178, 274 and note 6, 305

Great Basin Kingdom Revisited: Contemporary Perspectives, 127, 148, 165 note 2, 389 note 8
"Great Florence Fitout of 1861, The," 145
Great Republic: A History of the American People, The, 12
Greece, Mormonism in, 226
Greeley, Andrew M., 180, 231 note 7
Green, Arnold H., 5 note 11, 6 note 12
Green, Susette Fletcher, 226
Greenacre, Phyllis, 3
Greenslade, S. L., 231 note 7
Greg Kofford Books, xiii, 149, 248
Gregory, Fern D., 362 note 6
Gregory, Thomas J., 248
Greven, Philip J., Jr., 85
"'Gringo Jeringo': Anglo Mormon Missionary Culture in Bolivia," 216
Groberg, John H., 205
Groberg, Joseph H., 151, 159
Groberg, Lee, 133
Groesbeck, C. Jess, 3, 27
Gross, Robert A., 127
Grover, Mark L., xiv, 189, 211, 212, 213, 215, 227-28, 343, 364
"Growing Up in Pioneer Utah: Agonies and Ecstasies," 362
"Growth and Internationalization: The LDS Church since 1945," xiv
Guam, Mormonism in, 204, 207
Guarneri, Carl, 284 note 25
Guatemala, Mormonism in, 213, 215
"Guatemalan Hot/Cold Medicine and Mormon Words of Wisdom: Intercultural Negotiation of Meaning," 215
Gunn, Stanley R., 61, 75, 237
Gunnell, Wayne Cutler, 75
Gurley, Zenas H., Sr., 263, 268
Gurley, Zenas H., Jr., 271

H

Hadden, Jeffrey K., 203
Hafen, Ann W., 144, 152
Hafen, Bruce C., 338
Hafen, LeRoy R., 144, 152
Haglund, Richard Forsberg, 131 note 3, 341 note 18
Hale, Van, 132
Hale, Veda Tebbs, 339, 378 note 5
Hales, David A., 289 note 36, 345
Hales, Norma Derry, 345
Halford, Larry J., 157
Hall, Bruce W., 226
Hall, David, 172, 345
Hallwas, John E., 113, 117, 119, 120, 121, 127, 136, 243, 264
Ham, Wayne
 quoted, 265, 267, 268
 works by, 76, 238, 254, 267, 346
Hamblin, William J., 45, 47 note 9, 48-49, 131 note 3
Hamer, John, 111
Hamilton, Charles Mark, 163, 361
Hamilton, Marshall, 121, 123, 128
Hampshire, Annette P., 121
Han, In Sang, 218
Hancock, Levi, 108
handcart companies, 370
"Handcarts to Utah, 1856-1860," 144
Handcarts to Zion: The Story of a Unique Western Migration, 1856-1860, 144
Hands across the Water: The Story of the Polynesian Cultural Center, 204
Hands, W. O., 266
"Hanging by a Thread: Mormons and Watergate," 194
Hanks, Marion D., 385
Hanks, Maxine, 300, 301, 311 note 6
"Hans J. Zobell: Danish Seaman, Mormon Emigrant," 341 note 18
Hansen, Helynne H., 378 note 4
Hansen, Jennifer Moulton, 279 note 13
Hansen, Klaus J.
 about, 26, 234, 119
 works by, xi, xiii, 9-10, 12, 20 note 29, 25, 80, 114, 119, 120, 124, 126, 130, 149, 244, 248, 358
Hansen, Lorin K., 144
Hansen, Nadine, 283, note 21
Hansen, Terrence L., 213
Hardy, B. Carmon, 10, 82, 119, 158, 159, 160, 167, 172, 213, 279, 294, 296, 306, 313, 316, 343 note 20
Hardy, Grant, 71 note 8
Harker, Herbert, 387
Harline, Paula Kelly, 296
Harold B. Lee: Prophet and Seer, 333
Harold F. Silver: Western Inventor, Businessman, and Civic Leader, 338
Haroldsen, Edwin O., 224, 225
Harper, Laura, 223
Harper, Reid L., 135
Harper, Steven C., 12, 42, 219
Harrell, Charles R., 78
Harris, Claudia W., 210
Harris, James, 284
Harris, Jan, 357
Harris, Jenny Lynn, 193
Harris, John B., 196
Harris, Lacee, 342
Harris, Linda W., 297 note 48, 345
Harris, Martin, 61, 69, 74, 84, 85, 245, 328
Harris, R. Carl, 205
Harrison, Jerry N., 357
Hart, Darryl G., 131 note 4, 136 note 5
Hart, Jennie, 205
Hart, Newell, 162
Hartley, William G., 99, 106, 108, 111 note 23, 128, 135, 142, 145, 158, 172, 195, 338, 341, 342 note 19, 358, 362, 366, 392
Hartman, Mary S., 280 note 14
Harvard Encyclopedia of American Ethnic Groups, 18 note 20, 364
Harvesting the Light: The Paris Art Mission and the Beginning of Impressionism, 360
Harvey, Richard C., 204
"Has the Word of Wisdom Changed since 1833?," 78
Haseltine, James, 360
Haslam, Gerald, 364
Hatch, Charles M., 301
Hatch, Gary Layne, 341 note 18
Hatch, John P., 336
Hatch, Nathan O., 16, 27
Hatch, Nelle Spilsbury, 213
Hatch, Orrin, 340
Hatch, Tina, 195
Haupt, John, 339
Haupt, Jon, 6 note 11, 155, 387
Having Authority: The Origins and Development of Priesthood during the Ministry of Joseph Smith, 81, 238, 270
Hawaii, Mormonism in, 200, 204, 207
Hawkins, Paula, 340
Haws, Peter, 245, 246, 247
Hayfield, Barbara, 159
Haynes, Alan E., 151
Health and Medicine among the Mormons: Science, Sense, and Scripture, 363
"Hearken, O Ye People": Discourses on the Doctrine and Covenants, 79
Heartbeats of Colonia Diaz, 213
Heartfire, 375
HEARTS AFIRE (series), 394
Hearts Made Glad: The Charges of Intemperance against Joseph Smith the Mormon Prophet, 83
HEARTS OF THE CHILDREN (series), 383, 393
Heath, Harvard, 173
"'Heathen in Our Fair Land': Presbyterian Women Missionaries in Utah, 1870-90," 287 note 31
Heaton, Alma, 220
Heaton, Bill, 218
Heaton, H. Grant, 217
Heaton, Marie, 220
Heaton, Tim B., 184, 201, 210, 297 note 48, 357, 364
Heaton, William R., Jr., 219
Heavens Are Open: The 1992 Sperry Symposium on the Doctrine and Covenants and Church History, The, 221
Heavens Resound: A History of the Latter-day Saints in Ohio, 1830-1838, The, 54, 57, 84, 351-52
Heber C. Kimball: Mormon Patriarch and Pioneer, 62, 141, 309, 334, 343
"Heber J. Grant and the Utah Loan and Trust Company," 173, 331
Heber J. Grant: Man of Steel, Prophet of God, 173
"Heber J. Grant's European Mission, 1903-1906," 173
"Hebraisms in the Book of Mormon: A Preliminary Survey," 73
Hedrick, Granville, 232
Hedrickites, 247
Heeren, John, 283 note 19

Excavating Mormon Pasts

Hefner, Loretta L., 142 note 10, 284 note 25, 347
"'Heigh, Ho! I'm Seventeen': The Diary of a Teenage Girl," 362
Heinerman, Jacob, 83
Heinerman, John, 162, 196, 203, 362
"Heinrich Hug and Jacob Tobler: From Switzerland to Santa Clara, 1854-80," 162
"'Heirs According to the Promise': Observations on Ethnicity, Race and Identity in Two Factions of Nineteenth-Century Mormonism," 161
Heiss, Matthew K., 203, 220, 361
"Helping Teens Stay Strong," 184
Henderson, A. M., 230 note 5
Hendrickson, Virgina, 391
Henry Lunt: Biography and History of the Development of Southern Utah and Settling of Colonia Pacheco, Mexico, 213
Henry William Bigler: Soldier, Gold Miner, Missionary, Chronicler, 1815-1900, 142, 168, 341
Herald House/Herald Publishing House, 260, 266
Herald to the Saints: History of Herald Publishing House, A, 266
Herberg, Will, 22 and note 34, 231 note 7
"Here Is One Man Who Will Not Go, Dam'um': Recruiting the Mormon Battalion in Iowa Territory," 145
"Heritage and Tasks of Mormon Biography, The," 323 note 1, 324 note 4, 350
hermeticism, and Mormonism, 21, 28, 46, 48, 71, 130, 243
Hero or Traitor? A Biographical Study of Charles Wesley Wandell, 142, 270
"'Herself Moving Beside Herself, Out there Alone': The Shape of Mormon Belief in Virginia Sorensen's *The Evening and the Morning*," 378 note 4
Hicken, Don, 217
Hickman, Bill, 338
Hickman, Martin B., 311, 224
Hicks, Michael, 81, 361
Hicksite Separation: A Sociological Analysis of Religious Schism in Early Nineteenth Century America, The, 231 note 7
"'Hide and Seek': Children on the Underground," 161
Higbee, Chauncey L., 244
Higbee, Elias, 101
Higbee, Francis M., 244
Higbee, Marilyn, 279 note 13
Higdon, Barbara, 292
Higdon, Miriam Elizabeth, 80
"'High Treason and Murder': The Examination of Mormon Prisoners at Richmond, Missouri, in November 1838," 102
Hildreth, Steven A., 194
Hiles, Norma Derry, 262

Hill, Donald G., Jr., 194
Hill, Donna, 49, 60, 326
Hill, Gordon O., 84
Hill, Marvin
  about, 12, 84, 236, 240, 241, 309
  quoted, 30, 54
  works by, ix, 1, 10, 14, 27, 31-32, 34, 36, 60 note 2, 66, 68, 69, 72, 79, 83, 84, 103-4, 105, 106, 109, 121, 123, 124, 126, 130, 131, 240, 306, 324-26, 352
Hill, Samuel S., Jr., 37 note 6
Hillis, Bryan V., 231 note 11
Hilltop Where: An Informal History of Graceland College, The, 257
Hilton, G. F., 220
Hilton, Hope L., 338
Hinckley, Bryant S., 141 note 8, 212 note 5
Hinckley, Gordon B.
  about, 50, 217, 219, 220, 227, 333
  quoted, 63 note 5, 393
  works by, 217
Hinkle, George M., 98, 107, 240, 245, 248
Hinkle, Roscoe C., 230 note 4
Hinton, Wayne K., 174, 360
Hirschl, Thomas A., 297 note 48
Hirshson, Stanley P., 140 note 4, 329-31
"His Word Was as Good as His Note': The Impact of Justus Morse's Mormonism(s) on His Families," 272, 347
Historia de la Iglesia en Colombia: Suplemento para el Curso de Historia de la Iglesia [History of the Church in Colombia: Supplement for a History Course of the Church], 216
Historia de la Iglesia en Bolivia [History of the Church in Bolivia], 216
Historia de los Mormones en Argentina: Relatos de Pioneros [History of the Mormons in Argentina: Accounts of Pioneers], 215
Historia de los Santos de los Últimos Días en Paraguay: Relatos de Pioneros [History of the Latter-day Saints in Paraguay: Accounts of Pioneers], 215
Historia de los Santos de los Últimos Días en Uruguay: Relatos de Pioneros [History of the Latter-day Saints in Uruguay: Accounts of Pioneers], 215
Historia del Mormonismo en México, [History of Mormonism in Mexico], 213
"Historian as Entrepreneur: A Personal Essay," x
"Historians and Mormon Nauvoo, The," 130
Historians and the American West, xii, 273 note 1, 280 note 14
Historic Architecture of the Church of Jesus Christ of Latter-day Saints: A Survey of LDS Architecture in Utah: 1847-1930, 360
Historic Buildings in Ohio, 82

Historic Sites and Markers Along the Mormon and Other Great Western Trails, 143-44
"Historic Views of the Temple Lot," 90
historical fiction (LDS), xiv, 367-94
  resistance to, 389-91
"Historical Analysis of the Word of Wisdom, An," 78
Historical Atlas of Mormonism, The, 180
"Historical Background of the Doctrine and Covenants, The," 77
Historical Guide to the Mormon Battalion and Butterfield Trail, A, 145
"Historical Overview of the Mormons and Their Clothing, 1840-1850, A," 363
"Historical Relationship of Women and Priesthood, The," 283, note 21
"Historical Study of Vertical Mobility, The," 85
"Historical Study of Demographic Aspects of Urbanization in Utah, 1900-1960, A," 357
"Historical Survey of Representative Activities among the Mormons of Nauvoo, 1838-1845, A," 363
"Historical Theology and Theological History: Mormon Possibility," 130, 136
"Historicity of the Book of Mormon and the Use of the Sermon on the Mount in III Nephi, The," 257
"Historiography and the New Mormon History: A Historian's Perspective," 119
"History, Analysis, and Registry of Architectural Art Glass in Utah, A," 360
History and Feminism: A Glass Half Full, 280 note 14
"History and Functions of the Aaronic Priesthood and the Officers of Priest, Teacher, and Deacon in the Church of Jesus Christ of Latter-day Saints, 1829 to 1844," 81
"History and Memory in Virginia Sorensen's Danish Convert-Emigrant Novel, *Kingdom Come*," 341 note 18
"History and Mission in Tension: A View from Both Sides," 269
"History and the Mormon Scriptures," 76
History of a Valley: Cache Valley, Utah-Idaho, The, 355
History of Cache County, A, 355
History of Carbon County, A, 355
History of Colonia Dublán, The, 213
History of Illinois: From Its Commencement as a State in 1818 to 1847, A, 121
"History of Intercollegiate Basketball, Football, and Wrestling at Ricks College, The," 363
History of Iron County, A, 355
History of Joseph Smith, The, 113, 117

Index

"History of Kirtland Camp: Its Initial Purpose and Notable Accomplishments, A," 84
History of Louisa Barnes Pratt: The Autobiography of a Mormon Missionary Widow and Pioneer, The, 301, 341
History of Morgan County, A, 355
"History of Mormon Missions in the United States and Canada, 1830-1860, A," 9
"History of Mormon Exhibits in World Expositions," 218
"History of Mormon-Chinese Relations: 1849-1993, A," 218
History of Rich County, A, 355
History of Salt Lake County, A, 388
History of Sanpete County, A, 355
History of the Cairo Branch, Egypt, 1974-1985, 224
"History of the Church in Ireland since 1840," 210
"History of the Chuch in Japan, The," 218
History of the Church of Jesus Christ of Latter-day Saints, 51 note 13, 58-59, 84, 95 note 5, 96, 97, 105, 118, 324
RLDS edition, 118
"History of the Church of Jesus Christ of Latter-day Saints in Japan from 1948 to 1980, A," 217
"History of the Church of Jesus Christ of Latter-day Saints in Korea, 1950-1985, A," 218
"History of the Church of Jesus Christ of Latter-day Saints in Mexico, The," 213
History of the Church of Jesus Christ of Latter-day Saints in Singapore: Journey to Stakehood, 1964-1997, A, 219
"History of the Church of Jesus Christ of Latter-Saints in South America: 1945-1960, The," 215
"History of the Church of Jesus Christ of Latter-day Saints in Switzerland," 211
"History of the Danish Mission . . . 1850-1964, A," 211
"History of the Early Members of the Church of Jesus Christ of Latter-day Saints in Preston, Lancashire, England, The," 357
"History of the French Mission . . . 1850-1960, A," 211
"History of the Latter-day Saints in Clay County, Missouri, from 1833 to 1837, A," 105
"History of the Latter-day Saints in Northern Missouri from 1836 to 1839, A," 92, 97
"History of the Mormon Church," 117
History of the Mormons in Argentina, 364
"History of the Netherlands Mission . . . 1861-1966, A," 211
"History of the Norwegian Mission from 1851-1960, A," 211
"History of the Polynesian Cultural Center's Night Show, 1963-1983, A," 204
History of the Prophet Joseph Smith by His Mother, as Revised by George A. Smith and Elias Smith, 118
"History of the Recreational Program of the Church of Jesus Christ of Latter-day Saints, A," 363
"History of the St. George Temple," 361
"History of the Schools and Educational Programs of the Church of Jesus Christ of Latter-day Saints in Ohio and Missouri, 1831-1839, A," 78
"History of the Swedish Mission . . . 1905-1973," 211
History of the South African Mission, A, 221
"History of the South African Mission of the Church of Jesus Christ of Latter-day Saints: 1853-1970," 221
History of the Washington, D.C LDS Ward: From Beginnings (1839) to Dissolution (1979), 355
"History of Two Stories, A," 284 note 24
History of Utah, 1540-1886, 137 note 1, 114, 130
History of Utah, 1847-1869, 6, 146
History of Washington County, A, 355
History of Weber County, A, 355
"History: Sacred and Secular," 136
History's Apprentice: The Diaries of B. H. Roberts, 336
"History's Sequel: A Source Essay on Women in Mormon History," 302 note 67, 358
"Hoary-Headed Saints: The Aged in Nineteenth-Century Mormon Culture," 362
Hoffmann, E. T. A., 42
Hofmann, Mark W., x, 41, 42, 69, 388
Hogan, Mervin B., 45
Hoge, Dean R., 180
Hogge, Robert M., 333
"Holding Forth of Jeddy Grant, The," 151 note 15, 151
Holland, Jeffrey R., 63 note 5, 227
Holloman, Richard C., Jr., 217
Holm, Francis W., Sr., 307
Holt, Russ, 374
Holzapfel, Jeni Broberg, 279 note 13, 286 note 26, 302, 352
Holzapfel, Richard N., 133, 163, 172, 279 note 13, 286 note 26, 302, 352, 361
"Home Hungry Hearts," 153
home literature, 369-374, 377
"Home Literature," 369 note 1
"Homemaking Meetings," 284 note 24
Homer, Michael W., 44, 45, 133, 151, 155, 159, 211, 243
Homeward to Zion: The Mormon Migration from Scandinavia, 19, 144-45, 162
Homosexual Saints: The Community of Christ Experience, 271
homosexuality, 176, 194, 297-98, 300 note 61
Hong Kong, Mormonism in, 217, 218, 219
"Hong Kong: Pearl of the Orient," 219
"Honoring Leonard Arrington," 277
Hoopes, David S., 336
Hoopes, Roy, 336
Hope, Len, 385
Horman, Hermine B., 221
Horne, Alice Merrill, 345
Horne, Dennis B., 142, 336
Hoton (1832 dissident), 240
Hough, C. Merrill, 163
House Divided: Protestantism, Schism, and Secularization, A, 232 note 15
"House Divided: The John Johnson Family, A," 62
House without Walls, 383
"Houses with Two Fronts: The Evolution of Domestic Architectural Design in a Mormon Community," 162
"Housewives, Hussies, and Heroines, or the Women of Johnston's Army," 152
Houston, Gail Turley, 283 note 19, 390
"How Authentic Are Mormon Historic Sites in Vermont and New York?," 66
"How Common the Principle? Women as Plural Wives in 1860," 158, 296
"How International Is the Church in Japan?," 189, 218
"How Is Church Membership Divided as to Ages?," 183 note 5
"How Large Was the Population of Nauvoo?," 127
How Many Roads, 383
"How Mormon Is the Community of Christ," 136
"Howard Coray's Recollections of Joseph Smith," 59
Howard, F. Burton, 336
Howard, F. Burton, 336
Howard J. Stoddard: Founder, Michigan National Bank, 338
Howard, Richard P.
about, x, 240, 254, 262-63, 268, 270
quoted, 268, 308
works by, 54, 64, 74, 76, 77, 82, 83, 119, 120, 136, 233 note 16, 234, 241, 245, 267, 269, 283 note 21, 291 note 37
Howard W. Hunter, 333
Howe, Eber D., 3 and note 2, 4, 5, 40, 73
Howe, Susan Elizabeth, 223, 293, 339, 341 note 18, 378 note 4
Howell, Paul, 385

413

Hsiao, Candace Sheila Gutzman, 218
Huefner, Dixie Snow, 193, 298 note 52
Huff, Kent W., 88
Hugh B. Brown: His Life and Thought, 187, 336
Hugh Nibley: A Consecrated Life, 176, 339
Hughes, David L., 219
Hughes, Dean, 381-83, 393, 394
Hughes, Richard T., 34, 36, 54, 126
Hughes, William E., 357
Hulett, James, 304
Hullinger, Robert N., 71 note 9
Hulmston, John K., 145
Hungary, Mormonism in, 226
Hunsaker, Curtis B., 211
Hunt, Brian W., 208
Hunt, Dave, 17 note 19
Hunt, Larry E., 257
Hunter, Edward, 36 note 5
Hunter, Howard W., 203, 333
Hunter, Milton R., 146
Huntington, Dimick, 103
Huntington, Oliver, 36 note 5
Huntington, Zina Baker, 295, 345
Huntress, Keith, 123
Hurlburt, Philastus, 3 and note 2, 5
Hutchinson, Anthony A., 75, 76, 283, note 21
Hyde, John, Jr., 347
Hyde, Myrtle Stevens, 62, 141, 142
Hyde, Orson, 102, 103
Hyer, Paul V., 217
Hyrum Smith: A Life of Integrity, 61, 334
Hyrum Smith: Patriarch, 61, 334

I

I Have Chosen You, 391
"'I Know If I Don't Bear My Testimony, I'll Lose It': Why Mormon Women Bother to Speak at All," 287 note 30
"I Married a Family," 275 note 7
"I Speak from My Heart: The Story of a Black South African Woman," 223
"I-Thou-vs.-I-It Conversions: The Mormon Baseball Era," 210
"I Was An Hungered and Ye Gave Me Meat": Development and Relief Efforts of the LDS Church in a Troubled World, 219, 223
"I Was Called to Dixie": The Virgin River Basin, Unique Experiences in Mormon Pioneering, 146
Iannaccone, Laurence R., 297 note 48
"Idea of Pre-existence in the Development of Mormon Thought, The," 78
"Ideal Apostasy and Restoration, The," 37
"Identity and Boundary Maintenance: International Prospects for Mormonism at the Dawn of the Twenty-first Century," 203
"'If Only I Shall Have the Right Stuff': Utah Women in World War I," 174, 297 note 48
"'If Polygamy Is the Lord's Order, We Must Carry It Out,'" 295
"Illinois River Towns: Economic Units or Melting Pots," 126
Illusions of Innocence: Protestant Primitivism in America, 34, 36, 54, 126
Illustrated History of the Kirtland Temple, 260
"Illustrated Periodical Images of Mormons, 1850-1860," 155
"Image of Blacks within Mormonism as Presented in the *Church News,* The," 223
Images of Faith: Art of the Latter-day Saints, 360
"Immigrants and Their Gods: A New Perspective in American Religious History," 132
"Impact of the Mormon Migration on the Community of Kirtland, Ohio, 1830-1839, The," 357
"Imperfect Science: Brigham Young on Medical Doctors, The," 140
"Importance of Programs in Our Religious Community, The," 195
"Importuning for Redress," 105
"Improved Facilities Enhance 15-Year-Old Drama," 392
Improvement Era, 216, 217, 218
"'In Blessing We Too Were Blessed': Mormon Women and Spiritual Gifts," 287 note 30
"In God's Hands in Divided Germany," 211
"In His Own Language": Mormon Spanish Speaking Congregations in the United States, 162, 188, 366
"In Memoriam: Leonard J. Arrington," 389
In My Father's House, 298
In Old Nauvoo: Everyday Life in the City of Joseph, 126
In Sacred Loneliness: The Plural Wives of Joseph Smith, 82, 121, 244, 291, 295 note 44, 315, 343
In Search of Security: The Mormons and the Kingdom of God on Earth, 1830-1844, 22 note 35, 85
"In Search of the Historical Nephi: The Book of Mormon, 'Evangelicalisms' and Antebellum American Popular Culture, c. 1830," 14, 25-26
In Search of Joseph, 123
"In Search of Women's Language and Feminist Expression among Nauvoo Wives in *A Little Lower Than the Angels,*" 378 note 4
In Search of Steenie Bergman, 393
In Singapore and Other Asian Cities, 219
In the Eye of the Storm, 205
"In the Presence of the Past: Continuity and Change in Twentieth-Century Mormonism," 183
In the Strength of the Lord: The Life and Teachings of James E. Faust, 336
In the World: The Diaries of Reed Smoot, 173
In Their Own Words: Women and the Story of Nauvoo, 126
"In Their Own Behalf: The Politicization of Mormon Women and the 1870 Franchise," 160
In Their Own Words: Women and the Story of Nauvoo, 286, 352
"Inadvertent Disclosure: Autobiography in the Poetry of Eliza R. Snow," 306
"Incidence of Mormon Polygamy in 1880: 'Dixie' versus Davis Stake, The," 158, 316
"Incidental Effects of Church Activity on Development, Landscapes and Culture: An Example from Tonga," 207
Independence Temple (Community of Christ), 90, 263
"Independence Temple of Zion, The," 88
Independent Church, 240
Index to Early Caldwell County, Missouri, Land Records, 111 and note 22
India, Mormonism in, 217, 220, 386
"India: A Season of Sowing," 220
"India: A Synopsis of Cultural Challenges," 220
Indian origins, 30, 71-72
Indian Origins and the Book of Mormon: Religious Solutions from Columbus to Joseph Smith, 5 and note 7, 71 note 9
Indonesia, Mormonism in, 217, 219, 220
"Industrialization and Social Change: A Controlled Comparison of Two Utah Communities [American Fork and Santaquin]," 353
"Ineffable Made Effable: Rendering Joseph Smith's First Vision as Literature, The," 379
"Influence of the Frontier on Joseph Smith, The," 6
"Influence of Traditional British Social Patterns on LDS Growth in Southwest Britain, The," 210
Inouye, Henry K., Jr., 111 note 22, 265, 346
"'Inside-Outsider' in Zion, An," 292 note 40
Inside the Mind of Joseph Smith: Psychobiography and the Book of Mormon, 3, 27, 61, 326-27
insider/insider fiction, 370, 374-76
Insider's View of Mormon Origins, An, 42, 71 note 9
Institute of Mormon Studies, 66
"Institutional Role of Mormon Women, The," 297 note 48
International Affairs Office, 203

Index

International Church, The, 200
"International Diffusion of the Mormon Church," 201
"International Women's Year, 193, 298 note 52
internationalism and Mormonism, xiv, 20, 177-78, 187, 199-227
"Internationalization of the Church, The," 201
"Intolerable Zion: The Image of Mormonism in Nineteenth-Century American Literature," 6 note 11, 155, 387
Introvigne, Massimo, 17 note 19, 39-40, 40 note 7, 49-50, 345
"Inventing Mormon Identity in Tonga," 207
Inventing Mormonism: Tradition and the Historical Record, 44, 57
Investigating the Book of Mormon Witnesses, 61, 75
Invisible Man, The, 260
"Invisible Saint, The," 340
"Invisible Saint: Biography and Lesser Known Mormons, The," 340 note 16
Invisible Saints: A History of Black Americans in the Reorganized Church, 161, 260
Iowa Mormon Trail: Legacy of Faith and Courage, 128
"Iron City, Mormon Mining Town," 146
"Irony of Mormon History," x, 119
Irving, Gordon
  about, 203, 243
  works by, 76, 140, 172, 213, 353
"Is There no Help for the Widow's Son?," 45, 68
"Isaac McCoy and the Mormons," 96
"Isaac Trumbo and the Politics of Utah Statehood," 168
Ishikawa, Nancy Hiles, 346
Islam, and Mormonism, 5-6, 21
"Islands of Light [New Caledonia]," 207
Isn't One Wife Enough: The Story of Mormon Polygamy, 280, 294, 304
Israel, Mormonism in, 223, 223
"'It Seems Like Heaven Began on Earth': Joseph Smith and the Constitution of the Kingdom of God," 10, 244
"It's Your Misfortune and None of My Own": A New History of the American West, 79 note 14
Italy, Mormonism in, 211
Iversen, Joan Smyth, 159, 160, 286, 287 note 31, 293
Ivins, Anthony W., 304
Ivins, Charles, 244
Ivins, Stanley H., 304
Ivory Coast, Mormonism in, 221

J

"J. Golden Kimball: Private Life of a Public Figure," 336
J. Reuben Clark: The Church Years, 187
J. Reuben Clark: The Public Years, 336
"J. Spencer Cornwall: The Salt Lake Mormon Tabernacle Choir Years, 1935-1957," 362 note 6
Jack, Ronald C., 151
Jackson, Andrew, 14, 60
"Jackson County, 1831-1833: A Look at the Development of Zion," 90
Jackson County, Missouri Mormon Sites, 111 note 22
Jackson County. *See* Missouri period.
Jackson, Richard H., 145, 146
Jackson, Richard W., 162, 361
Jacksonian Economy, The, 14, 83
Jacksonian period, 72, 109, 117, 120, 121
"Jacob B. Backenstos: 'Defender of the Saints,'" 123
"Jacob Hamblin: Apostle to the Lamanites and the Indian Mission," 142
Jacobs, Henry, 295
Jacobson, Cardell K., 223
Jagger, Brett, 270
"James Blakeslee, the Old Soldier of Mormonism," 347
"James Colin Brewster: The Boy Prophet Who Challenged Mormon Authority," 241
"James Gordon Bennett's 1831 Report on 'The Mormonites,'" 59
James H. Moyle Oral History Program, 203, 220
"James J. Strang: The Prophet Who Failed," 248, 293
James, Jane Manning, 345, 383, 385
James, Kimberly Jensen, 295
James, Laurence P., 281 note 16
James, Samuel, 245, 248
"Jan Shipps and the Mormon Tradition," 119, 130
"Jane Manning James: Black Saint, 1847 Pioneer," 289 note 36, 344
Janetski, Joyce A., 360
Japan, Mormonism in, 217, 218
"Japan: Growing Light in the East," 218
"Japan: Land of the Rising Sun," 218
Jardine, Judith C. N., 224
Jardine, Leo A., 224
Jarvis, George K., 316
Jarvis, John C., 212
Jaynes, Julian, 3
"Jedediah and Heber Grant," 141 note 8
Jedediah M. Grant, 141 note 8
Jeffrey, Julie Roy, 295
Jeffries, Terry, 387
Jehlen, Myra, 280 note 14
Jehovah's Witnesses and Mormons, 16
Jenkins, Carri P., 225
Jennings, Warren A., 92, 96, 104

Jensen, Richard L., 132, 142, 155, 188, 348
Jepsen, Thomas C., 281 note 16
Jerusalem, Mormonism in, 224
"Jerusalem, the Muslims, and the Church," 223
Jerusalem: The Eternal City, 223
"Jesse Gause: Counselor to the Prophet," 62
"Jesse Gause: Joseph Smith's Little-Known Counselor," 62
Jessee, Dean C., x and note 3, 50 note 12, 58, 59, 64, 66, 69, 74, 102-3, 118, 123, 127, 140, 268, 329 note 10
Jessop, Craig, 362
Jews and Mormons, 14, 16
"Jiri and Olga Snederfler: A Closer Look at Two Czech Pioneers," 226
Johansson, Carl-Erik, 211
John A. Widtsoe: A Biography, 339
John Birch Society, 192, 333
John Doyle Lee: Zealot, Pioneer Builder, Scapegoat, 142, 177, 275
"John E. Page: An Apostle of Uncertainty," 62
"John Hyde Jr., Mormon Renegade," 157, 347
"John J. McClellan, Tabernacle Organist," 362 note 6
John R. Winder: Member of the First Presidency, Pioneer, Temple Builder, Dairyman, 338
"John Sharp and T. B. H. Stenhouse: Two Scottish Converts Who Chose Separate Paths," 160
John Stevens' Courtship: A Romance of the Echo Canyon War, 369
John Taylor: Nauvoo Journal, 127
John Taylor: The Last Pioneer, 141, 376
"John Taylor's Religious Preparation," 331 note 12
John Whitmer Historical Association, x, 117, 135, 253, 266, 269-70
John Whitmer Historical Association Monograph Series, 270
John Whitmer Historical Association Journal, 302
Johnson, Annie R., 213
Johnson, Benjamin F., 103
Johnson, Catherine M., 289 note 36
Johnson, Clark V., 90, 111 and note 22, 112, 213
Johnson, Curtis D., 47 and note 9, 48
Johnson, J. Randall, 210
Johnson, Jeffery Ogden, 192, 295, 321, 344, 362
Johnson, Joel, 36 note 5
Johnson, John M., 231 note 14
Johnson, Luke S., 102, 240
Johnson, Lyman E., 240
Johnson, Lyndon B., 340
Johnson, Paul E., 12 and note 17, 14, 47 and note 9, 48, 128
Johnson, R. Val, 207
Johnson, Sonia
  about, 281, 283, 301, 346, 348

415

works by, 193, 298-99
Jones, Arthur R., 363
Jones, Cleo, 386
Jones, Edward T., 32
Jones, Evelyn K., 213
Jones, Garth N., 189, 201, 220
Jones, Gerald E., 37
Jones, J. Talmage, 219
Jordan, Mormonism in, 223
Jorgensen, Bruce W., 377, 378 notes 4-5, 390
Jorgensen, Dan (scholar about Italy), 211
Jorgensen, Danny L.
about, 252, 272
quoted, 292
works by, xiv, 120, 231 note 14, 249, 252, 269, 341 note 18, 347
Jorgensen, Lynne Watkins, 135, 157, 174, 347, 357, 383
Joseph and Emma: Companions for Seventeen and a Half Years, 1827-1844, 307
"Joseph and His Brothers: Rivalry in Virginia Sorensen's *On This Star,*" 378 note 4
"Joseph, Brigham, and the Twelve: A Succession of Continuity," 135, 247
"Joseph F. Smith: From Impulsive Young Man to Patriarchal Prophet," 141 note 6
Joseph F. Smith: Patriarch and Preacher, Prophet of God, 331
Joseph Fielding Smith Institute for Latter-day Saint History, xi, 52, 58, 61, 193, 221, 284, 288, 366, 393 note 13
"Joseph/Hyrum Smith Funeral Sermons, The," 123
"Joseph Knight's Recollection of Early Mormon History," 59
Joseph Smith, 60, 328
"Joseph Smith, an American Muhammad?: An Essay on the Perils of Historical Analogy," 6 note 11
"Joseph Smith and Kabbalah: The Occult Connection," 45, 243
"Joseph Smith and Legal Process: In the Wake of the Steamboat *Nauvoo,*" 126
Joseph Smith and Masonry: No Help for the Widow's Son: Two Papers on the Influence of the Masonic Movement on Joseph Smith and his Mormon Church, 68
"Joseph Smith and Mysticism," 68, 243
"Joseph Smith and Process Theology," 78
Joseph Smith and the Beginnings of Mormonism, 4 note 3, 5 note 9, 49, 51, 54, 66, 69, 72, 131, 243, 326
"Joseph Smith and the 1826 Trial: New Evidence and New Difficulties," 68
"Joseph Smith and the Law of Consecration, 79, 88
"Joseph Smith and the Millenarian Time Table," 80
Joseph Smith and the Origins of the Book of Mormon, 61 note 4, 72
"Joseph Smith and the Plurality of Worlds Idea," 78
"Joseph Smith and the Presidency, 1844," 124
Joseph Smith and the Restoration: A History of the LDS Church to 1846, 57, 97, 309
"Joseph Smith and the Shaman's Vision: A Psychoanalytic Exploration of Mormonism," 3
Joseph Smith and World Government, 10, 80
"Joseph Smith as a Student of Hebrew," 78
"Joseph Smith, Brigham Young, and a Religious Tradition," 329 note 10
"Joseph Smith, Builder of Ideal Communities," 88
Joseph Smith Chronology, A, 60
Joseph Smith Revelations: Text & Commentary, The, 76-77
"Joseph Smith Revision and the Synoptic Problem: An Alternate View, The," 76
Joseph Smith, the First Mormon, 49
"Joseph Smith, the Mormons, and Antebellum Reform: A Closer Look," 328 note 9
"Joseph Smith III and the Art of Biography in the Reorganization," 346
"Joseph Smith III and the Kirtland Temple Suit," 82
"Joseph Smith III and the Mormon Succession Crisis, 1844-46," 135
Joseph Smith III: Pragmatic Prophet, 135, 157 and note 17, 233 note 16, 245, 260, 308, 345
"Joseph Smith Translation and Ancient Texts of the Bible, The," 76
"Joseph Smith: America's Hermetic Prophet," 45
"Joseph Smith: Candidate for President of the United States," 124
Joseph Smith: Martyr, Prophet of God, 309
"Joseph Smith: Mayor of Nauvoo," 124
"Joseph Smith: Prophet and Theologian," 307
Joseph Smith: Seeker after Truth, Prophet of God, 68 note 6, 309
Joseph Smith: The First Mormon, 60, 66, 326
"Joseph Smith: The Gift of Seeing," 74
Joseph Smith: The Making of a Prophet, 3, 27, 61, 328
Joseph Smith: The Man and the Seer, 309
"Joseph Smith: The Palmyra Seer," 42, 69, 74
"Joseph Smith: The Verdict of Depth Psychology," 3, 27
"Joseph Smith's Bainbridge, N.Y., Court Trials," 68
"Joseph Smith's Changing First Vision Accounts," 64
"Joseph Smith's Family Background," 44
"Joseph Smith's First Vision: The RLDS Tradition," 64
"Joseph Smith's First Vision: A Source Essay," 66
"Joseph Smith's First Vision: An Analysis of Six Contemporary Accounts," 268
Joseph Smith's First Vision: The First Vision in Historical Context, 66
"Joseph Smith's Introduction of Temple Ordinances and the 1844 Succession Question," 244
Joseph Smith's Kirtland: Eyewitness Accounts, 59, 352
Joseph Smith's New England Heritage: Influences of Grandfathers Solomon Mack and Asael Smith, 71
"Joseph Smith's New York Reputation Reappraised," 68, 71
Joseph Smith's New York Reputation Reexamined, 72
"Joseph Smith's Own Story of a Serious Childhood Illness," 59
Joseph Smith's Strange Account of the First Vision, 64
"Joseph Smith's Translation of the Bible and the Synoptic Problem," 76
"Joseph W. Musser: Dissenter or Fearless Crusader of Truth?," 321 note 7, 348
"Joseph's Measures': The Continuation of Esoterica by Schismatic Members of the Council of Fifty," 124
Journal of Book of Mormon Studies, 32
Journal of Discourses, 287 note 28
Journal of Mormon History, 203, 302
"Journal of Thomas Bullock," 127
Journals of Addison Pratt, The, 341
Journals of William E. McLellin, 1831-1836, The, 16 note 18, 49
Journey to the Great Salt Lake City, with a Sketch of the History, Religion, and Customs of the Mormons, A, 5
Journey to Zion: Voices from the Mormon Trail, 144, 286
Juanita Brooks: Mormon Woman Historian, 177 note 4, 293, 344 and note 21, 388
Judd, Mary G., 141 note 8
"Judicial Campaign against Polygamy and the Enduring Legal Questions, The," 159
"Judicial Prosecution of Prisoners for LDS Plural Marriage: Prison Sentences, 1884-1895," 159
"Judiciary and Common Law in Utah, 1850-1861, The," 151
Juntratip, Poinchair, 219
"Justice in the Black Hawk War: The

Index

Trial of Thomas Jose," 162

K

Kabbalah, 21 note 31, 45
Kagel, Brian, 191, 283 note 19, 288 note 35
Kahn, Roger, 348
Kalpakian, Laura, 329
Kamman, Michael, 85
Kane, Thomas L., 143
Kanosh (chief), 161
Katanuma, Seiji, 218
"Keeping Promises: The LDS Church Enters Bulgaria, 1990-1994," 226
Kelen, Leslie G., 161
Keller, Roger R., 220
Kellogg, Heather M., 298 note 53, 348
Kelly, Paula, 296
Kendall, Paul Murray, 350 and note 24
Kennedy, David M., 200, 203, 224
Kennedy, James H., 119
Kennedy, John F., 339, 340
Kennelly, Ardeth, 377
Kenney, Scott G., 59, 61, 141 note 6, 328
Kern, Louis J., 293, 319
Kerr, Howard, 21 note 31
Keyes, Ralph, 183
Kharakham, Wisit, 219
Kidnapped from That Land: The Government Raids on the Short Creek Polygamists, 170, 294, 321
Kidney, Walter C., 82
Kimball, Andrew E., Jr., 187, 333
Kimball, Edward L., 187, 333 and note 13, 344
Kimball, Heber C., 309, 334, 372
Kimball, J. Golden, xi, 336
Kimball, James L., Jr., 124
Kimball, James N., 336
Kimball, Richard Ian, 363
Kimball, Spencer W.
  about, 176, 178, 212, 221, 293, 333
  quoted, 200
  works by, 203, 344
Kimball, Stanley B., 58, 62, 74, 77, 114, 128, 132, 141, 143, 309, 334, 343
Kind Words: The Beginnings of Mormon Melody: A Historical Biography of the Life and Works of Ebenezer Beesley, Utah Pioneer Musician, Containing an Account from the Emigration of 1859 and the Evolution of Latter-day Saint Psalmody, 361
Kindred Saints: The Mormon Immigrant Heritage of Alvin and Kathryn Christensen, 341, 358
"King Follett Discourse: Joseph Smith's Greatest Sermon in Historical Perspective, The," 132
"King Follett Discourse: A Newly Amalgamated Text, The," 132
"King James Strang: Joseph Smith's Successor?," 248
King of Beaver Island: The Life and Assassination of James Jesse Strang, 248, 346
Kingdom and Community: The Social World of Early Christianity, 130
KINGDOM AND THE CROWN, THE (series), 372
Kingdom Come, 378
Kingdom in the West: The Mormons and the American Frontier, 149
Kingdom of God in America, The, 130
"Kingdom of God in Illinois: Politics in Utopia, The," 121
"Kingdom of God, the Council of Fifty, and the State of Deseret, The," 149
Kingdom of Matthias, The, 12 note 17, 14
"'Kingdom of Priests': Priesthood, Temple and Women in the Old Testament and in the Restoration," 283, note 21
Kingdom of Saint James: A Narrative of James J. Strang, the Beaver Island Mormon King, The, 248, 346
Kingdom of the Saints: The Story of Brigham Young and the Mormons, 8, 139 note 2
Kingdom on the Mississippi Revisited: Nauvoo in Mormon History, 113, 117, 119, 127, 243, 264
Kingdom or Nothing: The Life of John Taylor, Militant Mormon, The, 141, 170, 331, 376
"Kingdom Progresses in Africa, The," 220, 223
Kingdom Transformed: Themes in the Development of Mormon, A, 17
Kinkead, Joyce, 279 note 13
Kinney, Bruce, 5 note 11
Kirby, Dale Z., 211
Kiriakov family, 225
Kiribati, Mormonism in, 207
Kirtland Camp, 89
"Kirtland Crisis: The Division of 1837-1838, The," 84
"Kirtland Diary of Wilford Woodruff, The," 59
"Kirtland Economy Revisited: A Market Critique of Sectarian Economics, The," 14, 83, 352
Kirtland Elders' Quorum Record, 1836-1841, 59
Kirtland period, 5, 57, 61, 77-78, 97, 199, 234, 240-41, 311, 351-52
Kirtland Safety Society Anti-Banking Company, 83
"Kirtland Safety Society: The Stock Ledger Book and the Bank Failure, The," 83
Kirtland Temple. *See* temples.
"Kirtland Temple Suit and the Utah Church, The," 85
"Kirtland Temple, The," 82
Kirtland Temple: A Historical Narrative, The, 82, 260, 361
"Kirtland: A Stronghold for the Kingdom," 57
"Kirtland Temple: A Time of Transition, 1838-1880, The," 272
Knecht, William L., 32, 71
Knight, Gladys, 349
Knight, Gregory R., 127
Knight, Newel K., 36 note 5, 328
"Knowing Brother Joseph Again: The Book of Abraham, and Joseph Smith as Translator," 77
Knowledge and Understanding, 300 note 59
Knowles, Eleanor, 218, 333
Knowlton, Clark S., 289 note 36, 344
Knowlton, David C., 189, 213, 216
Komatsu, Adney Y., 217
Korea, Mormonism in, 217, 218
"Korea: Land of the Morning Calm," 218
Korean Saints: Personal Stories of Trial and Triumph, 1950-1980, The, 218
"Korean War and the Gospel, The," 218
Koritz, Alvin Karl, 151
Koury, Aleah J., 307
Kovick, Peter, 230 note 4
Krakauer, Jon, 153
Kramer, Neal, 390
Kraut, Ogden, 279 note 13
Kreitzer, Matthew E., 161, 342
"Kresimir Cosic Moves from Basketball to Diplomatic Courts," 225
"Kresimir Cosic of Yugoslavia," 225
Kuehne, Raymond M., 226
Kuhn, Thomas S., 69
Kunz, Philip R., 364
Kuta, Timothy J., 226

L

L'histoire de l'Eglise Mormone en Polynesie Francaise de 1844 à 1982 [The History of the Mormon Church in French Polynesia 1844-1982], 205
Laake, Deborah, 348
labor missionary program, 208
Labor of Love: The 1946 European Mission of Ezra Taft Benson, A, 224
Lafferty brothers, 153
Lair, Jim, 153
"Lamanism, Lymanism, and Cornfields," 145, 247
"Lamanite Mission, The," 96
Lamar, Howard R., 168
Lambert, Neal E., 64, 155, 369 note 1
Lamoni Wight: Life in a Mormon Splinter Colony on the Texas Frontier, 249
Lancaster, James E., 74
"Land Question at Adam-ondi-Ahman, The," 87 note 1
"Landmarks for LDS Woman: A Contemporary Chronology," 300 note 61

Excavating Mormon Pasts

Lange, Dorothea, 174
"Language Challenges Facing the Church of Jesus Christ of Latter-day Saints in Preaching the Gospel to 'Every Nation,'" 201
Laos, Mormonism in, 217
Larche, Douglas W., 233 note 17
Larsen, Dean L., 203
Larsen, Robert G., 188
Larsen, Sharyn H., 188
Larson, Andrew Karl, 141, 146, 334
Larson, Charles M., 77
Larson, Gustive O., 24, 146, 151, 158, 168, 311
Larson, Stan, 61 note 4, 74, 132, 174, 336
Larson, Wayne, 73
Last Mile of the Way, The, 383
"Last Months of Mormonism in Missouri: The Albert Perry Rockwood Journal, The," 102
Last Pioneer: John Taylor, a Mormon Prophet, The, 331
Latin America, Mormonism in, 203, 211, 212-13
"Latter-day Saint Prayer Circles," 158
Latter Day Saint Churches: An Annotated Bibliography, The, 240
"Latter Day Saint Movement: A Study in Survival, The," 247
"Latter Day Saint Scriptures and the Doctrine of Propositional Revelation," 74, 267
Latter-day Saint Century, The, 201
"Latter-day Saint Education in the Pacific Islands," 207
"Latter-day Saint Missions and Missionaries in Polynesia, 1844-1960," 205
"Latter-day Saint Prayer Circles," 244
"Latter-day Saint Servicemen in the Philippine Islands: A Historical Study of Their Religious Activities and Influences Resulting in the Official Organization of the Church of Jesus Christ of Latter-day Saints in the Philippines," 219
Latter-day Saint Social Life: Social Research on the LDS Church and Its Members, 184, 364
"Latter-day Saints in the Far West, 1847-1900, The," 139
Launius, Roger D.
 about, xiii, 86, 258-60, 265, 345
 quoted, 24, 31, 260, 262, 266-67
 works by, xiii, 37, 49 and note 10, 53, 57, 59, 61, 75, 82, 84, 92, 96, 97, 105, 113, 117, 119, 121, 123, 127, 128, 135, 136, 142, 157 and note 17, 158, 161, 164, 177, 183, 232, 233 note 16, 236, 241, 243, 245, 248, 249, 258, 263, 264, 266, 269, 273 note 1, 274 note 5, 291 note 38, 292 and note 39, 298 note 53, 307 note 5, 308, 339, 346, 361
"Lavina Fielding Anderson and the Power of a Church in Exile," 300 note 61
"Law of Adoption: One Phase of the Development of the Mormon Concept of Salvation, The," 243
Law, Reuben D., 205
Law, William and Wilson, 244, 347
Lawless, Elaine J., 287 note 30
Lawyer Looks at the Equal Rights Amendment, A, 193
Layton, Stanford J., 363
Layton, Tim, 73
"LDS Approaches to the Holy Bible," 76
"LDS Church and Higher Education in Mongolia, The," 219
"LDS Church as a New Religious Movement in Japan, The," 218
"LDS Church Authority and New Plural Marriages, 1890-1904," 160, 172, 293-94, 310-11
"LDS Church Finances from the 1803 to the 1990s," 195
"LDS Church Growth Today," 227 note 7
"LDS Church in the United States since 1945," xiv
"LDS Church Members in the U.S. and Canada: A Demographic Profile," 364
"LDS Church's Campaign against the Equal Rights Amendment, The," 193
LDS Ethnic Groups Oral History Project, 188
LDS Family Travel Guide: Independence to Nauvoo, The, 133
"LDS in Africa: Growing Membership Sees American Church with Unique Vision," 223
"LDS Intellectual Community and Church Leadership: A Contemporary Chronology, The," 191, 299 note 57, 300
"LDS International Trio, 1974-1997, An," 203
"LDS Position on the ERA: An Historical View," 298 note 52
"LDS Prospects in Italy in the Twenty-first Century," 211
LDS Roots in Egypt, 224
"LDS Sister Missionaries: An Oral History Response," 196
"Leadership of Mormon Missionary Efforts in Finland and Its Influence on Conversion Rates in the Finnish Mission, 1947-1969," 211-12
"'Leading Sisters': A Female Hierarchy in Nineteenth-Century Mormon Society, The," 281
Leading the Charge: Orrin Hatch and 20 Years of America, 340
Leaving Home, 292 note 42
Leaving the Fold: Candid Conversations with Inactive Mormons, 297 note 49
Lebanon, Mormonism in, 223
LeBaron, E. Dale, 220 and note 6, 221, 223, 343
LeCheminant, Wilford Hill, 152
"Lectures on Faith," 76, 78
"'Lectures on Faith': A Case Study in Decanonization, The," 78
Lee, George P., 342
"Lee Greene Richards: Portrait Painter," 360
Lee, Harold B., 194, 212, 217, 331
Lee, J. Bracken, 349
Lee, John D., 107, 275, 387
Lee, Lawrence B., 146
Lee, Mark S., 159
Lee, Rex D., 193
Legacy, 391
Legacy of Conquest: The Unbroken Past of the American West, The, 79 note 14
"Legacy of Early Latter-day Saint Women, The," 275
"Legacy of Mormon Furniture, The," 361
"'Legacy' Puts LDS Past on Wide Screen," 391 note 10
"Legend of Jessie Evans Smith, The," 297 note 48, 345
Legg, Philip R., 61, 75, 237, 333
"Legislating Morality: Reynolds vs. United States," 159
LeGrand Richards: Beloved Apostle, 338
Lehi in the Desert, 21
Lemon, James T., 128
Leonard, Glen M.
 about, 136
 quoted, 167, 172, 181, 187, 324, 331
 works by, xiii, 16, 53-54, 68, 83, 88, 92, 113, 114, 120, 121, 123, 124, 139, 142, 151, 153, 177, 186, 201, 234, 243, 305, 333, 343, 352
"Leonard J. Arrington: Reflections on a Humble Walk," 277
Leone, Mark P., xi, 18, 24, 149, 165, 181, 234, 324, 364
Lerner, Gerda, 280 note 14
LeRoy Robertson: Music Giant from the Rockies, 339
LeSueur, Stephen C., xiii, 90, 97, 99, 102, 103, 106, 107, 108, 110, 111, 112, 270
Let Contention Cease: The Dynamics of Dissent in the Reorganized Church of Jesus Christ of Latter Day Saints, 233 note 16, 263, 291 note 38
"Let 'Em Holler": A Political Biography of J. Bracken Lee, 349
Let the Artifacts Speak!, 123
"Letter Regarding the Acquisition of the Book of Abraham, A," 77
Letters from Exile: The Correspondence of Martha Hughes Cannon and Angus M. Cannon, 1886-1888, 279 note 13
Letters of Bernard DeVoto, The, 1 note 1
Letters of Brigham Young to His Sons, xi note 3, 140, 329 note 10
Letters of Catharine Cottam Romney, Plural Wife, 279 note 13

Index

"Level and Determinants of Burnout of Mormon Mothers in a Utah Suburban Town, The," 364
Lewis, David Rich, 85, 248
Lewis, Gale, 193
Lewis, James W., 148, 196, 355
Liahona, 223, 226
"Liahona High School, Its Prologue and Development to 1965," 207
Liahona High School (Tonga), 205, 207
"'Liberal Shall Be Blessed': Sarah M. Kimball, The," 283, 344
Liberating Women's History: Theoretical and Critical Essays, 280 note 14
Lieber, Constance L., 279 note 13, 287 note 30
Liebman, Robert C., 231 note 12
"Life and Contributions of Lyman Wight, The," 249
Life and Thought of Orson Pratt, The, 334
"Life at Iosepa, Utah's Polynesian Colony," 155
"Life behind Bars: Mormon Cohabs of the 1880s," 159
"Life in a Village Society, 1877-1920," 355
Life of Andrew Wood Cooley: A Story of Conviction, The, 142
Life of Joseph F. Smith, The, 141 note 6
Life of Joseph Fielding Smith: Tenth President of the Church, The, 331
Life of Lorenzo Snow, The, 141 note 6
LIFE WRITINGS OF FRONTIER WOMEN (series), 279 note 13, 301
life-stage history, 362-63
Like a Fire Is Burning, 370
Lim, Augusto A., 219
Limerick, Patricia Nelson, 79 note 14, 146 note 13
"Limits of Learning in Pioneer Utah, The," 163
Lindsey, Donald B., 283 note 19
Lindsey, Robert, 69 note 7
Line upon Line: Essays on Mormon Doctrine, 78, 158
Lineham, Peter, 364
Linford, Lawrence A., 149
Linford, Orma, 159, 317
Linn, William A., 5, 116, 119
"Lion and the Lady: Brigham Young and Emma Smith, The," 140, 264
Lion of the Lord: A Biography of Brigham Young, The, 140 note 4, 331
Lipson, Dorothy Ann, 25 note 39
"Literary Form and Historical Understanding: Joseph Smith's First Vision," 64
"Literature in the History of the Church: The Importance of Involvement," 279
Litster, Allen, 216
"Little Berlin: Swiss Saints of the Logan Tenth Ward," 162
"Little Bit of Heaven, A," 288 note 34
"'Little Books' from a Large Soul: The Private Poetry of Virginia Sorensen," 378 note 4
Little Known Schisms of the Restoration, 233
Little Lower than the Angels, A, 377, 378
Littlefield, Lyman O., 123
Lives of Service, 221, 223
Lives of the Saints in Southeastern Idaho: An Introduction to Mormon Pioneer Life Story Writing, 142
Lives of the Saints: Writing Mormon Biography and Autobiography, 324 note 6
"Living Histories: Selected Biographies from the Manhattan First Ward," 188
"'Living the Principle' of Plural Marriage: Mormon Women, Utopia, and Female Sexuality in the Nineteenth Century," 160, 293 note 43, 313
local history, 363
"Locations of Joseph Smith's Early Treasure Quests, The," 44
Lofgreen, Charlotte D., 219
Logan, Roger V., Jr., 153
Logue, Larry M., 17, 18 and note 22, 157, 161, 317, 353
Long, E. B., 151
"Long Promised Day Has Come: Vital Signs of Prophetic Leadership, The," 201
Lord's University: Freedom and Authority at BYU, The, 191, 283 note 19, 288 note 35
"Lords of Creation: Polygamy, the Abrahamic Household, and Mormon Patriarchy," 296, 306
Lore of Faith and Folly, 159
"Lorenzo Hill Hatch: Pioneer Bishop of Franklin," 142
Lorenzo Snow: Spiritual Giant, Prophet of God, 141 note 6, 331
Los Mormones en Chile, 1956-1986 [The Mormons in Chile], 216, 363
"Loss of Nerve, A," 80
"lost generation," 377
Lost Legacy: The Mormon Office of Presiding Patriarch, The, 176, 249, 293, 334
"Lost Tribes of Israel and the Book of Mormon, The," 71 note 9
Loving, Kimberly L., 85, 271
Lowe, Jay R., 81
Lowell L. Bennion: Teacher, Counselor, Humanitarian, 293, 339
Lozano Herrera, Agrícol, 213
Lubomurdrov, Carol Ann, 281 note 16
Luckmann, Thomas, 231 note 14
"Lucy Mack Smith," 61
"Lucy Mack Smith's 1829 Letter to Mary Smith Pierce," 74
Lucy's Book: A Critical Edition of Lucy Mack Smith's Family Memoir, 59, 291
Ludlow, Daniel H., 61 note 4
Ludlow, Victor L., 200
Lund, Anthon H., 336
Lund, Christopher C., 77
Lund, Gerald N.
about, 370-74, 379-80, 383, 393
quoted, 372-73
Lund, Jennifer L., 336, 341 note 18
Lundgren, Jeffrey, 271
Lundquist, John M., 63
Lundwall, N. B., 123
Lye, William, 221
"Lying for the Lord," 313
Lyman, Amasa M., 141, 347
Lyman, Amy Brown, 289
Lyman, Edward Leo, 142 and note 10, 146, 151, 160, 168, 291, 311, 347, 353
Lyman, Francis M., 142, 173
Lyman, Richard R., 388
Lyman, Stanford M., 231 note 14
Lynn, Karen, 88 and note 2
Lyon, David W., 123
Lyon, Joseph L., 123
Lyon, T. Edgar
about, 127, 135
works by, 66, 114, 132, 157, 243
Lyon, Tania Rands, 196
Lythgoe, Dennis L., 135, 161, 340, 349

M

Mabey, Rendell and Rachel, 221
Mack, Jason, 36
Mackay, Christin Craft, 272
Mackay, Lachlan, 272
MacKay, Kathryn L., 297 note 48
Mackinnon, William P., 152
"Madeline McQuown, Dale Morgan, and the Great Unfinished Brigham Young Biography," 339
Madelyn Cannon Stewart Silver: Poet, Teacher, Homemaker, 277, 344
Madison, Robert Ben, 161, 347
Madsen, Brigham D., 61 note 4, 73, 143, 162
Madsen, Carol Cornwall
about, 280, 284, 286, 305
works by, 126, 143, 144, 155, 159, 160, 170, 281 note 16, 281 note 17, 284 note 25, 287 note 27, 289, 302 note 67, 306, 344, 352, 358, 362
Madsen, Susan Arrington, 61, 143, 277, 344, 362
Madsen, Truman G., 66, 75, 131 note 3, 336
magic. *See* folk magic.
"Magic of the Great Salt Lake, The," 47 note 9
Magrath, C. Peter, 159
Mahmoudi, Kooros Mohit, 357
"Mahonri Young and the Church: A View of Mormonism and Art," 360
Mahonri Young: His Life and Art, 339, 360
de Amorim, Nádia Fernanda Maia,

419

216
Major, Jill C., 133
Majority Finds Its Past: Placing Women in History, The, 280 note 14
MAKERS OF CHURCH THOUGHT (series), 264-65, 346
"Making Money the Old-Fashioned Way: Banking Before the Civil War," 83
"Making of a Community: Blackfoot, Idaho, 1878-1910, The," 146
Making of a Mormon Apostle: The Story of Rudger Clawson, The, 336
"Making of British Saints in Historical Perspective, The," 210
"Making of King Strang: A Reexamination, The," 248
"Making of Saints: The Mormon Town as a Setting for the Study of Cultural Change, The," 148, 355
Making the Heartland Quilt: A Geographical History of Settlement and Migration in Early-Nineteenth-Century Illinois, 127
Making the Invisible Woman Visible, 280 note 14
Malaysia, Mormonism in, 217
Maldives, Mormonism in, 217
Malone, Michael P., xii, 273 note 1, 280 note 14
Mangrum, Richard Collin, 84, 149, 159, 167, 317
Mangum, Garth L., 174
Manifesto (1890), 165, 279, 303, 342
Manning, Isaac, 385
"Mantle Is Far, Far Greater Than the Intellect," ix
"Mantle of Joseph: Creation of Mormon Miracle, The," 135
"Mantle of the Prophet Joseph Passes to Brother Brigham: A Collective Spiritual Witness, The," 135
"Mantle of the Prophet: A Rhetorical Analysis of the Quest for Mormon Post-Martyrdom Leadership, 1844-1860, The," 233 note 17
Many Mansions, 377, 386
Marion G. Romney: His Life and Faith, 336
Mark E. Petersen: A Biography, 336
Market Revolution: Jacksonian America, 1815-1867, The, 12
"Marks of Success in American Mission Policies in Korea," 218
Marks, William, 245
Marquardt, H. Michael, 44, 57, 76, 88
Marquis, Kathleen, 160, 280 note 14, 313
Marriage in the Restoration, 307
Marriott, J. Willard, 339
Marriott, Robert L., 81
Marsh, Thomas B., 103, 107
Marshall Islands, Mormonism in, 207
Martin, Bill, 47 note 9, 48
"Martin Harris: Mormonism's Early Convert," 69, 75

"Martin Harris, The Honorable New York Farmer," 75
"Martin Harris, Witness and Benefactor to the Book of Mormon," 75
Martin, Thomas K., 357
Martins, Helvécio, 343
Martins, Marcus Helvécio, 216
Marty, Martin E., 12, 47 and note 9, 131 note 3, 136, 172, 181 note 4, 183, 329
Martyrdom Remembered: Reactions to the Assassination of the Prophet Joseph Smith, The, 123
"Mary Bennion Powell: Polygamy and Silence," 296, 342 note 19, 345
"Mary Fielding Smith: Her Ox Goes Marching On," 289 note 36
"Mary Teasdel, Yet Another American in Paris," 289 note 36
Mason, Biddy, 343, 385
Mason, James O., 220, 223
Mason, Marylee, 283 note 19
Masonry/anti-Masonry, and Mormonism, 5, 28, 30, 31, 42, 45
"Masonry and Ethan Smith's 'View of the Hebrews,'" 71
"Masonry and Mormonism: Nauvoo, Illinois, 1841-1847," 25-26
"Masons and Mormons: Released-Time Politics in Salt Lake City, 1930-56," 190
Massacre at Mountain Meadow: An American Legend and a Monumental Crime, 153
"Material Cultural Analysis of the Foundational History of Latter Day Saintism, 1827-1844, A," 271
"Material Culture: An Introduction and Guide to Mormon Vernacular," 361
Mather, Tina, 341 note 18
Matters of Conscience: Conversations with Sterling M. McMurrin on Philosophy, Education, and Religion, 339
Matthew Cowley, Man of Faith, 208
Matthews, Robert J., 76
"Mature Joseph Smith and Treasure Searching, The," 69
"Maturing of the Oak: The Dynamics of Latter-day Saint Growth in Latin America, The," 212
Maurois, Andre, 350 and note 23
Mauss, Armand L., 17, 20, 186, 192, 203, 298 note 52
Mavimbela, Julia, 223
Mavin, Richard, 210
May, Cheryll Lynn, 148, 196, 284 note 24, 355
May, Dean L.
  quoted, 19, 89
  works by, xi, 10, 17 note 20, 18, 79, 88, 144, 146, 148, 149, 196, 305, 353, 355, 357, 364
May, Rollo, 60 note 2
Maynard, Gregory, 92
Mazon, Maricio, 49 note 10

Mazur, Eric Michael, 24
McBrien, Dean D., 6
McClintock, James H., 146
McConkie, Bruce R., 200, 394
McCormick, W. J. Mck., 40
McCoy, Isaac, 96
McCune, Elizabeth Ann Claridge, 345
McFarland, Mary Ann Shumway, 196
McGary, Ellen Pratt, 168
McGavin, E. Cecil, 26, 117, 118, 233
McGuire, Meredith B., 230 note 5
McKay, David Lawrence, 331
McKay, David O., 173, 177, 191, 200, 207, 221, 299, 331, 333, 336, 342, 348, 394
McKay, Douglas, 155
McKiernan, F. Mark
  quoted, 258
  works by, 9, 57, 59, 62, 74 note 13, 75, 96, 114, 139, 245, 248, 257
McKinney, William, 181
McLaws, Monte B., 92
McLellan, John J., 362
McLellin, William E., 16, 245
McMurray, W. Grant
  about, 269-70, 345
  quoted, 268-69
  works by, 120, 135, 254, 268, 269
McMurrin, Sterling M., 20, 30, 179, 270, 339
McNeil, Byron J., 213
McPherson, Robert S., 153, 289 note 36
"Meaning of Revival Language in the Book of Mormon, The," 14
"Medicine and the Mormons: A Historical Perspective," 78
Medicine and the Mormons: An Introduction to the History of Latter-day Saint Health Care, 363
Meek, Shirleen, 207
"Meeting the Challenges of the Latter-day Saints in Vietnam," 219
"Meeting the Needs of the Worldwide Church: Significance of Recent Developments," 201
Meeting the Shadow: The Hidden Power of the Dark Side of Human Nature, 60 note 3
Mehr, Kahlile B., xiv, 203, 211, 224, 225, 226, 227, 295
Meinig, Donald W., 18
Melanesia, Mormonism in, 204, 207
Meldrum, Barbara Howard, 296
Melville, J. Keith, 151
"Membership Growth, Church Activity, and Missionary Recruitment," 203
Membership of the Church of Jesus Christ of Latter-day Saints, 1830-1848, 357 note 3
"Men of the Lot Smith Company, The," 152
Men with a Mission, 1837-1841: The Quorum of the Twelve Apostles in the

British Isles, 132
Mercer, Robert L., 223
"Mercy, Zina, and Kate: Virginia Sorensen's Strong Women in a Man's Society," 378 note 4
Mernitz, Susan Curtis, 72
Merrill, Byron R., 221
Merrill, Milton R., 173, 336
Merton, Robert, 231 note 8
Message of the Joseph Smith Papyri: An Egyptian Endowment, The, 77
"Messages from Two Cultures: Mormon Leaders in France, 1985," 211
Messenger and Advocate, (1834-37), 254
"Metamorphosis of the Kingdom of God: Toward a Reinterpretation of Mormon History, The," 120
Metcalf, Warren, 162
Metcalfe, Brent Lee, 22, 61 note 4, 72, 75
"Methods and Motives: Joseph Smith III's Opposition to Polygamy, 1860-90," 82, 158, 308
Mexico, Mormonism in, 178, 213-15
Meyer, Douglas K., 127
Meyer, Eduard, 5-6, 21
"Michael H. Chandler and the Pearl of Great Price Update," 77
"Michael H. Chandler and the Pearl of Great Price: 1986 Update," 77
Michaelson, Robert S., 116
Micronesia, Mormonism in, 204
"Middle Buddha," 218
Middle East, Mormonism in, 203, 220 223-24
Midgley, Louis C., ix, 30, 32, 63
Midwife's Tale: The Life of Martha Ballard, Based on Her Diary, 1785-1812, 277 note 11, 288
midwives, 288 and note 33
"Mighty Change in Mongolia, A," 219
"'Mighty Man was Brother Lot': A Portrait of Lot Smith, Mormon Frontiersman, A," 152
Mighty Missionary of the Pacific: The Building Program of The Church of Jesus Christ of Latter-day Saints, Its History, Scope, and Significance, 207
"Migration, Social Change and Mormonism in Portugal," 211
Miles, Carrie A., 297 note 48
militarism, 124-25, 194
Mill, John Stuart, 279
Millenarian World of Early Mormonism, The, 16, 21, 39
millennialism, 5, 28, 33, 39
Miller, Alta, 345
Miller, David E., 114, 116, 135, 139, 297 note 48
Miller, Della S., 114, 116, 124
Miller, George, 245, 246, 247, 249
Miller, Larry, 374
Miller, Reuben, 245
Miller, Timothy, 247
Millet, Robert L., 76, 78

Millhands and Preachers: A Study of Gastonia, 231 note 7
Mills, C. Wright, 230 note 5
Milner, Clyde A., II, 340 and note 17
"Milton and Irene Soares: Mormon Pioneers of Northeastern Brazil," 216
Milton, John, 31
Mind of the South, The, 18 note 21
"'Mine Angels Round About': Mormon Missionary Evacuation from Western Europe, 1939," 176
Mineau, Geraldine P., 158, 281 note 17, 357 and note 4, 362
Miner, Caroline Eyring, 344
"Minerva Teichert's Murals: The Motivation for Her Large-Scale Production," 360
Minerva!: The Story of an Artist with a Mission, 360
"Mini-Mission to India: A Year Teaching Eye Surgery, A," 220
"Ministering Angels: Single Women in Mormon Society," 297 note 48, 362-63
"Ministry of Anthon H. Lund, Scandinavian Apostle, The," 341 note 18
"Minnesota Mormons: The Cutlerites," 251
Mintz, Steven, 280 note 14
Minutemen and Their World, The, 127
"Miracle of the Rose and the Oak in Latin America," 213
"Missing Rib: The Forgotten Place of Queens and Priestesses in the Establishment of Zion, The," 283, note 21
Missing Stories: An Oral History of Ethnic and Minority Groups in Utah, 161
Mission to Mozambique: Impressions of the First Senior Missionaries Serving in Maputo, A, 221
"Mission to Paradise," 205
missionaries
about, 115, 132, 196, 201, 203, 208, 210, 217, 219, 221, 223, 270, 300 note 61, 386
finances of, 195
senior couples, 203, 223, 227
"Missionaries and Terror: The Assassination of Two Elders in Bolivia," 189
"Missionaries in the American Religious Marketplace: Mormon Proselyting in the 1830s," 12
"Missionary and Deseret Fiction," 370
"Missionary Couples in Eastern Europe," 203
"Missionary, Native, and General Authority Accounts of a Bolivian Conversion: The Creation of Sacred Mormon Myth," 216
"Missionary Work in the Philippines," 219
Missouri Folk Heroes of the Nineteenth Century, 75, 96
Missouri Mormon Frontier Foundation, 111 and note 24
Missouri period, 5, 61, 77, 87-112, 240-41, 258, 260, 271, 272, 338, 377
"Missouri Persecutions: Petitions for Redress," 112
"Missouri Persecutions: The Petition of Isaac Leany," 112
"Missouri Redress Petitions: A Reappraisal of Mormon Persecutions in Missouri, The," 111, 112
"Missouri's 1838 Extermination Order and the Mormons' Forced Removal to Illinois," 111 note 23
Mitchell, David, 219
"Mite to Bishop: RLDS Women's Financial Relationship to the Church," 292
Mitton, George L., 47 note 9, 48-49, 131 note 3
"Mobocracy and the Rule of Law: American Press Reactions to the Murder of Joseph Smith," 123
"Modernity and Conversion: Mormonism in Twentieth Century Japan," 218
"Modernization Arrested: Child-Naming and the Family in a Utah Town," 17, 161
Moessner, Hermann, 211
Moloney, Karen Marguerite, 300 note 61
money digging. *See* treasure seeking.
"'Money-Diggersville'—The Brief, Turbulent History of the Mormon Town of Warren," 1211
"Money-Digging Folklore and the Beginnings of Mormonism," 69
Mongolia, Mormonism in, 217, 219
"Mongolia: The Morning Breaks," 219
Monson, Farrell Ray, 221
Monson, Thomas S., 225
Montague, Terry Buhle, 176
Moore, Matthew S., 124
Moore, R. Laurence, 12, 14, 21 note 31
Moorman, Donald R., 152
Morain, William D., 3, 27, 60, 327
Moramona: The Mormons in Hawaii, 146, 204
Mordock, Christina, 364
"'More a Movement Than an Organization': Utah's First Encounter with Heresy, The Gladdenites, 1851-1854," 347
More Faith than Fear: The Los Angeles Stake Story, 188, 355
"More Nations than One," 200
More than One: Plural Marriage, a Sacred Heritage, a Promise for Tomorrow, 321
"More Than Meets the Eye: Concentration in the Book of Mormon," 73
More Wives Than One: Transformation of the Mormon Marriage System, 1840-

421

Excavating Mormon Pasts

1910, 25, 158, 168, 296, 316
Morgan, Dale
  about, xii, 1, 8, 176, 340
  quoted, 28, 233, 244, 251
  works by, 8 note 15, 19 note 27, 40, 146, 240, 248, 279
Mormon Alliance, 300 and note 62
Mormon America: The Power and the Promise, 196, 340, 349
Mormon Americana: A Guide to Sources and Collections in the United States, 58, 360 and note 5, 361
"Mormon Angles of Historical Vision: Some Maverick Reflections," xii
Mormon Battalion, 145, 168
"Mormon Battalion: Conflict between Religious and Military Authority, The," 145
Mormon Battalion: U.S. Army of the West, 1846-1848, The, 145
"Mormon Biography: Tracking the (Well-Written) LDS Life," 323 note 2, 324 note 3, 333, 338, 342, 343, 349
"Mormon Bride in the Great Migration, A," 145
"Mormon Carson Emigrant Trail in Western History, The," 145
Mormon Chronicle: The Diaries of John D. Lee, A, 275
"Mormon Church and the Spanish-American War: An End to Selective Pacifism, The," 172
Mormon Church: A Basic History, The, 393
"Mormon Church-State Confrontation in Nineteenth Century America, The," 80
Mormon Churches: A Comparison from Within, The, 307
"Mormon Concept of a Mother in Heaven: A Sociological Account of Its Origin and Development, The," 283 and note 19
"Mormon Concern over MX: Parochialism or Enduring Moral Theology," 194
Mormon Conflict, 1850-1859, The, 152
Mormon Corporate Empire, The, 196
"Mormon Cotton Mission in Southern Utah, The," 148
"Mormon Country a Century Ago: A Geographer's View," 139, 148
Mormon Culture: Four Decades of Essays on Mormon Society and Personality, 364
"Mormon Culture Region: Strategies and Patterns in the Geography of the American West, 1847-1964, The," 18
"Mormon Disenfranchisements of 1882 to 1892, The," 151, 159
"Mormon Divorce and the Statute of 1852: Questions for Divorce in the 1880s," 161
"Mormon Economy at Kirtland, Ohio, The," 83

"Mormon Education in Mexico: The Rise of the 'Sociedad Educativa y Cultural,'" 213
"Mormon Elders' Wafers: Images of Mormon Virility in Patent Medicine Ads," 155
Mormon Enigma: Emma Hale Smith, Prophet's Wife, "Elect Lady," Polygamy's Foe, 61, 243, 289-91, 289, 299, 302, 313, 315, 343
Mormon Experience: A History of the Latter-day Saints, The, 17, 24, 54, 64, 58, 120, 139, 167, 234, 305
"Mormon Experience in Missouri, 1830-1839," xiii, 110
"Mormon Experience in the Wisconsin Pineries, 1841-1845, The," 126, 132
"Mormon Experience: The Plains as Sinai, the Great Salt Lake as the Dead Sea, and the Great Basin as Desert-cum-Promised Land, The," 145
"Mormon Finance and the Mormon War," 149
Mormon Forum, 218
Mormon Graphic Image, 1834-1914: Cartoons, Caricatures, and Illustrations, The, 155
"Mormon Haters," 287
"Mormon Healer and Folk Poet: Mary Susannah Fowler's Life of 'Unselfish Usefulness,'" 344
"Mormon Heritage of Vardis Fisher, The," 339
"Mormon Hierarchy, 1832-1932: An American Elite, The," 358
Mormon Hierarchy: Extensions of Power, The, 191-92, 193, 195, 238 note 18, 297, 298 note 52, 301, 302 note 67, 358
Mormon Hierarchy: Origins of Power, The, 10, 81, 99, 101 note 11, 102, 103, 124, 135, 238, 245, 247, 301, 358
Mormon Historical Studies, 111
Mormon History, 24, 58, 302 note 67, 324 note 6
Mormon History Association, x, 4, 14, 18, 53, 42, 45, 68, 136, 135, 196, 249, 251, 296, 311, 340, 341, 342 note 19, 389, 387
Mormon Identities in Transition, 162, 203, 216, 220, 221, 366
"Mormon Ideology of Place: Cosmic Symbolism of the City of Zion, 1830-1846, The," 364
"Mormon Leaders in Politics: The Transition to Statehood in 1896," 151, 168
"Mormon Literature: Progress and Prospects," 360
Mormon Lives: A Year in the Elkton Ward, 196, 297 note 48, 355
"Mormon Lysistratas: Mormon Women in the International Peace Movement," 275

Mormon Mavericks: Essays on Dissenters, 301 note 64, 373
"Mormon Meetinghouse: Reflections on Pioneer Religious and Social Life in Salt Lake City, The," 162
"Mormon Memory, Mormon Myth, and Mormon History," 53
"Mormon Message in the Context of Maori Culture, The," 364
Mormon Midwife: The 1846-1888 Diaries of Patty Bartlett Sessions, 288 note 33, 301, 345
"Mormon Migration in the 1860s: The Story of the Church Trains," 145
"Mormon Migration into Texas, The," 249
Mormon Missionaries Enter Eastern Europe, 224, 226
"Mormon Missionary of the Nineteenth Century, The," 357
"Mormon Missionary Wives in Nineteenth Century Polynesia," 155, 286
Mormon Mother, A, 168, 277-79, 302, 344
"Mormon Motherhood: Official Images," 283
Mormon Murders: A True Story of Greed, Forgery, Deceit, and Death, The, 69 note 7
"Mormon Nauvoo from a Non-Mormon Perspective," 120
Mormon Neo-Orthodoxy: A Crisis Theology, 17, 189, 181
Mormon Odyssey: The Story of Ida Hunt Udall, Plural Wife, 279 note 13, 344
"Mormon Origins in New York: An Introductory Analysis," 66, 79
Mormon Pacific History Society, 204
Mormon Passage: A Missionary Chronicle, 196
"Mormon Past: Revealed or Revisited?, The," 119, 292 note 41
"Mormon Pavilion at Expo '70, The," 218
Mormon People: Their Character and Traditions, The, 148
"Mormon Persecutions in Missouri, 1833," 108
"Mormon Pioneers in Southern Germany," 211
"Mormon Political Involvement in Ohio," 80
"Mormon Polyandry in Nauvoo," 82 note 15, 82
Mormon Polygamous Families: Life in the Principle, 160, 244, 294, 319, 321, 340
"Mormon Polygamy in Mexico and Canada: A Legal and Historiographical Review," 316
"Mormon Polygamy: A Bibliography, 1900-1999," 170
"Mormon Polygamy: A Bibliography, 1977-92," 170, 296 note 46, 308, 358
"Mormon Polygamy: A Bibliography, 1900-2004," 296 note 46, 358

Index

Mormon Polygamy: A History, 82, 158, 170, 243, 294, 310, 311, 313

"Mormon Polygyny in the Nineteenth Century: A Theoretical Analysis," 158

Mormon Presence in Canada, The, 146, 316

"Mormon Priesthood Revelation and the São Paulo, Brazil Temple, The," 216

"Mormon Question Enters National Politics, 1850-1856, The," 152

Mormon Question in the 1849-1850 Statehood Debates," 151

"Mormon Question, 1850-1865: A Study in Politics and Public Opinion, The," 159

Mormon Question: Polygamy and Constitutional Conflict in Nineteenth-Century America, The, 25, 159, 296, 319

Mormon Reformation, 151-52, 304, 334

"Mormon Reformation, The," 151

"Mormon Reformation of 1856-1857, The," 151

"Mormon Reformation of 1856-1857: The Rhetoric and the Reality, The," 151

"Mormon Relief Society and the International Women's Year, The," 193, 298 note 52

"Mormon Religion in Nauvoo," 130

"Mormon Renegade: James Emmett at the Vermillion, 1846," 248

Mormon Role in the Settlement of the West, The, 146

"Mormon Satellite Settlements in Hancock County, Illinois, and Lee County, Iowa," 128

Mormon Settlement in Arizona, 146

"Mormon Settlement of Cassia County, Idaho, 1863-1921, The," 353

"Mormon Sexuality in Cross-Cultural Perspective," 364

Mormon Sisters: Women in Early Utah, 143, 277, 281 note 15, 286, 287, 302 note 67, 306, 344

"Mormon Society and Culture," xiv

Mormon Spirituality: The Latter-day Saints in Wales, 364

Mormon Struggle with Assimilation and Identity: Trends and Developments since Mid-Century, The," 20, 186

"Mormon Succession Crisis of 1844, The," 245-46, 268

"Mormon Suffrage Relationship: Personal and Political Quandaries, The," 160

"Mormon Temple in the American Rural Tradition, A," 82

"Mormon Theodemocracy: Theocratic and Democratic Elements in Early Latter-day Saint Ideology, 1827-1846," 80, 254

Mormon Thunder: A Documentary History of Jedediah Morgan Grant, 141 note 8, 334

"Mormon Town: One Man's West, A," 18, 355

"Mormon Trail Network in Iowa, 1838-1863: A New Look, The," 144 note 11

"Mormon Trail Network in Nebraska, 1846-1868: A New Look, The," 144 note 11

"Mormon Trail of 1846, The," 145

Mormon Trek West: The Journey of American Exiles, The, 144

"Mormon Values Set in Stone, Bronze," 392

"Mormon Village in Transition: Richfield, Utah, as a Case Study, The," 353

Mormon Village: A Pattern and Technique of Land Settlement, The, 146, 196

"Mormon Ward: Congregation or Community?, The," 196

Mormon Wards as Community, 198

"Mormon Way Stations, Garden Grove and Mt. Pisgah, The," 144

Mormon Woman's Forum Quarterly, 302

"Mormon Women and the Struggle for Definition: The Nineteenth Century Church," 286, 287 note 27

"Mormon Women and the Temple: toward a New Understanding," 286

"Mormon Women Have Had the Priesthood since 1843," 300, 301, 311 note 6

"Mormon Women in Southern Alberta: The Pioneer Years," 316

"Mormon Women: A Bibliography in Process, 1977-1985," 143, 302 note 67

Mormon Women's Forum, 193, 300

"Mormon Years of the Borglum Family, The," 349

"Mormon" Settlement on the Big Blue River, The, 111 note 22

"Mormon's Crickets and Gulls: A New Look at an Old Story," 392

"Mormondom's Lost Generation: The Novelists of the 1940s," 339, 377

Mormonen im Suedwesten Deutschland: Auf den Spuren Ihres Lebens und Ihrer Geschichte, Die [The Mormons in Southwest Germany: As Seen in the Marks of Their Lives and History], 210

"Mormonism and American Culture: Some Tentative Hypotheses," 1, 9, 12

"Mormonism and Maoism: The Church and People's China," 219

Mormonism and Masonry, 26

Mormonism and Music: A History, 81, 361

"Mormons and Politics in Illinois, 1839-1844," 121

Mormonism and the American Experience, xi, 3, 12, 24, 25, 234, 358

"Mormonism and the Challenge of the Mainline," 195

"Mormonism and the Dynamics of Dissent," 346

"Mormonism and the Equal Rights Amendment," 193

"Mormonism and the Occult Connection," 40 note 7

"Mormonism and the Puritan Connection: The Trial of Mrs. Anne Hutchinson and Several Persistent Questions Bearing on Church Governance," 33

"Mormonism in a Maori Village: A Study in Social Change," 208

"Mormonism in American Historiography: John L. Brooke's *The Refiner's Fire* and Competing Versions of Mormon Origins," 47 note 9

"Mormonism in Black Africa: Changing Attitudes and Practices, 1830-1981," 221

"Mormonism in Brazil: Religion and Dependency in Latin America," 215, 364

"Mormonism in Chile," 216

Mormonism in Conflict: The Nauvoo Years, 121

"Mormonism in France: The Family as a Universal Value in a Globalizing Religion," 212

"Mormonism in France: A Study of Cultural Exchange and Institutional Adaptation," 212

Mormonism in Germany: A History of the Church of Jesus Christ of Latter-day Saints in Germany between 1840 and 1970, 210

"Mormonism in Latin America: A Preliminary Historical Survey," 213

"Mormonism in Latin America: towards the Twenty-first Century," 213

"Mormonism in Modern Japan," 218

"Mormonism in New Zealand: A Historical Appraisal," 208, 364

"Mormonism in Secular Society: Changing Patterns in Official Ecclesiastical Rhetoric," 17, 181

"Mormonism in the Historical Setting of 19th Century America," 73

Mormonism in the Twentieth Century, 176

"Mormonism in the Twenty-first Century: Marketing for Miracles," 203

Mormonism in Transition: A History of the Latter-day Saints, 1890-1930, 17, 25, 165, 170, 178, 297, 311

Mormonism, Magic, and Masonry, 40

"Mormonism, the Maori, and Cultural Authenticity," 208

Mormonism Unvailed: Or, A Faithful Account of That Singular Imposition and Delusion, from Its Rise to the Present

Excavating Mormon Pasts

Time. With Sketches of the Characters of Its Propagators, and A Full, Detail of the Manner in which the Famous Golden Bible Was Brought Before the World, 3 note 2, 40, 73
Mormonism: A Faith for All Cultures, 20, 200, 211, 212, 218
"Mormonism: From Its New York Beginnings," 79
Mormonism: The Mohammedanism of the West, 5 note 11
Mormonism: The Story of a New Religious Tradition, xi, 19 note 28, 22, 28, 68, 130, 139, 234, 292
"Mormonism's 'Happy Warrior': Appreciating Leonard J. Arrington," 389-90
"Mormonism's Encounter with Spiritualism," 157
"Mormonism's Feminist Heretic," 346
"Mormonism's Negro Doctrine: An Historical Overview," 383
"Mormonites, The," 4 note 4
"Mormons," 18 note 20, 364
Mormons, The, 8, 10, 16, 22, 32, 116, 130, 139 note 2, 187, 236
"Mormons and California Gold," 146
Mormons and Cowboys, Moonshiners and Klansmen: Federal Law Enforcement in the South and West, 1870-1893, 159
Mormons and Gentiles: A History of Salt Lake City, 146, 353
Mormons and Jews, 20
Mormons and Muslims: Spiritual Foundations and Modern Manifestations, 6 note 12, 20
"Mormons and Native Americans: A Historical and Bibliographical Introduction," 161
"Mormons and Non-Mormon Divorce Patterns," 364
"Mormons and Slavery—A Closer Look, The," 161
"Mormons and the Bible in the 1830s, The," 76
Mormons and the Bible: The Place of the Latter-day Saints in American Religion, 16, 21, 34 note 4, 76
"Mormons and the Hula: The Polynesian Cultural Center in Hawaii," 204
"Mormons and the Law: The Polygamy Cases, The," 159, 317
"Mormons and the Morrisite War, The," 157
"Mormons and the Office of Indian Affairs: The Conflict Over Winter Quarters, 1846-1848, The," 144
Mormons and Their Historians, ix, 30, 339
Mormons at the Missouri, 1846-1852: "And We Should Die . . .," 144, 353
"Mormons Come to Canada, 1887-1902, The," 146

Os Mormons em Alagoas: Religião e Relações Raciais [The Mormons in Alagoas: Religion and Racial Relations], 216
Mormons for ERA, 299
Mormons in American History, The, 18 note 23, 32
"Mormons in Ireland, The," 210
Mormons in Mexico: The Dynamics of Faith and Culture, 178, 213, 315, 363
Mormons in Nevada, The, 146
"Mormons in Texas: The Ill-Fated Lyman Wight Colony, 1844-1858," 249, 347
Mormons in the Pacific: A Bibliography, 204
"Mormons in Victorian England," 357
Mormons in West Africa: New Terrain for the Sesquicentennial, 221
"Mormons of the Wisconsin Territory: 1835-1848, The," 128
"Mormons on the Warfront: The Protestant Mormons and Catholic Mormons of Northern Ireland," 210
"Mormons Who Did Not Go West: A Study of the Emergence of the Reorganized Church of Jesus Christ of Latter Day Saints," 245
"Mormons: Looking Forward and Outward, The," 179 note 3, 183, 187-88
Mormons' War on Poverty; A History of LDS Welfare 1830-1990, The, 174
Morning Breaks: Stories of Conversion and Faith in the Former Soviet Union, The, 225
"'Morning Fair, Roads Bad:' Geology, Topography, Hydrology, and Weather on the Iowa and Nebraska Mormon Trail, 1846-1847," 144
Morningstar, Connie, 361
Morris, Christopher, 127
Morris, Joseph, 347
Morris, Michael R., 207, 220
Morris, Robert J., 218
Morrison, Alexander B., 221, 223
Morton, Ermel J., 205
Moser, Stephen B., 363
Moss, James R., 200, 201, 208
Mother in Heaven, 283 and note 19, 299, 300-301
"Mother Tongue: Use of Non-English Languages in the Church of Jesus Christ of Latter-day Saints in the United States," 188
Mothers of the Prophets, 61, 277
"Mound Builders, Mormons, and William Cullen Bryant," 71 note 9
Mount Rushmore, 349
"'Mountain Common Law': The Extralegal Punishment of Seducers in Early Utah," 159
Mountain Meadows Massacre, 108, 142, 151-54, 178, 387

Mountain Meadows Massacre, The, xii, 153, 177, 274 and note 6, 275, 299, 302
Mountain Meadows Massacre: An Outlander's View, The, 153
Mountain Meadows Witness: The Life and Times of Bishop Phillip Klingensmith, 153, 338
Mouritsen, Maren M., 289 note 36
Mouritsen, Robert Glen, 81
Mouritsen, Russell H., 357
"Move South, The," 152
"Moving Possessions: An Analysis Based on Personal Documents from the 1847-1869 Mormon Migration," 145
Moyle, Henry D., 212, 336
Mueller, Mary Lou, 289 note 36
"Muhammad-Joseph Smith Comparison: Subjective Metaphor or a Sociology of Prophethood, The," 6 note 12
Muistamme, 211
Mulder, William
 about, 119
 quoted, 18 and note 23, 32
 works by, xii, 1 note 1, 19, 144, 159, 162, 341 note 18, 349, 352
Multiply and Replenish: Mormon Essays on Sex and Family, 298 note 51, 358
Mulvay, Jill C. *See* Derr, Jill Mulvay.
"Murder, Mayhem and Mormons: The Evolution of Law Enforcement on the San Juan Frontier, 1880-1900," 153
Murphy, Miriam B., 173, 174, 281 note 16, 289 note 36, 297 note 48
Murphy, Thomas W., 213, 215
Murray, Herbert F., 207
Museum of Church History and Art, 189
music, history of, 361-62
Musser, Amos Milton, 386
MX missile system, 186, 194
"My Best for the Kingdom": History and Autobiography of John Lowe Butler, A Mormon Frontiersman, 99, 106, 142, 338, 341
My Father, David O. McKay, 331
My Favorite Church History Stories, 394
"My Short Happy Life with *Exponent II*," 287 note 29
Myres, Sandra L., 280 note 14, 295 note 45
Mysteries of Godliness: A History of Mormon Temple Worship, The, 133, 243
"Mysteries of Mormonism, The," 47 note 9
"Mystics and Healers," 287
Myth Makers, The, 68 note 6

N

N. Eldon Tanner: His Life and Service, 336
Naifeh, Steven, 69 note 7

Index

Nam, Rhee Ho. *See* Rhee Honam.
Namier, Lewis, 357
"Nation in a Day: The Church in Guatemala, A," 215
National Aeronautical and Space Administration, 339
"National Culture, Personality, and Theocracy in the Early Mormon Culture of Violence," 101, 110, 153
National Defense University, 219
"National Perspectives of Utah's Statehood," 168
"National Women's Relief Society and the U.S. Sheppard-Towner Act, The," 284 note 25
Native Americans. *See* American Indians.
Naulu, Sosaih H., 207
Nauru, Mormonism in, 207
Nauvoo, 133
Nauvoo: A Place of Peace, a People of Promise, 92, 113, 124, 121, 135, 243, 352
"Nauvoo: A River Town," 126
"Nauvoo and the New Mormon History: A Bibliographical Survey," 113
"Nauvoo Charter: A Reinterpretation, The," 124
"Nauvoo: Dream and Nightmare," 114, 130
Nauvoo Expositor, 244-45
Nauvoo Fact Book: Questions and Answers for Nauvoo Enthusiasts, 133
"Nauvoo Heritage of the Reorganized Church," 119, 136, 245
Nauvoo: Kingdom on the Mississippi, 19 note 27, 49, 113, 114, 116-17, 124, 130, 243, 253-54, 307, 352
"Nauvoo Legion, 1840-1845: A Unique Military Organization, The," 124
"Nauvoo Neighborhood: A Little Philadelphia or a Unique City Set Upon a Hill, The," 126, 352
"Nauvoo Observed," 352
"Nauvoo of the Imaginations: A Book Review Essay, The," 136
"Nauvoo on My Mind," 117, 270
Nauvoo period, 5, 61, 104, 113-36, 234, 266
 dissent in, 232, 234, 241-51, 264
 in fiction, 374, 377, 383
 organizational developments, 237-38
Nauvoo Restoration Incorporated, 114, 116, 135
"Nauvoo Roots of Mormon Polygamy, 1841-46: A Preliminary Demographic Report," 244, 316, 343 note 20
"Nauvoo Stake, Priesthood Quorums, and the Church's First Wards," 135
"Nauvoo Teenager: Henry Sanderson," 362
Nauvoo Temple. *See* temples.
"Nauvoo Temple, The," 132
"Nauvoo Temple: 'A Monument of the Saints,'" 133
Nauvoo Temple: A Story of Faith, 133
Nauvoo the Beautiful, 118
Nauvoo: The City Beautiful, 133
Nauvoo: The City of Joseph, 114, 124
"Nauvoo West: The Mormons of the Iowa Shore," 128
"Nauvoo's Temple Square [1841-1999]," 133
Nealon, John S., 144
Nearly Everything Imaginable: The Everyday Life of Utah's Mormon Pioneers, 148, 362, 366
Needle, Jeffrey, 386
Neff, Andrew L., 6, 146
"Negro Slavery in Utah," 161
Neibaur, Alexander, 45
Neibuhr, H. Richard, 130
Neilson, Reid L., 228
Neither Black Nor White, 192
Nelson, Lee, 372 note 2
Nelson, Lowry, 19, 196, 146
Nelson, Russell M., 224
Nelson, Terry G., 217
Nepal, Mormonism in, 217
"Nephi's Outline," 73
Netherlands, Mormonism in, 211
Neuenschwander, Dennis B., 224
Neusner, Jacob, 132
"'New and Everlasting Covenant': An Approach to the Theology of Joseph Smith, A," 309
New Approaches to the Book of Mormon: Explorations in Critical Methodology, 22, 72, 75
"New B. H. Roberts Book Lacks Insight of his Testimony," 75
New Caledonia, Mormonism in, 204, 207
"New Climate of Liberation: A Tribute to Fawn McKay Brodie, 1915-1981, A," 30
New Commentary on the Doctrine and Covenants, A, 76
New Directions in American Religious History, 131 note 4, 136 note 5
"New Documents and Mormon Beginnings," 69
"New England Origins of Mormonism, The," xi, 9, 33, 79
"New England Origins of Mormonism Revisited, The," 33
New England puritanism, influence on Mormonism, 28, 33
New England Soul: Preaching and Religious Culture in Colonial New England, The, 132
New Era, 203
New Guinea, Mormonism in, 204
New Hebrides, Mormonism in, 204
"New Historical Synthesis: Women's Biography, The," 280 note 14
"New Light on an Old Hypothesis: The Ohio Origins of the Revelation on Eternal Marriage," 82, 310
"New Light on Mormon Origins from the Palmyra (N. Y.) Revival," 40, 66
"New Light on Old Egyptiana: Mormon Mummies, 1848-71," 77
"New Light on Old Difficulties: The Historical Importance of the Missouri Affidavits," 112
"New Light on the Mountain Meadows Caravan," 153
New Mormon History
 characteristics of, ix-xii, 24, 52, 113, 117, 128, 130, 137, 148, 177, 178, 187, 232, 234, 238, 253, 254, 273-74, 279, 301, 302, 323-24
 examples of, 274 note 6, 289
 future research topics, 23, 85-86, 110-12, 136, 163-64, 196-98, 227, 302, 362
 influence on fiction, 367-69, 376-90
 influences on, 30-32, 165, 176, 340
 interdisciplinarity of, 289, 295, 296
 primary sources, x, 58, 279, 301
 resistance to, 53, 184, 191, 294, 311, 389
"New Mormon History, The," ix, x, xi, note 2, 86, 119, 253
New Mormon History, The, xi, 36 note 6, 274 note 4, 281 note 17, 283 note 20, 292 note 41, 295
"New Mormon History: Historical Writing since 1950, The," 24
"'New Mormon History' Reassessed in Light of Recent Books on Joseph Smith and Mormon Origins, The," ix
New Mormon History: Revisionist Essays on the Past, The, 273 note 2, 392
"New Mormon Woman's History," xiv
"*New Northwest*, and *Woman's Exponent*: Early Voices for Suffrage, The," 288 note 32
"New Scholarship on Latter-day Saint Women in the Twentieth Century," 193
new social history, 57, 81, 85
"'New Social History' and the 'New Mormon History': Reflections on Recent Trends, The," 57, 164, 273 note 1, 292 note 39
"'New Translation' of the Bible, 1830-1833: Doctrinal Development during the Kirtland Era, The," 76
New Views of Mormon History: Essays in Honor of Leonard J. Arrington, 10, 28, 42, 53 note 1, 72, 148, 149, 158, 170, 188, 207, 274 note 4, 283 note 23, 284, 309, 353, 355
New Western History, 24, 183
"New Writers and Mormonism," ix note 1
New York period, 53-86, 59, 61
New Zealand, Mormonism in, 200, 207-8

425

Newell, Grandison, 102
Newell, L. Jackson, 288 note 35, 339
Newell, Linda King
  about, 299
  quoted, 342
  works by, 61, 81, 140, 243, 264, 283 and note 21, 289 note 36, 289-91, 315, 343, 344, 352
Newell, Lloyd D., 128
Newton, Marjorie, 142, 189, 207-8, 270, 364
Nibley, Hugh
  about, 31, 32
  works by, 21, 68 note 6, 73, 77
Nibley, Preston, 144 note 11
Nibley, Preston, 75
Nichols, Jeffrey, 25, 313
Niebuhr, H. Richard, 18, 230 note 5, 231 note 7
"Niels Bergeson: A Saint among Kings," 341 note 18
Nielson, Dean C., 363
Nielson, Reid L., xiv
Nigeria, Mormonism in, 221
"Nigeria and Ghana: A Miracle Precedes the Messengers," 223
Nightfall at Nauvoo, 376
"1968 Presidential Decline of George Romney: Mormonism or Politics, The," 340
"Nineteenth Century Cache Valley Folk Furniture: A Study of Form and Function," 361
"1989-90: The Curtain Opens," 226
Niue, Mormonism in, 205
Njeim, George, 307
"No Higher Ground: Objective History Is an Illusive Chimera," ix
No Ma'am, That's Not History: A Brief Review of Mrs. Brodie's Reluctant Vindication of a Prophet She Seeks to Expose, 31
No Man Knows My History: The Life of Joseph Smith the Mormon Prophet, xii, 1, 3, 5, 8, 10, 27, 28, 30, 49, 60, 63, 74 note 13, 119, 177, 234, 274, 275, 291, 304, 324, 327, 343 note 20
"No Toil Nor Labor Fear": The Story of William Clayton, 338
No Unhallowed Hand, 370
Noah, John, 240
Nolan, Max, 68, 243
"Non-Mormon Views of the Martyrdom: A Look at Some Early Published Accounts," 123
"Nonconformists of Leeds in the Early Victorian Era: A Study in Social Composition, The," 357
"North European Horizontal Log Construction in the Sanpete-Sevier Valleys," 162
"North from Zion: The Minnesota Cutlerites, 1864-1964," 251
Northcott, Herbert C., 315
Northern Marianas, Mormonism in, 207

Northern Voices: A Folk History of Mormonism among British Americans, 1830-1867, 12
Not By Bread Alone: The Journal of Martha Spencer Heywood 1850-1856, 275
"'Not Every Missourian Was a Bad Guy': Hiram G. Parks' 1839 Letter to James Sloan in Quincy, Illinois," 111 note 23
"Not Invited but Welcome: The History and Impact on Church Policy on Sister Missionaries," 196
"Note on the First Vision and Its Import in the Shaping of Early Mormonism, A," 66
"Notes on Mormon Polygamy," 304
Nothing More Heroic, 386
"'Nothing More Miraculous': The First Decade of Mormonism in Mongolia," 219
"Novels," 369
Novick, Peter, 280 note 14
Noyes, John Humphrey, 293
Numano, Jiro, 189, 218

O

"O My Father," 283
"'O What a Good Big World!': Virginia Sorensen's Letters from Denmark," 341 note 18
O'Brian, Robert, 204
O'Conner, Flannery, 321-22
O'Dea, Thomas
  about, 119, 236-38, 240, 241, 244
  quoted, 22-23, 190
  works by, 8, 10, 16, 32, 114, 116, 130, 139 note 2, 187
O'Donnal, John Forres, 215
O'Donovan, Rocky, 298 note 51
O'Driscoll, Jeffrey S., 61, 334
"Oak Tree Revisited: Brazilian LDS Leaders' Insights on the Growth of the Church in Brazil, The," 216
Oakland . . . A History, 186 note 6
Oaks, Dallin H., 123, 126, 179, 227, 244, 284, 393 note 13
Oatman, Lorenzo D., 245
"Obadiah Dogberry: Rochester Free-Thinker," 71 note 11
"Objectives of Mormon Economic Policy," 149
Obscure Believers: The Mormon Schism of Alpheus Cutler, 251, 347
occult. *See* folk magic.
"Occult Connection? Mormonism, Christian Science, and Spiritualism, The," 21 note 31
Occult in America: New Historical Perspectives, The, 21 note 31
Occultism: The True Origins of Mormonism, 40
"Odyssey of a Latter-day Prophet: Wilford Woodruff and the Manifesto of 1890, The," 141 note 5, 167,

160
"Odyssey of Sonia Johnson, The," 298 note 53
Of Woman Born, 280 note 14
"Off the Record: Telling the Rest of the Truth," 298 note 52
"Office of Associate President of the Church of Jesus Christ of Latter-day Saints, The," 81
"Official Declaration 2: Revelation on the Priesthood," 221
Ogden, D. Kelly, 223
Ohai, Jean B., 341 note 18
Ohio period, 53-86, 105
Olaiz, Hugo, 190
"Old Folks Day: A Unique Utah Tradition, The," 362
"Old Fox: Alpheus Cutler, The," 249
Old Mormon Nauvoo, 1839-1846: Historic Photographs and Guide, 133
Old Nauvoo: Everyday Life in the City of Joseph, 352
Old West–New West: Centennial Essays, 296
Oliver Cowdery: Second Elder and Scribe, 61, 75, 237
Oliver Cowdery: The Elusive Second Elder of the Restoration, 61, 75, 237, 333
"Oliver Cowdery's Kirtland, Ohio, Sketchbook," 59
Olmstead, Jacob W., 194
Olpin, Robert S., 360
Olsen, Steven L., 80, 364
Olson, Earl E., 77
Olson, Eric, 131
Oman, Richard G., 360 and note 5
Oman, Susan Staker. *See* Staker, Susan.
"On Becoming a Universal Church: Some Historical Perspectives," 20, 187, 201
"On Being a Mormon Historian (and Its Aftermath)," 53, 301 note 64, 311 note 6, 373
"On Conceptualization of Zion," 268
"On the Edge: Mormonism's Single Men," 362
On the Mormon Frontier: The Diary of Hosea Stout [1844-1861], 275
"On the Origin and Evolution of Religious Groups," 231 note 8
"On the Pacific Frontier: The Church in the Gilbert Islands," 204
On Their Own: Widows and Widowhood in the American Southwest, 1848-1939, 281 note 17, 362
On This Star, 377
On Wings of Faith, 224
One Fold and One Shepherd, 391
100 Years of Sports at Ricks College, 363
100 Years of Utah Painting, 360
"125 Years of Conspiracy Theories: Origins of the Utah Expedition of 1857-58," 152
"150 Years of Truth and Conse-

Index

quences about Mormon History," 142, 301
"One Lord, One Faith, Many Chat Rooms: Mormons, the Internet, and the Complexities of Open Spaces," 190
One More River to Cross, 383
One Side by Himself: The Life and Times of Lewis Barney, 1808-1894, 341
"'One Talk' in Papua New Guinea," 207
"Opening the Gates of Zion: Utah and the Coming of the Union Pacific Railroad," 148
oral histories, 196, 203, 220, 294, 304, 321, 333
Ord, Gayle Goble, 73
"Ordaining Women and Transformation from Sect to Denomination," 292
"Ordeal of Brigham Young Jr., The," 142 note 10
Order Is Love, The, 298
Ordered Love: Sex Roles and Sexuality in Victorian Utopias—the Shakers, the Mormons, and the Oneida Community, An, 293, 319
organizational developments, 80-81, 133-35, 194-95, 237, 254
"Organizational Development and Social Origins of the Mormon Hierarchy, 1832-1932: A Prosopographical Study," 358
Origin of Consciousness in the Breakdown of the Bicameral Mind, 3
"Original Book of Mormon Manuscripts, The," 74
Origins and History of the Mormons with Reflections on the Beginnings of Islam and Christianity, 6 note 12
Orrin Porter Rockwell: Man of God, Son of Thunder, 142, 338
Orson Hyde: Missionary, Apostle, Colonizer, 62, 141
Orson Hyde: The Olive Branch of Israel, 62, 141
"Orson Pratt-Brigham Young Controversies: Conflict within the Quorums, 1853-1868, The," 158
"Orson Pratt, Jr.: Gifted Son of an Apostle and an Apostate," 348
Orton, Chad M., 188, 355
Ostler, Barbara B., 360
Ostler, Blake, 73, 78
Ostling, Joan K., 196, 340, 349
Ostling, Richard N., 196, 340, 349
"Other Mormon Histories: Lamanite Subjectivity in Mexico," 213
Other Side of Heaven, The, 205
Otterstrom, Samuel M., 201
Ottley, Jerold, 362
Our Common Country: Family Farming, Culture, and Community in the Nineteenth-Century Midwest, 121, 352
"Our Foremothers and the 1870 Franchise," 283 note 23

Our Legacy of Faith: A Brief History of the Reorganized Church of Jesus Christ of Latter Day Saints, 54, 120, 234, 263
"Our Own Agenda: A Critique of the Methodology of the New Mormon History," ix
"Our Sacred Honor," 393
Out of Obscurity, Out of Captivity, Out of Darkness: The Church and Humanitarian Services in Former Yugoslavia and the Russian Empire, 224
"Out of Obscurity: The Emergence of the Church of Jesus Christ of Latter-day Saints in 'That Vast Empire' of Russia," 226
Out of Obscurity: The LDS Church in the Twentieth Century, 199 note 1, 200, 213, 215, 218, 221, 226
Out of the Black Patch: The Autobiography of Effie Marquess Carmack, Folk Musician, Artist, and Writer, 301
"Out of the Slot," 283 note 18
"Out of the Swan's Nest: The Ministry of Anthon H. Lund, Scandinavian Apostle," 336
Outreach International, 270
"Outside the Mormon Hierarchy: Alternative Aspects of Institutional Power," 284
outsider/outsider fiction, 374
Outsiders, 230 note 2
"Overt and Covert Politics: The Mormon Church's Anti-ERA Campaign in Virginia," 193
"Overworked Stereotypes or Accurate Images?: Images of Polygamy in *The Giant Joshua,*" 378 note 5
Owen, Paul L., 47 note 9
Owens, Kenneth N., 145
Owens, Lance, 45
Owens, Lance S., 44, 45, 47 note 9, 68, 131 note 3, 243
"Ownership of the Kirtland Temple: Legends, Lies, and Misunderstandings," 85, 271

P

Pace, D. Gene, 281 note 17
Pace, Glenn L., 223
Pacific, Mormonism in, 203-8
Packard, Sondra Bradford, 176
Packer, Boyd K., ix, 300-301, 311 note 6
Page, Hiram, 240, 244
Page, John E., 245
Pakistan, Mormonism in, 217
Palestine, Mormonism in, 223
Palmer, A. Delbert, 216
Palmer, Grant H., 42, 71 note 9
Palmer, Howard, 315-16
Palmer, Shirley, 218
Palmer, Spencer J.
about, 220
works by, 6 note 12, 20, 32, 71, 200 and note 2, 201, 217, 218, 221, 342

"Palmyra Revisited: A Look at Early Nineteenth Century America and the Book of Mormon," 72
Panek, Tracey E., 155
Pang, Beng L., 219
Panic of 1837, 14, 83, 241
Papanikolas, Helen Zeese, 161, 173, 342
Papers in Women's Studies: University of Michigan, 161
Papers of Joseph Smith, x-xi note 3, xi, 58
Papua New Guinea, Mormonism in, 207
"Paradox of Organization, The," 195
Paraguay, Mormonism in, 215
Paramore, James M., 311
parimutuel betting, 194
Parker, Douglas H., 159
Parkin, Darell L., 363
Parkin, Max H., 57, 80, 105, 106
Parkinson, Benson Young, 336, 369
"Parley P. Pratt in Winter Quarters and the Trail West," 145
Parrish, Alan K., 339, 341 note 18
Parrish, Warren, 240
Parry, Jay A., 219
Parson, Erin, 363
Parson, Robert E., 355
Parsons, Talcott, 18, 230 note 5, 231 note 8, 236
Partridge, Edward, 84
Partridge, Scott H., 83
Pascoe, Peggy, 284 note 24
Past before Us: Contemporary Historical Writing in the United States, The, 85
"Patriarchal Crisis of 1845, The," 135, 249
Patriarchs and Politics: The Plight of the Mormon Woman, 193, 283, 302
"Patrolling the Borders: Feminist Historiography and the New Historicism," 280 note 14
Patten, David W., 103, 107
"Patterns and Process of Growth, The," 201
"Patterns of Mormon Polygamy in 1880," 316
Patterson, Richard, 348
Paul, Charles Randall, 131 note 3
Paul, E. Robert, 78
Paulsen, David L., xiii, 52
"Peace Initiative: Using the Mormons to Rethink Culture and Ethnicity in American History," 146 note 13
Peaceable Kingdom, The, 377
Peacock, Ella, 345
Pearson, Carol Lynn, 298
Pearson, Lorene, 377
Peck, Elbert Eugene, 191
Peculiar People: Mormons and Same-Sex Orientation, 298 note 51
"Peculiar People: The Physiological Aspects of Mormonism, 1850-1875, A," 158
Pedraja, Carlos, 216

427

Pement, Isleta L., 265, 266
Penley, Kaija H., 211-12
Penny Tracts and Polemics: A Critical Analysis of Anti-Mormon Pamphleteering in Great Britain, 1837-1860, 155
Penrose, Romania B. Pratt, 345
People and Power of Nauvoo: Themes from the Nauvoo Experience, 133
People of Rimrock: A Study of Values in Five Cultures, 364
"People on the Mormon Frontier: Kanab's Families of 1874," 148, 353
"People Versus the Prophet: Joseph Smith and the Criminal Law in Illinois, The," 123
Peoples of Utah, The, 161, 342, 349
"Peopling the Upper Snake: The Second Wave of Mormon Settlement in Idaho," 353
"'Perfect Estopel': Selling the Nauvoo Temple, A," 133
"'Perfect Pattern': The Book of Mormon as a Model for the Writing of Sacred History, The," 131
"Peripheral Visions of the Mormon Mother God: Making the Invisible Visible," 300 note 60
Perkins, Keith W., 62, 133
"Perpetuation of a Myth: Mormon Danites in Five Western Novels, 1840-1890, The," 155
Perrin, Kathleen C., 205
Perrin, Yves A., 205
Perry, Anne S., 208
"Persistence of Mormon Community into the 1990s, The," 17, 188
"Persistent Idea of American Treasure Hunting, The," 69
"Personal Cost of the 1838 Mormon War in Missouri: One Mormon's Plea for Forgiveness, The," 111 note 23
Personal Writings of Joseph Smith, 50 note 12, 58
Personal Writings of Eliza Roxcy Snow, The, 281, 301, 343
"Personality and Motivation in Utah Historiography," 350
"Persons for All Seasons: Women in Mormon History," 275
Persuitte, David, 61 note 4, 72
Peru, Mormonism in, 216
Petersen, Boyd Jay, 176, 339
Petersen, LaMar, 83
Petersen, Lauritz G., 82
Petersen, Mark E., 218
Petersen, Melvin J., 77
Peterson, Charles S.
 quoted, 24, 389
 works by, 18, 127, 142, 146, 149, 152, 163, 176, 355, 388, 389 note 8
Peterson, Daniel C.
 quoted, 37, 48-49
 works by, 47 note 9, 131 note 3, 223
Peterson, Esther Eggertsen, 340, 345
Peterson, F. Ross, 340, 355

Peterson, Gary B., 355
Peterson, Gerald Joseph, 218
Peterson, H. Donl, 224
Peterson, John Alton, 162, 342
Peterson, Levi S.
 about, 388
 quoted, 344
 works by, 177 note 4, 293, 300 note 61, 344 and note 21
Peterson, Orlen C., 78
Peterson, Paul H., 78, 151
Peterson, William J., 145
Phelps, W. W., 69, 82, 105, 310
Philippines, Mormonism in, 207, 217, 219, 227
"Philippines: The Land of Joyous Service," 219
Philo T. Farnsworth: The Father of Television, 338
Philosophical Foundations of Mormon Theology, The, 270
Philosophy of a Future State, 30
Phonphongrat, Ruchirawan, 219
"Physical Evidence at the Carthage Jail," 123
"Picturing the Nauvoo Legion," 124
Pillar of Light, 370, 374, 379-80
"Pink *Dialogue* and Beyond, The," 277 note 11, 287 note 27
Pioneer in Guatemala, 215
"Pioneering in Chyulu, Kenya," 223
"Pioneering in Russia," 226
"Pioneering in South Korea," 218
"Pioneering in the Andes," 216
"Pioneering Women Physicians, 1847-1900," 281 note 16
"Pioneers in East Africa," 223
Pioneers in Every Land: Inspirational Stories of International Pioneers Past and Present, 201, 211, 216, 218, 221, 225
"Pioneers in Ivory Coast," 223
"Pioneers in Paraguay," 216
Pioneers in the Pacific Sesquicentennial Conference, 207
Pitcairn Island, Mormonism in, 205, 205
Pitman, Leon S., 361
"Pivotal Nauvoo Temple, The," 133
"Place of Joseph Smith in the Development of American Religion: A Historiographical Inquiry, The," 1, 5 note 7
Place over Time: The Continuity of Southern Distinctiveness, 18 note 21
"'Place Prepared': Joseph, Brigham, and the Quest for Promised Refuge in the West, A," 145
Places of Worship: 150 Years of LDS Architecture, 162, 361
Pladwell, E. S., 186 note 6
"'Plainer Translation': Joseph Smith's Translation of the Bible, A History and Commentary, A,* 76
"Plea to the Leadership of the Church: Choose Love Not Power, A," 191

plural marriage. *See* polygamy.
"Plural Marriage and Mormon Fundamentalism," 172
pluralism, and Mormonism, 19, 54, 59, 66, 72, 108-9, 130
"Plurality, Patriarchy, and the Priestess: Zina D. H. Young's Nauvoo Marriage," 306
Pluss, Caroline, 219
Poland, Mormonism in, 224
"Political and Social Realities of Zion's Camp, The," 84, 105
"Political Background of the Manifesto, The," 160
Political Deliverance: The Mormon Quest for Utah Statehood, 168, 311
"Political Interpretation of Mormon History, A," 10
Political Kingdom of God and the Council of Fifty in Mormon History, The, 10
"Political Kingdom of God as a Cause for Mormon-Gentile Conflict, The," 10
"Politicking against Polygamy: Joseph Smith III, the Reorganized Church, and the Politics of the Antipolygamy Crusade, 1860-1890," 158, 307 note 5, 308
politics, and Mormonism, 120-24, 149, 191-94, 244, 254, 353
Politics of American Religious Identity: The Seating of Senator Reed Smoot, Mormon Apostle, The, 25
Politics of Domesticity, Women, Evangelism, and Temperance in Nineteenth-Century America, 280 note 14
Politics of Religion and Social Change, The, 203
Poll, Richard D., 113, 117, 124, 139, 152, 159, 168, 174, 187, 191, 297 note 48, 336, 338
Pollock, Gordon Douglas, 12, 22 and note 35, 85
Polson, D. Michael, 162
"Polygamous Eyes: A Note on Mormon Physiognomy," 158
Polygamous Families in Contemporary Society, 295
"Polygamous Yet Monogamous: Cultural Conflict in the Writings of Mormon Polygamous Wives," 296
polygamy (LDS), xiv, 10, 120, 137, 139, 141 note 9, 158-60, 165, 167-68, 170, 178, 244, 274, 277, 287 note 31, 288, 293-96, 302-22, 369
 and Joseph Smith, 289, 291
 demographics, 304, 310, 315-17
 in fiction, 377
 in Nauvoo, 269, 291, 316, 372
 legal history, 317-19
 Ohio period, 81
 post-Manifesto, 170-72, 296
 social history, 319
 Strangite, 347
"Polygamy and Progress: The Reaction to Mormons in Canada,

Index

1887-1923," 316
"Polygamy and the Frontier: Mormon Women in Early Utah," 293
"Polygamy among James Strang and His Followers," 248
Polygamy Story: Fiction and Fact, The, 321 note 7
Polynesia, Mormonism in, 204, 205
"Polynesian Cultural Center: Reflections and Recollections, The," 204
"Polynesian Cultural Center: A Study of Authenticity, The," 204-5
Pope, Liston, 231 note 7
Porter, Larry C., 44, 66, 73, 88, 132, 208, 309
Portraits of Twelve Religious Communities, 148
Portugal, Mormonism in, 211
post-Manifesto polygamy, 301, 304, 310-13, 381
in fiction, 377-78, 386
Post, Stephen, 248
post-New Mormon History, characteristics of, 24
Pottmyer, Alice Allred, 298 note 53, 346, 348
Poulsen, Richard C., 123
Poulsen, Udell E., 210
Poverty and Progress: Social Mobility in a Nineteenth-Century City, 85
Powell, Allan Kent, 139, 176, 355
Power from On High: The Development of Mormon Priesthood, 81, 238
"'Power of Combination': Emmeline B. Wells and the National and International Councils of Women, The," 284
Praise to the Man, 370, 372
Pratt, Orson, 4, 48, 141 note 7, 329
Pratt, Parley P., 4, 5, 36 note 5, 104, 142
Pratt, Steven F., 142 note 10, 145
Pratte, P. Alfred, 205, 207
"Precarious Balance: The Northern Utes and the Black Hawk War, A," 162
Predators, Prey and Other Kinfolk: Growing Up in Polygamy, 298
PRELUDE TO GLORY (series), 393
Prelude to the Kingdom: Mormon Desert Conquest—A Chapter in American Cooperative Experience, 146
Prentice Alvin, 375
"Present at the Beginning: One Woman's Journey," 292
Presidents of the Church, 140, 173, 333
Price, Pamela, 82, 84
Price, Rex Thomas, 357
Price, Richard, 82, 84
Price, Sterling, 96
Priddis, Ronald, 191
"Priestess among the Patriarchs: Eliza R. Snow and the Mormon Female Relief Society, 1842-1877," 284 note 25
priesthood. *See* Africans/African Americans *and* women.
"Priesthood and Salvation: Is D&C 84 a Revelation for Women Too?," 283, note 21
"Priesthood Reorganization of 1877: Brigham Young's Last Achievement, The," 158
primitivism, and Mormonism, 5, 30
Prince, Gregory A., 81, 238, 270, 333
"Principle Revoked: A Closer Look at the Demise of Plural Marriage, The," 160, 292 note 41
"'Printed by Command of the King': James J. Strang's Book of the Law of the Lord," 248
Prisoner for Conscience' Sake: George Reynolds, 167
"Prisoners for Conscience Sake," 159
"Private versus the Public David O. McKay: Profile of a Complex Personality, The," 333
"Problem of the History of Religion in America, The," 131
"Problems and Opportunities of Missionary Work in Asia," 217
"Problems in Interpreting the Book of Mormon as History," 76, 267-68
"Professor Seixas, the Hebrew Bible, and the Book of Abraham," 78
Profile of Latter-day Saints of Kirtland, Ohio, and Members of Zion's Camp, 1830-1839, A, 357
"Profile of Mormon Missouri, 1834-1839, A," 112
"Profile of the Missionaries of the Church of Jesus Christ of Latter-day Saints, 1849-1900, A," 357
Progressive Era, 172
Prohibition. *See* Word of Wisdom.
Promises Made to the Fathers: Mormon Covenant Organization, 79, 131, 243, 319, 364
"Prophecies Regarding Japan," 218
"Prophet and the Presidency: Mormonism and Politics in Joseph Smith's 1844 Presidential Campaign, The," 124
Prophet Joseph: Essays on the Life and Mission of Joseph Smith, The, 44, 88
Prophet Joseph Smith: Essays on the Life and Mission of Joseph Smith, The, 309
Prophet Puzzle: Interpretive Essays on Joseph Smith, The, 328 and note 9
"Prophet Puzzle: Suggestions toward a More Comprehensive Interpretation of Joseph Smith, The," 36 note 6, 292, 328
"Prophetic Communitarianism: A Synthesis of Hermetic and Sociological Analyses of the Origins of Mormonism," 47 note 9
"Prosecution Begins: Defining Cohabitation in 1885, The," 159
prosopography, 281, 357-58
"Prosopography," 358
"Prospects for the Study of the Book of Mormon as a Work of American Literature," 73
Prostitution, Polygamy, and Power: Salt Lake City, 1847-1918, 25, 315
"'Protect the Children, Protect the Boys and Girls': Child Welfare Work in Utah, 1888-1920," 362
Protestant, Catholic, Jew: An Essay in American Religious Sociology, 231 note 7
Psychological and Ethical Aspects of Mormon Group Life, The, 16, 190
"Psychology of Religious Genius: Joseph Smith and the Origins of New Religious Movements," 3, 27, 319
"Public Image of Senator Reed Smoot, 1902-1932, The," 173
Publish Glad Tidings: Readings in Early Latter Day Saint Sources, 254
Pugsley, Sharon G., 358
"Puissant Procreator: The Comic Ridicule of Brigham Young, The," 155
Purdy, Virginia C., 280 note 14
Pure Church of Christ, 240
Puritan influence on Mormonism, 45-46, 88
Puritan New England and Mormonism, 131
Pursuit of the Millennium, The, 60 note 3
Pusey, Merlo J., 142 note 10, 331, 334
Putnam, Howard H., 362 note 6

Q

"Q-Sort Comparison between Cultural Expectations of Chinese and Cultural Perceptions of Returned Latter-day Saint Missionaries from the United States Who had Been Assigned to Chinese Missions, A," 218
Qatar, Mormonism in, 223
Quaife, Milo M., 248, 346
Qualities That Count: Heber J. Grant as Businessman, Missionary and Apostle, 331
"Quantitative Analysis of Behavioral Change in the Utah Frontier Fertility Transition: Women's Birth Cohorts, 1840-1899, A," 357 note 4
"Quest for a Restoration: The Birth of Mormonism in Ohio, The," 79
Quest for Empire: The Political Kingdom of God and the Council of Fifty in Mormon History, 80, 124, 126, 149, 244
"Quest for Refuge: An Hypothesis as to the Social Origins and Nature of the Mormon Political Kingdom," 79
Quest for Refuge: The Mormon Flight from American Pluralism, 10, 12, 27, 54, 60 note 2, 68, 79, 103, 126, 236
"Quest for Religious Authority and the Rise of Mormonism, The," 9, 27, 74 note 13, 79, 128, 130
Quest for the Gold Plates: Thomas Stuart

Ferguson's Archaeological Search for the Book of Mormon, 61 note 4
Quest: History and Meaning in Religion, The, 130
"Question for Religious Authority and the Rise of Mormonism, The," 22 note 33
Quicksand and Cactus: A Memoir of the Southern Mormon Frontier, 275
Quinn, D. Michael
  about, 41-42, 45, 47 note 9, 240, 270, 274 and note 3, 279, 300-301, 311 and note 6, 390
  quoted, xi-xii, 273 note 2
  works by, xi, 10, 21, 28, 36 note 6, 49, 53, 59, 62, 68, 69, 80, 81, 99, 101-2, 103-4, 105, 110, 124, 135, 139, 149, 153, 158, 160, 172, 176, 178, 187, 191, 192, 193, 194, 195, 210, 238, 243, 244, 245-47, 251, 268, 272, 274 note 4, 281 note 17, 283 note 20, 292 note 41, 293-94, 295, 297, 298 notes 51-52, 301 note 64, 302 note 67, 310-11, 336, 358, 373, 392
Quist, John, 62, 248, 346
"Quorum Called Out of the Kingdom, A," 80

R

"R. C. Evans: Boy Orator of the Reorganization," 346
Raber, Michael Scott, 353
race and Mormonism, 14, 216, 221, 223. *See also* African Americans.
"Rachel R. Grant: The Continuing Legacy of the Feminine Ideal," 289 note 36
Rahde, Heinz F., 6 note 12
Ralston, Russell A., 307
Ram in the Thicket: A History of the Mormon Battalion in the Mexican War, A, 145
Rampton, Calvin L., 192
Rarotonga, Mormonism in, 205
Ray Cheville: Explorer of Spiritual Frontiers, 346
Raynes, Marybeth, 298 note 51, 358, 363
"Reality of the Restoration and the Restoration Ideal in the Mormon Tradition, The," 36
"Reappraisal of a Classic [*Great Basin Kingdom*]," 127
"Rebels and Relatives: The Mormon Foundation of Spring Glen, 1878-90," 148
"Recent Writing on Utah and the Mormons," x
"Recent Writing on Mormon Nauvoo," 113, 352
Reconsidering No Man Knows My History: Fawn M. Brodie and Joseph Smith in Retrospect, 274 note 5, 275 note 9, 326
"Reconstruction of Mormon Theology: From Joseph Smith to Progressive Theology, The," 17, 157
Red Hills of November: A Pioneer Biography of Utah's Cotton Town, 146
"Red Peril, the Candy Maker, and the Apostle: David O. McKay's Confrontation with Communism, The," 333
Red Prophet, 375
Red Stockings & Out-Of-Towners: Sports in Utah, 363
Red Water, 387
Redd, Charles, 338
"Rediscovering the Context of Joseph Smith's Treasure Seeking," 41, 68
Redoubtable John Pack: Pioneer, Proselyter, Patriarch, The, 341
"Reed C. Durham, Jr.'s Astounding Research on the Masonic Influence on Mormonism," 45
"Reed Smoot, the LDS Church, and Progressive Legislation, 1903-1933," 173
Reed Smoot: Apostle in Politics, 173, 336
Reeves, Brian D., 362
"Reexamination of the Woodruff Manifesto in Light of Utah Constitutional History, A," 160, 168
Refiner's Fire: The Making of Mormon Cosmology, 1644-1844, The, xi, 20-21, 44, 45, 47-48, 69, 71, 130, 272
"Reflections on a Roundtable Colloquium Dealing with Joseph Smith's 1844 Campaign for U.S. President," 124
"Reflections on Establishing the Gospel in Eastern Europe," 224
Refuge: An Unnatural History of Family and Place, 297
"Refugee Converts: One Stake's Experience," 188
"Refugees Meet: The Mormons and Indians in Iowa," 161 note 18, 161
Regional Studies in Latter-day Saint History: British Isles, 210
Regional Studies in Latter-day Saint Church History: Europe, 212
Regional Studies in Latter-day Saint Church History: Illinois, 112, 124, 127, 132, 133
Regional Studies in Latter-day Saint Church History, Ohio, 57, 62
Regional Studies in Latter-day Saint Church History: Missouri, 90, 92, 112
"Reinventing Mormonism: Guatemala as Harbinger of the Future?," 215
"Reliability of Joseph Smith's History, The," 59, 118
"Relic of the Missouri Mormon Period: The Haun's Mill Stone at Breckenridge, Missouri, A," 111 note 23
Relief Society, 172-73, 174, 192, 194, 274, 284, 289, 295, 306, 333, 344, 393 note 13
in Nauvoo, 133-35, 269, 393
"Relief Society and Church Welfare: The Brazilian Experience," 189
"Relief Society and the Church, The," 393 note 13
"Relief Society Grain Storage Program, 1876-1940, The," 174
"Relief Society Origin Observed in Nauvoo," 393 note 13
"Religion and Change in a Mexican Village," 213
"Religion and Culture: A Persistent Problem," 4 note 4
"Religion and Economic Planning in the Far West: The First Generation of Mormons in Utah," 149
"Religion and Economics in Mormon History," 88, 149
Religion and Family Connection: Social Science Perspectives, The, 364
Religion and Sexuality: The Shakers, the Mormons, and the Oneida Community, xi, 27
Religion and Sexuality: Three American Communal Experiments of the Nineteenth Century, 10, 82, 158, 243-44, 293, 319
Religion and Society in Tension, 231 note 8
Religion and Society in the American West: Historical Essays, 284 note 25
"Religion and the Law: The Mormon Experience in the Nineteenth Century," 159
Religion, Feminism, and Freedom of Conscience: A Mormon/Humanist Dialogue, 300 note 59
Religion in Africa, 223
Religion in America: Or, an Account of the Origin, Relation to the State, and Present Condition of the Evangelical Churches in the United States, 14
"Religion in Nauvoo: Some Reflections," 121
Religion in the Modern World: From Cathedrals to Cults, 230 note 5
Religion in the Struggle for Power: A Study in the Sociology of Religion, 85
Religion: The Social Context, 230 note 5
religious radicalism, and Mormonism, 21
"Religious Accommodation in the Land of Racial Democracy: Mormon Priesthood and Black Brazilians," 215
"Religious Activities and Development in Utah, 1847-1910," 157
Religious Change in America, 180
Religious Movements in Contemporary America, 364
Religious Outsiders and the Making of Americans, 12, 14
"Religious Polity and Local Production: The Origins of a Mormon Town," 353
"Religious Schism in the Methodist

Index

Church: A Sociological Analysis of the Pine Grove Case," 231 note 7
Religious Sects: A Sociological Study, 230 note 3, 231 note 13
Religious Seekers and the Advent of Mormonism, 34, 37, 68, 79, 106
"'Remember Me in My Affliction': Louisa Beaman Young and Eliza R. Snow Letters, 1849," 279 note 13
"Remembering Leonard: Memorial Service, 15 February 1999," 389
"Remembering Nauvoo: Historiographical Considerations," 120
Remini, Robert V., 60, 327-28
Remy, Jules, 5
Rencher, Alvin C., 73
"'Render unto Caesar': State, Identity and Minority Religion in the German Democratic Republic, 1945-1989," 226
"Renegotiating Scylla and Charybdis: A New Look at Insider and Outsider Stereotypes of Mormonism," 390 note 9
"Reorganization in Nineteenth-Century America: Identity Crisis or Historiographical Problem?, The," 120
"Reorganized Church in Illinois, 1852-82: Search for Identity, The," 245
Reorganized Church of Jesus Christ of Latter Day Saints. *See* Community of Christ.
"Reorganized Church of Jesus Christ of Latter Day Saints: Moderate Mormons, The," 245, 257
"Reorganized Church, the Decade of Decision, and the Abilene Paradox," 269
'"Repent or Be Destroyed": The 1989 Cult Murders in Kirtland, Ohio,' 271
"Reply to Dr. Bushman, A," 66
"Report on the Orient," 217
republicanism and Mormonism, 14, 16
Rescue of the 1856 Handcart Companies, 144
"Response to Paul Toscano's 'A Plea to the Leadership of the Church: Choose Love Not Power,' A," 191
Restless: Memoirs of Labor and Consumer Activist Esther Peterson, 340
Restoration Movement: Essays in Mormon History, The, 9, 57, 114, 139, 245, 248, 257, 258
Restoration Scriptures: A Study of Their Textual Development, 74, 76-77, 254
Restoration Studies: A Collection of Essays about the History, Beliefs, and Practices of the Reorganized Church of Jesus Christ of Latter Day Saints (8 vols.), 80, 82, 90, 96, 257, 268-69, 292
Restored Church: A Brief History of the Growth and Doctrines of the Church of Jesus Christ of Latter-day Saints, The, 97, 118

"Re-Storying the Restoration: Gerald N. Lund's THE WORK AND THE GLORY Saga, and the Historical Novel," 370
"Retrospection: *Giant Joshua,*" 378 note 5
"Return of Thomas B. Marsh, The," 62
"Return to Carthage: Writing the History of Joseph Smith's Martyrdom," 123
"Reuben G. Miller: Turn of the Century Rancher, Entrepreneur, and Civic Leader," 338
"Reuben Miller: Recorder of Oliver Cowdery's Reaffirmations," 75
"Revelation on the Priesthood: The Dawning of a New Day in Africa," 221
Revelations of the Prophet Joseph Smith, The, 76, 309
"Reverend George Lane—Good 'Gifts,' Much 'Grace,' and Marked 'Usefulness,'" 66
"Re-Visioning Mormon History, The," 16, 126
"Revolution and Mormonism in Asia: What the Church Might Offer a Changing Society," 217
Revolutionary Brotherhood: Freemasonry and the Transformation of the American Social Order, 1730-1800, 25 note 39
Reynolds, Noel B., 72, 73
"Rhee Honam: Hallmarks of a Korean Pioneer," 218
Rich, Adrienne, 280 note 14
Rich among the Poor: Church, Firm, and Household among Small-Scale Entrepreneurs in Guatemala, 215
Rich, Charles C., 111
Rich, Leonard, 240, 245
Rich, Russell R., 71 note 11, 73, 139, 233, 347
"Richard L. Bushman—Scholar and Apologist," 1311
Richards, Franklin D., xi
Richards, J. Morris, 355
Richards, Paul C., 112
Richards, Willard, 36 note 5, 141
Richardson, David E., 372 note 2
Ricketts, Norma B., 145
Ricks, Joel E., 146, 355
Ricks, Kellene, 218
Ricks, Stephen D., 63, 82
Ridge, Martin, 329
"Riding Herd: A Conversation with Juanita Brooks," 274 note 4
"Riding on the Eagle's Wings: The Japanese Mission under American Occupation, 1948-52," 218
Riegal, O. W., 346
Riess, Jana Kathryn, 287 note 31
Rigby, Chris. *See* Arrington, Chris Rigby.
Rigdon, Sidney, 5, 57, 62, 73-74, 76, 79, 99, 103, 104, 105, 240, 241, 245,

247, 248
Riggs, Michael S., 96, 109, 111, 271, 347
Riley, Glenda, 144
Riley, I. Woodbridge, 3, 4, 5, 28, 30, 61
Rischin, Moses, ix, 119
"Rise and Decline of Mormon San Diego, The," 146
Rise and Fall of Nauvoo, The, 117
"Rise of a New World Faith, The," 180, 201
"Rise of Mormonism in the Burned-over District: Another View, The," 32, 79
"Rites of Passage: The Gathering as Cultural Credo," 144
Ritualization of Mormon History and Other Essays, 142 note 10
RLDS. *See* Community of Christ.
RLDS Beginnings to 1860, 54
"RLDS Views of Polygamy: Some Historiographical Notes," 82, 308
Road to Total Freedom: A Sociological Analysis of Scientology, The, 232 note 15
Roberts, Allen D., 69 note 7, 78, 355, 360, 388
Roberts, B. H.
about, 120, 131, 174, 388
quoted, 108
works by, 23, 58, 61 note 4, 73, 75, 97, 105, 117-18, 119, 324, 336, 369, 394
Roberts, Richard C., 174, 355
Robertson, Hilton A., 217
Robertson, Margaret C., 124
Robertson, R. J., 110
Robinson, Ann Marie, 204
ROBINSON FAMILY CHRONICLES, 372 note 2
Robinson, George W., 101, 103
Robinson, Louise Yates, 174
Robinson, Philemon B., Jr., 210
Robison, Elwin C., 82, 361
Rockwell, Orrin Porter, 92, 338, 374, 376
Rockwood, Albert P., 102, 103
Rocky Mountain Empire: The Latter-day Saints Today, 376
Rocky Mountain Saints: A Full and Complete History of the Mormons, from the First Vision of Joseph Smith to the Last Courtship of Brigham Young, The, 5, 119
Roderick, Lee, 340
Rodriguez, Derin Head, 201
Rodriguez, Joshua P., 378 note 4
Rodriguez, Laurie Illions, 378 note 4
Rogers, Eric Paul, 85
Rogers, Thomas F., 225
"Role of Christian Primitivism in the Origin and Development of the Mormon Kingdom: 1830-1844, The," 34, 36
Rollmann, Hans, 62, 74 note 13

431

Excavating Mormon Pasts

"Roman Catholic, Protestant and Latter-day Saint Missions in Thailand: An Historical Survey," 219
Romig, Ronald E., 22-24, 61, 75, 90, 96, 105, 106, 111 and note 22, 241, 272, 346
Romney, George, 340
Romney, Thomas C., 141 note 6
Roof, Wade Clark, 181
Rooker, C. Keith, 14, 83, 352
Roosevelt, Theodore, 173
Roots of Modern Mormonism, xi, 18, 24-25, 149, 165 note 1, 181, 234, 324, 364
Roozen, David A., 180
Roper, Roger, 355
Rose, Paul S., 217
Roth, Barry M., 361
Roughing It, 374
"Roundtable: The Question of the Palmyra Revival," 66
Rowley, Dennis, 59, 126, 132
Roy A. Cheville: Explorer of Spiritual Frontiers, 265
Royal Maccabees, 393
Ruch, Velma, 292
Ruckauer, Ulrich, 210
Rugh, Susan Sessions, 121, 128, 352
Rumors of War, 381
Ruoff, Norman D., 257
"Rural Life among Nineteenth-Century Mormons: The Woman's Experience," 281 note 16
Russell, Isaac, 240
Russell M. Nelson: Father, Surgeon, Apostle, 225, 338
Russell, William D.
about, 257, 291
works by, 76, 136, 248, 271, 291 note 38, 292
Russia, Mormonism in, 225
"Russia and the Restoration," 226
Russia and the Restored Gospel, 225
Russo, David J., 85
Rust, Richard Dilworth, 131 note 3
Ryan, Mary, 280 note 14

S

S. Dilworth Young: General Authority, Scouter, Poet, 336
Sacred and the Profane: The Nature of Religion, The, 130
"Sacred Connections: LDS Pottery in the Native American Southwest: Sources for Mormon Visual Arts," 360 note 5
"Sacred Departments for Temple Work in Nauvoo: The Assembly Room and the Council Chamber, The," 133
Sacred Geography, 31
Sacred Places: A Comprehensive Guide to Early LDS Historical Sites, 133
"Sacred Space and the Persistence of Identity: The Evolution and Meaning of an American Religious Utopia," 271
Sacred Stone: The Temple at Nauvoo, 133, 361
"Sacrifice to the Proper Gods," 378 note 4
Sadler, Richard W., 355
Safeway Stores, Inc., 195
Saffle, Sue Simmons, 293, 339, 341 note 18
Saga of the Book of Abraham, The, 77
Sagwitch: Shoshone Chieftain, Mormon Elder, 1822-1887, 342, 161
Sahkarov, Igor, 163
Saillant, John, 47 and note 9
Saint behind Enemy Lines, 225
Saintly Scoundrel: The Life and Times of Dr. John Cook Bennett, The, 347
Saints, 374
Saints and Soldiers, 394
"Saints and St. Louis, 1831-1857: An Oasis of Tolerance and Security, The," 128
Saints and the Union: Utah Territory during the Civil War, The, 151
"Saints and the San Francisco Earthquake [1906], The," 172
"Saints around the World: Strong Saints in Scotland, The," 210
Saints at War: Experiences of Latter-day Saints in World War II, 174
"Saints for All Seasons: Lavina Fielding Anderson and Bernard Shaw's Joan of Arc," 300 note 61
"Saints for These Latter Days," 47 note 9
"Saints in Fiji, The," 207
"Saints in France, The," 211
"Saints in Indonesia, The," 220
"Saints in Saigon: An End, a Beginning, The," 219
"Saints in Samoa, The," 205
"Saints in Southeast Asia," 220
"Saints, Sinners and Scribes: A Look at the Mormons in Fiction," 155
Saints, Slaves, and Blacks: The Changing Place of Black People within Mormonism, 161, 192
Saints without Halos: The Human Side of Mormon History, 142, 362
Salamander: The Story of the Mormon Forgery Murders, 69 note 7, 388
Salt Lake Temple. *See* temples.
"Salt Lake Temple and the Metaphors of Transformation, The," 361
Salt Lake Temple: Monument to a People, The, 163
"Salt Lake Temple: An Architectural Monograph, The," 361
"Salting of Mormon History, The," 47 note 9
Salvation and Protest: Studies of Social and Religious Movements, 232 note 15
Sam Brannan and the California Mormons, 348 note 22

Sam Brannan: Builder of San Francisco, 348 note 22
"'Samaritan Had Passed By': George Miller—Mormon Bishop, Trailblazer, and Brigham Young Antagonist, A," 2488
Same-Sex Dynamics among Nineteenth-Century Americans: A Mormon Example, 176, 298 note 51, 301
Samoa, Mormonism in, 205
Samoa Apia Mission History, 1888-1983, 205
"Samoan Saints: Samoans in the Mormon Village of Laie, Hawaii," 205
Sampson, D. Paul, 83
Samuel Brannan and the Golden Fleece, 348 note 22
"Samuel Brannan and His Forgotten, Final Years," 348
Samuel Claridge: Pioneering the Outposts of Zion, 341
"Samuel Woolley Taylor: Maverick Mormon Historian," 376
San Bernardino: The Rise and Fall of a California Community, 146, 355
San Pete Scenes: A Guide to Utah's Heart, 355
Sandberg, Karl C., 33, 77
Sandmel, Samuel, 48
Sandy City: The First Hundred Years, 355
"Sara Alexander: Pioneer Actress and Dancer," 289 note 36
"Sarah Elizabeth Carmichael: Poetic Genius of Pioneer Utah," 289 note 36
"Sarah M. Pratt: The Shaping of an Apostate," 141 note 9, 295, 348
Saunders, Richard L., 244, 339, 347
Scadron, Arlene, 281 note 17, 362
Scandinavia, Mormonism in, 19, 178, 211, 378
"Scandinavian Saga," 349
"Scapegoats and Scarecrows in Our Town: When the Interests of Church and Community Collide," 288 note 35
"Scattered Saints of Southwestern Iowa: Cutlerite-Josephite Conflict and Rivalry, 1855-1865, The," 249
Schapsmeier, Edward L., 192
Schapsmeier, Frederick H., 192
Scharffs, Gilbert W., 210, 225
Scherer, Mark A., xiv, 136, 232, 271, 272
Scherer, Ross P., 231 note 10
Schindler, Harold, 142, 338
schism. *See* dissent.
"Schism: An Overview," 229 note 1
Schism in the Early Church, 231 note 7
"Schism in the Sisterhood: Mormon Women and Partisan Politics, 1890-1900," 170, 284
Schmalz, Charles L., 148
School of the Prophets, 78
schoolteachers, 288

Index

"Schoolmarm All My Life": Personal Narratives from Frontier Utah, A, 279 note 13
Schow, Ron, 298 note 51
Schow, Wayne, 298 note 51
Schreiner, Alexander, 362, 362 note 6
Schroeder, Theodore, 313
Schwackhammer, Elijah, 245
Schweikart, Larry, 83
Schwimmer, Eric G., 208
Science, Religion, and Mormon Cosmology, 78
Scientific Study of Religion, The, 230 note 5
"Scots among the Mormons," 162
Scott, Ann Firor, 280 note 14, 306
Scott, Jeffrey, 394
Scott, Joan W., 280 note 14
Scott, Marvin B., 231 note 14
Scott, Patricia Lyn, 143, 170, 296 note 46, 302 note 67, 308, 358
Scott, Reva, 348 note 22
Scoundrel's Tale: The Samuel Brannan Papers, 348
Scowcroft, Brent, 340
Scowcroft, Richard, 377
"Scriptural Precedents for Priesthood," 283, note 21
Sculptor's Testimony in Bronze and Stone: The Sacred Sculpture of Avard T. Fairbanks, A, 360
"Sculptors," 360 note 5
"Scylla, Charybdis, and Achilles's Heels: Pitfalls in Writing Mormon Biography," 349
"Seabirds of Kiribati, The," 207
"Sealed in a Book: Preliminary Observations on the Newly Found Anthon Transcript," 74
Sealey, Shirley, 391
"Search for a Site: Selection of the Church College of Hawaii Campus," 205
"Search for Cultural Origins of Mormon Doctrines," xiii
Search for Sanctuary: Brigham Young and the White Mountain Expedition, 146
"Search for Truth and Meaning in Mormon History, The," 117, 273 note 2
"Searching Minds and Questioning Hearts: Protestantism and Social Context in Bolivia," 216
Searle, Don L., 210, 216, 218
Searle, Howard C., 1, 59, 151
Season of Joy, A, 370
Seasons of Faith and Courage: The Church of Jesus Christ of Latter-day Saints in French Polynesia, A Sesquicentennial History 1843-1993, 205
"Second American Revolution: Era of Preparation, The," 72
Second Century: Latter-day Saints in Great Britain, Volume I, 1937-1987, The, 208
"Secret History of Mormonism, The," 47 note 9, 51

Secret Ritual and Manhood in America, 25 note 39
Secrets Keep, 388
"Secrets of the Mormons," 329
sect, defined, 230 note 5
Sectarianism: Analyses of Religious and Non-Religious Sects, 232 note 15
Secular or Sectarian History? A Critique of *No Man Knows My History*," 30, 306, 309, 326
"Secular Smiths, The," 4, 68
secularism, and Mormonism, 16, 189-90, 210, 227
"Secularization, Higher Education, and Religiosity," 184
"Secularization Paradigm: A Systematization, The," 230 note 6
Seegmiller, Janet Burton, 141, 355
seekerism, and Mormonism, 34, 37
"Seeking the 'Remnant': The Native American during the Joseph Smith Period," 132, 161
Seely, Montell, 392
Seich, Eugene, 6 note 12
Seifrit, William C., 360
Seixas, Joshua, 78
"'Seizing Sacred Space': Women's Engagement in Early Mormonism," 287 note 30
Selected Collections from the Archives of the Church of Jesus Christ of Latter-day Saints, xi
"Selected Nauvoo Bibliography: Work since 1978," 352
"Self-Blame and the Manifesto," 160
Sellers, Charles, 12
Sells, Jeffery E., 192
"Selves and Others: A Study of Reflexivity and the Presentation of Culture in Touristic Display at the Polynesian Cultural Center," 204
"Senator Reed Smoot and Western Land Policy," 173
"Seniority in the Twelve: The 1875 Realignment of Orson Pratt," 141 note 7, 158
"'Separate but Equal?': The Advantages and Challenges of Separate Ethnic Wards and Branches," 162
"'Separate but Unequal': Schoolmarms of Utah, 1900-1905," 281 note 16
"September Six, The," 300 note 59
Sermon in the Desert: Belief and Behavior in Early St. George, A, 18 and note 22, 157, 317, 353
Sermons and Missionary Service of Melvin Joseph Ballard, 212 note 5
"Serving Where She Stands: Julia Mavimbela in Soweto," 223
Sesquicentennial Look at Church History, A, 201
"Sesquicentennial Reflections: A Comparative View of Mormon and Gentile Women on the Westward Trail," 144

Sessions, Gene A., 141 note 8, 151 note 15, 152, 334
Sessions, Patty Bartlett, 345
Set in Stone, Fixed in Glass: The Great Mormon Temple and Its Photographers, 163
settlement, Utah period, 145-48, 137-64, 174, 392
"Settlement of the Brigham Young Estate, 1877-1879, The," 140 note 3
SETTLEMENT SERIES, 393
"Settlements on the Muddy, 1865-1871: 'A God-forsaken Place,' The," 146
"Seven Ages of Thomas Lyne: A Tragedian among the Mormons, The," 347
Seven Days for Ruby, 393
Seventh Son, 375
"Seventies in the 1880s: Revelations and Reorganizing, The," 158
"Sex Roles, Marriage, and Childrearing at Mormon Nauvoo," 352
"Sexual Value-Behavior Congruence or Discrepancy: Coping of the Single Adult Mormon," 363
"Shades of Gray: Sonia Johnson's Life through Letters and Autobiography," 298 note 53, 348
Shakers, and Mormons, 14, 293
"Shaping of the Mormon Mind in New England and New York, The," 66, 79
Sharp, Thomas, 376
Shaw, Beverly L., 363
"Sheaves, Bucklers, and the State: Mormon Leaders Respond to the Dilemmas of War," 194
Sheldon, Carrel Hilton, 287
Shepard, William, 62, 123, 245, 347
Shepherd, Gary and Gordon, 17, 181, 196, 203
Shereer, James A. B., 348 note 22
Sherlock, Richard, 194
Shields, L. Grant, 201
Shields, Steven L.
  about, 240, 245
  works by, 234, 240, 244, 247, 263, 347
Shipley, Richard Lyle, 157 note 17, 157
Shipp, Ellis, 277, 289
Shipps, Jan
  about, 23, 24, 234, 292, 370
  quoted, 19, 22-23, 36, 49, 47, 49, 179, 181, 183, 187-88, 328-29
  works by, xi, 6 notes 14 and 18, 19 note 28, 28, 36 note 6, 53, 49, 68, 119, 130, 136, 139, 148, 160, 173, 196, 292 note 41, 300 note 59, 355
Ships, Saints, and Mariners: A Maritime Encyclopedia of Mormon Migration, 1830-1890, 144
Shirts, Kathryn H., 146, 283, note 21
Shirts, Morris A., 146
Shook, Charles E., 304

433

Excavating Mormon Pasts

Shopkeeper's Millennium: Society and Revivals in Rochester, New York, 1815-1837, A, 12, 128
Shoshoni Frontier and the Bear River Massacre, The, 162
Shot in the Heart, 349
Shumway, Eric B., 207, 343
Shumway, Larry V., 363
Shupe, Anson D., 196, 203
Shurtliff, Luman, 101
Siam (Thailand), Mormonism in, 217
Sideways to the Sun, 388
Sidney B. Sperry Symposium, 200, 201, 221
Sidney Rigdon: A Portrait of Religious Excess, 62, 248, 258, 334
"Sidney Rigdon: Post Nauvoo," 248
Siebert, John H., 90, 105, 106
Signature Books, 61, 378
"Significance of Joseph Smith's First Vision in Mormon Thought, The," 64
"Significance of 'O My Father' in the Personal Journey of Eliza R. Snow, The," 284
"Significance of Nauvoo for Latter-day Saints," 120
"Significance of the Frontier in American History, The," 79 note 14, 130
"Significance of Trivia, The," 288 note 34
Silent Courage, An Indian Story: The Autobiography of George P. Lee, a Navajo, 342
Sillito, John R., 279 note 13, 281 notes 16-17, 287 note 30, 301 note 64, 336, 373, 388
Sillitoe, Linda, 69 note 7, 190, 193, 298 note 52, 388
Silog, William, 18
Silver, Harold, 344
"'Similarity of Priesthood in Masonry': The Relationship between Freemasonry and Mormonism," 44, 133, 243
Simmonds, A. J., 157
"'Simply Folly': Stephen Post and the Children of Zion," 347
Since Cumorah: The Book of Mormon in the Modern World, 21, 73
"Since 1950: Creators and Creations of Mormon History," 53 note 1, 274 note 4
Since You Went Away, 381
Singapore, Mormonism in, 217, 219, 220
"Singapore Saints," 220
"Singing Saints: A Festival of Hymns and Hymnody, The," 270
"Single Cursedness: An Overview of LDS Authorities' Statements about Unmarried People," 363
Sister Saints, 143, 289, 306, 344
"Sister-Wives and Suffragists: Polygamy and the Politics of Woman Suffrage, 1870-1896," 160, 286
"Sisterhood and Sociability: The Utah Woman's Press Club, 1891-1928," 281 note 17
Sisters and Little Saints: One Hundred Years of Primary, 286
"Sisters at the Bar': Utah Women in Law," 159, 281 note 16
Sisters in Spirit: Mormon Women in Historical and Cultural Perspective, 281, 283, 286, 292 note 41, 306
"Sisters' Lives, Sisters' Voices: Neglected Reorganized Latter Day Saint Herstories," 292
"Six Intellectuals Disciplined for Apostasy," 300 note 59
"Sketches of the Sweet Singer: David Hyrum Smith, 1844-1904," 345
Skinner, Andrew C., 223
Smalling, Cyrus P., 240
Smart, Donna Toland, 288 note 33, 301, 345
Smart, M. Neff, 221
Smart, Paul F., 357
Smiley, Thomas, 31
Smith, Aaron, 245
Smith, Andrew, 347
Smith, Barbara B., 192-93
Smith, Becky Cardon, 133
Smith, Charone H., 226
Smith, D. Brent, 201, 211
Smith, Darron, 192
Smith, David Hyrum, 247, 291, 345
Smith, E. Gary, 135, 249, 293, 334
Smith, Elbert A., 307
Smith, Eldred G., 176, 293, 334
Smith, Emma Hale, 140, 264, 269, 289, 343
 in fiction, 376, 379
Smith, Ethan, 30, 32, 71
Smith, Everett, Jr., 201, 211
Smith, Frederick Madsen, 257-58, 262, 263, 346
Smith, G. Carlos, 220
Smith, George A., 142, 334
Smith, George Albert, 173, 199-200, 331, 334
Smith, George D., 53 note 1, 117, 244, 274 note 5, 300 note 59, 301 note 64, 311 note 6, 316, 343 note 20, 371
Smith, Grant T., 378 note 4
Smith, Gregory White, 69 note 7
Smith, Heman C., 118, 258
Smith, Henry A., 208
Smith, Hyrum, 4, 92, 104, 105, 106, 176, 244, 245, 246, 266, 379
Smith, Hyrum M., III, 141 note 6
Smith, Israel Alexander, 262
Smith, James E., 127
Smith, John Henry, 173, 334
Smith, Joseph, Jr., 50-51, 58-59, 176, 177, 199, 240, 266
 and Danites, 98-104
 and polygamy, 274, 295, 305-10, 313-35, 319, 343
 Bainbridge trial, 8
 biographies of, 262, 275, 324-29. *See also* individual titles.
 burial of, 266
 death of, 244
 in fiction, 372-73, 374-75, 379-81
 in Missouri, 104-7
 interpretations of, 3-4, 6, 27-30, 46-49, 60-76
 manuscript collections x-xi
Smith, Joseph, Sr., xiv, 36, 176, 334
Smith, Joseph, III
 about, 135, 158, 245, 246, 247, 260, 262, 289, 345
 presidency of, 263, 268, 271, 272
 quoted, 307
 works by, 118
Smith, Joseph F. (patriarch), 176
Smith, Joseph F. (president), ix, 140, 141, 172, 173, 194, 331, 344, 381, 385
Smith, Joseph Fielding (apostle/president)
 about, 97, 176, 218
 works by, 118, 141 note 6, 305, 331, 345
Smith, LeGrande W., 226
Smith, Linda H., 355
Smith, Lot, 152
Smith, Lucy Mack, 36, 59, 118
Smith, Melvin R., 114
Smith, Sylvester, 240
Smith, Thales, 226
Smith, Timothy L., 16, 73
Smith, W. Wallace, 262, 263, 271, 345
Smith, Wallace B., 345
Smith, William B., 176, 232, 245, 246, 247, 249, 345-46
Smith-Pettit Foundation, 61
Smith-Rosenberg, Carroll, 280 and note 14
"Smiths and Their Dreams and Visions, The," 27
Smoot, Reed, 173, 294, 336, 381
Smurthwaite, Michael B., 215
Snell, George, 377
Snow, Eliza R., 143, 193, 281, 283, 284, 287, 305, 343
 in fiction, 376
 works by, 193
Snow, Lorenzo, 36 note 5, 140, 141, 172, 331, 344
Snyder, Phillip A., 297 note 50
Snydergaard, Rex, 114
So Great a Cause, 370
"Soaring with the Gods: Early Mormons and the Eclipse of Religious Pluralism," 126
social history, 126-27, 351-66
social problems, and Mormonism, 189-90, 192
social science (LDS), 364
Social Accommodation in Utah, 289 note 36, 344
"Social Backgrounds and Characteristics of Those People Who

Index

Founded the Church of Jesus Christ (Cutlerite), The," 249
"Social Cleavage and Religious Conflict," 231 note 7
Social Construction of Reality: A Treatise in the Sociology of Knowledge, The, 231 note 14
"Social History of Camp Floyd, Utah Territory, 1858-1861, A," 153
"Social Movement Organizations: Growth, Decay and Change," 231 note 12
Social Order of a Frontier Community: Jacksonville, Illinois, 1825-70, The, 127
"Social Origins of Kirtland Mormons, The," 357
"Social Sources of Mormonism, The," 9, 32, 33, 73, 79
Social Sources of Denominationalism, The, 230 note 5, 231 note 7
Social System, The, 231 note 8
Social Teachings of the Christian Churches, The, 230 note 5
Social Theory and Social Structure, 231 note 8
socialists, and Mormonism, 14
Sociological Yearbook of Religion in Britain, A, 231 note 9
Sociology of Religion, The, 230 note 5
"Sociology of Schism, The," 231 note 9
Sociology of the Absurd, A, 231 note 14
"Socio-Political Factors Affecting the Growth of the Mormon Church in Argentina since 1925," 215
"Socioreligious Radicalism of the Mormon Church: A Parallel to the Anabaptists," 10, 21, 28
SODERBERG SAGA (series), 393
Sojourner in the Promised Land: Forty Years among the Mormons, 6 note 14, 24, 47, 53, 292
Solemn Covenant: The Mormon Polygamous Passage, 10, 82, 158, 160, 167, 172, 294, 313
Solomon, Dorothy Allred, 298
Solomon Islands, Mormonism in, 204, 207
"Some Comparative Perspectives on the Early Mormon Movement and the Church-State Question," 80
"Some Demographic Aspects of 100 Early Mormon Converts, 1830-1837," 357
"Some Historical Perspectives on the Mormon Response to the Great Depression," 174
"Some Problems in Translating Mormon Thought into Chinese," 218
"Some Reflections on the New Mormon History," x, xii, 30, 117, 121, 274 note 5
"Some Sociological Conclusions about Church Trends," 180
"Some Themes of Counter-Subversion: An Analysis of Anti-Masonic, Anti-Catholic, and Anti-Mormon Literature," 9, 73
"Something Extraordinary," 393 note 13
"'Something Was Wanting': The Meteoric Career of John Greenhow, Mormon Propagandist," 347
Sondrup, Steven, 388
Song of Joys: The Biography of Mahonri Macintosh Young: Sculptor, Painter, Etcher, A, 339, 360
"Sonia Johnson: Mormonism's Feminist Heretic," 298 note 53, 348
Sonne, Conway B., 144
Sorensen, Carole Gates, 161
Sorensen, Virginia, 293, 339, 345, 377-78 note 4, 386
Sorenson, John L., 73, 353, 364
"Sources on the History of the Mormons in Ohio, 1830-1838," 58
South Africa, Mormonism in, 220, 221
South America, Mormonism in, 212, 215-17
South/Southeast Asia. *See* Asia.
Southern Cross Saints: The Mormons in Australia, 208, 364
Southern Honor: Ethics and Behavior in the Old South, 18 note 21
Soviet Bloc, oral histories, 203
Spain, Mormonism in, 211
Spanish-American War (1898), 172, 178
Spaulding, Solomon, 73
Spaulding theory, and Book of Mormon, 4, 5, 28, 30, 73-74
"Spaulding Theory: Then and Now, The," 74
"Speaking for Themselves: LDS Ethnic Groups Oral History Project," 188
Speek, Vickie Cleverley, 248, 346
Spencer, Geoffrey F., 73, 76, 80, 130
Spencer W. Kimball: Twelfth President of the Church of Jesus Christ of Latter-day Saints, 187, 333
Spendlove, David C., 364
Spicer, Judith L. C., 357 note 4
Spillman, W. B. "Pat," 233 note 16, 263, 268, 291 note 38, 346
"Spiritual Paths after September 1993," 191
"Spiritual Searching: The Church on Its International Mission," 201
"Spit-Shined Shoes, Clear Decisions, and West German Mission Horror Stories," 226
Spitz, Lewis W., 136
Splinters of a Nation: German Prisoners of War in Utah, 176
"Spokes on the Wheel: Latter-day Saint Settlements in Hancock County, Illinois," 128
Sports in Zion: Mormon Recreation, 1890-1940, 363
"Spreading the Gospel in Indonesia: Organizational Obstacles and Opportunities," 189, 220
Sri Lanka, Mormonism in, 217
Stack, Peggy Fletcher, 47 note 9, 223, 391 note 10
Stahle, Shaun D., 392 note 11
St. Cook, Philip, 143
"'St. Peter's of the New World': The Salt Lake Temple and a New Public Image for Utah," 172
Staker, Susan, 286, 301 note 64, 373
Stalwarts South of the Border, 213
Stamps, Richard B., 219
Stand by My Servant Joseph: The Story of the Joseph Knight Family and the Restoration, 341
"Standing between Two Fires: Mormons and Prohibition, 1908-1917," 173
STANDING ON THE PROMISES (series), 383
Stanton, Max E., 205
Stark, Rodney, 180, 201, 231 notes 8 and 12
Stasi (East German secret police), 226
"State of Deseret, The," 146
"State-within-a-State Diplomacy: Mormon Missionary Efforts in Communist and Islamic Countries," 203
statehood, Utah, 151, 167, 168, 311
Stathis, Stephen W., 74
"Statistics on Suicide and LDS Church Involvement," 184
"Stealing at Mormon Nauvoo," 123
"Steamboat *Maid of Iowa:* Mormon Mistress of the Mississippi, The," 126
Steed, Mary Lou, 231 note 9
Stegner, Wallace, xii, 1 note 1, 139, 143, 145, 340
Stein, Stephen J., 47 and note 9, 131 note 3
Stellman, Louis J., 348 note 22
Stenhouse, Fanny, 143, 347
Stenhouse, T. B. H., 5, 119, 143, 347
"Stenhouses and the Making of a Mormon Image, The," 157, 347
"Stephen Post: From Believer to Dissenter to Heretic," 248
Sterling M. McMurrin Lecture Series, 270
"Sterling Moss McMurrin: A Philosopher in Action," 339
Stewart, David, 227 note 7
Stewart, John J., 331
"Still 'Side by Side': The Final Burial of Joseph and Hyrum Smith," 123, 266
Stoddard, S. B., 245
Stone, Barton, 36
Stone, Eileen Hallet, 161
Stone, Lawrence, 358
STORM TESTAMENT (series), 372 note 2

435

Story of Religions in America, 8 note 16
Story of the Church: A History of the Church of Jesus Christ of Latter Day Saints, and of Its legal Successor, the Reorganized Church, 97, 118, 262
Story of the Latter-day Saints, The, 16, 53, 68, 88, 113, 120, 139, 167, 172, 177, 181, 186, 201, 234, 305, 324, 331, 333, 343
Story of the Mormons: From the Date of Their Origin to the Year 1901, The, 5, 116, 119
Stott, Clifford L., 146
Stott, G. St. John, 331 note 12
Stout, Allen J., 101
Stout, Harry S., 131 note 4, 132, 136 note 5
Stout, Hosea, 36 note 5, 101, 275
Stowell, Josiah, 68, 69
"Strains, Conflicts and Schism in Protestant Denominations," 231 note 10
Strang, James Jesse, 245, 247, 248, 249, 346
"'Strange Mixture of Intellect': A Social History of Dale L. Morgan, 1933-42, The," 339
"'Strange Phenomena': Ernest L. Wilkinson, the LDS Church, and Utah Politics, A," 192
"Stranger in a Strange Land: A Personal Response to the 1984 Document," 292
"Strangers in a Strange Land: Heber J. Grant and the Opening of the Japanese Mission," 173, 331
Strangers in Paradox, 300
Strangites, 247, 248-49
Strategy of Social Protest, The, 231 note 12
"'Strength in Our Union': The Making of Mormon Sisterhood," 279 note 12, 283
"Strengths and Weaknesses of Virginia Sorensen's *On This Star,* The," 378 note 4
Stromberg, Lorie Winder, 274 note 3, 298 note 52, 300 note 61
"'Strong Minded Women': Desdemona Stott Beeson and Other Hard Rock Mining Entrepreneurs," 281 note 16
Struble, Patricia, 292
Structure of Scientific Revolutions, The, 69
Structure of Social Action, The, 231 note 8
"Struggle for Power in the Mormon Battalion, The," 145
Studies in Ethnomethodology, 231 note 14
Studies in Mormon History, 1830-1997: An Indexed Bibliography with A Topical Guide to Published Social Science Literature on the Mormons, 58, 302 note 67
Studies in Mormon History: A Bibliography, with Index, and a Guide to Further Research, 113

Studies of the Book of Mormon, 61 note 4, 73, 75
"Study of the General Conferences of the Church of Jesus Christ of Latter-day Saints, 1830-1901, A," 81
"Study of the Mormon Westward Migration between February 1846 and July 1847, with Emphasis on and Evaluation of the Factors that Led to the Mormons' Choice of Salt Lake Valley as the Site of their Initial Colony, A," 144
"Study of the Mormon Practice of Plural Marriage before the Death of Joseph Smith, A," 82, 310, 343 note 20
"Study of the Nature of and Significance of the Changes in the Revelations as Found in a Comparison of the Book of Commandments and Subsequent Editions of the Doctrine and Covenants, A," 77
"Study of the Origins of the Church of Jesus Christ of Latter-day Saints in the States of New York and Pennsylvania, 1816-1831, A," 57
"Study of Women at the University of Utah between 1941 and 1953, A," 357
Sturgis, Cynthia J., 353
"'Such Republicanism as This': John Corrill's Rejection of Prophetic Rule," 97, 241
suffrage. *See* women.
Sugar Creek: Life on the Illinois Prairie, 127
"Sugar House Ward: A Latter-day Saint Congregation," 148, 196, 355
Suksabjarern, Manoth, 219
Sumoi Calls, 210
Sunbonnet Sisters: The Stories of Mormon Women and Frontier Life, 143, 277, 344
Sunstone/Symposium, 191, 210, 388, 390
Supporting Saints: Life Stories of Nineteenth-Century Mormons, 142, 289 note 36, 323 note 1, 340 note 16, 361
"Survey of Nineteenth-Century Folk Architecture in the Mormon Culture Region, A," 361
Sutton, John R., 231 note 12
Sutton, Robert P., 126
Swanson, Vern G., 360
Swedenborgians, and Mormonism, 14
"Swedes in Grantsville, Utah, 1860-1900, The," 162
"'Sweet Counsel and a Sea of Tribulation': The Religious Life of the Women in Kirtland," 81, 352
Sweet, Northrop, 240
Sweet, William Warren, 8 and note 16
Swensen, James R., 174
Swetnam, Susan Hendricks, 142
Swinton, Heidi S., 133, 361
Swiss Temple, 342

Switzerland, Mormonism in, 211
Sword of Laban: Joseph Smith Jr. and the Dissociated Mind, 3, 27, 60, 327
Syfritt, Jacob, 245
"Symbol and Process: An Exploration into the Concept of Zion," 80
"Symposium of Former Mission Presidents, A," 217
Syria, Mormonism in, 223
Systematic Sociology on the Basis of the Beziehungslehre and Gebildelehre of Leopold Van Wiese, 230 note 5

T

Taber, Susan Buhler, 196, 297 note 48, 355
Tabernacle Choir, 224, 361
"Tabernacles for Waiting Spirits: Monogamous and Polygamous Fertility in a Mormon Town," 317
Tahiti, Mormonism in, 204
Taiwan, Mormonism in, 217, 218, 219
"Taiwan: Four Decades of Faith," 219
"Taiwan: Steep Peaks and Towering Faith," 219
Takagi, Shinji, 217-18
Takayama, K. Peter, 231 note 10
"Take Up Your Mission": Mormon Colonizing along the Little Colorado River, 1870-1900, 18, 146, 355
"Taking Flanders Too Seriously," 114
"Taking Stock: The 10th Anniversary of the Mormon Women's Forum," 300 note 61
"Taking the Gospel to Their Own People," 215
Talbot, Dan, 145
Talbot, Wilburn D., 81, 84
TALES OF ALVIN MAKER (series), 375
"Talk or Die," 386
Tambuli, 226
Taniguchi, Nancy Jacobus, 148
Tanner, Annie Clark, 168, 277, 344
Tanner, George S., 355
Tanner, Jerald and Sandra, 17 note 19, 40, 64
Tanner, Joseph M., 277, 279 note 12
Tanzania, Mormonism in, 223
Task Papers in LDS History, 213, 349
Tate, Charles D., Jr., 32
Tate, Lucille A., 338
Taves, Ernest H., 73, 137 note 1
Taylor, Alan, 34, 41, 68
Taylor, Janet ("Nettie") Maria Woolley, 280
Taylor, John, 36 note 5, 140, 170, 274, 331 and note 12, 344, 376, 385
Taylor, John W., 280
Taylor, P. A. M., x, 119, 144, 149, 151, 162
Taylor, Samuel Woolley
 about, 280, 377
 works by, 141, 170, 331, 376

Index

Taylor, Sandra C., 281 note 16
Taylor, William R., 18 note 21
Teachings of Gordon B. Hinckley, 50 note 11
Teichert, Shirley, 360
Telford, John, 133
"Telling the Nauvoo Story," 113
"Telling the Restoration Story: Gerald N. Lund's THE WORK AND THE GLORY Saga," 373
Temin, Peter, 14, 83
temples, 163, 201, 361
  Freiberg, 226
  Kirtland, 57, 82-83, 86, 260, 271, 361
  Korean, 217
  Nauvoo, 132-33, 243, 361
  Portland, 361
  Salt Lake, 163, 172, 361, 385
  Switzerland, 200
  theology, 139, 243, 244
  Tokyo, 218
"Temple Dedicated in Madrid, Spain," 381 note 6
"Temple for West Africa, A," 223
"Temple Lot Discoveries and the RLDS Temple," 90
Temple Manifestations, 83
Temple, Town, Tradition: The Collected Historical Essays of Lance D. Chase, 204
Temples to Dot the Earth, 201
"Ten Years in Camelot: A Personal Memoir," x, 389
Tending the Garden: Essays on Mormon Literature, 297 note 50, 339, 377
Tenney, Ammon M., 178
Terry, Keith, 77
"Terry Tempest Williams's *Refuge:* Sentimentality and Separation," 297 note 49
"Test of Faith: Jane Elizabeth James and the Origins of the Utah Black Community, A," 289 note 36, 344
"Test of Theories of Denominational Growth and Decline, A," 180
"Textual Variants in Book of Mormon Manuscripts," 74
Thailand, Mormonism in, 217, 219, 220
That Noble Dream: The Objectivity Question and the American Historical Profession, 230 note 4, 280 note 14
Thatcher, Elaine, 361
Thatcher, Linda, 61, 97, 142, 177, 236, 241, 248, 249, 264, 281 note 17, 298 note 53, 308, 346, 363
Thatcher, Moses, 142
Thayne, Emma Lou, 288, 345
"Themes in Latter Day Saint History," 120
theocracy, Mormonism as, 10, 80, 124
"Theological Crucibles: Social Movements in and of Religion," 231 note 12
Theological Foundations of the Mormon Religion, The, 270
theology, developments in, 30-31, 132, 241
"Theology of Thomas Dick and Its Possible Relation to That of Joseph Smith, The," 32
Theory of Religion, A, 231 note 12
Theory of Social and Economic Organizations, The, 230 note 5
"'There Goes Matilda': Millard County Midwife and Nurse," 289 note 36, 345
Thernstrom, Stephen, 18 note 20, 85, 364
"'These Licentious Days': Dancing among the Mormons," 363
These Were the Valiant, 372 note 2
'They Are My Friends': A History of the Joseph Knight Family, 1825-1850, 341
Things in Heaven and Earth: The Life and Times of Wilford Woodruff, a Mormon Prophet, 17, 62, 141, 167, 309, 331
This Is the Place: Brigham Young and the New Zion, 137 note 1
"This Was the Place: Utah and Mormons on an Olympic-sized Stage," 190
Thomas, Darwin L., 358, 364
"Thomas F. O'Dea on the Mormons: Retrospect and Assessment," 116
"Thomas Frazier: Vernacular Architect in Pioneer Utah," 361
Thomas, John C., 178
Thomas, John L., 12
"Thomas L. Kane and the Utah War," 152
"Thomas L. Kane: Ambassador to the Mormons," 152
Thomas, Madison H., 210
Thomas, Mark D., 14, 37, 61 note 4, 72
"Thomas W. Williams: Socialist in the Twelve," 346
Thompson, Brent G., 173
Thompson, Charles B., 245, 249
Thompson, John E., 99
Thomson, Dennis L., 223
Thornton, Roseland Bergeson, 341 note 18
Thornton, Willis, 80
Thorpe, Joseph, 109-10
Those Who Would Be Leaders (Offshoots of Mormonism), 233, 347
Thought of Orson Pratt, The, 62, 141
"Thoughts on Mormonism in Latin America," 189, 213
"Thoughts on the Mormon Scriptures: An Outsider's View of the Inspiration of Joseph Smith," 76
Three Frontiers: Family, Land, and Society in the American West, 1850-1900, xi, 18, 148, 353
"Three Mormon Women in the Cultural Arts," 283 note 23
Thy Gold to Refine, 370
Tice, Richard, 220
Tickemyer, Garland E., 78
"'Tidying Up Loose Ends?' The November 2000 Excommunication of Margaret Toscano," 301 note 63
"Time of Marriage: Monogamy and Polygamy in a Utah Town, A," 157, 317
"Time of Preparation: The Kirtland School of the Prophets, A," 78
"Times and Seasons of the Doctrine and Covenants, The," 181
Times and Seasons (1839-44), 254
Tinney, Thomas M., 77
To All the World: The Book of Mormon Articles from the Encyclopedia of Mormonism, 61 note 4
"To Be Free," 225
"To Be Native American—And Mormon," 3422
To Build, To Create, To Produce: Ephraim P. Ellison's Life and Enterprises, 1850-1939, 341, 342 note 19
"To Magnify Our Calling: A Response to Section 156," 292
"To Maintain Harmony: Adjusting to External and Internal Strifes, 1890-1930," 17, 170
To Rejoice as Women: Talks from the 1994 Brigham Young University Women's Conference, 226
"To Tell and Hear Stories: Let the Stranger Say," 390
"To the Koreans, and All the People of Asia," 200
"To Transform History: Early Mormon Culture and the Concept of Time and Space," 9
Tobler, Douglas F., 162, 210, 211, 226
Todd, Jay M., 77, 224
Toennies, Rudolf, 18
Together: A Love Story, 221
Tokelau, Mormonism in, 205
Tonga, Mormonism in, 205, 207
"Tonga: A Land of Believing People," 207
Tongan Saints: Legacy of Faith, 207, 343
Toone, Thomas E., 339, 360
Top, Brent L., 184, 212
Topping, Gary
  quoted, 28, 30, 350
  works by, xii, 31, 127, 176, 333, 340
Torgesen, Rolf, 341 note 18
Toronto, James A., 224
Toscano, Margaret Merrill, 283, note 21, 300 and notes 60 and 62, 301 and note 63
Toscano, Paul James, 191, 300 and note 62
Touchet, Francis Henry, 114
Toward a General Theory of Action, 231 note 8
"Toward a Reconstruction of Mormon and Indian Relations, 1847-1877," 161
"Toward the New Mormon History: An Examination of the Literature of

437

the Latter-day Saints in the Far West," xii, 273 note 1, 274 note 6
"Toward 2000: Mormonism in Australia," 208
Towards a Christian Republic: Antimasonry and the Great Transition in New England, 1826-1836, 25 note 39
Tracy, Shannon M., 123
Tragedy at Mountain Meadows, 153
trail histories, 54, 189, 377, 392-93
Trailing the Pioneers: A Guide to Utah's Emigrant Trails. 1829-1869, 144
Trails: toward a New Western History, 146 note 13
"Transformations of Power: Mormon Women's Visionary Narratives," 287 note 30
Transformation of the Mormon Culture Region, 24
translations, of Mormon scriptures, 201, 205, 220
"Transplanted to Zion: The Impact of British Latter-day Saint Immigration upon Nauvoo," 132
Trask, William R., 130
treasure seeking, 57, 63, 68-71, 74. *See also* folk magic.
"Treasure Seeking Then and Now," 44
trek to Utah, 54, 189, 377, 392-93
"Trek Stirs Imagination, Receives Vast Coverage," 392 note 11
"Trends in American Social History and the Possibilities of Behavioral Approaches," 85
Trennert, Robert A., Jr., 144
"Trial and Triumph in Thessaloniki: The Challenges of Opening Greece for the Preaching of the Gospel," 226
Trial Furnace: Southern Utah's Iron Mission, A, 146
"Trial of Faith," 370
Trial of Mary Lou, 393
"Trial of Sidney Rigdon: First Counselor to the Prophet Joseph Smith, The," 248
"Trial of the French Mission," 211
Trials of Discipleship: The Story of William Clayton—a Mormon, 142, 338
"Tribute to Stanley S. Ivins," 304 note 3
Trimble, Roxie D., 360
Troeltsch, Ernst, 18, 230 note 5
Trouble Enough: Joseph Smith and the Book of Mormon, 73
Troubled Waters, 383
True Church of Jesus Christ of Latter Day Saints (1844), 244
True Origin of Mormon Polygamy, The, 304
"'True Son of a True Father': Joseph Smith III and the Succession Question," 135, 268
"Truman Coe's 1836 Description of Mormonism," 59

"Truman Leonard: Pioneer Mormon Farmer," 142
"Truman O. Angell: Architect and Saint," 361
Trumbo, Isaac, 168
Truth and the Evidence, The, 307
"'Truth Will Prevail': The Rise of the Church of Jesus Christ of Latter-day Saints, 1837-1987,* 208, 370
"'Tryed and Purified as Gold,'" 279 note 13
Tsai, Shen-Luen, 205
Tschannen, Olivier, 230 note 6
Tuberville, Gus, 231 note 7
Tucker, J. Kent, 353
"Tudo Bem in Brazil," 216
Tullidge, Edward, 287, 347
Tullis, F. LaMond, 20, 178, 189, 200, 211, 212, 213, 315, 363
Tungate, Mel, 111
"Turbulent Coexistence: Duane Hunt, David O. McKay, and a Quarter-Century of Catholic-Mormon Relations, A," 333
Turkey, Mormonism in, 223
Turley, Richard E., Jr., 69 note 7, 153
Turn Again Home, 387
Turner, Frederick Jackson, 6, 7-8, 79 and note 14, 116, 130, 183
"Turner Thesis and the Mormon Frontier, The," 6
"Turner Thesis and Mormon Beginnings in New York and Utah, The," 9
Tuttle, A. Theodore, 212
Tuvalu, Mormonism in, 205
Tvedtnes, John A., 73
Twain, Mark, 374
Twentieth Century American West, 331
"Twentieth-Century Polygamy and Fundamentalist Mormons in Southern Utah," 172, 317
"Twenty-five Years: A Quarter Century after the Priesthood Revelation: Where Are We Now?," 192
"Twin Relic: A Study of Mormon Polygamy and the Campaign by the Government of the United States for Its Abolition, 1852-1890, The," 159
"Two Integrities: An Address to the Crisis in Mormon Historiography," 136
"'Two Legal Wives': Mormon Polygamy in Canada, the United States, and Mexico," 316
"Two Miss Cooks: Pioneer Professionals for Utah Schools, The," 283 note 23
"Two School Systems in Conflict: 1867-1890," 163
"Two Transparent Stones: The Story of the Urim and Thummim," 74
Tyler, Daniel, 36 note 5, 145
Tylor, Alice Felt, 6
Tyree, Alan D., 265, 346

U

Udall, Morris, 340
Udall, Stewart, 340
Uganda, Mormonism in, 223
Uhl, Edwin, 178
Ukraine, Mormonism in, 225
Ulrich, Laurel Thatcher, 277 and note 11, 283 note 18, 287, 286-89, 288 note 34
"Ultimate Taboos: Incest and Mormon Polygamy," 296, 313
"Uncertain Dynamics of LDS Expansion, 1950-2020, The," 203, 212 note 4
"Undefining 'Faithful Fiction' (The Sophic Stranger Rides Again With[out] His Evil Twin)," 390 note 9
Under the Banner of Heaven: A Story of a Violent Faith, 153
Under the Open Sky: Rethinking America's Western Past, 79 note 14
"Under the Sunbonnet: Mormon Women with Faces," 143, 281
Understanding Church Growth and Decline, 1950-1978, 180
Underwood, Grant
 about, 228
 quoted, 33, 37, 39, 48
 works by, xiv, 16, 21, 47 note 9, 72, 73, 126, 204, 208
"Uniforms and Equipment of the Black Hawk War and the Mormon War," 124
Unitarians, and Mormons, 14
United Nations, 191
United Order of Joseph Smith's Times, The, 88
Universalists and Mormons, 14
"Unparallel, An," 32
Unsettled People: Social Order and Disorder in American History, An, 85
Unsolicited Chronicler: An Account of the Gunnison Massacre, The, 153
Unto Every Nation: Gospel Light Reaches Every Land, 200
Unto the Islands of the Sea: A History of the Latter-day Saints in the Pacific, 204
"Update on Western Europe," 211
Ure, James W., 297 note 48
Ursenbach, Maureen. *See* Beecher, Maureen Ursenbach.
Ursprung und Geschichte der Mormonen, 6 note 12
Uruguay, Mormonism in, 212, 215, 216
"Uses of History: Sidney Rigdon and the Religious Historians, The," 62
"Utah Comes of Age Politically: A Study of the State's Policies in the Early Years of the Twentieth Century," 292 note 41
Utah county histories, 139, 355
Utah Expedition, 1857-1858: A Docu-

Index

mentary Account of the United States Military Movement under Colonel Albert Sidney Johnston and the Resistance by Brigham Young and the Mormon Nauvoo Legion, The, 152
Utah Folk Art: A Catalogue of Material Culture, 360
Utah Historians and the Reconstruction of Western History, xii, 28, 176, 340
Utah Historical Quarterly, 302, 304
 special women's issue, 281 note 16, 286
Utah in Demographic Perspective, 357
Utah in the 1990s: A Demographic Perspective, 297 note 48
"Utah Labor before Statehood," 149
"Utah National Guard in the Great War, 1917-18, The," 174
Utah Painting and Sculpture, 360
Utah Place Names: A Comprehensive Guide to the Origins of Geographic Names: A Compilation, 148 note 14, 148
Utah Remembers World War II, 176
Utah State Historical Society, 139, 355
"Utah Supreme Court Decides Polygamist Adoption Case," 317
"Utah Territorial Politics: 1874-1896," 151
Utah War, 151-53
"Utah Widowhood: A Demographic Profile," 281 note 17, 362
"Utah Women in World War I," 173
"Utah Writ Small: Challenge and Change in Kane County's Past," 355
Utah: The Right Place. The Official Centennial History, 139
"Utah's Anti-Polygamy Society, 1878-1884," 159
Utah's Audacious Stockman: Charlie Redd, 338
Utah's Black Hawk War, 162, 342
Utah's First Ladies, 143
Utah's Historic Architecture, 1847-1949, 360
Utah's History, 139, 297 note 48
"Utah's Peace Advocate, the 'Mormona': Elisa Rurer Musser," 281 note 16
"Utah's Pioneer Beet Sugar Plant: The Lehi Factory of the Utah Sugar Company," 148
"Ute Mode of War in the Conflict of 1865-68, The," 162
"Uttermost Parts of the Earth, The," 203

V

Van Beek, Laga, 158, 296
Van Beek, Walter E. A., 211
Van Cott, John W., 148 note 14, 148
Van Dusen, Increase M., 245, 347
Van Nest, Albert J., 240
Van Noord, Roger, 248, 346
Van Orden, Bruce A., 62, 155, 167, 177-78, 201, 210, 211, 224
Van Orden, Stephen, 226
Van Wagenen, Lola, 160, 286
Van Wagoner, Mary C., 348
Van Wagoner, Richard S.
 about, 328
 quoted, 30
 works by, 61, 62, 74, 78, 82 and note 15, 123, 141 note 9, 158, 170, 243, 248, 258, 294, 295, 310, 311, 313, 334, 348
Vanuatu, Mormonism in, 207
"Vanuatu: Gospel Growth in the Islands of the Sea," 207
Varner, James L., 123
Veterans Association for Service Activities Abroad, 219
Victims: The LDS Church and the Mark Hofmann Case, 69 note 7
"Victorian Pornographic Imagery in Anti-Mormon Literature," 155, 313
"Victory in Defeat—Polygamy and the Mormon Legal Encounter with the Federal Government," 159
Vietnam, Mormonism in, 194, 217, 219, 220
"Vietnam and the Restored Church," 219
Vietnam War, 184, 219
View of the Hebrews, and Book of Mormon, 28, 30, 31-32, 71
"*View of the Hebrews*: Substitute for Inspiration?," 32, 71
"Viewing Mormonism as Mainline," 181
Vinson, Michael, 281 note 16
Viper on the Hearth: Mormons, Myths, and the Construction of Heresy, The, 6 note 11
"Virginia Sorensen as the Founding Foremother of the Mormon Personal Essay," 378 note 4
"Virginia Sorensen: Literary Recollections from a Thirty-five Year Friendship," 378 note 4
Vlahos, Clare D., 64, 131 note 3, 263
Vogel, Dan
 about, 328
 quoted, 37
 works by, x, 3, 5 note 7, 22, 27, 34, 44, 59, 61 and note 4, 68, 71 note 9, 73, 76, 79, 106, 241, 328 and note 9
Vogt, Evon Z., 364
Voice of One Crying in the Wilderness: Sidney Rigdon, Religious Reformer, The, 62, 74 note 13, 248, 258
Voices in Harmony: Contemporary Women Celebrate Plural Marriage, 298
"Voices of Dissent: The History of the Reorganized Church of Jesus Christ of Latter Day Saints in Utah, 1863-1900," 157 and note 17
"Voices of Memory, The," 389
"Voyage of the *Brooklyn,* The," 144
Voyages of Faith: Explorations in Mormon Pacific History, 204, 205

W

"W. W. Phelps: His Ohio Contributions, 1835-1836," 62
Wade, Alton, 205
Wadsworth, Nelson B., 163
"Waging Holy War: Mormon-Congregationalist Conflict in Mid-Nineteenth-Century Hawaii," 155
Walden, David M., 207
Walker, John Philip, 8 note 15, 31, 176, 339
Walker, Ronald W.
 about, 19, 44, 69, 347
 quoted, 42, 324, 331, 333, 349, 350
 works by, 19 note 26, 24, 53 note 1, 58, 69, 74, 75, 113, 132, 140, 141 note 8, 148, 153, 157, 161, 173, 194, 224 note 6, 289 note 36, 302 note 67, 324 notes 4 and 6, 331, 355, 362, 366, 389-90
Walker, Steven C., 62, 73, 74, 78, 123
"Walker War: Defense and Conciliation as Strategy, The," 162
Walking in the Sand, 221
Walkowitz, Judith, 280 note 14
"Wall Comes Down, The," 225
"Wall to Defend Zion: The Nauvoo Charter, A," 124
Wallace, Arthur, 224
Wallis/Futuna, Mormonism in, 205, 205
Wallis, Roy, 232 and note 15
Walters, Luman, 42
Walters, Wesley P., 40, 44, 57, 64, 65, 68
Walton, Michael T., 78
"Waning of Mormon Kirtland, The," 84
ward/stake histories, 355, 363
"Ward Bishops and the Localizing of LDS Tithing, 1847-1856," 158
Ward, Margery W., 344
Ward, Maurine Carr, 111, 301
Wardle, Marian M. E., 360
Warenski, Marilyn, 193, 283, 302
"Warmth, Friendship, and Scholarship: The Life and Times of Virginia Hanson," 345
Warner, Edward A., 80, 254, 334
Warner, Keith C., 211
Warner, R. Stephen, 230 note 6
"Warnicke Family: A Prototype of Mormon Emigration from Scandinavia in the 1860s, The," 341 note 18
Warren, G. M., 374
"Wary Heart Becomes 'Unalterably Fix'd': Eliza R. Snow's Conversion to Mormonism, A," 143, 343
Washakie Letters of Willie Ottogary: Northwestern Shoshone Journalist and Leader, 1906-1929, The, 161, 342
Watanabe, Kan, 218

439

Waterman, Bryan, 191, 283 note 19, 288 note 35, 328 and note 9
Waters, Christine Croft, 281 note 16
Watson, Elden J., 121
Watson, Marianne, 298
Watt, Ronald G., 163, 355
Waugh, Alec, 377
Waugh, Richard A., 271
Waugh, Virginia. *See* Sorensen, Virginia.
Wayward Puritans, 230 note 2
Wayward Saints: The Godbeites and Brigham Young, 19 note 26, 69, 157, 347
"'We Took Our Change of Venue to the State of Illinois': The Gallatin Hearing and the Escape of Joseph Smith and the Mormon Prisoners from Missouri, April 1839," 111 note 23
We'll Find the Place: The Mormon Exodus, 1846-1848, 248
"'Weary Traveler': The 1848-1850 Diaries of Zina D. H. Young, A," 279 note 13
"Web of Trails: Bringing History Home, A," 342
Webb, Betty, 386
Weber, Georgia, 355
Weber, Max, 18, 230 note 5, 236, 237, 246 note 20, 293
Weight, Newell B., 81
Weintrub, Stanley, 350 note 23
Welch, Jay, 362
Welch, John C., 16 note 18, 32, 49, 61 note 4, 73, 75
Welch, Ruby, 208
Welch, Thomas W., 361
Welcoming the World: A History of Salt Lake County, 388
Weldon, Clair E., 74
Weldon, Roy E., 71
Weldon, Thomas, 6
Wells, Daniel H., 141, 284
Wells, Emmeline B., 143, 284, 288, 344
Welter, Barbara, 280 and note 14
Wennerlund, Bo G., 211
Werner, M. R., 8
West, Elliott, 161
West, Hugh, 311
West, Ray B., 8, 139 note 2
Westergren, Bruce N., 59, 78
"Western Mormon in Washington, D.C.: James C. Fletcher, NASA, and the Final Frontier, A," 339
Western Samoa, Mormonism in, 205
Westminster College of Salt Lake City: From Presbyterian Mission School to Independent College, 163
"Westward Migration of the Mormons, with Special Emphasis on Nauvoo," 116
"What about Heretics? An Analysis of the Causes of Schism," 231 note 7

"What Are the Occupations of Latter-day Saints?," 183 note 5
"What Are the Educational Attainments of the Latter-day Saints?," 183 note 5
"What Are You Doing Looking Up Here: Graffiti Mormon Style [at the MTC]," 196
"'What Has Become of Our Fathers?': Baptism for the Dead at Nauvoo," 133
"What of the Lectures on Faith?," 78
"What Sort of Priesthood for Women at Nauvoo?," 283, note 21
"What Were Joseph Smith's Sisters Like?" 61
"Whatever Happened to Maurine Whipple?," 378 note 5
Wheatley-Pesci, Meg, 283, note 21
Whelan, Shane L., 321
When Prophets Die: The Postcharismatic Fate of New Religious Movements, 247
When We Meet Again, 381
"When Will the Little Lady Come Out of the House?," 346
Where Nothing Is Long Ago: Memories of a Mormon Childhood, 377, 378
Where the Spirit Leads: American Denominations Today, 183
"Where Were the Moroni Visits?," 73
"Which Middle Ground," ix
Whipple, Maurine, 339, 377-78, 378 note 5
Whipple, Walter, 77
White, Jean Bickmore, 151, 168, 220, 286, 289
White, Leland D., 220
White, O. Kendall, Jr., 17, 181, 189, 193, 298 note 52
White, Richard, 79 note 14
Whitehurst, James, 204
Whitesides, Lynne Kanavel, 300
"Whither Reorganization Historiography?," 128
Whitley, Colleen, 140, 289, 345
Whitman, Omer (Greg) W., 123
Whitmer family, 99, 328
Whitmer, David, 61, 74, 84, 97, 105, 232, 245, 346
Whitmer, John, 59, 97, 105
Whitney, Helen Mar Kimball, 301-2
Whitney, Newel K., 284
Whitney, Orson F., 137 note 1, 369 and note 1
Whittaker, David J.
about, 324, 334, 340, 350
quoted, 37, 113, 324, 327, 340
works by, x, 24, 53 note 1, 58, 66, 102-3, 132, 142, 158, 161, 289 note 36, 302 note 67, 323 note 1, 324 note 6, 333, 340 note 16, 358, 360 and note 5, 361
Whittier, Charles H., 74
Whittle, G. Benson, 216
"Who Shall Raise the Children?: Vera Black and the Rights of Polygamous Utah Parents," 317
"Who Wrote the Book of Mormon? An Analysis of Wordprints," 73
"Wider Sisterhood: *Exponent II,* A," 288 note 32
Widow's Tale: The 1884-1896 Diary of Helen Mar Kimball Whitney, A, 301-2
"Widowhood among the Mormons: The Personal Accounts," 281 note 17, 362
Widtsoe, John A., 68 note 6, 183 note 5, 303 note 1, 309
Wiebe, Robert H., 12
Wight, Lyman, 103, 106-7, 232, 245, 246, 247, 249
Wightman, Philip C., 249
Wilcox, Linda P., 140, 283
"Wild Bill" Hickman and the Mormon Frontier, 338
Wilde, Anne, 298
Wilentz, Sean, 12 note 17, 14
Wiley, Peter, 196
"Wilford Woodruff and the Changing Nature of Mormon Religious Experience," 141 note 5, 167
"Wilford Woodruff and the Mormon Reformation, 1855-1857," 152
Wilford Woodruff's Journals: 1833-1898, 59
Wilkinson, Ernest L., 339
Willey, Dorothy G. Y., 362
"William A. Bringhurst: From Devout Latter-day Saint to Condemned California Killer, A Personal Confrontation with the Past," 342 note 19
"William B. Smith: The Persistent Pretender," 62, 249, 308, 346
"William B. Smith: 'A Wart on the Ecclesiastical Tree,'" 249, 308
"William E. McLellin: 'Mormonism's Stormy Petrel,'" 241
"William E. McLellin's Testimony of the Book of Mormon," 73
"William Harrison Folsom: Pioneer Architect," 361
"William Law: Nauvoo Dissenter," 244
"William Smith, 1811-1893: Problematic Patriarch," 62, 249, 346
"William Weeks: Architect of the Nauvoo Temple," 132
Williams, Clarissa Smith, 172
Williams, Frederick G., 62, 105, 215
Williams, J. D., 20 note 30
Williams, Roger, 36
Williams, Terry Tempest, 297 and note 49
Willing, Jennie Fowler, 5 note 11
Wilson, Bryan, 230 note 3, 231 note 13
Wilson, Douglas, 73
Wilson, John F., 80, 231 note 9
Wilson, Joni, 153
Wilson, Keith J., 215
Wilson, Laurie J., 211

Index

Wilson, Marian Robertson, 339
Wimmer, Larry T., 14, 83, 352
Wind, James P., 148, 196, 355
Winder, Lorie. *See* Stromberg, Lorie Winder.
Winder, Michael K., 172, 338
Windows on the Sea and Other Stories, 388
Winds of Change: Rapidly Growing Religious Groups in the Pacific Islands, 207
Wine-Dark Sea of Grass, The, 387
Wineera, Vernice, 204
"Wingfield Watson and the Reorganization," 347
Winkler, Albert, 162
Winn, Kenneth H.
  about, 97, 98
  quoted, 241
  works by, 16, 27, 54, 109, 121, 240
Winter Olympics (2002), 54, 190, 321, 392 note 11
Winter Quarters, 281
Winter Quarters: The 1846-1848 Life Writings of Mary Haskin Parker Richards, 301
Winter, Robert, 82
Wise, William, 153
"Without Purse or Scrip? Financing Latter-day Saint Missionary Work in Europe in the Nineteenth Century," 155, 196
Witnesses of the Book of Mormon, The, 75
"Witnesses through Trial and Triumph," 226
"Wives of Nineteenth-Century Mormon Bishops: A Quantitative Analysis," 281 note 17
Wolfinger, Henry J., 160, 168, 289 note 36, 344
"Woman and the Priesthood," 283, note 21
Woman of Destiny, A, 367, 374, 388
"Woman State School Superintendent: Whatever Happened to Mrs. McVicker?, A," 281 note 16
Woman's Exponent, 284, 288 and note 32, 305, 306, 344
"*Woman's Exponent:* Forty-Two Years of Speaking for Women, The," 288 note 32
"Woman's Place in Brigham Young's World," 283 note 23
Woman's View: Helen Mar Whitney's Reminiscences of Early Church History, A, 279 note 13, 302
Womanhood in America, 280 note 14
women, Community of Christ, 266, 269, 291-92
  and priesthood, 291-92
women, Cutlerite, 251
women, LDS, 143, 178, 358, 364
  and priesthood, 266, 274, 283 note 21, 287 note 27, 300-301, 311 note 6, 393 note 13
  biographies of, 343-45
  history of, 273-302
  institutional control of, 299-301
  traditional roles of, 189-90
women, non-LDS in Utah, 152, 287 note 31
"Women Alone: The Economic and Emotional Plight of Early LDS Women," 281 note 17, 363
Women and Authority: Re-Emerging Mormon Feminism, 300, 301, 311 note 6
"Women and Ordination: Introduction to the Biblical Context," 283, note 21
"Women and the Socialist Party in Utah, 1900-1920," 281 note 16
"Women as a Force in the History of Utah," 277
"Women: Changing Ideas and Institutions," 297 note 48
Women, Family, and Utopia: Communal Experiments of the Shakers, the Oneida Community, and the Mormons, 158, 293, 297 note 48, 302 note 67, 319
"Women in the West," 280 note 14, 295 note 45
"Women in Twentieth-Century Utah," 297 note 48
"Women in Winter Quarters," 281
Women of Covenant: The Story of Relief Society, 135, 174, 195, 284, 292, 302, 393 note 13
"Women of Fundamentalism: Short Creek, 1953, The," 295
Women of Mormondom, 287
Women of Nauvoo, 286 note 26, 352
Women of Principle: Female Networking in Contemporary Mormon Polygamy, 295
Women of Wisdom and Knowledge: Talks Selected from the BYU Women's Conferences, 223
"Women Scorned: Inside Utah's IWY Conference," 193
"Women Telegraph Operators on the Western Frontier," 281 note 16
"Women, the Mormon Family, and Class Mobility: Nineteenth-Century Victorian Ideology in a Twentieth-Century Church," 193
"Women Together: Kate Alexander's Search for Self in *The Evening and the Morning,*" 378 note 4
Women Vote in the West: The Woman Suffrage Movement, 1869-1896, 286
"Women's Place in Brigham Young's World," 306
"Women's Place Is in the Constitution: The Struggle for Equal Rights in Utah in 1895," 151
Women's Research Institute (BYU), 297 note 48
"Women's Response to Plural Marriage," 295
Women's Voices: An Untold History of the Latter-day Saints, 1830-1900, 279 note 13, 289, 306
"Women's Work on the Mormon Frontier," 281
Wood, Gordon S., 12, 14, 16, 27
Wood, Timothy L., 124
"Woodbury Years: An Insider's Look at Baseball Baptisms in Britain, The," 210
Woodford, Robert J., 62, 77
Woodman, Gene, 377
Woodruff, Abraham O., 294
Woodruff, Eliza Avery Clark, 294
Woodruff, Wilford, 36 note 5, 140-41, 167, 172, 309, 331, 344
Woods Cross: Patterns and Profiles of a City, 355
Woods, Fred E., 132, 200
Woodward, C. Vann, 18 note 21
Woodward, Mary Brown Firmage, 295, 306, 315, 345
Woodworth, Lucien C., 249
Woolley, Edwin D., 338
Woolley, Lorin, 170
"Word of God Is Enough: The Book of Mormon as Nineteenth-Century Scripture, The," 75
Word of God: Essays on Mormon Scripture, The, 73, 76
Word of Wisdom, 31, 173, 269
"Word of Wisdom in Early Nineteenth Century Perspective, The," 78
"Word of Wisdom: From Principle to Requirement, The," 157
Words of Joseph Smith: The Contemporary Accounts of the Nauvoo Discourses of the Prophet Joseph, The, xi note 3, 132
WORK AND THE GLORY, THE, 370-74, 372 note 2
"Work in Progress toward a New Paradigm for the Sociological Study of Religion in the United States," 230 note 6
Working the Divine Miracle: The Life of Apostle Henry D. Moyle, 174, 336
"Working Women of Salt Lake City: A Review of the *Utah Gazetteer,* 1892-93, The," 281 note 16
World and the Prophet, The, 19, 114
World War I, 172, 173-74, 178
World War II, 165, 174, 176, 178, 191, 195, 196, 199, 200, 205, 226, 270
  in fiction, 381-83, 394
  missionary work after, 207, 208
"Worship through Music Nigerian Style," 223
Worth Their Salt: Notable but Often Unnoted Women of Utah, 289, 345
Worth Their Salt, Too: More Notable but Often Unnoted Women of Utah, 289, 345
"Would-Be Saints: West Africa before the 1978 Priesthood Revelation," 221
Wrestling with the Principle: Readings on Polygamy from the Journal of Mormon History, 170, 296 note 46, 308, 358
Wright, Dennis A., 174
Wright, Evan P., 221
"Writing Mormon Biography," 333

note 13
"Writing of Joseph Smith's History, The," 59, 118
"Writing on the Mormon Past," 116
Writing on the Wall, The, 383
"Writing Women's Lives: A Bibliography on Writing Biographies on Women," 302 note 67
Writings of President Frederick M. Smith, The, 257
Wuthnow, Robert, 231 note 12
Wyatt-Brown, Bertram, 18 note 21
Wyatt, Gary, 158

X-Y

Xi, Feng, 218
Year of Decision: 1846, The, 6
Yinger, J. Milton, 85, 230 note 5
Yorgason, Blaine M., 393, 394
Yorgason, Brenton, 393
Yorgason, Ethan, 24
Yorgason, Laurence M., 357
"'You Nasty Apostates, Clear Out': Reasons for Disaffection in the Late 1850s," 157
Young, Biloine Whiting, 251, 347
Young, Brigham
 about, xiv, 139-40, 142, 161, 176, 217, 245, 246, 289, 287, 295, 336, 388
 and dissent, 232, 249
 and polygamy, 274, 295, 305, 307, 309, 343
 biographies of, 329-31
 in fiction, 372, 376
 leadership of, 245, 248, 347
 interpretations of, 6, 118
 quoted, 287, 303
Young, Brigham, Jr., 142
Young, Delworth Keith, 207
Young, S. Dilworth, 336
"Young Heber J. Grant and His Call to the Apostleship," 173, 331
"Young Heber J. Grant: Entrepreneur Extraordinary," 331
"Young Heber J. Grant's Years of Passage," 331
Young, Joseph, 336
Young, Kimball, 280, 304
Young, Lawrence A., 184, 201, 203, 212 note 4, 297 note 48, 364
Young, Levi Edgar, 6
Young, Mahonri Macintosh, 339
Young, Margaret Blair, 383-85
Young, Richard W., 174
Young, Zina Diantha Huntington Jacobs Smith, 284, 295 and note 44, 295, 345
Yuen, Tai Kwok, 220
Yurtinus, John F., 145

Z

Zald, Mayer N., 231 note 12
Zander, Wolfgang, 210, 211
Zanetsky, Irving I., 364
Zimmerman, Michael D., 192
"Zina Presendia Young Williams Card: Brigham's Daughter, Cardston's First Lady," 289 note 36
Zinsser, Judith P., 280 note 14
Zion in New Zealand: A History of the Church of Jesus Christ of Latter-day Saints in New Zealand, 1854-1977, 208
Zion in the Courts: A Legal History of the Church of Jesus Christ of Latter-day Saints, 1830-1900, 84, 159, 167, 317
"Zion Is Fled: The Expulsion of the Mormons from Jackson County, Missouri," 92
"Zion: The Structure of a Theological Revolution," 80
Zion's Camp, 97, 105, 258
Zion's Camp: Expedition to Missouri, 1834, 84, 105, 258, 260
"Zion's Rowdies: Growing Up on the Mormon Frontier," 161, 362
Zobell, Albert L., 152
Zucker, Louis C., 78
Zweig, Connie, 60 note 3

Also available from
Greg Kofford Books

Perspectives on Mormon Theology Series

Brian D. Birch and Loyd Ericson,
series editors

(forthcoming)

This series will feature multiple volumes published on particular theological topics of interest in Latter-day Saint thought. Volumes will be co-edited by leading scholars and graduate students whose interests and knowledge will ensure that the essays in each volume represent quality scholarship and acknowledge the diversity of thought found and expressed in Mormon theological studies. Topics for the first few volumes include: revelation, apostasy, atonement, scripture, and grace.

The *Perspectives on Mormon Theology* series will bring together the best of new and previously published essays on various theological subjects. Each volume will be both a valued resource for academics in Mormon Studies and an illuminating introduction to the broad and sophisticated approaches to Mormon theology.

Knowing Brother Joseph Again: Perceptions and Perspectives

Davis Bitton

Hardcover, ISBN: 978-1-58958-123-4

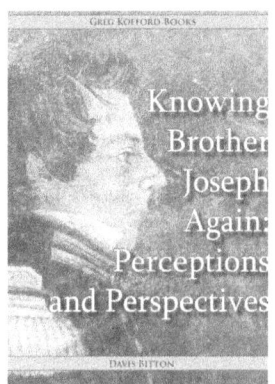

In 1996, Davis Bitton, one of Mormon history's preeminent and much-loved scholars, published a collection of essays on Joseph Smith under the title, *Images of the Prophet Joseph Smith*. A decade later, when the book went out of print, Davis began work on an updated version that would also include some of his other work on the Mormon prophet. The project was only partially finished when his health failed. He died on April 13, 2007, at age seventy-seven. With the aid of additional historians, *Knowing Brother Joseph Again: Perceptions and Perspectives* brings to completion Davis's final work—a testament to his own admiration of the Prophet Joseph Smith.

From Davis Bitton's introducton:

This is not a conventional biography of Joseph Smith, but its intended purpose should not be hard to grasp. That purpose is to trace how Joseph Smith has appeared from different points of view. It is the image of Joseph Smith rather than the man himself that I seek to delineate.

Even when we have cut through the rumor and misinformation that surround all public figures and agree on many details, differences of interpretation remain. We live in an age of relativism. What is beautiful for one is not for another, what is good and moral for one is not for another, and what is true for one is not for another. I shudder at the thought that my presentation here will lead to such soft relativism.

Yet the fact remains that different people saw Joseph Smith in different ways. Even his followers emphasized different facets at different times. From their own perspectives, different people saw him differently or focused on a different facet of his personality at different times. Inescapably, what they observed or found out about him was refracted through the lens of their own experience. Some of the different, flickering, not always compatible views are the subject of this book.

On the Road with Joseph Smith: An Author's Diary

Richard L. Bushman

Paperback, ISBN 978-1-58958-102-9

After living with Joseph Smith for seven years and delivering the final proofs of his landmark study, *Joseph Smith: Rough Stone Rolling* to Knopf in July 2005, biographer Richard Lyman Bushman went "on the road" for a year, crisscrossing the country from coast to coast, delivering addresses on Joseph Smith and attending book-signings for the new biography.

Bushman confesses to hope and humility as he awaits reviews. He frets at the polarization that dismissed the book as either too hard on Joseph Smith or too easy. He yields to a very human compulsion to check sales figures on Amazon.com, but partway through the process stepped back with the recognition, "The book seems to be cutting its own path now, just as [I] hoped."

For readers coming to grips with the ongoing puzzle of the Prophet and the troublesome dimensions of their own faith, Richard Bushman, openly but not insistently presents himself as a believer. "I believe enough to take Joseph Smith seriously," he says. He draws comfort both from what he calls his "mantra" ("Today I will be a follower of Jesus Christ") and also from ongoing engagement with the intellectual challenges of explaining Joseph Smith.

Praise for *On the Road With Joseph Smith*:

"The diary is possibly unparalleled—an author of a recent book candidly dissecting his experiences with both Mormon and non-Mormon audiences ... certainly deserves wider distribution—in part because it shows a talented historian laying open his vulnerabilities, and also because it shows how much any historian lays on the line when he writes about Joseph Smith."
-Dennis Lythgoe, *Deseret News*

"By turns humorous and poignant, this behind-the-scenes look at Richard Bushman's public and private ruminations about Joseph Smith reveals a great deal—not only about the inner life of one of our greatest scholars, but about Mormonism at the dawn of the 21st century."
-Jana Riess, co-author of *Mormonism for Dummies*

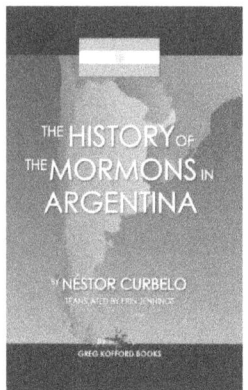

The History of Mormons in Argentina

Néstor Curbelo

English, ISBN: 978-1-58958-052-7

Originally published in Spanish, Curbelo's The History of the Mormons in Argentina is a groundbreaking book detailing the growth of the Church in this Latin American country.

Through numerous interviews and access to other primary resources, Curbelo has constructed a timeline, and then documents the story of the Church's growth. Starting with a brief discussion of Parley P. Pratt's assignment to preside over the Pacific and South American regions, continuing on with the translation of the scriptures into Spanish, the opening of the first missions in South America, and the building of temples, the book provides a survey history of the Church in Argentina. This book will be of interest not only to history buffs but also to thousands of past, present, and future missionaries.

Translated by Erin Jennings

Mormon Polygamous Families: Life in the Principle

Jessie L. Embry

Paperback, ISBN: 978-1-58958-098-5
Hardcover, ISBN: 978-1-58958-114-2

Mormons and non-Mormons all have their views about how polygamy was practiced in the Church of Jesus Christ of Latter-day Saints during the late nineteenth and early twentieth centuries. Embry has examined the participants themselves in order to understand how men and women living a nineteenth-century Victorian lifestyle adapted to polygamy. Based on records and oral histories with husbands, wives, and children who lived in Mormon polygamous households, this study explores the diverse experiences of individual families and stereotypes about polygamy. The interviews are in some cases the only sources of primary information on how plural families were organized. In addition, children from monogamous families who grew up during the same period were interviewed to form a comparison group. When carefully examined, most of the stereotypes about polygamous marriages do not hold true. In this work it becomes clear that Mormon polygamous families were not much different from Mormon monogamous families and non-Mormon families of the same era. Embry offers a new perspective on the Mormon practice of polygamy that enables readers to gain better understanding of Mormonism historically.

Penny Tracts and Polemics: A Critical Analysis of Anti-Mormon Pamphleteering in Great Britain, 1837–1860

Craig L. Foster

Hardcover, ISBN: 978-1-58958-005-3

By 1860, Mormonism had enjoyed a presence in Great Britain for over twenty years. Mormon missionaries experienced unprecedented success in conversions and many new converts had left Britain's shores for a new life and a new religion in the far western mountains of the American continent.

With the success of the Mormons came tales of duplicity, priestcraft, sexual seduction, and uninhibited depravity among the new religious adherents. Thousands of pamphlets were sold or given to the British populace as a way of discouraging people from joining the Mormon Church. Foster places the creation of these English anti-Mormon pamphlets in their historical context. He discusses the authors, the impact of the publications and the Mormon response. With illustrations and detailed bibliography.

The Gift and Power: Translating the Book of Mormon

Brant A. Gardner

Hardcover, ISBN: 978-1-58958-131-9

From Brant A. Gardner, the author of the highly praised *Second Witness* commentaries on the Book of Mormon, comes *The Gift and Power: Translating the Book of Mormon*. In this first book-length treatment of the translation process, Gardner closely examines the accounts surrounding Joseph Smith's translation of the Book of Mormon to answer a wide spectrum of questions about the process, including: Did the Prophet use seerstones common to folk magicians of his time? How did he use them? And, what is the relationship to the golden plates and the printed text?

Approaching the topic in three sections, part 1 examines the stories told about Joseph, folk magic, and the translation. Part 2 examines the available evidence to determine how closely the English text replicates the original plate text. And part 3 seeks to explain how seer stones worked, why they no longer work, and how Joseph Smith could have produced a translation with them.

Second Witness:
Analytical and Contextual Commentatry on the Book of Mormon

Brant A. Gardner

Second Witness, a new six-volume series from Greg Kofford Books, takes a detailed, verse-by-verse look at the Book of Mormon. It marshals the best of modern scholarship and new insights into a consistent picture of the Book of Mormon as a historical document. Taking a faithful but scholarly approach to the text and reading it through the insights of linguistics, anthropology, and ethnohistory, the commentary approaches the text from a variety of perspectives: how it was created, how it relates to history and culture, and what religious insights it provides.

The commentary accepts the best modern scholarship, which focuses on a particular region of Mesoamerica as the most plausible location for the Book of Mormon's setting. For the first time, that location—its peoples, cultures, and historical trends—are used as the backdrop for reading the text. The historical background is not presented as proof, but rather as an explanatory context.

The commentary does not forget Mormon's purpose in writing. It discusses the doctrinal and theological aspects of the text and highlights the way in which Mormon created it to meet his goal of "convincing . . . the Jew and Gentile that Jesus is the Christ, the Eternal God."

Praise for the *Second Witness* series:

"Gardner not only provides a unique tool for understanding the Book of Mormon as an ancient document written by real, living prophets, but he sets a standard for Latter-day Saint thinking and writing about scripture, providing a model for all who follow. . . . No other reference source will prove as thorough and valuable for serious readers of the Book of Mormon."
     -Neal A. Maxwell Institute, Brigham Young University

1. 1st Nephi: 978-1-58958-041-1
2. 2nd Nephi–Jacob: 978-1-58958-042-8
3. Enos–Mosiah: 978-1-58958-043-5
4. Alma: 978-1-58958-044-2
5. Helaman–3rd Nephi: 978-1-58958-045-9
6. 4th Nephi–Moroni: 978-1-58958-046-6
Complete set: 978-1-58958-047-3

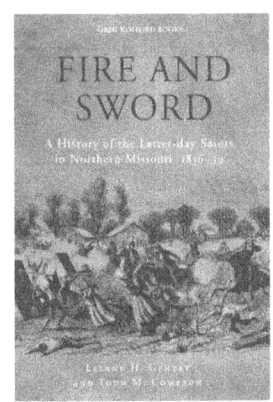

Fire and Sword: A History of the Latter-day Saints in Northern Missouri, 1836-39

Leland Homer Gentry
and Todd M. Compton

Hardcover, ISBN: 978-1-58958-103-6

Many Mormon dreams flourished in Missouri. So did many Mormon nightmares.

The Missouri period—especially from the summer of 1838 when Joseph took over vigorous, personal direction of this new Zion until the spring of 1839 when he escaped after five months of imprisonment—represents a moment of intense crisis in Mormon history. Representing the greatest extremes of devotion and violence, commitment and intolerance, physical suffering and terror—mobbings, battles, massacres, and political "knockdowns"—it shadowed the Mormon psyche for a century.

Leland Gentry was the first to step beyond this disturbing period as a one-sided symbol of religious persecution and move toward understanding it with careful documentation and evenhanded analysis. In Fire and Sword, Todd Compton collaborates with Gentry to update this foundational work with four decades of new scholarship, more insightful critical theory, and the wealth of resources that have become electronically available in the last few years.

Compton gives full credit to Leland Gentry's extraordinary achievement, particularly in documenting the existence of Danites and in attempting to tell the Missourians' side of the story; but he also goes far beyond it, gracefully drawing into the dialogue signal interpretations written since Gentry and introducing the raw urgency of personal writings, eyewitness journalists, and bemused politicians seesawing between human compassion and partisan harshness. In the lush Missouri landscape of the Mormon imagination where Adam and Eve had walked out of the garden and where Adam would return to preside over his posterity, the towering religious creativity of Joseph Smith and clash of religious stereotypes created a swift and traumatic frontier drama that changed the Church.

"Swell Suffering":
A Biography of Maurine Whipple

Veda Tebbs Hale

Paperback, ISBN: 978-1-58958-124-1
Hardcover, ISBN: 978-1-58958-122-7

Maurine Whipple, author of what some critics consider Mormonism's greatest novel, *The Giant Joshua,* is an enigma. Her prize-winning novel has never been out of print, and its portrayal of the founding of St. George draws on her own family history to produce its unforgettable and candid portrait of plural marriage's challenges. Yet Maurine's life is full of contradictions and unanswered questions. Veda Tebbs Hale, a personal friend of the paradoxical novelist, answers these questions with sympathy and tact, nailing each insight down with thorough research in Whipple's vast but under-utilized collected papers.

Praise for *"Swell Suffering"*:

"Hale achieves an admirable balance of compassion and objectivity toward an author who seemed fated to offend those who offered to love or befriend her. . . . Readers of this biography will be reminded that Whipple was a full peer of such Utah writers as Virginia Sorensen, Fawn Brodie, and Juanita Brooks, all of whom achieved national fame for their literary and historical works during the mid-twentieth century"
—Levi S. Peterson, author of *The Backslider* and *Juanita Brooks: Mormon Historian*

Modern Polygamy and Mormon Fundamentalism: The Generations after the Manifesto

Brian C. Hales

Paperback, ISBN: 978-1-58958-109-8

Winner of the John Whitmer Historical Association's Smith-Pettit Best Book Award

This fascinating study seeks to trace the historical tapestry that is early Mormon polygamy, details the official discontinuation of the practice by the Church, and, for the first time, describes the many zeal-driven organizations that arose in the wake of that decision. Among the polygamous groups discussed are the LeBaronites, whose "blood atonement" killings sent fear throughout Mormon communities in the late seventies and the eighties; the FLDS Church, which made news recently over its construction of a compound and temple in Texas (Warren Jeffs, the leader of that church, is now standing trial on two felony counts after his being profiled on America's Most Wanted resulted in his capture); and the Allred and Kingston groups, two major factions with substantial membership statistics both in and out of the United States. All these fascinating histories, along with those of the smaller independent groups, are examined and explained in a way that all can appreciate.

Praise for *Modern Polygamy and Mormon Fundamentalism*:

"This book is the most thorough and comprehensive study written on the sugbject to date, providing readers with a clear, candid, and broad sweeping overview of the history, teachings, and practices of modern fundamentalist groups."
—Alexander L. Baugh, Associate Professor of Church History and Doctrine, Brigham Young University

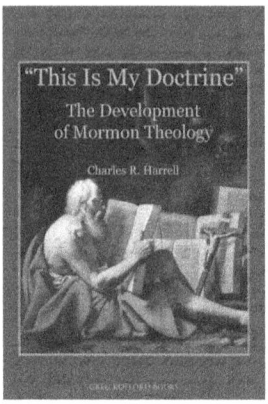

"This is My Doctrine": The Development of Mormon Theology

Charles R. Harrell

Hardcover, ISBN: 978-1-58958-103-6

The principal doctrines defining Mormonism today often bear little resemblance to those it started out with in the early 1830s. This book shows that these doctrines did not originate in a vacuum but were rather prompted and informed by the religious culture from which Mormonism arose. Early Mormons, like their early Christian and even earlier Israelite predecessors, brought with them their own varied culturally conditioned theological presuppositions (a process of convergence) and only later acquired a more distinctive theological outlook (a process of differentiation).

In this first-of-its-kind comprehensive treatment of the development of Mormon theology, Charles Harrell traces the history of Latter-day Saint doctrines from the times of the Old Testament to the present. He describes how Mormonism has carried on the tradition of the biblical authors, early Christians, and later Protestants in reinterpreting scripture to accommodate new theological ideas while attempting to uphold the integrity and authority of the scriptures. In the process, he probes three questions: How did Mormon doctrines develop? What are the scriptural underpinnings of these doctrines? And what do critical scholars make of these same scriptures? In this enlightening study, Harrell systematically peels back the doctrinal accretions of time to provide a fresh new look at Mormon theology.

"This Is My Doctrine" will provide those already versed in Mormonism's theological tradition with a new and richer perspective of Mormon theology. Those unacquainted with Mormonism will gain an appreciation for how Mormon theology fits into the larger Jewish and Christian theological traditions.

LDS Biographical Encyclopedia

Andrew Jenson

Hardcover, ISBN: 978-1-58958-031-2

In the Preface to the first volume Jenson writes, "On the rolls of the Church of Jesus Christ of Latter-day Saints are found the names of a host of men and women of worth—heroes and heroines of a higher type—who have been and are willing to sacrifice fortune and life for the sake of their religion. It is for the purpose of perpetuating the memory of these, and to place on record deeds worthy of imitation, that [this set] makes its appearance."

With over 5,000 biographical entries of "heroes and heroines" complete with more than 2,000 photographs, the *LDS Biographical Encyclopedia* is an essential reference for the study of early Church history. Nearly anyone with pioneer heritage will find exciting and interesting history about ancestors in these volumes.

Andrew Jenson was an assistant historian for the Church of Jesus Christ of Latter-day Saints from 1897 to 1941.

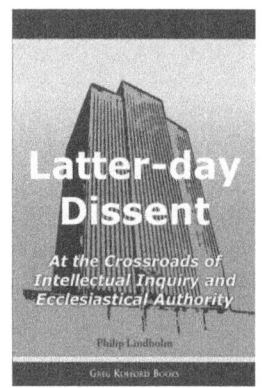

Latter-Day Dissent: At the Crossroads of Intellectual Inquiry and Ecclesiastical Authority

Philip Lindholm

Paperback, ISBN: 978-1-58958-128-9

This volume collects, for the first time in book form, stories from the "September Six," a group of intellectuals officially excommunicated or disfellowshipped from the LDS Church in September of 1993 on charges of "apostasy" or "conduct unbecoming" Church members. Their experiences are significant and yet are largely unknown outside of scholarly or more liberal Mormon circles, which is surprising given that their story was immediately propelled onto screens and cover pages across the Western world.

Interviews by Dr. Philip Lindholm (Ph.D. Theology, University of Oxford) include those of the "September Six," Lynne Kanavel Whitesides, Paul James Toscano, Maxine Hanks, Lavina Fielding Anderson, and D. Michael Quinn; as well as Janice Merrill Allred, Margaret Merrill Toscano, Thomas W. Murphy, and former employee of the LDS Church's Public Affairs Department, Donald B. Jessee.

Each interview illustrates the tension that often exists between the Church and its intellectual critics, and highlights the difficulty of accommodating congregational diversity while maintaining doctrinal unity—a difficulty hearkening back to the very heart of ancient Christianity.

A House for the Most High: The Story of the Original Nauvoo Temple

Matthew McBride

Hardcover, ISBN: 978-1-58958-016-9

This awe-inspiring book is a tribute to the perseverance of the human spirit. *A House for the Most High* is a groundbreaking work from beginning to end with its faithful and comprehensive documentation of the Nauvoo Temple's conception. The behind-the-scenes stories of those determined Saints involved in the great struggle to raise the sacred edifice bring a new appreciation to all readers. McBride's painstaking research now gives us access to valuable first-hand accounts that are drawn straight from the newspaper articles, private diaries, journals, and letters of the steadfast participants.

The opening of this volume gives the reader an extraordinary window into the early temple-building labors of the besieged Church of Jesus Christ of Latter-day Saints, the development of what would become temple-related doctrines in the decade prior to the Nauvoo era, and the 1839 advent of the Saints in Illinois. The main body of this fascinating history covers the significant years, starting from 1840, when this temple was first considered, to the temple's early destruction by a devastating natural disaster. A well-thought-out conclusion completes the epic by telling of the repurchase of the temple lot by the Church in 1937, the lot's excavation in 1962, and the grand announcement in 1999 that the temple would indeed be rebuilt. Also included are an astonishing appendix containing rare and fascinating eyewitness descriptions of the temple and a bibliography of all major source materials. Mormons and non-Mormons alike will discover, within the pages of this book, a true sense of wonder and gratitude for a determined people whose sole desire was to build a sacred and holy temple for the worship of their God.

Discourses in Mormon Theology: Philosophical and Theological Possibilities

Edited by
James M. McLachlan and Loyd Ericson

Hardcover, ISBN: 978-1-58958-103-6

A mere two hundred years old, Mormonism is still in its infancy compared to other theological disciplines (Judaism, Catholicism, Buddhism, etc.). This volume will introduce its reader to the rich blend of theological viewpoints that exist within Mormonism. The essays break new ground in Mormon studies by exploring the vast expanse of philosophical territory left largely untouched by traditional approaches to Mormon theology. It presents philosophical and theological essays by many of the finest minds associated with Mormonism in an organized and easy-to-understand manner and provides the reader with a window into the fascinating diversity amongst Mormon philosophers. Open-minded students of pure religion will appreciate this volume's thoughtful inquiries.

These essays were delivered at the first conference of the Society for Mormon Philosophy and Theology. Authors include Grant Underwood, Blake T. Ostler, Dennis Potter, Margaret Merrill Toscano, James E. Faulconer, and Robert L. Millet

Praise for *Discourses in Mormon Theology*:

"In short, *Discourses in Mormon Theology* is an excellent compilation of essays that are sure to feed both the mind and soul. It reminds all of us that beyond the white shirts and ties there exists a universe of theological and moral sensitivity that cries out for study and acclamation."
        -Jeff Needle, Association for Mormon Letters

Modern Mormonism: Myths and Realities

Robert L. Millet

Paperback, ISBN: 978-1-58958-127-2

What answer may a Latter-day Saint make to accusations from those of other faiths that "Mormons aren't Christians," or "You think God is a man," and "You worship a different Jesus"? Not only are these charges disconcerting, but the hostility with which they are frequently hurled is equally likely to catch Latter-day Saints off guard.

Now Robert L. Millet, veteran of hundreds of such verbal battles, cogently, helpfully, and scripturally provides important clarifications for Latter-day Saints about eleven of the most frequent myths used to discredit the Church. Along the way, he models how to conduct such a Bible based discussion respectfully, weaving in enlightenment from LDS scriptures and quotations from religious figures in other faiths, ranging from the early church fathers to the archbishop of Canterbury.

Millet enlivens this book with personal experiences as a boy growing up in an area where Mormons were a minuscule and not particularly welcome minority, in one-on-one conversations with men of faith who believed differently, and with his own BYU students who also had lessons to learn about interfaith dialogue. He pleads for greater cooperation in dealing with the genuine moral and social evils afflicting the world, and concludes with his own ardent and reverent testimony of the Savior.

Exploring Mormon Thought Series

Blake T. Ostler

In VOLUME ONE, *The Attributes of God*, Blake T. Ostler explores Christian and Mormon notions about God. ISBN: 978-1-58958-003-9

In VOLUME TWO, *The Problems of Theism and the Love of God*, Blake Ostler explores issues related to soteriology, or the theory of salvation. ISBN: 978-1-58958-095-4

In VOLUME THREE, *Of God and Gods*, Ostler analyzes and responds to the arguments of contemporary international theologians, reconstructs and interprets Joseph Smith's important King Follett Discourse and Sermon in the Grove, and argues persuasively for the Mormon doctrine of "robust deification." ISBN: 978-1-58958-107-4

Praise for the *Exploring Mormon Thought* series:

"These books are the most important works on Mormon theology ever written. There is nothing currently available that is even close to the rigor and sophistication of these volumes. B. H. Roberts and John A. Widtsoe may have had interesting insights in the early part of the twentieth century, but they had neither the temperament nor the training to give a rigorous defense of their views in dialogue with a wider stream of Christian theology. Sterling McMurrin and Truman Madsen had the capacity to engage Mormon theology at this level, but neither one did."

—Neal A. Maxwell Institute, Brigham Young University

Hugh Nibley: A Consecrated Life

Boyd Jay Petersen

Hardcover, ISBN: 978-1-58958-019-0

Winner of the Mormon History Association's Best Biography Award

As one of the LDS Church's most widely recognized scholars, Hugh Nibley is both an icon and an enigma. Through complete access to Nibley's correspondence, journals, notes, and papers, Petersen has painted a portrait that reveals the man behind the legend.

Starting with a foreword written by Zina Nibley Petersen and finishing with appendices that include some of the best of Nibley's personal correspondence, the biography reveals aspects of the tapestry of the life of one who has truly consecrated his life to the service of the Lord.

Praise for *A Consecrated Life*:

"Hugh Nibley is generally touted as one of Mormonism's greatest minds and perhaps its most prolific scholarly apologist. Just as hefty as some of Nibley's largest tomes, this authorized biography is delightfully accessible and full of the scholar's delicious wordplay and wit, not to mention some astonishing war stories and insights into Nibley's phenomenal acquisition of languages. Introduced by a personable foreword from the author's wife (who is Nibley's daughter), the book is written with enthusiasm, respect and insight. . . . On the whole, Petersen is a careful scholar who provides helpful historical context. . . . This project is far from hagiography. It fills an important gap in LDS history and will appeal to a wide Mormon audience."
—Publishers Weekly

"Well written and thoroughly researched, Petersen's biography is a must-have for anyone struggling to reconcile faith and reason."
—Greg Taggart, Association for Mormon Letters

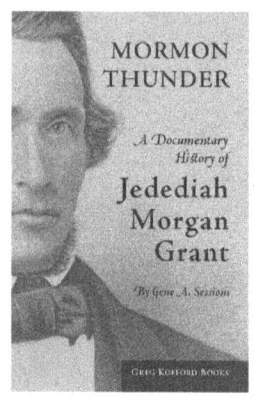

Mormon Thunder: A Documentary History of Jedediah Morgan Grant

Gene A. Sessions

Paperback, ISBN: 978-1-58958-111-1

Jedediah Morgan Grant was a man who knew no compromise when it came to principles—and his principles were clearly representative, argues Gene A. Sessions, of Mormonism's first generation. His life is a glimpse of a Mormon world whose disappearance coincided with the death of this "pious yet rambunctiously radical preacher, flogging away at his people, demanding otherworldliness and constant sacrifice." It was "an eschatological, pre-millennial world in which every individual teetered between salvation and damnation and in which unsanitary privies and appropriating a stray cow held the same potential for eternal doom as blasphemy and adultery."

Updated and newly illustrated with more photographs, this second edition of the award-winning documentary history (first published in 1982) chronicles Grant's ubiquitous role in the Mormon history of the 1840s and '50s. In addition to serving as counselor to Brigham Young during two tumultuous and influential years at the end of his life, he also portentously befriended Thomas L. Kane, worked to temper his unruly brother-in-law William Smith, captained a company of emigrants into the Salt Lake Valley in 1847, and journeyed to the East on several missions to bolster the position of the Mormons during the crises surrounding the runaway judges affair and the public revelation of polygamy.

Jedediah Morgan Grant's voice rises powerfully in these pages, startling in its urgency in summoning his people to sacrifice and moving in its tenderness as he communicated to his family. From hastily scribbled letters to extemporaneous sermons exhorting obedience, and the notations of still stunned listeners, the sound of "Mormon Thunder" rolls again in "a boisterous amplification of what Mormonism really was, and would never be again."

Hearken, O Ye People: The Historical Setting of Joseph Smith's Ohio Revelations

Mark Lyman Staker

Hardcover, ISBN: 978-1-58958-113-5

2010 Best Book Award - John Whitmer Historical Association

2011 Best Book Award - Mormon History Association

More of Mormonism's canonized revelations originated in or near Kirtland than any other place. Yet many of the events connected with those revelations and their 1830s historical context have faded over time. Mark Staker reconstructs the cultural experiences by which Kirtland's Latter-day Saints made sense of the revelations Joseph Smith pronounced. This volume rebuilds that exciting decade using clues from numerous archives, privately held records, museum collections, and even the soil where early members planted corn and homes. From this vast array of sources he shapes a detailed narrative of weather, religious backgrounds, dialect differences, race relations, theological discussions, food preparation, frontier violence, astronomical phenomena, and myriad daily customs of nineteenth-century life. The result is a "from the ground up" experience that today's Latter-day Saints can all but walk into and touch.

Praise for *Hearken O Ye People*:

"I am not aware of a more deeply researched and richly contextualized study of any period of Mormon church history than Mark Staker's study of Mormons in Ohio. We learn about everything from the details of Alexander Campbell's views on priesthood authority to the road conditions and weather on the four Lamanite missionaries' journey from New York to Ohio. All the Ohio revelations and even the First Vision are made to pulse with new meaning. This book sets a new standard of in-depth research in Latter-day Saint history."
-Richard Bushman, author of *Joseph Smith: Rough Stone Rolling*

"To be well-informed, any student of Latter-day Saint history and doctrine must now be acquainted with the remarkable research of Mark Staker on the important history of the church in the Kirtland, Ohio, area."
-Neal A. Maxwell Institute, Brigham Young University

The Wasp

Hardcover, ISBN: 978-1-58958-050-3

A newspaper published in Nauvoo from April 16, 1842, through April 26, 1843, *The Wasp* provides a crucial window into firsthand accounts of the happenings and concerns of the Saints in Nauvoo. It was initially edited by William Smith, younger brother of Joseph Smith. William was succeeded by John Taylor as editor and Taylor and Wilford Woodruff as printers and publishers. Some of the main stories covered in the newspaper are the August 1842 elections where local candidates endorsed by the Mormons easily won against their opponents, the fall from grace of John C. Bennett, the attempt by the state of Missouri to extradite Joseph Smith as an accessory in the attempted murder of Lilburn W. Boggs, and the Illinois legislature's effort to repeal the Nauvoo charter.

With a foreword by Peter Crawley putting the newspaper in historical context, this first-ever reproduction of the entire run of the *The Wasp* is essential to anyone interested in the Nauvoo period of Mormonism.

www.ingramcontent.com/pod-product-compliance
Lightning Source LLC
Chambersburg PA
CBHW082057230426
43670CB00017B/2878